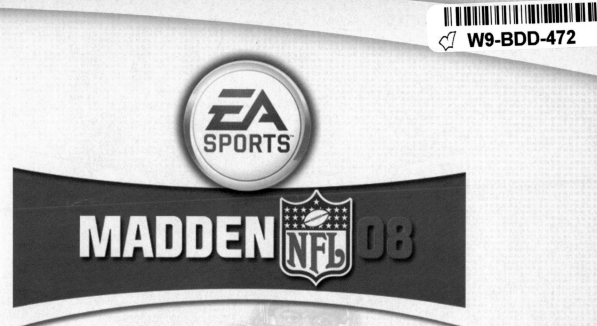

PRIMA Official Game Guide

Prima Games
A Division of Random House, Inc.

3000 Lava Ridge Court
Roseville, CA 95661
1-800-733-3000
www.primagames.com

Product Manager: Mario De Govia

The Prima Games logo is a registered trademark of Random House, Inc., registered in the United States and other countries. Primagames.com is a registered trademark of Random House, Inc., registered in the United States. Prima Games is a division of Random House, Inc.

© 2007 Electronic Arts Inc. Electronic Arts, EA, EA SPORTS and the EA SPORTS logo are trademarks or registered trademarks of Electronic Arts Inc. in the U.S. and/or other countries. All Rights Reserved. The mark "John Madden" and the name, likeness and other attributes of John Madden reproduced on this product are trademarks or other intellectual property of Red Bear, Inc. or John Madden, are subject to license to Electronic Arts Inc., and may not be otherwise used in whole or in part without the prior written consent of Red Bear or John Madden. © 2007 NFL Properties LLC. Team names/logos are trademarks of the teams indicated. All other NFL-related trademarks are trademarks of the National Football League. Officially Licensed Product of PLAYERS INC. Visit WWW.NFLPLAYERS.COM. All other trademarks are the property of their respective owners.

Please be advised that the ESRB Ratings icons, "EC", "E", "E10+", "T", "M", "AO", and "RP" are trademarks owned by the Entertainment Software Association, and may only be used with their permission and authority. For information regarding whether a product has been rated by the ESRB, please visit www.esrb.org. For permission to use the Ratings icons, please contact the ESA at esrblicenseinfo.com.

Important:
Prima Games has made every effort to determine that the information contained in this book is accurate. However, the publisher makes no warranty, either expressed or implied, as to the accuracy, effectiveness, or completeness of the material in this book; nor does the publisher assume liability for damages, either incidental or consequential, that may result from using the information in this book. The publisher cannot provide information regarding game play, hints and strategies, or problems with hardware or software. Questions should be directed to the support numbers provided by the game and device manufacturers in their documentation. Some game tricks require precise timing and may require repeated attempts before the desired result is achieved.

ISBN: 9780-7615-5725-8

Library of Congress Catalog Card Number: 2005925099
Printed in the United States of America

07 08 09 10 LL 10 9 8 7 6 5 4 3 2 1

Strategy Guide Createdy By:
Kaizen Media Group™

President: Howard Grossman
Writers: The Sports Video Gamers
Design/Production: Tim Davis
Production Assistance: Hg, Craig Keller, Troy Silver, and Holly Davis

EA SPORTS Fantasy Footbal section written by the Prima Crew: Jeff Barton, Don Tica, James Knight, Fernando Bueno, Brandon Smith, Andy Rolleri, Chris Rojas, Paul Giacomotto, Dan Ransom

EA SPORTS MADDEN NFL 08
CONTENTS

GAME MODES

Welcome to *Madden NFL 08*. This has got to be the best time of the year for gridiron fans with Fantasy Football, NFL & College games, and of course *Madden NFL 08*! *Madden NFL 08* brings a bunch of under-the-hood changes including improved DB AI, Auto-Motion plays, Hit Stick 2.0 and Player Weapons.

Prima Guides is back with The Official Strategy Guide to *Madden NFL 08*. Our guides grow each year to provide you with a more in depth look at the greatest sports franchise around.

GETTING STARTED

Here we'll go over the nuts and bolts of *Madden NFL 08*.

PLAY NOW

Jump right into play without wasting another minute. When you have some friends over or just want to get in a quick battle against the CPU, select the Play Now option and get going. Choose your team, weather, stadium, let it all hang out.

The results and stats of Play Now games are saved with your profile allowing you to gain points to unlock *Madden* Cards for your collection. See the *Madden* Cards chapter for a complete breakdown of the challenges and rewards.

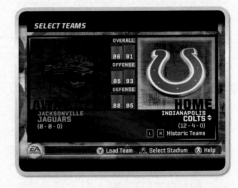

MADDEN NFL 08 ONLINE

The CPU can put up a good fight, but once you get the hang of things you'll quickly find yourself putting a beat down on the computer. For the ultimate in competition, nothing beats going head-to-head with another living, breathing opponent. For more on online play, refer to the online section of this guide.

TOURNAMENT MODE

If you want to get in a tournament with a group of friends then this is the way to go. You have Double Elimination, Single Elimination, Double Round Robin, and Round Robin modes. You can have up to 16 players and even throw a Fantasy Draft to start things off.

RUSHING ATTACK

Rushing Attack is a great way to improve your stick skills. It is also a way to get a quick dose of competition if you don't have time for a full game. We guarantee that if you spend time in Rushing Attack you will see your skills at running and tackling dramatically improve in real games.

TWO-MINUTE DRILL

In this mode you can simulate the end of game frenzy as you dash down the field trying to score as often as you can. This is an excellent tool for working on your clock management and no-huddle offense. Call quick hot routes to change up your play and rack up as many points as possible.

Once you press Start, you'll have 2:00 on the clock and the ball at your own 20-yard line. The clock starts as soon as you snap the ball. Get out of bounds to stop the clock and save time. You can also play this game in head-to-head mode where you and a buddy take turns playing offense and defense.

PRACTICE MODE

Top players spend the majority of their time here. Unless you spend serious time in this mode (also called the Lab), you will never reach your peak as a *Madden NFL 08* baller. Take your team and favorite playbook and hit the field. Run your plays against all different types of defenses to see how they work best. As the season evolves and new go-to plays come out, you can go into practice mode to figure out how to defend them best.

Normal – Offense vs Defense

Offense Only – Only your offense will show up on the field

Kickoff – Practice your special teams plays

MINI-GAMES

Mini-Camp is the best method to improve your stick skills and become a better player. Earning a GOLD on the higher levels will unlock special *Madden* Cards.

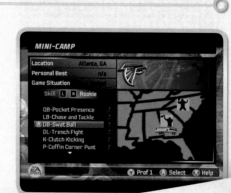

GAME MODES

CREATE A PLAYBOOK

This feature is for all the would-be offensive and defensive coordinators of the world. Scheme and devise a playbook with all of your favorite go-to plays. Or you can start with the playbook of your choice and just edit it to your liking.

The first step is to create a formation. You have complete control over the placement of each player. Using the grid, place each player in the starting point for your formation. When you're happy with the formation, you'll be prompted to rename it.

When you're finished with the play, test it against randomly selected offensive or defensive formations. If you spot bugs or weak spots in the play, go back to the drawing board and tweak it up.

CREATE A PLAYER

The first step in creating a player is to fill in the Information and Appearance screens to shape your player into an NFL star. Become the next Dan Marino, develop a lock-down corner, or create the next impact playmaker.

On the Build screen, you can fine-tune your player's appearance. Go for the ripped, broad-shouldered look, or be a fat and flabby master of the team buffet.

The Equipment screen lets you customize your player's gear. You can change things like ankle tape, eye paint, elbow pads, and more. Make your guys look unique and distinct.

The Attributes section is where you set your player's skill level. Max out all your attributes to become the greatest of all time.

CREATE A TEAM

If you want to put a team in your own city, this is the place you want to go. Choose the logo, nickname, city, state, abbreviation, team rosters, and climate for your new team.

On the Design Stadium screen you can build your stadium from the ground up. Add tunnels, extra seating, sky boxes and even make it a dome. When the stadium is finished, advance to the Uniform Editor and design your team's apparel. You can go with a classic look, or light up the field with a crazy color mix.

CREATE A FAN

For the hardcore fan, nothing beats being able to go to a game and get dressed up to root for the home team. Create a Fan allows you to do just that, but *Madden NFL 08* style. Once your fan has been created, you will see him cheering in the stands whenever you make a big play. You can add foam hands, crazy face paint, and even pick their clothes for them.

HISTORIC TEAMS

Back again are Historic Teams. You can play All-Star Teams for each franchise, or dip into some of the greatest teams of all time. You get some right of the box, but others you have to unlock wth *Madden* Cards. They allow you to play "what if" type games. Go back in time and play some of the greatest games ever. The players do not have their actual names, but you can edit them if you want optimum realism.

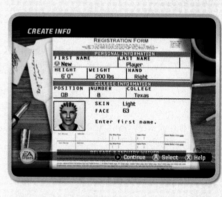

NFL SUPERSTAR MODE

This is your chance to become a living legend and be enshrined in the Hall of Fame forever. You can create your player, customize his look, and then take him from the NFL Draft to superstardom. See the NFL Superstar section for a complete breakdown of this game mode.

FRANCHISE MODE

Take control of every aspect of your franchise. You are the Owner, General Manager, Coach and Player all rolled into one. You manage everything from the price of hot dogs to which player your team will take as the number one draft pick. Play through 30 seasons as you lead your franchise to the championship. See the Franchise section for a complete breakdown of this game mode.

FANTASY CHALLENGE

Leverage your Fantasy Football knowledge by drafting the ultimate NFL dream team. Play through four competition levels with your fantasy squad in hope of winning challenges, increasing your salary cap, and adding new superstars to your team.

NEW FEATURES

THE PLAYER WEAPONS

The biggest new gameplay feature added to *Madden NFL 08* is called Player Weapons. This new gameplay feature allows NFL Elite Players to distinguish themselves from the standard NFL player. If a team has a shutdown corner such as Bronco's Champ Bailey, then he uses his Player Weapons ability to shut down the receiver lined up across from him.

HOW PLAYER WEAPONS ARE USED

There is no limit to the amount of Player Weapons a team can have. For instance, a team like the Chargers is loaded with players that have Player Weapons abilities, whereas a team such as the Lions isn't. This makes playing the loaded Player Weapons teams a lot easier to play than the less loaded teams.

The best way to utilize a player's Player Weapons ability is to play to that player's strength. For instance, if your team has a Player Weapon that is a power back, such as Jamal Lewis, you wouldn't want to try to run him outside; instead, you would want to pound him between the tackles to maximize his Player Weapons ability.

PLAYER WEAPONS MENU

If you want to view all the Player Weapons in the game, go to the Features menu screen and then click on Player Weapons. There, you can view and get a detailed description of each Player Weapon.

VIEW TEAM'S PLAYER WEAPONS IN THE ROSTER MENU

To view each player for each team that has a Player Weapon ability, go to the Features menu screen, and then click on Rosters. From there, you can view each team's players that have a Player Weapon ability. In the screen shot, notice Patriots' quarterback Tom Brady's Player Weapon icon is a Star. This means he is a Franchise Quarterback.

ON THE FIELD

Once on the field, you can view each team's Player Weapons by using the Player Weapons cam. To do this, press down on the Left Thumbstick. All the players on the field that have Player Weapons will appear. This is nice because it shows you each match-up.

PLAYER WEAPONS LIST

(Current Generation Consoles)

There are a total of 26 Player Weapons that you will find throughout the game (see chart at the right). You will find at least 2 Player Weapons categories for each position. For instance, A QB has a total of four Player Weapons categories. They are Precision Passer, Cannon Arm, Scrambler, and Franchise Quarterback. For a more detailed explanation, go to the Player Weapons Menu Screen.

Current Generation Player Weapons

#	Player Weapons
1	Playmaker
2	Precision Passer
3	Cannon Arm
4	Scrambler
5	Franchise Quarterback
6	Power Back
7	Elusive Back
8	Speed Back
9	Run Blocker
10	Pass Blocker
11	Road Blocker
12	Force of Nature
13	Heavy Hitter
14	Containment Corner
15	Quick Corner
16	Big Hitter
17	Coverage Safety
18	Hit Man
19	Feature Back
20	Go-to Guy
21	Deep Threat
22	Possession Receiver
23	Shutdown Corner
24	Pass Rusher
25	Run Stopper
26	Defensive Enforcer

Next Generation Player Weapons

#	Player Weapons	#	Player Weapons	#	Player Weapons
1	Smart QB	8	Quick Recevier	17	Big Hitter
2	Cannon Arm QB	9	Possesion Receiver	18	Brick Wall Defender
3	Accurate QB	10	Spetacular Catch Receiver	19	Finesse Move D-Lineman
4	Speed QB	11	Hands	20	Power Move D-Lineman
5	Elusive Back	12	Shutdown Corner	21	Crushing Run Blocker
6	Power Back	13	Smart Corner	22	Pass Blocker
7	Stiff Arm Ball Carrier	14	Press Coverage Corner	23	Accurate Kicker
		15	Smart Safety	24	Big Foot Kicker
		16	Smart Linebacker	25	Speed

COACH CAM PLAY ART

Offensive and defensive coach cam art is nothing new to this game. It's been around for some time now. However, in *Madden NFL 08*, the Tiburon team added a little twist to it. How many times have you wanted to look at your pass routes or defensive assignments while playing offline with a friend, but couldn't because you didn't want to reveal the play you were calling? In *Madden NFL 08*, you can now do that by pressing the coach cam button, then up, down, left, or right on the R3 Button. This also can be used to bluff your opponent into thinking you are running a different play by showing him your offensive or defensive play cam art.

OFFENSIVE COACH CAM ART

Real Play Art	Show Pass	Show Run	Show Play Action
	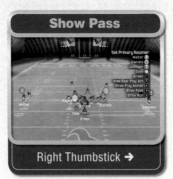		
Right Thumbstick ↑	Right Thumbstick →	Right Thumbstick ↓	Right Thumbstick ←

By pressing the coach cam button and up on the Right Thumbstick, you will show your opponent the real offensive play you are calling.

By pressing the coach cam button and right on the Right Thumbstick, you will bluff your opponent into thinking you are running a pass play.

By pressing the coach cam button and down on the Right Thumbstick, you will bluff your opponent into thinking you are running a run play.

By pressing the coach cam button and left on the Right Thumbstick, you will bluff your opponent into thinking you are running a play action pass play.

DEFENSIVE COACH CAM ART

Real Play Art	Show Man Coverage	Show Blitz	Show Zone
			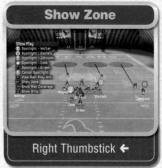
Right Thumbstick ↑	Right Thumbstick →	Right Thumbstick ↓	Right Thumbstick ←

By pressing the coach cam button and up on the Right Thumbstick, you will show your opponent the real defensive play you are calling.

By pressing the coach cam button and right on the Right Thumbstick, you will bluff your opponent into thinking you are calling man coverage.

By pressing the coach cam button and down on the Right Thumbstick, you will bluff your opponent into thinking you are calling a blitz.

By pressing the coach cam button and left on the Right Thumbstick, you will bluff your opponent into thinking you are calling zone.

NEW FEATURES

AUTO MOTION

Back in *Madden NFL 2000*, there were several plays on the offensive side of the ball in which motion was pre-scripted. In *Madden NFL 08*, that same type of motion has been implemented. What makes auto motion effective is that it often allows a player going in motion to get an extra step on the defender in pass coverage, because the player in motion is already at full speed just as the ball is being snapped. Auto motion can also be effective in the running game by sending a receiver in motion to seal off a defender to the inside, allowing the ball carrier to get outside.

Auto Motion plays are indicated by a receiver having a green route or block assignment. For instance, if you look at the following screen shot ❶, notice that the split end's drag route is green.

This means he will be sent automatically in motion before the ball is snapped ❷. Colts' receiver Reggie Wayne is sent in motion from the right side.

❸ The auto motion allows for Wayne to get an extra step on the defender in coverage. In the screen shot, we make the catch for a five yard pick up, thanks to Wayne being sent in auto motion.

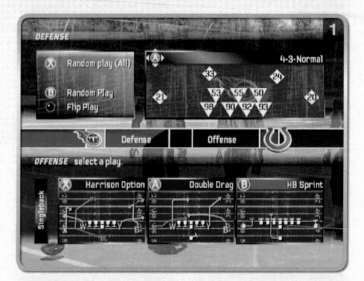

AUTO MOTION **TIP**

① Most auto motion formations have at least two similar looking plays. For instance, if you were to look at the Singleback Deuce formation of the Colts' playbook, you would find the Double Drag and HB Sprint. Both plays send Reggie Wayne in motion to the right. The reason for this is to keep your opponent from knowing which play you are running.

NEW FEATURES

RECEIVER CONTROL

Receiver control allows for the human-controlled user to take control of any eligible receiver on the field before the snap and run, and then actually run that receiver's pass route once the ball is snapped. This gives the human-controlled user even more control over his passing game, because if the defense calls a blitz, the pass route can be shortened, allowing the CPU-controlled quarterback to throw the ball earlier and avoid being sacked.

HOW IT WORKS

To take control of any eligible receiver, Use the same method for lead blocking. Press (the B button) for the Xbox or (the ● button) for the PS2 before the snap. Cycle through the receivers until you find the one you want to take control of. Once the ball is snapped, run the designed pass route for that receiver.

In the first screen, we take control of the rookie Lion's receiver Calvin Johnson.

The play calls for him to run a curl route. Once the ball is snapped, we run a curl route by taking control of him.

We curl back about 10 yards down the field and call for the ball. To do this, we press the Ⓛ Trigger on the Xbox or for PS2, the [L2] button.

The CPU-controlled quarterback will now throw us the ball.

We make the catch for an eight yard pick up.

RECEIVER CONTROL TIP

① While in control of the receiver, you are at the mercy of the CPU-controlled quarterback. There are times he will throw the ball to another receiver before you have a chance to call for the ball. Hopefully, if the CPU-controlled QB does decide to throw ball to another receiver, he will read the coverage correctly and make the right throw.

RECEIVER CONTROL TIP

① You don't have to run the receiver's exact pass route while in control of him. If you choose to, you can run any other route. For instance, if you see a hole in the pass coverage, you can run your receiver to that that area and call for the ball. However, the CPU quarterback does not seem to be accurate and tends to lose some power on his throws. This is quite apparent on deep pass routes.

NEW FEATURES

NEW FEATURES/DEFENSE

HIT STICK 2.0

The Hit Stick was introduced in *Madden NFL 05*, and made playing defense fun. It used to be that by flicking up or down on the Right Thumbstick, a player would put a high, bone-crushing hit on the ball carrier and possibly force a fumble. In *Madden NFL 08*, EA Sports Tiburon has added another twist to what is now called Hit Stick 2.0. Now, not only can the player press up on the Right Thumbstick to deliver a high blow, but they can also go for the legs by flicking the Right Thumbstick down. This works particularly well against bigger running backs.

DEFENDING THE **HIGH PASS**

In *Madden NFL 07*, the high-precision quick pass was the most successful way to move the ball. Slants, curls, hitches, and several other pass routes could be delivered high with great success by throwing the ball quickly.

Most top players found that the best way to counter the high pass was to use the Hit Stick to knock the ball out of a receiver's hands as he was attempting to make the catch. Although the high-precision quick pass has been toned down, it can still be effective against man and zone coverage. By learning to use the Hit Stick at the proper time, you can knock the ball out of the receiver's hands, and make your opponent think twice about using it all game long.

CREATING **FUMBLES**

We have already shown how effective the Hit Stick can be in jarring the ball free from receivers, but it also can be used to force fumbles. In the first screen, the defender closes in on the ball carrier. In the second screen, the Hit Stick is used. The defender delivers a vicious blow that causes the ball carrier to fumble the ball.

HIGH RISK **HIGH REWARD**

Using the Hit Stick properly can lead to turnovers and broken-up passes, but it also comes with risks. Don't get in the habit of always using it as your main way to tackle and break up passes. This is particularly true when playing online, where lag becomes an issue. By selling out to use the Hit Stick, there is a good possibility that you may miss the ball carrier or receiver completely. If this happens, the player with the ball can go all the way for an easy six points.

SMART ZONES

RECEIVER SPOTLIGHT

Smart Zones is a brand new defensive individual hot route that has been added to *Madden NFL 08*. It allows the player controlling the defense to drop any defender(s) back in pass coverage near the first down marker or goal line. If the offense is in a crucial third or fourth down situation where they must pass to pick up a first down, putting a defender in a smart zone is a good decision because it will make it that much more difficult to pick up the first down.

By pressing up twice on the Right Thumbstick while in control of the defender you want to put in a smart zone, you will see a red circle coming from the player.

❶ Notice that in the first screen shot, we come out in the Nickel 3-3-5 Cover 3. The middle linebacker is playing a hook zone. Even though he is dropping back in zone coverage, he does not drop back far enough to swat away a pass near the first down marker.

❷ By pressing the Right Thumbstick up twice, the middle linebacker now drops back near the first down marker.

❸ Because the middle linebacker drops back in a smart zone, the quarterback cannot throw to his primary receiver over the middle near the first down marker.

❹ He is forced to look elsewhere or be sacked.

Receiver Spotlight allows the human-controlled user to put special attention (before and after the snap) on a receiver that threatens to beat the pass coverage called.

❶ For instance, Cowboys' tight end Jason Witten has been torching our defense all game long by running a deep post route. We decide we need to pay extra attention to him by using the Receiver Spotlight feature. To do this, we press the Right Thumbstick on the Xbox or the R2 Button on the PS2, and then the receiver's pass icon. In this case, Witten's pass icon is a Y. He is now spotlighted. *Note:* You will not actually see a spotlight or anything on the field that receiver is actually being covered.

❷ Once the ball is snapped, the defenders in the area of the spotlighted receiver will aggressively try to cover him. Notice that Witten is surrounded by Giants defenders. The QB forces the pass to Witten, despite the tight pass coverage. The result is an interception.

RECEIVER SPOTLIGHT TIPS

❶ Even when a receiver has been spotlighted, it doesn't mean that he won't still make the catch. You still have to call the right pass coverage to keep the receiver from making the catch. For instance, if a receiver runs a quick out and you call a defense where no defenders are, he is going to be open, regardless of whether he's been spotlighted or not.

❷ Whenever a receiver is spotlighted, it opens other passing lanes for other receivers. What we mean by this is defenders will break off their coverage responsibilities to go cover the spotlighted receiver when he is in their area. If another receiver comes in the same area, the defenders won't go cover that receiver; instead, they will stick to the spotlighted receiver.

NEW FEATURES

OFFENSIVE STRATEGY

OFFENSE STRATEGY / **RUNNING GAME**

Several new moves and animations have been added this year to improve the running game. With all of these new moves and animations, this year's running game is the strongest the series has ever seen.

RUNNING MOVES

Before we get to some of the different types of run plays that are in the game, we need to get you up to speed on the running controls. Jukes, stiff arms, speed burst, cover up, and dive buttons are important controls to learn if you want your rushing attack to succeed.

COVER UP

If your ball carrier is having a problem coughing up the ball whenever he is hit, learn to use the cover up button. Chances are if the ball carrier covers up the ball, it will not be stripped or knocked out of his hands. Another advantage of using the cover up button is that he lowers his shoulders and often knocks defenders over. It's not as effective as the Highlight Stick when it comes to breaking tackles, but it's safer to use because the ball carrier tends to keep the rock off the turf.

SPIN MOVE

The spin move has always been one of the most efficient running moves in this game to pick up yardage. By learning when to use it, you can turn what looks to be a short gain into something that makes the evening sports newscast. Most top players learn when to properly use the spin while in practice mode or in rushing attack.

This year you can perform two different types of spin moves. Tap the spin button for a quick spin move. The ball carrier spins around quickly and often puts the defender(s) out of position to make the tackle. The drawback of using the quick spin is if the defender is not fooled, he can make the tackle. The power spin takes the ball carrier longer to spin around, but he has a better chance of breaking the tackle even if the defender is in position to make the tackle. Learn when to use each type of spin move.

In these two screen shots, we show us covering up the ball as we go through the hole. The linebacker tries to strip the ball, but because we are covering the ball, he is unable to strip the ball away.

Notice that the linebacker is closing in on our running back. By timing when to use the spin button, we are able avoid the linebacker and keep trucking down the field.

QUICK RUNNING TIPS

1. Overusing the speed burst button applies to all positions. It's just more prevalent with the running backs, because they tend to get the ball the most.

2. Avoid running towards the sideline as much as possible; instead, keep moving straight up the field for positive yardage.

3. Learn when to use all the running moves. It can make the difference between picking up no yardage at all or picking up large chunks.

4. Use the Highlight Stick to break and avoid tackles based on the ball carrier's attributes.

OFFENSIVE STRATEGY

JUKE MOVE

In *Madden NFL 2008*, the juke move is back with a vengeance because of the sheer number of animations that can be pulled off. For example, by pressing left and right quickly on the Right Thumbstick, the ball carrier performs a devastating move that leaves defenders grasping at air.

The back juke returns in *Madden NFL 2008*. This juke move was not used as much as some of the other jukes, but if you do it at the right time, defenders will mistime their tackle. This especially holds true when a human is in control of the defender and hits the hit stick or tackle button.

Another juke animation move we have seen is the ability to slash through the open holes inside. In previous versions of this game, using the juke move inside tackles did not always provide positive results. Often the ball carrier would get stuck behind offensive linemen and could not pick up yardage. Thanks to the ability to slash through the line of scrimmage by pressing softly left or right on the right thumbstick, you now can slash the ball carrier between offensive linemen to pick up positive yardage with ease.

STIFF ARM

The stiff arm has been in the series for a long time. For all of you old school veterans who have played this game before the juke and spin move were added to the game, you know the stiff arm was used the most outside of the speed burst. Ball carriers with high break tackle ratings benefit the most from a well-timed stiff arm. If it's performed correctly, the ball carrier puts his non-football-carrying hand out and shoves the would-be tackler to the turf. To throw a stiff arm, press left or right on the stiff arm buttons.

SPEED BURST MOVE

The speed burst button is by far the most-used rushing control. Whether you are running outside to escape defenders or running the ball inside to get through the hole quickly, you can bet that the speed burst is being used. The key to using the speed burst button is knowing the proper time to use it. For example, if you are running some type of counter play to the outside, don't use the speed burst button too early or you risk overlapping your pulling guard.

If you do, it defeats the whole purpose of the guard pulling outside to be your lead blocker. Another factor to consider when using the speed burst button is maneuverability. Whenever the speed burst is held down, you lose some ability to move your ball carrier. It may not seem significant, but when you are trying to make a quick cut, that lack of maneuverability can mean the difference between picking up a few yards or taking the rock to the house for a score.

One last consideration is fatigue. The more the speed burst button is used, the quicker the ball carrier gets tired. If you have a running back with a high stamina rating, this may not be a big deal. But if your running back has a low stamina rating and his backup is not very good, it can have a negative effect.

Notice in the screenshots as we come to line of scrimmage, there is not much room for us to squeeze our running back through. By using use the juke move, we are able to dart through the hole and break into the secondary for a huge pick up.

In the first screen shot, the linebacker has a good position to make the tackle on our running back. Just as our running back is about to be tackled, we throw him a stiff arm. This allows us to break the tackle and pick up extra yards.

In the first screen shot, we have yet to press the Speed Burst button. We do not want to outrun our lead blocker. We wait for our blocker to engage the strong safety. Once he does, we then press down on the Speed Burst button and get outside quickly where have plenty of room to run for daylight.

Offensive Strategy

HIGHLIGHT STICK

The Truck Stick was introduced in *Madden NFL 06*. This allowed the user-controlled ball carrier to run over defenders by moving the Right Thumbstick up. For big, powerful running backs such as Larry Johnson, this was great because it enabled him to knock over smaller defenders. However, for smaller running backs such as Warrick Dunn, the Truck Stick was not that much of a factor. They didn't have the strength or break tackle ratings to effectively use it.

In *Madden NFL 07*, EA Tiburon decided to make the stick work for both types of backs. Instead of the Truck Stick, it was called the Highlight Stick.

In *Madden NFL 08*, the Highlight Stick is back for yet another season. For those of you who are new to this game or haven't been using the Highlight Stick, you will want to jump on the bandwagon, because it is the most effective way to move the ball on the ground (outside of having great stick control).

If the running back is a big bruising type, he will run defenders over when you press up on the Right Thumbstick. If the running back is smaller, he will look to work around the defender once you press up on the right thumbstick. Of course, not every running back is going to be able to run over or around defenders. A lot of what happens on the field is based on ratings or luck.

There are 20 different animations for the big running backs and 20 different animations for smaller running backs. Chances are that you will see several different types of Highlight Stick animations when playing *Madden NFL 08*. This helps keeps the running game looking fresh.

HIGHLIGHT STICK TIPS

1. Some backs, such as Steven Jackson and LaDainian Tomlinson, can perform both big and small running animations. These types of backs are most effective because they can do all the moves to avoid being brought down.

2. There is a downside to using the Highlight Stick too much, and that's fumbling the ball. If your running back has a lower carry rating, be cautious when using the Highlight Stick too frequently. If you notice that your running back is coughing up the ball way too often, lay off the Highlight Stick and rely on the normal running controls.

LEAD BLOCKING CONTROL

Last year, Lead Blocking Control was added to the game with mixed results. Some players really like being able to take control of a fullback, tight end, or offensive linemen to lead block for the running back. Others would rather just stay in control of the running back during the duration of the play, because they don't want to have rely on the CPU-controlled running back to find the open holes. In any event, Lead Blocking Control is in *Madden NFL 08*.

LEAD BLOCKING **CONTROL MENU**

If you decide to use Lead Blocking Control, you first must decide which Blocking Control options you want to use. To get to the Blocking Control options, pause the game, and then go to Settings and choose Game Play. Next pick Blocking Control. There you will find four options. Each setting has a different effect on how the game plays. Each setting can be toggled on/off. We have listed these four settings, plus a brief description of how they affect your game.

Auto Switch Back — off by default

When this setting is turned on and you are in control of the blocker, you automatically switch to the ball carrier if a successful block is thrown. If the setting is turned off, you can control the lead blocker for as long as you like, but you must hit the switch player button to take control of the ball carrier.

Blocking Slowdown — off by default

With this turned on, the game slows down momentarily when the user-controlled lead blocker engages a defender and triggers a block. With this turned off, the game speed does not change, even if you connect on a crushing block.

Switch Slowdown — off by default

With this turned on, the game slows down momentarily when you switch from the lead blocker back to the ball carrier. With this turned off, you instantly switch to the ball carrier with no slowdown at all.

Blocking View — Zoomed In is on by default

With this setting on Zoom In, the game camera is zoomed in closer to the lead blocker (closer to a first-person view). With it set to Normal, the game camera is in the default camera view when lead blocking.

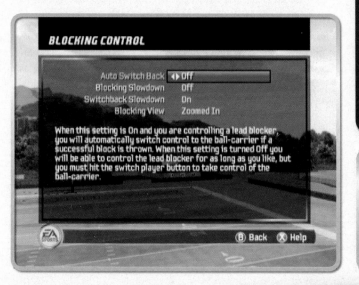

LEAD BLOCKING CONTROL **TIPS**

1. If you want to take control of the ball carrier and pretend you are going to block with him before the snap, you can. As soon as the ball is snapped, you switch from blocker to ball carrier automatically.

2. If you decide to call a pass play, you can still take control of a player to block with before the snap. This is a good way to bluff your opponent into thinking run. As soon as the ball is snapped, you are automatically switched to the quarterback.

3. Taking control of pulling offensive linemen seems to be more beneficial than taking control of the offensive linemen who do not pull. When we take control of offensive linemen who don't pull, we normally end up blocking the defender lined up across from us. We might as well just let the CPU-controlled offensive linemen do that, and instead take control of the fullback to lead him through the hole unless you want to Turn Block Left or Right.

4. Don't get yourself out of position to get the block. If you feel like you are losing control of the blocker, switch to the ball carrier and let the CPU take control of the blocker.

5. On the other hand, if you see the CPU-controlled ball carrier not going through the correct hole, switch off the blocker quickly and take control of the ball carrier to get him to go through the open hole.

6. You cannot switch back and forth between the blocker and ball carrier more than once. Once you switch to the ball carrier, all run blocking controls are turned off and run controls are turned on.

7. Use the Speed Burst button to get the blocker out in front quicker. This works best with a pulling offensive linemen or fullback who is lead blocking to the outside.

OFFENSIVE STRATEGY

17

INSIDE RUNNING PLAYS

EA Tiburon did an excellent job of achieving the ability to run the ball inside in *Madden NFL 07*. In *Madden NFL 08*, nothing has changed. Being able to pound the rock inside is a must. You may not have much success with it in the earlier stages of the game, but if you stick with it, the defense will wear down. You will start to notice your running back picking up more chunks of yardage. Nothing is more satisfying in football than knowing you have the defense back on its heels because it has no way of stopping the pound inside.

In this section, we'll take a look at some of our favorite inside plays from the Rams' playbook.

SPLIT BACKS NORMAL **HB BLAST**

You don't see many players calling running plays from the Split Backs Normal. However, that does not mean there aren't any good run plays from it. The Off Tackle, FB Dive, and HB Counter are all good run plays to call from this formation. There is another run play we like to call: the HB Blast. Just like the Singleback Big HB Slam, it gets the ball carrier to the line of scrimmage and through the hole.

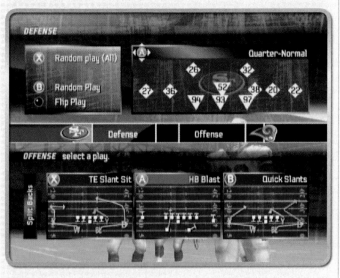

❶ The play is designed to have the running back run between the left guard and left tackle. It also has the potential to have the running back spin to the outside and run for daylight.

❷ In the second screen, we bust through the line of scrimmage between the left guard and left tackle. We are able to pick up 7 yards before being brought down.

STRONG NORMAL **FB DIVE**

This is another inside run play that many top players have set in their audibles. Though the FB Dive may be fairly simple, it's one of the most consistent run plays with which to pick up positive yardage. Most top players will package or sub in a number 2 running back in at fullback to get a better runner.

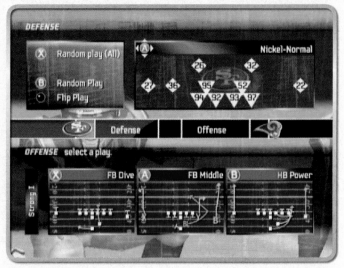

❶ For this example, we have called the Strong I Normal FB Dive. The play is designed to have the fullback between the center and right guard.

❷ Because the fullback lines up so close to the line of scrimmage, it takes no time to get through the hole quickly and into the second line of defense.

SINGLEBACK BIG **HB SLAM**

If you asked any top player what one of the best run plays in the game is, they will tell you that it is the Singleback Big HB Slam. It's a quick-hitting run play that gets the running back through the hole quickly and in the second level of defense. This play picks up consistent yardage and is a staple run play in many of the top players' offensive audibles.

The Singleback Big HB Slam is designed to have the ball carrier run though hole between the center and left guard. However, the beauty of this play is that it does not always have to be run in this exact way.

❶ For example, in the first screen shot, the hole between the center and left guard is sealed up. As we are getting the ball, we look for an open hole along the offensive line.

❷ We spot an opening between the left guard and left tackle.

❸ We slip through the hole and into the second level of defense. Expect to consistently pick up at least 3 yards. Sometime it might be less and sometimes it may be more.

SINGLEBACK 4WR SPREAD **HB DIVE**

One of the big trends we saw online in *Madden NFL 07* was that more and more players were running the ball inside from spread formations. One of the most frequently called run plays from a spread formation is the HB Dive out of the Singleback 4WR Spread. What makes this play so effective is that the defense is forced to cover the slot receivers with smaller defensive backs.

Most players on defense will call Dime or Quarter formations to match up with all the speed on the field. The problem with that is it leaves five defenders in the box to defend the run. As long as the five offensive linemen hold their blocks on the defenders in front of them, there will be plenty of inside running room.

❶ In the first screen shot, look at how much running room we have to run through with our running back.

❷ Once through the line, we press the sprint button.

❸ By the time the strong safety reacts, we have already picked up 7 yards.

INSIDE RUNNING **TIPS**

① Find inside run plays that get the ball carrier to and through the line of scrimmage quickly. Avoid inside run plays where it takes time to develop.

② The higher the running back's break tackle ratings, the better chance he has of breaking a few tackles as he pounds his way through the line of scrimmage.

③ Decide if you like to run the ball inside with or without a fullback. Some players prefer to have a lead blocker, and others prefer not to have a lead blocker. Both have their pros and cons, you just need to decide which suits your style.

OFFENSIVE STRATEGY

19

OUTSIDE RUNNING PLAYS

Having a fast running back that can get to the outer perimeter quickly is the key ingredient to having a successful outside running attack. It also requires some stick skill and knowledge on how to set up blocks with your blockers. If you don't have speed, stick, and knowledge, it becomes a serious challenge to establish an outside running game on the higher difficulty levels.

In this section, we'll give you some tips and plays that will hopefully improve your perimeter run game.

I-FORM NORMAL FB FK HB TOSS

This play has been used more both online and offline over the last few years. It is particularly effective against man coverage. Often, the defenders will bite on the fake to the fullback, freeing the halfback to take a toss from the quarterback going in the opposite direction. With the defenders going in the wrong direction, there is plenty of room for the halfback to find running room.

❶ What makes the FB FK HB Toss so effective is that frequently, the defenders will bite on the fake hand-off to the fullback.

❷ With them converging on the fullback to make the tackle, the quarterback is tossing the ball to the halfback, who is running outside.

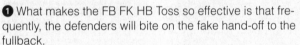

❸ With the outside receivers running fake streaks, they draw their men, plus the safeties (if in deep zone coverage) away from the halfback.

❹ As long as the halfback has any type of speed, he is going to pick up a good chunk of yardage before any defender is in position to make a tackle. In the fourth screen, notice that we have already picked up 7 yards before defenders even get close. By the time we are actually tackled, we have picked up 12 yards.

SINGLEBACK TIGHT DOUBLE HB STRETCH

Ever since the stretch play was put in this game a few years ago, it has becomes one of the most popular outside run plays among top players. This is because any time it is run, the ball carrier has potential for a big play.

❶ For this example, we have called the Singleback Tight Doubles HB Stretch out of the Saints' playbook. This play has our running back taking the hand-off and looking to run outside to the right side of the field.

❷ As long as the right tackle and tight end seal off their men from getting to the outside, we will find plenty of running room in the open field.

❸ A running back such as the Saints' shifty Reggie Bush makes it quite hard for just one defender to bring him down, when the Highlight Stick is used to avoid the would-be tackler.

❹ We pick up 15 yards before finally being brought down.

Offensive Strategy

20

MISDIRECTION PLAYS

During the 2006 season, misdirection plays saw a huge improvement in how the run blocking sets up. It seemed like every other play was some type of misdirection run play online. In previous years, that just wasn't the case. Because offensive linemen did not block correctly, these types of run plays were not a factor in most players' offensive playbooks. In *Madden NFL 07*, the blocking was better than ever, making misdirection run plays a great choice when running the ball. Nothing much has changed in *Madden NFL 08*; the run blocking is just as effective as ever.

❶ In the screen above, notice that the running back starts off by going to the right. The middle linebacker mimics the running back by going in the same direction.

❷ The running back then changes direction and goes left.

❸ The middle linebacker is now a step or two behind and pretty much out of position to make a play.

❹ With the tight end and right guard pulling to the left, they get in front to block defenders downfield.

❺ Our running back has enough speed to turn the corner and run straight up the field for a big pick up.

DRAWS AND DELAYS

Draws and delays have been improved over the last few seasons. More and more players have been using them to run the ball, mainly because players on defense like to drop 11 men in pass coverage. That's another reason why draws and delays were used so much in *Madden NFL 07*. The offensive line will sell the pass to the defense, and defenders will abandon their run pursuit to come after the quarterback. Just as the defenders close in on the quarterback, he hands the ball off to a running back that squirts up the middle for a nice gain. In this section, we take a look at a few of our favorite misdirection and draw plays.

❶ Normally, we prefer quick hitting inside run plays, but if we catch our opponent dropping defensive linemen into pass coverage, we like to call a draw or two to keep him honest.

❷ In the second screen shot, the quarterback drops back as if he is going to pass. He quickly hands off to the running back.

❸ Once we take control of him, we dart through the open hole.

❹ We pick up 8 yards before being tackled by the opposing linebacker.

OFFENSE STRATEGY / **PASSING GAME**

To be successful in the passing game you must learn different pass route combinations, learn what the different pass coverage types are and how to attack them. In this section of book, we give you the keys to becoming a winning passer.

QB VISION CONE

For better or worse, the QB Vision is back again in *Madden NFL 08*, but this time, you don't have to use it unless you choose an All *Madden* level. Then it's a must. If you play on All Pro levels or lower, it does have a slight effect on how accurately the pass is thrown.

HOW TO **TURN IT ON**

Xbox Example

If you elect to have it on, it can be turned on in the following ways:

• Go to the Gameplay settings and turn it on.

• Turn it on during actual gameplay by switching the primary receiver before the snap (optional setting must be turned on).

• Pull ® after the ball is snapped (optional setting must be turned on).

• Press the Right Thumbstick ® or ® after the ball is snapped (optional setting must be turned on).

HOW THE **VISION CONE WORKS**

Xbox Example

Once the QB Vision Cone has been activated, there are two ways to move the cone around on the field. The first way: hold down ® and then press the receiver's pass icon to lock the passing cone on the receiver you want to pass to. The second way: press the Right Thumbstick (®) and direct the passing cone to the area you want to throw ball to. Of those two ways, the ® Trigger is the most accurate way to direct the Vision Cone.

Hopefully, this section will give you a clear-cut idea of which QB Vision Cone style suits you best. Keep in mind that in *Madden NFL 08*, you don't have to use the QB Vision Cone to pass the ball. If you want to go back to the conventional way of throwing the ball, you can. The biggest difference between the QB Vision Cone and the conventional way is that you get a slight accuracy boost when using the QB Vision Cone

RIGHT **TRIGGER**

Strengths

- Allows the user-controlled quarterback to lock onto a receiver without having to move the right thumbstick.

- Works better than the Right Thumbstick when the quarterback's Vision Cone is not very wide.

- Easier to move the quarterback while in the pocket.

- Lessens the learning curve for the Vision Cone.

Weaknesses

- Takes longer to throw the ball. The user must press the intended receiver's pass icon to lock on, and then press it again to make the pass.

- The user cannot get rid of the ball as quickly on short passes after the snap as compared to when the Right Thumbstick is used.

- Not much of a challenge for hard-core players.

RIGHT **THUMBSTICK**

Strengths

- Allows the user to scan the field for the open receiver without holding the Right Trigger.

- You have a better chance to beat the blitz because you don't have to push the pass receiver's pass icon twice to throw the ball.

- Works best with high awareness QBs because their cones are bigger.

Weaknesses

- Harder to lock onto a particular receiver.

- Quarterbacks with lower awareness ratings have smaller Vision Cones, thus making it almost impossible to establish a consistent passing game.

- Moving the quarterback while trying to aim the Vision Cone with the Right Thumbstick is very difficult.

- Too difficult for casual players.

QB VISION **TIPS**

1. Learn to use the Vision Cone to influence how safeties play pass coverage. Often, they will follow the cone. Lock onto a receiver, then, as the safeties go to cover the receiver, switch the cone to another receiver and make the throw. This is very effective when one receiver is running a post route and another receiver is running a corner. Lock onto the receiver running the post first, then once the safeties go cover him, switch to the receiver running the corner route and make the throw.

2. Hold the R Trigger (®) down the whole time that you are looking for the open receiver and reading the pass coverages. This allows you to select the receiver more quickly.

3. Different skill levels determine how big the QB's Vision Cone will be. When playing on Rookie level, the QB's Vision Cone is considerably bigger than on All *Madden*.

4. The QB Vision Cone does not affect short pass route such as flats, slants, drags, and quick outs. This means you can throw the ball to a receiver without the Vision Cone on them, without sacrificing too much accuracy.

5. You can center the QB Vision Cone before the snap by holding down the R Trigger (®) and pressing the snap button. Once you do this, there won't be a primary receiver highlighted when the ball is snapped.

6. When rolling out with the quarterback with the speed burst button pushed down, the Vision Cone will not lock onto a receiver. Instead, it goes toward the sideline. You need to release the speed burst button, then lock onto a receiver to make the throw. It takes a few seconds for the Vision Cone to move to your receiver. Those few seconds may not be enough time to make the throw without being sacked.

OFFENSIVE STRATEGY

QB PRECISION PLACEMENT

Since being introduced in *Madden NFL 06*, QB Precision Placement has been one of the better passing features added to the game because it allows the user to take control of the quarterback to throw more precise passes to the receivers.

There are four basic directions in which to throw the ball to a receiver when using the QB Precision Placement: high, low, outside, or inside. Each has its strengths and weaknesses. In this section, we will take a look at all four of them.

OFFENSIVE STRATEGY

High Pass

Press ↑ on the D-pad or Left Thumbstick.

Of the four basic directions, the high pass is the most used. It is still highly effective against man coverage, but not nearly as effective against zone.

Strengths

- Great against man coverage.
- Gets the ball over the top of the defensive linemen where they cannot knock it down.
- Good for throwing the deep lob pass.

Weaknesses

- Is not nearly as effective as it was in *Madden NFL 06* against zone coverage.
- Quarterbacks with low accuracy ratings tend to sail the ball over the top of receivers. If a defender is behind the receiver, there's a good chance the pass will be picked off.
- The receiver leaves himself hung out to dry when going up for the ball. In *Madden NFL 08*, defenders tend to pop receivers as they go up for the pass. This often knocks the ball loose, or worse yet, injures the receiver.

Low Pass

Press ↓ on the D-pad or Left Thumbstick.

Of the four basic directions, the low pass is the least used. That's not to say the low pass does not have its uses in *Madden NFL 08*, because it does; it's just a matter of knowing when to throw the low pass.

Strength

- Keeps the ball low where only the receiver can get it.

Weaknesses

- The quarterback needs a clear throwing lane to make the throw. If the low pass is made with a defensive lineman in the throwing lane, the pass may be knocked down.
- The receiver often has to come back to make the catch. For instance, if you need 8 yards for a first down, you may not get it if the receiver comes back 2 yards to catch the low pass.

Outside Pass

Press ← or → on the D-pad or Left Thumbstick.

On routes where receivers run toward the sideline or the flag, use the QB Precision Placement to throw the pass outside.

Strength

- Use the outside pass when throwing to receivers running routes toward the sideline.

Weakness

- Quarterbacks with low accuracy ratings tend to lead the receiver too much. Often, the receiver cannot get to the spot on time or a defender is in position to make the pick.

Inside Pass

Press ← or → the D-pad or Left Thumbstick.

The inside pass works the same as the outside pass when using the QB Precision Placement. The only difference is you lead the pass inside rather than to the outside.

Strength

- Use the inside pass when throwing to receivers running routes toward the middle.

Weakness

- Quarterbacks with low accuracy ratings tend to lead the receiver too far inside. Often, the receiver cannot get to the spot on time or a defender is in position to make the pick.

QB PRECISION PLACEMENT TIPS

1. On top of the four main precision passes that can be thrown, there are four others you may want to try:

    High Out, Low Out, High In, and **Low In**.

2. No matter which direction the ball is thrown when using the QB Precision Placement, the harder you press down in the direction you want the ball to go, the more the pass will lead the receiver.

SMART ROUTES

Smart routes are back again for another season. They allow the user to make a receiver's pass route shorter or longer depending on where the first down marker/goal line is on the field.

HOW SMART ROUTES WORK

To use a smart route, press the hot route button, the receiver's pass icon and then press ↓ on the R3 Button.

❶ Notice that in the first screen shot, we come out in the Singleback Trips Bunch Curls Attack from out the Bills playbook. Receiver Lee Evans lines up at the flanker in the cluster of the receivers on the right. He is running what we like to call a slant hook at about 7 yards depth. If we need more than 7 yards, we could smart route his pass route, so he can run it to the first down marker.

❷ We also make one more pre-snap adjustment, and that's to send Josh Reed on a streak. We do this to clear out room for Evans underneath.

❸ We throw the ball to Evans while he is running the slant portion of his route.

❹ We take control of him and make a user catch. We pick up 15 yards before being tackled. If we had not smart routed Evans, we might have only picked up 6 to 8 yards.

HOT ROUTES

Hot routes and playmaker pass routes have become a big part of every top player's offensive game plan around the country. You can run a complete offensive system based on hot routes and playmaker routes if you understand how each one works. A lot of players can run any type of offensive playbook, because they know how to use hot routes and playmaker routes effectively. These players can call just about any play and still move the ball efficiently.

Streak	Curl	Out	In

Hot Route Button + ↑ on the D-pad.	Hot Route Button + ↓ on the D-pad.	Hot Route Button + → on the D-pad.	Hot Route Button + ← on the D-pad.

Best for:
When the receiver is matched up with a slower defensive back in one-on-one coverage. Once the receiver gets a few steps on the defensive back, throw the ball.

Best for:
When the defense is playing any type of man coverage. Once the receiver curls back, throw a high pass to him.

Best for:
When the defense plays soft zone. Once the receiver makes his cut toward the sideline, make the throw. Don't be late on the throw or it may be picked off.

Best for:
When the defense plays any type of man coverage. Once the receiver breaks over the middle, make the throw.

OFFENSIVE STRATEGY

HOT **ROUTES**

Continued

Slant

PS2: Hot Route Button + L2 or R2 for RBs and TEs

Xbox: Hot Route Button + BLK or WHT button for RBs and TEs

Best for:
Blitzing defenses. Wait for the blitzing defender to vacate his area. Once he does, throw a high bullet pass if the receiver has inside position.

Pass Block

PS2: Hot Route Button + L1 or R1 for RBs and TEs

Xbox: Hot Route Button + L or R Trigger for RBs and

Best for:
When the defense has called a blitz.

Fade

PS2: Hot Route Button + Right Thumbstick ↑

Xbox: Hot Route Button + R

Best for:
Defenses that are in bump-n-run man coverage. Look for the receiver once he breaks down the field. If you take control of the receiver as the ball is coming down, you can jump high for the ball if timed right.

Drag

Both: Hot Route Button + Right Thumbstick → or ← depending on where the receiver is lined up.

Best for:
Defenses that are in bump-n-run man coverage. Once the receiver breaks the jam, he often gets inside position on the defender. Once he does, make the throw.

Flat

Both: Hot Route Button + Right Thumbstick → or ← depending on where the receiver is lined up.

Best for:
Defenses that are playing soft zone coverage. If no receivers are open deep, look for the receiver in the flat.

Screen

Both: Hot Route Button + Right Thumbstick ↓ when the receiver is running the play's primary pass route.

Best for:
Defenses that are playing soft zone coverage. If no receivers are open deep, wait a few seconds and throw to the receiver running the screen.

HOT ROUTES **TIPS**

1. Use hot routes to set up different route combinations. For instance, say you call a play from the Singleback Normal Slot. The split end runs a 10 yard curl route and the slot runs a corner route. By hot routing the split end on a streak, you have changed the route from a curl/slant to a curl/streak.

2. Many top players around the country use hot routes as one of the primary means to attack through the air. Learn how to use them effectively. It will help make your passing offense that much more potent.

SLIDE PROTECTION

Slide protection returns again to *Madden NFL 08*. Here is a quick overview of how it works. Pressing the slide protection button allows you to adjust your pass protection schemes on the fly. Slide protection was put in the game to help counter the blitz in the passing game, but it can be used in the run game also. It may not always be effective, but in some run plays it can help create running lanes for the ball carrier. Below we take a look at the four protection adjustments that can be made.

Slide Protection Out

Press the slide protection button, and then press the D-pad or Left Thumbstick ↑.

Strengths

- Puts the offensive line in a better position to counter the defensive line when it has been spread out.
- Good to use to respond when defense is showing blitz from the outside because the offensive line protects out.

Weaknesses

- The quarterback is at greater risk of being sacked from the inside pass rush.
- If the defense overloads the middle of the offensive line, the line won't be able to block all the pass rushers.

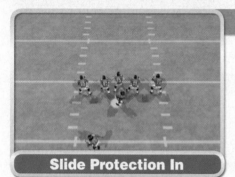

Slide Protection In

Press the slide protection button, and then press the D-pad or Left Thumbstick ↓.

Strengths

- Puts the offensive line in a better position to counter the defensive line when it has been pinched in.
- If the defense overloads the middle of the offensive line, the offensive linemen can block all the pass rushers because they slide protect in.

Weaknesses

- The quarterback is at greater risk of being sacked from the outside pass rush.
- If the defense overloads the outside on both sides to blitz, the offensive linemen won't be able to block all the pass rushers because they slide protect in.

Slide Protection Left

Press the slide protection button, and then press the D-pad or Left Thumbstick ←.

Strengths

- Puts the offensive line in a better position to counter the blitz when the defense overloads the left side of the offensive line.
- Use if you plan on rolling the quarterback out to the right. It helps keep the backside pass rush off the quarterback.

Weaknesses

- The quarterback is not protected from the right side of the defensive line if the defense brings the blitz
- If the defense puts multiple defenders on the right side of the offensive line, don't use the slide protection left.

Slide Protection Right

Press the slide protection button, and then press the D-pad or Left Thumbstick →.

Strengths

- Puts the offensive line in a better position to counter the blitz when the defense overloads the right side of the offensive line.
- Use if you plan on rolling the quarterback out to the left. It helps keep the backside pass rush off the quarterback.

Weaknesses

- The quarterback is not protected from the left side of the defensive line if the defense brings the blitz.
- If the defense puts multiple defenders on the left side of the offensive line, don't use the slide protection right.

OFFENSIVE STRATEGY

27

OFFENSIVE STRATEGY

PASS ROUTES

To be successful when throwing the ball, you need to know what each pass route's strengths and weaknesses are. The best way to learn pass routes is to spend time in practice mode (the lab). Run plays over and over just like a real quarterback does during training camp and through film room study. In this section of the book, we take a look at some of the different pass routes you will see in the game, and teach you how to use them to perfection.

SHORT PASS ROUTES

Teams that run the West Coast Offense throw a lot of short pass routes. The quarterback must be able to make good reads and quick decisions. If he can do that, he can steadily move the offense down the field with high percentage passes and control the clock. Yards after the catch (YAC) are the key to running the short passing game. Once the receiver makes the catch, he can turn a short pass into a huge gain by using his speed and agility to pick up yardage. In this section, we look at a few essential short pass routes that we feel are important to learn when running the short passing game.

Flat

Whether it's a running back, tight end, or receiver who is running it, the flat route is one of more reliable pass routes in the entire game.

Short Slant

The short (quick) slant is highly effective against both man and zone coverage. If the pass is timed perfectly to the intended receiver, it can be one of the most electrifying pass routes.

Curl

Of all the short pass routes in the game, the curl route is the one you want to learn first. Against man coverage (even if bump-n-run is called), this is the most effective short pass route you can call.

Drag

If your opponent likes to play bump-n-run man as his base coverage, then try running some plays that have a receiver running a drag route.

Pivot

This is another route that works well against man coverage. The receiver will first break towards the middle, then pivot and break back towards the sideline. The mesh concept uses this route.

Dig

The dig (quick in) is a rock-solid pass route to call against any type of man coverage. The receiver runs straight up the field about five yards and then cuts toward the middle.

Quick Out

Any team that runs the West Coast Offense will run this route several times during the game. Great route to call if the defense is playing normal or loose man coverage.

Screen

A lot of teams that run the West Coast Offense use the screen to beat the blitz. The Packers and Eagles both do an excellent job of setting up screens to their backs to pick up yardage.

Slant Hook

This short pass route is also highly effective against both man and zone coverage, because this route has two points where the ball can be thrown to the receiver.

Swing

Swing routes are an extension of toss run plays. The running back breaks wide out of the backfield.

MEDIUM PASS ROUTES

Now that you have a better understanding of how some of the short pass routes work in *Madden NFL 08*, it's time to open things up a little bit more by looking at three medium pass routes that will help you improve your pass game. These pass routes take a little longer to develop than the shorter pass routes we've just shown, so you may need an extra pass blocker if the defense sends the blitz.

Comebacks

There are several plays in the game where the receiver drives 10-12 yards down the field, then comes back toward the quarterback about 2 yards. These pass routes are known as comebacks. They work best against man coverage or soft zone coverage.

Cross

One of the better medium pass routes in the game is the crossing route. It is most effective when two receivers run crossing routes from opposite directions, especially if the defense plays man coverage.

Post

There are two types of post routes in this game: the post and the deep post. The post route is a good route to run with a receiver lined up in the slot or a tight end.

DEEP PASS ROUTES

Short and medium routes may be the cornerstone of your passing game, but the deep ball is what gets the fans out of their seats. With the improved defensive back play over the past few years, just running streaks won't do. You have to be a little more creative if you want to complete the long ball. Using QB Precision Placement, stick control, route combinations, and mismatches will enable you to go deep.

Corner

If you have been playing this game over the past several years, you know that corner routes are the most efficient pass routes in the game. Some players still base their entire offense around this one route.

Streak

Of all the deep pass routes in the game, this one may be used most because of the home run threat. It's also used to clear out room for underneath pass routes.

Fade

Over the last few years the fade hot route route has probably been the most-used deep route besides the streak and corner routes. This route is really effective if you have solid stick control.

Out 'n Ups

Another deep pass route that has caught fire with top players who played in the *Madden* Challenge and online over the last few years is the Out-n-Ups. In conjunction with the pump fake, this route is highly effective against zone coverage because it often gets the safeties to bite, leaving the receiver open once he breaks up the field.

PATTERN COMBINATIONS

Route combinations are the foundation of a solid passing game. Without route combinations, defense would be able to shut down most passing attacks. That's why it is so important to know which pass route combinations work and don't work against different pass coverages.

WHAT ARE PATTERN COMBINATIONS?

Pattern combinations are based on a passing tree that all offensive coordinators have in their playbooks. All of the trees use the same basic numbering system; even-numbered routes are directed toward the middle of the field, while odd-numbered routes head for the sidelines. The tree allows the offensive coordinator and quarterback to communicate pass plays to the rest of the skills position players. Without the tree, there would be communication problems.

PASSING TREE ROUTE NAMES

Number	Route Name
1	Quick Out
3	Deep Out
5	Flag Route
7	Shoot Route
9	Streak Route

Number	Route Name
2	Slant Route
4	Drag Route
6	Curl Route
8	Post Route

☐ Odd ▨ Even

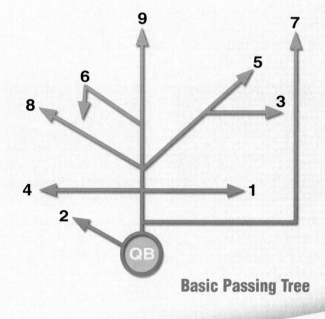

Basic Passing Tree

THREE POPULAR *MADDEN NFL 08* **ROUTE COMBINATIONS**

In this section of the book, we are going to take a look at three of the more popular pass route combinations you will find top players using in *Madden NFL 08*.

Streak / Corner

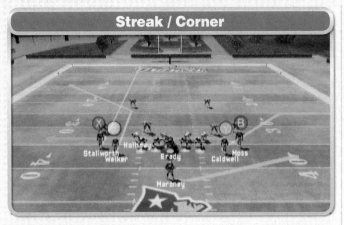

The Streak/Corner pattern combination is another one that many top players use to beat most zone coverages in the game.

In the screen shot above, we hot route Donté Stallworth on a streak. Slot receiver Wes Welker is running a corner route.

❶ Once the ball is snapped, we read Cover 3 coverage by watching the free safety rotate over the deep middle of the field.

❷ The right corner back and free safety go cover Stallworth running the streak.

❸ This allows Welker to get open once he breaks to the corner.

❹ We take control of Welker and make the catch for a 25 yard pick-up.

Flat / Curl

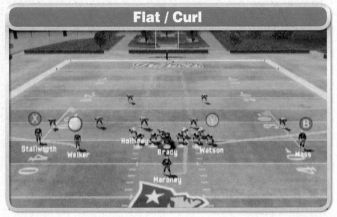

The Flat Curl pattern combination is the most simple one you will find in this game. It's a very simple run and read. Notice that on both sides of the field we have a flat/curl pattern combination.

We are going to concentrate on the one with Patriots' tight end Ben Watson and flanker Randy Moss. Watson is running the flat, while Moss is running the curl.

❶ Once the ball is snapped, we read the pass coverage; the safeties show a Cover 2 shell look. The left corner back plays flat. The pass coverage is Cover 2 zone.

❷ This tells us that Watson will be covered in the flat by the left corner back, and we must shift our focus to Moss.

❸ We could throw a bullet pass between the left corner back and strong safety to Moss before he curls back.

❹ Or we can play it safe and wait for him to curl back. The key to making this pass is to throw to the outside, and away from the linebacker dropping back in a hook zone near Moss. It's a tight passing window, but we still complete the pass to Moss for a 10 yard pick-up.

Post Corner / Streak

The Post Corner/Streak pattern combination is another one that can be used to attack Cover 2 and Cover 3 zone coverage. Notice there is no receiver running a streak route at this point.

❶ We take control of Patriots' running back Laurence Maroney and motion him out to the left so he lines up in the slot. We then hot route him on a streak. We now have our Post Corner/Streak pattern combination.

❷ Once the ball is snapped, Maroney will force the free safety to cover him because he is the receiver running the deepest route on left side of the field.

❸ Once Stallworth breaks to the corner, we throw him a high bullet pass.

❹ We make the catch and pick up 20 yards.

OTHER **COMBINATIONS** FOR PRACTICE MODE

Fade / Streak

Great against Cover 2 and Cover 3 zone coverage. Come out in the I- Form Normal. Hot route the tight end on a streak and hot route the flanker on a fade route. Look for the flanker deep down the sideline.

Dig / Streak / Flat

Works well against any zone coverage. Come in the Single-back Normal. Hot route the split end on a dig route, the slot on a streak. Motion the running back to the left and hot route him on a flat route. Once the ball is snapped, look for the running back in the flat first; if he is not open, look for the split end running the dig route.

Streak / Streak / Streak / Streak / Flat

Run this against any zone. Come out in Shotgun 4WR. Hot route the four receivers on streaks. Send the running back in motion to one side. Hot Route him on a flat route. Once the ball is snapped, read the coverage. If it's Cover 2 or Cover 3 zone, look to go deep. The numbers favor the offense. If it's Cover 4, look to dump the pass off to the running back in the flat.

PATTERN COMBINATIONS TIP

❶ The best way to learn how to set up pattern combinations is to go into practice mode and try different pass plays against different zone defenses. Use the default design of the play and see how pattern combination works. If it doesn't work, try adding hot routes and then try again. That is quickest way to learn different pattern combinations in *Madden NFL 08.*

OFFENSIVE STRATEGY

PULLING RUNNING BACK ROUTES

In *Madden NFL 07*, there was an undocumented way to pull pass running back routes from play to play. Many of the top players in the EA Sports *Madden* Challenge knew how to do this, but most casual players did not. What makes pulling running back routes so useful is that it allows you to pretty much take any running back pass route from one and move it over to another.

HOW IT WORKS

❶ Before getting on the field, you will want to add a play(s) of your choice to your offensive audibles. For instance, for this example, we put the Strong I Normal WR Option in our offensive audibles.

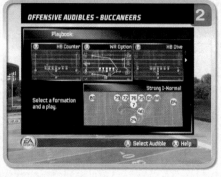

❷ Next, we come out on the field in the Strong I Normal TE Option. Notice that the Buccaneers' running back Carnell Williams is running an angle route. We want to pull that route from the Strong I Normal TE Option into the Strong I Normal WR Option.

❸ To do this, we first audible into the Strong I Normal WR Option. We hot route receivers Michael Clayton and Joey Galloway on streaks. This step is optional. It has no effect on pulling running back routes. We just do it to clear room for tight end Anthony Becht running the crossing route and for Williams.

❹ To actually pull Williams's angle route, we press the hot route button, and then up on the on the Dpad. We then repeat this same step. We now have pulled Williams's angle route from the TE Option to the WR Option. Also notice that we pulled the fullback's delayed flat route.

❺ Once the ball is snapped, we look for Becht or Williams over the middle.

❻ We make the catch while in control of Williams for an 8 yard pick-up.

PULLING RUNNING BACK ROUTES TIP

① There are some running back routes you cannot pull from play to play. You will want to spend some time in practice mode learning which routes can and cannot be pulled.

OFFENSIVE STRATEGY

CALL PLAY ACTION FROM ANY PASS PLAY

Another undocumented gem that was added to the offensive side of the ball in *Madden NFL 07* was the ability to call play action from just about any pass play in the game. This made defending the offense that much harder because if the human player knew what he was doing, the player on defense couldn't just sit back on defense and defend the pass. He had respect the run because he never knew if play action was going to be used or not.

HOW CALLING PLAY ACTION FROM PASS PLAY

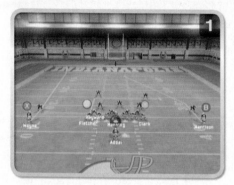

❶ In the first screen shot, we come out in the Singleback Deuce Ace TE Drag out of the Colts' playbook. Peyton Manning's go-to guy Marvin Harrison is lined up at flanker and is running a deep post route. Notice that there is no play action in this play.

❷ To turn Singleback Deuce Ace TE Drag into a play action play, press the hot route button, and then press up on the D-pad. The play now has play action in it. Notice that running back Joseph Addai is now running a pass route.

❸ Once the ball is snapped, Manning play fakes to Addai.

❹ After the play fake, we take control of Manning and start looking down the field.

❺ We spot Harrison deep down the field with one on one coverage, so we throw him the ball.

❻ We take control of Harrison, make the catch, and go in for the score.

CALL PLAY ACTION FROM ANY PASS PLAY TIP

❶ **There are situations where you cannot call play action from any pass play. If the formation does not have a play action play in it to begin with, then you won't be able to call play action. For instance, let's say you call a play from the Singleback 4WR Flex, but there is no actual play action play in the formation. You could not change any of the pass plays from that formation into play action.**

OFFENSIVE STRATEGY

UNDERSTANDING PASS COVERAGES 101

COVER 1

Cover 1 has one of the safeties dropping to the deep middle of the field as the ball is snapped and playing zone coverage. He is responsible for guarding the deep middle and providing assistance to the corners on deep sideline routes. The majority of the time, the FS acts as the center fielder unless he is involved in double coverage on the left side. The corner backs and the other safety play man-to-man coverage.

The key to reading the Cover 1 defense is to read the safeties after the snap of the ball. If one of them goes to the deep middle, and the other plays man, then the pass coverage is Cover 1. Another name you may hear thrown out at you is Man Free, which is just another way to say Cover 1.

Strengths

- With man-to-man all around, this technique provides tight coverage with help to the deep middle. The SS can cheat up, giving this play strong run support to his side. Usually, one of the linebackers is free to blitz, creating a four to five man rush.

Weaknesses

- There is very little underneath help, so crossing routes & pick routes can be very effective against this scheme. If the deep safety bites on play action there is a good chance for a deep gain. The corners get very little help on out routes in this defense.

COVER 2

In Cover 2, both safeties will drop deep as the ball is snapped and play zone coverage. They can provide assistance to the corners on deep sideline routes. The coverage underneath can be zone or man. For instance, the Bears like to play a lot of Tampa 2. This type of Cover 2 coverage has the safeties playing 2 deep coverage, while the defenders underneath play hook zones and the flats; this is except for the middle linebacker, who actually drops back deep over the middle to decrease the weakness of a traditional Cover 2 zone defense.

2 Man Under is another type of Cover 2 coverage, but this time it can have up to five defenders playing man coverage underneath. A lot of top players use this coverage as their base defensive scheme.

Strengths

- This coverage scheme is strong against the short passing game, as it allows for up to 5 underneath zones if desired. The CB can move up and jam the receivers at the line, disrupting the timing of the play. The short flats areas can be pretty well locked down, additionally.

Weaknesses

- This scheme can be vulnerable against fades and deep middle routes. A post corner route can also cause trouble for this scheme. Strong side run support is weaker than in the Cover 1, as the SS must play the pass first. You need to have strong defensive line that can get pressure on the QB. If the defensive line cannot get pressure, average college quarterbacks will pick the Cover 2 apart.

COVER 3

When Cover 3 pass coverage is called, three defensive backs will drop deep as the ball is snapped, and play zone coverage. This can be both corners and one of the safeties, or both safeties with one corner. For most players that like to call zone coverage, Cover 3 is the one most used. This is mainly because there are several plays in the game that have Cover 3 coverage, but it also brings the heat on the quarterback. You will find several zone blitz schemes that have Cover 3 coverage.

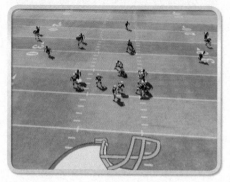

Strengths

• Three men in deep zones help cover the entire width of the field. You can get good strong side run support if the SS is not involved in the 3 deep coverage. You have the ability to rush either a safety or CB at times and still get good deep coverage.

Weaknesses

• Flood routes to either side can be difficult to defend with this scheme. If the defense attacks with 4 players vertically, you can get out-manned at the point of attack. Flats attack to the side with the CB in deep coverage, and in routes over the middle are effective against this scheme. You will often hear the words 3 Deep Zone coverage associated with the Cover 3 defense.

COVER 4

In a Cover 4 pass defense (also known as quarters), all 4 defensive backs drop deep with the instructions to let no one get behind them. Also known as a four across, this defense blankets the entire deep part of the field. The linebackers & nickel or dime backs can play either short zones or man-to-man, depending on the play call.

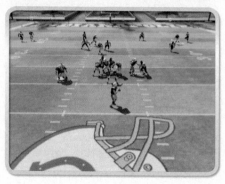

Strengths

• This defense provides excellent deep coverage. Against 2 WR sets, the safeties can provide double coverage on the deep routes. The corners can jam at the line knowing they have help from the safeties over the top.

Weaknesses

• The flats areas to either side are vulnerable in this scheme. Safeties can be fooled by play action causing a break down deep. Sending multiple receivers to one side can nullify the benefits of over the top double coverage. Screen passes to the receivers also work against the Cover 4. The only pass rush is from the defensive line. The QB may have plenty of time in the pocket to pick apart the defense. Your best bet is to run it on 3rd and long passing situations.

DEFENSIVE STRATEGY

Note: All control commands are preformed with the Xbox Controller.

INDIVIDUAL DEFENSE HOT ROUTE

Since being introduced in *Madden NFL 05*, Individual Defensive Hot Routes have been the main way for top players to play defense. The reason for this is most of the top players will come out in a handful of defenses, and use Individual Defensive Hot Routes and make adjustments based on what their opponent is doing on the offensive side of the ball. For example, many of the top players will come out in some type of 2 Man Under and playmaker both defensive ends to play buzz zones. Sure, there is only a two man rush from the defensive tackles, but the coverage is pretty tight all over the field. The hope is that one of the defensive tackles will get to the quarterback. Some may even sub defensive ends in at

defensive tackle, so they can get a better pass rush on the quarterback. A good example of this would be to come out in Dime Normal 2 Man Under, sub the two defensive ends in at the two defensive tackle spots, and then package in both two linebackers at defensive end. This is actually a pretty effective defense. Some top players will go so far as to drop all their defenders into pass coverage. Some players call this cheese and others say it is part of football. There are counters to this type of scheme, but it still can be hard to find an open receiver down the field. In this section of the book, we'll take a look at all of the Individual Defensive Hot Routes, including a new one that has been added (Smart Zone).

Flat (Light Blue)

While the defender is selected, press → on the Right Thumbstick.

If your opponent is abusing the flats, hot route a defender to the flat to take away his bread and butter.

When to use:

- Use it to stop the outside run. Often defenders get out quicker because their assignment is to play the flats.

- When the offense is abusing the flats with running backs or tight ends. Play-makering a defensive end to play the flats can be an effective strategy, but it takes away from your pass rush.

- Use it to stop athletic quarterbacks from rolling out of the pocket. If the quarterback tries to take off, the defender covering the flat is normally in position to make a play before any damage is done.

When not to use:

- If the offense is pounding the rock inside.

- If another defender is already defending the flats. There is no reason to have two defenders covering the same area of the field.

- If your opponent tends to run more of a vertical offense and does not use the flats.

Curl Flat Zone (Purple)

While the defender is selected, press → twice on the Right Thumbstick.

It's a good choice against corner routes run by slot receivers. The curl flat zone is probably the most-used playmaker adjustment.

When to use:

- Against corner routes, use the curl flat zone defensive hot route in conjunction with shading safeties toward the sideline. This one-two combination is

very effective in stopping corner and post corner routes.

- It is not as effective as the flats coverage defensive hot route, but the curl flat zone can be used to stop passes to running backs and tight ends in the flat. Normally the receiver will make the catch but not pick up any extra yardage because the defender can close in a hurry to make the tackle.

- If you are playing Cover 2 zone, use it to put a defender in between the cornerback playing the flat and the safety playing the deep half of the field. There's a soft spot in the Cover 2 zone coverage where the receiver is open between the cornerback and safety. By assigning a defender to cover the curl flat zone, you can take away that soft spot. There are a few defenses in the game where this is already done for you, such as the Nickel 3-3-5 Cover 2.

When not to use:

- If your opponent likes to run the ball inside, don't make this adjustment. By calling curl flat zones, you put the defenders out of position to stop the run.

- If the defense you called has the defenders already dropping into the curl flat zones, there is no need to make this call.

- If your opponent likes to run drags, crosses, ins, slants, and deep post routes, stay away from this adjustment.

Blitz (Orange Arrow)

While the defender is selected, press ↓ once on the Right Thumbstick.

Adding an extra defender to blitz can be beneficial to stop the run or to bring the heat on the quarterback. A lot of top players create heat by hot routing a defender or two to blitz on the same side, while dropping players into zone on the other side. Usually the player controlling the quarterback gets confused, and is either sacked or forces a pass into tight coverage where a defender picks off the pass.

When to use:

- If the offense is showing a run up the middle or to the outside when you do not have a defense called to properly stop the play.

- Use it to overload one side of the defensive line. Sending more pass rushers than the offensive line can protect against often results in the quarterback having to throw quicker than he may want. This can lead to interceptions and/or sacks.

- The defensive line can also be hot routed to blitz. Hot routing linemen to blitz changes the way they pass rush the quarterback.

When not to use:

- Do not blitz a defender when he is supposed to be covering a specific area of the field, unless you have another defender to take on that vacated space.

- Do not blitz if your opponent likes to go max protect. You will just get picked up and leave holes in your secondary.

QB Spy (Orange Circle)

While the defender is selected, press ← once on the R Thumbstick.

Ever since the defensive Quarterback Spy hot route was put in the game in 2005, players on offense have had a harder time taking off and running with the quarterback to pick up yardage.

When to use:

- Use it to counter against athletic quarterbacks who like to take off and run the ball.

- Use it to defend against drag and crossing routes over the middle. Even though the defender is spying the quarterback, he is often in position to guard against passes over the middle.

When not to use:

- Do not spy the quarterback if he is a pure pocket passer, unless you plan to use it to stop drags and crossing routes.

- Do not put a defender in QB Spy if he is in man coverage on a receiver, unless it's a fullback.

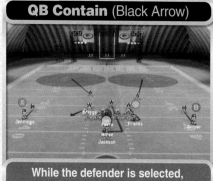

QB Contain (Black Arrow)

While the defender is selected, press ↓ twice on the R Thumbstick.

Having containment on the quarterback forces him to think twice about taking off. The defender will not rush the quarterback initially unless the quarterback takes off out of the pocket.

When to use:

- Use it to keep the quarterback in the pocket.

- Use it as a counter to players who step up and then step back in the pocket with the quarterback.

When not to use:

- If the offense is running the ball with a halfback or fullback, this can hurt your defense.

DEFENSIVE STRATEGY

Hook Zone (Yellow Circle)

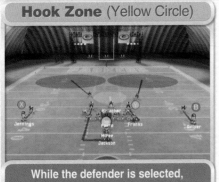

While the defender is selected, press ↑ once on the Right Thumbstick.

This option allows any defender to play hook zones. Drop defensive linemen and linebackers over the short to mid middle of the field to take away circle and angle routes run by running backs. Playmaker a safety to play a hook zone to take away quick slants and make your opponent pay for not reading the safeties after the snap.

When to use:

- Use the hook zone coverage to drop a defensive lineman into the area vacated by the blitzing linebacker. This lets you rush a quicker linebacker without sacrificing too much pass coverage underneath. This is really effective when dropping a defensive tackle over the middle while you attack the outside of the line with your middle linebacker.

- Drop multiple defensive linemen inside the red zone to take away short passes over the middle.

- Drop linebackers into hook zones when playing man coverage on the outside.

- Often your opponent will read man and look to throw inside, where a linebacker is waiting to pick off the pass.

- Use hook zones to stop drags and crossing routes.

When not to use:

- If your opponent tends to avoid the short middle of the field, then this call is a waste. The CPU AI will attack you if you leave the middle open, but not every human opponent will. If that's the case, there is no point in covering the middle; instead, use your defenders to cover routes on the outside.

- Do not use in third and long situations or at end of half or game situations.

- Chances are that your opponent will not look to throw passes underneath, knowing he or she won't pick up enough yardage.

Smart Zone (Red Circle)

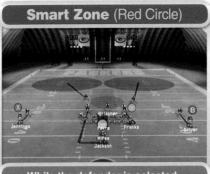

While the defender is selected, press ↑ twice on the Right Thumbstick.

The Smart Zone is a brand new defensive individual hot route that has been added to *Madden NFL 08*. It drops a defender back in zone coverage near the first down marker. This makes it more difficult for the opposing quarterback to throw a pass near the first down maker.

When to use:

- In crucial third and fourth down situations when the offense must pass to pick up the first down.

- Use when the offense is near the goal line and must pass to get in. Instead of the defender(s) dropping back to the first down marker, they will drop back near the goal line.

When not to use:

- In short yardage running situations. You don't want your linebackers dropping, you want them to go forward to plug up running lanes.

- In end half or end of game situations where the offense must throw past the first down marker to score.

Deep Zone (Dark Blue)

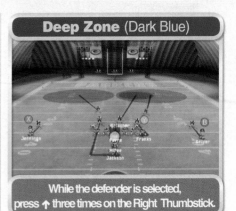

While the defender is selected, press ↑ three times on the Right Thumbstick.

Use this defensive playmaker hot route to take away the deep ball. Any defender can be hot routed to drop into the deep zones of the field.

When to use:

- Against players who like to use the long ball as their main source to move the ball down the field.

- In third and long situations when offense has no other alternative to pick up a first down.

- When you have a defensive back covering deep, but without having to play man coverage. Works best when your defensive back is slower than the receiver across from him.

When not to use:

- Does not do a good job at covering underneath pass routes such as quick outs, ins, slants, curls, hitches, hooks, and screens.

DEFENSIVE AUDIBLE SHIFTS

One of the great things about playing defense is the ability to change how the defenders line up before the snap or who they cover after the snap. Defensive shifts are not new to the game, but they are still just as effective as they were when first put into the game. Here is a breakdown of all the defensive shifts in the game.

Spread Defensive Line

Press ↓ on the Defensive Line Audible button and then press ↑ on the D-pad or Left Thumbstick to spread the defensive line out.

Strengths

- Gives the defensive ends to get a better pass rush angle on the quarterback.
- Puts defensive ends in better position to stop the outside run.
- Does a good job at keeping athletic quarterbacks from taking off out of the pocket.

Weaknesses

- Not very strong against the inside run.
- Must have fast defensive ends to maximize pass rush from the outside angle.

Pinch Defensive Line

Press ↓ on the Defensive Line Audible button and then press ↓ on the D-pad or Left Thumbstick to pinch the defensive line in.

Strengths

- Stout against the inside runs.
- Better pass rush up the gut.
- Creates inside gaps for the linebackers to shoot through.

Weaknesses

- Defensive ends are limited in their pass rush.
- Does not contain the athletic quarterback.
- Defensive linemen cannot defend the outside run as well.

Shift Defensive Line Left

Press ↓ on the Defensive Line Audible button and then press ← on the D-pad or Left Thumbstick to shift the defensive line left.

Strengths

- Generates pressure from the weak side by overloading the offensive line.
- Puts defensive linemen in better position to defend against weak side runs.
- Decent against the inside run.

Weaknesses

- Pressure from the strong side is not as intense.
- Defensive linemen are not in good position to defend against strong side runs.

Shift Defensive Line Right

Press ↓ on the Defensive Line Audible button and then press → on the D-pad or Left Thumbstick to shift the defensive line right.

Strengths

- Creates pressure from the strong side by overloading the offensive line.
- Puts defensive linemen in better position to defend against strong side runs.
- Decent against inside runs.

Weaknesses

- Pressure from the opposite side is not as effective.
- Defensive linemen are not in good position to defend against weak side runs.

PLAYMAKER STICK DEFENSIVE LINE SHIFT AUDIBLES

Crash Out

To have the defensive line crash out, press the Defensive Line Audible button, and then press ↑ on the Right Thumbstick.

Crash In

To have the defensive line crash in, press the Defensive Line Audible button, and then press ↓ on the Right Thumbstick.

Crash Left

To have the defensive line crash left, press the Defensive Line Audible button, and then press ← on the Right Thumbstick.

Crash Right

To have the defensive line crash right, press the Defensive Line Audible button, and then press → on the Right Thumbstick.

DEFENSIVE STRATEGY

DEFENSIVE STRATEGY

LB AUDIBLE SHIFTS

Pinch Linebackers In

Press ↓ on the LB Audible button and then press ↓ on the D-pad or Left Thumbstick to spread the linebackers out.

Strengths

- Puts linebackers in a better position to be able to stop the inside run.
- Puts linebackers in better position to put pressure on the quarterback up the middle.

Weaknesses

- Linebackers do not defend against the outside run as well.
- Linebackers are not in position to defend multiple receiver sets.
- Not as well-suited to contain the athletic quarterback.

Spread Linebackers Out

Press ↓ on the LB Audible button and then press ↑ on the D-pad or Left Thumbstick to spread the linebackers out.

Strengths

- The outside linebackers have better pass rush angles to get pressure on the QB.
- Allows outside linebackers to take better angles at stopping the outside run.
- Spreading the linebackers out puts them closer to cover the slot receiver.
- Puts linebackers in better position to keep the athletic quarterback in the pocket.

Weaknesses

- Puts the OLBs out of position to stop the inside run.

Shift Linebackers Left

Press ↓ on the LB Audible button and then press ← on the D-pad or Left Thumbstick to spread the linebackers out.

Strengths

- The right outside linebacker has an improved pass rush angle to put pressure on the quarterback.
- Good for stopping the weak side toss and pitch plays.
- Does a decent job against inside runs.

Weaknesses

- Weak against the inside run.
- LOLBs pass rush angle is somewhat sacrificed.
- Weak at containing athletic quarterbacks to the strong side.

Shift Linebackers Right

Press ↓ on the LB Audible button and then press → on the D-pad or Left Thumbstick to spread the linebackers out.

Strengths

- The left outside linebacker has an improved pass rush angle to the quarterback.
- Good at stopping the strong side toss.
- Does a decent job against inside runs.

Weaknesses

- Weak against the inside run.
- ROLBs pass rush angle is somewhat sacrificed.
- Weak at containing athletic quarterbacks to the weak side.

PLAYMAKER STICK LINEBACKER SHIFT AUDIBLES

ROLB & LOLB Blitz

To send both the ROLB and LOLB on a blitz, press the LB Audible button and then press ← on the Right Thumbstick. Again, press the LB Audible, and this time press → on the Right Thumbstick. The ROLB and LOLB will now blitz. This is faster than individually selecting the linebackers and assigning them to blitz.

LOLB Blitz, Hook Zone

To have the LOLB blitz with the MLB and ROLB dropping back in hook zones underneath, press the LB Audible button, and then press ↑ on the Right Thumbstick. Next, press the LB Audible again, and then press → on the Right Thumbstick. The LOLB will now blitz, while the MLB and ROLB play hook zones underneath.

ROLB Blitz, Hook Zone

To have the ROLB blitz with the MLB and LOLB dropping back in hook zones underneath, press the LB Audible button, and then press ↑ on the Right Thumbstick. Next, press the LB Audible again, and then press ← on the Right Thumbstick.

All LB Blitz

To send all the linebackers on a blitz, press the LB Audible button and then press ↓ on the Right Thumbstick.

All LB Hook Zone

To put all linebackers into hook zones, press the LB Audible and ↑ on the Right Thumbstick.

COVERAGE AUDIBLE SHIFTS

Loose Coverage

Press the Coverage Audible button and then press ↑ on the D-pad or Left Thumbstick.

Strengths
- Puts the corner backs and safeties in a deeper alignment before the snap to be in better position to defend against the deep pass.
- Corner backs that play loose coverage are less likely to be blocked on outside runs.

Weaknesses
- Quick outs, slants, hitches, and WR screens work well against this type of coverage.

Tight Coverage

Press the Coverage Audible button and then press ↓ on the D-pad or Left Thumbstick.

Strengths
- Defensive backs jam receivers at the line of scrimmage.
- Impedes the timing between the quarterback and receiver on routes such as slants.

Weaknesses
- Defensive backs can easily be beaten deep unless they have a good acceleration rating.
- Not as good against run support.

Crowd the Box

Press the Coverage Audible button and then press ← on the D-pad or Left Thumbstick.

Strengths
- Enhances inside run support.
- Provides opportunities for safeties to put pressure on the quarterback by shooting through the gaps.

Weaknesses
- Weak against outside runs.
- Safeties are suspect against the deep pass.
- Safeties tend to bite on play action more often than if in normal or loose coverage.

Man Shift Coverage Audible

Press the Coverage Audible button and then press → on the D-pad or Left Thumbstick.

Strengths
- Puts the defensive backs in better position to cover receivers in the man coverage. Also applies to LBs.
- Quicker to use than manually moving defenders into place.

Weaknesses
- A good human player on offense will be able to pre-read pass coverage assignments based on how defenders line up.

Safeties Shading the Sidelines

Press the Coverage Audible button and then press ↑ on the D-pad or Right Thumbstick.

Strengths
- Works against corner and post corner routes.
- Use it to defend against streak and fade routes run by the outside receivers.

Weaknesses
- Deep post routes can exploit this type of coverage.
- Seam routes run by tight ends can be deadly against this type of coverage.

Safeties Shading the Deep Middle

Press the Coverage Audible button and then press ↓ on the D-pad or Right Thumbstick.

Strengths
- Works best at defending deep post routes.
- Defends the deep middle of the field against seam routes by tight ends.

Weaknesses
- Corner and post corner routes will exploit this type of coverage.
- Safeties will have to make up more ground to cover streaks run by the outside receivers.

Safeties Left Deep Zone

Press the Coverage Audible button and then press ← on the D-pad or Right Thumbstick.

Strengths
- The safeties cheat to the left side of the deep zone.
- If your opponent has an elite receiver lined up on the left side of the field, shade your safeties to his side. This will force the quarterback to look to the other side to find an open receiver.

Weaknesses
- Coverage is sacrificed on the deep right zone.

Safeties Right Deep Zone

Press the Coverage Audible button and then press → on the D-pad or Right Thumbstick.

Strengths
- Cheats the safeties to the right side of the deep zone.
- Shade your safeties to your opponents's elite receiver side of the field. This forces the quarterback to look to the other side to find an open receiver.

Weaknesses
- Coverage is sacrificed on the deep left zone.

DEFENSIVE STRATEGY

DEFENDING THE RUN

We cannot get far defensively if we cannot defend the run. When we cannot stop the run, a host of other things goes awry. We constantly find ourselves guessing what the offense is doing, rather than anticipating intelligently. A strong rushing attack opens up the door for the play action game, leading to a host of big plays. In this tutorial, we will look at defending the inside run, the outside run, and defending counters and the draw play.

DEFENDING THE INSIDE RUN

4-3 Normal

4-3 Under

46 Normal

This is the base 4-3 that most teams use. The structure of this front is weak because of two interior bubbles, as well as the off tackle hole.

This is a stronger 4-3 front that only has one interior bubble. It is also good against the off tackle runs.

This is a version of the 46 front. It brings one safety down into the box to create an eight man front. Three interior bubbles lie in this front.

46 Bear

This is the version of the 46 created by legendary defensive coordinator Buddy Ryan that led the Chicago Bears to an NFL Title.

3-4 Normal

3-4 Over

3-4 Solid

This is the base front for the 3-4. Both offensive guards are uncovered, and thus there are two bubbles that weaken the structure of this front.

The nose tackle shades the center and the right defensive end shades the right guard in this front. Two bubbles still exist in the interior.

The solid front eliminates interior bubbles in the defense. The off tackle hole is the primary concern.

DEFENDING THE OUTSIDE RUN

Defending the outside run is a lot easier than defending the inside run. The defense responds quicker to tosses and fake dive pitches than to isolations and slams, as you will notice from the interior run defense write-up above. The goal is to use fronts to bounce the runner outside to the pursuit.

DEFENDING THE COUNTER

The most powerful run play in the game for the last three years has been the counter play. Once this train gets going, watch out. One of the best ways to slow the brakes on counter plays is to defend them from the inside out. Getting out in front on a counter play is not a great idea. You will more likely than not get pancaked by the offensive lineman leading the charge. Let's look at defending the counter play.

DEFENDING THE PASS

Defending the pass is a critical part in the overall scheme of playing defense. You must be able to defend the run and pass with consistency if you plan on winning your share of games. After all, as the saying goes, "Offense wins games; defense wins championships." There are a few things that we must do in order to have a solid pass defense. Let's go into a few fundamental rules before getting into the basic strategy of pass defense.

PASS DEFENSE RULES AND TIPS

- The defensive line must generate a pass rush. If the defensive linemen can get to the quarterback without having any help, it allows for more defenders to drop back in pass coverage. Also, the defensive backs don't have to hold their coverages as long when the rush is there.

- If your corner backs are slower than the receivers lined up across from them, always have at least one safety dropping back in deep coverage to help defend the deep pass.

- Mix zones and man coverage to keep the opposing quarterback from getting too comfortable.

- Use defensive individual hot routes to create different coverage schemes on the fly.

- When calling blitz schemes where there is no safety help deep, be sure your cornerbacks are able to cover their man by themselves. There are only a handful of corner backs in the game that fit this description.

- If you plan on bringing the heat, it's best to call bump-n-run coverage and jam the receivers, so they get out on the pass routes as fast as they can. Plus, it gives the pass rushers extra time to get to the quarterback.

- If your team doesn't have fast corner backs, but you still plan on blitzing, try calling zone blitz schemes. That way, you still get solid pass coverage deep, in addition to getting a pass rush.

- Next, the defense needs to make sure that they cover all areas or zones of the field as much as possible. Obviously, there are going to be times where this is not possible, due to a defensive play that has been called.

- The defensive line must also get their hands in the air when the quarterback is getting ready to pass. Doing this prevents clear looks through the passing lanes and increases the chance of a tipped pass and/or a blind throw by the quarterback.

- When rushing the passer, the defensive ends must be aware of maintaining containment of the quarterback without creating running lanes for the quarterback to exploit if the play breaks down. The QB contain feature and improved pursuit logic makes this possible.

- Most top players control a safety to defend the deep pass; they don't worry about the underneath passes so much. The reason they control a safety the most is because they don't want to give up the big play; plus, its a lot harder to defend quick passes underneath than it is to defend long passes down the field.

- The quickest way to learn to use the swat button is go into mini camp mode and select DB-Swat Ball. Don't worry about your score; just concentrate on swatting the ball down.

PASS DEFENSE CONTROLS

When playing *Madden NFL 08*, there are a few basic controls to learn in order to stay consistent against the pass. Most top players have these controls mastered, making them very difficult to throw on.

Swat Button

The DB swat button is the first of the pass defense buttons that a *Madden NFL Football* pass defender must be able to use to guard against the pass. This button allows a player to swat the ball down and is a most effective way to defend all types of passes. The key to using the swat button is timing and getting the right angle to swat the pass down.

Jump/Intercept Button

The next button a player needs to learn is the jump/intercept button. This button allows a player to contest the pass and try to intercept the ball. Combined with the DB swat, this will have a defense secondary feared by many of their opponents. The downside of using the jump/intercept button is if you go for a pick and miss,

chances are you will give up more yardage than if you had played it safe.

Strafe Button

The last button that needs to be learned to defend the pass is the strafe button. This button allows the player on defense to take control of a defender, and then get squared up between the receiver and ball. If done right, you can press the strafe button, the jump/intercept button and pick off the pass. This combination works

particularly well when in control of a safety.

DEFENDING **PASS ROUTES**

Now that we have talked about pass defense rules and pass defense controls, it's time to take a look at five different passcoverages that can be called to defend different types of pass routes in *Madden NFL 08*.

CORNER **PASS ROUTE**

❶ The best way to defend corner routes outside of manually defending them is to call defense where defenders drop back in the curl flats zone (purple zone). Every defensive playbook has plays designed with them, plus you can always hot route a defender(s) into zones if you choose to. For example, the Nickel Normal Quarters Safe has the nickel back and left outside linebacker dropping back in the curl flat zones on both sides of the field.

❷ With the left outside linebacker dropping back in the curl flat zone, and the left cornerback dropping back a deep blue zone, the slot receiver running the corner to the right of the field is well-covered.

❸ The left outside linebacker is in perfect position to either knock or pick off the pass. There is no way the receiver is going to make the catch.

SLANT **PASS ROUTE**

❶ In *Madden NFL 06*, it seemed like everyone was using the slant route because of the high quick pass. In *Madden NFL 07*, the slant route was toned down and was not nearly as effective. The key to defending it when playing man coverage is not to call bump-n-run coverage. Instead, play normal man coverage and the cornerbacks will do the job for you.

❷ The quarterback throws a high bullet pass to the split end, but the right cornerback cuts in front of him once the ball is snapped.

❸ The split has no chance to make the catch because the right cornerback is between him and the ball.

CURL PASS ROUTE

❶ Most top players don't like to play a lot of Cover 2 Zone because of the fear of being beat deep, but it does have its uses in *Madden NFL 08*. It's one of the better defenses to call to defend the quick pass, or in this case, curl routes.

❷ The split end is running a curl route on the left side. The right CB will jam him at the line of scrimmage.

❸ The right outside linebacker drops back in a hook zone and drifts over toward the split end. The quarterback tries to thread the needle...

❹ ...but he is picked off by the right outside linebacker.

STREAK PASS ROUTE

❶ The best way to defend the streak is to call 2 Man Under coverages and fan the safeties out by pressing the coverage audible button and then up on the Right Thumbstick. This will put their deep coverage closer to the sidelines.

❷ The flanker is running a streak down the right sideline. The left cornerback and strong safety are in coverage.

❸ The flanker is bracketed by them both. The left cornerback plays underneath him, while the safety plays over the top.

❹ With the flanker covered, he won't be able to make the catch. We take control of the left cornerback and swat the pass away.

TE POST PASS ROUTE

❶ The tight end post is another route that can be difficult to defend, especially if the offense has an elite tight end. In the screen shot above, the middle linebacker drops back in a hook zone and the free safety rotates towards the middle. One would think this coverage would be good for defending a tight end post. That assumption would be wrong.

❷ What we like to do is hot route the middle linebacker so that he plays man coverage on the tight end. To do this, press the coverage audible button while in control of the middle

linebacker, then press the tight end's pass icon, and then right on the D-pad. The tight end will now be in man coverage on the tight end.

❸ Once the ball is snapped, the middle linebacker will cover the tight end, but play underneath him once the tight end breaks over the middle. The free safety will play over the top.

❹ The middle linebacker is in perfect position to knock the pass away from the tight end.

DEFENSIVE STRATEGY

45

THE BLITZ

Different types of blitzing schemes were developed in the golden age of the NFL. In today's game, NFL Defensive Coordinators use these same concepts while adding new ones to give quarterbacks different looks. Some defensive coordinators will use a zone blitz scheme; others will use a man coverage blitz scheme, and others use both. They all have one common goal: to get after the quarterback. In *Madden NFL 08*, you are the team's defensive coordinator. Knowing the nuts and bolts of how and when to blitz will improve your defense dramatically.

THE **FIVE OBJECTIVES** OF A BLITZING **DEFENSE**

Sacks make the ESPN highlights during Sports Center, but the defense doesn't fail when missing the sack. Being able to produce heat that makes the quarterback uneasy in the pocket is effective because it causes him to throw more quickly than he wants. The quarterback is more likely to throw errant passes that can lead to interceptions.

Even if the quarterback is able to make the correct read, avoid the heat, and get the pass off, his throws will be significantly shorter than if he had time in the pocket. By forcing the quick throw, the receivers will not be able to run their pass routes as far down the field, and will often come up short of the first down marker.

❶ Sack the quarterback.

❷ Cause the QB to throw incomplete passes.

❸ Force turnovers – pressure him into throwing interceptions and hit him in order to cause fumbles.

❹ In long yardage situations, make the quarterback throw shorter passes to beat the blitz.

❺ Dictate the tempo of the game.

DOWNFALLS OF **UTILIZING THE BLITZ**

• Unless the defense is zone blitzing, it usually requires some type of man to man coverage. Often, defensive backs will be left in one-on-one coverage with limited safety help.

• It increases the chance for a big play if the offensive line and backs are able to pick up the blitz.

• Athletic quarterbacks who escape the pocket can break containment and scramble for huge chunks of yardage.

• Defenders wear out faster if they are continually sent on a blitz. Be sure to package in different defenders to keep players fresh.

MADDEN NFL 08 — EFFECTIVE **BLITZING TIPS**

❶ In *Madden NFL 06*, random blitz assignments were added to the game. A defender that is assigned to blitz a particular gap may not always do what the play diagram shows. This was done to counter nanos (instant heat). When setting up a defense in practice mode, keep in mind that your blitz may not work twice in a row because the defenders will randomly blitz different gaps.

❷ For best results, put your **fastest defensive personnel** out on the field when blitzing the quarterback. The more speed the defender has, the quicker he will get to the quarterback.

❸ First, set up blitz packages in practice mode. Once you feel comfortable, try them in a real game situation. A blitz that works in practice mode may not always work the same way in regular game mode. You don't want to play a human online to find if your blitz you thought works. The best way to learn to set up blitz packages is to put one controller on your team and the other controller on the other. Once on the field, set up the defense and then run the play to see if it works. If it does, then you know you can run it against a human opponent online or offline.

❹ Learn to **manually blitz a defender** if he is playing zone or man coverage. You can generate even more heat on the quarterback than a default blitz defense.

❺ Once you find blitz set-ups you like that works, **be sure to run them against multiple formations** to see if they are effective or not.

❻ If your opponent smells a blitz, he can use the slide protection feature to counter your blitz set-up. That's why it is important to set up blitz packages against the four slide protection adjustments that can be used. **Repetition is imperative when learning how to set up blitz packages.** Some will take time to set up.

❼ We cannot stress how important it is to **use instant replay** to see how the pass protection works against the blitz. This also applies to playing the CPU. Often the CPU will set up a blitz through the use of shifts, and will be able to get after the quarterback quickly. If you see a blitz by the CPU that comes in quickly, save it for further review.

DEFENSIVE STRATEGY

WHERE PRESSURE COMES FROM

There are generally four types of blitz schemes that attack from different areas on the field in *Madden NFL 08*. Pressure from both outside sides, overloading one side, up the gut pressure, and from all areas. We show an example of each from the Ravens' defensive playbook.

PRESSURE FROM **BOTH OUTSIDE SIDES**

Pressure from both outsides of the field can come from two linebackers, two inside defensive backs, two corner backs, or a combination of both. Most players that use this type of blitz scheme put their fastest defensive players in the blitzing outside positions to bring the heat.

❶ The 3-4 Normal OLB Dogs Fire from the Ravens' playbook is a good example of how outside pressure works from both sides. With outside linebackers Terrell Suggs and Jarret Johnson, both bring the heat. We have spread the linebackers to give them both better pass rush angles at the quarterback.

❷ The key to them getting pressure is to use their speed to get past the offensive tackles. Suggs is one of the better blitzing linebackers in the game.

❸ Suggs blows right past the left tackle and then goes straight for the quarterback.

❹ The result is a sack.

OVERLOAD **ONE SIDE**

Overloading one side with multiple blitzing defenders is the most common blitz scheme you will find in the game. By blitzing multiple defenders to attack one side the offensive, it pretty much guarantees that at least one or more defenders are going to get pressure on the quarterback. This is because there are not enough offensive linemen to account for all pass rushers blitzing from the overloaded side.

❶ The 46 Normal Swap Blitz 1 is a perfect example of how effective overloading one side with blitzing defenders can be. Strong safety Dawan Landry and left outside linebacker Jarret Johnson are both blitzing from the right side of the offensive line.

❷ Once the ball is snapped, they both take outside pass rush angles.

❸ The right tackle is overwhelmed because of the multiple pass rushers coming from his side. Not only are Landry and Johnson coming in on a blitz, but he must also deal with left end Trevor Pryce, who is already a menace as a pass rusher.

❹ The right tackle picks up Johnson, but allows Landry and Pryce to come through. The quarterback has no chance to avoid being sacked, and is brought down to the turf.

DEFENSIVE STRATEGY

WHERE PRESSURE **COMES FROM**

Continued

UP THE GUT **PRESSURE**

A few years ago, up the gut pressure was by far the most popular way to get pressure on the quarterback. However, once random blitz gap angles were added to *Madden NFL 06*, top players began to shy away from this type of pressure because there was a good chance the blitz wouldn't work and they didn't want to give up the big play.

❶ The 46 Normal Mike Blitz sends middle linebacker Ray Lewis in on a blitz between the center and right guard.

❷ Because of random blitz angles, he may or not take the correct blitz assignment. Because of this, a lot of players will take control of the blitzing defender and manually blitz themselves to make sure the defender blitzes through the correct gap. In the screen shot above, that's what we are doing; we are controlling Lewis and making sure he goes through the right gap.

❸ Once through the gap, we can either release Lewis or stay in control of him and go after the quarterback.

❹ We get home with Lewis and sack the quarterback.

FROM ALL **AREAS**

The final blitz scheme we want to show is one that many players will use, especially right when *Madden NFL Football* is released, to bring the heat from all areas of the field. They want to see if their opponent can handle the pressure or not early in the game. If they can't handle the pressure, you can bet he will keep bringing the pressure until his opponent can counter it.

❶ The Nickel 1-1-5 Prowl Bird Fire 3 is a great example of a blitz from all areas of the field that many players will use. This blitz scheme sends a total of 8 pass rushers after the quarterback. Sure, there several areas on the field in which to throw the ball to beat the blitz, but the quarterback must be fast. If not, he is going to get sacked within 2-3 seconds after the snap.

❷ With all the defenders attacking different areas of the offensive line, it's impossible to block them all.

❸ The quarterback has nowhere to go because of the pressure from the outside and up the gut.

❹ The result is a sack.

DEFENSIVE FORMATIONS BREAKDOWN

4-3 Normal

The 4-3 Normal defense is comprised of 4 down linemen and 3 linebackers. The 4-3 defense does not have to rely on blitzing as much as some of the other defenses do, and is fairly decent at stopping both the run and the pass.

Strengths

Able to stop the running game without having to blitz heavily. Fairly decent at stopping both the run and the pass with the base personnel grouping.

Weaknesses

Extremely weak against spread, shotgun style offenses. Also weak stopping outside running plays.

4-3 Over

The 4-3 Over defense is the same as the 4-3 with the difference being the placement of the linemen and linebackers. Here, the defensive line is shifted over to the tight end side of the formation (also known as the strong side), with the strong side linebacker lined up between the guard and the tackle on that same side.

Strengths

Works well defending against runs to the strong side both inside and out. Still able to stop the pass effectively without blitzing.

Weaknesses

Extremely weak against runs to the weak side, both inside and out. Still weak against defending spread, shotgun style offenses.

4-3 Under

4-3 Under is essentially the opposite of 4-3 Over. Here, the defense is shifted towards the weak side of the offense with the weak side linebacker between the weak side guard and tackle.

Strengths

This defense works well defending against weak side runs, and is still able to stop the pass effectively without being forced to blitz.

Weaknesses

Extremely weak defending against runs to the strong side, both inside and out. Still weak against defending spread, shotgun style offenses.

3-4 Normal

The 3-4 defense consists of 3 down linemen and 4 linebackers as opposed to the 4-3's 4 down linemen and 3 linebackers. The 3-4 defense relies heavily on big, strong defensive linemen to clog holes, and quick, athletic-type linebackers to react quickly. This style of defense requires heavy blitzing to make up for the lack of a missing lineman upfront to stop both the run and the pass.

Strengths

Able to disguise blitzes better due to having an extra linebacker. Able to stop spread offenses through the use of blitzing. Also works well defending runs that go outside.

Weaknesses

Very vulnerable to runs right up the gut, especially out of tight formations. Still isn't great at defending spread offenses with multiple receivers. Also, many linebackers can't keep up with the speed of receivers, which will limit your playcalling.

DEFENSIVE STRATEGY

DEFENSIVE STRATEGY

3-4 Over

The 3-4 Over defense is the same as the 3-4 defense, with the only difference being that the defensive line is shifted over towards the strong side of the offensive line, and the linebackers are shifted towards the weak side.

Strengths

Similar to the 3-4 Normal, the 3-4 Over allows you to be able to disguise blitzes. Also, this defense is able to stop the run better toward the strong side.

Weaknesses

Very weak against runs toward the weak side, both inside and out. Must blitz in order to keep the offense guessing and off-balance.

3-4 Under

The 3-4 Under is pretty much the opposite of 3-4 Over in that the defense is shifted towards the weak side of the formation.

Strengths

Still able to disguise blitzes well. Works well defending runs toward the weak side.

Weaknesses

Very weak against runs toward the strong side of the formation. Must still blitz in order for this defense to be successful.

3-4 Solid

The 3-4 Solid defense has the defensive line shifted in and the line backers shifted over on the outside shoulders of the defensive ends.

Strengths

Takes away the inside running game, thanks to the close alignment of the defensive line and the alignment of the linebackers. Still able to mix up blitzes well.

Weaknesses

Very weak against runs to the outside in either direction. Must blitz with base personnel against spread offenses.

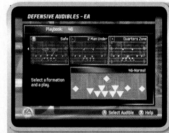

4-6 Normal

The 4-6 Normal defense focuses on stopping the running game by bringing down the strong safety into a linebacker position. Usually, teams that use this defense have a physical type of strong safety, known for making hard hits.

Strengths

Very effective at stopping all forms of run due to eight players being in the box. Works well against tight offensive formations. Allows the strong safety to be able to contain tight ends lined up on the line of scrimmage in the passing game.

Weaknesses

Extremely ineffective at stopping a spread passing attack. Lack of deep help in the secondary. Limited to what you can do defensively as far as playcalling goes.

4-6 Bear

The 4-6 Bear defense moves both of the OLBs down to the line of scrimmage, essentially making six defensive linemen. The SS is now playing as a LB, while the MLB slides over to become more of an OLB.

Strengths

Useful in short yardage situations when you don't want to go with a goal line defense. Works well against tight offensive formations and is exceptional at stopping the run.

Weaknesses

Horrible at defending passes. No help deep in the secondary. Extremely weak against spread offensive sets.

Nickel Normal

The Nickel Normal defense substitutes one linebacker out for a 5th defensive back. Usually used against three receiver sets.

Strengths

Able to defend three receiver sets well without sacrificing linebacker support in the running game. Fairly decent at stopping the run.

Weaknesses

Unable to effectively defend against offensive sets with more than three receivers. Not effective against tight offensive formations, especially runs up the middle.

Nickel Strong

Strengths

Works well defending against three receiver sets. The closeness of the free safety allows him to help out in the running game more.

Weaknesses

Essentially puts the corner on the weak side of the offensive set on an island by himself. Unable to effectively defend against offensive sets with more than three receivers.

Nickel 3-3-5

Similar to Nickel Normal, except now, instead of there being four down linemen, there are three. There are also three linebackers and five defensive backs. Both safeties are now back to their traditional positions.

Strengths

Defends against runs from shotgun sets to the outside. Still effective against three receiver sets.

Weaknesses

Weak against runs to the inside, especially from under center offensive formations. Still weak against offensive sets with more than three receivers.

Nickel 1-5-5

Similar to Nickel Normal, except now, there's only one down lineman. There are now five linebackers and five defensive backs, thus allowing for more speed on the field.

Strengths

Effective against the run game from spread offensive formations. With more speed on the field, you're able to be a little more creative in your playcalling. Can better defend against offensive sets with more than one defender compared to previous other Nickel formations.

Weaknesses

Horrible at defending runs right up the gut. Linebackers aren't as fast as receivers, so you may be forced to run a little more zone than you're comfortable doing.

Nickel 2-4-5

Similar to Nickel Normal, except now, there are only two down defensive linemen and four linebackers.

Strengths

Effective against the run from spread formations, more so than Nickel 1-5-5. Can better defend against offensive sets with more than three WRs.

Weaknesses

Not great when defending against runs right up the gut. May still have to play more zone coverage when going against offensive sets with more than three WRs.

DEFENSIVE STRATEGY

Similar to Nickel 1-5-5 except now, nobody is down in a stance; everyone is standing up.

Nickel 1-5-5 Prowl

Strengths

Able to confuse offenses with this look. Able to blitz from all sorts of areas.

Weaknesses

Horrible at defending runs right up the gut. Forces you to play more zone coverage than you would probably want to against formations with more than three receivers.

Used primarily in passing situations. The defense has four down linemen, one linebacker, and six defensive backs. The term dime comes from being one coin higher than Nickel. Typically used against offensive sets with four wide receivers.

Dime Normal

Strengths

Works well defending against passes from multiple receiver sets. Extra defensive back allows you to play more man if you want to. Provides adequate protection against deep balls.

Weaknesses

Doesn't fare too well against tight offensive formations. Bad at defending the run from most offensive formations.

Similar to Dime Normal, except now there's more of an emphasis on coverage in the flats. Both safeties are moved down closer to the line of scrimmage as well as the extra defensive backs (the dime and nickel backs).

Dime Flats

Strengths

Defends against the flats well as the name would suggest. Useful in third and short type situations where there are more than three receivers.

Weaknesses

Horrible at defending against tight offensive formations, especially running plays from them. Lack of help deep.

Similar to Dime Normal except now there are only 3 down linemen and two linebackers to go along with the six defensive backs.

Dime 3-2-6

Strengths

Defends against the run better than the other Dime sets. Useful for when there's a threat for the offense to run when they are in spread formation sets. Safeties provide adequate coverage deep.

Weaknesses

Still weak against runs up the middle. Weak against power run formations in general.

Similar to Quarter Normal except now all three safeties are playing deep.

Quarter 3 Deep

Strengths

Even better against the deep ball than Quarter Normal. Works well against Hail Mary-type plays when you know the offense is throwing deep like at the end of a half.

Weaknesses

Even worse against the run game compared to Quarters Normal.

Used primarily in extreme passing situations, when you know for a fact the offense is passing. Quarter refers to there being seven defensive backs, usually with one of them being an extra safety.

Quarter Normal

Strengths

Extremely effective against the deep ball.

Weaknesses

Not ideal to use against power run formations. Horrible at defending against the run in general.

MORE DEFENSIVE GAMEPLAY FEATURES

Here are some other defensive game features for *Madden NFL 08* that you will be sure to want to know and learn before playing the computer or playing a live human being.

DELAYED BUMP-N-RUN

Many top players already know about delayed bump-n-run coverage, but for those of you who are new to *Madden NFL Football*, here is a nice feature to throw at your opponent that can help disrupt their passing game.

❶ First, come out in any zone coverage defense and call bump-n-run coverage.

❷ Next, audible to any man defense. Notice that the cornerbacks line up at a normal depth across from the receiver they are covering.

❸ Once the ball is snapped, the defenders will now jam the receivers across from them. In this case, it's the right cornerback jamming the split end.

ALTERNATE HOOK ZONE

Many players like to use drags to effectively move down the field by throwing low risk passes. You can stop them in their tracks by using the alternate hook zone. Here is how.

❶ Notice that we have three defenders playing normal hook zones. We can change that by taking control of them and using the hot route hook zone.

❷ To do this, take control of the defender you want to put in the alternate hook zone. Once the defender has been hot routed into a hook zone, take control of him and move him 1 yard in any direction. His hook zone will now change. Instead of him dropping back like in normal hook zone, he will now stay put.

❸ This puts him in perfect position to cover any drag routes that come his way. He often will even bump the receiver running the drag route.

DEFENSIVE STRATEGY

53

DEFENSIVE ASSIGNMENTS

Defensive Assignments were first added to *Madden NFL 05* to help counter match-up problems that occurred in previous editions. For example, back in *Madden NFL 04*, if a player moved his top receiver into the slot, a third or fourth defensive back would cover him. The only way to change your coverage on him was to pause the game and move him inside through the use of the defensive depth chart or formation sub menu. That was a lot of micromanagement that most players were not up to.

With the addition of Defensive Assignments, that type of micromanagement is not needed. For instance, if the offense has a top-notch receiver, you can put your top cornerback on him to keep him in check. Not only can you assign your top corner back, you can assign any defender (except defensive linemen) on any receiver, halfback, fullback, or tight end. For instance, if your opponent likes to package or sub his top receiver into the slot, your top cornerback can be assigned to cover him no matter where the receiver lines up.

Defensive Assignments Pros & Cons

+ Pros

• Being able to match up specific defenders on specific receivers.

• Takes away your opponent's ability on offense to get unrealistic match-ups.

• Allows for more creativity and flexibility for the defense when calling man coverage.

− Cons

• It shows whether the defense is playing man or zone coverage and also leads to defenders playing out of position. For example, the left outside linebacker and strong safety switch positions. The left outside linebacker now plays the strong safety position and the strong safety now plays the left outside linebacker spot because he is in man coverage on the tight end.

• If man lock coverage is turned off, the defender assigned to that particular receiver will not follow. Instead, the defender will slide in to cover the slot or tight end. For example, say the offense comes out in the Split Backs 3WR and the defense comes out in the Dime Normal Man Under. If man lock is turned off and if the receiver on the far right is sent in motion, the defender covering him will slide in to cover the slot. The defensive back lined up inside on the left now slides out to cover the receiver in motion. Often this creates a mismatch that favors the offense.

DEFENSIVE ASSIGNMENTS TIPS

The obvious way to use the defensive assignments feature would be to have your top cornerback covering your opponent's top receiver. If you just use this feature for that one reason, then you are missing out on its other benefits. Here are few things you may want to consider adding to your defensive coverage schemes when assigning defensive coverage.

1. Put your top defensive back on a lower-rated receiver. That way, you limit your opponent's ability to throw to that side of the field. Now you can roll your pass coverage to the other side of the field and focus on defending your opponent's top receiver.

2. If the halfback is the main target in your opponent's pass game, consider assigning your top linebacker or defensive back on him. That way, you limit the primary threat and force him to throw to other receivers on the field.

3. If you are playing against teams with an elite tight end, such as the Chargers' Antonio Gates, assign a linebacker or safety who has good coverage skills to him.

RUN/PASS COMMIT

Back in *Madden NFL 04*, the Run/Pass Commit feature was added to the game to improve the play of the defense. In *Madden NFL 08*, it's back once again. If you press down on the Right Thumbstick within a second of the snap, the defenders commit to the run. If you press up on the Right Thumbstick within a second of the snap, the defenders commit to the pass. This feature helps turn every down into more of a chess match, as the user controlling the defense tries to

anticipate the offense's next move. If the offense has called a play action play and you decide to commit to the run, be prepared to get burned deep. If play action is called and you press the Right Thumbstick up, there is a better chance the safeties won't bite on the play fake. If the offense has called a draw play and you decide to commit to the pass, the ball carrier can get past the initial contact and rip off a good chunk of yardage.

Another addition to Run/Pass Commit feature is the ability to crash the defenders to the left or right of the line of scrimmage. If you can anticipate the run's direction, this feature gets them in position quicker to make the tackle. Press left on the Right Thumbstick to make the defenders crash to the left side. Press right on the Right Thumbstick to make the defenders crash to the right side. Be careful of teams that run a lot of counter plays, as they will hurt you if you guess incorrectly.

MAN LOCK ON/OFF

In *Madden NFL 05*, EA added the capability to turn man coverage on and off for the human-controlled defense. When the man lock on/off feature is used, it makes it harder for offensive players to distinguish between man and zone coverage.

In *Madden NFL 08*, man lock on and off is back again. At the play call screen, press the L1 button for the PS2 (Ⓛ trigger on the Xbox), and man lock coverage is turned on. Press the R1 button for the PS2 (Ⓡ trigger on the Xbox), and man lock coverages turned off. Man lock on and off coverage can also be reset while on the field. When man lock is off at the play call screen and you decide you want man lock on once the teams break the huddle, just press the coverage audible (▲ for PS2, Ⓨ for Xbox), and then press the D-pad or Left Thumbstick →. The defenders will now be in man lock coverage on. If you want to turn it off again, press the coverage audible (▲ for PS2, Ⓨ for Xbox), and then press the D-pad or Left Thumbstick →.

Put CBs in Man Coverage Without Taking Control of Them

Here is another nifty feature that you can use to fool your opponent into thinking you're in zone coverage, when really it's man/zone.

❶ Notice that we are in control of the right inside LB.

❷ The defense called is the 3-4 Normal Cover 3. The RCB is supposed to drop in deep zone coverage.

❸ By pressing the coverage audible, then receiver's pass icon, and then Ⓡ trigger or Ⓛ trigger on the Xbox or R1 button or L1 button the PS2 controller, we can put the right corner back in man coverage without ever actually taking control of him.

CHICAGO BEARS

Division: NFC North | **Home Field:** Soldier Field | **Type:** Open | **Capacity:** 61,500 | **Surface:** Grass

TEAM STRATEGY

COACHING PROFILE

Lovie Smith

- **Head Coaching Year:** 4th
- **Experience:** Defensive coordinator for St.Louis Rams (2001-2003).

Smith became the Bears' head coach in January of 2004. Since taking over, he has a winning percentage of .596. His overall record is 31-21. He became the first African-American head coach to lead his team to a Super Bowl.

TEAM RANKINGS

Scoring	2nd
Passing Offense	14th
Rushing Offense	15th
Passing Defense	11st
Rushing Defense	5th
Turnovers	4th

RATINGS HISTORY

Category	'07	'06	'05	'04
Overall	87	73	79	82
Offense	87	66	78	81
Defense	89	76	79	84

Bold = Highest Year

82
FIVE-YEAR
AVERAGE

2006 STANDINGS

Wins	Losses	Ties	PF	PA	Home	Road	vs. AFC	vs. NFC	vs. Div
13	3	0	427	255	6-2	1-3	2-2	11-1	5-1

TEAM OVERVIEW

The Bears had a magical run to the Super Bowl, but were unable to come home with the trophy. Grossman will have the opportunity to put some of his demons behind him this season. If he can be more consistent and take care of the ball, the Bears should be in fine shape.

Cedric Benson will be the man this year at running back. He is more of a bruiser than a speed guy, which fits in with Chicago's persona. Muhammad is a capable hands guy and Berrian provides serious deep speed.

Let's not forget Devin Hester and his 100 speed rating as well. Get him as many touches as possible. Urlacher and Briggs anchor a strong defense that has very few (if any) weaknesses.

SCOUTING REPORT

STRENGTHS

Description	Maximizing Potential	Tips for Opponents
The Bears have one of the stronger offensive lines to run behind. You must pound the ball.	Road-grader Olin Kreutz is one of the top centers in the game. Look to run the ball up behind him.	Stack eight and nine defenders in the box to stop the Bears' rushing and force the pass.
The Bears' d-line is one of the strongest in the game. They have plenty of speed to get to the opposing QB.	DT Tommie Harris uses his strength and speed to push the pocket inside so the DEs can attack outside.	Don't let Harris penetrate up the middle. Use slide protection and hot routes to slow him down.
The Bears' backers are fast at getting to ball carriers.	Use Urlacher's speed and awareness to shut down the run.	Avoid running the ball in his area. If you do, be sure to put a hat on him.

WEAKNESSES

Description	Minimizing Risks	Tips for Opponents
Rex Grossman is prone to making mistakes in the pass game because of his poor decision making.	Last season he threw 20 interceptions. Don't get in third and long situations.	You should bring the heat on Grossman and force him to throw the ball quicker than he wants to.
Bears' safety Adam Archuleta is suspect against the deep ball due to lack of speed.	Consider putting in a faster safety to replace Archuleta if you run a lot of Cover 2 Zone.	Look to go up top if the Bears play their traditional Cover 2 Buc scheme.

Overall Rating **88**
Offense **87**
Defense **90**

OFF-SEASON **UPGRADES**

Type	Round	First Name	Last Name	School/Team	Positon	Height	Weight
Free Agent	N/A	Anthony	Adams	San Francisco 49ers	DT	6'0"	229
Trade	N/A	Adam	Archuleta	Washington Redskins	S	6'0"	223
Draft	1st	Greg	Olsen	Miami (Florida)	TE	6'4"	252
Draft	2nd	Dan	Bazuin	Central Michigan	DE	6'3"	265
Draft	3rd	Garrett	Wolfe	Northern Illinois	RB	5'7"	177

FANTASY **OUTLOOK**

Star Player: Cedric Benson
Round of Draft: 2nd

Benson will see an increase in the amount of touches he receives as he has locked down the starting role at running back. Mark him down for 1,200 yards plus as long as the injury bug doesn't bite him.

Star Player: Bernard Berrian
Round of Draft: 10th

Last season Berrian broke out as the Bears' big play receiver by posting a career-best six touchdown catches. If Rex Grossman has a more consistent season, Berrian's numbers will be even higher.

5-YEAR **PLAYER PROGRESSION**

First Name	Last Name	Position	'07 Overall	'08 Overall	'09 Overall	'10 Overall	'11 Overall
Brian	Urlacher	LB	98	99	99	99	99
Tommie	Harris	DT	97	97	98	99	99
Cedric	Benson	HB	86	89	91	93	95
Greg	Olsen	TE	83	83	83	83	83
Devin	Hester	WR	75	76	77	77	78

FRANCHISE MODE
STRATEGY

The Bears are getting old up front and will need to get young sooner than later. Look to draft young offensive linemen in the early rounds of the 2008 draft. Adding another receiver would also be beneficial.

Key Franchise Info

Team Salary: $96.8M
Cap Room: $12.2M
Key Rival:
• **Green Bay** Packers
NFL Icons: Brian Urlacher
Philosophy:
• Offense: Vertical Passing
• Defense: Disrupt Passing
Prestige: Very High
Team Needs:
• Offensive Line (future)
• Receivers
Highest Paid Players:
• Cedric Benson
• Brian Urlacher
Up and Coming Players:
• Greg Olsen
• Michael Okwo

ROSTER AND **PACKAGE TIPS**   KEY PLAYER SUBSTITUTIONS

• **Position:** 3DRB
• **Substitution:** Garrett Wolf
• **When:** Global
• **Advantage:** Wolf is the Bears' best receiver out of the backfield. His speed and catching rating are both higher than the two halfbacks in front of him.

• **Position:** WR
• **Substitution:** Devin Hester
• **When:** Global
• **Advantage:** With a 100 speed rating, Hester has to be on the field as much as possible. Having him line up in the slot will put the fear in the defense.

• **Position:** TE
• **Substitution:** Greg Olsen
• **When:** Global
• **Advantage:** Default Desmond Clark is a solid starter at tight end, but Olsen's speed makes him a vertical threat down the middle of the field.

• **Position:** QB
• **Substitution:** Brian Griese
• **When:** Global
• **Advantage:** If starter Rex Grossman struggles, sub Griese in to give the offense a spark. Grossman has a stronger arm, but Griese is a tad more accurate.

CHICAGO BEARS / OFFENSE

OFFENSIVE STAR PLAYER #87

Muhsin Muhammad — Wide Receiver (WR)

Key Attributes

Acceleration	85
Awareness	90
Catching	93
Speed	86

Last season, **Muhammad** was very productive, despite the erratic play at the quarterback position. He managed to haul in **60** receptions and **five** touchdowns. He was the Bears' leading receiver in yardage with 863 yards. He uses his 6'2" frame to shield smaller defensive backs and make the catch. Despite catching only five touchdown passes, Muhammad is still a primary target inside the red zone. Expect him to have a more productive season in '08.

Player Weapons: Possession Receiver/Hands

RECOMMENDED OFFENSIVE AUDIBLE PACKAGES

I Form-Twin WR	Singleback-Normal Slot	Singleback-Twin TE	Singleback-4WR Spread	Singleback-4WR Spread
WR Corner	Slot Cross	HB Dive	HB Wheel	HB Cutback

OFFENSIVE PLAYCOUNTS

Quick Pass:	12	Screen Pass:	18	Pinch:	16
Standard Pass:	89	Hail Mary:	2	Counter:	17
Shotgun Pass:	22	Inside Handoff:	32	Draw:	17
Play Action Pass:	57	Outside Handoff:	15		

TEAM TRIVIA

Chicago Bears Facts

Turn the page for the answers.

1. What was original name of the Bears franchise?
2. Who was the founder and first coach of the Bears?
3. What Bears player was named the Offensive Rookie of the year for 2001?

OFFENSIVE FORMATIONS

Singleback	Strong I
Big	Normal
Twin TE	3WR
Normal Slot	Twin TE
Strong TE Flip	**Weak I**
Trips Bunch	Normal
4WR Spread	Twin WR
Trey Open	**Shotgun**
Empty 5WR	2RB 3WR
I-Form	Normal
Normal	Trips TE
Twin WR	4WR
3WR	
Split Backs	
3WR	

OFFENSIVE STRENGTH CHART

- ○ : OVR less than 80
- ○ : OVR between 80-89
- ● : OVR 90 or greater
- ○ : Player Weapons

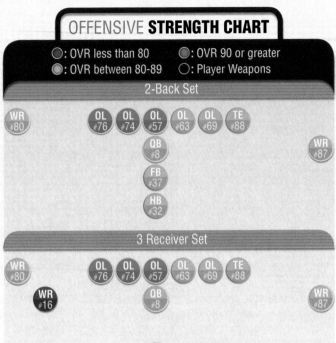

2-Back Set / 3 Receiver Set

OFFENSIVE ROSTER LIST Current/Next Gen

Pos.	#	First Name	Last Name	Overall	Player Weapons
C	57	Olin	Kreutz	98	Road Blocker/Pass Blocker
C	65	Patrick	Mannelly	65	
C	68	Anthony	Oakley	63	
FB	37	Jason	McKie	86	
FB	47	Bryan	Johnson	85	
HB	32	Cedric	Benson	86	
HB	29	Adrian	Peterson	78	
HB	25	Garrett	Wolfe	73	
K	9	Robbie	Gould	93	Accurate Kicker
LG	74	Ruben	Brown	90	Run Blocker/Pass Blocker
LG	60	Terrence	Metcalf	81	
LT	76	John	Tait	90	Road Blocker
LT	78	John	St. Clair	75	
QB	8	Rex	Grossman	85	Cannon Arm/Cannon Arm QB
QB	14	Brian	Griese	82	
QB	18	Kyle	Orton	75	
RG	63	Roberto	Garza	85	
RG	67	Josh	Beekman	75	
RT	69	Fred	Miller	87	
RT	75	Mark	LeVoir	70	
TE	88	Desmond	Clark	86	
TE	82	Greg	Olsen	83	
TE	85	John	Gilmore	69	
WR	87	Muhsin	Muhammad	87	Possession Receiver/Hands
WR	80	Bernard	Berrian	86	Deep Threat/Speed
WR	16	Mark	Bradley	78	
WR	81	Rashied	Davis	76	Deep Threat
WR	23	Devin	Hester	75	Deep Threat/Speed

I Form-Normal

Muhammad Opt.

Shotgun-Trips

Slot Attack

Singleback-Twin TE

PA TE Attack

Mushin Muhammad is an imposing receiver for many smaller defenders to deal with. Use the Option route to take advantage of his size and speed.

The Shotgun-Trips Slot Attack will allow him to play from the slot and use his size to take advantage of a smaller nickel back or linebacker.

The Singleback Twin TE PA TE Attack is perfect for Mushin Muhammad. Not only do we have a comeback route but it is helped out with play action.

The I Form Muhammad Option is used to let our flanker beat the defense in one of three routes, the hook, corner or streak.

This play is designed to send crossing routes at the defense in hopes of beating the defense with faster receivers as they cross.

The Singleback-Twin TE PA TE Attack is designed to get the ball to our tight end after drawing the defense in on the play action run fake.

Against man coverage shown above Muhammad will run the hook route. When he is even with the cornerback throw the ball to his outside shoulder.

Muhammad is a perfect receiver to send across the middle of the field. He has great hands and perfect size to go in there and battle.

When we see that Muhammad has sold the go route to the cornerback and he broke to the come back, it is now time to throw the ball.

The outside throw will allow Muhammad to break back to the ball and avoid the defense.

He catches the ball in the middle of the field, in the area that is voided by the defense.

Muhammad is too much for any defender when running a comeback route, so keep this play handy.

TEAM STRATEGY

59

CHICAGO BEARS / DEFENSE

DEFENSIVE STAR PLAYER #54

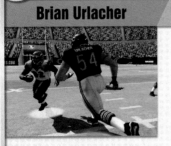

Brian Urlacher   Linebacker (MLB)

Key Attributes

Awareness	93
Speed	88
Strength	77
Tackle	94

A rare physical specimen, **Urlacher** is able to take over a game by himself at the middle linebacker position. Urlacher is the heart and soul of the Bears' defense. Last season, he singlehandedly won a game against the Cardinals by coming up with big plays late in the game. Urlacher led the team in total tackles during the '06-'07 season with **142**. He also managed to pick off **three** passes.

Player Weapons: Defensive Enforcer / Smart Linebacker, Big Hitter, Brick Wall Defender

RECOMMENDED DEFENSIVE AUDIBLE PACKAGES

4-3-Normal	4-3-Over	4-3-Under	Nickel-3-3-5	Dime-Flat
Double QB Spy	Zone Pistol 3	Over 3 Strong	Under Slice 7	Zone Blitz

DEFENSIVE PLAYCOUNTS

Man Coverage:	36	Cover 3 Zone:	18	Combo Blitz:	11
Man Zone:	30	Deep Zone:	15	Goal Line:	15
Combo Coverage:	8	Man Blitz:	36	Special Teams:	12
Cover 2 Zone:	18	Zone Blitz:	53		

TEAM TRIVIA

Chicago Bears Facts
Answers:

1 Decatur Staleys

2 George Halas

3 Anthony Thomas

DEFENSIVE FORMATIONS

4-3	Nickel
4-3-Normal	Nickel-3-3-5
4-3-Over	Nickel-Normal
4-3-Under	**Quarter**
46	Quarter-Normal
46-Bear	
Dime	
Dime-3-2-6	
Dime-Flat	
Dime-Normal	

DEFENSIVE STRENGTH CHART

○ : OVR less than 80   ● : OVR 90 or greater
◐ : OVR between 80-89   ○ : Player Weapons

4-3 Base Defense

FS #30   SS #20

CB #33   LB #55   LB #54   LB #92   CB #31

RE #96   DT #99   DT #91   LE #93

Dime Defense

FS #30   SS #20

CB #33   CB #24   LB #54   CB #21   CB #31

RE #96   DT #99   DT #91   LE #93

DEFENSIVE ROSTER LIST Current / Next Gen

Pos.	#	First Name	Last Name	Overall	Player Weapons
CB	31	Nathan	Vasher	90	Quick Corner / Smart Corner
CB	33	Charles	Tillman	89	Press Coverage Corner
CB	24	Ricky	Manning	84	
CB	21	Dante	Wesley	74	
DT	91	Tommie	Harris	97	Run Stopper / Finesse Move, Power Move D-Lineman
DT	99	Tank	Johnson	83	
DT	73	Anthony	Adams	77	
FS	30	Mike	Brown	90	
FS	38	Danieal	Manning	83	
LE	93	Adewale	Ogunleye	92	Pass Rusher / Finesse Move D-Lineman
LE	71	Israel	Idonije	66	
LOLB	92	Hunter	Hillenmeyer	79	
LOLB	58	Darrell	McClover	69	
LOLB	94	Brendon	Ayanbadejo	67	
MLB	54	Brian	Urlacher	98	Defensive Enforcer / Smart LB, Big Hitter, Brick Wall Defender
MLB	59	Rod	Wilson	70	
P	4	Brad	Maynard	87	
RE	96	Alex	Brown	88	Pass Rusher
RE	97	Mark	Anderson	87	
RE	79	Dan	Bazuin	76	
ROLB	55	Lance	Briggs	95	Heavy Hitter / Big Hitter, Brick WallI Defender
ROLB	62	Michael	Okwo	75	
ROLB	53	Leon	Joe	65	
SS	20	Adam	Archuleta	81	
SS	46	Chris	Harris	75	Big Hitter

4-3-Normal

2 Man Under

4-3-Over

Blizzard Blitz

4-3-Over

Safety Blitz

Brian Urlacher is a force on our defense and because of his ability we can use base defenses with the same effectiveness of more exotic blitz defenses.

Urlacher is one of the best blitzing linebackers in football. He has a high motor and is determined to bring his target down.

Everyone knows how good Urlacher is against the run, but he is just as good when defending the pass. This plays shows how good he is in coverage.

The 4-3 Normal 2 Man Under is a base defense. This is a perfect fit for Urlacher because it allows him to attack the offense no matter what they do.

The Blizzard Blitz is created to release chaos against the offense. The defense comes with reckless abandon and is looking for whoever has the ball.

This play is designed to bring pressure on the offense by blitzing both safeties, while leaving Urlacher in underneath zone coverage.

The offense decides to run the ball, and Urlacher takes to much pride to allow any rushing yards on his defense.

The defensive tackle engages the left guard and leaves a blitzing lane for Urlacher. This has to be one of the scariest things a quarterback can see.

While the pressure is attacking the offense, Urlacher is roaming the underneath zone and guarding against a pass to the tight end.

The play is over just as soon as it startes. We expect this when Brian is on the field.

Urlacher wastes no time shooting the vacant "A" gap and is on the quarterback immediately for the sack.

Urlacher makes the offense pay for throwing the ball into a zone he is covering.

TEAM STRATEGY

CINCINNATI BENGALS

Division: AFC North | **Stadium:** Paul Brown Stadium | **Type:** Open | **Capacity:** 65,535 | **Surface:** Turf

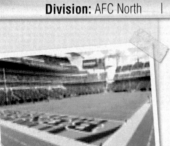

2006 STANDINGS

Wins	Losses	Ties	PF	PA	Home	Road	vs. AFC	vs. NFC	vs. Div
8	8	0	373	331	4-4	4-4	6-6	2-2	4-3

TEAM OVERVIEW

With assets at every position, the Bengals are a passer's dream come true. Unfortunately, their defense has not been up to the task the last few years, which has led to only mediocre regular season results.

Chad Johnson is a gamebreaker at WR. His speed and route running make him almost impossible to handle one-on-one. Houshmandzadeh is the beneficiary of these double teams, and usually runs free on his side of the field.

Geathers provided a pass rush spark for 10.5 sacks last season. The secondary should be a lot better than their league-worthy pass defense showed last year. At least their ratings show some promise.

COACHING PROFILE

Marvin Lewis

- **Head Coaching Year:** 5th
- **Experience:** Defensive coordinator for the Ravens (1996-2001)

On January 14, 2003, Lewis became the ninth coach in Bengals history. Since taking over for the Bengals, he has yet to have a sub .500 season. In his four seasons with the team, Lewis has compiled a 35-29 regular season record.

TEAM RANKINGS

Scoring	8th
Passing Offense	6th
Rushing Offense	28th
Passing Defense	31st
Rushing Defense	15th
Turnovers	6th

RATINGS HISTORY

Category	'07	'06	'05	'04
Overall	89	84	83	72
Offense	92	85	86	75
Defense	85	76	74	69

Bold = Highest Year

83
FIVE-YEAR AVERAGE

SCOUTING REPORT

STRENGTHS

Description	Maximizing Potential	Tips for Opponents
The Bengals passing game is one of the most potent in the game with Carson Palmer at the helm.	Look to get the ball downfield to Chad Johnson and T.J. Houshmandzadeh.	Defend the deep pass first. As effective as the Bengals' run game can be, you must defend the pass.
Rudi Johnson often gets overlooked because of the Bengals' passing game.	If the defense decides to defend the pass first, use Johnson in the run game.	Don't get caught bringing eight and nine defenders in the box to stop the run.
DE Justin Smith is an underrated pass rusher.	Develop schemes that allow Smith to come in cleanly.	If Smith is causing havoc, put a TE on him to force him outside.

WEAKNESSES

Description	Minimizing Risks	Tips for Opponents
The Bengals' secondary is rather weak. They were tied for last in pass defense in 2006.	TE Reggie Kelly is known for run and pass blocking skills, not for pass catching.	Don't waste extra defenders to defend the Bengals' tight ends. Use them to double up the WRs.
As good as the Bengals' passing attack is, they don't have a true threat at tight end to attack the seams.	Blitzing may not be the best. Allow the Bengals' defensive linemen to apply the pressure.	If the Bengals do decide to blitz, look to exploit the secondary by going deep.

TEAM STRATEGY

Overall Rating **88**
Offense **91**
Defense **83**

OFF-SEASON **UPGRADES**

Type	Round	First Name	Last Name	School / Team	Positon	Height	Weight
Released	N/A	Edgerton	Hartwell	Atlanta Falcons	LB	6'1"	250
Free Agent	N/A	Michael	Myers	Denver Broncos	DT	6'2"	300
Free Agent	N/A	Alex	Stepanovich	Arizona Cardinals	C	6'4"	312
Draft	1st	Leon	Hall	Michigan State	CB	5'11"	193
Draft	2nd	Kenny	Irons	Auburn	RB	5'11"	195

FANTASY **OUTLOOK**

⭐ **Star Player:** Carson Palmer
Round of Draft: 2nd

Palmer has too much talent around him at receiver to expect much of a decline from his '06 numbers. Expect him to put up another 3,800 plus yards and 28 touchdowns this season.

⭐ **Star Player:** Chad Johnson
Round of Draft: 2nd

With fellow receiver Chris Henry riding the pine for the first eight games due to a league suspension, Johnson will be in prime position to pick up the extra catches, yards, and touchdowns.

5-YEAR **PLAYER PROGRESSION**

First Name	Last Name	Position	'07 Overall	'08 Overall	'09 Overall	'10 Overall	'11 Overall
Chad	Johnson	WR	98	99	99	99	98
Carson	Palmer	QB	97	98	99	99	99
Justin	Smith	DE	87	87	87	88	87
Robert	Geathers	DE	86	85	86	85	85
Leon	Hall	CB	80	80	81	81	81

FRANCHISE MODE **STRATEGY**

The Bengals' linebacker unit is the team's most pressing need especially at left outside linebacker. Drafting at least one with speed in the early rounds of the 2008 draft will improve the Bengals pass rush.

Key Franchise Info

Team Salary: $82.2M
Cap Room: $26.7M
Key Rival:
• **Cleveland** Browns
NFL Icons: Chad Johnson
Philosophy:
• Offense: Vertical Passing
• Defense: Disrupt Passing
Prestige: Medium
Team Needs:
• Linebackers
• Defensive Line
Highest Paid Players:
• Carson Palmer
• Chad Johnson
Up and Coming Players:
• Domata Peko
• Leon Hall

TEAM STRATEGY

ROSTER AND **PACKAGE TIPS** — KEY PLAYER SUBSTITUTIONS

• **Position:** HB
• **Substitution:** Chris Perry
• **When:** Passing Plays
• **Advantage:** Perry's speed and catch ratings are higher than starter Rudi Johnson. This makes Perry a big threat in the passing game.

• **Position:** WR
• **Substitution:** Chris Henry
• **When:** Global
• **Advantage:** Real NFL off-the-field issues don't apply on the cyber football field. Move Henry to the number three spot on the Bengals' depth chart.

• **Position:** LOLB
• **Substitution:** Landon Johnson
• **When:** Global
• **Advantage:** On the team's depth chart, Johnson sits behind starter Ed Hartwell at ROLB. Even when he moves to LOLB, he is still better than the team's default starter.

• **Position:** PR
• **Substitution:** Deltha O'Neal
• **When:** Global
• **Advantage:** O'Neal is by far the Bengals' best punt return man. With his 94 speed rating, he has a great chance to take the ball back for a score.

CINCINNATI BENGALS / **OFFENSE**

OFFENSIVE **STAR PLAYER** #9

Carson Palmer — Quarterback (QB)

Key Attributes

Awareness	92
Speed	56
Throwing Power	97
Throwing Accuracy	96

After sustaining a major knee injury in the AFC Playoffs in 2005, **Palmer** bounced back in 2006 to post his biggest yardage total by throwing for **4,035** yards. At 6'5", Palmer is able to see over the defensive line and look for the open receiver. His quick release allows him to get the ball off quickly and avoid being sacked. Going into the 2007 season, Palmer ranks among the elite quarterbacks in the NFL.

Player Weapons: Franchise Quarterback / Smart QB, Accurate QB, Cannon Arm QB

RECOMMENDED OFFENSIVE **AUDIBLE PACKAGES**

I Form-Normal	Singleback-Normal	Singleback-Twin TE	Shotgun-2RB 3WR	Shotgun-4WR
Short Slants	Slot Pivot	WR Drag	Double Slant	Curl Flats

OFFENSIVE **PLAYCOUNTS**

Quick Pass:	11	Screen Pass:	16	Pinch:	16
Standard Pass:	91	Hail Mary:	1	Counter:	17
Shotgun Pass:	20	Inside Handoff:	32	Draw:	17
Play Action Pass:	61	Outside Handoff:	15		

TEAM **TRIVIA**

Cincinnati Bengals Facts

Turn the page for the answers.

1. What Bengals receiver caught two TDs in Super Bowl XVI?

2. What lanky wide receiver did the Bengals draft with their second round pick in 1980?

3. What innovative Bengals coach was credited with inventing the no-huddle offence?

OFFENSIVE **FORMATIONS**

Singleback	Strong I
Big Wing	Normal
Twin TE	Twin WR
Normal	3WR
Slot Strong	**Weak I**
Trips Bunch	Close
Tight Slots	Twin WR
4WR Flex	**Shotgun**
Trips WR	2RB 3WR
I Form	Normal
Normal	4WR
Twin WR	Trips
Split Backs	
Normal	
3WR	

OFFENSIVE **STRENGTH CHART**

- ○: OVR less than 80
- ●: OVR 90 or greater
- ●: OVR between 80-89
- ○: Player Weapons

2-Back Set

WR #84 — OL #76 — OL #64 — OL #53 — OL #63 — OL #71 — TE #82 — WR #85
QB #9
FB #31
HB #32

3 Reciever Set

WR #84 — OL #76 — OL #64 — OL #53 — OL #63 — OL #71 — TE #82 — WR #85
WR #15 — QB #9
HB #32

OFFENSIVE **ROSTER LIST** Current / Next Gen

Pos.	#	First Name	Last Name	Overall	Player Weapons
C	53	Eric	Ghiaciuc	81	
C	69	Alex	Stepanovich	76	
FB	31	Jeremi	Johnson	90	
HB	32	Rudi	Johnson	91	Power Back / Power Back, Stiff Arm BC
HB	23	Chris	Perry	81	
HB	30	Kenny	Irons	79	
HB	33	Kenny	Watson	73	
K	17	Shayne	Graham	94	Accurate Kicker
LG	77	Andrew	Whitworth	73	
LG	64	Ben	Wilkerson	73	
LT	76	Levi	Jones	91	Pass Blocker
LT	70	Adam	Kieft	68	
QB	9	Carson	Palmer	97	Franchise QB / Smart QB, Cannon Arm QB, Accurate QB
QB	11	Doug	Johnson	71	
QB	3	Jeff	Rowe	67	
RG	63	Bobbie	Williams	82	
RG	79	Stacy	Andrews	70	
RT	71	Willie	Anderson	95	Road Blocker / Crushing Run Blocker
RT	75	Scott	Kooistra	75	
TE	82	Reggie	Kelly	81	
TE	80	Ronnie	Ghent	70	
WR	85	Chad	Johnson	98	Go-To Guy / Quick, Possession, Spectacular Catch Receiver, Hands
WR	84	T.J.	Houshmandzadeh	92	Possession Receiver / Quick, Possesion Receiver, Hands
WR	15	Chris	Henry	85	
WR	88	Tab	Perry	75	
WR	83	Antonio	Chatman	74	
WR	16	Glenn	Holt	73	

Singleback-Normal

TE Post

Singleback-Trips Bunch

Smash Slot Post

Strong I-3WR

Deep Cross

Plays such as Singleback-Normal TE Post show off Carson Palmer's ability to place balls where only his receiver can catch them.

This is a play that displays Palmer's ability to hit the deep corner route with accuracy.

A final play that shows off Palmer's ability to thread the needle between defenders is the Strong I-3WR Deep Cross.

The play contains three deep routes and two short routes.

Singleback-Trips Bunch Smash Slot post is another play that contains the post and the corner routes.

Call this play If you need more protection against the pass rush but would like to emphasize the same routes to show off Palmer's precision passing.

Once you drop back with Palmer, look for your slot receiver on the corner route or the tight end on the post route.

Send the outside flanker on a streak. The streak route is added because it runs one defender off deep and opens up the corner route to the outside.

As you drop back with Palmer, you will have more protection against the blitz due to the backs picking up defenders.

Palmer has a knack for putting the ball on his wide receiver and away from any defenders lurking to defend the pass.

Throw the ball to the outside to your receiver on the corner route for the big play.

Palmer's accuracy is so keen that he can hit his favorite target, Chad Johnson, in traffic.

TEAM STRATEGY

CINCINNATI BENGALS / DEFENSE

DEFENSIVE STAR PLAYER #91

Robert Geathers — Defensive End (RE)

Key Attributes	
Speed	80
Strength	73
Awareness	72
Tackling	74

In his third season with the Bengals, **Geathers** made a huge impact on the defensive side of the ball by leading the team in sacks, with **10.5**. During his three NFL seasons, he has improved his pass rush ability, which has made him a force to be reckoned with. Geathers will see more double teams this season, but as long as he works hard, he will be a productive pass rusher that the opposing offense will have to reckon with.

Player Weapon: None

RECOMMENDED DEFENSIVE AUDIBLE PACKAGES

4-3-Normal	4-3-Over	46-Bear	46-Normal	Dime-3-2-6
Buzz Duo	Bengal 3 Fire	Wall Stunt	Safe 4 Zip	QB Trap

DEFENSIVE PLAYCOUNTS

Man Coverage:	41	Cover 3 Zone:	23	Combo Blitz:	23
Man Zone:	37	Deep Zone:	22	Goal Line:	15
Combo Coverage:	12	Man Blitz:	49	Special Teams:	12
Cover 2 Zone:	14	Zone Blitz:	57		

TEAM TRIVIA

Cincinnati Bengals Facts

Answers:

1. Dan Ross
2. Cris Collinsworth
3. Sam Wyche

DEFENSIVE FORMATIONS

4-3	Nickel
4-3-Normal	Nickel-3-3-5
4-3-Over	Nickel-Normal
4-3-Under	**Quarter**
46	Quarter-Normal
46-Bear	Quarter-3 Deep
46-Normal	
Dime	
Dime-3-2-6	
Dime-Flat	
Dime-Normal	

DEFENSIVE STRENGTH CHART

○: OVR less than 80 ●: OVR 90 or greater
◐: OVR between 80-89 ◯: Player Weapons

4-3 Base Defense

FS #40 — SS #28
CB #22 — LB #56 — LB #51 — LB #93 — CB #24
RE #90 — DT #94 — DT #97 — LE #98

Dime Defense

FS #40 — SS #28
CB #22 — CB #29 — LB #51 — CB #25 — CB #24
RE #90 — DT #94 — DT #97 — LE #98

DEFENSIVE ROSTER LIST — Current / Next Gen

Pos.	#	First Name	Last Name	Overall	Player Weapons
CB	24	Deltha	O'Neal	86	Quick Corner
CB	22	Johnathan	Joseph	85	Quick Corner / Speed
CB	29	Leon	Hall	80	
CB	25	Keiwan	Ratliff	79	
CB	27	Greg	Brooks	69	
DT	97	John	Thornton	86	
DT	96	Michael	Myers	79	
DT	94	Domata	Peko	79	
DT	67	Kenderick	Allen	71	
FS	40	Madieu	Williams	86	
FS	43	Ethan	Kilmer	74	
LE	98	Bryan	Robinson	80	
LE	68	Jonathan	Fanene	73	
LE	92	Frostee	Rucker	72	
LOLB	99	David	Pollack	77	
LOLB	93	Rashad	Jeanty	77	
MLB	51	Odell	Thurman	84	
MLB	50	Ahmad	Brooks	76	
MLB	58	Caleb	Miller	75	
P	19	Kyle	Larson	82	
RE	90	Justin	Smith	87	
RE	91	Robert	Geathers	86	
ROLB	56	Ed	Hartwell	86	Heavy Hitter / Big Hitter
ROLB	59	Landon	Johnson	85	
SS	28	Dexter	Jackson	84	
SS	26	Marvin	White	72	

TEAM STRATEGY

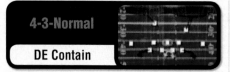

4-3-Normal	4-3-Normal	Dime-3-2-6
DE Contain	Zip Gut Shoot	QB Contain

Robert Geathers shows a solid first step and displays decent lateral speed. Plays like this show off Geathers's footwork to contain the quarterback.

A play that highlights Geathers's ability in space and lateral movement is the 4-3-Normal Zip Gut Shoot.

A final play that emphasizes Geathers's ability to play in space and cover the pass is the Dime-3-2-6 DB Contain.

Robert Geathers is a big hitter. He is not a great pass rusher. The 4-3-Normal DE Contain sends him on a containment pass rushing lane toward the quarterback.

This play drops the defensive ends back into coverage in the hook/curl area. It's good play that baits the QB into a quick throw to the tight end.

The Dime-3-2-6 DB Contain drops both defensive ends into flats coverage. This is a good play to contain those quick passes to the running backs in the flats.

On the snap, rather than going up the field, Geathers will go outside and then turn up the field and delay his pass rush.

Geathers drops into coverage where he can mirror the tight end and other players that happen to run in his area.

Geathers drops into the flat area and mirrors the running back as he makes his way out of the backfield on the swing route.

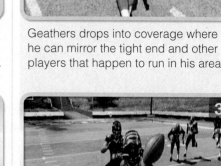

There he will wait to see if the quarterback makes a move. If the QB runs in his direction, he is there to make the big hit.

Because of his height, Geathers can knock down quick passes and leap to knock down high passes.

He easily defends. If he had better hands, he would be running this one back for six points.

TEAM STRATEGY

BUFFALO BILLS

Division: AFC East | **Stadium:** Ralph Wilson Stadium | **Type:** Open | **Capacity:** 73,967 | **Surface:** AstroPlay

TEAM STRATEGY

COACHING PROFILE

Dick Jauron

- **Head Coaching Year:** 8th
- **Experience:** Detroit Lions defensive coordinator (2004-2005)

He took his third head coaching job when he became the 14th coach of the Buffalo Bills on Jan. 23, 2006. In his first year with the team, he lead the Bills to a 7-9 record. He enters season two with a career record of 43-58.

TEAM RANKINGS

Scoring	23rd
Passing Offense	28th
Rushing Offense	27th
Passing Defense	7th
Rushing Defense	28th
Turnovers	23rd

RATINGS HISTORY

Category	'07	'06	'05	'04
Overall	84	78	82	83
Offense	82	77	78	82
Defense	87	94	93	79

Bold = Highest Year

82
FIVE-YEAR
AVERAGE

2006 STANDINGS

Wins	Losses	Ties	PF	PA	Home	Road	vs. AFC	vs. NFC	vs. Div
7	9	0	300	311	4-4	3-5	5-7	2-2	3-3

TEAM OVERVIEW

The Bills are going through a serious youth movement after losing veterans Nate Clements, London Fletcher, and Willis McGahee during the off-season. They will continue to push their power rushing attack, handing the keys to backfield over to Marshawn Lynch.

Lynch has good speed and agility and should be able to carry the load with Anthony Thomas providing a solid back up QB. J.P. Losman is improving, but doesn't have many assets to throw to at WR.

The Bills ran numerous rookies on defense last year. This should pay off in year two as they come back with great experience. You should get good pressure from the line with RE Aaron Schobel leading the way.

SCOUTING REPORT

STRENGTHS

Description	Maximizing Potential	Tips for Opponents
Lee Evans is a perennial #1 wide receiver. A year ago he exploded with 82 receptions for 1,292 yards.	Look for Evans as much as possible. Look for him in the short game as well as in the vertical attack.	Know where Evans is on all downs. Use bracketing schemes and double coverage on Evans.
Donte Whitner is an up-and-coming safety with 104 tackles and 1 interception last season.	Whitner's game is to bring the pain to both wide receivers and running backs.	Do not lead your wide receivers to Whitner or else they may be seeing stars.
Simpson started as a rookie in the Bills' secondary.	Simpson has good speed to run with receivers	Stay out of the middle unless you want your WRs hurt.

WEAKNESSES

Description	Minimizing Risks	Tips for Opponents
The Bills lost most of their premier athletes on defense including Fletcher, Spikes and Clements.	Angelo Crowell becomes the key man at linebacker, but he's no London Fletcher.	Establish the run early and often against this weak front seven to get Whitner and/or Simpson in the box.
The Bills do not have defensive linemen who can get to the quarterback consistently.	You must call blitz packages to apply pressure; otherwise the opposing quarterback will be able to pick your secondary apart.	Send all five receivers out on pass patterns until the Bills can prove they can get a consistent pass rush on your quarterback.

Overall Rating **83**
Offense **83**
Defense **84**

OFF-SEASON UPGRADES

Type	Round	First Name	Last Name	School/Team	Positon	Height	Weight
Free Agent	N/A	Derrick	Dockery	Redskins	G	6'6"	345
Trade	N/A	Darwin	Walker	Eagles	DT	6'3"	294
Free Agent	N/A	Langston	Walker	Raiders	T	6'8"	345
Draft	1	Marshawn	Lynch	California	RB	5'11"	217
Draft	2	Paul	Posluszny	Penn State	LB	6'1"	237

FANTASY OUTLOOK

⭐ **Star Player:** Lee Evans
Round of Draft: 4th

In his final seven games, Evans had a total of 12 touchdown receptions, making him a hot commodity for the '08 season. As long as J.P. Losman doesn't slip, Evans will post even higher numbers.

⭐ **Star Player:** J.P. Losman
Round of Draft: 13th

The lightbulb went on for Losman in the second half of the season. He had 13 of his 19 touchdown passes during that stretch. We would not draft him as a fantasy starter, but he makes a for a solid backup.

5-YEAR PLAYER PROGRESSION

First Name	Last Name	Position	'07 Overall	'08 Overall	'09 Overall	'10 Overall	'11 Overall
Aaron	Schobel	DE	92	93	93	96	97
Lee	Evans	WR	90	92	92	93	93
J.P.	Losman	QB	81	81	79	79	78
Marshawn	Lynch	HB	82	82	82	82	83
Angelo	Crowell	LB	86	89	89	89	89

FRANCHISE MODE STRATEGY

Look to upgrade depth at receiver. Outside of Lee Evans, the Bills don't have any other receiver that defenses have to scheme for. An upgrade at right guard needs to be addressed in the draft or free agency.

Key Franchise Info

Team Salary: $71.7M
Cap Room: $37.2M
Key Rival:
• Miami Dolphins
NFL Icons: None
Philosophy:
• Offense: Ball Control
• Defense: Force the Pass
Prestige: Very Low
Team Needs:
• Offensive Line
• Linebacker
Highest Paid Players:
• Derrick Dockery
• Donte Whitner
Up and Coming Players:
• Marshawn Lynch
• Donte Whitner

TEAM STRATEGY

ROSTER AND PACKAGE TIPS — KEY PLAYER SUBSTITUTIONS

• **Position:** WR
• **Substitution:** Roscoe Parrish
• **When:** Global
• **Advantage:** By moving Parrish up to the number three receiver on the depth chart, you add speed in the slot when coming out in the 3WR formations.

• **Position:** TE
• **Substitution:** Kevin Everett
• **When:** Global
• **Advantage:** This may seem a little picky, but the Bills' offense can use all the receivers they can when throwing the ball. Move Everett to the number two spot on the depth chart. He has decent speed, plus solid hands.

• **Position:** DT
• **Substitution:** Darwin Walker
• **When:** Global
• **Advantage:** Walker is clearly the Bills' best defensive tackle. He needs to be on the field at all times because of the pressure he can apply up the middle as a pass rusher.

• **Position:** LOLB
• **Substitution:** Keith Ellison
• **When:** Global
• **Advantage:** This move is based purely on speed. Ellison's speed rating is an 83. Default LOLB Mario Haggan's speed rating is a 77. More speed means better pass coverage and pass rushing.

BUFFALO BILLS / OFFENSE

OFFENSIVE **STAR PLAYER** #83

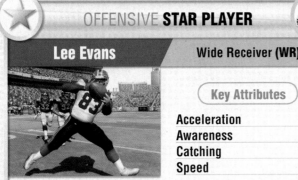

Lee Evans — Wide Receiver (WR)

Key Attributes	
Acceleration	99
Awareness	84
Catching	88
Speed	98

Evans will have to really take the offense on his shoulders this year with the departure of RB Willis McGahee. He is confident enough to handle the task, and with the way that he and J.P. Losman have been hooking up on the deep ball, Bills' fans are reminded of Kelly and Reed on the field. Evans has proven himself as one of the best deep threats in the league. With his speed, he will force double coverage or man with a safety rolling to his side.

Player Weapons: Deep Threat / Speed

OFFENSIVE **STRENGTH CHART**

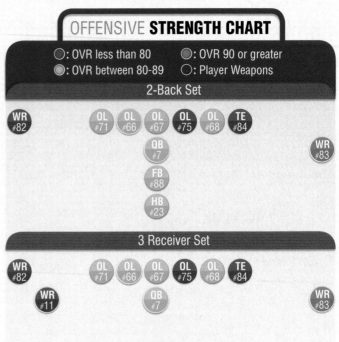

○: OVR less than 80   ●: OVR 90 or greater
◉: OVR between 80-89   ○: Player Weapons

2-Back Set

WR #82 · OL #71 · OL #66 · OL #67 · OL #75 · OL #68 · TE #84 · WR #83 · QB #7 · FB #88 · HB #23

3 Receiver Set

WR #82 · OL #71 · OL #66 · OL #67 · OL #75 · OL #68 · TE #84 · WR #83 · WR #11 · QB #7 · HB #23

RECOMMENDED OFFENSIVE **AUDIBLE PACKAGES**

I Form-Normal	Weak I-Normal	Strong I-Normal	Singleback-Trips Bunch	Shotgun-4WR
HB Slam	PA Boot LTttt	Counter Lead	Slants Slot Flat	HB Flare

OFFENSIVE **PLAYCOUNTS**

Quick Pass:	16	Screen Pass:	13	Pinch:	17
Standard Pass:	94	Hail Mary:	1	Counter:	16
Shotgun Pass:	34	Inside Handoff:	34	Draw:	14
Play Action Pass:	51	Outside Handoff:	16		

TEAM **TRIVIA**

Buffalo Bills Facts

Turn the page for the answers.

❶ Who was the team's head coach before Marv Levy?

❷ In what Super Bowl did Scott Norwood's field goal go wide right?

❸ Who was the quarterback that led the Bills in the biggest comeback in NFL history?

OFFENSIVE **FORMATIONS**

Singleback	Strong I
Big	Normal
Twin TE	3WR
Normal Slot	H Pro
Slot Strong	**Weak I**
Trips Bunch	Normal
Tight Slots	Twin WR
4WR	**Shotgun**
Flip Trips	2RB 3WR
I Form	4WR
Normal	5WR
Close	
3WR	
Split Backs	
3WR	

OFFENSIVE **ROSTER LIST** Current / Next Gen

Pos.	#	First Name	Last Name	Overall	Player Weapons
C	67	Melvin	Fowler	80	
C	65	Jason	Whittle	77	
FB	88	Ryan	Neufeld	80	
HB	23	Marshawn	Lynch	82	
HB	28	Anthony	Thomas	80	
HB	31	Dwayne	Wright	76	
HB	36	Shaud	Williams	74	
K	9	Rian	Lindell	90	Accurate Kicker
LG	66	Derrick	Dockery	86	Run Blocker / Crushing Run Blocker
LG	62	Aaron	Merz	66	
LT	71	Jason	Peters	88	
LT	73	Kirk	Chambers	64	
QB	7	J.P.	Losman	81	Cannon Arm
QB	16	Craig	Nall	77	
QB	5	Trent	Edwards	71	
RG	75	Duke	Preston	74	
RG	60	Brad	Butler	73	
RT	68	Langston	Walker	80	
RT	79	Terrance	Pennington	70	
TE	84	Robert	Royal	79	
TE	85	Kevin	Everett	73	
TE	86	Brad	Cieslak	71	
WR	83	Lee	Evans	90	Deep Threat / Speed
WR	81	Peerless	Price	79	
WR	11	Roscoe	Parrish	79	Deep Threat
WR	82	Josh	Reed	79	

Singleback-Normal Slot

Slot Cross

Lee Evans is a big play receiver, and with that comes a lot of attention from the defense. Use the package system to move Lee Evans to the slot.

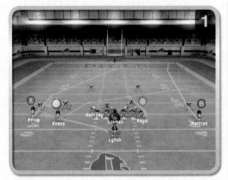

The Slot Cross is a play that is designed to beat the defense over the middle with a crossing route, while sending the outside receivers on vertical routes.

Evans is the slot receiver, and as the quarterback rolls out, he spots him running across the field and free of any defenders.

Evans's speed is more of a problem for the defense if they have to cover him on a crossing route.

Split Backs-3WR

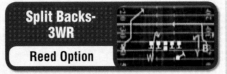

Reed Option

Evans is not known as a perfect route runner but if he gets the ball in stride, then the defenders can just start walking off the field.

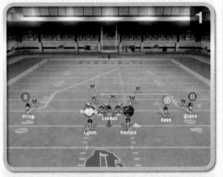

The 3WR Reed Option is a play that is designed with two great routes. This play has a seam post and a seam cross by Evans.

The quarterback looks over the defense and, as soon as the quarterback sees Evans break inside, he releases the ball.

The defense has to respect Evans's speed, so this route is practically always open.

Weak I-Twin WR

Royal Option

Earlier, Lee Evans was in the slot by package, but this time he is given the opportunity to work the inside because of the play call.

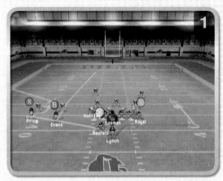

The offensive play is designed to work the left side of the field with a "C" route by the split end and a seam route by Lee Evans.

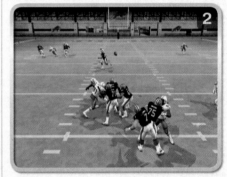

Anytime Evans is matched up in man-to-man coverage with one defender, that is a winning situation for the offense.

The elite receivers have abilities that separate them from everyone else.

BUFFALO BILLS / **DEFENSE**

TEAM STRATEGY

DEFENSIVE **STAR PLAYER** #20

Donte Whitner	Strong Safety (SS)

Key Attributes

Awareness	68
Strength	65
Tackling	82
Speed	92

Whitner is a young, hard-hitting safety who proved that he was ready for the mental and physical challenges that is required to be a starter in the NFL. He made an impressive showing with **107** tackles in his rookie season. In his second year in the NFL, and as a starter, he should start to see offensive schemes and designs quicker and help him add to his top-five finish in tackles for his team.

Player Weapon: Coverage Safety

DEFENSIVE **AUDIBLE PACKAGES**

4-3-Normal	4-3-Over	Nickel-3-3-5	Nickel-Strong	Quarters-Normal
Buzz Weak	Zone Blitz	CB Sting Blitz	FS Snake Blitz 3	DB Strike 1

DEFENSIVE **PLAYCOUNTS**

Man Coverage:	41	Cover 3 Zone:	23	Combo Blitz:	23
Man Zone:	37	Deep Zone:	22	Goal Line:	15
Combo Coverage:	12	Man Blitz:	49	Special Teams:	12
Cover 2 Zone:	14	Zone Blitz:	57		

TEAM **TRIVIA**

Buffalo Bills Facts

Answers:

❶ Hank Bullough

❷ Super Bowl XXV

❸ Frank Reich

DEFENSIVE **FORMATIONS**

4-3	Nickle
4-3-Normal	Nickel-3-3-5
4-3-Over	Nickel-Normal
4-3-Under	Nickel-Strong
Dime	**Quarter**
Dime-Flat	Quarter-Normal
Dime-Normal	Quarter-3 Deep

DEFENSIVE **STRENGTH CHART**

- ◯: OVR less than 80
- ◉: OVR 90 or greater
- ◕: OVR between 80-89
- ◯: Player Weapons

4-3 Base Defense

FS #30   SS #20

CB #44   LB #51   LB #55   LB #53   CB #24

RE #94   DT #98   DT #96   LE #92

Dime Defense

FS #30   SS #20

CB #44   CB #25   LB #55   CB #26   CB #24

RE #94   DT #98   DT #96   LE #92

DEFENSIVE **ROSTER LIST** Current / Next Gen

Pos.	#	First Name	Last Name	Overall	Player Weapons
CB	24	Terrence	McGee	85	Quick Corner
CB	44	Jason	Webster	81	
CB	25	Kiwaukee	Thomas	77	
CB	26	Ashton	Youboty	76	
CB	33	Jabari	Greer	69	
DT	96	Darwin	Walker	86	
DT	98	Larry	Tripplett	85	
DT	77	Tim	Anderson	77	
DT	95	Kyle	Williams	76	
DT	97	John	McCargo	75	
FS	30	Ko	Simpson	80	
FS	29	John	Wendling	75	
LE	90	Chris	Kelsay	83	
LE	92	Ryan	Denney	83	
LOLB	53	Mario	Haggan	77	
LOLB	58	Roy	Manning	69	
MLB	55	Angelo	Crowell	86	
MLB	52	John	DiGiorgio	61	
P	8	Brian	Moorman	94	Big Foot Kicker
RE	94	Aaron	Schobel	92	Power Move D-Lineman
RE	93	Anthony	Hargrove	77	
ROLB	51	Paul	Posluszny	82	Playmaker
ROLB	56	Keith	Ellison	76	
ROLB	57	Josh	Stamer	70	
SS	20	Donte	Whitner	88	Coverage Safety
SS	27	Coy	Wire	71	

Nickel-Normal	
Engage 8	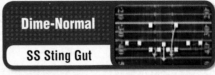

Whitner came on strong last year and showed that he can bring the wood as he did in college. Make sure to get Whitner involved in the blitz game.

The Engage 8 is a jailbreak defense. This defense brings pressure from everywhere, and with eight men blitzing, someone is bound to get through.

When the play starts and the quarterback is still in his drop, Whitner is already across the line of scrimmage and on a beeline to the QB.

As soon as the quarterback gets turned around on his rollout, Whitner meets him and crushes him.

Dime-Normal	
SS Sting Gut	

Whitner is a solid blitzer and plays the run well. If the offense tries to run, he will make sure they understand it's not going to happen.

This is a man defense that has flat coverage. This play is also great if a team has a safety who can come up and disrupt the offense.

The offense decides to run the ball. Donte plays the run perfectly, and does not get so far ahead that he would leave a cut back lane.

When he gets to the running back, he drops him where he stands. There will be no rushing yards.

Dime-Normal	
Cover 3	

There has been a lot of attention on Whitner's ability defending the run. He is also solid in pass coverage. Any offense that tests him will pay a price.

The Dime Cover 3 is a defense used to cover the field with a 3-deep zone while also covering both flats. Whitner is assigned to robber coverage.

In robber coverage, Whitner will not run with the streak route, but he will defend against it as long as it is in his area.

The quarterback throws the ball to the slot receiver, but Donte uses his skills to intercept the pass.

TEAM STRATEGY

73

DENVER BRONCOS

Division: AFC West	**Stadium:** Invesco Field at Mile High	**Type:** Open	**Capacity:** 76,125	**Surface:** Grass

2006 STANDINGS

Wins	Losses	Ties	PF	PA	Home	Road	vs. AFC	vs. NFC	vs. Div
9	7	0	319	305	4-4	5-3	8-4	1-3	3-3

COACHING PROFILE

Mike Shanahan

- **Head Coaching Year:** 14th
- **Experience:** Shanahan was an assistant with Denver (1984-1987, 1989-1991) and San Francisco (1992-1994)

He became the fifth head coach to lead his team to back-to-back Super Bowl championships in 1997 and 1998 while coaching the Broncos legend John Elway.

TEAM STRATEGY

TEAM RANKINGS

Scoring	17th
Passing Offense	25th
Rushing Offense	8th
Passing Defense	21st
Rushing Defense	12th
Turnovers	17th

RATINGS HISTORY

Category	'07	'06	'05	'04
Overall	**89**	74	80	80
Offense	88	**90**	77	82
Defense	**90**	80	89	77

Bold = Highest Year

82
FIVE-YEAR
AVERAGE

TEAM OVERVIEW

Despite having one of the top rosters in the league, the Broncos didn't sit back on their laurels in the off-season. Jay Cutler is firmly entrenched as the starter at QB, with Plummer traded/retired to the Bucs. Cutler has a rocket arm and enough accuracy to remind diehards of the Legend, #7.

With Tatum Bell gone, Travis Henry steps into the mix at running back. He is a strong back and should work well with Shanahan's system. Javon Walker and Rod Smith get the job done at WR.

The Broncos have the best corner back in the game with Champ Bailey. Combine him with FS John Lynch and CB Dre Bly, and opposing teams are going to have a tough time moving the ball through the air against this unit.

SCOUTING REPORT

STRENGTHS

Description	Maximizing Potential	Tips for Opponents
The Broncos signed former Bills' and Titans' running back Travis Henry to carry the load at running back.	Use Henry to pound the ball at the opposing defense. Then use play action to confuse the defense.	Don't let Henry get going on the ground. Make him a priority to stop.
Javon Walker was the team's most explosive receiver with 1,084 receiving yards last year.	With his size and strength, use Walker as your go-to receiver.	Walker doesn't have great speed, but that doesn't mean he can be left in one-on-one coverage.
Champ Bailey is known throughout the NFL as the best corner.	Have Bailey cover the opposing offense's top receiver.	Don't throw toward Bailey unless there is no other option.

WEAKNESSES

Description	Minimizing Risks	Tips for Opponents
Jay is still learning how to be an effective quarterback. He can be pressured into making mistakes.	Use play action to keep the defense honest. By doing so, the defense is less likely to call blitz packages.	In third and long, bring the pressure on the young Cutler to force him into making mistakes.
The Broncos' lackluster pass rush from the defensive line was evident in 2006.	Get rookie defensive end Jarvis Moss in the line-up to rush the quarterback.	If the line is unable to apply pressure, attack the Broncos when they blitz.

Overall Rating 88
Offense 88
Defense 89

OFF-SEASON UPGRADES

Type	Round	First Name	Last Name	School/Team	Positon	Height	Weight
Trade	N/A	Dre'	Bly	Detroit Lions	CB	5'9"	188
Free Agent	N/A	Daniel	Graham	New England Patriots	TE	6'3"	257
Free Agent	N/A	Travis	Henry	Tennessee Titans	RB	5'9"	215
Draft	1st	Jarvis	Moss	Florida	DE	6'6"	251
Draft	2nd	Tim	Crowder	Texas	DE	6'4"	271

FANTASY OUTLOOK

Star Player: Travis Henry
Round of Draft: 1st

The Broncos traditionally have had one of the top running games in the league. Henry is expected to get a heavy workload as the team's featured running back. There is very little reason to think he won't deliver.

Star Player: Javon Walker
Round of Draft: 5th

As long as Jay Cutler performs well at quarterback, Walker will post the fantasy type numbers we all expect from a go to receiver. Anything less than 1,200 receiving will be a disappointment.

5-YEAR PLAYER PROGRESSION

First Name	Last Name	Position	'07 Overall	'08 Overall	'09 Overall	'10 Overall	'11 Overall
Champ	Bailey	CB	99	99	98	95	91
Javon	Walker	WR	93	94	95	97	98
Dre'	Bly	CB	90	87	84	81	-
Jay	Cutler	QB	86	86	90	89	89
Marcus	Thomas	DT	77	77	78	78	77

FRANCHISE MODE STRATEGY

Travis Henry is still a workhorse at running back, but the Broncos need to start grooming a future starter. If a stud running back falls your way in the first round of the '08 draft, snag him.

Key Franchise Info

Team Salary: $84.2M
Cap Room: $24.7M
Key Rival:
• **Oakland** Raiders
NFL Icons: Champ Bailey
Philosophy:
• Offense: West Coast
• Defense: Contain Passing
Prestige: Medium
Team Needs:
• Defensive Line
• Running Back (Future)
Highest Paid Players:
• Champ Bailey
• Javon Walker
Up and Coming Players:
• Marcus Thomas
• Elvis Dumervil

ROSTER AND PACKAGE TIPS — KEY PLAYER SUBSTITUTIONS

• **Position:** WR
• **Substitution:** Rod Smith
• **When:** Global
• **Advantage:** Smith is not as fast as he once was, but still has one the best set of hands in the league. Move him to the number two spot on the depth and use him as a possession receiver.

• **Position:** WR
• **Substitution:** Brandon Stokley
• **When:** Global
• **Advantage:** Stokley is still a solid slot receiver. His speed and hands ratings are slightly higher than Brandon Marshall's, making for a good target down near the goal line.

• **Position:** RE
• **Substitution:** Elvis Dumervil
• **When:** Global
• **Advantage:** Dumervil has a 79 speed rating, which is seven points higher than default starter Ebenezer Ekuban. This makes him a better threat as a pass rusher.

• **Position:** PR
• **Substitution:** Champ Bailey
• **When:** Anytime a big play needs a kick return.
• **Advantage:** Obviously, you don't want to have Bailey returning punts every time, but you will be hard-pressed to find a kick returner who changes the game on one play.

DENVER BRONCOS / OFFENSE

OFFENSIVE STAR PLAYER #6

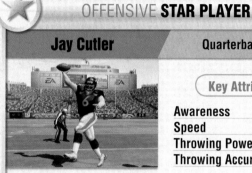

Jay Cutler — Quarterback (QB)

Key Attributes

Awareness	71
Speed	68
Throwing Power	95
Throwing Accuracy	88

Last season, **Cutler** was on the bench learning the ins and outs of being an NFL Quarterback. Midway through the season, Cutler was off the bench and starting. By the end of season, he clearly belonged under center in the NFL. His future looks bright because of his cannon of an arm and his ability to make plays in and out of the pocket. Expect Cutler to have a breakout season and lead the Broncos into the playoffs.

Player Weapons: Cannon Arm / Cannon Arm QB

RECOMMENDED OFFENSIVE AUDIBLE PACKAGES

Singleback-Big	Singleback-Normal Slot	Weak I-Normal	Shotgun-Normal	Shotgun-Normal
FL Corner	Strong Stretch	PA Boot Slide	TE Out-N-Up	PA Slot Post

OFFENSIVE PLAYCOUNTS

Quick Pass:	16	Screen Pass:	7	Pinch:	12
Standard Pass:	85	Hail Mary:	1	Counter:	19
Shotgun Pass:	33	Inside Handoff:	32	Draw:	6
Play Action Pass:	40	Outside Handoff:	22		

TEAM TRIVIA

Denver Broncos Facts

Turn the page for the answers.

1. Which major league baseball team drafted John Elway?

2. Which of the Broncos' widereceivers were know as 'The Three Amigos'?

3. Who was the first Broncos RB to win Rookie-of-the-Year?

OFFENSIVE FORMATIONS

Singleback	Strong I
Big	Normal
Big Twin WR	Twin WR
Twin TE WR	Big Tight
Normal	**Weak I**
Normal Slot	Normal
Base Flex	Twin WR
Empty Trey	Close
I Form	Tight Twins
Normal	**Shotgun**
Twin WR	Normal Slot
Close	Empty Trey
Big	5WR
Normal	
3WR	

OFFENSIVE STRENGTH CHART

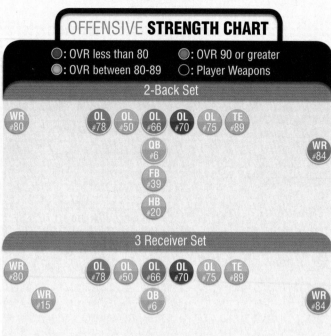

- ○: OVR less than 80
- ◉: OVR 90 or greater
- ◑: OVR between 80-89
- ○: Player Weapons

2-Back Set

WR #80, OL #78, OL #50, OL #66, OL #70, OL #75, TE #89, WR #84, QB #6, FB #39, HB #20

3 Receiver Set

WR #80, OL #78, OL #50, OL #66, OL #70, OL #75, TE #89, WR #15, QB #6, WR #84, HB #20

OFFENSIVE ROSTER LIST Current / Next Gen

Pos.	#	First Name	Last Name	Overall	Player Weapons
C	66	Tom	Nalen	92	Run Blocker
C	65	Mark	Fenton	70	
FB	39	Kyle	Johnson	87	
FB	26	Paul	Smith	79	
HB	20	Travis	Henry	88	
HB	30	Mike	Bell	81	
HB	37	Cecil	Sapp	78	
K	1	Jason	Elam	95	Accurate Kicker
LG	50	Ben	Hamilton	89	
LG	62	Chris	Myers	71	
LT	78	Matt	Lepsis	90	Run Blocker
LT	64	Erik	Pears	72	
QB	6	Jay	Cutler	86	Cannon Arm / Cannon Arm QB
QB	8	Patrick	Ramsey	77	
RG	70	Montrae	Holland	76	
RG	73	Chris	Kuper	74	
RT	75	Adam	Meadows	81	
RT	74	Ryan	Harris	73	
TE	89	Daniel	Graham	86	
TE	82	Stephen	Alexander	79	
TE	88	Tony	Scheffler	79	
WR	84	Javon	Walker	93	Go-To Guy / Quick, Possesion, Spectacular Catch Receiver, Hands
WR	80	Rod	Smith	84	
WR	15	Brandon	Marshall	83	
WR	14	Brandon	Stokley	81	
WR	87	David	Kircus	75	
WR	11	Quincy	Morgan	74	

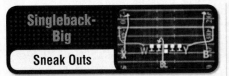

Singleback-Big
Sneak Outs

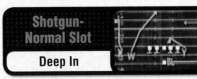

Shotgun-Normal Slot
Deep In

Shotgun-Empty Trey
Hi Lo Read

QB Jay Cutler can make all the throws with good velocity and precision. Plays such as this show off his ability to throw the deep ball with precision.

Another play that shows off Cutler's strong arm and ability to make precision passes is the Shotgun-Normal Slot Deep In.

A final play that shows off Cutler's play-making ability and his physical tools as a quarterback is the Shotgun-Empty Trey Hi Lo Read.

Jay Cutler has a rocket arm that is fitted for the deep ball. The streak route does a good job of showing off the potential of his arm.

It is all about the deep routes with Cutler. Not only can he throw the streak, but he can also throw the Deep In route with some consistency.

This play has everything you would want to show off Cutler's abilities. It has the Deep In route as well as the streak route.

Drop back in the pocket with Cutler. If you see you have a one-on-one match up on the outside, throw the ball up and deep and let your receivers track it down.

As you drop back with Cutler on this play, look for the flanker to make his move across the middle. Make sure that a linebacker is not sitting underneath.

Drop back with Cutler. If you get a blitz on this play, watch the safety. If he blitzes, throw the streak because you will have one one-on-one on the outside.

WR Javon Walker uses his speed to catch up to the deep pass by Cutler and burn the secondary for the big one.

Once the flanker gets clear, deliver him a bullet over the middle and keep the chains moving.

Cutler gets off the deep pass and allows his big target Javon Walker to run under the pass for the big gain.

TEAM STRATEGY

DENVER BRONCOS / **DEFENSE**

TEAM STRATEGY

DEFENSIVE **STAR PLAYER** **#24**

Champ Bailey — Cornerback (CB)

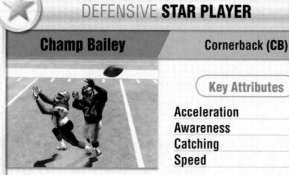

Key Attributes	
Acceleration	98
Awareness	97
Catching	82
Speed	98

Bailey is one of the best cornerbacks in the game. QB don't normally test his side of the field in fear that Bailey may pick the pass off and go in for the score. He has the ability to lock down an opponent's number one receiver. As good as he is in pass coverage, he also isn't afraid to stick his nose in to help against the run game. Last season, he had **86** tackles, which tied him for third on the team.

Player Weapons: Shutdown Corner/Shutdown Corner, Smart Corner, Press Coverage Corner, Speed

RECOMMENDED DEFENSIVE **AUDIBLE PACKAGES**

4-3-Normal	4-3-Over	Dime-Flat	Nickel-3-3-5	Nickel-Normal
Hog Buck 3	Zone Blitz	1 Man DB Strike	Man-QB Spy	9 Velcro

DEFENSIVE **PLAYCOUNTS**

Man Coverage:	41	Cover 3 Zone:	23	Combo Blitz:	23
Man Zone:	37	Deep Zone:	22	Goal Line:	15
Combo Coverage:	12	Man Blitz:	49	Special Teams:	12
Cover 2 Zone:	14	Zone Blitz:	57		

TEAM **TRIVIA**

Denver Broncos Facts

Answers:

1 Yankees

2 Jackson, Johnson, and Nattiel

2 Bobby Humphrey

DEFENSIVE **FORMATIONS**

4-3	Nickle
4-3-Normal	Nickel-3-3-5
4-3-Over	Nickel-Normal
4-3-Under	Nickel-Strong
Dime	**Quarter**
Dime-Normal	Quarter-Normal
Dime-Flat	Quarter-3 Deep

DEFENSIVE **STRENGTH CHART**

◒: OVR less than 80	●: OVR 90 or greater
◐: OVR between 80-89	○: Player Weapons

4-3 Base Defense

FS #47, SS #25
CB #32, LB #52, LB #55, LB #57, CB #24
RE #91, DT #99, DT #61, LE #76

Dime Defense

FS #47, SS #25
CB #32, CB #22, LB #55, CB #41, CB #24
RE #91, DT #99, DT #61, LE #76

DEFENSIVE **ROSTER LIST** Current/Next Gen

Pos.	#	First Name	Last Name	Overall	Player Weapons
CB	24	Champ	Bailey	99	Shutdown Corner/Shutdown, Smart, Press Coverage Corner, Speed
CB	32	Dre'	Bly	90	Shutdown Corner/Shutdown Corner
CB	22	Domonique	Foxworth	83	Quick Corner
CB	41	Karl	Paymah	75	
DT	61	Gerard	Warren	85	
DT	99	Alvin	McKinley	83	
DT	77	Marcus	Thomas	77	
DT	97	Demetrin	Veal	74	
DT	94	Amon	Gordon	66	
FS	47	John	Lynch	96	Big Hitter/Smart Safety, Big Hitter, Brick Wall Defender
FS	42	Sam	Brandon	77	
LE	76	Kenard	Lang	86	
LE	60	John	Engelberger	80	
LE	96	Tim	Crowder	78	
LOLB	57	Warrick	Holdman	83	
LOLB	54	D.D.	Lewis	78	
MLB	55	D.J.	Williams	90	Playmaker/Big Hitter, Brick Wall Defender
MLB	58	Nate	Webster	79	
P	10	Todd	Sauerbrun	86	
RE	92	Elvis	Dumervil	82	
RE	91	Ebenezer	Ekuban	82	
RE	95	Jarvis	Moss	81	
ROLB	52	Ian	Gold	90	Playmaker
ROLB	53	Louis	Green	69	
SS	25	Nick	Ferguson	86	
SS	40	Curome	Cox	75	

4-3-Normal
Free Fire

4-3-Normal
Cover 3

Dime-Normal
1 Man CB Snake

Plays such as the 4-3-Normal Free Fire allow the defense to be aggressive as Champ Bailey shows off his ability.

One play that allows Bailey to show off his transitional quickness and ability to read and recover from double moves is the 4-3-Normal Cover 3.

A final play that highlights Bailey's top speed is the Dime-Normal 1 Man CB Snake. Flip the play so that Bailey becomes the pass rusher.

Champ Bailey is a shutdown CB that allows you to run a high risk/high reward type of defense. This play is a risky blitz that sends six pass rushers after the QB.

Not only can Bailey play man and press man coverage at the highest level, he can also play the short and deep zone.

Finally, Bailey is a tremendous blitzer. His speed allows him to get to the quarterback rather quickly.

Champ can come up on Cover 0 Blitzes such as the Free Fire and play press coverage. He reroutes the wide receiver here.

Bailey does an excellent job of mirroring post routes. He gets his hips around without hesitation.

Bailey is quick to hit the edge on cornerback blitzes using his athleticism and skill to easily get past the offensive line.

Even when he presses the wide receiver, Bailey's instincts are keen. He also reads the route and uses his speed to stay out in front of the wide receiver.

When the ball gets there, Bailey is also there to break up the play. Bailey is rarely fooled by transition routes such as the post.

Once he gets into the back field, he is a smart tackler and knows how to bring the QB down to the turf.

TEAM STRATEGY

79

CLEVELAND BROWNS

Division: AFC North | **Stadium:** Cleveland Browns Stadium | **Type:** Open | **Capacity:** 73,200+ | **Surface:** Grass

2006 STANDINGS

Wins	Losses	Ties	PF	PA	Home	Road	vs. AFC	vs. NFC	vs. Div
4	12	0	238	356	2-6	2-6	3-9	1-3	0-6

TEAM STRATEGY

TEAM OVERVIEW

The Browns are still picked to be in the AFC North cellar this year, but they do have some interesting players that make this a fun team to run with in *Madden NFL 08*. The big question is: how long will it be before Brady Quinn takes over the starting role for this squad?

Whoever the quarterback is, they have some pieces to work with. Kellen Winslow is a force at TE and will find himself the beneficiary of serious mismatches with opposing linebackers. Braylon Edwards is no slouch at WR, either.

The strength of the defense is at the safety position with Sean Jones. He has big play potential and many scouts believe that he will be a future star. Andra Davis is a solid MLB, but much of the defense is a little suspect.

COACHING PROFILE

Romeo Crennel

- **Head Coaching Year:** 3rd
- **Experience:** New England Patriots defensive coordinator (2001-2004)

Crennel became the head coach of the Cleveland Browns on February 8, 2005. Before becoming the Browns' coach, he helped the Patriots win three championship rings as defensive coordinator.

TEAM RANKINGS

Scoring	30th
Passing Offense	23rd
Rushing Offense	8th
Passing Defense	21st
Rushing Defense	12th
Turnovers	17th

RATINGS HISTORY

Category	'07	'06	'05	'04
Overall	**85**	62	65	67
Offense	**86**	67	69	67
Defense	**86**	70	68	67

Bold = Highest Year

73
FIVE-YEAR
AVERAGE

SCOUTING REPORT

STRENGTHS

Description	Maximizing Potential	Tips for Opponents
Browns' tight end Kellen Winslow had his best season as a pro by catching 89 passes for 875 yards.	Winslow is an imposing specimen at tight end. Take advantage of his speed and athleticism.	Winslow needs to be covered by a fast, athletic linebacker or safety.
Braylon Edwards came into his own last season by posting his best yardage total with 884 yards.	Edwards is the Browns' best outside receiver. He has good height, making him a good red zone target.	Although Edwards is the team's best receiver, he still needs a quarterback throw him the ball.
Wimbley is Cleveland's biggest threat to put pressure on the QB.	Call defensive plays that allow Wimbley to get after the passer.	Be sure to account for Wimbley with hot route blocks.

WEAKNESSES

Description	Minimizing Risks	Tips for Opponents
Inconsistent quarterback play from Charlie Frye stunted the growth of the Browns' offense in 2006.	We would start Quinn to begin improving his ratings.	Regardless of who the starting quarterback is, bring tons of pressure until he proves he can beat it.
The Cleveland corners struggled last season to defend the pass and it won't be much better in '07.	Try to avoid leaving the Browns' corners exposed in one-on-one situations.	The Browns do not have any type of lockdown corner on their roster, attack both sides of the field.

Overall Rating **85**
Offense **85**
Defense **86**

OFF-SEASON UPGRADES

Type	Round	First Name	Last Name	School/Team	Positon	Height	Weight
Free Agent	N/A	Jamal	Lewis	Baltimore Ravens	RB	5'11"	245
Free Agent	N/A	Mike	Adams	San Francisco 49ers	S	5'11"	185
Free Agent	N/A	Antwan	Peek	Houston Texans	LB	6'3"	250
Draft	1st	Joe	Thomas	Wisconsin	OT	6'6"	313
Draft	1st	Brady	Quinn	Notre Dame	QB	6'3"	226

FANTASY OUTLOOK

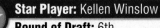 **Star Player:** Kellen Winslow
Round of Draft: 6th

Winslow posted solid numbers in 06 and will look to increase them in 07. However, that all depends on the quarterback play. If it's inconsistent like it was last year, then Winslows numbers will not see much improvement.

Star Player: Braylon Edwards
Round of Draft: 10th

Edwards falls in the same category as Winslow does. For him to improve on his receptions, yardage, and touchdown totals, the Browns' quarterback play must be more consistent.

5-YEAR PLAYER PROGRESSION

First Name	Last Name	Position	'07 Overall	'08 Overall	'09 Overall	'10 Overall	'11 Overall
Kellen	Winslow	TE	93	93	95	96	97
Braylon	Edwards	WR	88	89	90	91	92
Karemion	Wimbley	LB	87	89	88	87	88
Jamal	Lewis	HB	86	84	81	78	-
Joe	Thomas	T	85	84	83	81	79

FRANCHISE MODE STRATEGY

The Browns can use help all over the field. Another receiver needs to be added to improve the passing game. A defensive end with speed will help the team's lack of a pass rush.

Key Franchise Info

Team Salary: $81.4M
Cap Room: $27.5M
Key Rival:
• Pitsburg Steelers
NFL Icons: Jamal Lewis
Philosophy:
• Offense: Vertical Passing
• Defense: Disrupt Passing
Prestige: Very Low
Team Needs:
• Running Back
• Defensive Line
Highest Paid Players:
• Eric Steinbach
• Braylon Edwards
Up and Coming Players:
• Brady Quinn
• Joe Thomas

TEAM STRATEGY

ROSTER AND PACKAGE TIPS — KEY PLAYER SUBSTITUTIONS

• **Position:** QB
• **Substitution:** Brady Qiunn
• **When:** Franchise Mode
• **Advantage:** If you plan on playing franchise mode with the Browns, you might as well get Quinn some reps. He is not as fast as starter Charlie Frye, but he is slightly more accurate.

• **Position:** FB
• **Substitution:** Alan Ricard
• **When:** Global
• **Advantage:** The Browns need all the help they can get when it comes to running the ball. Alan Ricard is the team's best blocking fullback and will help open running lanes.

• **Position:** WR
• **Substitution:** Tim Carter
• **When:** Global
• **Advantage:** The Browns can use all the speed they can get. Smith is the team's faster receiver, making him a perfect fit lining up in the slot.

• **Position:** RG
• **Substitution:** Kevin Shaffer
• **When:** Global
• **Advantage:** Shaffer's overall rating is 10 points higher than starter Seth McKinney. With a 96 run blocking, it would not be wise to have Shaffer starting somewhere along the offensive line.

CLEVELAND BROWNS / OFFENSE

OFFENSIVE **STAR PLAYER** #17

Braylon Edwards — Wide Receiver (WR)

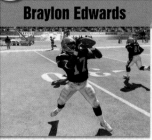

Key Attributes

Acceleration	94
Awareness	72
Catching	87
Speed	93

Edwards has yet to reach his full potential since coming into the league in 2005. A lot of that has to do with inconsistency at the quarterback position. Despite this fact, he still managed to lead the team last season in yardage and touchdown catches. At 6'3", he uses his well-built body and leaping ability to out-jump and out-muscle smaller defensive backs. Look for more big plays from Edwards as he continues to improve.

Player Weapons: Deep Threat / Spectacular Catch Receiver

OFFENSIVE **STRENGTH CHART**

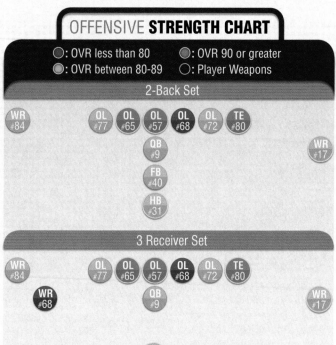

○: OVR less than 80   ○: OVR 90 or greater
●: OVR between 80-89   ○: Player Weapons

2-Back Set

WR #84, OL #77, OL #65, OL #57, OL #68, OL #72, TE #80, QB #9, FB #40, HB #31, WR #17

3 Receiver Set

WR #84, OL #77, OL #65, OL #57, OL #68, OL #72, TE #80, WR #68, QB #9, WR #17, HB #31

RECOMMENDED OFFENSIVE **AUDIBLE PACKAGES**

I Form- Normal	I Form- Normal	Singleback- Normal Slot	Singleback- Slot Cross	Shotgun-4WR
SE Post Flag	PA TE Dig	HB Counter Trap	FL Middle	Circle

OFFENSIVE **PLAYCOUNTS**

Quick Pass:	17	Screen Pass:	21	Pinch:	15
Standard Pass:	77	Hail Mary:	1	Counter:	20
Shotgun Pass:	23	Inside Handoff:	27	Draw:	15
Play Action Pass:	27	Outside Handoff:	12		

TEAM **TRIVIA**

Cleveland Browns Facts

Turn the page for the answers.

1. What name was originally chosen in a newspaper poll as the nickname for the Browns?

2. Which year of his career did Jim Brown not lead the league in rushing?

3. The Cleveland Browns are notorious for what section of the stadium?

OFFENSIVE **FORMATIONS**

Singleback	Near
Big Twin WR	Pro
Twin TE WR	**Full House**
Normal Slot	Normal Wide
Slot Strong	**Strong I**
Trips Bunch	Normal
4WR Flex	Twin TE
Empty 5WR	**Weak I**
I Form	Normal
Normal	3WR
Twin WR	**Shotgun**
Close	2RB 3WR
Split Backs	4WR
Pro	
3WR	

OFFENSIVE **ROSTER LIST** Current / Next Gen

Pos.	#	First Name	Last Name	Overall	Player Weapons
C	57	LeCharles	Bentley	90	
C	66	Hank	Fraley	84	
FB	40	Alan	Ricard	82	
FB	47	Lawrence	Vickers	77	
HB	31	Jamal	Lewis	86	Power Back / Power Back, Stiff Arm BC
HB	35	Jerome	Harrison	74	
HB	29	Jason	Wright	71	
K	4	Phil	Dawson	88	
LG	65	Eric	Steinbach	92	Pass Blocker / Pass Blocker
LG	62	Lennie	Friedman	76	
LT	77	Kevin	Shaffer	88	
LT	73	Joe	Thomas	85	Pass Blocker / Pass Blocker
QB	9	Charlie	Frye	81	
QB	10	Brady	Quinn	77	
QB	3	Derek	Anderson	73	
RG	68	Seth	McKinney	76	
RG	67	Fred	Matua	73	
RT	72	Ryan	Tucker	85	
RT	71	Kelly	Butler	76	
TE	80	Kellen	Winslow	93	Quick, Possession Receiver
TE	82	Steve	Heiden	77	
TE	87	Darnell	Dinkins	75	
WR	17	Braylon	Edwards	88	Deep Threat / Spectacular Catch Receiver
WR	84	Joe	Jurevicius	83	
WR	86	Tim	Carter	76	
WR	81	Travis	Wilson	76	
WR	16	Joshua	Cribbs	68	

Singleback-Normal Slot
Edwards Option

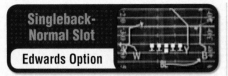

Braylon Edwards has the frame and speed to out-muscle and outrun most of today's cornerbacks.

The option route here for Edwards is a comeback route, a post, or a streak. He will choose the best route possible based on the defensive coverage.

Here, Edwards sees he has one-on-one coverage with Steelers' corner back Deshea Townsend, and chooses to run the streak.

He beats Townsend to the inside and is he is able to make the big play catch for the offense.

Singleback-Trips Bunch
Edwards Option

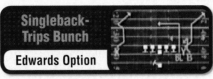

One play that shows off Edwards's craftiness to get open in the middle of the field is the Singleback-Trips Bunch Edwards Option.

This is another play that gives Edwards the freedom to choose his route based on the coverage employed by the defense.

On this play, Edwards selects from an in route, an out route, or a comeback route. This is a nice way to emphasize different routes with the same player.

He catches the ball on the in route and is able to get some yards after the catch due to his coverage read on the defense.

Singleback-Empty 5WR
Slot Flats

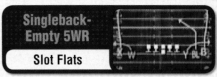

A final play that shows off Edwards's deep speed and big catch ability is the Singleback-Empty 5WR Slot Flats.

Braylon Edwards is a big game wide receiver that can run the streak route and be a force deep down the field.

He runs the streak and is covered by two corner backs. But this is no security blanket for the defense. He was drafted for these situations.

Even when double covered, Edwards is still able to use his body and go up and snag the football.

TEAM STRATEGY

CLEVELAND BROWNS / **DEFENSE**

TEAM STRATEGY

DEFENSIVE **STAR PLAYER** #95

Kamerion Wimbley — Linebacker (ROLB)

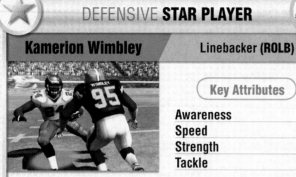

Key Attributes	
Awareness	72
Speed	84
Strength	77
Tackle	86

Wimbley burst onto the scene during his rookie season by posting a team-high **11** sacks. He has quick feet that allow him to quickly get around slower offensive tackles. Once he blows by them, he goes straight to the quarterback. He still needs to improve his run support, but that will come in time as he grows stronger. He has great skill as an NFL linebacker and will likely make a few Pro Bowls during the course of his career.

Player Weapons: Playmaker / Finesse Move D-Lineman

RECOMMENDED DEFENSIVE **AUDIBLE PACKAGES**

3-4-Normal	3-4-Over	3-4-Solid	Dime-Normal	Nickel-3-3-5
2 Deep MLB Spy	Sting Pinch Zone	Clamp Double Go	SS Gut Blitz	CB Fox Blitz 3

DEFENSIVE **PLAYCOUNTS**

Man Coverage:	46	Cover 3 Zone:	24	Combo Blitz:	10
Man Zone:	36	Deep Zone:	16	Goal Line:	15
Combo Coverage:	9	Man Blitz:	48	Special Teams:	12
Cover 2 Zone:	24	Zone Blitz:	60		

TEAM **TRIVIA**

Cleveland Browns Facts

Answers:

1 Panthers

2 1962

3 The Dawg Pound

DEFENSIVE **FORMATIONS**

3-4	Nickle
3-4-Normal	Nickel-3-3-5
3-4-Over	Nickel-Normal
3-4-Under	Nickel-Strong
3-4-Solid	**Quarter**
Dime	Quarter-Normal
Dime-3-2-6	Quarter-3 Deep
Dime-Normal	

DEFENSIVE **STRENGTH CHART**

○: OVR less than 80 ●: OVR 90 or greater
●: OVR between 80-89 ○: Player Weapons

4-3 Base Defense

FS #21   SS #26

CB #28   LB #95   LB #54   LB #55   CB #23

RE #99   DT #90   DT #95   LE #96

Dime Defense

FS #21   SS #26

CB #28   CB #25   LB #54   CB #39   CB #23

RE #98   DT #91   DT #92   LE #99

DEFENSIVE **ROSTER LIST** Current / Next Gen

Pos.	#	First Name	Last Name	Overall	Player Weapons
CB	23	Gary	Baxter	85	
CB	28	Leigh	Bodden	82	
CB	25	Kenny	Wright	80	
CB	39	Daven	Holly	79	
CB	33	Jereme	Perry	72	
CB	24	Eric	Wright	71	
DT	92	Ted	Washington	86	Run Stopper / Power Move D-Lineman
DT	91	Shaun	Smith	76	
DT	78	Ethan	Kelley	75	
DT	96	Babatunde	Oshinowo	70	
FS	21	Brodney	Pool	85	
FS	20	Mike	Adams	75	
LE	99	Orpheus	Roye	84	
LE	75	Simon	Fraser	69	
LOLB	55	Willie	McGinest	86	
LOLB	90	David	McMillan	69	
MLB	54	Andra	Davis	90	Heavy Hitter / Brick Wall Defender
MLB	58	D'Qwell	Jackson	84	
MLB	51	Chaun	Thompson	78	
MLB	94	Leon	Williams	77	
P	15	Dave	Zastudil	83	
RE	98	Robaire	Smith	82	
RE	93	Orien	Harris	71	
ROLB	95	Kamerion	Wimbley	87	Playmaker / Finesse Move D-Lineman
ROLB	52	Matt	Stewart	78	
SS	26	Sean	Jones	88	Coverage Safety
SS	27	Justin	Hamilton	66	

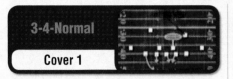

3-4-Normal

Cover 1

3-4-Over

Cross Fire 3

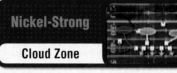

Nickel-Strong

Cloud Zone

Kamerion Wimbley combines speed, quickness, and closing speed to be a force off the edge.

Another play that shows off his excellent pass rushing skills from the edge is the 3-4-Over Cross Fire 3.

Wimbley also has the ability to drop into coverage in zone situations and defend passes with his change of direction skills.

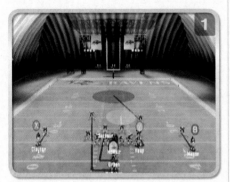

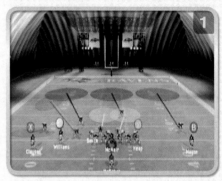

Kamerion Wimbley has good speed to blitz the edge. The 3-4-Normal Cover 1 is a good defensive scheme to use to get the most out of his speed rushing ability.

Another play that allows Wimbley to shine from the edge is the 3-4-Over Cross Fire 3. The blitz uses an inside twist stunt by the inside linebackers.

Wimbley has adequate coverage skills to drop back into zone coverage and defend the short and intermediate routes over the middle.

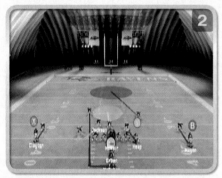

Shift the defensive line toward Wimbley. Next, hot blitz Wimbley and the inside linebacker on Wimbley's side (Davis). Spread the linebackers.

On this blitz, just shift the defensive line toward Wimbley so that the offensive tackle will have to deal with what is in front of him.

As Wimbley drops back into coverage, he will mirror the nearest wide receiver. In this case, that's Ravens' slot receiver Demetrius Williams.

The decoy of a blitz by the ILB allows Wimbley to charge the edge and move into the backfield to lay the smack down on the quarterback.

The inside stunt causes the tackle to look to block inside. Wimbley is allowed to hit the edge cleanly and fly to the quarterback.

Wimbley is able to jump in front of the pass meant for Williams, and create a big play.

TEAM STRATEGY

TAMPA BAY BUCCANEERS

Division: NFC South | **Stadium:** Raymond James Stadium | **Type:** Open | **Capacity:** 66,000+ | **Surface:** Grass

TEAM STRATEGY

COACHING **PROFILE**

Jon Gruden

- **Head Coaching Year:** 10th
- **Experience:** Oakland Raiders head coach (1998-2001)

Jon Gruden has had a long fall from grace since winning Super Bowl XXXVII. He led the Bucs to a 4-12 finish in 2006. He could find himself walking the plank if the Bucs suffer another losing season.

TEAM **RANKINGS**

Scoring	31st
Passing Offense	26th
Rushing Offense	28th
Passing Defense	19th
Rushing Defense	17th
Turnovers	30th

RATINGS **HISTORY**

Category	'07	'06	'05	'04
Overall	87	75	80	91
Offense	85	76	81	80
Defense	89	88	86	97

Bold = Highest Year

84
FIVE-YEAR AVERAGE

2006 **STANDINGS**

Wins	Losses	Ties	PF	PA	Home	Road	vs. AFC	vs. NFC	vs. Div
4	12	0	300	311	4-4	3-5	5-7	2-2	3-3

TEAM **OVERVIEW**

This team is going to be interesting this season. Vince Young has a huge burden on his shoulders as the cover guy for *Madden NFL 08* and the franchise hope for the Tennessee Titans. Unfortunately, he doesn't have much help on offense so if they win, it'll be because he makes it happen.

Madden NFL 08 players will be drawn to Young for his mobility and rocket arm. When they see what he has to work with, they will probably bail out on this team. David Givens is the only real asset on a team short on speed at receiver.

The Titans have one star on defense in Keith Bulluck. He better make plays all over the field because the right side of the defensive line isn't going to give him any room.

SCOUTING **REPORT**

STRENGTHS

Description	Maximizing Potential	Tips for Opponents
Even though the Bucs defense is getting up there in age, they're still one of the best units around.	Ronde Barber and Derrick Brooks continue to be the centerpiece of the defense.	Try to isolate free safety Will Allen and attack him deep. He's really the only chink in the Bucs' defense.
Defensive ends Simeon Rice and rookie Gaines Adams demand constant attention from the offense.	Both players can end a drive or halt any momentum the offense can get quickly with a sack.	To counter the Bucs' speed, run at them. What the Bucs have in speed, they lack in strength.
Joey Galloway is still blazingly fast.	Galloway's speed can impact the game immensely.	Put your best corner on Galloway at all times.

WEAKNESSES

Description	Minimizing Risks	Tips for Opponents
Other than Galloway, the Bucs don't have any real threats at receiver. Load the box up to stop the run.	Use your running game to grind the games out. Don't rely on the pass to get it done.	Load up the box and force the Bucs to pass.
The Bucs just can't seem to settle on a starting quarterback. This year, Jeff Garcia is at the helm.	Garcia is far from his pro bowl days, and doesn't have the arm strength that he used to.	Blitz and load the box up to prevent any type of play action from developing downfield.

OFF-SEASON UPGRADES

Type	Round	First Name	Last Name	School / Team	Positon	Height	Weight
Free Agent	N/A	Kevin	Carter	Dolphins	DE	6'6"	305
Free Agent	N/A	Jeff	Garcia	Eagles	QB	6'1"	200
Free Agent	N/A	Cato	June	Colts	LB	6'0"	227
Draft	1	Adam	Gaines	Clemson	DE	6'5"	260
Draft	2	Arron	Sears	Tennessee	T	6'4"	328

FANTASY OUTLOOK

⭐ **Star Player:** Carnell Williams
Round of Draft: 3rd

Williams did not have the production like he did his rookie season. Much of that had to do with injuries along the offensive line and inconsistent play from the quarterback position.

⭐ **Star Player:** Joe Galloway
Round of Draft: 7th

Galloway is getting up there in age, but he still has plenty of speed to break away once the catch is made. With Jeff Garcia stepping in the starting role at quarterback, Galloway's numbers should be better.

5-YEAR PLAYER PROGRESSION

First Name	Last Name	Position	'07 Overall	'08 Overall	'09 Overall	'10 Overall	'11 Overall
Jeff	Garcia	QB	82	-	-	-	-
Carnell	Williams	HB	88	89	91	91	90
Cato	June	LB	89	89	90	92	92
Ronde	Barber	CB	96	94	92	89	-
Gaines	Adams	DE	84	83	83	82	82

FRANCHISE MODE STRATEGY

Jeff Garcia is more than capable of running the Buccaneers' version of the West Coast Offense for a season or two. However, if a franchise QB should land in your draft spot, go ahead and pull the trigger.

Key Franchise Info

Team Salary: $100.2M
Cap Room: $87.5M
Key Rival:
• New Orleans Saints
NFL Icons: Derrick Brooks
Philosophy:
• Offense: West Coast
• Defense: Contain Passing
Prestige: Medium
Team Needs:
• Reciever
• Offensive Line
Highest Paid Players:
• Gaines Adams
• Derrick Brooks
Up and Coming Players:
• Davin Joseph
• Arron Sears

TEAM STRATEGY

ROSTER AND PACKAGE TIPS — KEY PLAYER SUBSTITUTIONS

• **Position:** TE
• **Substitution:** Jerramy Stevens
• **When:** Global
• **Advantage:** Starter Anthony Becht is a good run and pass blocker, but he is not very productive in the passing game. Move Jerramy Stevens up to the number one spot if you plan on passing more than running. If not, leave Becht where he is.

• **Position:** LE
• **Substitution:** Gaines Adams
• **When:** Global
• **Advantage:** The Buccaneers did not draft Adams as a number one pick to ride the pine. Move him over LE and let him do what he does best: rush the quarterback.

• **Position:** DT
• **Substitution:** Kevin Carter
• **When:** Global
• **Advantage:** Carter can play inside or outside. Because the Buccaneers already set at both defensive spots, move Carter inside where he can get push up the middle.

• **Position:** CB
• **Substitution:** Phillip Buchanon
• **When:** Teams with fast receivers
• **Advantage:** Buchanon is not a better corner than Brian Kelly, but he does have speed to keep with the faster receivers in the game.

TAMPA BAY BUCCANEERS / OFFENSE

OFFENSIVE STAR PLAYER #84

Joey Galloway	Wide Receiver (WR)

Key Attributes

Acceleration	97
Awareness	90
Catching	87
Speed	97

How does a 35-year-old receiver continue to perform and prove that he is the number 1 receiver? If you want to know the answer, take a look at the Bucs on Sundays in the fall. **Joey Galloway** has had back to back **1,000** yard seasons, and is making the younger Michael Clayton look like a bust. Galloway found his way into the end zone seven times last season. Hopefully, with more consistent play from the QB position, he will have 3 1,000 yard seasons.

Player Weapons: Deep Threat / Speed

RECOMMENDED OFFENSIVE AUDIBLE PACKAGES

I Form-Big	Split Backs-3WR	Strong-Normal	Singleback-4WR Flex	Singleback-Bunch TE
HB Lead Dive	2 Jet FL Drive	PA Counter Flat	Slot Cross	Corner Stop

OFFENSIVE PLAYCOUNTS

Quick Pass:	13	Hail Mary:	1	Counter:	15
Standard Pass:	122	Inside Handoff:	31	Draw:	15
Shotgun Pass:	54	Outside Handoff:	15	FB Run:	10
Screen Pass:	10	Pinch:	17		

TEAM TRIVIA

Tampa Bay Buccaneers Facts

Turn the page for the answers.

❶ Who was the first Tampa Bay Buccaneer in the Pro Football Hall of Fame?

❷ Who was originally awarded the ownership rights for the Tampa Bay franchise?

❸ Who was the first head coach for the Bucs?

OFFENSIVE FORMATIONS

Singleback	I Form
Big	Normal
Twin TE WR	Twin WR
Normal	Big
Slot Strong	**Split Backs**
Bunch TE	3WR
Trips Bunch	**Strong I**
Flip Trips	Normal
Tight	3WR
4WR Flex	Twin TE
Empty Bunch	**Weak I**
Empty 4WR	Normal
Empty 5WR	Twins WR

OFFENSIVE STRENGTH CHART

○: OVR less than 80	◉: OVR 90 or greater
◉: OVR between 80-89	○: Player Weapons

OFFENSIVE ROSTER LIST Current / Next Gen

Pos.	#	First Name	Last Name	Overall	Player Weapons
C	76	John	Wade	85	
C	66	Nick	Mihlhauser	67	
FB	40	Mike	Alstott	86	
FB	35	B.J.	Askew	82	
HB	24	Carnell	Williams	88	Elusive Back
HB	32	Michael	Pittman	81	
HB	33	Kenneth	Darby	75	
HB	34	Earnest	Graham	71	
K	3	Matt	Bryant	84	Big Foot Kicker
LG	72	Dan	Buenning	84	
LG	73	Matt	Lehr	83	
LT	79	Luke	Petitgout	86	Pass Blocker
LT	69	Anthony	Davis	78	
QB	7	Jeff	Garcia	82	
QB	2	Chris	Simms	77	
QB	5	Bruce	Gradkowski	71	
RG	75	Davin	Joseph	87	
RG	67	Arron	Sears	78	
RT	65	Jeremy	Trueblood	79	
RT	70	Donald	Penn	61	
TE	86	Jerramy	Stevens	83	
TE	81	Alex	Smith	81	
TE	88	Anthony	Becht	78	
WR	84	Joey	Galloway	88	Deep Threat / Speed
WR	80	Michael	Clayton	79	
WR	19	Ike	Hilliard	78	
WR	89	David	Boston	77	
WR	85	Maurice	Stovall	77	

Singleback-Slot Strong	Singleback-Bunch TE	Singleback-Empty Bunch
Clayton Option	**PA Draw Pass**	**Clayton Option**

 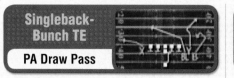 

Michael Clayton is a smart wide receiver who runs good crisp routes and knows how to get separation.

A good play that shows off Clayton's ability to run crisp routes and get separation from defenders is the Singleback-Bunch TE PA Draw Pass.

A final play that shows off Clayton's intelligence at reading coverages is the Singleback-Empty Bunch Clayton Option.

  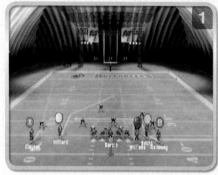

The Singleback-Slot Strong Clayton Option allows wide receiver Michael Clayton to choose the best route based on the defensive coverage.

This play contains a delay route that helps on a rollout by the QB to the left, and a crossing route which Clayton runs over the middle.

On this option route, Clayton chooses three primary routes: streak, comeback, and the slant.

Clayton recognizes the Cover 2 Zone by the Saints, as the corner back steps forward to the flats while the safety moves out to the deep ½ area of the field.

We send the outside WR on a fade route. On the snap, Clayton will make his way across the formation on the crossing route, putting the defender in his pocket.

On this play from the scrimmage, Clayton reads the coverage as a deep zone. Thus, he chooses to run the comeback route underneath the coverage.

He chooses to go one on one with speed safety Daniel Bullocks, and use his physical ability to get higher than the defender and snag the football.

As the QB rolls with Clayton to the left, he notices the separation and delivers the football down the sideline. This is a nice change-up play.

QB Jeff Garcia hits him on the comeback route and now Clayton has all kinds of room to run.

TEAM STRATEGY

TAMPA BAY BUCCANEERS / DEFENSE

TEAM STRATEGY

DEFENSIVE STAR PLAYER #20

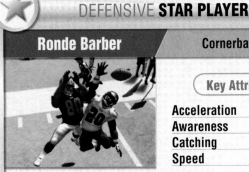

Ronde Barber — Cornerback (CB)

Key Attributes

Acceleration	95
Awareness	97
Catching	78
Speed	88

Ronde is everything on defense that his brother was to the Giants on offense. He is an extremely tough and determined defender. He plays well above his physical size. He is a clever corner and was selected to the Pro Bowl again mainly because of his performance against the Philadelphia Eagles. His three interceptions are not much to brag about, but two of the three went for touchdowns against the Eagles.

Player Weapons: Containment Corner/Smart Corner, Press Coverage Corner

DEFENSIVE AUDIBLE PACKAGES

4-3-Normal	4-3-Over	Dime-Normal	Nickel-3-3-5	Nickel-Normal
Nece Blitz	Zone Blitz	MLB Pistol 1	Wide Tite Crash	Flat Four

DEFENSIVE PLAYCOUNTS

Man Coverage:	36	Cover 3 Zone:	18	Combo Blitz:	11
Man Zone:	30	Deep Zone:	15	Goal Line:	15
Combo Coverage:	8	Man Blitz:	36	Special Teams:	12
Cover 2 Zone:	18	Zone Blitz:	53		

TEAM TRIVIA

Tampa Bay Buccaneers Facts

Answers:

❶ Lee Roy Selmon

❷ Tom McCloskey

❸ John McKay

DEFENSIVE FORMATIONS

4-3	Nickel
4-3-Normal	Nickel-3-3-5
4-3-Over	Nickel-Normal
4-3-Under	**Quarter**
Dime	Quarter-Normal
Dime-Normal	
Dime-Flat	
Dime-3-2-6	

DEFENSIVE STRENGTH CHART

- ◯: OVR less than 80
- ◯: OVR 90 or greater
- ◉: OVR between 80-89
- ◯: Player Weapons

4-3 Base Defense

FS #26, SS #23, CB #25, LB #55, LB #51, LB #59, CB #20, RE #97, DT #98, DT #95, LE #93

Dime Defense

FS #26, SS #23, CB #25, CB #31, LB #51, CB #22, CB #26, RE #97, DT #98, DT #95, LE #93

DEFENSIVE ROSTER LIST — Current/Next Gen

Pos.	#	First Name	Last Name	Overall	Player Weapons
CB	20	Ronde	Barber	96	Containment Corner/Smart Corner, Press Coverage Corner
CB	25	Brian	Kelly	87	
CB	31	Phillip	Buchanon	77	Quick Corner
CB	22	Sammy	Davis	76	
CB	29	Alan	Zemaitis	72	
DT	95	Chris	Hovan	86	
DT	98	Ryan	Sims	79	
DT	96	Ellis	Wyms	78	
FS	26	Will	Allen	80	
FS	36	Tanard	Jackson	74	
LE	93	Kevin	Carter	86	Run Stopper
LE	94	Greg	Spires	83	
LOLB	59	Cato	June	89	
LOLB	56	Ryan	Nece	79	
MLB	51	Barrett	Ruud	80	
MLB	52	Antoine	Cash	66	
P	9	Josh	Bidwell	85	
RE	97	Simeon	Rice	92	Pass Rusher
RE	90	Gaines	Adams	84	Pass Rusher
RE	58	Patrick	Chukwurah	75	
RE	92	Charles	Bennett	70	
ROLB	55	Derrick	Brooks	94	Defensive Enforcer/Smart Linebacker, Brick Wall Defender
ROLB	50	Jamie	Winborn	76	
ROLB	58	Quincy	Black	73	
SS	23	Jermaine	Phillips	87	
SS	38	Sabby	Piscitelli	79	

4-3-Over		Dime-Normal		Nickel-Normal	
Cover 2		**2 Deep Blitz**		**CB Fox Blitz**	

Ronde Barber shows excellent transitional movement and change of direction skills. He is at his best in zone coverage.

Barber is a top playmaker for the Tampa Bay Buccaneers defense. This is one play that allows him to show off his playmaking ability.

A final play that allows Ronde Barber to make plays off of the edge and show his closing speed is the Nickel-Normal CB Fox Blitz.

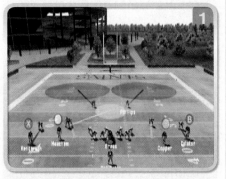

Ronde Barber is perfectly fitted for Cover 2 Zone coverage. He does an excellent job of playing the flat to intermediate areas of the field.

Barber has been one of the better blitzing corner backs in the league the last few years. Use this play to get Barber after the quarterback.

The Nickel-Normal CB Fox Blitz sends Barber on the pass rush from the right flat area. We move him in manually just a tad so he can get a better jump.

He does a good job of pressing and rerouting the wide receiver off the line of scrimmage, and then quickly turning his hips to defend his area.

Sub Barber in at dime back. Go to the formation subs and make Barber the #4 cornerback in the Dime formation. On the snap, Barber will hit the edge.

On the snap, Barber will bypass all of the traffic inside with the defensive and offensive linemen, and make his way around the edge.

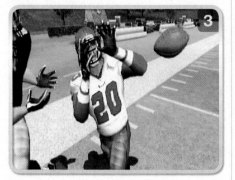

If there is no immediate threat in the flats area, Barber will drop back and defend passes in the intermediate area.

Once an experienced vet like Barber gets into the backfield, he knows how to bring the QB down to the turf.

He gets on top of the QB in a hurry, and shows why he is still one of the league's top blitzing corners.

TEAM STRATEGY

91

ARIZONA CARDINALS

Division: AFC West | **Stadium:** Sun Devil Stadium | **Type:** Open | **Capacity:** 73,379 | **Surface:** Grass

TEAM STRATEGY

COACHING PROFILE

Ken Whisenhunt

- **Head Coaching Year:** 1st
- **Experience:** Three years as offensive coordinator for Steelers (2004-2006).

On January 14, 2007 the Arizona Cardinals hired Whisenhunt as their new head coach. He is known throughout the league for his creative offensive play calling. He played four years (1985- 1988) as a tight end for the Atlanta Falcons.

TEAM RANKINGS

Scoring	19th
Passing Offense	10th
Rushing Offense	20th
Passing Defense	30th
Rushing Defense	16th
Turnovers	12th

RATINGS HISTORY

Category	'07	'06	'05	'04
Overall	**87**	76	66	65
Offense	**88**	78	70	65
Defense	**85**	79	67	67

Bold = Highest Year

76
FIVE-YEAR
AVERAGE

2006 STANDINGS

Wins	Losses	Ties	PF	PA	Home	Road	vs. AFC	vs. NFC	vs. Div
5	11	0	314	389	3-5	2-6	0-4	5-7	4-2

TEAM OVERVIEW

Coach Ken Whisenhunt takes the helm at Arizona and he should be excited about his personnel. Leinart has a year under his belt, and with decent accuracy, he should be a strong contributor this season. He has no shortage of targets with Boldin, Fitzgerald, and Johnson lined up out wide.

Edgerrin James isn't quite the powerhouse that he was at Indy, but then again he hasn't had Peyton Manning lined up in front of him the last couple of years. With the emergence of Leinart and the wide receivers, he should have a solid season.

The Cards may make a move to a 3-4 defense. Whatever they do, they need to improve on last year's work. SS Adrian Wilson is their biggest star, and with a slow supporting cast, he had better be on his toes in the secondary.

SCOUTING REPORT

STRENGTHS

Description	Maximizing Potential	Tips for Opponents
Cardinal receiver's Anquan Boldin and Larry Fitzgerald form one of the top tandems in the NFL.	Get the ball into both of their hands as much as possible. Both are playmakers.	Pick your poison. Unless your team has two lock-down corners, one of them is going to become open.
Matt Leinart showed last season he could be a starting NFL quarterback by passing for 2,547 yards.	He doesn't have the strongest arm, but he has enough to zip in there. He has a lot of tools to work with.	The Cards have many assets at their disposal, so blitzing Leinart may not always be best.
Pro Bowl safety Adrian Wilson is one of best in the game.	Develop schemes that put Wilson up near the line to blitz.	If you see Wilson up tight, leave in extra blockers.

WEAKNESSES

Description	Minimizing Risks	Tips for Opponents
The Cardinals' offensive line played inconsistently for most of last season.	When passing the ball, use three and five step drops to get rid of the ball quickly.	If your team has a good front four who can put pressure on the QB, then there is no reason to blitz.
Arizona does not have a lockdown cornerback on their team.	Call defenses that put at least one safety back in deep coverage to help prevent the deep play.	The Cardinals' top two corners can be exposed by going deep with receivers with speed.

Overall Rating **86**
Offense **86**
Defense **85**

OFF-SEASON **UPGRADES**

Type	Round	First Name	Last Name	School/Team	Positon	Height	Weight
Free Agent	N/A	Ralph	Brown	Cleveland Browns	CB	5'10"	185
Free Agent	N/A	Mike	Gandy	Buffalo Bills	OL	6'4"	310
Free Agent	N/A	Roderick	Hood	Philadelphia Eagles	CB	5'11"	196
Draft	1st	Levi	Brown	Penn State	OT	6'4"	328
Draft	2nd	Alan	Branch	Michigan	DT	6'6"	331

FANTASY **OUTLOOK**

⭐ **Star Player:** Larry Fitzgerald
Round of Draft: 3rd

At 6-3, Fitzgerald makes a great target inside the red zone. The problem though is Matt Leinart needs to throw it his way. Fitzgerald only got in the end zone six times last season, the lowest total of his career.

⭐ **Star Player:** Anquan Boldin
Round of Draft: 4th

Boldin posted big time fantasy numbers as far as yardage totals are concerned with 1,203 yards. However, his touchdown numbers were not so great. He only got into the end zone four times.

5-YEAR **PLAYER PROGRESSION**

First Name	Last Name	Position	'07 Overall	'08 Overall	'09 Overall	'10 Overall	'11 Overall
Adrian	Wilson	S	96	97	98	95	92
Anquan	Boldin	WR	94	94	96	93	93
Larry	Fitzgerald	WR	94	94	95	96	96
Matt	Leinart	QB	85	87	90	89	90
Alan	Branch	DT	78	78	79	77	77

FRANCHISE MODE **STRATEGY**

They are set on offense at the skill positions in the future except for a running back. They eventually will need one to replace the aging Edgerrin James. A center and right guard also should be in your plans.

Key Franchise Info

Team Salary: $94.3M
Cap Room: $14.6M
Key Rival: St. Louis Rams
NFL Icons: Edgerrin James
Philosophy:
• Offense: Ball Control
• Defense: Force the Pass
Prestige: Very Low
Team Needs:
• Offensive Line
• Linebackers
Highest Paid Players:
• Larry Fitzgerald
• Edgerrin James
Up and Coming Players:
• Alan Branch
• Leonard Pope

ROSTER AND **PACKAGE TIPS**   KEY PLAYER SUBSTITUTIONS

• **Position:** FB
• **Substitution:** Obafemi Ayan Badejo
• **When:** Passing Situations
• **Advantage:** There is really no way you can package in Ayan Badejo in fullback without actually subbing him. If you plan on throwing more than running, then you should make this substitution.

• **Position:** LB
• **Substitution:** Gerald Hayes
• **When:** Passing Situations
• **Advantage:** When coming out in nickel, dime, and quarter formations, be sure to package Hayes out. Although he is solid against the run, he doesn't have the speed to drop back in pass coverage.

• **Position:** ROLB
• **Substitution:** Darryl Blackstock
• **When:** Global
• **Advantage:** Blackstock's overall ratings is two points lower than starter Calvin Pace. Plus, his speed rating is seven points higher. It just makes sense to us to have him in the lineup.

• **Position:** PR
• **Substitution:** Steve Breaston
• **When:** Global
• **Advantage:** Breaston needs to get on the field as much as possible to showcase his speed. He won't see much time at receiver, but he should see a lot of time as a punt returner.

TEAM STRATEGY

ARIZONA CARDINALS / **OFFENSE**

OFFENSIVE **STAR PLAYER** #81

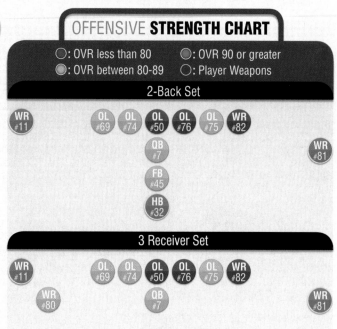

Anquan Boldin	Wide Receiver (WR)

Key Attributes

Acceleration	92
Awareness	87
Catching	94
Speed	89

Boldin uses his big body to consistently make plays over the middle. Last season, he led the team with **1,203** yards and **83** receptions. He does not have deep speed, but he runs precise routes that allow him to be a big time asset on offense and a threat to pick up crucial first downs. With improved quarterback play, pass protection, and a solid run game, Boldin should improve on stats this season.

Player Weapons: Go-To Guy / Stiff Arm BC, Possesion Receiver, Quick Receiver, Specatular Catch Receiver

RECOMMENDED OFFENSIVE **AUDIBLE PACKAGES**

I Form-Normal	Shotgun-4WR	Singleback-Normal Slot	Singleback-Normal Slot	Shotgun-2RB 3WR
Cross In	FL Hook	Ins Left	HB Counter Trap	HB Screen

OFFENSIVE **PLAYCOUNTS**

Quick Pass:	12	Screen Pass:	12	Pinch:	10
Standard Pass:	80	Hail Mary:	1	Counter:	21
Shotgun Pass:	46	Inside Handoff:	33	Draw:	17
Play Action Pass:	15	Outside Handoff:	11		

TEAM **TRIVIA**

Arizona Cardinals Facts

Turn the page for the answers.

❶ Who became the first Cardinal to catch passes for over 1,500 yards in one season?

❷ How many playoff appearances did the Cardinals make during their years as the Phoenix Cardinals, from '88 to '93?

OFFENSIVE **FORMATIONS**

Singleback	Strong I
Big	Normal
Big Twin WR	Normal Flex
Twin TE WR	**Weak I**
Big 3TE	Normal
Normal	Tight Twins
Normal Slot	**Shotgun**
Slot Strong	2RB 3WR
Trips Bunch	Normal Offset Wk
4WR	Slot Strong
I Form	Slot Strg HB Wk
Normal	4WR
Twin WR	
Big	

OFFENSIVE **STRENGTH CHART**

○ : OVR less than 80   ● : OVR 90 or greater
● : OVR between 80-89   ○ : Player Weapons

2-Back Set

3 Receiver Set

OFFENSIVE **ROSTER LIST**   Current / Next Gen

Pos.	#	First Name	Last Name	Overall	Player Weapons
C	50	Al	Johnson	77	
C	60	Nick	Leckey	75	
FB	45	Terrelle	Smith	88	
FB	30	Obafemi	Ayanbadejo	80	
HB	32	Edgerrin	James	92	Feature Back / Stiff Arm BC
HB	31	Marcel	Shipp	78	
HB	28	J.J.	Arrington	74	
K	1	Neil	Rackers	89	Big Foot Kicker
LG	74	Reggie	Wells	84	
LG	67	Milford	Brown	77	
LT	69	Mike	Gandy	81	
LT	79	Oliver	Ross	77	
QB	7	Matt	Leinart	84	
QB	13	Kurt	Warner	81	
RG	76	Deuce	Lutui	76	
RG	61	Elton	Brown	73	
RT	75	Levi	Brown	82	
RT	72	Brandon	Gorin	76	
TE	82	Leonard	Pope	77	
TE	89	Ben	Patrick	75	
WR	11	Larry	Fitzgerald	94	Go-To Guy / Quick, Possesion, Spectacular Catch Receiver, Hands
WR	81	Anquan	Boldin	94	Go-To Guy / Stiff Arm BC, Quick, Possesion, Spectacular Catch, Hands
WR	80	Bryant	Johnson	84	
WR	18	Steve	Breaston	71	
WR	15	Michael	Spurlock	70	
WR	19	LeRon	McCoy	67	
WR	87	Sean	Morey	67	

Singleback-Big
Boldin Option

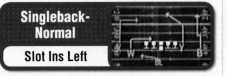

Singleback-Normal
Slot Ins Left

Singleback-Big
HB Blast

Anquan Boldin has size, plays tough as nails, and makes big plays over the middle for the Arizona Cardinals' offense.

Another play that highlights Boldin's ability to play in the middle of the field is the Singleback-Normal Slot Ins Left.

A final play that highlights Boldin's toughness is the Singleback Big HB Blast. This play highlights Boldin's ability to block.

Option routes are perfect for a possession wide receiver like Anquan Boldin. Use the Singleback-Big Boldin option as a go-to play when looking for him.

The Singleback-Normal Slot Ins Left sends Boldin on a deep In route over the middle and allows him to use his physical skills.

Wide receivers have multiple roles with a football team. Singleback Big-HB Blast allows Boldin to use his big body as a blocker.

One of Boldin's options on this play is the skinny post route that almost looks like a slant route. Boldin will choose this route if the coverage allows it.

Boldin will take off as if he is going vertical, and then cut on the in route and make his way across the middle.

Motion Boldin into the formation and hike the football before he reaches the tight end. Then watch him seal the corner back inside.

Leinart is able to hit him in the middle of the field behind the linebackers for a nice pick-up on the play.

This is a good route to run with a big body wide receiver like Boldin, as he can take the punishment and dish it out over the middle.

This allows the running back to get outside and pick up some additional yardage on the run play.

TEAM STRATEGY

95

ARIZONA CARDINALS / **DEFENSE**

DEFENSIVE **STAR PLAYER** #58

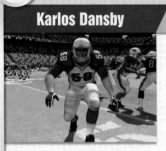

Karlos Dansby	Linebacker (LOLB)

Key Attributes

Awareness	83
Speed	85
Strength	73
Tackle	86

Last season, **Dansby** made a huge splash at outside linebacker for the Cardinals. He notched a team high of **8.5** sacks. He also had **82** total tackles, which placed him fourth on the team. Because of a lack of team depth at middle linebacker, he will move inside. The question remains, does he have the bulk to hold up for the whole season? If the defensive tackles up front keep blockers off of him, he should have a solid season.

Player Weapon: None

RECOMMENDED DEFENSIVE **AUDIBLE PACKAGES**

4-3-Normal	4-3-Over	4-3-Under	4-3-Under	Nickel-Normal
OLB Fire 3	SS Blitz	Buzz Duo	4 Deep DT Stunt	Quarter Half

DEFENSIVE **PLAYCOUNTS**

Man Coverage:	41	Cover 3 Zone:	23	Combo Blitz:	23
Man Zone:	37	Deep Zone:	22	Goal Line:	15
Combo Coverage:	12	Man Blitz:	49	Special Teams:	12
Cover 2 Zone:	14	Zone Blitz:	57		

TEAM **TRIVIA**

Arizona Cardinals Facts
Answers:

❶ Roy Green

❷ Zero

DEFENSIVE **FORMATIONS**

4-3	Nickle
4-3-Normal	Nickel-3-3-5
4-3-Over	Nickel-Normal
4-3-Under	Nickel-Strong
Dime	**Quarter**
Dime-Flat	Quarter-Normal
Dime-Normal	Quarter-3 Deep

DEFENSIVE **STRENGTH CHART**

- ○: OVR less than 80
- ◉: OVR between 80-89
- ◉: OVR 90 or greater
- ○: Player Weapons

4-3 Base Defense

FS #42   SS #24

CB #26   LB #97   LB #54   LB #58   CB #21

RE #92   DT #70   DT #90   LE #56

Dime Defense

FS #42   SS #24

CB #26   CB #25   LB #54   CB #22   CB #21

RE #92   DT #70   DT #90   LE #56

DEFENSIVE **ROSTER LIST** Current / Next Gen

Pos.	#	First Name	Last Name	Overall	Player Weapons
CB	21	Antrel	Rolle	84	
CB	26	Roderick	Hood	82	
CB	25	Eric	Green	79	
CB	22	Matt	Ware	73	
DT	90	Darnell	Dockett	87	
DT	70	Kendrick	Clancy	80	
DT	78	Alan	Branch	78	
DT	98	Gabe	Watson	72	
FS	42	Terrence	Holt	81	
FS	47	Aaron	Francisco	78	
LE	56	Chike	Okeafor	85	
LE	91	Rodney	Bailey	75	
LOLB	58	Karlos	Dansby	87	
LOLB	59	Brandon	Johnson	69	
MLB	54	Gerald	Hayes	85	Heavy Hitter
MLB	52	Monty	Beisel	78	
MLB	53	Buster	Davis	71	
P	10	Scott	Player	93	
RE	92	Bertrand	Berry	90	Finesse Move D-Lineman
RE	94	Antonio	Smith	67	
ROLB	97	Calvin	Pace	74	
ROLB	55	Darryl	Blackstock	72	
SS	24	Adrian	Wilson	96	Big Hitter
SS	37	Hanik	Milligan	66	

4-3-Under
Sam Shoot Fire 2

Dansby has solid instincts and is a playmaker at the strong side LB position. He is a good run and pass defender that excels in space.

Karlos Dansby has the speed to rush and cover for the Cardinals' defense. The 4-3-Under Sam Shoot Fire 2 features his pass rushing ability.

To get Dansby after the quarterback, shift the line toward him. Then hot blitz him with the linebacker audibles and spread the linebackers.

Dansby will get around the edge and into the backfield, and attack the passer. He has rare closing speed that many cannot escape.

Nickel-3-3-5
2 Deep Man Under

A good play that shows off Dansby's ability to play in space. Flip it so that Dansby is the linebacker that drops to the hook/curl area.

The Nickel-3-3-5 2 Deep Man Under allows you to drop your best coverage outside linebacker into zone coverage in the curl/hook area.

We call the play flipped since Dansby is our best coverage linebacker. He will drop back over the middle and cover the intermediate routes.

He will help on any pass that comes into his area. He allows his instincts to take over and the results are always in favor of the defense.

Nickel-3-3-5
Cover 2 Pinch

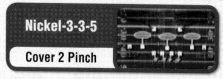

A final play that shows off Dansby's ability to play in space is the Dime Normal Cover 2 Pinch.

Dansby is an every down linebacker, and his skills are needed on the field if the Cardinals are to put up a fight. Use him in the Dime with the LOLB sub Package.

By allowing Dansby to drop into zone using the Cover 2 Pinch, he can cover the crossing routes that many teams and players like to run.

Dansby breaks on the football and creates big plays for his defense if given the opportunity

TEAM STRATEGY

SAN DIEGO CHARGERS

Division: AFC West | **Stadium:** Qualcomm Stadium | **Type:** Open | **Capacity:** 70,561 | **Surface:** Grass

TEAM STRATEGY

COACHING PROFILE

Norv Turner

- **Head Coaching Year:** 10th
- **Experience:** Turner has served as head coach of the Washington Redskins and the Oakland Raiders.

Turner was hired on February 19, 2007 as the head coach of the San Diego Chargers. He was the offensive coordinator for the Dallas Cowboys during two of their championships runs in the early 90s.

TEAM RANKINGS

Scoring	1st
Passing Offense	16th
Rushing Offense	1st
Passing Defense	13th
Rushing Defense	7th
Turnovers	3rd

RATINGS HISTORY

Category	'07	'06	'05	'04
Overall	86	86	62	78
Offense	89	88	75	77
Defense	86	77	65	77

Bold = Highest Year

80
FIVE-YEAR
AVERAGE

2006 STANDINGS

Wins	Losses	Ties	PF	PA	Home	Road	vs. AFC	vs. NFC	vs. Div
14	2	0	492	303	8-0	6-2	10-2	4-0	5-1

TEAM OVERVIEW

The cupboards are full with this team. They have the most complete lineup from top to bottom in the NFL, and are a blast to play with in *Madden NFL 08*. Philip Rivers stepped up nicely last year, and is a solid QB in the game. He's very accurate with sufficient arm strength to get it done.

The Chargers have all kinds of assets for head coach Norv Turner to work with. Antonio Gates is one of the true game changers, with overwhelming size and speed at the TE position. And let's not forget MVP running back LaDainian Tomlinson.

The defense runs a stingy 3-4 scheme with Jamal Williams collapsing offensive lines in the middle. The corners are solid, and Marriman is a beast at linebacker.

SCOUTING REPORT

Description	STRENGTHS	
	Maximizing Potential	**Tips for Opponents**
LaDainian Tomlinson set the NFL single season record for the most TDs with 31.	Get Tomlinson the ball anytime around the goal line. His break tackles and speed rating makes him a lock.	You can be 99% sure that Tomlinson is going to get the ball down near the goal line. Load up the box.
TE Antonio Gates continues to be one of the top players at his position.	Have Gates run deep post routes to expose slower linebackers. Use his height advantage to snag the ball.	Call defenses where two defenders bracket Gates. This will force Rivers to look elsewhere.
Shawne Merriman's speed makes him a danger to the quaterback.	Develop blitz schemes to put Merriman to use.	Be aware of where Merriman lines up on the field.

Description	WEAKNESSES	
	Minimizing Risks	**Tips for Opponents**
The Chargers do not have a go-to receiver on the outside that can be relied on when Gates is not open.	Consider packaging Tomlinson out wide in crucial situations. He is an accomplished receiver.	If Tomlinson is lined up outside at receiver, consider rotating pass coverage to his side.
The Chargers' safeties are the defense's only real weak link. Neither starter has great ball hawking skills.	Don't bring the safeties down in the box to defend the run. The Chargers' front seven can handle things	If the Chargers do line up near the line of scrimmage, consider calling play action.

OFF-SEASON **UPGRADES**

Type	Round	First Name	Last Name	School/Team	Positon	Height	Weight
Draft	1st	Craig	Davis	Louisiana State	WR	6'1"	207
Draft	2nd	Eric	Weddle	Utah	S	5'11"	200
Draft	3rd	Anthony	Waters	Clemson	LB	6'3"	245
Draft	4th	Scott	Chandler	Iowa	TE	6'7"	257
Draft	5th	Legedu	Naanee	Boise State	WR	6'2"	225

FANTASY **OUTLOOK**

Star Player: LaDainian Tomlinson
Round of Draft: 1st

If you happen to get the number 1 overall pick in your league fantasy draft, you won't find a better selection than LT. Last season he got into the end zone a whopping 31 times and rushed for leading 1,815 yards.

Star Player: Antonio Gates
Round of Draft: 4th

As far as tight ends go when it comes to fantasy value, Gates is the top. Last season he got into the end zone 9 times, plus had over 900 yards receiving.

5-YEAR **PLAYER PROGRESSION**

First Name	Last Name	Position	'07 Overall	'08 Overall	'09 Overall	'10 Overall	'11 Overall
LaDainian	Tominson	HB	99	99	99	99	95
Shawne	Merriman	LB	98	99	99	99	99
Antonio	Gates	TE	97	99	99	99	99
Philip	Rivers	QB	88	90	91	94	95
Craig	Davis	WR	79	79	79	79	81

FRANCHISE MODE **STRATEGY**

The Chargers are pretty much stacked at all positions on offense, except for receiver. If there is go-to receiver available in the 08 draft, don't let him slip by.

Key Franchise Info

Team Salary: $84.2M
Cap Room: $24.7M
Key Rival:
• Oakland Raiders
NFL Icons: LaDainian Tomlinson
Philosophy:
• Offense: West Coast
• Defense: Contain Passing
Prestige: Very Good
Team Needs:
• Receiver
• Safety
Highest Paid Players:
• LaDainian Tomlinson
• Philip Rivers
Up and Coming Players:
• Craig Davis
• Scott Chandler

ROSTER AND **PACKAGE TIPS**   KEY PLAYER SUBSTITUTIONS

• **Position:** WR
• **Substitution:** Vincent Jackson
• **When:** Global
• **Advantage:** Jackson's size is hard to ignore. He has the body of a tight end, but the speed of a receiver. That's why we move in as the Chargers' number one receiver.

• **Position:** WR
• **Substitution:** Craig Davis
• **When:** Global
• **Advantage:** Despite being rookie, Davis is ready to step in at the team's number two receiver. His speed rating is two point higher than Vincent Jackson and Eric Parker.

• **Position:** MLB
• **Substitution:** Brandon Siler
• **When:** Global
• **Advantage:** Stephen Cooper is adequate against the run, but he lacks speed to drop back in pass coverage. That's we suggest moving Siler into the send MLB on the depth chart.

• **Position:** CB
• **Substitution:** Antonio Cromartie
• **When:** Global
• **Advantage:** Cromartie is faster than Drayton Florence, and also has a higher catch rating. With those two ratings alone, he could even move into the number one slot.

TEAM STRATEGY

99

SAN DIEGO CHARGERS / OFFENSE

OFFENSIVE STAR PLAYER #21

LaDainian Tomlinson Halfback (HB)

Key Attributes

Acceleration	98
Agility	98
Break Tackle	91
Speed	96

What else can possibly be said about one of the greatest running backs ever to play the game? Last season, **Tomlinson** managed to get in the end zone a single season record **31** times (28 on the ground, 3 through the air). On top of that, he led the league in rushing and won the NFL's Most Valuable Player Award. There is no reason to think that he will slow down this season.

Player Weapons: Feature Back / Elusive Back, Power Back, Stiff Arm BC

RECOMMENDED OFFENSIVE AUDIBLE PACKAGES

I Form-Normal	I Form-Normal	Singleback-Big	Shotgun-4WR	Shotgun-2RB 3WR
HB Slam	PA FB Flat	HB Dive	Curl Flats	RB Circles

OFFENSIVE PLAYCOUNTS

Quick Pass:	14	Screen Pass:	9	Pinch:	14
Standard Pass:	75	Hail Mary:	1	Counter:	21
Shotgun Pass:	19	Inside Handoff:	32	Draw:	11
Play Action Pass:	29	Outside Handoff:	9		

TEAM TRIVIA

San Diego Chargers Facts

Turn the page for the answers.

1 What college did Chargers running back LaDainian Tomlinson attend?

2 Which team did the Chargers defeat in the 1994 AFC Championship Game to advance to Super Bowl XXIX?

3 What stadium did the Chargers play in from 1961 to 1966?

OFFENSIVE FORMATIONS

Singleback	Split Backs
Big	3WR
Twin TE	Strong I
Twin TE WR	Normal
Normal Slot	Twin WR
Slot Strong	Normal Flex
Base Flex	Twin TE
4WR Spread	**Weak I**
Flip Trips	Normal
Trey Open	Close
I Form	**Shotgun**
Normal	2RB Flex
Twin WR	2RB 3WR
Twin TE	4WR

OFFENSIVE STRENGTH CHART

- ○: OVR less than 80
- ●: OVR 90 or greater
- ●: OVR between 80-89
- ○: Player Weapons

2-Back Set

WR #88 — OL #73 OL #68 OL #61 OL #79 OL #70 OL #85 — WR #83
QB #17
FB #41
HB #21

3 Receiver Set

WR #88 — OL #73 OL #68 OL #61 OL #79 OL #70 OL #85 — WR #83
WR #84
QB #17
HB #21

OFFENSIVE ROSTER LIST Current / Next Gen

Pos.	#	First Name	Last Name	Overall	Player Weapons
C	61	Nick	Hardwick	90	Run Blocker / Crushing Run Blocker
C	65	Cory	Withrow	70	
FB	41	Lorenzo	Neal	98	Crushing Run Blocker
FB	34	Andrew	Pinnock	71	
HB	21	LaDainian	Tomlinson	99	Feature Back / Elusive Back, Power Back, Stiff Arm BC
HB	33	Michael	Turner	87	Speed Back / Power Back
HB	43	Darren	Sproles	77	Elusive Back
K	10	Nate	Kaeding	91	
LG	68	Kris	Dielman	93	Road Blocker / Cushing Run Blocker
LG	63	Scott	Mruczkowski	66	
LT	73	Marcus	McNeill	94	Road Blocker / Crushing Run Blocker, Pass Blocker
LT	72	Roman	Oben	81	
QB	17	Philip	Rivers	88	Precision Passer / Accurate QB
QB	7	Billy	Volek	81	
QB	6	Charlie	Whitehurst	73	
RG	79	Mike	Goff	90	Run Blocker
RG	66	Jeromey	Clary	71	
RT	70	Shane	Olivea	88	Run Blocker
RT	71	Cory	Lekkerkerker	65	
TE	85	Antonio	Gates	97	Quick Receiver, Spectacular Catch Receiver, Hands
TE	87	Scott	Chandler	78	
TE	86	Brandon	Manumaleuna	76	
WR	88	Eric	Parker	81	
WR	83	Vincent	Jackson	81	Deep Threat
WR	84	Craig	Davis	79	
WR	80	Malcom	Floyd	77	
WR	81	Kassim	Osgood	74	
WR	82	Greg	Camarillo	68	

Singleback-Big
HB Counter

RB LaDainian does everything well. He is quick to the hole and has great vision. Plays such as this Counter show off LT's ability to get outside.

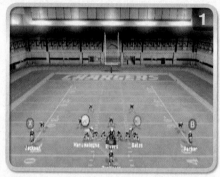

Singleback-Big HB Counter is one of the best running plays in the entire game. What better way to use it than with the best running back in the game.

The right guard will pull to the left and clear the way for LT. If any defender shows blitz, the guard will take him.

As LT follows the blocks, he may find a lane inside, but there will also be one outside. Get LT on the perimeter and it is a big problem for the defense.

Singleback-Base Flex
HB Slant 18

The Singleback-Base Flex HB Slant 18 is a good stretch running play and spreads the defense out and opens up running lanes.

Fullback Lorenzo Neal lines up at wide out on this play. He comes in motion into the backfield to lead block for LT prior to the snap of the football.

Neal and the RG will lead block. Follow them both and watch how they blow up defenders and cave them inside, creating an outside rushing lane.

Get outside and take it to the house. The Singleback-Base Flex HB Slant 18 is a good play to build an offense from.

Shotgun-2RB Flex
HB Wheel

LT has deceptive speed and soft hands. This is one play that shows off his ability to get open in the passing attack and pull in the football.

This play uses the speed of the HB on a deep wheel route. This play was built with getting a match-up advantage in mind.

Send LT in motion to the left and hike the football while he is in motion. This gives you the advantage, especially if LT is being covered by a linebacker.

LT will fly up the field on the wheel route. Throw the deep pass and let LT do the rest of the work.

SAN DIEGO CHARGERS / DEFENSE

DEFENSIVE STAR PLAYER #56

Shawne Merriman — Linebacker (LOLB)

Key Attributes

Awareness	83
Speed	87
Strength	86
Tackle	90

Despite only playing in 12 games last season, **Merriman** posted a league-leading **17** sacks. He has managed to come up with **63** tackles and one interception. With his catlike speed, he is able to get the quarterback before he has any time to get rid of the ball. In just his third year, he ranks among the top outside linebackers in the game. Look for him to post the same type of sack numbers in '07.

Player Weapons: Defensive Enforcer / Big Hitter, Brick Wall Defender, Finesse Move D-Lineman, Power Move D-Lineman

RECOMMENDED DEFENSIVE AUDIBLE PACKAGES

3-4-Normal	3-4-Over	3-4-Solid	Dime-Normal	Nickel-2-4-5
2 Deep MLB Spy	Cross Fire 3	Clamp Double Go	DB Contain	CB Fox Blitz

DEFENSIVE PLAYCOUNTS

Man Coverage:	46	Cover 3 Zone:	24	Combo Blitz:	10
Man Zone:	36	Deep Zone:	16	Goal Line:	15
Combo Coverage:	9	Man Blitz:	48	Special Teams:	12
Cover 2 Zone:	24	Zone Blitz:	60		

TEAM TRIVIA

San Diego Chargers Facts
Answers:
1. Texas Christian
2. The Pittsburgh Steelers
3. Balboa Stadium

DEFENSIVE FORMATIONS

3-4	Nickle
3-4-Normal	Nickel-3-3-5
3-4-Over	Nickel-2-4-5
3-4-Under	**Quarter**
3-4-Solid	Quarter-Normal
Dime	Quarter-3 Deep
Dime-3-2-6	
Dime-Normal	

DEFENSIVE STRENGTH CHART

- OVR less than 80
- OVR between 80-89
- OVR 90 or greater
- Player Weapons

4-3 Base Defense

FS #20, SS #27, CB #31, LB #95, LB #57, LB #56, CB #23, RE #99, DT #97, DT #76, LE #93

Dime Defense

FS #20, SS #27, CB #31, CB #29, LB #57, CB #28, CB #23, RE #99, DT #97, DT #76, LE #93

DEFENSIVE ROSTER LIST — Current / Next Gen

Pos.	#	First Name	Last Name	Overall	Player Weapons
CB	23	Quentin	Jammer	87	Quick Corner / Press Coverage Corner
CB	31	Antonio	Cromartie	84	
CB	29	Drayton	Florence	81	
CB	28	Steve	Gregory	74	
DT	76	Jamal	Williams	97	Force of Nature / Power Moe D-Lineman
DT	97	Ryon	Bingham	68	
DT	91	Brandon	McKinney	65	
FS	20	Marlon	McCree	86	Big Hitter
FS	32	Eric	Weddle	78	
K	10	Nate	Kaeding	91	
LE	93	Luis	Castillo	90	Run Stopper / Power Move D-Lineman
LE	98	Derreck	Robinson	70	
LOLB	56	Shawne	Merriman	98	Defensive Enforcer / Big Hitter, Brick Wall Defender, Finesse Move, Power Move D-Lineman
LOLB	52	Carlos	Polk	70	
MLB	57	Matt	Wilhelm	74	
MLB	54	Stephen	Cooper	71	
MLB	59	Brandon	Siler	70	
MLB	53	Anthony	Waters	68	
P	5	Mike	Scifres	80	
RE	99	Igor	Olshansky	84	Run Stopper
RE	74	Jacques	Cesaire	76	
ROLB	95	Shaun	Phillips	85	Playmaker
ROLB	92	Marques	Harris	70	
SS	27	Bhawoh	Jue	75	
SS	42	Clinton	Hart	74	

3-4-Over
Cross Fire Chuck

3-4-Under
Strong Blitz

Nickel-2-4-5
2 Man Under

To get the beast that is Shawne Merriman to take over the game, call 3-4-Over Cross Fire Chuck. It brings serious heat against the passing game.

Another blitz out of the 3-4 that sends Merriman flying is the 3-4-Under Strong Blitz. We call this one against two running back formations.

Merriman is simply the most dominant pass rusher in the game. This is a safe coverage play that allows him to show how dominant he is.

The only adjustment we make to this play is to shift the defensive line to the right side of the football field, toward Shawne Merriman.

A few adjustments need to be made for this play. First, shift the defensive line to the right, then hot blitz Merriman and spread the linebackers.

The Nickel-2-4-5 2 Man Under is a pretty safe defense to call and one most teams use as a base coverage. There are two safeties to help on the deep pass.

This shift ensures that Merriman will get a free release on the snap of the football. When this happens, only terrible things can occur for the offense.

Merriman brings the thunder from the edge. He gets up to full speed very quickly and bears down on the QB.

Two things need to be done to make this play an effective pass rushing play. First, spread the defensive line. Second, spread the linebackers.

Great things occur for the Chargers' defense, as Merriman brings the quarterback down in the backfield for a sack.

Another sack for the thundering linebacker from San Diego. Merriman can do wonderful things for your pass rush.

Now watch Merriman work on the opposing team's offense.

TEAM STRATEGY

103

KANSAS CITY CHIEFS / OFFENSE

OFFENSIVE **STAR PLAYER** #27

Larry Johnson — Halfback (HB)

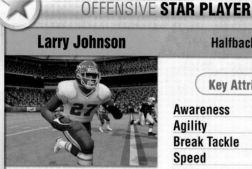

Key Attributes

Awareness	91
Agility	90
Break Tackle	97
Speed	93

As a pure north-south runner, **Johnson** does not waste time with fancy footwork. Instead, he uses his big body to pound out tough yardage inside. That's not to say that Johnson can't break off long runs, because he can. Once he gets in the open field, smaller defenders have a hard time bringing him down by themselves. Another portion of his game that is often overlooked is his ability to catch the ball out of the backfield.

Player Weapons: Feature Back / Power Back, Stiff Arm BC

OFFENSIVE **STRENGTH CHART**

○: OVR less than 80   ◉: OVR 90 or greater
◉: OVR between 80-89   ○: Player Weapons

2-Back Set

3 Receiver Set

RECOMMENDED OFFENSIVE **AUDIBLE PACKAGES**

Singleback-Normal Slot	Singleback-Normal Slot	Shotgun-4WR	Singleback-Normal	Shotgun-4WR
HB Stretch	WR Drag	HB Flat	FL Middle	Chiefs Cross

OFFENSIVE **PLAYCOUNTS**

Quick Pass:	8	Screen Pass:	17	Pinch:	14
Standard Pass:	80	Hail Mary:	1	Counter:	14
Shotgun Pass:	35	Inside Handoff:	33	Draw:	19
Play Action Pass:	34	Outside Handoff:	16		

TEAM **TRIVIA**

Kansas City Chiefs Facts

Turn the page for the answers.

1. The Kansas City Chiefs were originally known as what team?

2. Who was the first Chiefs running back to lead the NFL in rushing yardage for a season?

3. Which former Chiefs head coach played quarterback for San Jose State?

OFFENSIVE **FORMATIONS**

Singleback	Strong I
Big	Twin WR
Big Twin WR	Normal Flex
Twin TE	Twin WR
Twin TE WR	**Weak I**
Normal Slot	Normal
Slot Strong	Twin WR
Trips TE	**Shotgun**
Trips Bunch	2RB Flex
4WR	4WR
Flip Trips	5WR
I Form	
Normal	
Twin WR	
Big	
Twin TE	

OFFENSIVE **ROSTER LIST** Current / Next Gen

Pos.	#	First Name	Last Name	Overall	Player Weapons
C	62	Casey	Wiegmann	92	
C	64	Rudy	Niswanger	69	
FB	43	Greg	Hanoian	70	
FB	46	Boomer	Grigsby	68	
HB	27	Larry	Johnson	97	Feature Back / Power Back, Stiff Arm BC
HB	31	Priest	Holmes	82	
HB	26	Michael	Bennett	76	Speed Back / Speed
K	8	Justin	Medlock	76	
LG	54	Brian	Waters	96	Road Blocker / Crushing Run Blocker
LG	67	Chris	Bober	82	
LT	77	Damion	McIntosh	78	
LT	79	Kevin	Sampson	72	
QB	10	Trent	Green	83	
QB	11	Damon	Huard	80	
QB	12	Brodie	Croyle	75	
RG	76	John	Welbourn	82	Run Blocker
RG	61	Tre	Stallings	69	
RT	60	Chris	Terry	77	
RT	71	Will	Svitek	67	
TE	88	Tony	Gonzalez	96	Possession Receiver / Possesion, Quick Receiver, Hands
TE	89	Jason	Dunn	79	
TE	84	Kris	Wilson	76	
WR	87	Eddie	Kennison	85	
WR	82	Dwayne	Bowe	81	Deep Threat
WR	18	Samie	Parker	77	
WR	85	Rod	Gardner	75	
WR	80	Jeff	Webb	74	

I Form-Twin TE

HB Counter Str

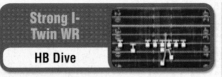

Strong I-Twin WR

HB Dive

Singleback-Twin TE

Kennison Option

HB Larry Johnson is a downhill North/South runner that runs with a mean streak. This play shows Johnson's ability to punish a defense.

One play that shows off Johnson's tough runner attitude and North/South running style is the Strong I-Twin WR.

Johnson has soft hands, which makes for a good receive threat.

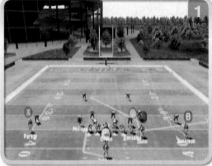

This is a strong running play for one of the strongest running backs in the game. It is designed to get him to the edge and let him use his strength.

Another running play to get Johnson going for the Chiefs is the Strong I-Twin WR HB Dive. This is power football at its finest.

This play that is designed for wide receiver Eddie Kennison. However, Johnson can be used on this play to pick up yards.

Follow the blocks of the fullback and the right guard on this play as they lead around the edge and deliver punishing blows.

The fullback will lead the way. The task here is simple. Follow the fullback right up the gut and punish the defense.

Johnson will run a circle route out of the backfield. This route is a good route against the zone, as well as a quick dump against the blitz.

Get outside and run to daylight. Once you are out here with Larry Johnson, there are not many defenders that will want to go toe to toe with you.

As you move up the middle, navigate Johnson through the traffic and pick up extra yards. Before you know it, you will be delivering blows to the safeties.

Johnson pulls it in. Use the short pass over the middle to get Johnson some receptions.

TEAM STRATEGY

107

KANSAS CITY CHIEFS / DEFENSE

DEFENSIVE STAR PLAYER #59

Donnie Edwards — Linebacker (ROLB)

Key Attributes

Awareness	74
Speed	79
Strength	77
Tackle	84

Donnie Edwards returns to the Chiefs starting line up after spending five productive years at middle linebacker in San Diego. In the Chiefs scheme he will move outside where he can use his speed to get after the quarterback and to drop back in pass coverage. As long as he is protected he will be able to flow to the ball and make plays all over the field.

Player Weapons: Heavy Hitter / Smart Linebacker

RECOMMENDED DEFENSIVE AUDIBLE PACKAGES

4-3-Normal	4-3-Normal	4-3-Under	Dime-3-2-6	Nickel-3-3-5
Hog Buck 3	Zip Shoot Gut	Mike Fire	2 Deep LB Blitz	Overload Blitz

DEFENSIVE PLAYCOUNTS

Man Coverage:	41	Cover 3 Zone:	23	Combo Blitz:	23
Man Zone:	37	Deep Zone:	22	Goal Line:	15
Combo Coverage:	12	Man Blitz:	49	Special Teams:	12
Cover 2 Zone:	14	Zone Blitz:	57		

TEAM TRIVIA

Kansas City Chiefs Facts

Answers:

1. Dallas Texans

2. Christian Okoye

3. Dick Vermeil

DEFENSIVE FORMATIONS

4-3	Nickle
4-3-Normal	Nickel-3-3-5
4-3-Over	Nickel-Normal
4-3-Under	**Quarter**
46	Quarter-Normal
46-Normal	
Dime	
Dime-3-2-6	
Dime-Flat	
Dime-Normal	

DEFENSIVE STRENGTH CHART

○: OVR less than 80   ◑: OVR 90 or greater
◑: OVR between 80-89   ○: Player Weapons

4-3 Base Defense

FS #25   SS #49

CB #24   LB #59   LB #50   LB #56   CB #23

RE #69   DT #95   DT #92   LE #91

Dime Defense

FS #25   SS #49

CB #24   CB #20   LB #50   CB #45   CB #23

RE #69   DT #95   DT #92   LE #91

DEFENSIVE ROSTER LIST — Current / Next Gen

Pos.	#	First Name	Last Name	Overall	Player Weapons
CB	23	Patrick	Surtain	92	Containment Corner / Shutdown Corner
CB	24	Ty	Law	91	Containment Corner / Smart Corner
CB	20	Benny	Sapp	72	
CB	45	Marcus	Maxey	69	
DT	92	James	Reed	82	
DT	95	Ron	Edwards	79	
DT	70	Alfonso	Boone	74	
DT	93	Tank	Tyler	74	
FS	25	Greg	Wesley	84	Big Hitter
FS	44	Jarrad	Page	73	
LE	91	Tamba	Hali	86	
LE	90	Turk	McBride	78	
LOLB	56	Derrick	Johnson	87	Playmaker
LOLB	53	Kris	Griffin	69	
LOLB	55	Rich	Scanlon	69	
MLB	50	Napoleon	Harris	80	
MLB	52	William	Kershaw	68	
P	2	Dustin	Colquitt	82	
RE	69	Jared	Allen	88	Finesse Move D-Lineman
RE	96	Jimmy	Wilkerson	72	
ROLB	59	Donnie	Edwards	94	Heavy Hitter / Smart Linebacker
ROLB	99	Kendrell	Bell	83	
ROLB	97	Keyaron	Fox	73	
SS	49	Bernard	Pollard	78	
SS	47	Jon	McGraw	76	

TEAM STRATEGY

DEFENSE / KEY DEFENSIVE PLAYS

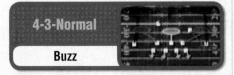

4-3-Normal

Buzz

This play is solid against base offensive twin receiver sets when the ball must be thrown. Edwards drops back in a buzz zone (curl/flat).

He first looks defend any receiver that comes in his area of the field. Notice the Broncos WR is starting to break toward the corner.

Edwards is in position defend the pass because his speed and awareness allow him to cover even some of the better receivers in the league.

With the ball coming down, Edwards jumps and swats the ball away for an incomplete pass.

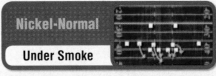

Nickel-Normal

Under Smoke

A good defense to get him a few sacks from the Nickel Normal Front is Nickel Normal Under Smoke.

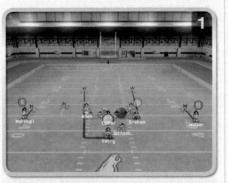

This play is designed to have Edwards blitz between the left guard and left tackle.

In the screen shot, we show Edwards taking an outside blitz angle. The left tackle tries to block him, but doesn't have the agility or speed to keep up.

The quarterback is unable to find an open receiver down the field and is sacked by Edwards.

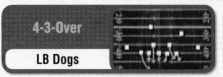

4-3-Over

LB Dogs

The 4-3 Over LB Dogs is a perfect run blitz that showcases Edwards's ability to diagnose what offense is doing before and after the snap.

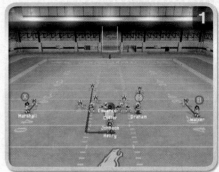

We like to shift the linebackers to the left side of the offensive line if we believe our opponent likes to run to that side. This puts Edwards in better spot to tackle.

The offense has called the I Form Fk FB HB Toss play. Edwards sniffs it out and goes straight after the ball carrier.

The ball carrier has no chance to escape.

TEAM STRATEGY

INDIANAPOLIS COLTS

Division: AFC South | **Stadium:** RCA Dome | **Type:** Dome | **Capacity:** 57,890 | **Surface:** Turf

TEAM STRATEGY

COACHING PROFILE

Tony Dungy

- **Head Coaching Year:** 12th
- **Experience:** Buccaneers head coach (1996-2001).

Tony Dungy was named head coach of the Colts on Jan. 22, 2002. In the five years that he has led the team, he has a regular season record of 60-20. He has a unique, soft-spoken style of coaching that seems to work well with his team.

TEAM RANKINGS

Scoring	2nd
Passing Offense	2nd
Rushing Offense	18th
Passing Defense	2nd
Rushing Defense	32nd
Turnovers	30th

RATINGS HISTORY

Category	'07	'06	'05	'04
Overall	90	90	**94**	75
Offense	91	**99**	98	87
Defense	**87**	69	78	65

Bold = Highest Year

88
FIVE-YEAR AVERAGE

2006 STANDINGS

Wins	Losses	Ties	PF	PA	Home	Road	vs. AFC	vs. NFC	vs. Div
12	4	0	427	360	8-0	4-4	9-3	3-1	3-3

TEAM OVERVIEW

Peyton Manning got the monkey off his back and picked up that elusive Super Bowl title. The Colts have been one of the most consistent regular season performers over the last five years, and with a strong returning cast on offense, things should be business as usual.

How can you not like the Colts' receiving core? Pro bowlers Reggie Wayne and Marvin Harrison bookend a wicked passing attack. Rookie Anthony Gonzalez will have to step up in the slot to keep things working.

The Colts have a nasty front four that can flat get after the QB. They have some issues at cornerback, but superstar FS Bob Sanders can lend a hand and shade over to help out with coverage.

SCOUTING REPORT

STRENGTHS

Description	Maximizing Potential	Tips for Opponents
Let's face it, Peyton Manning is the cream of the crop when talking about quarterbacks.	All Manning did two years ago was rewrite the touchdown passes thrown record.	As cool as Manning is, at times, he can be flustered when the defense shows blitzes from all over.
Receivers Reggie Wayne and Marvin Harrison are arguably the leagues best tandem in the league.	Harrison is paving the way for his induction into Canton while Wayne is making a viable case on his own.	Your best bet is to get to Manning, because there's no stopping these two.
Free safety Bob Sanders is a top tier safety.	Without Sanders last year, the Colts were horrible on D.	Use play action to try to suck him in.

WEAKNESSES

Description	Minimizing Risks	Tips for Opponents
The Colts did have one of the worst run-stopping defenses in the league last year for a reason.	Starting linebackers Rocky Boiman, Gary Brackett, and Freddie Keiaho accumulated 165 tackles combined.	Put pressure on the linebackers by running right at them and forcing them to make tackles.
The Colts like to run a lot of Cover 2 looks and force receivers inside so that their safeties can help over top.	The Colts' corners are OK, but become even better when you add Bob Sanders to the equation.	Try spreading the Colts out horizontally by using multiple receiver sets to get them out of their Cover 2 shell.

Overall Rating **91**
Offense **93**
Defense **85**

OFF-SEASON **UPGRADES**

Type	Round	First Name	Last Name	School/Team	Positon	Height	Weight
Free Agent	N/A	Rick	DeMulling	Lions	G	6'0"	304
Free Agent	N/A	Mike	Seidman	Panthers	TE	6'4"	261
Draft	1	Anthony	Gonzalez	Ohio State	WR	6'0"	195
Draft	2	Tony	Ugoh	Arkansas	G	6'5"	305
Draft	3	Daymeion	Hughes	California	CB	5'10"	192

FANTASY **OUTLOOK**

 Star Player: Peyton Manning
Round of Draft: 1st

Manning will be the first quarterback taken off the board. If no elite running back falls to you by the time it's your turn, and Manning is still on the board, snag him up.

Star Player: Marvin Harrison
Round of Draft: 2nd

As long as Manning is tossing him the rock, Harrison will continue to put up top receiving fantasy numbers. He had only three games last season, in which he put up less than 50 yards.

5-YEAR **PLAYER PROGRESSION**

First Name	Last Name	Position	'07 Overall	'08 Overall	'09 Overall	'10 Overall	'11 Overall
Peyton	Manning	QB	99	99	99	97	97
Marvin	Harrison	WR	97	-	-	-	-
Bob	Sanders	S	97	97	99	99	99
Dwight	Freeney	DE	96	96	99	99	99
Anthony	Gonzalez	WR	79	79	79	79	81

FRANCHISE MODE **STRATEGY**

Repeat after us: linebackers, linebackers, linebackers. The Colts are in serious need of playmakers at linebackers. We suggest at least drafting with your first three draft selections.

Key Franchise Info

Team Salary: $95.1M
Cap Room: $13.8M
Key Rival:
• Tennesse Titans
NFL Icons:
Peyton Manning
Philosophy:
• Offense: West Coast
• Defense: Contain Passing
Prestige: Very High
Team Needs:
• Linebacker
• Defensive Back
Highest Paid Players:
• Peyton Manning
• Marvin Harrison
Up and Coming Players:
• Anthony Gonzalez
• Daymeion Hughes

ROSTER AND **PACKAGE TIPS**   KEY PLAYER SUBSTITUTIONS

• **Position:** LG
• **Substitution:** Rick Demulling
• **When:** Global
• **Advantage:** Because the Colts are a passing team, having DeMulling start over Ryan Lilja makes more sense to us. Throw in the fact DeMulling has a higher overall rating.

• **Position:** LOLB
• **Substitution:** #55
• **When:** Global
• **Advantage:** The Colts are in dire need of speed at the linebacker position. Having their rookie linebacker sitting on the bench is not in your best interest. Move him into the starting role at LOLB.

• **Position:** MLB
• **Substitution:** Rob Morris
• **When:** Global
• **Advantage:** Normally we don't like to take away speed at any position, but this substitution must be made for the sake of the team. Have Morris start at MLB and move Gary Brackett to ROLB.

• **Position:** ROLB
• **Substitution:** Gary Brackett
• **When:** Global
• **Advantage:** Because speed is more important at outside linebacker than middle linebacker, Brackett is best suited to move the ROLB until you can build the Colts' linebacker's unit up.

INDIANAPOLIS COLTS / OFFENSE

OFFENSIVE STAR PLAYER #18

Peyton Manning
Quarterback (QB)

Key Attributes

Awareness	99
Speed	59
Throwing Power	96
Throwing Accuracy	98

Perfection best describes **Peyton Manning**, not only when speaking about his play on the field, but also in the way he attacks preparation. Manning is considered one of the smartest offensive minds in football and that's even compared to coaches. Manning focused last season on taking exactly what defenses gave him. He capped off a **4,397** yard passing season and **31** touchdowns with a Super Bowl win and the Super Bowl MVP.

Player Weapons: Franchise Quarterback / Smart QB, Accurate QB, Cannon Arm QB

RECOMMENDED OFFENSIVE AUDIBLE PACKAGES

Singleback-Deuce	Singleback-Dice	Singleback-4WR	Singleback-4WR Stack	Shotgun-Normal Slot
FL Drag Clearout	Safety Bait	HB Spint	Slot Cross	Deep In

OFFENSIVE PLAYCOUNTS

Quick Pass:	10	Screen Pass:	19	Pinch:	13
Standard Pass:	58	Hail Mary:	1	Counter:	14
Shotgun Pass:	63	Inside Handoff:	28	Draw:	18
Play Action Pass:	64	Outside Handoff:	17		

TEAM TRIVIA

Indianapolis Colts Facts

Turn the page for the answers.

❶ Which league did the Colts play in before joining the NFL in 1950?

❷ Baltimore defeated Dallas in Super Bowl V. Who kicked the winning field goal?

❸ What was the name of the owner who moved the Colts to Indianapolis?

OFFENSIVE FORMATIONS

Singleback	Strong I
Deuce	Normal
Big Twin WR	Jumbo
Dice	**Shotgun**
Normal Slot	2RB 3WR
Slot Strong	Normal
4WR Stack	Normal Slot
4WR	Slot Strong
I Form	Slot Strg HB Wk
Normal	4WR
Big	
Split Backs	
3WR	

OFFENSIVE STRENGTH CHART

○ : OVR less than 80   ◑ : OVR 90 or greater
◐ : OVR between 80-89   ○ : Player Weapons

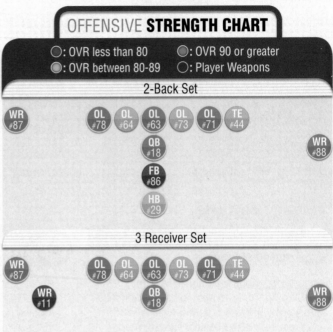

2-Back Set

3 Receiver Set

OFFENSIVE ROSTER LIST Current/Next Gen

Pos.	#	First Name	Last Name	Overall	Player Weapons
C	63	Jeff	Saturday	96	Pass Blocker / Pass Blocker
C	57	Dylan	Gandy	73	
FB	86	Ben	Utecht	79	
HB	29	Joseph	Addai	88	Elusive Back
HB	36	Kenton	Keith	72	
HB	25	DeDe	Dorsey	70	
K	4	Adam	Vinatieri	98	Accurate Kicker
LG	64	Rick	DeMulling	83	Pass Blocker
LG	65	Ryan	Lilja	81	
LT	78	Tarik	Glenn	96	Pass Blocker
LT	74	Charlie	Johnson	68	
QB	18	Peyton	Manning	99	Franchise Quarterback / Smart QB, Accurate QB, Cannnon Arm QB
QB	12	Jim	Sorgi	70	
QB	16	John	Navarre	66	
RG	73	Jake	Scott	83	
RG	69	Matt	Ulrich	70	
RT	71	Ryan	Diem	90	Pass Blocker
RT	67	Tony	Ugoh	75	
RT	75	Michael	Toudouze	65	
TE	44	Dallas	Clark	85	
TE	81	Bryan	Fletcher	78	
WR	88	Marvin	Harrison	97	Go-To Guy / Possesion Receiver, Spectacular Catch Receiver, Hands
WR	87	Reggie	Wayne	94	Possesion, Quick, Spectacular Catch Receiver, Hands
WR	11	Anthony	Gonzalez	79	
WR	85	Aaron	Moorehead	73	
WR	10	Terrence	Wilkins	72	

Singleback-Deuce PA	Strong I-Normal	Shotgun-Normal
Double Posts	**FL Drag**	**Deep In**

 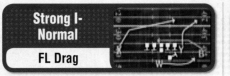 

Peyton Manning is the best because he prides himself on performing every aspect of his game at a perfect level. He is a threat on every passing play.

Manning has become such an efficient quarterback because he spreads the ball around the field and does not just look to Marvin all the time.

When teams try to blitz Peyton Manning, many times he will drop back into the Shotgun formation and just pick them apart with machinelike precision.

The play is designed with a play action fake to the running back, as so many of the Colts passing plays do.

The play is designed to pull the defensive coverage to the right with a crossing route, corner route while sneaking the flanker against the flow on a drag.

The play is designed to attack the defense vertically but it has quick developing routes in it that will help beat the blitz if the defense brings heat.

Peyton Manning to Marvin Harrison is often heard over the PA system. Manning always finds his #1 receiver and is looking his way on this play.

The defense has man coverage on the flanker which makes the corner route to the tight end and the swing route to the half back are promising options.

It is clear to see that the middle of the field is the best option. Both the slot and the tight end are open down the field.

Manning delivers a perfectly thrown ball to Harrison on the streak route down the right sideline.

The perfect decision in this situation would be to take the corner route because it is farther down field.

The pass to the TE is the safest and higher percentage choice because he is underneath the coverage.

TEAM STRATEGY

INDIANAPOLIS COLTS / **DEFENSE**

DEFENSIVE **STAR PLAYER** #**21**

Bob Sanders	Safety (FS)

Key Attributes

Awareness	88
Strength	65
Tackle	86
Speed	93

There aren't too many safeties in the NFL that are game changers and leaders on the team, but if you look at the Colts' defense, the leader of the group is **Bob Sanders**. How often has it been said that if you want to stop the run, make sure you have a safety. Bob Sanders took a horrible, run-stopping defense and made them a shut down squad. His leadership turned the Colts' weakness into a strength and carried them through the playoffs and onto a Super Bowl victory.

Player Weapons: Hit Man / Smart Safety

RECOMMENDED DEFENSIVE **AUDIBLE PACKAGES**

4-3-Normal	4-3-Over	4-3-Under	Dime-3-2-6	Nickel-3-3-5
Mid Rush	Dbl TE Bracket	Over 3 Strong	Cov 1 FS Robber	Monster Blitz

DEFENSIVE **PLAYCOUNTS**

Man Coverage:	36	Cover 3 Zone:	18	Combo Blitz:	11
Man Zone:	30	Deep Zone:	15	Goal Line:	15
Combo Coverage:	8	Man Blitz:	36	Special Teams:	12
Cover 2 Zone:	18	Zone Blitz:	53		

TEAM **TRIVIA**

Indianapolis Colts Facts

Answers:

1 All-America Football Conference

2 Jim O`Brien

3 Robert Irsay

DEFENSIVE **FORMATIONS**

4-3	Nickle
4-3-Normal	Nickel-3-3-5
4-3-Over	Nickel-Normal
4-3-Under	**Quarter**
Dime	Quarter-Normal
Dime-3-2-6	
Dime-Normal	

DEFENSIVE **STRENGTH CHART**

- ◯ : OVR less than 80
- ◑ : OVR between 80-89
- ● : OVR 90 or greater
- ◯ : Player Weapons

4-3 Base Defense

FS #21   SS #41

CB #26   CB #20   LB #58   LB #50   CB #28

RE #93   DT #97   DT #92   LE #98

Dime Defense

FS #21   SS #41

CB #26   CB #20   LB #58   CB #27   CB #28

RE #93   DT #97   DT #92   LE #98

DEFENSIVE **ROSTER LIST** Current / Next Gen

Pos.	#	First Name	Last Name	Overall	Player Weapons
CB	28	Marlin	Jackson	84	
CB	26	Kelvin	Hayden	79	
CB	20	Daymeion	Hughes	77	
CB	27	Tim	Jennings	73	
CB	34	T.J.	Rushing	65	
DT	92	Anthony	McFarland	88	Run Stopper
DT	97	Corey	Simon	86	Run Stopper
DT	79	Raheem	Brock	81	
DT	90	Dan	Klecko	77	
DT	72	Quinn	Pitcock	75	
FS	21	Bob	Sanders	97	Hit Man / Smart Safety
FS	43	Matt	Giordano	71	
LE	98	Robert	Mathis	90	Pass Rusher / Finesse Move D-Lineman
LE	91	Josh	Thomas	78	
LOLB	50	Rocky	Boiman	73	
MLB	58	Gary	Brackett	85	
MLB	94	Rob	Morris	83	
P	17	Hunter	Smith	88	
RE	93	Dwight	Freeney	96	Force of Nature / Finesse Move D-Lineman
RE	96	Bo	Schobel	72	
ROLB	54	Freddie	Keiaho	69	
ROLB	53	Keith	O'Neil	67	
SS	41	Antoine	Bethea	86	
SS	42	Brannon	Condren	72	

Dime-Normal

FS Blitz

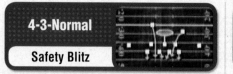

4-3-Normal

Safety Blitz

Nickel-Normal

Wham Lurk

Bob Sanders can set the tone with a free safety blitz. He is the heart and soul of the Colts defense and makes the defense dominant against the run.

Bob Sanders keeps the pressure on here with another safety blitz. He has a background of being a successful blitzer that can give us more options.

Bob Sanders is just as scary versus the pass and receivers are always looking over their shoulders to find out where he is.

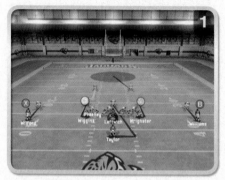

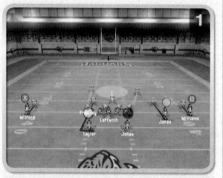

The defense is designed to make use of the blitzing and run stopping ability of Bob Sanders. It calls for him to blitz around the outside.

The defense is designed to get Bob Sanders and the strong safety down in the box to add pressure to the offensive play call.

This defense is designed to put Sanders in a Robber Zone and let him roam between the seams and break up anything coming his way.

The play starts and Sanders is running up to defend the run. He has to read the way the running back attacks the line of scrimmage before committing.

The look is the same for Sanders in this play. Teams still believe the Colts are weak against the run but Sanders is there to set them straight.

Even when Sanders is not delivering a crushing blow he can still make an impact. He defends the pass and prevents the receiver from making the catch.

Sanders makes the right read and explodes up field to tackle the running back in the back field.

Sanders is known as a big hitter. He comes up and lays the hammer on the running back.

The batted ball is intercepted by the LB, but it was all started because of the deflection by Sanders.

TEAM STRATEGY

DALLAS COWBOYS

Divsion: NFC East | **Stadium:** Texas Stadium | **Type:** Partial Dome | **Capacity:** 65,675 | **Surface:** Turf

2006 STANDINGS

Wins	Losses	Ties	PF	PA	Home	Road	vs. AFC	vs. NFC	vs. Div
9	7	0	425	350	4-4	5-3	3-1	6-6	2-4

TEAM OVERVIEW

Fortunately, you don't have to worry about T.O.'s state of mind when playing the game. Without drama, the Cowboys have tons of skill to get the job done. Romo is improved and has several good throwing options with T.O., Terry Glenn, and Jason Witten.

Halfback Marion Barber is more of a bruiser than a speed guy. The Cowboys should be able to pound it between the tackles and go up to to Owens and Glenn off of play action.

DeMarcus Ware gives the Cowboys great flexibility on defense. He can rush the passer with ferocity and has enough speed to get by in coverage. Hard-hitting Roy Williams patrols the middle and will drop the hammer on any receivers coming into his area.

SCOUTING REPORT

STRENGTHS

Description	Maximizing Potential	Tips for Opponents
Terrell Owens is hands down the best receiver in the game. Get him the football often.	Try to get Terrell Owens in one-on-one situations. There are few corners in the game that can cover Owens.	Go ahead and decide to double-team Terrell Owens and make your opponent go to another receiver.
Julius Jones and Marion Barber are proving that a two-headed rushing attack may not be a bad thing.	The combined rushing of Jones and Barber will open the door for Romo to play action and go deep to T.O.	Try to bring pressure with your front four and do not bite on play action passes which will lead to big plays.
The Cowboys' defense is loaded.	The Cowboys can get good pressure from the d-line.	Run the ball and force them to put eight in the box.

WEAKNESSES

Description	Minimizing Risks	Tips for Opponents
Despite Tony Romo doing a decent job for a benched QB, the verdict is still out on him.	Rely on establishing the run early in the game. Do not depend on Tony Romo winning the game for you.	Bring the pressure on Tony Romo. He is a young quarterback that is still learning the position.
The secondary of the Cowboys is still susceptible to the big play.	The front seven of the Cowboys are strong, but if the rush is met, opposing QBs will be able to work.	Establish the run early so you can use play action to test the Cowboys' weak secondary.

TEAM STRATEGY

COACHING PROFILE

Wade Phillips

- **Head Coaching Year:** 6th
- **Experience:** Atlanta Falcons interim head coach (2003). San Diego Chargers defensive coordinator (2004-2006).

Wade Phillips became the coach of the Cowboys on February 8, 2007. He will rely on his five years of head coaching experience and 30 years of coaching experience to handle the many personalities on this team.

TEAM RANKINGS

Scoring	4th
Passing Offense	5th
Rushing Offense	13th
Passing Defense	24th
Rushing Defense	10th
Turnovers	15th

RATINGS HISTORY

Category	'07	'06	'05	'04
Overall	**88**	73	78	75
Offense	**86**	78	66	65
Defense	85	79	**94**	82

Bold = Highest Year

80
FIVE-YEAR
AVERAGE

OFF-SEASON **UPGRADES**

Type	Round	First Name	Last Name	School/Team	Position	Height	Weight
Free Agent	N/A	Leonard	Davis	Cardinals	T	6'6"	366
Free Agent	N/A	Ken	Hamlin	Seahawks	S	6'2"	209
Free Agent	N/A	Brad	Johnson	Vikings	QB	6'5"	225
Draft	1	Anthony	Spencer	Purdue	LB	6'3"	266
Draft	2	James	Marten	Boston College	T	6'7"	303

FANTASY **OUTLOOK**

 Star Player: Terrell Owens
Round of Draft: 3rd

With as many catches as Owens dropped in '07, he still managed to put up elite numbers as a receiver. Last season, he led the league in touchdown receptions with 13.

Star Player: Terry Glenn
Round of Draft: 8th

Glenn doesn't get the publicity that Owens gets, but he does earn solid numbers season after season. He managed to go over the 1,000 yard mark for the fourth time in his career.

5-YEAR **PLAYER PROGRESSION**

First Name	Last Name	Position	'07 Overall	'08 Overall	'09 Overall	'10 Overall	'11 Overall
Terrell	Owens	WR	95	92	90	-	-
Roy	Williams	S	94	95	96	96	96
DeMarcus	Ware	LB	92	92	92	92	92
Tony	Romo	QB	84	84	88	90	90
Anthony	Spencer	LB	79	80	80	80	81

FRANCHISE MODE **STRATEGY**

The Cowboys have two of the more talented receivers in the game, but both Terrell Owens and Terry Glenn are getting up there in age. Slot receiver Patrick Crayton is solid, but there is nothing behind him.

Key Franchise Info

Team Salary: $92.5M
Cap Room: $16.4M
Key Rival:
• Washington Redskins
NFL Icons: Terrell Owens
Philosophy:
• Offense: Ball Control
• Defense: Force the Pass
Prestige: Medium
Team Needs:
• Running Back
• Defensive Line
Highest Paid Players:
• Leonard Davis
• Terence Newman
Up and Coming Players:
• Sam Hurd
• Anthony Spencer

TEAM STRATEGY

ROSTER AND **PACKAGE TIPS** KEY PLAYER SUBSTITUTIONS

• **Position:** HB
• **Substitution:** Marion Barber
• **When:** Red Zone
• **Advantage:** Barber is a powerful inside runner. Anytime he gets the ball near the end zone, it's almost a lock he is going to get in.

• **Position:** FB
• **Substitution:** Lousaka Polite
• **When:** Global
• **Advantage:** We can't see any reason why Polite should not be the Cowboys' starter at FB. He has better hands and is a better pass/run blocker than Oliver Hoyte.

• **Position:** MLB
• **Substitution:** Bobby Carpenter
• **When:** Global
• **Advantage:** If you plan on blitzing Cowboys' linebackers up the middle, then you have to get Carpenter. His speed rating is too fast to ignore. Beside, he also makes for an excellent pass overage defender.

• **Position:** PR
• **Substitution:** Tyson Thompson
• **When:** Global
• **Advantage:** Thompson is one of the faster Cowboys on the team, so it is good judgment to have him as the team's punt returner.

DALLAS COWBOYS / **OFFENSE**

OFFENSIVE **STAR PLAYER** #81

Terrell Owens	Wide Receiver (WR)

Key Attributes

Acceleration	96
Awareness	90
Catching	89
Speed	93

Forget all of the negatives that you hear about **T.O.** He continues to dominate his position and is still considered the best overall receiver in the game. T.O. had a so-so year (in his eyes), and he still led the NFL with **13** receiving touchdowns, and racked up **85** receptions for **1,180** yards. He is coming into his second year with the Cowboys and his **eleventh** overall with a smile on his face because he knows Jerry Jones has his back.

Player Weapons: Go-To Guy / Quick Receiver, Stiff Arm BC

RECOMMENDED OFFENSIVE **AUDIBLE PACKAGES**

I Form-Normal	I Form-Close	Strong-Normal	Singleback-Big Twin WR	Shotgun-4WR
HB Slam	HB Stretch	Comet Pass	Posts	Circle

OFFENSIVE **PLAYCOUNTS**

Quick Pass:	17	Screen Pass:	19	Pinch:	14
Standard Pass:	79	Hail Mary:	1	Counter:	15
Shotgun Pass:	34	Inside Handoff:	31	Draw:	18
Play Action Pass:	52	Outside Handoff:	17		

TEAM **TRIVIA**

Dallas Cowboys Facts

Turn the page for the answers.

1. In which Super Bowl did the Dallas Cowboys have their first victory?

2. Which three Super Bowls in the 1990's did the Cowboys win?

3. In which NFL season did Emmitt Smith break Walter Payton's record for career rushing yards?

OFFENSIVE **FORMATIONS**

Singleback	Full House
Big Twin WR	Normal Wide
Twin TE	**Strong I**
Normal Slot	Normal
Slot Strong	Twin TE
Trips Bunch	**Weak I**
4WR	Normal
Trey Open	Twin WR
Empty 5WR	**Shotgun**
I Form	2RB 3WR
Normal	4WR
Close	
Twin WR	

OFFENSIVE **STRENGTH CHART**

○ : OVR less than 80 ● : OVR 90 or greater
● : OVR between 80-89 ○ : Player Weapons

2-Back Set

WR #83 — OL #76 — OL #63 — OL #65 — OL #70 — OL #75 — TE #82 — WR #81

QB #9

FB #39

HB #24

3 Receiver Set

WR #83 — OL #76 — OL #63 — OL #65 — OL #70 — OL #75 — TE #82

WR #84 — QB #9 — WR #81

HB #24

OFFENSIVE **ROSTER LIST** Current / Next Gen

Pos.	#	First Name	Last Name	Overall	Player Weapons
C	65	Andre	Gurode	89	
C	67	Joe	Berger	60	
FB	39	Lousaka	Polite	80	
FB	46	Oliver	Hoyte	72	
HB	24	Marion	Barber	87	Power Back
HB	21	Julius	Jones	86	
HB	28	Tyson	Thompson	71	Speed Back
K	7	Martin	Gramatica	80	
LG	63	Kyle	Kosier	85	
LG	71	Cory	Procter	63	
LT	76	Flozell	Adams	89	Run Blocker / Crushing Run Blocker
LT	72	Doug	Free	77	
LT	77	Pat	McQuistan	69	
QB	9	Tony	Romo	84	
QB	14	Brad	Johnson	80	
RG	70	Leonard	Davis	89	Run Blocker / Crushing Run Blocker
RG	62	Marco	Rivera	87	Run Blocker
RT	75	Marc	Colombo	82	Run Blocker
RT	79	James	Marten	73	
RT	69	Jim	Molinaro	64	
TE	82	Jason	Witten	90	
TE	88	Anthony	Fasano	78	
WR	81	Terrell	Owens	95	Go-To Guy / Quick Receiver, Stiff Arm BC
WR	83	Terry	Glenn	89	Possession Receiver / Quick Receiver, Pass Blocker, Hands
WR	84	Patrick	Crayton	82	Hands
WR	17	Sam	Hurd	73	
WR	19	Miles	Austin	68	
WR	86	Isaiah	Stanback	65	

Singleback-Big Twin WR

Owens Option

Split Back Pro

Witten Option

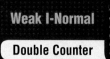

Weak I-Normal

Double Counter

A receiver with his talent must be given the opportunity to work a defender over. One of the best ways to do this is with an option route.

Size, strength, and speed are so much of a concern for DBs when they line up against T.O. that they can be taken advantage of on every play.

T.O. can easily move a defender out of the way and clear a good running lane for the back. This aspect of his game must be utilized.

This play is used to let T.O. work his magic from the slot position, where he can find a favorable match-up because of his size.

The play is designed to get the tight end the ball on the option route, but with T.O. running a comeback route, he is still the best option.

The Double Counter is a run play that use misdirection to allow the offense to beat an overly aggressive defense.

The defense will always overplay, TO. and on an option route, that usually means the corner will fear the deep pass first and leave the hook route open.

The defense remains cautious, and because of this, when T.O. makes his break back to the ball, he already has good distance from the defender.

The back uses the counter action to get the defense going one way, and then when he cuts back, T.O. has the perfect blocking angle on the corner.

If the defense plays off, the result of the play will always end with T.O. catching the ball.

He will make the defense pay every time if they do not play him perfectly

After T.O. holds the block, he releases and can now go upfield to get another block.

TEAM STRATEGY

119

DALLAS COWBOYS / **DEFENSE**

DEFENSIVE **STAR PLAYER** #94

DeMarcus Ware	Linebacker (ROLB)

Key Attributes

Awareness	76
Speed	86
Strength	78
Tackle	90

At 6'4" and 257 pounds, **DeMarcus Ware** should not be able to move as well as he does. He is extremely athletic and has become the dominant linebacker on the Cowboys' team. Last season, he racked up **11.5** sacks, and over his first two seasons, he has compiled **19.5** sacks and **104** tackles. Look for those numbers to increase at an even faster pace now that Ware will be in an aggressive, Wade Phillips-style defense that likes to let the linebackers get after it.

Player Weapons: Playmaker / Finesse Move D-Lineman

RECOMMENDED DEFENSIVE **AUDIBLE PACKAGES**

3-4-Normal	3-4-Over	3-4-Under	Dime-3-2-6	Nickel-3-3-5
OLB Dogs Fire	Trio Sky Zone	Weak Blitz 3	2 Deep Scalp	2 Deep Robber

DEFENSIVE **PLAYCOUNTS**

Man Coverage:	46	Cover 3 Zone:	24	Combo Blitz:	10
Man Zone:	36	Deep Zone:	16	Goal Line:	15
Combo Coverage:	9	Man Blitz:	48	Special Teams:	12
Cover 2 Zone:	24	Zone Blitz:	60		

TEAM **TRIVIA**

Dallas Cowboys Facts

Answers:

1 VI.

2 XXVII, XXVIII, and XXX

3 2002-2003.

DEFENSIVE **FORMATIONS**

3-4	Nickel
3-4-Normal	Nickel-3-3-5
3-4-Over	Nickel-Normal
3-4-Solid	Nickel-Strong
3-4-Under	**Quarter**
Dime	Quarter-3 Deep
Dime-3-2-6	Quarter-Normal
Dime-Normal	

DEFENSIVE **STRENGTH CHART**

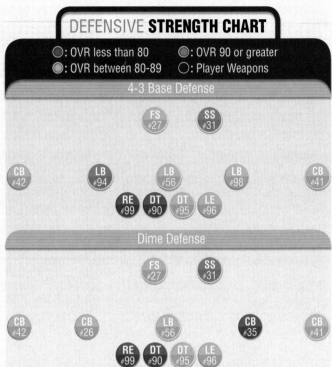

- ○ : OVR less than 80
- ◉ : OVR between 80-89
- ● : OVR 90 or greater
- ○ : Player Weapons

4-3 Base Defense

FS #27 SS #31

CB #42 LB #94 LB #56 LB #98 CB #41

RE #99 DT #90 DT #95 LE #96

Dime Defense

FS #27 SS #31

CB #42 CB #26 LB #56 CB #35 CB #41

RE #99 DT #90 DT #95 LE #96

DEFENSIVE **ROSTER LIST** Current / Next Gen

Pos.	#	First Name	Last Name	Overall	Player Weapons
CB	41	Terence	Newman	89	Quick Corner
CB	42	Anthony	Henry	86	
CB	26	Aaron	Glenn	80	
CB	35	Jacques	Reeves	72	
CB	33	Nathan	Jones	67	
DT	95	Jason	Ferguson	85	Run Stopper
DT	90	Jay	Ratliff	73	
DT	92	Montavious	Stanley	69	
FS	27	Ken	Hamlin	86	Big Hitter / Big Hitter
FS	25	Pat	Watkins	79	
FS	29	Keith	Davis	76	
LE	96	Marcus	Spears	84	
LE	72	Stephen	Bowen	69	
LOLB	98	Greg	Ellis	83	
LOLB	93	Anthony	Spencer	79	
MLB	56	Bradie	James	86	Heavy Hitter
MLB	51	Akin	Ayodele	84	
MLB	54	Bobby	Carpenter	79	Playmaker
P	1	Mat	McBriar	93	Big Foot Kicker
RE	99	Chris	Canty	79	
RE	97	Jason	Hatcher	76	
ROLB	94	Demarcus	Ware	92	Playmaker / Finesse Move D-Lineman
ROLB	57	Kevin	Burnett	76	
SS	31	Roy	Williams	94	Big Hitter / Big Hitter, Brick Wall Defender
SS	37	Abram	Elam	72	

3-4-Solid

Sting Pinch

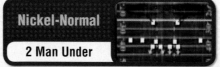

Nickel-Normal

2 Man Under

Dime-3-2-6

2 Deep Scalp

There aren't too many linebackers that pose a threat to an offensive game plan like Demarcus Ware does. He has great size and a motor that never stops.

Ware is not only a good blitzer, he is also a good pass defender. At 6'4" and fast, he is like a super wide receiver on defense.

Ware loves the green light to go get the quarterback. He has the skill and determination, so let him impose his will and alter the offensive game plan.

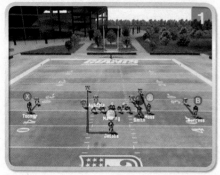

The Sting Pinch is designed to bring serious pressure on the offense by blitzing six defenders. Ware is at the end of the line in a 2-point stance.

The 2 Man Under is a base defense that is used to play things safe and see what the offense's plan of attack is.

This defense calls for Ware to blitz the left "B" gap. He will take the gap if it is open, or shoot right off of the defensive end.

This is not good for the offense. They left no one in to protect against Ware on the outside, and he is about to unload on the quarterback.

The offense thinks they have a mismatch with their RB being covered by Ware. Not a problem; the defense feels this is a match-up in their favor.

When the ball is hiked, the guard turns toward Ware to shut the "B" gap down. He stays close to the defensive end and has a clear blitz lane.

A few more hits like this, and the second string QB will have to start warming up.

Ware swats the ball down and lets it be known that it ain't sweet over here.

Ware delivers another devastating hit on the quarterback and the backup is warming up.

TEAM STRATEGY

MIAMI DOLPHINS

Division: AFC East | **Stadium:** Dolphins Stadium | **Type:** Open | **Capacity:** 75,000 | **Surface:** Grass

2006 **STANDINGS**

Wins	Losses	Ties	PF	PA	Home	Road	vs. AFC	vs. NFC	vs. Div
6	10	0	260	283	4-4	2-6	3-9	3-1	1-5

TEAM **OVERVIEW**

Miami is a team in transition this season. New coach Cam Cameron takes over an offense that has underperformed for quite a while. Step one will be to solidify things at QB. If they can get consistent play here, they have a number of skills that they can put into play.

Ronnie Brown is a very solid Dolphins back. With good speed, agility and break tackle ratings, he can get the job done. The problem for the Dolphins is their offensive line. Not much to like here.

Defensively, the Dolphins sport one of the best linebacking groups in the game. Zach Thomas and Joey Porter can roam the middle with the versatile Jason Taylor providing pressure on the QB.

COACHING **PROFILE**

Cam Cameron

- **Head Coaching Year:** 9th
- **Experience:** San Diego Chargers head coach (1997-2001), Miami Dolphins offensive coordinator (2002-2006).

The Dolphins plan to change their ways on offense this season under the direction of Cam Cameron. He was given the head coaching job on January 19, 2007, and brings with him experience of running the Chargers' offense.

TEAM **RANKINGS**

Scoring	29th
Passing Offense	13th
Rushing Offense	22nd
Passing Defense	5th
Rushing Defense	8th
Turnovers	13th

RATINGS **HISTORY**

Category	'07	'06	'05	'04
Overall	88	70	81	91
Offense	88	67	86	82
Defense	85	79	88	94

Bold = Highest Year

83 FIVE-YEAR **AVERAGE**

TEAM STRATEGY

SCOUTING **REPORT**

STRENGTHS

Description	Maximizing Potential	Tips for Opponents
The Dolphins finished last in the AFC East a year ago, but Taylor was a bright spot.	Use rip and swim moves with Taylor to get through blocks and put pressure on the QB.	Identify Jason Taylor prior to every snap. On pass plays, use an extra blocker if need be.
Chris Chambers is often overlooked at the wide receiver position.	Chambers is a burner. He does a great job against press man coverage.	Chris Chambers is the go-to guy at wide receiver for the Dolphins. He has all of the skills to be great.
Ronnie Brown was another bright spot for Miami.	Mix in different types of runs with Brown.	Swarm the football and get several players around him.

WEAKNESSES

Description	Minimizing Risks	Tips for Opponents
The Dolphins do not boast a stellar cast in the secondary. They are decent in coverage schemes.	The safeties are better suited to cover and play deep in a 2-deep look. The CBs do not have top end speed.	If you catch the Dolphins with only one deep safety or with no safety deep, get vertical.
Thomas is one of the best run defenders. However he lacks speed to cover backs out of the backfield in the passing game.	Thomas doesn't have the speed to keep up with faster runningbacks, it's best not to have him in the lineup in obvious passing downs.	If your team has a fast runningback, try to get him matched up with Thomas to expose his lack of speed.

Overall Rating 84
Offense 84
Defense 85

OFF-SEASON **UPGRADES**

Type	Round	First Name	Last Name	School/Team	Position	Height	Weight
Trade	N/A	Trent	Green	Chiefs	QB	6'3"	217
Free Agent	N/A	Joey	Porter	Steelers	LB	6'3"	250
Free Agent	N/A	Cory	Schlesinger	Lions	FB	6'0"	247
Draft	1	Ted	Ginn Jr	Ohio State	WR	6'0"	180
Draft	2	John	Beck	Brigham Young	QB	6'0"	216

FANTASY **OUTLOOK**

Star Player: Ronnie Brown
Round of Draft: 2nd

With stability now at quarterback with Trent Green, Brown should be able to set career bests across the board, especially with Ricky Williams out of the picture.

Star Player: Chris Chambers
Round of Draft: 6th

Chambers did not put up the All Pro numbers in '06 like he did in '05. In fact, he only caught four touchdown passes and went over the 66 yard mark just one time.

5-YEAR **PLAYER PROGRESSION**

First Name	Last Name	Position	'07 Overall	'08 Overall	'09 Overall	'10 Overall	'11 Overall
Zach	Thomas	LB	97	96	96	-	-
Jason	Taylor	LB	95	92	91	-	-
Chris	Chambers	WR	88	88	88	88	87
Ronnie	Brown	HB	89	91	91	92	92
Ted	Ginn Jr.	WR	80	80	82	82	84

FRANCHISE MODE **STRATEGY**

The Dolphins need help at several positions along the offensive line. Look to draft a few guards and center in the '08 draft. On the defensive side of the ball, a few fresh bodies at defensive tackle are also needed.

Key Franchise Info

Team Salary: $84.7M
Cap Room: $24.2M
Key Rival:
• Buffalo Bills
NFL Icons: Jason Taylor
Philosophy:
• Offense: Ball Control
• Defense: Force the Pass
Prestige: Very Low
Team Needs:
• Offensive Line
• Defensive Line
Highest Paid Players:
• Jason Taylor
• Chris Chambers
Up and Coming Players:
• Ted Ginn Jr.
• Samson Satele

TEAM STRATEGY

ROSTER AND **PACKAGE TIPS** KEY PLAYER SUBSTITUTIONS

• **Position:** WR
• **Substitution:** Ted Ginn Jr.
• **When:** Global
• **Advantage:** With a 98 speed rating, Ginn can stretch the field and help open up pass routes underneath. He doesn't have much strength, so it might be a problem if the defense calls bump-n-run coverage.

• **Position:** RG
• **Substitution:** L.J. Shelton
• **When:** Global
• **Advantage:** It may not be a natural spot, for Shelton moving to the right guard is an upgrade. He is serviceable until a better replacement is added through the draft or free agency.

• **Position:** RT
• **Substitution:** Mike Rosenthal
• **When:** Global
• **Advantage:** With Shelton moving inside, Rosenthal should fit nicely as the starter at RT. He is more mobile than Shelton and that's major plus if a fast defense lines up across from him.

• **Position:** 3DRB
• **Substitution:** Lorenzo Booker
• **When:** Third down situations
• **Advantage:** Booker is a slightly better receiver out of the backfield than Ronnie Brown. That's the only reason we make this move, alone to the fact that it gives Brown a rest.

MIAMI DOLPHINS / OFFENSE

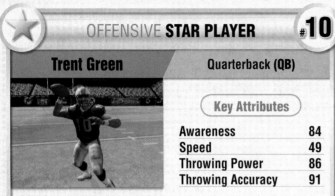

OFFENSIVE STAR PLAYER   #10

Trent Green	Quarterback (QB)

Key Attributes

Awareness	84
Speed	49
Throwing Power	86
Throwing Accuracy	91

How can you make up for not taking Brady Quinn in this year's draft? Easy—you get **Trent Green** from the Chiefs for a fifth round pick. With the addition of Green, the Dolphins get leadership that has been missing for years. We are not going to jinx him by mentioning D.M., but that's how long it's been. Look for an improved offensive unit with Trent Green in charge. He will not only revive Chris Chambers's numbers, but also help develop rookie QB John Beck.

Player Weapon: None

OFFENSIVE STRENGTH CHART

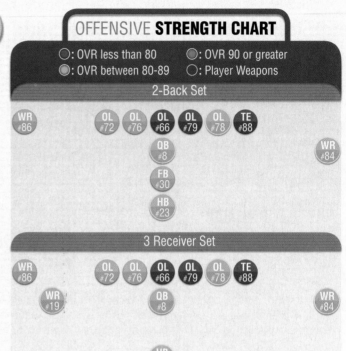

◯: OVR less than 80   ◉: OVR 90 or greater
◉: OVR between 80-89   ◯: Player Weapons

2-Back Set

WR #86 — OL #72 — OL #76 — OL #66 — OL #79 — OL #78 — TE #88 — WR #84
QB #8
FB #30
HB #23

3 Receiver Set

WR #86 — OL #72 — OL #76 — OL #66 — OL #79 — OL #78 — TE #88
WR #19 — QB #8 — WR #84
HB #23

RECOMMENDED OFFENSIVE AUDIBLE PACKAGES

I Form-Normal	I Form-Twin TE	Strong I-Normal	Singleback-Big Wing	Shotgun-Normal Slot
HB Blast	FB Fake HB Toss	HB Off Tackle	PA TE Corner	QB Sonya Check

OFFENSIVE PLAYCOUNTS

Quick Pass:	16	Screen Pass:	10	Pinch:	13
Standard Pass:	71	Hail Mary:	1	Counter:	17
Shotgun Pass:	47	Inside Handoff:	27	Draw:	13
Play Action Pass:	25	Outside Handoff:	11		

TEAM TRIVIA

Miami Dolphins Facts

Turn the page for the answers.

❶ What pro baseball team drafted Dolphin QB Dan Marino first?

❷ Which receiver owns the Dolphins record for longest TD reception in the Super Bowl?

❸ What team ended the streak of consecutive Dolphins wins in 1973?

OFFENSIVE FORMATIONS

Singleback	Strong I
Big	Normal
Big Twin WR	**Weak I**
Twin TE	Normal
Twin TE WR	**Shotgun**
Big Wing	2RB 3WR
Normal	Normal Slot
Normal Slot	Slot Strong
Slot Strong	Wing Trips
Trips Bunch	4WR
I Form	5WR
Normal	
Twin WR	
3WR	
Twin TE	

OFFENSIVE ROSTER LIST Current / Next Gen

Pos.	#	First Name	Last Name	Overall	Player Weapons
C	66	Rex	Hadnot	79	
C	68	Johnathan	Ingram	70	
FB	30	Cory	Schlesinger	86	
HB	23	Ronnie	Brown	89	Feature Back / Power Back
HB	20	Lorenzo	Booker	76	
HB	28	Jesse	Chatman	75	Speed Back
K	3	Jay	Feely	85	
LG	76	Chris	Liwienski	82	
LG	64	Samson	Satele	78	
LT	72	Vernon	Carey	82	
LT	67	Joe	Toledo	68	
QB	8	Daunte	Culpepper	85	Cannon Arm / Cannon Arm QB
QB	9	John	Beck	74	
QB	17	Cleo	Lemon	72	
RG	79	Anthony	Alabi	75	
RG	73	Dan	Stevenson	69	
RT	78	Mike	Rosenthal	84	Run Blocker
RT	70	L.J.	Shelton	80	
TE	88	David	Martin	79	
TE	87	Justin	Peelle	73	
WR	84	Chris	Chambers	88	Deep Threat
WR	86	Marty	Booker	82	
WR	19	Ted	Ginn Jr.	80	Deep Threat / Speed
WR	82	Derek	Hagan	77	
WR	80	Kelly	Campbell	77	
WR	81	Az-Zahir	Hakim	72	

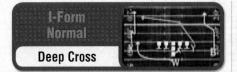

I-Form Normal

Deep Cross

Shotgun-2RB 3WR

Slot Drag

Singleback-Trips Bunch

PA Waggle

Green is a great decision maker at the quarterback position, and has pinpoint accuracy. The Deep Cross is a great play to get things started.

When a team has a quarterback that is not mobile, the best option is the Shotgun formation. Trent Green works well out of the Shotgun.

The PA Waggle is a perfect way to get Trent Green out of the pocket while still protecting him and giving him down-field targets to beat the defense.

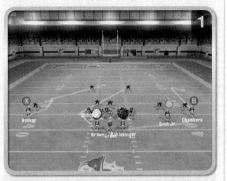

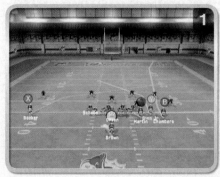

The Deep Cross is a play used to stretch the defense vertically, and in doing so, also sends the tight end on a deep cross.

The Slot Drag is a well designed play. This play makes use of the backs out of the backfield, a drag route, a comeback, and a seam post.

Use this play for a rollout in it for the quarterback. Green can use this to keep the defense from setting thier target on him.

While Trent is back in the pocket and sur-veying the field, he reads man and short zone coverage over the middle and has to look elsewhere.

As Green scans the field, he has multiple options open. He can take the deep comeback to the right or the slot on the drag.

With Trent out of the pocket, the defense has to stretch with him, and in doing so, they are leaving areas open for passes.

Green fires a pass to the flanker as he breaks inside for a completion.

Green gets the ball to rookie Ted Ginn Jr. and lets him use speed to blow by the defense.

Trent Green fires a pass to the backside receiver as he runs his crossing route.

TEAM STRATEGY

MIAMI DOLPHINS / DEFENSE

DEFENSIVE STAR PLAYER #99

Jason Taylor	Linebacker (ROLB)

Key Attributes

Awareness	94
Speed	84
Strength	78
Tackle	89

Taylor did something that goes against the logic of the NFL. The NFL's highest values are supposed to be youth, speed, and strength, but in his 10th season and at age 32, Taylor became the NFL's Defensive Player of the Year. He is still very much a threat off the edge and totaled **13.5** sacks in last year's campaign. Taylor may even increase his production this year, with the addition of Joey Porter to the defense.

Player Weapon: Defensive Enforcer

RECOMMENDED DEFENSIVE AUDIBLE PACKAGES

3-4-Normal	3-4-Solid	4-3-Normal	4-3-Under	Nickel-3-3-5
MLB Cross Fire	Wide Blitz	Thunder Smoke	Mid Gut Rush	Heat

DEFENSIVE PLAYCOUNTS

Man Coverage:	35	Cover 3 Zone:	19	Combo Blitz:	14
Man Zone:	36	Deep Zone:	19	Goal Line:	15
Combo Coverage:	10	Man Blitz:	37	Special Teams:	12
Cover 2 Zone:	20	Zone Blitz:	56		

TEAM TRIVIA

Miami Dolphins Facts
Answers:

1 Kansas City Royals

2 Jimmy Cefalo

3 Oakland Raiders

DEFENSIVE FORMATIONS

3-4	Dime
3-4-Normal	Dime-3-2-6
3-4-Over	Dime-Flat
3-4-Solid	Dime-Normal
4-3	**Nickel**
4-3-Normal	Nickel-3-3-5
4-3-Under	Nickel-Normal
46	**Quarter**
46-Bear	Quarter-3 Deep
46-Normal	Quarter-Normal

DEFENSIVE STRENGTH CHART

○: OVR less than 80   ◉: OVR 90 or greater
◉: OVR between 80-89   ○: Player Weapons

4-3 Base Defense

FS #24   SS #26

CB #29   LB #99   LB #54   LB #55   CB #25

RE #91   DT #96   DT #94   LE #98

Dime Defense

FS #24   SS #26

CB #29   CB #21   LB #54   CB #22   CB #25

RE #91   DT #96   DT #94   LE #98

DEFENSIVE ROSTER LIST   Current / Next Gen

Pos.	#	First Name	Last Name	Overall	Player Weapons
CB	25	Will	Allen	83	Quick Corner / Speed
CB	29	Travis	Daniels	79	
CB	21	Andre	Goodman	74	
CB	22	Michael	Lehan	71	
DT	94	Keith	Traylor	83	Run Stopper
DT	96	Paul	Soliai	74	
DT	62	Fred	Evans	67	
FS	24	Renaldo	Hill	83	
FS	32	Jason	Allen	80	Coverage Safety
LE	98	Matt	Roth	78	
LE	90	Rodrique	Wright	72	
LOLB	55	Joey	Porter	94	Defensive Enforcer / Big Hitter, Finesse Move D-Lineman, Brick Wall Defender
LOLB	51	Robert	McCune	75	
MLB	54	Zach	Thomas	97	Heavy Hitter / Smart Defender, Brick Wall Defender
MLB	52	Channing	Crowder	85	Heavy Hitter
MLB	59	Donnie	Spragan	76	
MLB	56	Derrick	Pope	63	
P	6	Ryan	Flinn	58	
RE	91	Vonnie	Holliday	83	Run Stopper
RE	95	Chase	Page	74	
ROLB	99	Jason	Taylor	95	Defensive Enforcer / Finesse Move D-Lineman
ROLB	93	Akbar	Gbaja Biamila	66	
SS	26	Travares	Tillman	80	
SS	37	Yeremiah	Bell	78	
SS	44	Cameron	Worrell	64	

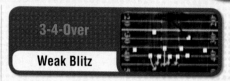

Nickel-3-3-5
Double X

4-3-Normal
LB Contain

3-4-Over
Weak Blitz

For the first time in his career, Jason Taylor is being moved to outside linebacker. This will now have him playing like a DeMarcus Ware.

Even though Jason Taylor is now playing outside linebacker, he can be used the same way he was as a defensive end.

Because of Taylor's speed and quickness, he must be used in the blitz game. With him in a two-point stance he gives the defense a lot of versatility.

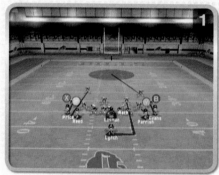

The Double X is a defense that is used to double-team the opponent's split end receiver. Jason Taylor is assigned to a delay blitz.

This play is a zone defense. With the whole field protected by zone, the outside linebackers will force the opposing QB to stay in the pocket.

The weak blitz attacks the offense by bringing Taylor off of the edge. The intent is that he will get to the quarterback. He rarely disappoints.

Jason Taylor's size is a mis-match for a tight end to try and block him. Taylor just levels the end and waits to deal with the running back.

The play starts with the quarterback trying to stretch the pocket. This is a no-no and it makes Taylor play the quarterback more aggressively.

The two point stance gives Taylor a brand new advantage, and when he drops his hips to get around the end, the quarterback doesn't see him coming.

When the back gets closer, Taylor puts an end to the play behind the line of scrimmage.

The QB pays the price as Taylor jumps on him and takes him down for the sack.

Taylor delivers a crushing blow to the quarterback as he takes him down for a sack.

TEAM STRATEGY

PHILADELPHIA EAGLES

| Division: NFC East | Stadium: Lincoln Financial Field | Type: Open | Capacity: 68,532 | Surface: Grass |

2006 STANDINGS

Wins	Losses	Ties	PF	PA	Home	Road	vs. AFC	vs. NFC	vs. Div
10	6	0	398	328	5-3	5-3	1-3	9-3	5-1

TEAM OVERVIEW

The 2006 campaign didn't end exactly as the Eagles would have hoped, but with a couple of tweaks, they should be right on top of things in the NFC. Donovan McNabb will be back at full strength and has a dangerous combination of mobility, accuracy, and throwing power.

McNabb is aided on offensive by versatile back Brian Westbrook. Westbrook is fast, agile, and a great receiver out of the backfield—just what you want out of your West Coast RB. Kevin Curtis was signed to provide a deep threat and experience to the receiving corps.

Philadelphia's attacking style of defense remains in place led by the hard-hitting Brian Dawkins. He teams up with Lito Sheppard and a solid group of linebackers to anchor this stingy unit.

SCOUTING REPORT

STRENGTHS

Description	Maximizing Potential	Tips for Opponents
Donovan McNabb is still the man in Philadelphia. He is a dual threat with a cannon arm and good legs.	Since McNabb does not have a star at receiver. He has to distribute the ball more to move the offense.	Do not let McNabb get in a rhythm. Keep the pressure on and force him out of the pocket.
Brian Westbrook is probably the most underrated back in the game. He is quick and elusive.	Use him coming out of the backfield as he is a nice safety valve when everyone is covered downfield.	Get Westbrook into the flow of the offense early. This will not allow McNabb to use play action.
Brian Dawkins is still the heart of the Eagles' defense.	Allow Brian Dawkins to cover the opponent's best receiver.	Do not throw toward Brian Dawkins unless you must.

WEAKNESSES

Description	Minimizing Risks	Tips for Opponents
The Eagles do not have a go-to receiver. With the exodus of T.O., the Eagles' receivers must step up.	The acquisition of Kevin Curtis from the Rams should bolster the Eagles' receiving corp.	There is no need to double cover any Eagles' receivers, which means the opposing defenses will blitz often.
The Eagles' defense is susceptible to the big play. Call plays that will challenge their the deep coverage.	Try not to leave the corners in one-on-one situations. Have Brian Dawkins playing over the top.	Establish your running game early, which will force the Eagles to shift their defensive focus.

COACHING PROFILE

Andy Reid

- **Head Coaching Year:** 9th
- **Experience:** Green Bay Packers offensive line coach (1995-1996), Green Bay Packers quarterbacks coach (1997-1998).

Andy Reid has put together a 80-48 regular season record since becoming the Eagles head coach on January 11, 1999. He is known as an even keel.

TEAM RANKINGS

Scoring	11th
Passing Offense	19th
Rushing Offense	7th
Passing Defense	28th
Rushing Defense	14th
Turnovers	17th

RATINGS HISTORY

Category	'07	'06	'05	'04
Overall	89	96	95	91
Offense	88	91	93	87
Defense	90	93	89	86

Bold = Highest Year

92 FIVE-YEAR AVERAGE

TEAM STRATEGY

Overall Rating **90**
Offense **90**
Defense **89**

OFF-SEASON **UPGRADES**

Type	Round	First Name	Last Name	School/Team	Position	Height	Weight
Free Agent	N/A	Kevin	Curtis	Rams	WR	5'11"	186
Release	N/A	Montae	Reagor	Colts	DT	6'3"	285
Free Agent	N/A	Takeo	Spikes	Bills	LB	6'2"	242
Draft	2	Kevin	Kolb	Houston	QB	6'3"	220
Draft	2	Victor	Abiamiri	Notre Dame	DE	6'5"	271

FANTASY **OUTLOOK**

⭐ **Star Player:** Brian Westbrook
Round of Draft: 1st

Westbrook recorded career bests in receptions, carries, and rushing yards in '06. However, as with any smaller running back in the league, you have to wonder how long he can keep it up without getting injured.

⭐ **Star Player:** Donovan McNabb
Round of Draft: 5th

Before McNabb got injured, he was putting up MVP-type numbers. Provided that he is able to avoid the injury bug, he has to be considered a top-10 fantasy quarterback.

5-YEAR **PLAYER PROGRESSION**

First Name	Last Name	Position	'07 Overall	'08 Overall	'09 Overall	'10 Overall	'11 Overall
Donovan	McNabb	QB	95	97	97	96	96
Brian	Westbrook	HB	94	97	99	97	96
Brian	Dawkins	S	97	97	94	92	-
Reggie	Brown	WR	85	85	85	86	86
Kevin	Kolb	QB	73	73	74	74	75

As always, the Eagles need help at receiver. Grabbing one in the first two rounds of the '08 draft would be wise. At outside linebacker is another position that also needs to be addressed in the early rounds.

Key Franchise Info

Team Salary: $94.8M
Cap Room: $14.1M
Key Rival:
• Dallas Cowboys
NFL Icons: Donovan McNabb
Philosophy:
• Offense: West Coast
• Defense: Disrupt Passing
Prestige: High
Team Needs:
• Receiver
• Linebacker
Highest Paid Players:
• Donovan McNabb
• Jevon Kearse
Up and Coming Players:
• Brodrick Bunkley
• Tony Hunt

TEAM STRATEGY

ROSTER AND **PACKAGE TIPS**   KEY PLAYER SUBSTITUTIONS

• **Position:** HB
• **Substitution:** Correll Buckhalter
• **When:** Red Zone
• **Advantage:** Brian Westbrook is a fine HB, but when it comes to getting into the end zone near the red zone, he doesn't have the bulk. That's why we suggest packaging in Buckhalter when those types of situations come up.

• **Position:** FB
• **Substitution:** Matt Schobel
• **When:** Global
• **Advantage:** When we compared the ratings between starter Thomas Tapen and Schobel, we decide that Schobel made more sense to start at FB, despite his default being TE.

• **Position:** RE
• **Substitution:** Darren Howard
• **When:** Run Defense
• **Advantage:** If your opponent is running all over your defense, try moving Howard into the starter's role at RE. He has more bulk than default starter Trent Cole.

• **Position:** LOLB
• **Substitution:** Omar Gaither
• **When:** Global
• **Advantage:** Gaither has no chance at starting at ROLB because Takeo Spikes is in front of him, but over at LOLB, he is an instant upgrade as a starter.

PHILADELPHIA EAGLES / OFFENSE

OFFENSIVE STAR PLAYER #36

Brian Westbrook	Halfback (HB)

Key Attributes

Acceleration	99
Agility	98
Break Tackle	80
Speed	94

Known as the ultimate player, **Brian Westbrook** proved last season that if you give him the ball, he can carry the load. Westbrook racked up **1,217** rushing yards and **7** touchdowns. It doesn't end there; he also added **77** pass receptions for **699** yards and **4** touchdowns. He may be the key factor in getting Donovan McNabb back to full strength by keeping some of the load off of his shoulders.

Player Weapons: Feature Back / Elusive Back, Hands

RECOMMENDED OFFENSIVE AUDIBLE PACKAGES

Singleback-Big	Singleback-Flip Trips	Singleback-Normal	Singleback-Trips Bunch	Singleback-Empty 5WR
HB Stretch	Angle	HB Screen	FL Out Stop	Slot Angle Post

OFFENSIVE PLAYCOUNTS

Quick Pass:	12	Screen Pass:	16	Pinch:	12
Standard Pass:	107	Hail Mary:	1	Counter:	16
Shotgun Pass:	13	Inside Handoff:	31	Draw:	16
Play Action Pass:	36	Outside Handoff:	10		

TEAM TRIVIA

Philadelphia Eagles Facts

Turn the page for the answers.

1. Eagles' great Wilbert Montgomery ended his career with what team?

2. Former Eagles QB Ron Jaworski attended what college?

3. What college did former Eagles' defensive end Reggie White attend?

OFFENSIVE FORMATIONS

Singleback	Split Backs
Big	Normal
Twin TE	**Near**
Normal	Normal
Slot Strong	3WR
Trips Bunch	**Strong I**
Flip Trips	Normal
Trey Open	3WR
4WR Flex	**Weak I**
Empty 5WR	Normal
I Form	Twins WR
Normal	**Shotgun**
3WR	2RB 3WR
Twin TE	Empty Trey Stack

OFFENSIVE STRENGTH CHART

⬤ : OVR less than 80	⬤ : OVR 90 or greater
⬤ : OVR between 80-89	◯ : Player Weapons

2-Back Set

WR #80 — OL #72 — OL #79 — OL #67 — OL #73 — OL #69 — TE #82 — WR #86
QB #5
FB #38
HB #36

3 Receiver Set

WR #80 — OL #72 — OL #79 — OL #67 — OL #73 — OL #69 — TE #82 — WR #86
WR #84 — QB #5
HB #36

OFFENSIVE ROSTER LIST Current / Next Gen

Pos.	#	First Name	Last Name	Overall	Player Weapons
C	67	Jamaal	Jackson	85	
C	59	Nick	Cole	64	
FB	38	Thomas	Tapeh	74	
HB	36	Brian	Westbrook	94	Feature Back / Elusive Back, Hands
HB	28	Correll	Buckhalter	79	
HB	23	Ryan	Moats	76	
HB	29	Tony	Hunt	75	
K	2	David	Akers	91	
LG	79	Todd	Herremans	82	
LG	62	Max	Jean-Gilles	74	
LT	72	William	Thomas	93	Road Blocker / Crushing Run Blocker, Pass Blocker
LT	74	Winston	Justice	75	
QB	5	Donovan	McNabb	95	Franchise QB / Cannon Arm QB
QB	10	Kelly	Holcomb	79	
QB	14	A.J.	Feeley	74	
QB	4	Kevin	Kolb	73	
RG	73	Shawn	Andrews	95	Run Blocker / Crushing Run Blocker
RG	71	Scott	Young	68	
RT	69	Jon	Runyan	90	Run Blocker / Crushing Run Blocker
RT	68	Patrick	McCoy	62	
TE	82	L.J.	Smith	87	
TE	89	Matt	Schobel	79	
TE	88	Mike	Bartrum	69	
WR	86	Reggie	Brown	85	Deep Threat
WR	80	Kevin	Curtis	84	Deep Threat
WR	84	Hank	Baskett	78	
WR	83	Greg	Lewis	76	
WR	81	Jason	Avant	74	

TEAM STRATEGY

Near-3WR		Singleback-Trips Bunch		Singleback-Slot Strong	
HB Inside		**HB Counter**		**HB Screen**	

Brian Westbrook has been begging to prove that he is a capable running back and able to carry the load of 20 plus carries a game.

Because Brian Westbrook is so good in the passing game, when the Eagles line up in passing sets he is always thought of as an option.

Because Brian Westbrook is the ultimate player, his pass catching ability must be showcased. He hauled in 77 receptions last season.

This play allows Brian Westbrook to take an inside hand off, and use his vision to read the block and get up field.

The HB Counter from the bunch is used to attack the defense at its weak side and take advantage of the fewer defenders on that side.

Use the screen play from the Slot Strong to attack the strong side of the formation. The flanker and slot receivers will try to clear the right flat.

This is a quick developing run play and as soon as Westbrook has the ball, he is in the hole and ready to get to the second level.

The counter works well and Westbrook has good blocking with only one defender to beat. It is a known fact that he makes the first man miss.

With the ball in his hand on the edge and two dominating blockers in front of him, this is a great look for the offense.

Westbrook is not a power back, but he makes up for it by being explosive through the hole.

Westbrook jukes inside and eludes the initial defender. He is racing upfield to get more from the defense.

With Westbrook's speed, this play can be run anywhere on the field with success.

PHILADELPHIA EAGLES / DEFENSE

DEFENSIVE **STAR PLAYER** #26

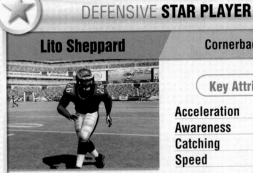

Lito Sheppard	Cornerback (CB)

Key Attributes

Acceleration	94
Awareness	92
Catching	78
Speed	92

It's strange seeing a name other than Brian Dawkins when talking about the Eagles' defense, but **Lito Sheppard** was a savior for the team on defense last year. He finished the year with an impressive 6 interceptions, none more crucial than the game-saving end zone interception against the Panthers that kept the Eagles pushing for the playoffs. He is quietly becoming one of the better cornerbacks in the NFC.

Player Weapons: Containment Corner / Shutdown Corner, Smart Corner

RECOMMENDED DEFENSIVE **AUDIBLE PACKAGES**

4-3-Normal	4-3-Over	4-3-Over	Nickel-3-3-5	Nickel-3-3-5
Eagle Crunch 3	Bluff Stack Tear	Over 3 Strong	Man Lock Spy	Under 7 Slice

DEFENSIVE **PLAYCOUNTS**

Man Coverage:	41	Cover 3 Zone:	23	Combo Blitz:	23
Man Zone:	37	Deep Zone:	22	Goal Line:	15
Combo Coverage:	12	Man Blitz:	49	Special Teams:	12
Cover 2 Zone:	14	Zone Blitz:	57		

TEAM **TRIVIA**

Philadelphia Eagles Facts

Answers:

1. Detroit Lions

2. Youngstown State

3. Tennessee

DEFENSIVE **FORMATIONS**

4-3	Nickel
4-3-Normal	Nickel-3-3-5
4-3-Over	Nickel-Normal
4-3-Under	Nickel-Strong
Dime	**Quarter**
Dime-Flat	Quarter-3 Deep
Dime-Normal	Quarter-Normal

DEFENSIVE **STRENGTH CHART**

- ●: OVR less than 80
- ●: OVR between 80-89
- ●: OVR 90 or greater
- ○: Player Weapons

4-3 Base Defense

FS #20   SS #37

CB #24   LB #51   LB #54   LB #57   CB #26

RE #90   DT #97   DT #98   DT #93

Dime Defense

FS #20   SS #37

CB #24   CB #21   LB #54   CB #22   CB #26

RE #90   DT #97   DT #98   DT #93

DEFENSIVE **ROSTER LIST** Current / Next Gen

Pos.	#	First Name	Last Name	Overall	Player Weapons
CB	26	Lito	Sheppard	94	Containment Corner / Shutdown Corner, Smart Corner
CB	24	Sheldon	Brown	89	Containment Corner
CB	21	William	James	79	
CB	22	Joselio	Hanson	69	
DT	98	Mike	Patterson	85	
DT	97	Brodrick	Bunkley	84	
DT	91	Ian	Scott	81	
DT	94	Montae	Reagor	79	
FS	20	Brian	Dawkins	97	Hit Man / Big Hitter, Smart Safety
FS	30	C.J.	Gaddis	74	
LE	93	Jevon	Kearse	89	Pass Rusher / Finesse Move D-Lineman
LE	75	Juqua	Thomas	78	
LE	95	Jerome	McDougle	76	
LOLB	57	Chris	Gocong	79	
LOLB	55	Stewart	Bradley	73	
MLB	54	Jeremiah	Trotter	91	Heavy Hitter / Brick Wall Defender, Smart Defender
MLB	96	Omar	Gaither	81	
P	8	Dirk	Johnson	79	
RE	58	Trent	Cole	86	
RE	90	Darren	Howard	86	
RE	78	Victor	Abiamiri	75	
ROLB	51	Takeo	Spikes	91	Heavy Hitter / Big Hitter
ROLB	50	Matt	McCoy	79	
SS	37	Sean	Considine	83	
SS	27	Quintin	Mikell	70	

TEAM STRATEGY

Lito Sheppard has become one of the better corner in the NFL and has shown that he can keep his game at a high level on a consistent basis.

Lito is a solid corner for the Eagles, and when a defense has a great cover corner on the outside, they can use base-like defenses to set their scheme.

Lito is so good versus the run and the pass, why not give him a shot in the blitz game? He has great speed and is a solid tackler.

This defense is a Cover 3. It has Lito Sheppard and the opposite cornerback playing deep thirds, and they will keep all the receiver routes inside of them.

The 2 Man Under is a base defense, it lets a team get a feel for what the offense is trying to do.

This defense is used to allow Lito Sheppard his opportunity to get after the quarterback and bring pressure from the edge.

This is great fundamental coverage being played by Lito. He is keeping the receiver in front of him and looking into the backfield to read the QB's release.

If there is no pass threat in front of Lito, then he will come up and play a role in run support.

At the snap, Lito shoots in and has the quarterback in his sights. He is also relying on some element of surprise.

Lito is able to intercept the pass because of the solid fundamentals he used on the play.

Lito is a great run support corner and he shows it here.

The quarterback doesn't see Lito blitzing in and this results in a sack for Lito.

TEAM STRATEGY

ATLANTA FALCONS

Division: NFC South | **Stadium:** Georgia Dome | **Type:** Dome | **Capacity:** 71,149 | **Surface:** Turf

COACHING PROFILE

Bobby Petrino

- **Head Coaching Year:** 1st
- **Experience:** Auburn University offensive coordinator (2002), University of Louisville head coach (2003-2006).

Bobby Petrino was hired by the Falcons on Jan. 7, 2007, to replace Jim Mora Jr. Petrino comes in with a 41-9 record that he earned while coaching the Cardinals. He is known as one of the best offensive minds in football.

TEAM RANKINGS

Scoring	25th
Passing Offense	32nd
Rushing Offense	1st
Passing Defense	29th
Rushing Defense	9th
Turnovers	8th

RATINGS HISTORY

Category	'07	'06	'05	'04
Overall	**89**	85	84	83
Offense	**89**	80	86	85
Defense	**90**	82	77	79

Bold = Highest Year

86
FIVE-YEAR AVERAGE

2006 STANDINGS

Wins	Losses	Ties	PF	PA	Home	Road	vs. AFC	vs. NFC	vs. Div
7	9	0	292	328	3-5	4-4	2-2	5-7	3-3

TEAM OVERVIEW

Michael Vick will still be at the helm of the Dirty Birds in *Madden NFL 08*, which will still make them a top choice for gamers. His speed is off the charts and every defense must scheme for him on each and every snap of the ball. His accuracy is poor, but his arm strength is off the charts.

Joe Horn was brought in to give Vick a reliable target, as Jenkins and White have not been up to the task. Crumpler is still a reliable receiver over the middle and can be counted on to help move the chains.

The Falcons can count on their defensive line and speed at linebacker to control the action up front. Unfortunately, with the exception of DeAngelo Hall and Lawyer Milloy, the secondary has some serious issues.

SCOUTING REPORT

STRENGTHS

Description	Maximizing Potential	Tips for Opponents
With Michael Vick, Warrick Dunn and Jerious Norwood, the Falcons have a serious run game.	Getting the running game started with Atlanta should be a primary focus, especially to the right side.	Make it a point to stop the Falcons' running game and force Vick to pass. Don't forget to contain him.
TE Alge Crumpler is one of the elite tight ends in the league and is a force to be reckoned with..	Crumpler should be the primary target any time he goes out for a route.	Most safeties in the league will have trouble containing Crumpler. Try using bracket coverage on him.
CB DeAngelo Hall is one of the fastest guys in the league.	Hall led the Falcons last season in interceptions with four.	Look for your secondary receivers instead.

WEAKNESSES

Description	Minimizing Risks	Tips for Opponents
QB Michael Vick has the worst throwing accuracy rating of all the starting quarterbacks in the league.	Vick's speed can only do so much for him. His threat to run is probably more dangerous than to pass.	Contain Vick and make him stay in the pocket to force him to pass and take away his running threat.
The Falcons lack a big play receiver. The addition of Joe Horn helps, but he's lost a step or two.	Last season's starters Michael Jenkins and Roddy White caught a combined 69 passes for 942 yards.	Focus your defense to concentrate on Crumpler. None of the Falcons' receivers have the speed to hurt you.

OFF-SEASON **UPGRADES**

Type	Round	First Name	Last Name	School / Team	Position	Height	Weight
Released	N/A	Joey	Harrington	Dolphins	QB	6'4"	220
Released	N/A	Joe	Horn	Saints	WR	6'1"	213
FreeAgent	N/A	Ovie	Mughelli	Ravens	FB	6'1"	255
Draft	1	Jamal	Anderson	Arkansas	DE	6'6"	288
Draft	2	Justin	Blalock	Texas	T	6'3"	320

FANTASY **OUTLOOK**

★ **Star Player:** Michael Vick
Round of Draft: 6th

Vick has never really put up eye-popping numbers as a passer. However, where his fantasy numbers have come from is his legs. As long as his off-the-field problems don't bite him, he will again be a top-10 fantasy quarterback.

★ **Star Player:** Alge Crumpler
Round of Draft: 8th

Crumpler does not rank among the elite fantasy tight ends in the game, but he does produce solid numbers, making him a good pick once the top three tight ends have come off the board.

5-YEAR **PLAYER PROGRESSION**

First Name	Last Name	Position	'07 Overall	'08 Overall	'09 Overall	'10 Overall	'11 Overall
Michael	Vick	QB	89	91	94	95	95
Warrick	Dunn	HB	89	86	-	-	-
Michael	Jenkins	WR	83	84	88	89	88
Rod	Coleman	DT	94	94	93	92	90
Jamal	Anderson	DE	81	82	84	87	87

FRANCHISE MODE **STRATEGY**

The Falcons can use help at left guard and at free safety. If one or both positions have a top notch player in the draft when it's your turn to select, go ahead and nab them.

Key Franchise Info

Team Salary: $82.1M
Cap Room: $26.8M
Key Rival:
• New Orleans Saints
NFL Icons: Michael Vick
Philosophy:
• Offense: West Coast
• Defense: Contain Passing
Prestige: Medium
Team Needs:
• Receiver
• Linebacker
Highest Paid Players:
• Michael Vick
• Keith Brooking
Up and Coming Players:
• Jamaal Anderson
• Chris Houston

TEAM STRATEGY

ROSTER AND **PACKAGE TIPS**   KEY PLAYER SUBSTITUTIONS

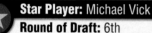

• **Position:** HB
• **Substitution:** Jerious Norwood
• **When:** Short Yardage
• **Advantage:** There really isn't much of a difference between Warrick Dunn and Norwood when it comes to ratings, except strength and break tackle ratings. As you know, both of those ratings play an important role in getting into the end zone when near the goal line.

• **Position:** WR
• **Substitution:** Joe Horn
• **When:** Global
• **Advantage:** Horn doesn't have great speed, but he needs to be on the field as much as possible because he is a reliable pass catcher. That's why we prefer to have him as our number one receiver.

• **Position:** WR
• **Substitution:** Roddy White
• **When:** Global
• **Advantage:** White is the team's fastest receiver, so he needs to be on the field as the number two receiver to help stretch the defense. With him running deep routes, it will allow Joe Horn to work underneath with more room.

• **Position:** FS
• **Substitution:** Jimmy Williams
• **When:** Global
• **Advantage:** One of the big problems with the Falcons' pass defense is that the safeties give up a lot of speed. Williams's 93 speed rating should help cover up some of the problems.

ATLANTA FALCONS / **OFFENSE**

TEAM STRATEGY

OFFENSIVE **STAR PLAYER** #28

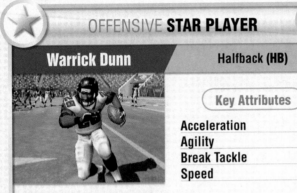

Warrick Dunn	Halfback (HB)

Key Attributes

Acceleration	97
Agility	97
Break Tackle	66
Speed	95

The former NFL Man of the Year is still a dominant force in the run. **Dunn** comes into his tenth year in the league fresh off of a 1,140 rushing yard performance in 2006, where he also tallied **4** touchdowns. Depending on the outcome of the Michael Vick situation, Dunn could be looked upon to carry even more of the workload to offset those missing yards. Dunn can also be used in the passing game, as he used to when in Tampa.

Player Weapons: Elusive Back / Elusive Back

RECOMMENDED OFFENSIVE **AUDIBLE PACKAGES**

I Form-Normal	I Form-Tight Twins	Singleback-4WR	Singleback-Flip Triops	Shotgun-5WR
HB Sweep	HB Screen	HB Wheel	Corner Flat	Hitch Corners

OFFENSIVE **PLAYCOUNTS**

Quick Pass:	8	Screen Pass:	21	Pinch:	16
Standard Pass:	73	Hail Mary:	1	Counter:	15
Shotgun Pass:	34	Inside Handoff:	31	Draw:	16
Play Action Pass:	34	Outside Handoff:	15		

TEAM **TRIVIA**

Atlanta Falcons Facts

Turn the page for the answers.

❶ In which stadium did the Falcons win their first regular season game ever?

❷ What college did QB Steve Bartkowski attend?

❸ What was the Falcons' first season in the NFL?

OFFENSIVE **FORMATIONS**

Singleback	Weak I
Big	Normal
Twin TE	Twin WR
Normal	**Shotgun**
Slot Strong	2RB Flex
4WR Falcon	Normal
Flip Trips	Trips TE
I Form	Slot Strong
Normal	Trips
Twin WR	4WR Spread
3WR	5WR
Strong I	
Normal	
Twin TE	

OFFENSIVE **STRENGTH CHART**

- ○ : OVR less than 80
- ● : OVR 90 or greater
- ● : OVR between 80-89
- ○ : Player Weapons

2-Back Set

WR #12   OL #72   OL #63   OL #62   OL #65   OL #74   TE #83   WR #87

QB #7

FB #34

HB #28

3 Receiver Set

WR #12   OL #72   OL #63   OL #62   OL #65   OL #74   TE #83   WR #87

WR #84   QB #7

HB #28

OFFENSIVE **ROSTER LIST**   Current / Next Gen

Pos.	#	First Name	Last Name	Overall	Player Weapons
C	62	Todd	McClure	91	Run Blocker
C	77	Tyson	Clabo	73	
FB	34	Ovie	Mughelli	90	Crushing Run Blocker
HB	28	Warrick	Dunn	89	Elusive Back / Elusive Back
HB	32	Jerious	Norwood	84	Speed Back
HB	42	Jamal	Robertson	72	
K	4	Billy	Cundiff	76	
K	2	Aaron	Elling	75	
LG	63	Justin	Blalock	79	
LG	68	Toniu	Fonoti	74	
LT	72	Wayne	Gandy	88	Pass Blocker
LT	70	Frank	Omiyale	66	
QB	7	Michael	Vick	89	Franchise Quarterback / Cannon Arm QB, Speed QB
QB	13	Joey	Harrington	76	
QB	3	D.J.	Shockley	71	
RG	65	Kynan	Forney	90	Pass Blocker
RG	73	Leander	Jordan	80	
RG	64	P.J.	Alexander	67	
RT	74	Todd	Weiner	90	Road Blocker
RT	76	Quinn	Ojinnaka	71	
TE	83	Alge	Crumpler	92	Possession Receiver
TE	85	Dwayne	Blakley	69	
TE	88	Martrez	Milner	66	
WR	87	Joe	Horn	86	Possession Receiver / Hands
WR	12	Michael	Jenkins	83	
WR	84	Roddy	White	78	
WR	19	Laurent	Robinson	77	
WR	86	Brian	Finneran	76	

Singleback-Normal	Singleback-4WR	Shotgun-2RB Flex
Horn Option	**Falcon Slot Option**	**Corner Flats**

Joe Horn is a route running machine that explodes off the line of scrimmage with power.

This is another play that shows off Horn's quickness and explosiveness as he runs routes.

This play highlights Horn's ability to get separation and make catches.

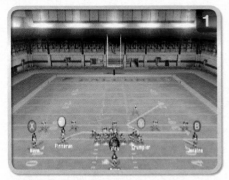

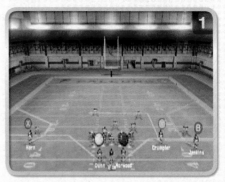

The option route gives the wide receiver control over which route he will run. He will read the coverage to tell him the best route for the situation.

Joe Horn has lost some speed over the years. He is not the burner that he once was, but he can still be dangerous on short and intermediate routes.

This play allows Horn to run one of the best deep routes that fits his style of play. This play has Horn running a corner route.

Horn reads this coverage as an all out blitz with three deep defenders. Thus he makes a move to the inside on the slant route.

The Singleback-4WR Falcon Slot Option sends Horn on a Deep In route. Horn sells the vertical threat, then rounds his route off in the In.

Horn's first move is to the inside. He sells this move to the cornerback. Then he makes his move back to the outside as he moves to the corner.

He gets open quickly, allowing quarterback Michael Vick to release the pass and avoid being sacked by oncoming defenders.

While he has lost some speed, he still can get up off the ground and use his body to shield the corner back as he comes down with the catch.

Once Horn establishes position in front of a cornerback, it's almost a guaranteed catch.

ATLANTA FALCONS / **DEFENSE**

DEFENSIVE **STAR PLAYER** #21

DeAngelo Hall	Cornerback (CB)

Key Attributes

Acceleration	98
Awareness	78
Catching	80
Speed	98

Young and unproven, **DeAngelo Hall** is still one of the fastest cornerbacks in football and is a great cover corner. Hall can turn and run with any receiver in man-to-man coverage, and loses nothing in zone coverage. He had a solid 2006 season, and finished with the lead on his team for interceptions with **4**. His play didn't go unnoticed as he made his first appearance in the Pro Bowl.

Player Weapons: Quick Corner / Speed

RECOMMENDED DEFENSIVE **AUDIBLE PACKAGES**

4-3-Normal	4-3-Over	4-3-Under	Dime-Normal	Nickel-3-3-5
Buzz Weak	Zone Blitz Swap	Bonzai Blitz	1 Man CB Snake	2 Man Hang Spy

DEFENSIVE **PLAYCOUNTS**

Man Coverage:	41	Cover 3 Zone:	23	Combo Blitz:	23
Man Zone:	37	Deep Zone:	22	Goal Line:	15
Combo Coverage:	12	Man Blitz:	49	Special Teams:	12
Cover 2 Zone:	14	Zone Blitz:	57		

TEAM **TRIVIA**

Atlanta Falcons Facts

Answers:

❶ Yankee Stadium

❷ University of California

❸ 1966

DEFENSIVE **FORMATIONS**

4-3	Nickel
4-3-Normal	Nickel-3-3-5
4-3-Over	Nickel-Normal
4-3-Under	Nickel-Strong
Dime	**Quarter**
Dime-Flat	Quarter-3 Deep
Dime-Normal	Quarter-Normal

TEAM STRATEGY

DEFENSIVE **STRENGTH CHART**

◑: OVR less than 80 ◯: OVR 90 or greater
◕: OVR between 80-89 ○: Player Weapons

4-3 Base Defense

Dime Defense

DEFENSIVE **ROSTER LIST** Current / Next Gen

Pos.	#	First Name	Last Name	Overall	Player Weapons
CB	21	DeAngelo	Hall	93	Quick Corner / Speed
CB	23	Chris	Houston	79	
CB	29	Lewis	Sanders	76	
CB	20	Allen	Rossum	70	Quick Corner / Speed
DT	75	Rod	Coleman	94	Power Move D-Lineman
DT	90	Grady	Jackson	83	Run Stopper
DT	95	Jonathan	Babineaux	75	
FS	25	Chris	Crocker	79	
FS	24	Jimmy	Williams	77	
LE	98	Jamaal	Anderson	81	
LE	92	Chauncey	Davis	73	
LE	94	Josh	Mallard	71	
LOLB	59	Michael	Boley	81	
LOLB	50	Marcus	Wilkins	62	
MLB	56	Keith	Brooking	91	Heavy Hitter / Brick Wall Defender
MLB	52	Jordan	Beck	71	
P	9	Michael	Koenen	82	Big Foot Kicker
RE	55	John	Abraham	92	Pass Rusher / Finesse Move D-Lineman
RE	91	Paul	Carrington	73	
ROLB	51	Demorrio	Williams	84	Playmaker
ROLB	54	Stephen	Nicholas	73	
SS	36	Lawyer	Milloy	87	
SS	26	Omare	Lowe	67	

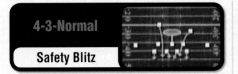

4-3-Normal

Safety Blitz

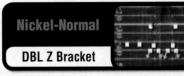

Nickel-Normal

DBL Z Bracket

Nickel-3-3-5

CB String Blitz

Cornerback Deangelo Hall does a good job of exploding out of cuts and turning and running with wide receivers.

This highlights the advantage of having DeAngelo Hall on the Falcons' defensive unit.

Another great play to show off cornerback Deangelo Hall's speed is the Nickel-3-3-5 CB Sting Blitz.

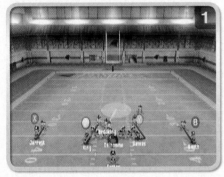

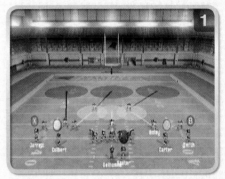

The Safety Blitz out of the 4-3-Normal front is a high risk, high reward play that sends both safeties after the quarterback.

Another thing that Hall's speed allows the Falcons' defense to do is double up on specific receivers. To do this, call the Nickel-Normal DBL Z Bracket.

The last strategy that Hall allows the Falcons' defense to use is the corner blitz.

DeAngelo Hall allows the Falcons to run this type of scheme, as he does a good job of pressing his man at the line of scrimmage.

Because Hall can stay with his man and shut down his side of the field, the defense can take one of its safeties and double a problem WR.

Hall will get a good jump on the quarterback. Be sure to spread the line so that the defensive ends can engage the offensive tackles.

Not only does Hall disrupt the receiver's timing with the quarterback, but he jumps certain routes well and makes big plays.

This strategy keeps the quarterback guessing and in a great deal of trouble.

Hall gets around the edge and meets his teammate in the backfield, and both sandwich the quarterback.

TEAM STRATEGY

SAN FRANCISCO 49ERS

| Division: NFC West | Stadium: Monster Park | Type: Dome | Capacity: 70,000 | Surface: Turf |

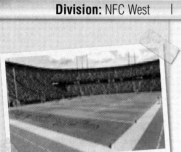

TEAM STRATEGY

COACHING PROFILE

Mike Nolan

- **Head Coaching Year:** 3rd
- **Experience:** Baltimore Ravens defensive coordinator (2002-2004).

Nolan was named the 15th head coach in 49ers history on January 19, 2005. He coached at the collegiate level at Stanford University, Rice University, and LSU before moving on to the National Football League.

TEAM RANKINGS

Scoring	24th
Passing Offense	29th
Rushing Offense	6th
Passing Defense	26th
Rushing Defense	19th
Turnovers	23rd

RATINGS HISTORY

Category	'07	'06	'05	'04
Overall	83	67	66	88
Offense	84	81	69	90
Defense	83	69	71	84

Bold = Highest Year

78 FIVE-YEAR AVERAGE

2006 STANDINGS

Wins	Losses	Ties	PF	PA	Home	Road	vs. AFC	vs. NFC	vs. Div
7	9	0	298	412	4-4	3-5	2-2	5-7	3-3

TEAM OVERVIEW

The 49ers fell apart in the 90s when they ran into cap troubles. With that problem well behind them, they had plenty of cash to make a splash in the free agent market. Nate Clements comes in to lock down the corner position, holding what could be the richest defensive free agent contract ever.

Alex Smith should be much more comfortable under center, especially with up-and-comer Frank Gore lined up behind him. He has good targets in Vernon Davis, Darrell Jackson, and Ashley Lelie.

Clements is the lone star on defense, but most of the other guys offer decent support. Banta Cain was a surprise last year with 5.5 sacks, and Patrick Willis could have a big impact with his speed at MLB.

SCOUTING REPORT

STRENGTHS

Description	Maximizing Potential	Tips for Opponents
Frank Gore is the team's best offensive guy. Last season, he rushed for almost 1,700 yards.	Don't underestimate Gore's rushing ability. Find plays that have him running behind LG Larry Allen.	First and foremost, Gore must be stopped. Call run blitz schemes to slow Gore down.
Brandon Moore is the 49ers' best playmaker at linebacker. He led the team in sacks and tackles in '06.	Moore needs to be on the field at all times: defending the run, playing the pass, or blitzing the QB.	You must neutralize Moore if you plan on having success on offense. Call plays that avoid running his way.
The 49ers' cornerback position is in good hands.	Clements has good speed and doesn't always need from safeties to be successful.	Harris is an easy target to attack deep if left alone.

WEAKNESSES

Description	Minimizing Risks	Tips for Opponents
Despite quarterback Alex Smith having a solid season in '06, he still has much to learn about being a QB.	Pound Gore to set up manageable third down short yardage situations.	Load the box up to stop Gore and force Smith to beat you with his arm.
The 49ers' defensive line is not much of a threat to bring pressure on the quarterback.	You will have to rely on the 49ers' linebackers to get pressure on the quarterback.	Watch for blitzing outside linebackers, since that's where the 49ers are going to get most of their pressure.

OFF-SEASON **UPGRADES**

Type	Round	First Name	Last Name	School/Team	Position	Height	Weight
Free Agent	N/A	Nate	Clemons	Buffalo Bills	CB	6'0"	209
Free Agent	N/A	Ashley	Lelie	Atlanta Falcons	WR	6'3"	200
Free Agent	N/A	Michael	Lewis	Philadelphia Eagles	S	6'1"	222
Draft	1st	Patrick	Willis	Mississippi	LB	6'1"	240
Draft	2nd	Joe	Staley	Central Michigan	T	6'5"	302

FANTASY **OUTLOOK**

⭐ **Star Player:** Frank Gore
Round of Draft: 1st

Gore had a breakout year in his second season in the league by rushing for 1,695 yards. Despite all the yardage he racked up, he only got into the end zone eight times. With that being said, he still is a first round choice.

⭐ **Star Player:** Alex Smith
Round of Draft: 11th

Smith made huge strides in his second season behind center by posting 2,890 yards and tossing 16 touchdowns. Those numbers are not spectacular, but they do make Smith worth a late round draft pick.

5-YEAR **PLAYER PROGRESSION**

First Name	Last Name	Position	'07 Overall	'08 Overall	'09 Overall	'10 Overall	'11 Overall
Nate	Clements	CB	93	93	95	93	90
Frank	Gore	HB	92	93	98	99	99
Vernon	Davis	TE	86	87	89	91	92
Patrick*	Willis	LB	85	88	93	96	99
Alex	Smith	QB	84	90	91	93	96

FRANCHISE MODE **STRATEGY**

The 49ers offense is in good shape because of the young talent that is in place, but the defensive side of ball could use some help. Look to draft a defensive tackle if one comes available in the first or second round.

Key Franchise Info

Team Salary: $78.3M
Cap Room: $30.6
Key Rival:
• St. Louis Rams
NFL Icons: None
Philosophy:
• Offense: West Coast
• Defense: Contain Passing
Prestige: Low
Team Needs:
• Defensive Line
• Linebackers
Highest Paid Players:
• Nate Clements
• Alex Smith
Up and Coming Players:
• Patrick Willis
• Jason Hill

TEAM STRATEGY

ROSTER AND **PACKAGE TIPS** — KEY PLAYER SUBSTITUTIONS

• **Position:** RE
• **Substitution:** Melvin Oliver
• **When:** Global
• **Advantage:** In the 3-4 defensive scheme, you need strength up front to stop the run. Melvin Oliver's strength rating of 86 is eight points higher than current starter Marques Douglas's.

• **Position:** NT
• **Substitution:** Isaac Sopoaga
• **When:** Global
• **Advantage:** Sopoaga has a four point advantage when it comes to OVR ratings over the other DTs; plus his 95 strenght rating allows him to clog holes and get off blockers up front.

• **Position:** FS
• **Substitution:** Dashon Goldson
• **When:** Global
• **Advantage:** Goldson has a two point higher catch rating at 63 than current starter Mark Roman, meaning he's more likely to get picks than Roman is.

• **Position:** PR
• **Substitution:** Jason Hill
• **When:** Global
• **Advantage:** Hill's OVR rating is two points higher than current starter Maurice Hicks's. Not to mention Hill's 92 speed. That extra speed could prove to be beneficial in the return game.

141

SAN FRANCISCO 49ERS / OFFENSE

OFFENSIVE **STAR PLAYER** #21

Frank Gore	Halfback (HB)

Key Attributes

Acceleration	93
Agility	93
Break Tackle	91
Speed	92

One of the more underrated runningbacks in the NFL is **Frank Gore**. This may be due to the fact that he plays on a team that hasn't been very good over the last few years. In '06, Gore ranked third in the league in rushing yardage with a total of **1,695** yards. He also managed to get in the end zone **8** times on the ground. As the 49ers' passing offense improves, you can bet that Gore's numbers will increase.

Player Weapon: Power Back

OFFENSIVE **STRENGTH CHART**

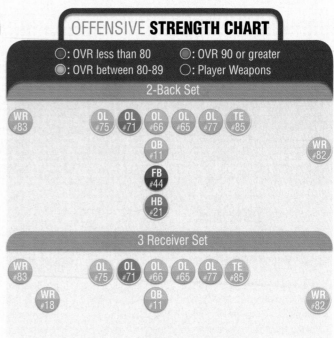

○: OVR less than 80   ◉: OVR 90 or greater
◑: OVR between 80-89   ⬡: Player Weapons

2-Back Set

WR #83 | OL #75 | OL #71 | OL #66 | OL #65 | OL #77 | TE #85 | QB #11 | FB #44 | HB #21 | WR #82

3 Receiver Set

WR #83 | OL #75 | OL #71 | OL #66 | OL #65 | OL #77 | TE #85 | WR #18 | QB #11 | WR #82 | HB #21

RECOMMENDED OFFENSIVE **AUDIBLE PACKAGES**

I Form-Normal	I Form-Normal	Singleback-Normal	Singleback-Slot Strong	Singleback-4WR
HB Blast	Mid Attack	HB Plunge	FL Drag	WR Post Flags

OFFENSIVE **PLAYCOUNTS**

Quick Pass:	31	Screen Pass:	8	Pinch:	11
Standard Pass:	73	Hail Mary:	2	Counter:	13
Shotgun Pass:	36	Inside Handoff:	35	Draw:	8
Play Action Pass:	25	Outside Handoff:	8		

TEAM **TRIVIA**

San Francisco 49ers Facts

Turn the page for the answers.

❶ In what year were the 49ers admitted into the NFL?

❷ How many Super Bowls have the 49ers won?

❸ The most prolific play in San Francisco history, known as "The Catch," was between which two 49er players?

OFFENSIVE **FORMATIONS**

Singleback	Strong I
Big	Normal
Big Twin WR	Twin WR
Twin TE WR	**Weak I**
Normal	Normal
Slot Strong	Close
4WR	Twin WR
Empty Trey	Twin TE
I Form	**Shotgun**
Normal	Normal
Twin WR	Slot Strong
3WR	Trips Bunch
Big	4WR
Split Backs	
Normal	

OFFENSIVE **ROSTER LIST** Current / Next Gen

Pos.	#	First Name	Last Name	Overall	Player Weapons
C	66	Eric	Heitmann	85	
C	69	Tony	Wragge	68	
FB	44	Moran	Norris	74	
HB	21	Frank	Gore	92	Power Back
HB	24	Michael	Robinson	78	
HB	43	Maurice	Hicks	75	
K	6	Joe	Nedney	88	
LG	71	Larry	Allen	91	Run Blocker / Crushing Run Blocker
LG	78	Patrick	Estes	71	
LT	75	Jonas	Jennings	85	Run Blocker
LT	74	Joe	Staley	79	
QB	11	Alex	Smith	84	
QB	12	Trent	Dilfer	79	
QB	13	Shaun	Hill	67	
RG	65	Justin	Smiley	83	
RG	64	David	Baas	80	
RT	77	Kwame	Harris	82	
RT	68	Adam	Snyder	78	
TE	85	Vernon	Davis	86	Deep Threat
TE	46	Delanie	Walker	69	
WR	82	Darrell	Jackson	89	Possession Receiver / Quick Receiver
WR	18	Ashley	Lelie	80	
WR	83	Arnaz	Battle	80	
WR	89	Jason	Hill	78	Deep Threat
WR	88	Taylor	Jacobs	75	
WR	84	Bryan	Gilmore	73	

Weak I-Twin TE
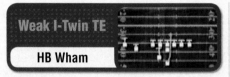
HB Wham

Running back Frank Gore runs with a good pad level and always keeps his legs moving.

Frank Gore is a straight-ahead, punishing power runner that also possesses a host of moves to send the defense packing.

This play will go straight up the middle. There is nothing fancy about this play; it's just straight, smashmouth football, Gore-style.

Navigate through the traffic and pick up extra yards. The HB Wham uses Gore's power to punish the defense.

I Form-Big

HB Counter

Gore also has above average speed once he gets into the open field. This is a play that shows off his speed.

This play uses his physicality on the defense and is designed for Gore to get outside.

Once Gore receives the football, follow the blocks to the outside. Patience is key here. Do not outrun the blocking.

Once outside, turn on the afterburners. Gore has the power to pound it inside, as well as the speed to get outside and be a problem on the perimeter.

Singleback-Big

Jackson Option

Gore shows a great work ethic and the attitude to constantly improve.

This play is designed for wide out Daryl Jackson. He runs an option route on the play. Gore runs an auto-motion route that has big play potential as well.

Prior to the snap, Gore will motion to the left of the formation. Alex Smith will hike the football before Gore sets out wide.

Gore works behind the LBs and in the deep middle. Hit him with the pass to Gore defenders to the turf.

TEAM STRATEGY

SAN FRANCISCO 49ERS / DEFENSE

DEFENSIVE STAR PLAYER #56

Brandon Moore — Linebacker (MLB)

Key Attributes

Awareness	77
Speed	78
Strength	79
Tackle	85

On a team short of defensive playmakers, **Moore** stepped up last season to be one of them. He registered **93** total tackles and **6.5** sacks. In both of those categories, he led the team. At 6'1" and 242 pounds, his strength and quickness allow him to get to the ball carrier quickly. Moore is now in his 6th season and can help rebuild a once proud 49ers' defense.

Player Weapon: None

RECOMMENDED DEFENSIVE AUDIBLE PACKAGES

3-4-Normal	3-4-Over	3-4-Solid	Dime-Normal	Nickel-3-3-5
2 Deep MLB Spy	Cross Fire 3	Clamp Double Go	Quarters Spy	LB Rams Dogs

DEFENSIVE PLAYCOUNTS

Man Coverage:	46	Cover 3 Zone:	24	Combo Blitz:	10
Man Zone:	36	Deep Zone:	16	Goal Line:	15
Combo Coverage:	9	Man Blitz:	48	Special Teams:	12
Cover 2 Zone:	24	Zone Blitz:	60		

TEAM TRIVIA

San Francisco 49ers Facts

Answers:

1. 1950

2. Five

3. Joe Montana and Dwight Clark

DEFENSIVE FORMATIONS

3-4	Nickel
3-4-Normal	Nickel-3-3-5
3-4-Over	Nickel-Normal
3-4-Solid	Nickel-Strong
3-4-Under	**Quarter**
Dime	Quarter-3 Deep
Dime-3-2-6	Quarter-Normal
Dime-Normal	

DEFENSIVE STRENGTH CHART

- ○: OVR less than 80
- ◕: OVR between 80-89
- ●: OVR 90 or greater
- ○: Player Weapons

4-3 Base Defense

FS #26 SS #32

CB #27   LB #95   LB #50   LB #99   CB #22

RE #94   DT #93   DT #90   LE #97

Dime Defense

FS #26 SS #32

CB #27   CB #36   LB #50   CB #30   CB #22

RE #94   DT #93   DT #90   LE #97

DEFENSIVE ROSTER LIST Current / Next Gen

Pos.	#	First Name	Last Name	Overall	Player Weapons
CB	22	Nate	Clements	93	Shutdown Corner / Press Coverage Corner, Shutdown Corner
CB	27	Walt	Harris	88	Containment Corner / Smart Corner
CB	36	Shawntae	Spencer	81	
CB	30	Donald	Strickland	75	
CB	20	B.J.	Tucker	65	
DT	90	Isaac	Sopoaga	77	
DT	93	Ronald	Fields	74	
DT	76	Joe	Cohen	73	
DT	92	Aubrayo	Franklin	73	
FS	26	Mark	Roman	79	
FS	38	Dashon	Goldson	76	
LE	97	Bryant	Young	86	Power Move D-Lineman
LE	96	Melvin	Oliver	78	
LE	91	Ray	McDonald	77	
LOLB	99	Manny	Lawson	80	Playmaker
LOLB	98	Parys	Haralson	75	
MLB	50	Derek	Smith	88	Playmaker
MLB	52	Patrick	Willis	85	Big Hitter
MLB	56	Brandon	Moore	82	
MLB	53	Jeff	Ulbrich	80	
P	4	Andy	Lee	85	
RE	94	Marques	Douglas	84	
RE	63	Damane	Duckett	73	
ROLB	95	Tully	Banta-Cain	82	
ROLB	54	Roderick	Green	65	
ROLB	58	Jay	Moore	62	
SS	32	Michael	Lewis	84	Big Hitter
SS	28	Keith	Lewis	76	

3-4-Over
Sting Pinch

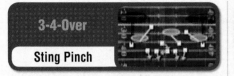

Cornerback Nate Clements is a pure man coverage defender that is physical and aggressive.

Nickel-3-3-5
CB Fox Blitz 3

Clements can get to top speed in a hurry. He is explosive and very physical.

3-4-Normal
2 Man Under

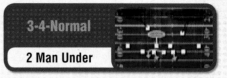

Clements also has excellent change of direction skills and hitting power.

The 3-4-Over Sting Pinch is a very risky defense to call because it has no deep backfield help. The corners are stuck on an island.

The Nickel-3-3-5 CB Fox Blitz 3 sends the nickelback and the left cornerback on the pass rush after the quarterback.

Players show their worth when they do extraordinary things within normal plays.

Nate Clements gives a level of comfort in calling this play, due to his ability to press WRs at the line and then keep up with them down the field.

Clements gets a jump from the right side of the screen. He has deep help behind him, so coverage is not a problem.

Clements follows the wide receiver at first due to the receiver selling pass. But he quickly diagnoses the counter play and makes his way to the football.

Clements's shutdown ability allows for the 49ers' pass rush to swarm the quarterback and take him down for a loss.

He meets his teammate at the quarterback where they both make a sandwich. They pop each other a high five for doing damage to the quarterback.

When he arrives there, he shows why he is the best tackling CB.

TEAM STRATEGY

145

NEW YORK GIANTS

Divison: NFC East | **Stadium:** Giants Stadium | **Type:** Open | **Capacity:** 80,062 | **Surface:** Turf

TEAM STRATEGY

COACHING **PROFILE**

Tom Coughlin

- **Head Coaching Year:** 12th
- **Experience:** Boston College head coach (1991-1993), Jacksonville Jaguars head coach (1995-2002).

He was hired on January 6, 2004. Since then he has a record of 25-23. He could be in his last year as the team's coach, so he made sure to get new coordinators on O/D so he can go down swinging.

TEAM **RANKINGS**

Scoring	11th
Passing Offense	19th
Rushing Offense	17th
Passing Defense	28th
Rushing Defense	14th
Turnovers	17th

RATINGS **HISTORY**

Category	'07	'06	'05	'04
Overall	**89**	72	70	83
Offense	**89**	74	67	80
Defense	**89**	78	78	79

Bold = Highest Year

80
FIVE-YEAR **AVERAGE**

2006 **STANDINGS**

Wins	Losses	Ties	PF	PA	Home	Road	vs. AFC	vs. NFC	vs. Div
8	8	355	355	362	3-5	5-3	1-3	7-5	1-5

TEAM **OVERVIEW**

With their personnel, the Giants should be able to run a power fun/vertical passing style of attack. Brandon Jacobs and Reuben Droughns can both tote the leather with power. Jacobs is especially difficult to take down.

Eli Manning must continue to improve if this team's offense is going to flourish. He has the ratings to get the ball to Shockey and Plaxico Burress. Burress is a match-up nightmare for most short corners.

The Giants have great bookend pass rushers in Strahan and Umenyiora. They should be able to get after the QB. They had better, because the corners are not the strong points of this defense.

SCOUTING **REPORT**

STRENGTHS

Description	Maximizing Potential	Tips for Opponents
Even though Tiki Barber has left the team, the tandem of Jacobs and Droughns should be tough enough.	The offensive line has quietly become very solid behind Shaun O'Hara at center.	Do not hesitate to stack eight or nine defenders in the box. Force Eli Manning into hurrying his throws.
The Giants defensive line still can wreak havoc as led by All Pro defensive end Michael Strahan.	Rely on the combined outside rush of Strahan and Umenyiora to free up players in coverage.	Do not be afraid to run right at Strahan. One nice juke move and you could be off to the races.
The linebackers for the Giants are quick and explosive.	Antonio Pierce is a big hitter.	If you run up the middle watch out for Pierce.

WEAKNESSES

Description	Minimizing Risks	Tips for Opponents
Eli Manning has yet to prove he belongs in the Manning family. He makes poor decisions at times.	Eli started off the 2006 campaign on fire but fizzled close to the end of last season.	Blitz, blitz, and blitz. Force Eli Manning to beat you with his arm.
The Giant's secondary is nothing to write home about.	Always play a 2 Man Under type defense to have your safeties protect your CBs.	Look to go deep as often as you can to expose the Giants' weak secondary.

	Overall Rating	87
	Offense	86
	Defense	87

OFF-SEASON UPGRADES

Type	Round	First Name	Last Name	School/Team	Position	Height	Weight
Release	N/A	Marcus	Bell	Lions	DT	6'2"	325
Trade	N/A	Reuben	Droughns	Browns	RB	5'11"	220
Free Agent	N/A	Kawika	Mitchell	Chiefs	LB	6'1"	253
Draft	1	Aaron	Ross	Texas	CB	6'1"	193
Draft	2	Steve	Smith	USC	WR	6'0"	197

FANTASY OUTLOOK

Star Player: Brandon Jacobs
Round of Draft: 3rd

With Jacobs entrenched as the team's featured runningback in the Big Apple, he is poised to put up big time fantasy numbers. If the top three runningbacks are not on the draft board come time to draft, seriously consider him.

Star Player: Jeremy Shockey
Round of Draft: 5th

Shockey will be one of the first three tight ends to come off the draft board at draft time. If Eli Manning can pick up the pace, Shockey could become the top fantasy tight end.

5-YEAR PLAYER PROGRESSION

First Name	Last Name	Position	'07 Overall	'08 Overall	'09 Overall	'10 Overall	'11 Overall
Osi	Umenyiora	DE	90	90	91	91	90
Jeremy	Shockey	TE	92	94	96	97	97
Plaxico	Burress	WR	90	91	92	92	93
Eli	Manning	QB	86	89	91	92	92
Aaron	Ross	CB	80	83	83	85	85

FRANCHISE MODE STRATEGY

On draft day, look to pick up at least one defensive tackle in the early rounds of the draft. Selecting a free safety who has speed will be also prove beneficial in the future.

Key Franchise Info

Team Salary: $80.6M
Cap Room: $28.3M
Key Rival:
• Dallas Cowboys
NFL Icons: Michael Strahan
Philosophy:
• Offense: Establish Runs
• Defense: Shut Down Runs
Prestige: Medium
Team Needs:
• Linebacker
• Defensive Back
Highest Paid Players:
• Eli Manning
• Kareem McKenzie
Up and Coming Players:
• Steve Smith
• Barry Cofield

ROSTER AND PACKAGE TIPS — KEY PLAYER SUBSTITUTIONS

• **Position:** WR
• **Substitution:** Steve Smith
• **When:** Global
• **Advantage:** Smith's 92 speed rating will allow him to stretch the field vertically, giving the Giants and quarterback Eli Manning another tool on the field.

• **Position:** CB
• **Substitution:** Aaron Ross
• **When:** Global
• **Advantage:** Ross's speed rating of 90 will allow him to catch up to receivers should he get burned. Plus, he's slightly taller than starter Corey Webster.

• **Position:** PR
• **Substitution:** Aaron Ross
• **When:** Global
• **Advantage:** Ross has a 98 OVR rating as a return man, which is thirteen points higher than starter Sinorice Moss's, which should solidify the return game.

• **Position:** MLB
• **Substitution:** Reggie Torbor
• **When:** Global
• **Advantage:** As an MLB, Torbor's rating of 67 is four points higher than Chase Blackburn's, giving the Giants a better overall MLB as the fourth linebacker.

TEAM STRATEGY

PRIMAGAMES.COM

NEW YORK GIANTS / OFFENSE

OFFENSIVE STAR PLAYER #10

Eli Manning	Quarterback (QB)

Key Attributes

Awareness	85
Speed	61
Throwing Power	91
Throwing Accuracy	86

This year, it's all about **Eli**. He will have to prove that he can make the team win without Tiki Barber around. Manning has had his moments where he shines like the New York skyline, but he has had to do it on a game-to-game basis. Last season he threw for **3,244** yards, **24** touchdowns, and **18** interceptions. He should also benefit this year because he had a star receiver and tight end at minicamp, which is virtually unheard of for the Giants.

Player Weapon: None

RECOMMENDED OFFENSIVE AUDIBLE PACKAGES

I Form Normal	I Form Twin TE	Strong I Twin WR	Singleback Slot Strong	Shotgun Trips Bunch
HB Slash	PA HB Curl	WR Smash	TE Flat Slant	Spacing Switch

OFFENSIVE PLAYCOUNTS

Quick Pass:	13	Screen Pass:	8	Pinch:	13
Standard Pass:	80	Hail Mary:	1	Counter:	19
Shotgun Pass:	25	Inside Handoff:	33	Draw:	15
Play Action Pass:	27	Outside Handoff:	10		

TEAM TRIVIA

New York Giants Facts

Turn the page for the answers:

1. Where did Giants QB Phil Simms play college football?

2. Who was named MVP in the Giants' Super Bowl XXV victory over the Buffalo Bills?

3. Between what years did Hall of Famer Fran Tarkenton play for the Giants?

OFFENSIVE FORMATIONS

Singleback	Full House
Big	Normal Wide
Big Wing	**Strong I**
Twin TE	Normal
Normal Slot	Twin WR
Slot Strong	**Weak I**
4WR Flex	Normal
Flip Trips	Twin TE
Empty 4WR	**Shotgun**
I Form	Normal Offset Wk
Normal	Trips Bunch
Twin WR	Slot Strong TE Flip
Close	
Twin TE	

OFFENSIVE STRENGTH CHART

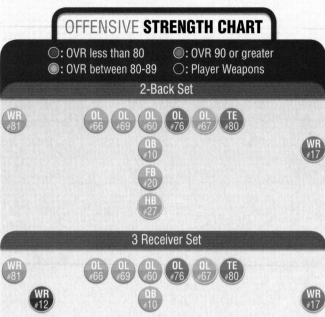

- ○: OVR less than 80
- ●: OVR 90 or greater
- ●: OVR between 80-89
- ○: Player Weapons

2-Back Set

3 Receiver Set

OFFENSIVE ROSTER LIST Current / Next Gen

Pos.	#	First Name	Last Name	Overall	Player Weapons
C	60	Shaun	O'Hara	84	
C	65	Grey	Ruegamer	77	
FB	20	Jim	Finn	85	
HB	27	Brandon	Jacobs	85	Power Back / Power Back
HB	22	Reuben	Droughns	82	
HB	34	Derrick	Ward	72	
K	1	Lawrence	Tynes	84	
LG	69	Rich	Seubert	80	
LT	66	David	Diehl	81	
LT	79	Guy	Whimper	72	
QB	10	Eli	Manning	86	
QB	2	Anthony	Wright	78	
QB	8	Tim	Hasselbeck	72	
QB	13	Jared	Lorenzen	63	
RG	76	Chris	Snee	90	
RG	64	Matt	Lentz	69	
RT	67	Kareem	McKenzie	87	Run Blocker
RT	71	Jon	Dunn	72	
TE	80	Jeremy	Shockey	92	Possesion, Quick Receiver
TE	89	Kevin	Boss	77	
WR	17	Plaxico	Burress	90	Spectacular Catch Receiver
WR	81	Amani	Toomer	83	
WR	12	Steve	Smith	76	Deep Threat / Possession Receiver, Quick Receiver, Speed, Hands
WR	85	David	Tyree	75	
WR	83	Sinorice	Moss	74	Deep Threat
WR	87	Darius	Watts	73	
WR	15	Michael	Jennings	72	

Singleback-Slot Strong

TE Flat Slant

It can feel like the weight of the world is on your shoulders if you're an NFL quarterback. The success of the Giants rests on Eli Manning performance.

Increase the chance of success with Eli by using plays that free up his playmakers.

Eli has great poise in the pocket when the play works as it should. It is also pretty easy to remain when Shockey is your go-to target.

Eli sees Shockey seperating from the defender on his crossing route and gets him the ball.

Singleback-Normal Slot

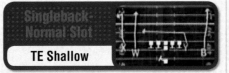

TE Shallow

Eli has many tools from the Giants offense at his disposal. A good QB will make sure he uses all his skills to keep the offense moving the chains.

The TE Shallow is used to get the tight end working across the middle; it also allows the offense to stretch the field with 2 streak routes.

Eli sees the mis-match on the outside with Plaxico going against a smaller defender. He will use this option every time he has this match up.

Arm strength and touch are what's needed to complete the deep ball. Eli delivers a perfect throw to Plaxico.

Singleback-Big

PA Waggle

One aspect of Eli's game that can really cause problems for the defense is the play action.

Use the PA Waggle to attack the defense with passing routes to the left while giving a play action run fake to the right.

Eli gives such a good ball fake that the outside linebacker for the defense bites on the fake and abandons the blitz to go tackle the back.

With the extra time in the pocket Eli gets the ball to the tight end.

TEAM STRATEGY

NEW YORK GIANTS / DEFENSE

⭐ DEFENSIVE STAR PLAYER #72

Osi Umenyiora	Defensive End (RE)

Key Attributes

Awareness	72
Speed	84
Strength	73
Tackle	77

The Giants have two of the best defensive ends in football, and **Umenyiora** is showing that he will carry the load when Strahan is no longer around. Osi had an injury-plagued season that saw him out due to a torn hip flexor, but he did manage to finish the year with a team-leading **6** sacks. With a healthy 2007 season approaching, Umenyiora should be back to his 2005 form where he had **14.5** sacks.

Player Weapons: Pass Rusher / Finesse Move D-Lineman

RECOMMENDED OFFENSIVE AUDIBLE PACKAGES

4-3-Normal	4-3-Over	4-3-Under	Dime-Normal	Nickel-3-3-5
Mid Rush	Fire Man	Buzz Duo	Pierce Blitz	CB Dogs Blitz

OFFENSIVE PLAYCOUNTS

Quick Pass:	13	Screen Pass:	8	Pinch:	13
Standard Pass:	80	Hail Mary:	1	Counter:	19
Shotgun Pass:	25	Inside Handoff:	33	Draw:	15
Play Action Pass:	27	Outside Handoff:	10		

TEAM TRIVIA

New York Giants Facts

Answers:

1️⃣ Morehead State

2️⃣ Ottis Anderson

3️⃣ 1967-71

DEFENSIVE FORMATIONS

4-3	Nickel
4-3-Normal	Nickel-3-3-5
4-3-Over	Nickel-Normal
4-3-Under	Nickel-Strong
Dime	**Quarter**
Dime-Flat	Quarter-3 Deep
Dime-Normal	Quarter-Normal

DEFENSIVE STRENGTH CHART

○: OVR less than 80	◉: OVR 90 or greater
◉: OVR between 80-89	○: Player Weapons

4-3 Base Defense

FS #47 — SS #28

CB #23 — LB #55 — LB #58 — LB #97 — CB #29

RE #72 — DT #99 — DT #98 — LE #92

Dime Defense

FS #47 — SS #28

CB #23 — CB #25 — LB #58 — CB #31 — CB #29

RE #72 — DT #99 — DT #98 — LE #92

DEFENSIVE ROSTER LIST Current / Next Gen

Pos.	#	First Name	Last Name	Overall	Player Weapons
CB	29	Sam	Madison	87	Containment Corner
CB	23	Corey	Webster	81	
CB	31	Aaron	Ross	80	
CB	25	R.W.	McQuarters	80	
DT	98	Fred	Robbins	80	
DT	99	Marcus	Bell	79	
DT	94	William	Joseph	78	
DT	96	Barry	Cofield	78	
DT	73	Jay	Alford	72	
FS	47	Will	Demps	82	
FS	37	James	Butler	71	
LE	92	Michael	Strahan	93	Force of Nature / Power Move D-Lineman
LE	95	Adrian	Awasom	73	
LOLB	97	Mathias	Kiwanuka	84	
LOLB	53	Reggie	Torbor	77	
LOLB	51	Zac	DeOssie	69	
MLB	58	Antonio	Pierce	95	Defensive Enforcer / Smart Linebacker, Brick Wall Defender
MLB	57	Chase	Blackburn	63	
P	18	Jeff	Feagles	79	
RE	72	Osi	Umenyiora	90	Pass Rusher / Finesse D-Lineman
RE	91	Justin	Tuck	75	
ROLB	55	Kawika	Mitchell	83	
ROLB	59	Gerris	Wilkinson	78	
SS	28	Gibril	Wilson	90	
SS	33	Jason	Bell	70	
SS	26	Michael	Stone	69	

4-3-Normal

Thunder Smoke

Nickel-Normal

DE Contain

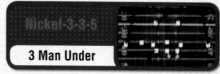

Nickel-3-3-5

3 Man Under

The Giants are lucky to have two of the better defensive ends in football. Osi Umenyiora is starting to show that he is the future of the defense.

With an athletic DE like Osi Umenyiora, defenses are now letting the ends contain and use their athleticism to deal with some of the fast quarterbacks.

Osi Umenyiora is a great control pass rusher, meaning he can rush the passer with out breaking containment. He demonstrates that here.

Let Umenyiora rush the passer using a wide angle rush. This can be used versus the passing and run game.

Use Umenyiora to prevent the QB from breaking the pocket and getting outside. This defense is also good at stopping running plays.

The 3-3-5 3 Man Under is a play that is designed to play a 3 deep zone with man coverage underneath. This defense also maximizes Umenyiora ability.

Umenyiora is a quick defender off of the ball and his speed lets him blow by many offensive tackles that he faces. Here, it isn't even a contest.

Because Umenyiora is assigned to play contain it doesn't matter if the QB or the runningback has the ball. He will not let either break contain.

When the play starts, Umenyiora is shown taking an outside rush angle. He is under control and looking to make sure the back doesn't sneak out.

The outside rush suits Umenyiora's skills and is the reason the defense can celebrate the sack.

When the back got to the edge, Umenyiora shed the block and made the tackle.

Whenever the defense needs a big play on the quarterback, they can look to Osi Umenyiora.

TEAM STRATEGY

JACKSONVILLE JAGUARS

| Division: AFC South | Stadium: Alltel Stadium | Type: Open | Capacity: 73,000 | Surface: Turf |

TEAM STRATEGY

COACHING PROFILE

Jack Del Rio

- **Head Coaching Year:** 5th
- **Experience:** Baltimore Ravens linebackers coach (1999-2000), Carolina Panthers defensive coordinator (2001-2002).

Jack Del Rio is coming into his fifth season with the Jacksonville Jaguars with a 34-30 career record. His team finished 8-8 last season. However, due to injuries through the year, he gets a mulligan.

TEAM RANKINGS

Scoring	9th
Passing Offense	24th
Rushing Offense	3rd
Passing Defense	10th
Rushing Defense	4th
Turnovers	15th

RATINGS HISTORY

Category	'07	'06	'05	'04
Overall	**87**	84	81	75
Offense	87	79	**88**	75
Defense	**88**	85	80	75

Bold = Highest Year

83
FIVE-YEAR
AVERAGE

2006 STANDINGS

Wins	Losses	Ties	PF	PA	Home	Road	vs. AFC	vs. NFC	vs. Div
8	8	0	371	274	6-2	2-6	5-7	3-1	2-4

TEAM OVERVIEW

The Jags top-five defensive unit have carried them the last couple of seasons. The big question this year is: can the offense step up and carry its share of the load? Del Rio is settled on Leftwich as his signal caller, but if he doesn't come through, the Jags will be watching the playoff parade go by.

The running game is the offense's strength with veteran Fred Taylor and bowling ball Maurice Jones-Drew sharing the load. Both guys have good speed and can mow down would-be tacklers.

On defense, the Jags are stingy against the run with Mike Peterson and emerging LOLB Daryl Smith leading the way. Cornerback Rashean Mathis can hold down his side of the field against even against the elite receivers.

SCOUTING REPORT

STRENGTHS

Description	Maximizing Potential	Tips for Opponents
John Henderson and Marcus Stroud are two of the best defensive tackles in the game.	Henderson and Stroud were key cogs in the Jags' 4th rated rush defense last season.	If you're going to use play action, be cautious of these two and be sure to try to keep a back or tight end.
The Jags also had the second best defense last season in terms of total yards allowed per game.	A huge reason for that defense was the play of Jacksonville's secondary.	You're going to have to use a stiff running game to force the safeties into helping. Then use play action.
One-two back combinations seem to be the new fad.	Jones-Drew and Taylor accumulated 2000 plus yards in '06.	Hit Taylor hard and often as he is injury prone.

WEAKNESSES

Description	Minimizing Risks	Tips for Opponents
With inconsistencies at QB due to injuries, the Jags' passing attack was abysmal last season.	The Jags wound up with the 25th worst passing offense last season with only 191 yards per game.	Load up the box on the Jags and force them to pass the ball. Be sure to cover Jones when you do!
The Jags tried to fill a need and a hole at the same time by drafting Reggie Nelson in this year's draft.	It seems as if Nelson will get a crack at starting as a rookie this season.	Exploit Nelson in the secondary by playing to his over-aggressive style.

Overall Rating 86
Offense 85
Defense 88

OFF-SEASON UPGRADES

Type	Round	First Name	Last Name	School/Team	Position	Height	Weight
Free Agent	N/A	Kevin	McCadam	Panthers	S	6'01"	219
Free Agent	N/A	Dennis	Northcutt	Browns	WR	5'11"	171
Free Agent	N/A	Tony	Pashos	Ravens	T	6'6"	320
Draft	1	Reggie	Nelson	Florida	S	6'0"	198
Draft	2	Justin	Durant	Hampton	LB	6'1"	230

FANTASY OUTLOOK

Star Player: Maurice Jones-Drew
Round of Draft: 2nd

Jones-Drew is supposed to be the Jaguars' featured back, but he is not that big and may not be able to handle the pounding for a full season. If you take Jones-Drew, then consider taking Taylor.

Star Player: Fred Taylor
Round of Draft: 6th

Taylor is not supposed to be the team's go-to back, but with Jones-Drew's small-frame body, Taylor will still get his share of carriers, especially around the goal line.

5-YEAR PLAYER PROGRESSION

First Name	Last Name	Position	'07 Overall	'08 Overall	'09 Overall	'10 Overall	'11 Overall
Byron	Leftwich	QB	82	82	80	81	80
Fred	Taylor	HB	89	85	81	-	-
Matt	Jones	WR	83	83	82	82	82
John	Henderson	DT	96	98	99	99	98
Reggie	Nelson	S	83	82	81	82	82

FRANCHISE MODE STRATEGY

Both David Garrard and Byron Leftwich are solid quarterbacks, but the question with both of them is: can they lead the Jaguars to Super Bowl? If you feel they can't, then look for a franchise QB in the draft.

Key Franchise Info

Team Salary: $97.4M
Cap Room: $11.5M
Key Rival:
• Indianapolis Colts
NFL Icons: Fred Taylor
Philosophy:
• Offense: Establish Run
• Defense: Shut Down Runs
Prestige: Medium
Team Needs:
• Receiver
• Linebacker
Highest Paid Players:
• John Henderson
• Brian Williams
Up and Coming Players:
• Dee Web
• Marcedes Lewis

TEAM STRATEGY

ROSTER AND PACKAGE TIPS — KEY PLAYER SUBSTITUTIONS

• **Position:** QB
• **Substitution:** David Garrard
• **When:** Global/Mobility
• **Advantage:** At 70, Garrard has a twenty point speed rating advantage (over Byron Leftwich), which should allow you to be more mobile in the pocket.

• **Position:** HB
• **Substitution:** Maurice Jones-Drew
• **When:** Global
• **Advantage:** Jones-Drew's speed and versatility allow him to be a threat in both the running and the passing game. Plus, he's got a better BTK rating at 93 than Fred Taylor.

• **Position:** WR
• **Substitution:** Matt Jones
• **When:** Global
• **Advantage:** Jones, with a rating of 83 OVR, is the best-rated receiver for the Jags. Not to mention his 93 speed, which will help the Jags stretch the field.

• **Position:** LE
• **Substitution:** Bobby McCray
• **When:** Global
• **Advantage:** At 84 OVR, Bobby McCray is three points higher than Paul Spicer. McCray's speed also allows him to be a threat in any passing situation.

JACKSONVILLE JAGUARS / OFFENSE

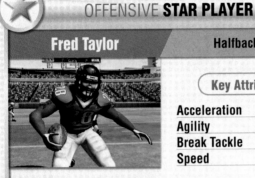

OFFENSIVE **STAR PLAYER** #28

Fred Taylor — Halfback (HB)

Key Attributes

Acceleration	94
Agility	93
Break Tackle	86
Speed	93

After being labled as injury prone, and getting past his prime, **Fred Taylor** silenced his critics with a **1,146** rushing yards and **5** touchdown season. Not only is that a good thing for the Jaguars, but he proved to be durable even in his eight season, by carrying the ball **231** times. Taylor is an imposing back and with his speed, he can take it to the house on any given down.

Player Weapon: None

OFFENSIVE **STRENGTH CHART**

- ◯: OVR less than 80
- ◉: OVR 90 or greater
- ◉: OVR between 80-89
- ◯: Player Weapons

2-Back Set

WR #11 | OL #74 | OL #67 | OL #63 | OL #65 | OL #79 | TE #85 | WR #18
QB #9
FB #33
HB #28

3 Receiver Set

WR #11 | OL #74 | OL #67 | OL #63 | OL #65 | OL #79 | TE #85 | WR #18
WR #19
QB #9
WR #18
HB #28

RECOMMENDED OFFENSIVE **AUDIBLE PACKAGES**

I Normal-Normal	Weak I-Normal	Singleback-Big	Singleback-Spread	Shotgun-2RB 3WR
HB Counter	TE Fade	HB Counter Trap	PA HB Streak	Slot Cross

OFFENSIVE **PLAYCOUNTS**

Quick Pass:	11	Screen Pass:	13	Pinch:	12
Standard Pass:	81	Hail Mary:	1	Counter:	16
Shotgun Pass:	52	Inside Handoff:	28	Draw:	12
Play Action Pass:	33	Outside Handoff:	19		

TEAM **TRIVIA**

Jacksonville Jaguars Facts
Turn the page for the answers.

1. The Jaguars joined the NFL in 1995. Which other team also came into the NFL that year?
2. Who was the Jaguars' first-ever NFL draft pick?
3. In 2001, who was the defensive coordinator?

OFFENSIVE **FORMATIONS**

Singleback	Strong I
Big	Normal
Twin TE WR	3WR
Big 3TE	Jumbo
Normal Slot	**Weak I**
Slot Strong	Normal
4WR Spread	Twin WR
I Form	**Shotgun**
Normal	2RB 3WR
Twin WR	Slot Strg HB Wk
Twin TE	Trips Bunch
Split Backs	4WR
Normal	5WR
3WR	

OFFENSIVE **ROSTER LIST** Current/Next Gen

Pos.	#	First Name	Last Name	Overall	Player Weapons
C	63	Brad	Meester	90	
C	61	Dan	Connolly	63	
FB	33	Greg	Jones	87	
FB	36	Derrick	Wimbush	70	
HB	32	Maurice	Jones-Drew	89	Speed Back/Elusive Back, Power Back
HB	28	Fred	Taylor	89	
HB	34	Alvin	Pearman	75	
HB	22	LaBrandon	Toefield	75	
K	10	Josh	Scobee	84	
LG	67	Vince	Manuwai	89	Crushing Run Blocker
LG	62	Dennis	Norman	64	
LT	69	Khalif	Barnes	85	
LT	74	Maurice	Williams	85	
QB	7	Byron	Leftwich	82	Cannon Arm/Cannon Arm QB
QB	9	David	Garrard	82	
QB	5	Quinn	Gray	72	
RG	65	Chris	Naeole	90	Run Blocker
RG	73	Stockar	McDougle	81	
RT	79	Tony	Pashos	82	
RT	76	Richard	Collier	62	
TE	85	Jermaine	Wiggins	83	
TE	87	George	Wrighster	82	
TE	89	Marcedes	Lewis	80	
WR	18	Matt	Jones	83	Deep Threat/Spectacular Catch Receiver
WR	11	Reggie	Williams	81	
WR	19	Ernest	Wilford	80	
WR	86	Dennis	Northcutt	77	
WR	81	Mike	Walker	72	

TEAM STRATEGY

Singleback-Big 3TE
HB Smash

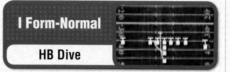
I Form-Normal
HB Dive

Shotgun-4WR
HB Screen

Fred Taylor is a special runningback. He has a rare combination of speed and size. There aren't too many defenders that can bring him down one-on-one.

Fred Taylor is a problem for the defense when running between the tackles. He is a load to bring down no matter what defender steps in his path.

Taylor is solid in the running game, so much so that many people forget just how good he is at catching the ball out of the backfield.

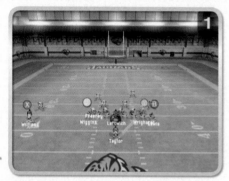

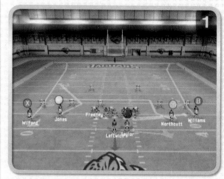

The HB Smash gets Fred Taylor the ball on an off-tackle run. With extra blocking to the right side he is assured of big yards.

This play has Taylor follow his fullback straight ahead into the left "A" gap. This play uses him in to pound the ball.

The HB Screen is used to hit the defense with both the long ball, if they over play the screen, or short if they run with the streaking receivers.

Taylor has great vision, and when running this play he needs to keep his eyes down-field to read the blocks that he has set up.

When the play begins, the left guard and tackle open a big hole for Taylor to run through as he follows his fullback's lead into the hole.

Once Taylor has the ball in his hands and the screen blockers are in position, he can take advantage of the blockers and use his speed in open space.

Taylor uses his speed to hit the sideline and take off.

Taylor will always pick up positive yards when running him with the I Form-Normal HB Dive.

Taylor benefits from the blocks being set for him while he moves the ball down field.

TEAM STRATEGY

JACKSONVILLE JAGUARS / **DEFENSE**

DEFENSIVE **STAR PLAYER** #98

John Henderson — Defensive Tackle (DT)

Key Attributes

Awareness	83
Speed	62
Strength	95
Tackle	93

Building a solid defense starts up front. The Jaguars are led on the defensive line by **John Henderson**. At 6'5" and 285 pounds, he is one of the reasons why the Jags finished last season ranked second in the league for yards allowed. His play up front makes it possible for other players such as LB Mike Peterson and CB Rashean Mathis to shine. Henderson will no doubt continue to disrupt any offensive line that his team is playing against.

Player Weapons: Run Stopper / Power Move D-Lineman

RECOMMENDED DEFENSIVE **AUDIBLE PACKAGES**

4-3-Normal	4-3-Over	4-3-Under	Dime-3-2-6	Nickel-3-3-5
OLB Fire 3	LB Contain	Sam Shoot Fire 2	QB trap	Man Lock Spy

DEFENSIVE **PLAYCOUNTS**

Man Coverage:	36	Cover 3 Zone:	18	Combo Blitz:	11
Man Zone:	30	Deep Zone:	15	Goal Line:	15
Combo Coverage:	8	Man Blitz:	36	Special Teams:	12
Cover 2 Zone:	18	Zone Blitz:	53		

TEAM **TRIVIA**

Jacksonville Jaguars Facts

Answers:

1. Carolina Panthers
2. Tony Boselli
3. Dom Capers

DEFENSIVE **FORMATIONS**

4-3	Nickel
4-3-Normal	Nickel-3-3-5
4-3-Over	Nickel-Normal
4-3-Under	Nickel-Strong
Dime	**Quarter**
Dime-3-2-6	Quarter-3 Deep
Dime-Normal	Quarter-Normal

DEFENSIVE **STRENGTH CHART**

○ : OVR less than 80   ◑ : OVR 90 or greater
◑ : OVR between 80-89   ○ : Player Weapons

4-3 Base Defense

FS #42   SS #20

CB #29   LB #55   LB #54   LB #52   CB #27

RE #97   DT #98   DT #99   LE #95

Dime Defense

FS #42   SS #20

CB #29   CB #21   LB #54   CB #31   CB #27

RE #97   DT #98   DT #99   LE #95

DEFENSIVE **ROSTER LIST** Current / Next Gen

Pos.	#	First Name	Last Name	Overall	Player Weapons
CB	27	Rashean	Mathis	95	Shutdown Corner / Press Coverage Corner, Shutdown Corner, Smart Corner
CB	29	Brian	Williams	87	
CB	21	Terry	Cousin	78	
CB	31	Scott	Starks	75	
CB	23	Dee	Webb	70	
CB	37	Bruce	Thornton	64	
DT	98	John	Henderson	96	Run Stopper / Power Move D-Lineman
DT	99	Marcus	Stroud	96	Run Stopper / Power Move D-Lineman
DT	92	Rob	Meier	79	
FS	42	Reggie	Nelson	83	
FS	43	Gerald	Sensabaugh	81	
LE	95	Paul	Spicer	81	
LE	94	Jeremy	Mincey	75	
LOLB	52	Daryl	Smith	87	
LOLB	51	Clint	Ingram	81	
LOLB	58	Jorge	Cordova	73	
MLB	54	Mike	Peterson	91	Defensive Enforcer / Brick Wall Defender, Smart Linebacker
MLB	50	Tony	Gilbert	70	
P	3	Adam	Podlesh	78	
RE	97	Reggie	Hayward	88	
RE	93	Bobby	McCray	84	
ROLB	55	Nick	Greisen	79	
ROLB	53	Pat	Thomas	75	
SS	20	Donovin	Darius	89	Big Hitter / Big Hitter
SS	47	Kevin	McCadam	71	

Nickel-Normal

Double Slot

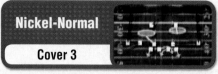

Nickel-Normal

Cover 3

Nickel-Strong

FS Snake Blitz 3

The life of a defensive tackle is one of anonymity. Henderson is a force on the line and one of the main reasons the Jaguars defense is so successful.

There are ways to get John Henderson more involved in the defense. He has the strength and quickness to wreck havoc on an offense if used on a stunt.

Henderson plays beyond his size, and when he can't get to the QB he defends the ball by getting his hands up.

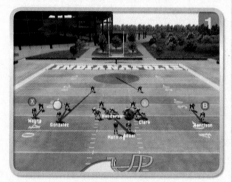

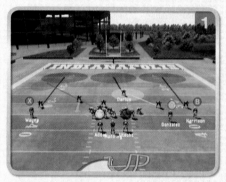

This play is called to prevent the offense from being able to go to their slot receiver by assigning the nickelback and safety to cover him.

This defense lets John Henderson use his quickness on a line stunt that will shoot him around the strong side defensive tackle.

The FS Snake Blitz 3 is uses John Henderson on angle rush inside. He is needed to create a lane for the blitzing linebacker.

Henderson provides a great opportunity for the linebacker to shoot the gap that is created when he engages with the offensive lineman.

Henderson loops around the defensive tackle and is on his way into the backfield. He can now use his power to bull rush the opposing lineman.

Henderson is in a heated battle with the center and instead of letting the center take him out of the play he looks to see where the QB is going.

The linebacker is able to make the play because of the perfect play of John Henderson.

John Henderson is a big man and he delivers a crushing blow as he sacks the quarterback.

He keeps himself alive on the play and bats the ball down to prevent a sure completion.

TEAM STRATEGY

157

NEW YORK JETS

| Division: AFC East | Stadium: Giants Stadium | Type: Open | Capacity: 80,062 | Surface: Turf |

2006 STANDINGS

Wins	Losses	Ties	PF	PA	Home	Road	vs. AFC	vs. NFC	vs. Div
10	6	0	316	295	4-4	6-2	7-5	3-1	4-2

TEAM OVERVIEW

The Jets surprised everybody in the league when they posted their 10-6 record and playoff appearance last year. Things are sure to be a bit tougher this season, but the Jets did make some moves to improve. Thomas Jones comes in to supply some security at the HB position.

Pennington returns healthy, and that is a big boon for Jets' fans. If you are a Jets fan , you'll appreciate his accurate arm and adequate velocity. Laveranues Coles provides the main threat for a WR core that is full of speed.

The middle of the field is pretty strong on defense, with Vilma at MLB and Kerry Rhodes at the SS spot. Things are a bit dicey up front, however, as your defensive ends don't provide much speed off the edges.

TEAM STRATEGY

COACHING PROFILE

Eric Mangini

- **Head Coaching Year:** 2nd
- **Experience:** New England Patriots defensive backs coach (2000-2004), New England Patriots defensive coordinator (2005).

In his rookie year as the Jets' head coach, Eric Mangini turned a 4-12 team into a 10-6 playoff team. His attention to detail and superior game day decision-making gained him the respect of his team.

TEAM RANKINGS

Scoring	18th
Passing Offense	17th
Rushing Offense	20th
Passing Defense	14th
Rushing Defense	24th
Turnovers	17th

RATINGS HISTORY

Category	'07	'06	'05	'04
Overall	**85**	81	80	83
Offense	85	**86**	85	85
Defense	84	**86**	72	75

Bold = Highest Year

83
FIVE-YEAR
AVERAGE

SCOUTING REPORT

STRENGTHS

Description	Maximizing Potential	Tips for Opponents
Jerricho Cotchery made a name for himself last season making spectacular catches and plays for the Jets.	Cotchery is dangerous over the middle. He is a tough player and a classic possession receiver.	Do not allow Cotchery to get matched up on a linebacker or even a safety, unless you have a top cover guy.
With Curtis Martin leaving, the Jets signed Thomas Jones.	Get Thomas Jones running downhill quickly on stretch plays and counters. Try to stay outside the tackles.	Early in his career, Jones had issues with holding onto the football. Use the hit stick on him and jar it loose.
After his rookie season, many began to hail Jonathan Vilma as the new Ray Lewis.	Vilma has outstanding quickness and agility. He is also great in pursuit.	Be aware of where Vilma is at all times, even in the passing game.

WEAKNESSES

Description	Minimizing Risks	Tips for Opponents
The Jets' run defense ranked 24th last season. Things do not look much better for them this season.	When the Jets' linebackers are not rushing the passer, they are very vulnerable in coverage.	Hobson and Thomas lack the speed and quickness to match up with receivers and backs. Attack them!
The CBs are good at defending the short to intermediate pass routes, but they don't have the speed to defend deeper routes.	Avoid blitzing as much as possible. If you must blitz, least leave one safety to play over the top to help defend against the deep pass.	Look to go deep any time the Jets cornerbacks are left in one-on-one coverage.

OFF-SEASON **UPGRADES**

Type	Round	First Name	Last Name	School/Team	Position	Height	Weight
Trade	N/A	Thomas	Jones	Bears	RB	5'11"	220
Free Agent	N/A	David	Bowens	Dolphins	DE	6'3"	265
Free Agent	N/A	Kenyon	Coleman	Cowboys	DE	6'5"	295
Draft	1	Darrelle	Revis	Pittsburgh	CB	6'4"	204
Draft	2	David	Harris	Michigan	LB	6'2"	243

FANTASY **OUTLOOK**

★ **Star Player:** Thomas Jones
Round of Draft: 2nd

For some reason, Jones tends to get overlooked when it comes time for the Fantasy Draft. With him now entrenched as the Jets' starting runningback, he is poised to put up his best career numbers.

★ **Star Player:** Jerricho Cotchery
Round of Draft: 7th

During the last 10 games of the '06 season, Cotchery caught fire by catching at least five balls per game. He won't be the first receiver to come off the board, but he also won't be the last.

5-YEAR **PLAYER PROGRESSION**

First Name	Last Name	Position	'07 Overall	'08 Overall	'09 Overall	'10 Overall	'11 Overall
Chad	Pennington	QB	88	90	91	90	90
Thomas	Jones	HB	88	88	85	82	-
Kerry	Rhodes	S	95	96	96	97	99
Jonathan	Vilma	LB	94	94	96	97	97
Darrelle	Revis	CB	81	82	84	85	85

FRANCHISE MODE **STRATEGY**

Not every team utilizes the tight end in the passing game. If you plan on doing so while playing the Jets, then you will definitely want to consider a fast one with hands in the early rounds of the draft.

Key Franchise Info

Team Salary: $93.9M
Cap Room: $15.0M
Key Rival:
• New England Patriots
NFL Icons: None
Philosophy:
• Offense: Ball Control
• Defense: Force the Pass
Prestige: Low
Team Needs:
• Running Back (Depth)
• Defensive Line
Highest Paid Players:
• Chad Pennington
• Dewayne Robertson
Up and Coming Players:
• Darrelle Revis
• David Harris

TEAM STRATEGY

ROSTER AND **PACKAGE TIPS** KEY PLAYER SUBSTITUTIONS

• **Position:** 3DBR
• **Substitution:** Thomas Jones
• **When:** Global
• **Advantage:** Jones's AWR rating is 14 points higher than Leon Washington's; plus his catch rating is slightly better, allowing him to be a receiving threat out of the backfield.

• **Position:** RE
• **Substitution:** Eric Hicks
• **When:** Passing Situations
• **Advantage:** With an SPD rating of 73, Hicks is the fastest end on the Jets roster. Putting him in on passing situations will give the Jets a speed rusher off the end.

• **Position:** MLB
• **Substitution:** David Harris
• **When:** Global
• **Advantage:** Harris's 83 speed will allow him to be able to cover better than Victor Hobson, which could be pivotal in your coverage scheme.

• **Position:** PR
• **Substitution:** Justin Miller
• **When:** Global
• **Advantage:** As a return man, Miller's rating of 99 can't get any better. His 95 SPD rating will also allow him to be a threat to run one back every time.

NEW YORK JETS / **OFFENSE**

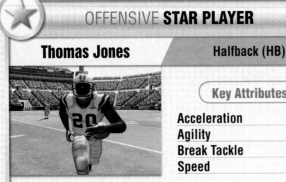

OFFENSIVE **STAR PLAYER** #20

Thomas Jones — Halfback (HB)

Key Attributes

Acceleration	92
Agility	90
Break Tackle	88
Speed	90

Ask any quarterback how important it is to have a good running game, and what it does for the offense. The Jets get a boost to the offense with the addition of **Thomas Jones** and his workhorse-like ability. Jones gained over **1,200** yards last season and had six trips to the end zone. He will indeed have a better season with the Jets, because now he won't see eight in the box every down.

Player Weapon: None

OFFENSIVE **STRENGTH CHART**

◯: OVR less than 80   ●: OVR 90 or greater
�: OVR between 80-89   ◯: Player Weapons

2-Back Set

WR #89 — OL #60 — OL #66 — OL #74 — OL #65 — OL #68 — TE #86 — WR #87
QB #10
FB #37
HB #20

3 Receiver Set

WR #89 — OL #60 — OL #66 — OL #74 — OL #65 — OL #68 — TE #86 — WR #87
WR #81
QB #10
HB #20

RECOMMENDED OFFENSIVE **AUDIBLE PACKAGES**

I Form-Big	Weak I-Twins	Singleback-Tight Flex	Singleback-Trips Bunch	Shotgun-Slot Strong
HB Counter	TE Shallow	HB Slam	Delta Sit	Post Corner

OFFENSIVE **PLAYCOUNTS**

Quick Pass:	9	Screen Pass:	11	Pinch:	16
Standard Pass:	75	Hail Mary:	1	Counter:	17
Shotgun Pass:	32	Inside Handoff:	34	Draw:	9
Play Action Pass:	27	Outside Handoff:	9		

TEAM **TRIVIA**

New York Jets Facts

Turn the page for the answers.

❶ Which Jets quarterback was known as "Broadway Joe?"

❷ What Super Bowl did Joe Namath guarantee the Jets would win?

❸ Who was the only Jet in the 20th century to score four touchdowns in a single game?

OFFENSIVE **FORMATIONS**

Singleback	Strong I
Big	Normal
Big Twin WR	Twin WR
Big Wing	Normal Flex
Normal	Twin TE
Slot Strong	**Weak I**
Trips Bunch	H Pro
Tight Flex	H Twins
Base Flex	**Shotgun**
4WR	Normal Offset Wk
I Form	Slot Strong
Normal	4WR
Twin WR	
Big	

OFFENSIVE **ROSTER LIST**  Current / Next Gen

Pos.	#	First Name	Last Name	Overall	Player Weapons
C	74	Nick	Mangold	88	
C	71	Wade	Smith	77	
FB	37	Darian	Barnes	77	
HB	20	Thomas	Jones	88	
HB	29	Leon	Washington	82	
HB	32	Cedric	Houston	76	
K	1	Mike	Nugent	84	
LG	66	Pete	Kendall	85	
LG	61	Adrien	Clarke	71	
LT	60	DBrickashaw	Ferguson	87	Pass Blocker
LT	79	Adrian	Jones	79	
QB	10	Chad	Pennington	88	Precision Passer / Accurate QB
QB	11	Kellen	Clemens	76	
QB	8	Marques	Tuiasosopo	74	
RG	65	Brandon	Moore	87	
RG	78	Ed	Blanton	72	
RT	68	Anthony	Clement	80	
RT	76	Na'Shan	Goddard	64	
TE	86	Chris	Baker	79	
TE	88	Sean	Ryan	74	
WR	87	Laveranues	Coles	91	Go-To Guy / Possession Receiver, Hands, Speed
WR	89	Jerricho	Cotchery	85	Hands
WR	81	Justin	McCareins	74	Deep Threat
WR	17	Tim	Dwight	73	
WR	83	Chansi	Stuckey	73	
WR	16	Brad	Smith	72	

I Form-Twin WR
HB Slash

I Form-Normal
HB Dive

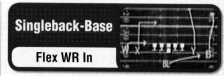

Singleback-Base
Flex WR In

With Thomas Jones in the backfield for the Jets, they can get back to the smash mouth football that they played when Curtis Martin was there.

Jones is a back that played in an offense where every team knew they had to run, and he still produced. This is a sign of a special player.

Current NFL backs are smaller, faster, and have great hands. Make sure to take advantage of Jones' hands and use him in the passing game.

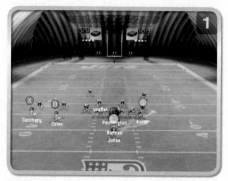

The HB Slash is designed similar to a stretch play. With Jones running this play, he will follow the fullback and use his speed to get more yards.

The HB Dive is a straight ahead, smashmouth running play. This play fits the style of Thomas Jones, as this is what he was known for in Chicago.

The WR In is used to stretch the right side of the field with vertical routes and then send crossing routes to clear the quick flat route for Jones.

Once the ball is in Jones' hands, the rest is simple. He already has blocks set up and his fullback is free to lead him around the corner.

When the play starts, Jones sees that he does not really have any work to do here to do. The offensive line opens a monster hole for him to run through.

Right away after the ball is snapped and the outside receivers run the defensive backs out of the flat, the quarterback delivers the ball to Jones in the flat.

The play works as planned, and Jones gets to the outside easily and has turned upfield.

Jones just plows forward, and reaches the second level carrying a linebacker on his way downfield.

Jones turns upfield, jukes the linebacker and picks up 5 yards on the play.

TEAM STRATEGY

NEW YORK JETS / DEFENSE

DEFENSIVE STAR PLAYER #51

Jonathan Vilma — Linebacker (MLB)

Key Attributes

Awareness	88
Speed	85
Strength	72
Tackle	95

Even with **Jonathan Vilma** having a sophomore slump in his second season, he still has the potential to perform as well as he did in his rookie season. Last season was his first year in the 3-4, and given his talent level, he should be able to make the needed off-season adjustments to get comfortable in the defense. Just imagine how good Vilma will be when he adds more knowledge of the defense to that **113** tackle total from last season.

Player Weapons: Playmaker / Brick Wall Defender, Smart LB

DEFENSIVE STRENGTH CHART

- ○: OVR less than 80
- ◑: OVR between 80-89
- ●: OVR 90 or greater
- ○: Player Weapons

4-3 Base Defense

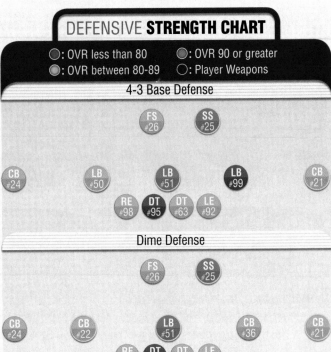

Dime Defense

RECOMMENDED DEFENSIVE AUDIBLE PACKAGES

3-4-Normal	3-4-Over	3-4-Over	3-4-Under	Dime-3-2-6
Drop Zone	Corss Fire Chuck	Clamp Double Go	Weak Blitz 3	DB Contain

DEFENSIVE PLAYCOUNTS

Man Coverage:	46	Cover 3 Zone:	24	Combo Blitz:	10
Man Zone:	36	Deep Zone:	16	Goal Line:	15
Combo Coverage:	9	Man Blitz:	48	Special Teams:	12
Cover 2 Zone:	24	Zone Blitz:	60		

TEAM TRIVIA

New York Jets Facts

Answers:

❶ Joe Namath

❷ Super Bowl III

❸ Wesley Walker

DEFENSIVE FORMATIONS

3-4	Nickel
3-4-Normal	Nickel-1-5-5
3-4-Over	Nickel-1-5-5 Prowl
3-4-Solid	Nickel-3-3-5
3-4-Under	Nickel-Normal
Dime	**Quarter**
Dime-3-2-6	Quarter-3 Deep
Dime-Normal	Quarter-Normal

DEFENSIVE ROSTER LIST — Current / Next Gen

Pos.	#	First Name	Last Name	Overall	Player Weapons
CB	21	Andre	Dyson	86	Quick Corner
CB	36	David	Barrett	81	
CB	22	Justin	Miller	81	Quick Corner / Speed
CB	24	Darrelle	Revis	81	
CB	30	Drew	Coleman	68	
CB	31	Hank	Poteat	67	
DT	63	Dewayne	Robertson	86	
DT	95	C.J.	Mosley	73	
DT	91	Sione	Pouha	72	
FS	26	Erik	Coleman	83	
FS	33	Eric	Smith	74	
LE	92	Shaun	Ellis	88	Power Move D-Lineman
LE	77	Eric	Hicks	84	
LE	93	Kenyon	Coleman	73	
LOLB	99	Bryan	Thomas	78	
LOLB	58	Matt	Chatham	69	
MLB	51	Jonathan	Vilma	94	Playmaker / Brick Wall Defender, Smart Linebacker
MLB	54	Victor	Hobson	83	
MLB	55	Brad	Kassell	79	
MLB	52	David	Harris	77	
MLB	56	Anthony	Schlegel	74	
P	7	Ben	Graham	87	Big Foot Kicker
RE	67	Kimo	vonOelhoffen	82	Run Stopper
RE	98	Bobby	Hamilton	82	
ROLB	50	Eric	Barton	89	Heavy Hitter
ROLB	96	David	Bowens	76	
SS	25	Kerry	Rhodes	95	
SS	42	Rashad	Washington	74	

3-4-Under

Weak Blitz

3-4-Solid

Trio Sky Zone

Nickle-3-5-5

3 Deep

When a team has a playmaker like Jonathan Vilma, it's not necessary to send him in on a blitz. His read-and-react assignment is perfect

It doesn't take too long into the game before Jonathan Vilma wants to get behind the line of scrimmage and make a play. He is a great blitzer.

Vilma can also be used in pass coverage. He is a solid pass defender, and plays that drop him into coverage are a real asset to the defense.

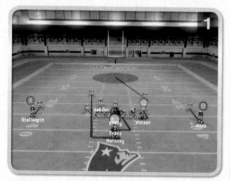

The defense is designed to bring pressure from the weak side. The right linebackers will blitz while Vilma and the free safety will bracket-cover the backs.

The Trio Sky Zone is a defense that is designed to play the left side of the field heavily and prevent a deep throw this way.

This play is a max zone coverage that blankets the field. Vilma is responsible for playing the middle underneath zone and will prevent any completions.

As the quarterback makes his way to hand off the ball, Jonathan Vilma has already recognized the run and shot through the strong side "A" gap.

When the offense puts the play in motion, the defense is dropping into coverage and Vilma is getting low as he charges around the right outside.

As the receivers work their way open, Vilma is sitting on that zone and is watching the tight end. He will punish him if he comes in his zone.

His great playmaking instincts lead him into the backfield, and he is able to stop the runningback.

The quarterback doesn't have enough time to adjust for Vilma. The result is a quarterback sack.

Vilma makes the interception and is off to the races as he tries to score.

TEAM STRATEGY

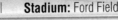

DETROIT LIONS

| Division: NFC North | Stadium: Ford Field | Type: Dome | Capacity: 65,000 | Surface: Turf |

2006 STANDINGS

Wins	Losses	Ties	PF	PA	Home	Road	vs. AFC	vs. NFC	vs. Div
3	13	0	305	398	2-6	1-7	1-3	2-10	0-6

TEAM OVERVIEW

Rod Marinelli calls the shots, but the offense is Mike Martz's playground. When things run smoothly, a Martz offense can be scarily good. When they don't, it can be really ugly. Martz has plenty of tools to work with, but it remains to be seen if the Lions can protect the ball.

Yet another first round wide receiver draft pick brings Calvin Johnson to the Lions.

He is the real deal and teamed up with Roy Williams and Mike Furrey, Kitna is not lacking for throwing options.

The Lions struggled to stop anybody last year, despite have some decent pieces. Shaun Rogers is back and will need to get into dominating form if the Lions are to see success on the defensive side of the ball in *Madden NFL 08*.

COACHING PROFILE

Rod Marinelli

- **Head Coaching Year:** 2nd
- **Experience:** Tampa Bay Buccaneers defensive line coach (1996-2001).

Marinelli was named the Lions' 24th head coach on January 19, 2006. He is known for getting the best out of his players. In six of the ten seasons that he coached the defensive line for the Bucs, the unit ranked number-one in total sacks.

TEAM RANKINGS

Scoring	21st
Passing Offense	7th
Rushing Offense	32rd
Passing Defense	25th
Rushing Defense	11th
Turnovers	29th

RATINGS HISTORY

Category	'07	'06	'05	'04
Overall	84	78	79	70
Offense	85	80	84	65
Defense	85	74	81	73

Bold = Highest Year

79 FIVE-YEAR AVERAGE

SCOUTING REPORT

STRENGTHS

Description	Maximizing Potential	Tips for Opponents
Roy Williams and Calvin Johnson form one of the best young receiving tandems in the league.	Come out in formations where Williams and Johnson are lined up on the same side. Have one of them run a deep route.	Don't get beat deep. Have a safety play over-the-top coverage to force the ball to be thrown underneath.
On top of the Lions having Williams and Johnson, there is plenty of depth right behind them.	Furrey is the perfect receiver to have lined up in the slot. Find plays that maximize his talents.	With Williams and Johnson lined up on the outside, you can't afford to concentrate too much on Furrey.
Cory Redding was the Lions' best pass rusher.	Redding will get his share of penetration up the gut.	You may need to slide protect to stop Redding.

WEAKNESSES

Description	Minimizing Risks	Tips for Opponents
The Lions' offensive line is the team's weak link on the offensive side of the ball.	If you decide to employ four receiver sets, run plays with at least one or two receivers running short routes.	Anytime the Lions go four wide, blitz the quarterback. The Lions' offensive line cannot protect him.
The Lions traded their best cornerback to the Broncos, leaving an already thin secondary thinner.	Call defenses where safeties play over-top such as 2 Man Under coverage schemes.	Bryant does have the speed, to keep up with most receivers. However, Fisher does not.

TEAM STRATEGY

OFF-SEASON **UPGRADES**

Type	Round	First Name	Last Name	School/Team	Position	Height	Weight
Trade	N/A	Tatum	Bell	Denver Broncos	RB	5'11"	213
Free Agent	N/A	T.J.	Duckett	Washington Redskins	RB	6'0"	254
Type	N/A	Edwin	Mulitalo	Baltimore Ravens	G	6'3"	350
Draft	1st	Calvin	Johnson	Georgia Tech	WR	6'4"	237
Draft	2nd	Drew	Stanton	Michigan State	QB	6'3"	235

FANTASY **OUTLOOK**

Star Player: Roy Williams
Round of Draft: 4th

With Calvin Johnson lining up on the opposite side of Williams, he will be less likely to see double-team coverage. This should result in increases in both receiving yardage and touchdown production.

Star Player: Calvin Johnson
Round of Draft: 6th

He is in the perfect position to have an outstanding rookie season. The Lions' passing offense has potential to be one of better ones as long as Jon Kitna can put up the same yardage as he did last season.

5-YEAR **PLAYER PROGRESSION**

First Name	Last Name	Position	'07 Overall	'08 Overall	'09 Overall	'10 Overall	'11 Overall
Shaun	Rogers	DT	95	95	96	96	92
Roy	Williams	WR	93	94	95	95	94
Kevin	Jones	HB	87	87	87	87	86
Calvin	Johnson	WR	87	87	87	87	86
Jon	Kitna	QB	84	86	-	-	-

FRANCHISE MODE STRATEGY

John Kitna is a solid quarterback, but he lacks the arm strength to get the ball downfield to his talented receivers. If a franchise quarterback should fall in your lap in the first round, show him the money.

Key Franchise Info

Team Salary: $86.8M
Cap Room: $22.1M
Key Rival:
• Green Bay Packers
NFL Icons: None
Philosophy:
• Offense: Vertical Passing
• Defense: Disrupt Passing
Prestige: Very Low
Team Needs:
• Quarterback (Future)
• Defensive Back
Highest Paid Players:
• Calvin Johnson
• Damien Woody
Up and Coming Players:
• Calvin Johnson
• Brian Calhoun

ROSTER AND **PACKAGE TIPS** — KEY PLAYER SUBSTITUTIONS

• **Position:** HB
• **Substitution:** Kevin Jones
• **When:** Global
• **Advantage:** Jones is the Lions' best halfback; plus, his 78 AWR rating is the best among halfbacks. You should have a better all-around running game with Jones in.

• **Position:** RT
• **Substitution:** Rex Tucker
• **When:** Global
• **Advantage:** Tucker's 85 AWR rating is 17 points higher than starter George Foster's, meaning he's more likely to pick up blitzes and stunts than Foster is.

• **Position:** MLB
• **Substitution:** Teddy Lehman
• **When:** Global
• **Advantage:** Lehman's SPD rating of 84 is seven points higher than Paris Lenon's, allowing him to be able to cover faster players better than Lenon can.

• **Position:** CB
• **Substitution:** Stanley Wilson
• **When:** Global
• **Advantage:** Wilson's 94 SPD rating will allow you to play more bump-n-run coverage and not have to pay for it should a receiver break loose.

TEAM STRATEGY

DETROIT LIONS / **OFFENSE**

OFFENSIVE **STAR PLAYER** #11

Roy Williams	Wide Receiver (WR)

Key Attributes

Acceleration	92
Awareness	86
Catching	91
Speed	93

It took three seasons for Williams to show why the Lions drafted him with their first round pick in 2004. In 2006, he led the team with **82** receptions and **1,310** yards. Williams uses his physical tools to out-man defensive backs trying to cover him. With a good combination of speed, strength, and size, he causes mismatches no matter what defender tries to cover him. In Mike Martz's wide open attack, the sky is the limit for Williams.

Player Weapons: Go-To Guy/Spectacular Catch Receiver, Hands

RECOMMENDED OFFENSIVE **AUDIBLE PACKAGES**

I Form-Normal	I Form-Twin WR	Weak-Normal	Singleback-Tight Slots	Shotgun-4WR
SE Post Flag	HB Blast	PA Boot LT	Lions Corners	WR Post Corner

OFFENSIVE **PLAYCOUNTS**

Quick Pass:	14	Screen Pass:	7	Pinch:	13
Standard Pass:	93	Hail Mary:	2	Counter:	23
Shotgun Pass:	12	Inside Handoff:	33	Draw:	9
Play Action Pass:	22	Outside Handoff:	6		

TEAM **TRIVIA**

Detroit Lions Facts

Turn the page for the answers.

1. In what year did the Lions have their first Thanksgiving Day game?
2. In what year did the Lions win their first NFL Championship?
3. Lions runningback greats Barry Sanders and Billy Sims both wore the same number. What was it?

OFFENSIVE **FORMATIONS**

Singleback	Split Backs
Big	Normal
Twin TE	3WR
Normal	**Strong I**
Normal Slot	Normal
Trips Bunch	3WR
Tight Slots	H Pro
Base Flex	**Weak I**
4WR Spread	Normal
Trips WR	Twin WR
I Form	3WR
Normal	**Shotgun**
Twin WR	4WR
3WR	
Twin TE	

OFFENSIVE **STRENGTH CHART**

○: OVR less than 80   ◉: OVR 90 or greater
◉: OVR between 80-89   ○: Player Weapons

2-Back Set

3 Receiver Set

OFFENSIVE **ROSTER LIST** Current/Next Gen

Pos.	#	First Name	Last Name	Overall	Player Weapons
C	51	Dominic	Raiola	84	
C	67	Blaine	Saipaia	68	
FB	24	Shawn	Bryson	85	
HB	34	Kevin	Jones	87	Speed Back/Stiff Arm BC
HB	28	Tatum	Bell	82	Speed Back
HB	45	T.J.	Duckett	78	Power Back
HB	29	Brian	Calhoun	75	Speed Back
K	4	Jason	Hanson	92	Accurate Kicker
LG	64	Edwin	Mulitalo	88	Run Blocker
LG	66	Stephen	Peterman	68	
LT	76	Jeff	Backus	88	
LT	73	Jonathan	Scott	72	
QB	8	Jon	Kitna	84	
QB	5	Drew	Stanton	72	
QB	6	Dan	Orlovsky	71	
RG	65	Damien	Woody	91	Run Blocker
RG	71	Manuel	Ramirez	74	
RT	74	Rex	Tucker	84	
RT	72	George	Foster	82	Run Blocker
TE	89	Dan	Campbell	81	
TE	80	Eric	Beverly	75	
TE	82	Casey	Fitzsimmons	70	
WR	11	Roy	Williams	93	Go-To Guy/Specatular Catch Receiver, Hands
WR	87	Mike	Furrey	87	Hands
WR	81	Calvin	Johnson	87	Deep Threat/Specatular Catch Receiver
WR	84	Shaun	McDonald	76	
WR	18	Eddie	Drummond	73	

Singleback-Big
Fl Stretch

It is a must to throw the ball to Roy Williams on a streak. This player has good speed, good hands, and great height.

Attack the defense with multiple vertical routes. The primary route is to Roy and is sure to demonstrate his breakaway ability.

The CB made a crucial mistake and looked into the backfield when a pump fake was given. Roy has already put distance between him and the corner.

Roy goes up and gets the ball at its highest point and prevents the defense from defending the pass.

Singleback-Tight Doubles
Shallow Cross

The most common thing is to see a big receiver like Roy Williams running down the field, but he is also a beast working the middle of the field.

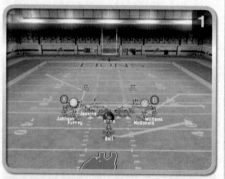

Use this play to beat man and zone coverage by using crossing routes. Roy's size and speed make this a perfect way to get him open.

When Williams clears the defenders, either because he finds a void in the coverage or he pulls away from a defender, the QB will get him the ball.

With the ball in his hands, it's going to be a foot race to the end zone.

Singleback-Trips Bunch
FL Out Stop

There are certain routes that are requirements when using a receiver with the size and speed of a Roy Willams. Hook, curls, CB, post, and outs all qualify.

This play is used to attack a defense that wants to defend with zone coverage. Roy Williams is a receiver that will not be slowed by zone coverage.

When the receivers break to the outside, the defense will jump the quick out and the corner route. This will make the Roy Williams route the best option.

This is more of a possession catch but Roy is always determined to get into the end zone.

TEAM STRATEGY

DETROIT LIONS / **DEFENSE**

TEAM STRATEGY

DEFENSIVE **STAR PLAYER**   #**50**

Ernie Sims	Linebacker (ROLB)

Key Attributes

Awareness	70
Speed	86
Strength	77
Tackle	90

In just his first season, **Sims** made his presence felt on the defensive end of the ball, leading the team in total tackles with **125**. He is not a very big linebacker, but he uses his explosive playmaker ability to make plays all over the field. His motor is always on high and that makes him a disruptive force in the 4-3 Tampa 2 that the Lions run. Look for him to lead the team in tackles again in '07.

Player Weapons: Playmaker / Big Hitter, Brick Wall Defender

RECOMMENDED DEFENSIVE **AUDIBLE PACKAGES**

4-3-Normal	4-3-Over	4-3-Under	Dime-3-2-6	Dime-Normal
Buzz Weak	Zone Blitz	Man Flats	2 Deep LB Blitz	Lehman Blitz

DEFENSIVE **PLAYCOUNTS**

Man Coverage:	36	Cover 3 Zone:	18	Combo Blitz:	11
Man Zone:	30	Deep Zone:	15	Goal Line:	15
Combo Coverage:	8	Man Blitz:	36	Special Teams:	12
Cover 2 Zone:	18	Zone Blitz:	53		

TEAM **TRIVIA**

Detroit Lions Facts

Answers:

1. 1934
2. 1935
2. The number 20

DEFENSIVE **FORMATIONS**

4-3	Nickel
4-3-Normal	Nickel-3-3-5
4-3-Over	Nickel-Normal
4-3-Under	Nickel-Strong
Dime	**Quarter**
Dime-3-2-6	Quarter-3 Deep
Dime-Normal	Quarter-Normal

DEFENSIVE **STRENGTH CHART**

○: OVR less than 80   ◉: OVR 90 or greater
◉: OVR between 80-89   ○: Player Weapons

4-3 Base Defense

Dime Defense

DEFENSIVE **ROSTER LIST**   Current / Next Gen

Pos.	#	First Name	Last Name	Overall	Player Weapons
CB	25	Fernando	Bryant	82	Quick Corner
CB	21	Travis	Fisher	79	
CB	31	Stanley	Wilson	76	
CB	33	A.J.	Davis	75	
CB	23	Keith	Smith	73	
DT	92	Shaun	Rogers	95	Run Stopper / Power Move D-Lineman
DT	78	Cory	Redding	88	
DT	75	Shaun	Cody	78	
DT	77	Jon	Bradley	71	
DT	62	Cleveland	Pinkney	69	
FS	27	Daniel	Bullocks	79	
FS	42	Gerald	Alexander	73	
LE	91	Dewayne	White	83	
LE	95	Jared	DeVries	73	
LE	94	Ikaika	Alama-Francis	72	
LOLB	97	Boss	Bailey	83	Playmaker
LOLB	59	Alex	Lewis	80	
MLB	53	Paris	Lenon	79	
MLB	54	Teddy	Lehman	75	
P	2	Nick	Harris	86	
RE	98	Kalimba	Edwards	81	
RE	93	Corey	Smith	69	
ROLB	50	Ernie	Sims	89	Playmaker / Big Hitter, Brick Wall Defender
ROLB	55	Donte	Curry	71	
SS	26	Kenoy	Kennedy	82	Playmaker / Big Hitter
SS	44	Idrees	Bashir	72	

Nickel-3-3-5

DE Contain

Nickel-3-3-5

2 Deep Robber

Nickel-Strong

FS Snake Blitz 3

Ernie Simms is always on go. If someone on the defense needs to make a play he is going to make sure he answers the call.

Playmakers make plays against the run, and pass. Ernie Simms is a playmaker and because of this it's not a stretch to ask him to defend the pass.

Simms is a great blitzing LB. He has a seek-and-destroy mindset and will take down any opponent he sees.

This defense is designed to prevent the quarterback from breaking the pocket. The DE Contain has also become known as a way to defend the run.

This defense lets Simms play the robber zone where he can eliminate any route in the seam or post area.

The defense is a zone blitz. It is used to create pressure and cause confusion with the zone coverage. Simms will handle the pressure.

The offense runs the ball and Simms attacks the run perfectly. He has his outside arm and shoulder free, preventing the RB from getting outside.

Simms is shown in the robber zone. Even with the tight end behind him, a good zone defender will not vacate his zone because of the initial threat.

To get the needed result the linebackers on the defense should be shifted to the right. After doing this, Ernie Simms will shoot through the "A" gap.

Because of Simms' technique, he shuts the run down at the line of scrimmage.

Simms makes a spectacular interception as he leaps to snag the ball out of the air.

Whenever Ernie Simms gets a clean blitz lane on any opposing quarterback, it's lights-out time.

TEAM STRATEGY

169

GREEN BAY PACKERS

Division: NFC North | **Stadium:** Lambeau Field | **Type:** Open | **Capacity:** 72,601 | **Surface:** Grass

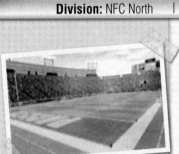

2006 STANDINGS

Wins	Losses	Ties	PF	PA	Home	Road	vs. AFC	vs. NFC	vs. Div
8	8	0	301	366	3-5	5-3	1-3	7-5	5-1

TEAM OVERVIEW

You can't talk about the Packers without mentioning their forever starter, Brett Favre. He still has plenty of zip on his arm even though his accuracy has dipped a bit over the years. He is still a playmaker and can manage the game with legendary precision.

The rubber is really going to meet the road when it comes to the running game. The Pack is going to struggle here with the departure of Ahman Green. Morency is going to have to step up.

The defense improved dramatically last season. A.J. Hawk is a force at MLB, and the Pack have two solid corners in Harris and Woodson. Kampman provides a good speed rush off the edge to put pressure on the opposing quarterback.

SCOUTING REPORT

STRENGTHS

Description	Maximizing Potential	Tips for Opponents
Brett Favre enters his 17th season as the Packers' quarterback. He still has great arm strength.	Use it to your advantage by frequently airing the ball out deep while looking for the big play.	Favre has a tendency to overthrow to his receivers because his accuracy rating is not what it once was.
Veteran Donald Driver and second year receiver Greg Jennings give the Packers a solid receiver duo.	Look for Driver in crucial down situations. His catch rating allows him to snag most balls thrown his way.	You can bet that ball is going be thrown towards Driver when the Packers need to pick up a first down.
A.J. Hawk is a force to be reckoned with.	Come up with schemes that use his playmaking ability.	If he looks like he is going to blitz, roll away from him.

WEAKNESSES

Description	Minimizing Risks	Tips for Opponents
With Ahman Green gone, the Packers don't have a go-to back who can get the job done consistently.	Your best bet to get any type of run production is to use the run-by-committee attack.	Don't bother stacking the box with extra run defenders. Instead, leave them back to stop deep passes.
The Packers' offensive line is not as strong as it was during the Super Bowl years in the 90s.	Your best bet for any type of ground success is to run behind right tackle Mark Tauscher.	Because the Packers' offensive line is not that strong, you should be able to get penetration.

COACHING PROFILE

Mike McCarthy

- **Head Coaching Year:** 2nd
- **Experience:** New Orleans Saints offensive coordinator (2000-2004), San Francisco 49ers offensive coordinator (2005).

McCarthy was named the 14th head coach in Packers history on January 12, 2006. He is best known for his knowledge of the West Coast offense. he compiled an 8-8 record his first season.

TEAM RANKINGS

Scoring	22nd
Passing Offense	8th
Rushing Offense	23rd
Passing Defense	17th
Rushing Defense	13th
Turnovers	17th

RATINGS HISTORY

Category	'07	'06	'05	'04
Overall	87	80	87	83
Offense	87	94	91	92
Defense	86	70	74	71

Bold = Highest Year

85
FIVE-YEAR
AVERAGE

OFF-SEASON **UPGRADES**

Type	Round	First Name	Last Name	School / Team	Position	Height	Weight
Free Agent	N/A	Frank	Walker	Giants	CB	5'10"	197
Draft	1st	Justin	Harrell	Tennessee	DT	6'4"	305
Draft	2nd	Brandon	Jackson	Nebraska	RB	5'10"	210
Draft	3rd	James	Jones	San Jose State	WR	6'1"	207
Draft	3rd	Aaron	Rouse	Virginia Tech	SS	6'4"	225

FANTASY **OUTLOOK**

Star Player: Donald Driver
Round of Draft: 6th

Driver quietly puts up solid fantasy numbers year after year. Over the last 48 games, he has gone over the 100-yard mark 12 times. Last season he had at least 90 yards in 11 of 16 games.

Star Player: Brett Favre
Round of Draft: 8th

Some will argue that Favre is not a top-flight fantasy quarterback any longer, but even at his age, he still can zip the ball in. Last season he threw for 3,885 yards. Not bad for a 37-year-old quarterback.

5-YEAR **PLAYER PROGRESSION**

First Name	Last Name	Position	'07 Overall	'08 Overall	'09 Overall	'10 Overall	'11 Overall
Donald	Driver	WR	93	94	95	93	-
Brett	Favre	QB	89	-	-	-	-
Charles	Woodson	CB	89	87	86	84	82
A.J.	Hawk	LB	89	89	91	91	93
Brandon	Jackson	HB	80	80	80	80	80

FRANCHISE MODE **STRATEGY**

Brett Favre has to retire at some point during his career. You must decide if you want to put your trust in Aaron Rogers or look for another quarterback in the draft. Hey, we didn't say drafting would be easy.

Key Franchise Info

Team Salary: $87.7M
Cap Room: $21.2M
Key Rival:
• Chicago Bears
NFL Icons: Brett Favre
Philosophy:
• Offense: Establish Run
• Defense: Shut Down Runs
Prestige: Very Low
Team Needs:
• Quarterback (Future)
• Running Back
Highest Paid Players:
• Brett Favre
• Charles Woodson
Up and Coming Players:
• Brandon Jackson
• David Clowney

ROSTER AND **PACKAGE TIPS** — KEY PLAYER SUBSTITUTIONS

• **Position:** HB
• **Substitution:** Vernand Morency
• **When:** Global
• **Advantage:** Morency not only has a better OVR rating than Brandon Jackson at 82, but he's also got better ratings in SPD, AWR, and CTH.

• **Position:** RE
• **Substitution:** Kabeer Gbaja-Biamila
• **When:** Global
• **Advantage:** Gbaja-Biamila's SPD rating of 81 is fifteen points higher than Cullen Jenkins's, and gives the Packers a significant boost to their pass rush defense.

• **Position:** PR
• **Substitution:** Robert Ferguson
• **When:** Global
• **Advantage:** Ferguson's 91 SPD rating will allow him to be a game breaker in the return game. Not to mention he's got a five point edge in OVR rating over Charles Woodson.

• **Position:** HB
• **Substitution:** DeShawn Wynn
• **When:** Short Yardage
• **Advantage:** Weighing in at 232 pounds and having an STR rating of 71 allows Wynn to be able to be the back that can pound the rock in short yardage situations.

TEAM STRATEGY

GREEN BAY PACKERS / OFFENSE

OFFENSIVE STAR PLAYER #4

Brett Favre — Quarterback (QB)

Key Attributes

Awareness	88
Speed	53
Throwing Power	98
Throwing Accuracy	88

Entering his **16**th season as quarterback, **Brett Favre** remains one of single best callers in the game. At 37, he still hasn't lost his fast ball. Last season, he managed to throw for **3,885** yards. With young talent around him, he will make one more run at trying to lead the Packers into the playoffs and Super Bowl. For him to be able to do this, he will need to cut down on throwing interceptions.

Player Weapons: Cannon Arm / Cannon Arm QB

RECOMMENDED OFFENSIVE AUDIBLE PACKAGES

I Form-Big	Strong I-Twin	Singleback-4WR Flex	Singleback-Trips Bunch	Shotgun-Normal
Counter Lead	Toss Strong	Slot Cross	Packers Smash	Packers Cross

OFFENSIVE PLAYCOUNTS

Quick Pass:	11	Screen Pass:	15	Pinch:	14
Standard Pass:	80	Hail Mary:	1	Counter:	17
Shotgun Pass:	25	Inside Handoff:	33	Draw:	20
Play Action Pass:	40	Outside Handoff:	8		

TEAM TRIVIA

Green Bay Packers Facts

Turn the page for the answers.

1. Founded by Curly Lambeau and George Calhoun, the Green Bay Packers team went professional and joined the AFPA (later NFL) in which year?

2. The Packers set an NFL franchise record for having 13 consecutive non-losing seasons. Which season did their streak stop?

OFFENSIVE FORMATIONS

Singleback	Split Backs
Big Win	Normal
Big 3TE	**Strong I**
Twin TE	Normal
Twin TE WR	Twin TE
Normal Slot	**Weak I**
Slot Strong	Normal
Trips Bunch	Twin WR
Tight Doubles	Twin TE
4WR Flex	**Shotgun**
Empty Bunch	2RB 3WR
I Form	Normal
Normal	4WR
Twin WR	
Big	

OFFENSIVE STRENGTH CHART

- ○ : OVR less than 80
- ◉ : OVR 90 or greater
- ◉ : OVR between 80-89
- ○ : Player Weapons

OFFENSIVE ROSTER LIST   Current / Next Gen

Pos.	#	First Name	Last Name	Overall	Player Weapons
C	63	Scott	Wells	83	
C	70	Tyson	Walter	72	
FB	40	Brandon	Miree	78	
HB	34	Vernand	Morency	82	
HB	32	Brandon	Jackson	80	
HB	42	DeShawn	Wynn	74	
K	2	Mason	Crosby	82	
K	16	Dave	Rayner	81	Big Foot Kicker
LG	73	Daryn	Colledge	79	
LG	64	Tony	Palmer	66	
LT	76	Chad	Clifton	91	Road Blocker
LT	78	Allen	Barbre	70	
QB	4	Brett	Favre	89	Cannon Arm / Cannon Arm QB
QB	12	Aaron	Rodgers	76	
QB	7	Ingle	Martin	71	
RG	72	Jason	Spitz	74	
RG	62	Junius	Coston	67	
RT	65	Mark	Tauscher	92	Road Blocker
RT	71	Kevin	Barry	79	
TE	88	Bubba	Franks	81	
TE	86	Donald	Lee	76	
TE	44	Clark	Harris	73	
WR	80	Donald	Driver	93	Go-To Guy / Possesion Receiver, Quick Receiver, Hands
WR	85	Greg	Jennings	84	Deep Threat
WR	87	Robert	Ferguson	78	
WR	82	Ruvell	Martin	75	
WR	89	James	Jones	75	
WR	11	David	Clowney	73	

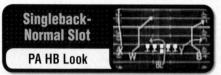

Singleback-Normal Slot

PA HB Look

Shotgun-2RB 3WR

Post Flags

Singleback-Tight Doubles

PA Rollout

Bret Favre is a living legend at quarterback. There is no aspect of his game that can't be used to benefit the offense.

He can really show off his pinpoint passing accuracy when running this play.

One way to increase passing yards and a QB's completion percentage is by using a play-action rollout pass.

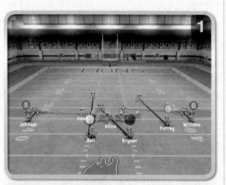

The play is used to get the play action fake to the back to get him open on his out route, while also clearing out the middle of the defense.

The Shotgun-2RB 3WR Post Flags is used to take advantage of aggressive corners who like to play man-to-man coverage.

This play usues a play action fake to the runningback to show misdirection, while getting Favre to move the pocket and further stretch the defense.

Bret Favre is the original play action king out of the current NFL quarterbacks. He fakes the ball to the halfback and gets the defense to bite.

As soon as the outside receiver makes his inside move to show the post route to the defense, the ball is put in the air.

While Favre is rolling out he has three options down field. The flanker and split end are both open and the slot is open on his deep crossing route.

Favre delivers the ball to the slot receiver for an easy catch over the middle.

The ball is put in a spot where only the receiver can make a play on the ball.

Favre takes the crossing route as his option and completes the down field pass.

TEAM STRATEGY

GREEN BAY PACKERS / DEFENSE

DEFENSIVE STAR PLAYER #50

A.J. Hawk — Linebacker (ROLB)

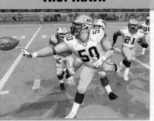

Key Attributes

Awareness	78
Speed	87
Strength	73
Tackle	85

In just his first season at linebacker for the Packers, **Hawk** made an instant impact by leading the Packers in total tackles with **121**. On top of that, he had **3.5** sacks and **2** interceptions. With his speed and his ability to find the ball carrier, Hawk is a human-seeking missile looking to destroy the opposition. Look for him to improve on his tackles and sacks totals as he gets more comfortable in the Packers 4-3 scheme.

Player Weapons: Playmaker / Brick Wall Defender

RECOMMENDED DEFENSIVE AUDIBLE PACKAGES

4-3-Normal	4-3-Over	Dime-Flat	Nickel-3-3-5	Nickel-Normal
Hog Buck 3	SS Blitz	DB Blitz	CB Dogs Blitz	9 Velcro

DEFENSIVE PLAYCOUNTS

Man Coverage:	41	Cover 3 Zone:	23	Combo Blitz:	23
Man Zone:	37	Deep Zone:	22	Goal Line:	15
Combo Coverage:	12	Man Blitz:	49	Special Teams:	12
Cover 2 Zone:	14	Zone Blitz:	57		

TEAM TRIVIA

Green Bay Packers Facts

Answers:

① 1921

② 2005

DEFENSIVE FORMATIONS

4-3	Nickel
4-3-Normal	Nickel-3-3-5
4-3-Over	Nickel-Normal
4-3-Under	Nickel-Strong
Dime	**Quarter**
Dime-3-2-6	Quarter-3 Deep
Dime-Flat	Quarter-Normal
Dime-Normal	

DEFENSIVE STRENGTH CHART

○: OVR less than 80   ●: OVR 90 or greater
●: OVR between 80-89   ○: Player Weapons

4-3 Base Defense / Dime Defense

DEFENSIVE ROSTER LIST Current / Next Gen

Pos.	#	First Name	Last Name	Overall	Player Weapons
CB	31	Al	Harris	93	Shutdown Corner / Press Coverage Corner, Shutdown Corner, Smart Corner
CB	21	Charles	Woodson	89	Containment Corner / Press Coverage Corner, Smart Corner
CB	43	Patrick	Dendy	73	
CB	41	Frank	Walker	72	
CB	27	Will	Blackmon	71	
DT	99	Corey	Williams	87	
DT	79	Ryan	Pickett	82	
DT	91	Justin	Harrell	80	
DT	90	Colin	Cole	76	
FS	36	Nick	Collins	82	Coverage Safety
FS	25	Marviel	Underwood	74	
LE	74	Aaron	Kampman	93	Pass Rusher / Power Move D-Lineman
LE	57	Jason	Hunter	66	
LOLB	51	Brady	Poppinga	80	
LOLB	35	Korey	Hall	71	
MLB	56	Nick	Barnett	89	Heavy Hitter
MLB	52	Abdul	Hodge	76	
P	9	Jon	Ryan	84	Big Foot Kicker
RE	94	Kabeer	Gbaja Biamila	86	
RE	77	Cullen	Jenkins	83	
ROLB	50	A.J.	Hawk	89	Playmaker / Brick Wall Defender
ROLB	59	Tracy	White	73	
SS	22	Marquand	Manuel	76	
SS	29	Tyrone	Culver	72	
SS	37	Aaron	Rouse	71	

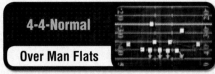

Nickel-3-3-5
Double X

A.J. Hawk has a real nose for the ball and the Double X is a play that will allow Hawk's tenacity to shine through.

The Double X play doubles up the X receiver. The play is a Cover 1 defense with man around and with A.J. Hawk on a delayed blitz.

Even though the play calls for a blitz, Hawk sees that the offense has come out running the ball and he stays in good relationship to the back.

Hawk blows the runningback up in the backfield before he gets to the corner.

4-4-Normal
Over Man Flats

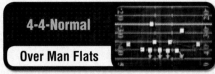

If proof is needed to show how good A.J. Hawk is against the pass, look no further than his stat sheet. He had two interceptions last year.

The Man Flats defense is made to take away the quick pass to the runningback or the quick slant pass to the outside receivers.

Hawk has the speed to run with many of the running backs in *Madden NFL 08* when they turn routes up field. He is in perfect position here.

A.J. goes up and gets the ball out of the air like a receiver is taught.

4-3-Over
LB Dogs

A.J. Hawk can be moved around on the defense. This is done is by calling an over defensive front. This brings a whole new dimension to the defense.

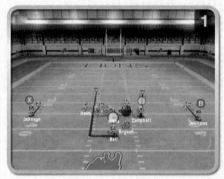

This defense is designed with one thing in mind: pressure. The play calls for a seven man blitz but the pressure will feel stronger from the right side.

When the offense snaps the ball, Hawk benefits from his alignment on the end of the defensive line. He gets in clean with no blockers to delay him.

Any offense that does not account for A.J. Hawk should expect to see their QB sacked.

TEAM STRATEGY

CAROLINA PANTHERS

Division: NFC South | **Stadium:** Bank of America Stadium | **Type:** Open | **Capacity:** 73,298 | **Surface:** Grass

2006 STANDINGS

Wins	Losses	Ties	PF	PA	Home	Road	vs. AFC	vs. NFC	vs. Div
8	8	0	270	305	4-4	4-4	2-2	6-6	5-1

TEAM OVERVIEW

The Panthers aren't getting any younger, so the time for them to win is now. Their stars are back healthy and they should make a solid run at the playoffs. They have two options now at QB. Delhomme has better accuracy, but Carr has a stronger arm.

The Panthers have playmaker Steve Smith at the wide out spot, which will allow them to spread the field and back the defense off the line. Williams and Foster can get it done in the run game if they have room.

Kris Jenkins and Julius Peppers bring the pain up front and should dominate their side of the line. The linebackers are quick and the corners should be able to hang with all but the fastest receivers in the game.

SCOUTING REPORT

STRENGTHS

Description	Maximizing Potential	Tips for Opponents
Receiver Steve Smith is one of the best, if not the best, receiver in the game today.	Smith's speed makes him a big play threat whenever he's on the field. He also has great hands.	The defense must know where Smith is lined up at all times. Be sure to use bracket coverage on him.
With Julius Peppers and Kris Jenkins leading the way, the Panthers have one of the best defenses.	The Panthers were tied for 6th last season in sacks at 41, with Peppers accounting for a team high 13.	Keep tight ends and backs in to help out blocking Peppers, and double team whenever you can.
Delhome's accuracy plus Smith's speed is very dangerous.	Don't be afraid to attack deep, the QB is accurate.	Mix up your coverages to confuse Delhomme.

WEAKNESSES

Description	Minimizing Risks	Tips for Opponents
Even though Carolina is known for their passing game, tight end Jeff King is not known for his catching.	The Panthers have no threat to exploit the seams unless they go to formations with three or more receivers.	Focus your attention on the receivers on the field and don't really worry about the tight ends.
As good as HB DeShaun Foster has been or has the potential to be, it seems as if he's always getting hurt.	He split carries last season with then rookie DeAngelo Williams to cut down on his workload.	Hit Foster often and hard. Use the hit stick if at all possible and try to knock him out of the game.

COACHING PROFILE

John Fox

- **Head Coaching Year:** 6th
- **Experience:** Defensive coordinator for the New York Giants (1997-2001).

John Fox has a career record of 41 and 30 since becoming the Panthers Head Coach on Jan. 25, 2002. He has gotten the Carolina fan base used to winning by taking them to two NFC Championship games and one Super Bowl.

TEAM RANKINGS

Scoring	27th
Passing Offense	15th
Rushing Offense	24th
Passing Defense	4th
Rushing Defense	11th
Turnovers	23rd

RATINGS HISTORY

Category	'07	'06	'05	'04
Overall	**90**	85	93	75
Offense	**89**	87	89	72
Defense	90	87	**99**	77

Bold = Highest Year

86 FIVE-YEAR AVERAGE

TEAM STRATEGY

OFF-SEASON **UPGRADES**

Type	Round	First Name	Last Name	School / Team	Position	Height	Weight
Released	N/A	David	Carr	Houston Texans	QB	6'3"	230
Free Agent	N/A	Deke	Cooper	San Francisco 49ers	S	6'2"	210
Free Agent	N/A	Chad	Lavalais	Atlanta Falcons	NT	6'1"	293
Draft	1st	Jon	Beason	Miami	LB	6'0"	237
Draft	2nd	Dwayne	Jarrett	USC	WR	6'4"	219

FANTASY **OUTLOOK**

★ Star Player: Steve Smith
Round of Draft: 2nd

Smith had a down year, by his standards, in '06. The decline in numbers was mainly due to multiple hamstring ailments. Now that he is healthy again, expect him to put up at least 1,300 yards and 10 touchdowns in '07.

★ Star Player: Jake Delhomme
Round of Draft: 12th

Delhomme did not put up the type of fantasy numbers one might expect from him. In fact, he only threw for 2,805 yards, his lowest total in the four years. Despite that, he is still a solid number 2 quarterback.

5-YEAR **PLAYER PROGRESSION**

First Name	Last Name	Position	'07 Overall	'08 Overall	'09 Overall	'10 Overall	'11 Overall
Jake	Delhomme	QB	86	88	87	86	85
Steve	Smith	WR	98	99	99	99	98
Julius	Peppers	DE	98	99	99	99	99
Mike	Rucker	DE	89	89	87	87	87
Jon	Beason	LB	83	83	83	84	84

FRANCHISE MODE **STRATEGY**

The Panthers can use some help at both starting guard positions. We wouldn't draft in the first round, but if one falls in the 2nd or 3rd rounds, make the effort to draft one. Another position needed is at strong safety.

Key Franchise Info

Team Salary: $87.0M
Cap Room: $21.9M
Key Rival:
• Tampa Bay Buccaneers
NFL Icons: None
Philosophy:
• Offense: Establish the Run
• Defense: Shut Down Runs
Prestige: Medium
Team Needs:
• Linebacker
• Defensive Back
Highest Paid Players:
• Jake Delhomme
• Julius Peppers
Up and Coming Players:
• Dwayne Jarrett
• Richard Marshall

TEAM STRATEGY

ROSTER AND **PACKAGE TIPS** — KEY PLAYER SUBSTITUTIONS

• **Position:** FB
• **Substitution:** Jeff King
• **When:** Global
• **Advantage:** Even though King is a TE, his rating as a FB is two points higher than current starter Brad Hoover's. Plus, he's got better hands which can help in the passing game.

• **Position:** WR
• **Substitution:** Drew Carter
• **When:** Global
• **Advantage:** Carter's 94 SPD rating as a slot receiver will allow him to stretch the field and take some of the focus off of Steve Smith in the passing game.

• **Position:** CB
• **Substitution:** Kevin Lucas
• **When:** Global
• **Advantage:** Lucas's 79 AWR rating helps him read routes more easily, thus allowing him to make better plays on the ball.

• **Position:** SS
• **Substitution:** Deke Cooper
• **When:** Global
• **Advantage:** Cooper is a better fit as a strong safety and will help secure an otherwise weak secondary. His speed will allow him to recover from any mistakes.

CAROLINA PANTHERS / OFFENSE

OFFENSIVE STAR PLAYER #89

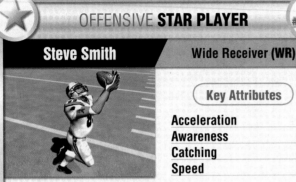

Steve Smith — Wide Receiver (WR)

Key Attributes

Acceleration	99
Awareness	89
Catching	95
Speed	97

The Panthers have arguably the most feared receiver in the NFL. Some receivers have big bodies and use their size, while others are smaller and more agile. **Smith** is a small, explosive receiver who plays like a big man and will go after the ball no matter where it is on the field. He had another outstanding year, and put up **1,166** yards and **8** touchdowns on **83** receptions. Don't forget that Smith is also equally a threat when lined up on punt return.

Player Weapons: Go-To Guy / Possession Receiver, Quick Receiver, Hands, Speed

RECOMMENDED OFFENSIVE AUDIBLE PACKAGES

I Form-Normal	Singleback-Big	Singleback-Normal	Singleback-4WR	Shotgun-5WR Tight
Cross In	Ace Post	Streaks	FL Corner	Wide Corners

OFFENSIVE PLAYCOUNTS

Quick Pass:	24	Screen Pass:	7	Pinch:	10
Standard Pass:	78	Hail Mary:	1	Counter:	26
Shotgun Pass:	31	Inside Handoff:	33	Draw:	10
Play Action Pass:	16	Outside Handoff:	11		

TEAM TRIVIA

Carolina Panthers Facts
Turn the page for the answers.

1. What team did the Panthers defeat to win their first game in the regular season, in their first season of 1995?

2. Who was the first player ever drafted by the Carolina Panthers?

3. Who was the team's first head coach?

OFFENSIVE FORMATIONS

Singleback	Strong I
Big	H Pro
Big Wing	H Twins
Twin TE WR	H TE Flip
Normal Slot	H Twin TE
Slot Strong	**Weak I**
Panther Trips	H Pro
4WR	H Twins
Empty 5WR	H Wing TE
I Form	H Twin TE
Normal	**Shotgun**
Strg Twin TE	4WR Spread
Split Backs	5WR Tight
3WR	Empty TE Flip
Big	Empty Trey Stack

OFFENSIVE STRENGTH CHART

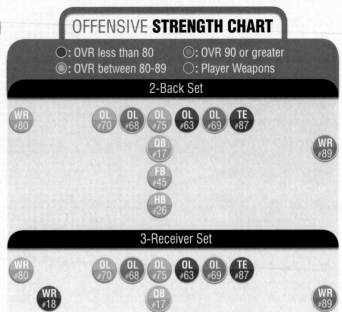

○: OVR less than 80   ○: OVR 90 or greater
◉: OVR between 80-89   ○: Player Weapons

2-Back Set
WR #80 — OL #70, OL #68, OL #75, OL #63, OL #69, TE #87 — WR #89 — QB #17 — FB #45 — HB #26

3-Receiver Set
WR #80 — OL #70, OL #68, OL #75, OL #63, OL #69, TE #87 — WR #18 — QB #17 — WR #89 — HB #26

OFFENSIVE ROSTER LIST — Current / Next Gen

Pos.	#	First Name	Last Name	Overall	Player Weapons
C	75	Justin	Hartwig	84	
C	65	Ryan	Kalil	82	
FB	45	Brad	Hoover	80	
HB	26	DeShaun	Foster	85	
HB	34	DeAngelo	Williams	84	Elusive Back / Elusive Back
HB	37	Nick	Goings	78	
HB	32	Eric	Shelton	74	
K	4	John	Kasay	90	Big Foot Kicker
LG	68	Mike	Wahle	94	
LG	66	Will	Montgomery	61	
LT	70	Travelle	Wharton	83	
LT	79	Rashad	Butler	73	
QB	17	Jake	Delhomme	86	Precision Passer
QB	8	David	Carr	83	
RG	71	Evan	Mathis	79	
RG	63	Geoff	Hangartner	79	
RG	76	D'Anthony	Batiste	69	
RT	69	Jordan	Gross	92	Road Blocker / Pass Blocker
RT	73	Jeremy	Bridges	78	
TE	87	Jeff	King	78	
TE	84	Michael	Gaines	73	
WR	89	Steve	Smith	98	Go-To Guy / Possession, Quick Receiver, Hands, Speed
WR	80	Dwayne	Jarrett	80	Spectacular Catch
WR	83	Keary	Colbert	73	
WR	18	Drew	Carter	73	
WR	81	Chris	Horn	72	
WR	10	Ryne	Robinson	71	

OFFENSE / KEY OFFENSIVE PLAYS

Weak I-H Pro

Smith Option

Singleback-Normal

PA Rollout

Singleback-Slot Strong

WR Drag

Steve Smith is a crisp route runner that excels in the intermediate and short areas. He also has the speed to take it deep.

PA Rollout displays Smith's ability to be explosive and burn the defense deep.

This play shows Smith's tenacity and tough man attitude over the middle.

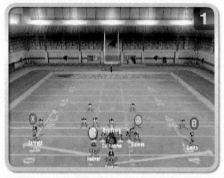

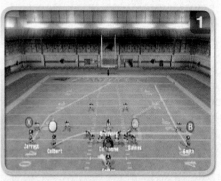

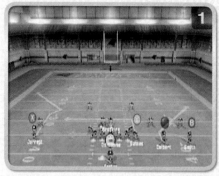

Most starting receivers in the game will have plays that allow them to choose the best route for the situation they are in.

A player like Steve Smith allows the Panthers' offense to be very creative.

WR Drag sends the primary receiver on a ball control route across the middle of the football field.

In this situation, Steve Smith chooses to run an out route. He stops here and comes back toward the football and makes the play.

On this play, the running back and the quarterback must do a believable job of selling the run so that the defense will bite.

Steve Smith is a good choice to run ball control routes like the drag. He will get free from most defenders and be available to receive the pass.

In classic Steve Smith fashion, he shakes the first defender. Now the defense has a big problem—a six-point problem.

Once the quarterback locates Smith running one-on-one with any defender, it is time to cash in for six points.

These routes allow Smith to use his speed and arsenal of moves to pick up yards after the catch.

TEAM STRATEGY

CAROLINA PANTHERS / **DEFENSE**

DEFENSIVE **STAR PLAYER** #90

Julius Peppers — Defensive End (LE)

Key Attributes

Awareness	77
Speed	87
Strength	84
Tackle	76

Peppers is the best player on the Panthers' defense, and could perhaps be called the best defensive end in football. He registered **13** sacks last season, and has had 10 sacks in four of his first five seasons. This puts him in elite company, as only **eight** other players have achieved this mark since sacks became a stat. He is also a threat in pass defense because he has the speed to run with backs and tight ends.

Player Weapons: Force of Nature / Big Hitter, Finesse Move D-Lineman

DEFENSIVE **STRENGTH CHART**

○: OVR less than 80   ●: OVR 90 or greater
◑: OVR between 80-89   ○: Player Weapons

4-3 Base Defense

Dime Defense

RECOMMENDED DEFENSIVE **AUDIBLE PACKAGES**

4-3-Normal	4-3-Over	4-3-Under	Nickel-3-3-5	Nickel-Normal
Slant 1 OLB Fire	Man Flats	Over 3 Strong	Double X	Over Storm Brave

DEFENSIVE **PLAYCOUNTS**

Man Coverage:	41	Cover 3 Zone:	23	Combo Blitz:	23
Man Zone:	37	Deep Zone:	22	Goal Line:	15
Combo Coverage:	12	Man Blitz:	49	Special Teams:	12
Cover 2 Zone:	14	Zone Blitz:	57		

TEAM **TRIVIA**

Carolina Panthers Facts
Answers:
1 New York Jets
2 Kerry Collins
3 Dom Capers

DEFENSIVE **FORMATIONS**

4-3	Nickel
4-3-Normal	Nickel-3-3-5
4-3-Over	Nickel-Normal
4-3-Under	Nickel-Strong
Dime	**Quarter**
Dime-Flat	Quarter-3 Deep
Dime-Normal	Quarter-Normal

DEFENSIVE **ROSTER LIST** Current / Next Gen

Pos.	#	First Name	Last Name	Overall	Player Weapons
CB	20	Chris	Gamble	88	Quick Corner
CB	21	Ken	Lucas	88	Quick Corner
CB	31	Richard	Marshall	82	
CB	25	Christian	Morton	67	
DT	77	Kris	Jenkins	94	Defensive Enforcer / Power Move D-Lineman
DT	99	Máake	Kemoeatu	87	Run Stopper
DT	92	Damione	Lewis	81	
DT	94	Kindal	Moorehead	77	
FS	30	Mike	Minter	86	Big Hitter
FS	35	Deke	Cooper	78	
LE	90	Julius	Peppers	98	Force of Nature / Big Hitter, Finesse Move D-Lineman
LE	96	Dave	Ball	66	
LOLB	58	Thomas	Davis	84	
LOLB	49	Tim	Shaw	78	Playmaker
LOLB	57	Brandon	Jamison	64	
MLB	55	Dan	Morgan	89	Defensive Enforcer
MLB	59	Adam	Seward	68	
P	7	Jason	Baker	89	
RE	93	Mike	Rucker	89	
RE	95	Charles	Johnson	78	
RE	74	Stanley	McClover	71	
ROLB	52	Jon	Beason	83	
ROLB	53	Náil	Diggs	82	
ROLB	50	James	Anderson	76	
SS	33	Nate	Salley	71	
SS	29	Cam	Newton	61	

TEAM STRATEGY

DEFENSE / **KEY DEFENSIVE PLAYS**

4-3-Normal	Nickel-Normal	4-3-Normal
2 Man Under	**QB Contain**	**Zip Shoot Gut**

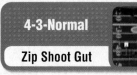

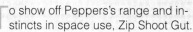

Panthers DE Julius Peppers has outstanding range. Plays such as the this show off Peppers's ability to shake blocks and get to the football.

This shows off Peppers's lateral mobility and his ability to play in zone coverage.

To show off Peppers's range and instincts in space use, Zip Shoot Gut.

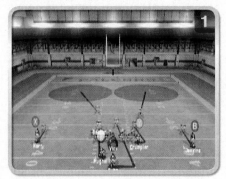
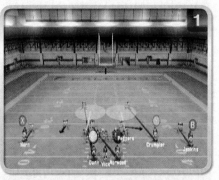

This is the base defensive front and coverage of many NFL teams. Front four pressure is essential for this defense to be successful.

Julius Peppers is a freakish athlete. Not only can he rush the passer, but he can also drop back into coverage and defend passing routes.

This play gets Peppers to use his outstanding quickness and big play ability against the opposing team's passing attack.

We like to control Peppers on this play and use a host of defensive line moves to defeat pass blockers and put fear into the heart of the quarterback.

The Nickel-Normal QB Contain gets Peppers to drop back into the curl area and guard the short and intermediate routes.

Peppers drops back into the curl/hook zone area on this play and defends the intermediate passing routes. He is not fooled by cross up patterns.

Once we get off the block, we beeline toward the quarterback and force him up into the pocket where our teammates take him out.

He jumps any routes that cross his face. Julius Peppers makes plays on the football that some linebackers cannot make.

Peppers's instincts take over as he makes a big play on the ball and gives the ball back to his offense.

TEAM STRATEGY

NEW ENGLAND PATRIOTS

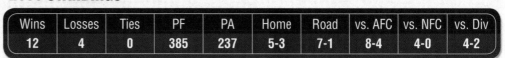

Division: AFC East | **Stadium:** Gillette Stadium™ | **Type:** Open | **Capacity:** 68,000 | **Surface:** Grass

COACHING PROFILE

Bill Belichick

- **Head Coaching Year:** 8th
- **Experience:** Belichick owns a 10-1 mark in the postseason.

Belichick is considered the best head coach in the NFL. He is the only coach in NFL history to lead his team to three Super Bowl wins in a four-year period. Since he took over in 2000, he has compiled a record of 75-39.

TEAM RANKINGS

Scoring	7th
Passing Offense	12th
Rushing Offense	12th
Passing Defense	12th
Rushing Defense	5th
Turnovers	4th

RATINGS HISTORY

Category	'07	'06	'05	'04
Overall	90	97	**99**	88
Offense	89	**93**	90	82
Defense	88	96	**99**	88

Bold = Highest Year

93
FIVE-YEAR
AVERAGE

2006 STANDINGS

Wins	Losses	Ties	PF	PA	Home	Road	vs. AFC	vs. NFC	vs. Div
12	4	0	385	237	5-3	7-1	8-4	4-0	4-2

TEAM OVERVIEW

After falling just short of another Super Bowl appearance in 2006, the Patriots took a radically different approach to the off-season with the signings of several big splash fee agents. LB Adalius Thomas, WRs Randy Moss, Donté Stallworth, and Kelly Washington all join the Pats lineup.

With Randy Moss lined up at receiver, the Patriots are sure to be one of the go-to teams for Madden players all around the country. It's hard to resist a team featuring the accurate Tom Brady and explosive Moss.

Defensively, the Patriots remain solid. With a secondary anchored by Asante Samuel and the aging but still effective Rodney Harrison, the Pats should be able to keep good passing teams on lockdown.

SCOUTING REPORT

STRENGTHS

Description	Maximizing Potential	Tips for Opponents
The Patriots lost a great deal on offense last season, particularly at the wide receiver position.	With new talent at the wide receiver position in Randy Moss and Donte Stallworth, test the deep coverage.	Be aware of Brady's accuracy and deep ball. It might be best to have safety help over the top.
Randy Moss has had disappointing seasons in Oakland and is looking to rebound.	Moss is still one of the most, if not the most dangerous wide receiver in the game.	Moss has a tag team partner in Stallworth, it might not be such a smart move to press these guys.
Maroney sat behind Dillon in his rookie campaign but came on strong.	Get Maroney the ball on counters and sweeps so he can get into the open field.	Maroney is a back that can do it all. Swarm the football when he has it.

WEAKNESSES

Description	Minimizing Risks	Tips for Opponents
It is tough to find weaknesses with a team that is constantly contending for the title year in and out.	Teddy Bruschi and Mike Vrabel are no longer young guns. If man coverage is the scheme watch out.	Use formation shifts and motion to get them manned up on a faster player.
Ellis Hobbs will get most of the attention due to fact that teams will look to avoid throwing towards Asante Samuel side of the field.	If Hobbs gets beat consistently, rotate the pass coverage to his side. This will put extra defenders in position to help defend the pass.	Look to attack Hobbs early and often until he shows he can cover his side of the field.

Overall Rating **92**
Offense **91**
Defense **91**

OFF-SEASON UPGRADES

Type	Round	First Name	Last Name	School / Team	Position	Height	Weight
Trade	N/A	Randy	Moss	Oakland Raiders	WR	??	??
Free Agent	N/A	Tory	James	Cincinnati Bengals	CB	??	??
Free Agent	N/A	Donté	Stallworth	Philadelphia Eagles	WR	??	??
Draft	1st	Brandon	Meriweather	Miami	S	5'11"	195
Draft	4th	Kareem	Brown	Miami	DT	6'4"	290

FANTASY OUTLOOK

⭐ **Star Player:** Laurence Maroney
Round of Draft: 1st

With Corey Dillon out of the picture, Maroney's fantasy value has sky rocketed. Throw in the fact that Tom Brady now has assets at receiver, and opposing defenses cannot load the box to stop Maroney.

⭐ **Star Player:** Randy Moss
Round of Draft: 3rd

Moss was a bust in Oakland as far as fantasy numbers go. With him now in a New England Patriots' uniform and with Tom Brady throwing him the ball, Moss should at least have 1,200 yards receiving and 10 touchdowns.

5-YEAR PLAYER PROGRESSION

First Name	Last Name	Position	'07 Overall	'08 Overall	'09 Overall	'10 Overall	'11 Overall
Tom	Brady	QB	98	98	99	99	99
Richard	Seymour	DE	97	97	98	99	99
Randy	Moss	WR	94	93	93	91	91
Laurence	Maroney	HB	87	89	90	91	91
Brandon	Meriweather	FS	77	82	82	81	82

FRANCHISE MODE STRATEGY

The Patriots have great talent at middle linebacker, but Mike Vrable, Teddy Bruschi, and Junior Seau are all getting older. Look to draft at least one middle linebacker with speed in the first two rounds for the future.

Key Franchise Info

Team Salary: $96.7M
Cap Room: $12.3M
Key Rival:
• Miami Dolphins
NFL Icons: Tom Brady
Philosophy:
• Offense: West Coast
• Defense: Contain Passing
Prestige: Very High
Team Needs:
• Offensive Line
• Defensive Line
Highest Paid Players:
• Tom Brady
• Adalius Thomas
Up and Coming Players:
• Brandon Meriweather
• James Sanders

TEAM STRATEGY

ROSTER AND PACKAGE TIPS — KEY PLAYER SUBSTITUTIONS

• **Position:** FB
• **Substitution:** Kyle Brady
• **When:** Global
• **Advantage:** TE Kyle Brady has an overall rating of 87 at FB, 4 points higher than Heath Evans. Brady is also a better blocker and should pave the road as a lead blocker.

• **Position:** TE
• **Substitution:** David Thomas
• **When:** Global
• **Advantage:** Thomas's SPD rating of 78 will allow him to stretch the defense along the seams in two TE sets, and is a better receiver than Kyle Brady.

• **Position:** RT
• **Substitution:** Stephen Neal
• **When:** Global
• **Advantage:** Neal has an 80 OVR rating when lined up as an RT. He's also a better all around blocker than current starter Nick Kaczur. If you make this substitution, move Kaczur to RG.

• **Position:** SS
• **Substitution:** Brandon Meriweather
• **When:** Global
• **Advantage:** Meriweather's SPD rating of 90 will add extra speed to the secondary when calling plays from the Quarter Normal and Quarter 3 Deep formations.

NEW ENGLAND PATRIOTS / **OFFENSE**

TEAM STRATEGY

OFFENSIVE **STAR PLAYER** #12

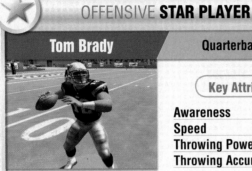

Tom Brady	Quarterback (QB)

Key Attributes

Awareness	98
Speed	60
Throwing Power	92
Throwing Accuracy	96

When you look up the word "leader" in the dictionary, don't be surprised if you see a picture of **Tom Brady**. Not only is this man a leader on the field, but when he wants to help the team in free agency, he gets management to rework his contract. So when the Patriots are destroying defense this season, look no further than Brady for having a part in bringing Donté Stallworth and Randy Moss to the team.

Player Weapons: Franchise QB / Accurate QB, Smart QB

RECOMMENDED OFFENSIVE **AUDIBLE PACKAGES**

I Form-Big	Singleback-Empty 4WR	Singleback-Empty 5WR	Shotgun-Empty Trey Stack	Shotgun-5WR
HB Slam	TE Angle Post	Cross Ups	Middle Corner Post	Deep Post

OFFENSIVE **PLAYCOUNTS**

Quick Pass:	7	Screen Pass:	12	Pinch:	14
Standard Pass:	78	Hail Mary:	1	Counter:	19
Shotgun Pass:	48	Inside Handoff:	30	Draw:	16
Play Action Pass:	52	Outside Handoff:	17		

TEAM **TRIVIA**

New England Patriots Facts

Turn the page for the answers.

❶ Before becoming the New England Patriots, what was the team's first name?

❷ In what season did the Patriots make their first Super Bowl appearance?

❸ What year were the Patriots instated into the AFL?

OFFENSIVE **FORMATIONS**

Singleback	Strong I
Big	Normal
Big Twin WR	Jumbo
Twin TE	**Weak I**
Big 3TE	Normal
Normal Slot	Twin Te
Tight Slots	**Shotgun**
4WR Spread	Normal
Empty 4WR	Slot Strong TE Flip
Empty 5WR	4WR
I Form	Twin TE Trips
Normal	5WR
Twin TE	Empty Trey Stack
Big	

OFFENSIVE **STRENGTH CHART**

- ○: OVR less than 80
- ◐: OVR between 80-89
- ●: OVR 90 or greater
- ○: Player Weapons

2-Back Set

WR #18 | OL #72 | OL #70 | OL #67 | OL #61 | OL #77 | OL #84 | WR #11
QB #12
FB #44
HB #39

3-Receiver Set

WR #18 | OL #72 | OL #70 | OL #67 | OL #61 | OL #77 | OL #84
WR #83 | QB #12 | WR #11
HB #39

OFFENSIVE **ROSTER LIST** Current / Next Gen

Pos.	#	First Name	Last Name	Overall	Player Weapons
C	67	Dan	Koppen	88	Pass Blocker
C	64	Gene	Mruczkowski	65	
FB	44	Heath	Evans	83	
HB	39	Laurence	Maroney	87	Power Back / Power Back, Stiff Arm BC
HB	34	Sammy	Morris	79	
HB	33	Kevin	Faulk	79	Elusive Back
K	3	Stephen	Gostkowski	80	
LG	70	Logan	Mankins	88	
LG	71	Russ	Hochstein	80	
LT	72	Matt	Light	90	Pass Blocker
LT	65	Wesley	Britt	70	
QB	12	Tom	Brady	98	Franchise Quarterback / Accurate QB, Smart QB
QB	16	Matt	Cassel	75	
RG	61	Stephen	Neal	87	
RG	74	Billy	Yates	65	
RT	77	Nick	Kaczur	79	
RT	68	Ryan	O'Callaghan	74	
TE	84	Benjamin	Watson	88	
TE	88	Kyle	Brady	81	
TE	86	David	Thomas	75	
WR	11	Randy	Moss	94	Deep Threat / Spectacular Catch, Speed
WR	18	Donte	Stallworth	86	Deep Threat / Speed
WR	87	Reche	Caldwell	82	
WR	83	Wes	Welker	82	Possession Receiver
WR	10	Jabar	Gaffney	79	
WR	15	Kelley	Washington	78	Deep Threat
WR	17	Chad	Jackson	77	

Shotgun-Twin TE Trips
Moss Option

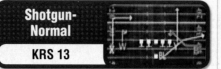

Shotgun-Normal
KRS 13

Shotgun-5WR
WR Drag

Tom Brady is the best QB in football. Demonstrated here is his greatness in the shotgun.

Tom Brady does not play favorites, all of his receivers work hard to get open because they know that he will get the ball to them if they're open.

Brady doesn't have a weakness in his game; he is an solid competitor and doesn't show any outward flaws. We've noticed he is a fan of the 5WR set.

The Moss Option is designed to get Moss the ball, but at the same time, this play gives Brady the whole field to work with.

The KRS 13 is a play designed with auto motion and it is a play that is used to have Moss as a decoy to gte other route open.

The 5WR, WR Drag is a play that is de-signed to attack the defense at multiple levels across the middle of the field.

Being a smart QB is understanding what the defense should expect. Brady knows that with Moss open in the left flat, the defense is focused there first.

The auto motion by Moss led the corner back inside, and when the ball was hiked, Brady immediately saw the void in the flat.

As the play develops, Brady is scanning the field and is amazed at how wide open the defense has left the middle of the field.

Instead of taking Moss on the play, he fires a completion to the tight end cross-ing the middle.

Brady sits back and watches as the run-ner advances the ball farther up field for a first down.

He hits the inside slot receiver Gaff-ney on the drag route as it nears the sideline.

TEAM STRATEGY

185

NEW ENGLAND PATRIOTS / DEFENSE

DEFENSIVE STAR PLAYER #93

Richard Seymour — Defensive End (RE)

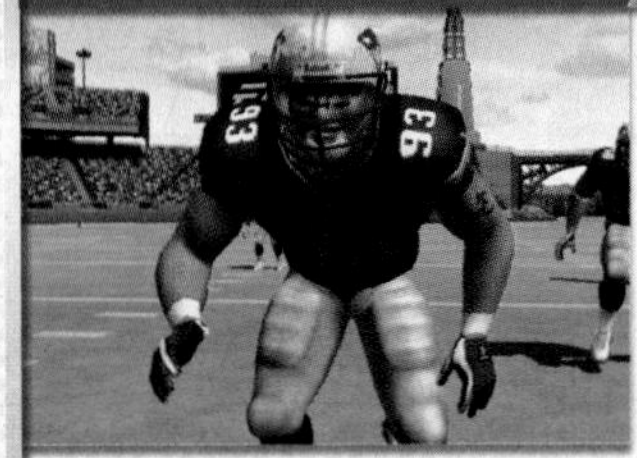

Key Attributes

Awareness	91
Speed	71
Strength	92
Tackle	88

The Patriots have one of the best defensive ends in all of football. **Seymour** makes it possible for the Patriots to be a dominating force on defense, helping them set a franchise record for points allowed in 2006. Even though the team is not big on personal stats, Seymour commands the defensive line and forces opposing offenses to double and triple team him. He will continue to be the reason why the Pats have arguably the best defensive line in football.

Player Weapons: Force of Nature/Power Move D-Lineman

DEFENSIVE STRENGTH CHART

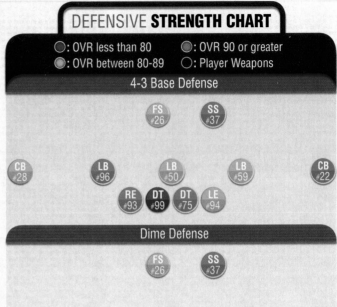

●: OVR less than 80 ●: OVR 90 or greater
●: OVR between 80-89 ○: Player Weapons

4-3 Base Defense

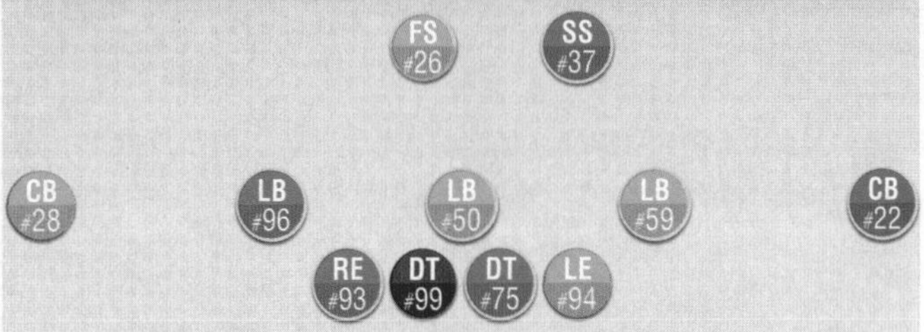
FS #26
SS #37
CB #28
LB #96
LB #50
LB #59
CB #22
RE #93
DT #99
DT #75
LE #94

Dime Defense

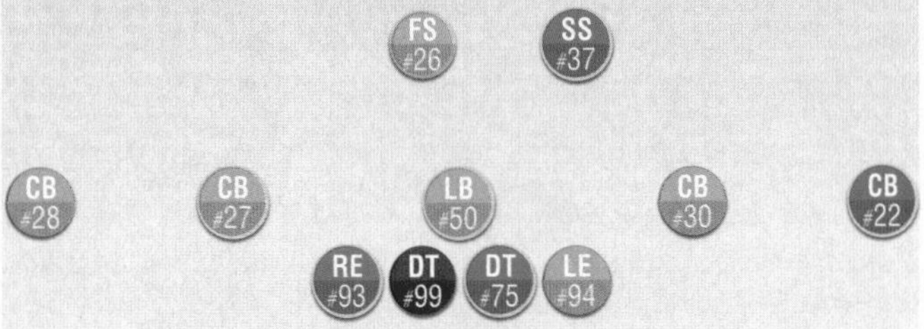
FS #26
SS #37
CB #28
CB #27
LB #50
CB #30
CB #22
RE #93
DT #99
DT #75
LE #94

RECOMMENDED DEFENSIVE AUDIBLE PACKAGES

3-4-Normal	3-4-Normal	3-4-Over	3-4-Solid	3-4-Under
Cover 1 Robber	2 Deep MLB Spy	Pats Fire 3	Clamp Swap Razor	Scalp Silver Fire

DEFENSIVE PLAYCOUNTS

Man Coverage:	47	Cover 3 Zone:	25	Combo Blitz:	19
Man Zone:	37	Deep Zone:	19	Goal Line:	15
Combo Coverage:	9	Man Blitz:	50	Special Teams:	12
Cover 2 Zone:	26	Zone Blitz:	55		

TEAM TRIVIA

New England Patriots Facts

Answers:

1. Boston Patriots
2. 1985
2. 1960

DEFENSIVE FORMATIONS

3-4	Nickel
3-4-Normal	Nickel-1-5-5
3-4-Over	Nickel-1-5-5 Prowl
3-4-Under	Nickel-2-4-5
3-4-Solid	**Quarter**
Dime	Quarter-3 Deep
Dime-3-2-6	Quarter-Normal
Dime-Normal	

DEFENSIVE ROSTER LIST

Current/Next Gen

Pos.	#	First Name	Last Name	Overall	Player Weapons
CB	22	Asante	Samuel	95	Shutdown Corner/Press Coverage, Smart, Shutdown Corner
CB	28	Tory	James	85	
CB	27	Ellis	Hobbs	84	Quick Corner
CB	30	Chad	Scott	81	
CB	21	Randall	Gay	79	
CB	23	Willie	Andrews	71	
DT	75	Vince	Wilfork	92	Run Stopper/Power Move D-Lineman
DT	99	Mike	Wright	71	
DT	90	Le Kevin	Smith	69	
FS	26	Eugene	Wilson	87	Coverage Safety
FS	38	Brandon	Meriweather	82	
LE	94	Ty	Warren	89	
LE	95	Kareem	Brown	70	
LOLB	59	Rosevelt	Colvin	88	Playmaker
LOLB	58	Pierre	Woods	69	
MLB	50	Mike	Vrabel	89	Heavy Hitter
MLB	54	Tedy	Bruschi	87	Smart Linebacker
MLB	55	Junior	Seau	84	Smart Linebacker
MLB	53	Larry	Izzo	74	
P	8	Josh	Miller	87	
RE	93	Richard	Seymour	97	Force of Nature/Power Move D-Lineman
RE	97	Jarvis	Green	84	
ROLB	96	Adalius	Thomas	95	Defensive Enforcer/Finesse Move D-Lineman
ROLB	52	Eric	Alexander	75	
SS	37	Rodney	Harrison	92	Strong Safety/Big Hitter, Brick Wall Defender, Smart Safety
SS	36	James	Sanders	75	

DEFENSE / **KEY DEFENSIVE PLAYS**

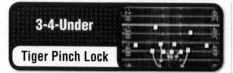

3-4-Under
Tiger Pinch Lock

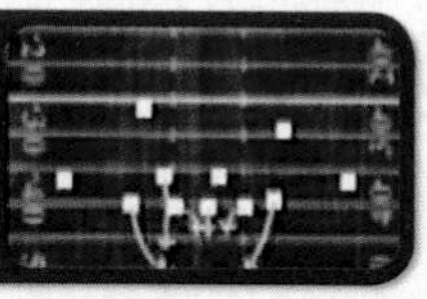

Richard Seymour is dominant force at defensive end. People feel the Patriots are a plug and play team, but Seymour does make the defense better.

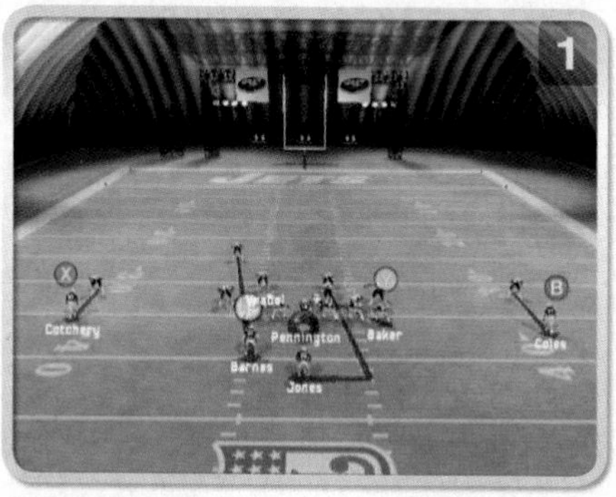

This is a defense that uses Seymour in a line stunt to help free him and get him on the inside shoulder, and moving upfield on an offensive lineman.

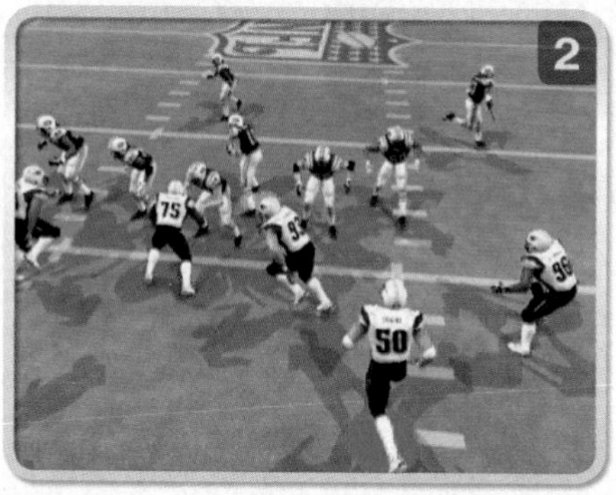

When the offense hikes the ball, Seymour has made his move inside and has really already gained a step on the offensive linemen. Bad news for the offense.

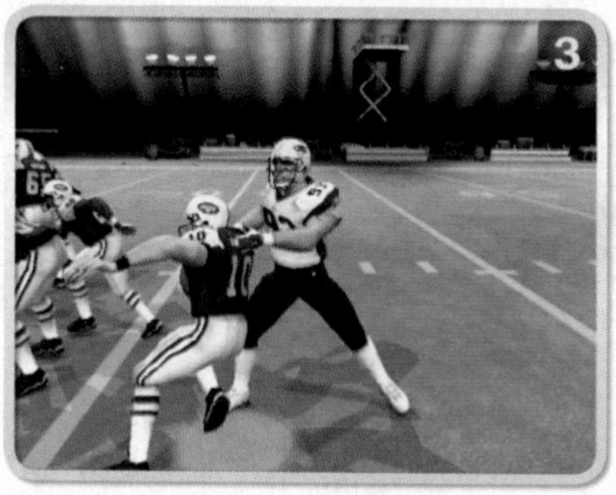

Once Seymour has a step on any offensive lineman, then the quarterback needs to run for his life.

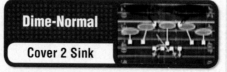

Dime-Normal
Cover 2 Sink

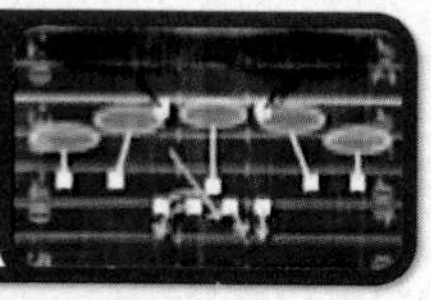

Richard Seymour is the Patriots best defensive lineman, so they will stunt him and rush him to provide him with opportunities to exploit the offense.

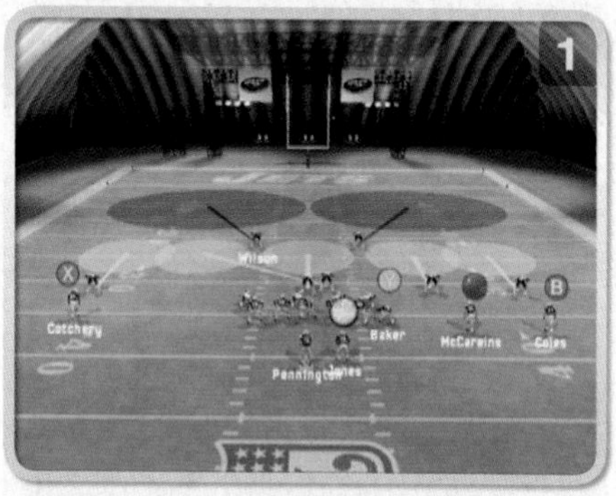

This is a line stunting defense that allows the Patriots' defense the chance to take advantage of Richard Seymour's pass rushing ability.

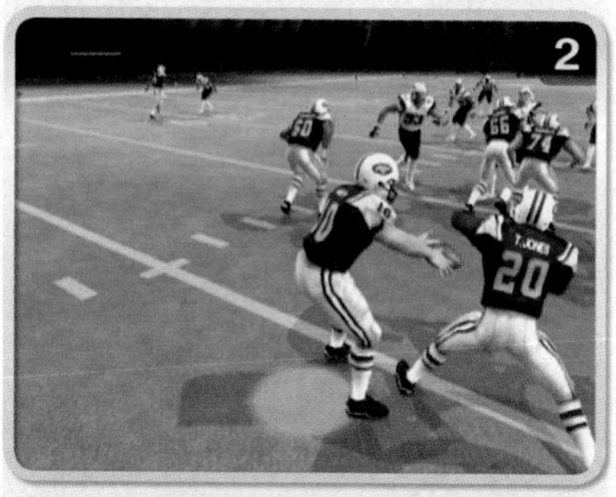

When the play begins, Seymour gets a clean jump off the snap and sees that the offense wants to run the ball.

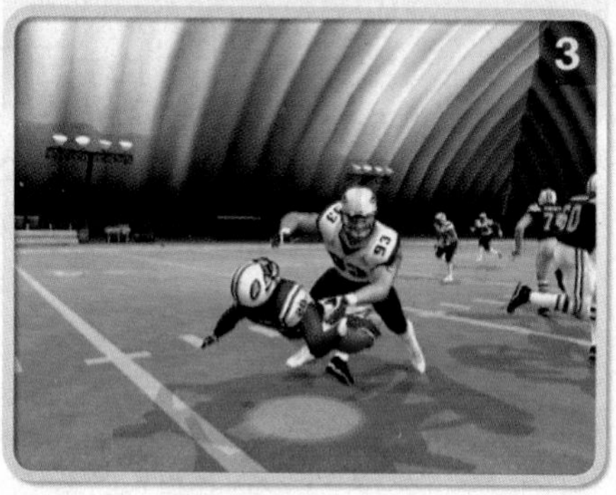

Seymour got a great jump on the line stunt and was in perfect position to make a devastating play.

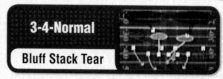

3-4-Normal
Bluff Stack Tear

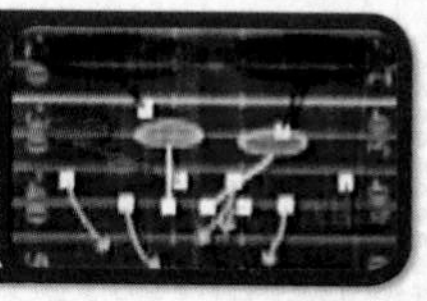

This defense is designed as a zone blitz. It ask Richard Seymour and the nose tackle to drop back in underneath coverage.

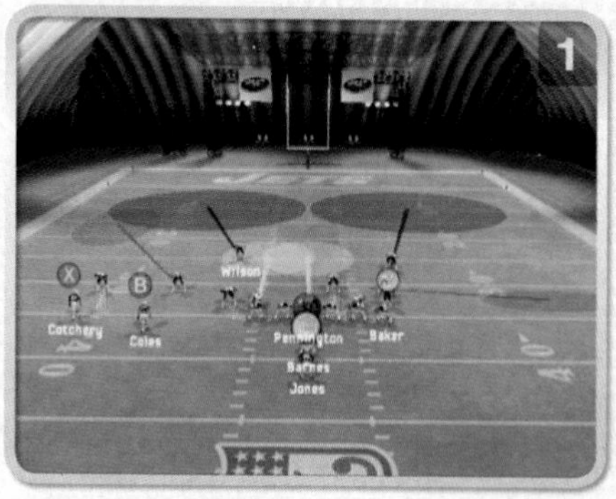

This defense is designed as a zone blitz. It asks Richard Seymour and the nose tackle to drop back in underneath coverage.

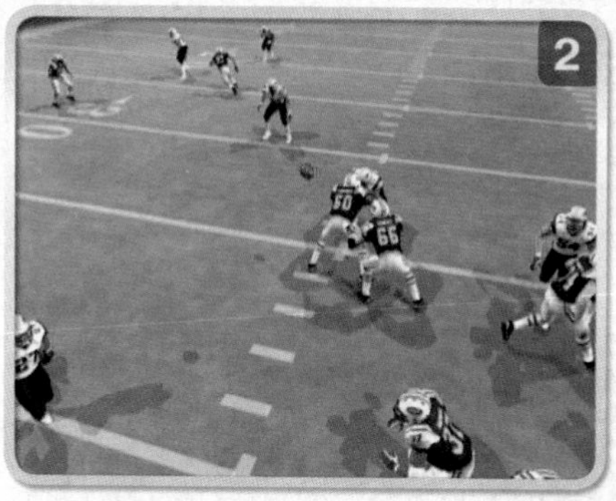

The offense sees an opening and will try to get the ball to the receiver. Already, the receiver looks to be frozen because Seymour is in the area.

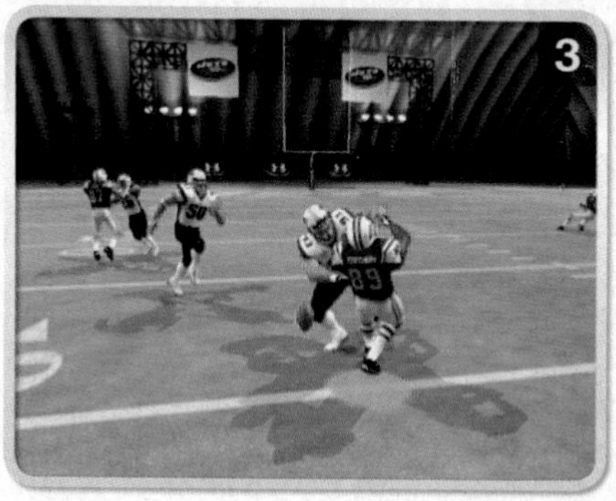

When the ball arrives, so does Seymour and it is not a pretty sight.

OAKLAND RAIDERS

Division: AFC West | **Stadium:** McAfee Coliseum | **Type:** Open | **Capacity:** 63,132 | **Surface:** Grass

2006 STANDINGS

Wins	Losses	Ties	PF	PA	Home	Road	vs. AFC	vs. NFC	vs. Div
7	9	0	300	311	4-4	3-5	5-7	?-?	3-3

TEAM OVERVIEW

Since their Super Bowl appearance in the '02 season, the Raiders have been on a downhill tear. Rookie JaMarcus Russell will have the daunting task of trying to put points on the board with a weak offensive line and no legitimate deep threats.

Now that Randy Moss is gone, the Raiders have gone from being a Madden favorite to a forgotten team. There's not much to get excited about here, unless Jerry Porter can get back to form and have an impact.

Defense showed some signs of life last year coming in 3rd overall in yards allowed and first against the pass. The pass rush coming from speedy Derrick Burgess and two solid corners should keep you in games. Now you just have to figure out how to score.

COACHING PROFILE

Lane Kiffin

- **Head Coaching Year:** 1st
- **Experience:** University of Southern California offensive coordinator (2004–2006),

Kiffin was named the 16th head coach in Raiders history on Jan. 22, 2007, becoming the youngest head coach in the NFL. Kiffin joined the USC staff in 2001 as the tight ends coach.

TEAM RANKINGS

Scoring	32nd
Passing Offense	31st
Rushing Offense	29th
Passing Defense	1st
Rushing Defense	25th
Turnovers	32nd

RATINGS HISTORY

Category	'07	'06	'05	'04
Overall	86	81	77	**94**
Offense	88	88	69	**98**
Defense	83	67	**86**	82

Bold = Highest Year

FIVE-YEAR **AVERAGE**

SCOUTING REPORT

STRENGTHS

Description	Maximizing Potential	Tips for Opponents
DE Derrick Burgess has been a disruptive force to opposing quarterbacks over the last two seasons.	Get Burgess matched up with weaker offensive tackles. This will allow him to use his speed.	If Burgess is getting to your QB more often than you like, you will need to leave an extra pass blocker in.
MLB Morrison and SOLB Howard have made a positive impact on the Raiders' pass coverage.	When running any type of Nickel package, make sure you have both Morrison and Howard on the field.	Try using play action with the fullback leaking out of the backfield. Look for the fullback in the flat.
The Raiders' secondary was vastly improved in '05.	Asomugha is a solid lock-down corner.	Look deep' as he is just a bit slow.

WEAKNESSES

Description	Minimizing Risks	Tips for Opponents
RT Robert Gallery hasn't been the anchor on the offensive line that the Raiders thought he would be.	Gallery doesn't have the awareness or pass blocking ability to hold up against the best rushers.	Try overloading Gallery's side with multiple pass rushers. Force the offense to use multiple blockers.
With Moss moving on to New England, the Raiders do not have a legiti number-one receiver.	Just a few years ago, Jerry Porter was the team's go-to receiver. With Moss gone, he takes over again.	With Moss gone, there is no reason not to press the receivers on every down.

OFF-SEASON **UPGRADES**

Type	Round	First Name	Last Name	School / Team	Position	Height	Weight
Free Agent	N/A	Cooper	Carlisle	Denver Broncos	G	6'5"	295
Trade	N/A	Josh	McCown	Detroit Lions	QB	6'4"	213
Trade	N/A	Mike	Williams	Detroit Lions	WR	6'4"	229
Draft	1st	JaMarcus	Russell	Louisiana State	QB	6'6"	263
Draft	2nd	Zach	Miller	Arizona State	TE	6'5"	259

FANTASY **OUTLOOK**

Star Player: LaMont Jordan
Round of Draft: 8th

If you pick Jordan you should consider selecting Dominic Rhodes soon after. Jordan is expected to be the starter, but he will share the load with Rhodes. That means less carries and fewer chances to score.

Star Player: Ronald Curry
Round of Draft: 10th

With Randy Moss gone, Curry is expected to become the Raiders go to receiver. However, he shouldn't be even considered until the later rounds because the quarterback situation is somewhat up in the air.

5-YEAR **PLAYER PROGRESSION**

First Name	Last Name	Position	'07 Overall	'08 Overall	'09 Overall	'10 Overall	'11 Overall
Derrick	Burgess	DE	93	94	96	96	96
Namdi	Asomugha	CB	93	93	95	95	97
Fabian	Washington	CB	89	90	89	90	90
Michael	Huff	S	87	90	90	90	91
JaMarcus	Russell	QB	83	84	84	84	84

FRANCHISE MODE **STRATEGY**

The good news is the Raiders have some talent on the defensive line, so there is no need to draft players on that side of ball. The bad news is, the Raiders need a lot of help on the offensive side.

Key Franchise Info

Team Salary: $89.3M
Cap Room: $19.6M
Key Rival:
• Denver Broncos
NFL Icons: None
Philosophy:
• Offense: West Coast
• Defense: Contain Passing
Prestige: Very Low
Team Needs:
• Receiver
• Offensive Line
Highest Paid Players:
• JaMarcus Russel
• Robert Gallery
Up and Coming Players:
• Zack Miller
• JaMarcus Russell

TEAM STRATEGY

ROSTER AND **PACKAGE TIPS** — KEY PLAYER SUBSTITUTIONS

• **Position:** LG
• **Substitution:** Jake Grove
• **When:** Global
• **Advantage:** Grove's 76 OVR and 83 PBK rating will help solidify the offensive line, especially with the passing game.

• **Position:** C
• **Substitution:** Jeremy Newberry
• **When:** Global
• **Advantage:** Newberry's 84 OVR rating makes him the best lineman on the Raiders roster, making him a key figure in the pass and running game.

• **Position:** RG
• **Substitution:** Cooper Carlisle
• **When:** Global
• **Advantage:** Carlisle's PBK and RBK ratings are higher than Kevin Boothe's, and help make the offensive line as a whole better.

• **Position:** PR
• **Substitution:** Johnnie Lee Higgins
• **When:** Global
• **Advantage:** At 96 OVR as a return man, Higgins is a better fit as a returner than Chris Carr. Plus, his CAR and BTK ratings are better than Carr's.

OAKLAND RAIDERS / **OFFENSE**

OFFENSIVE **STAR PLAYER** #2

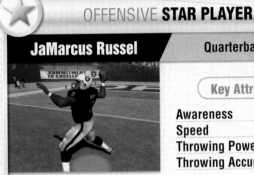

JaMarcus Russel	Quarterback (QB)

Key Attributes

Awareness	58
Speed	74
Throwing Power	99
Throwing Accuracy	82

Normally we wouldn't put a rookie in as a star profile, but when you are the number 1 overall draft pick in the NFL, and viewed as a savior to a once proud franchise, we feel we can make an exception to the rule. **Russell** has all the physical tools to succeed as an NFL Quarterback. He is going to take his lumps while learning on the job during his first season, but he is ready for it.

Player Weapons: Cannon Arm / Cannon Arm QB

RECOMMENDED OFFENSIVE **AUDIBLE PACKAGES**

I Form-Normal	Weak I-Close	Singleback-Big Wing	Singleback-Normal Slot	Singleback-Tight
HB Middle	TE Fade	TE Cross	Slot Cross	Strike Post

OFFENSIVE **PLAYCOUNTS**

Quick Pass:	17	Screen Pass:	11	Pinch:	11
Standard Pass:	95	Hail Mary:	1	Counter:	16
Shotgun Pass:	6	Inside Handoff:	32	Draw:	11
Play Action Pass:	21	Outside Handoff:	11		

TEAM **TRIVIA**

Oakland Raiders Facts

Turn the page for the answers.

1. What was the first year the team was known as the Los Angeles Raiders?

2. In which Super Bowl did John Madden coach the Raiders to a win?

3. Which Raider was named MVP of Super Bowl XVIII?

OFFENSIVE **FORMATIONS**

Singleback	Split Backs
Big	Flex Close
Big Wing	**Strong I**
Twin TE	Normal
Normal Slot	Twin WR
Slot Strong	**Weak I**
Offset Strong	Normal
Trips Bunch	Close
Tight	Twin WR
Empty 4WR	Tight Twins
I Form	Twin TE
Normal	**Shotgun**
Twin WR	2RB 3WR
3WR	
Twin TE	

OFFENSIVE **STRENGTH CHART**

○: OVR less than 80   ◉: OVR 90 or greater
◑: OVR between 80-89   ○: Player Weapons

2-Back Set

WR #8   OL #65   OL #79   OL #60   OL #66   OL #74   OL #85   WR #84
QB #2
FB #36
HB #34

3-Receiver Set

WR #8   OL #65   OL #79   OL #60   OL #66   OL #74   OL #85   WR #84
WR #80   QB #2   WR #84
HB #34

OFFENSIVE **ROSTER LIST** Current / Next Gen

Pos.	#	First Name	Last Name	Overall	Player Weapons
C	60	Jeremy	Newberry	84	
C	64	Jake	Grove	81	
FB	36	Justin	Griffith	91	
FB	32	Zack	Crockett	86	
HB	34	LaMont	Jordan	86	
HB	33	Dominic	Rhodes	83	Elusive Back
HB	25	Justin	Fargas	79	Speed Back
HB	43	Michael	Bush	79	
K	11	Sebastian	Janikowski	84	Big Foot Kicker
LG	79	Paul	McQuistan	73	
LG	69	Ben	Claxton	67	
LT	65	Barry	Sims	81	
LT	75	Mario	Henderson	69	
QB	2	JaMarcus	Russell	82	Cannon Arm / Cannon Arm QB
QB	12	Josh	McCown	79	
QB	16	Andrew	Walter	75	
RG	66	Cooper	Carlisle	82	
RG	67	Kevin	Boothe	73	
RT	76	Robert	Gallery	77	
RT	74	Cornell	Green	77	
TE	45	Zach	Miller	76	
TE	85	John	Madsen	76	
TE	86	Randal	Williams	72	
WR	84	Jerry	Porter	82	Deep Threat
WR	8	Travis	Taylor	80	
WR	89	Ronald	Curry	79	
WR	80	Doug	Gabriel	79	
WR	15	Johnnie Lee	Higgins	75	

TEAM STRATEGY

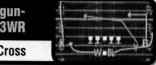

Singleback-Big
Raider Fade

Singleback-Big
Wing PA Boot Lt

Shotgun-2RB 3WR
Slot Cross

JaMarcus Russell has the best pure arm in the game, even as a rookie.

As a rookie, Russell should find some success in running plays that get him out of the pocket and keep him moving.

Russell displays a knack for fitting the ball into tight spots. Plays such as this display his ability to move with the passing route and thread the needle.

JaMarcus Russell has a long journey ahead of him, as he takes over the reins as quarterback for the Oakland Raiders.

The Singleback-Big Wing PA Boot Lt has Russell sell the run fake and then roll out to the left side.

Raiders' coaches will have to call passing plays that allow Russell to move out of the pocket, as well as move with receiver routes.

As he drops back in the pocket, he spots a one-on-one match up.

While on the left side, he finds his tight end on the intermediate crossing route down the field for a nice gain.

The Shotgun-2RB 3WR Slot Cross sends the slot receiver on the crossing route to the left. Russell can move with this route.

Use Russell's arm and throw the ball out in front of wide receiver Jerry Porter; let him go chase the ball for the big catch.

Use this play action play to keep the defense off-balance.

Once the receiver is clear, Russell can make the pass to slot receiver Taylor to move the chains.

TEAM STRATEGY

OAKLAND RAIDERS / **DEFENSE**

DEFENSIVE **STAR PLAYER** #56

Derrick Burgess — Defensive End (RE)

Key Attributes

Awareness	85
Speed	82
Strength	75
Tackle	79

Burgess doesn't get press as one of the top pass rushers at defensive end like some of the other high profile players do. If you look at his sack totals over the last two seasons, he has registered a total of **27**. That ranks him among the top sack artists in the NFL. He plays with a non-stop motor and never takes a play off. He has the speed to get around most offensive tackles and go after the quarterback.

Player Weapons: Force of Nature / Finesse Move D-Lineman

DEFENSIVE **STRENGTH CHART**

- ●: OVR less than 80
- ●: OVR between 80-89
- ●: OVR 90 or greater
- ○: Player Weapons

4-3 Base Defense

FS #30, SS #24
CB #27, LB #53, LB #52, LB #54, CB #21
RE #56, DT #90, DT #99, LE #93

Dime Defense

FS #30, SS #24
CB #27, CB #22, LB #52, CB #35, CB #21
RE #56, DT #90, DT #99, LE #93

RECOMMENDED DEFENSIVE **AUDIBLE PACKAGES**

4-3-Normal	4-3-Under	4-3-Under	Dime-Flat	Nickel-3-3-5
Mid Rush	Edge Sting	Zone Blitz	Zone Man X	Man QB Spy

DEFENSIVE **PLAYCOUNTS**

Man Coverage:	41	Cover 3 Zone:	23	Combo Blitz:	23
Man Zone:	37	Deep Zone:	22	Goal Line:	15
Combo Coverage:	12	Man Blitz:	49	Special Teams:	12
Cover 2 Zone:	14	Zone Blitz:	57		

TEAM **TRIVIA**

Oaklnad Raiders Facts
Answers:

1. 1982
2. Super Bowl XI
3. Marcus Allen

DEFENSIVE **FORMATIONS**

4-3	Nickel
4-3-Normal	Nickel-3-3-5
4-3-Over	Nickel-Normal
4-3-Under	Nickel-Strong

Dime	Quarter
Dime-Normal	Quarter-3 Deep
Dime-Flat	Quarter-Normal

DEFENSIVE **ROSTER LIST** Current / Next Gen

Pos.	#	First Name	Last Name	Overall	Player Weapons
CB	21	Nnamdi	Asomugha	93	Containment Corner / Shutdown Corner
CB	27	Fabian	Washington	89	Quick Corner / Speed
CB	22	Duane	Starks	78	
CB	35	N/A	N/A	76	
CB	26	Stanford	Routt	75	Quick Corner / Speed
CB	23	Chris	Carr	66	
DT	99	Warren	Sapp	89	Finesse Move D-Lineman
DT	90	Terdell	Sands	82	
DT	77	Anttaj	Hawthorne	69	
FS	30	Stuart	Schweigert	86	Coverage Safety
FS	40	Jarrod	Cooper	74	
LE	93	Tommy	Kelly	83	
LE	91	Tyler	Brayton	81	
LOLB	54	Sam	Williams	81	
LOLB	57	Ricky	Brown	61	
MLB	52	Kirk	Morrison	88	Brick Wall Defender
MLB	55	Robert	Thomas	75	
P	9	Shane	Lechler	98	Big Foot Kicker
RE	56	Derrick	Burgess	93	Force of Nature / Finesse Move D-Lineman
RE	96	Quentin	Moses	77	
ROLB	53	Thomas	Howard	85	
ROLB	50	Isaiah	Ekejiuba	67	
SS	24	Michael	Huff	87	Coverage Safety
SS	29	Darnell	Bing	72	
SS	39	Eric	Frampton	67	

DEFENSE / **KEY DEFENSIVE PLAYS**

4-3-Normal	**4-3-Under**	**Nickel-Normal**
Zip Shoot Gut	**Bonzai Blitz**	**Velcro 9**

Derrick has uncanny instincts and plays like he belongs on the field. This displays his instincts to jump passes in the intermediate area.

Burgess has a nonstop motor, good speed, and a quick first step off the edge.

Burgess has developed into an elite pass rusher and big playmaker in all facets of the game.

The 4-3-Normal Zip Shoot Gut allows Derrick Burgess to show his talent as a pass defender as he drops into the hook curl area.

The Bonzai Blitz is a very high-risk/high reward call. It is an eight man pass rush that leaves only three players in coverage.

Burgess can also be used in multiple ways in the Nickel Package. He can be used to rush the passer or can be dropped into coverage.

On the snap, rather than rushing the passer, Burgess drops out into coverage and mirrors the receiver closest to his area.

Burgess gets loose on this play when we shift the defensive line to the left. With a left line shift, he lines up outside of the offensive tackle.

This play drops him into the curl/hook zone area. This is especially good against three wide receiver sets with a slot receiver to his side.

He will sit on the crossing routes, curl routes, and many of the intermediate in routes.

On the snap, he gets a free rush at the QB. Most will try to escape him, but will end up running into someone else. His speed off the edge makes that possible

He has leaping ability and is a ball magnet. Use this play as a change of pace.

ST. LOUIS RAMS

| Division: NFC West | Stadium: Edward Jones Dome | Type: Dome | Capacity: 66,000 | Surface: Turf |

COACHING PROFILE

Scott Linehan

- **Head Coaching Year:** 2nd
- **Experience:** Miami Dolphins offensive coordinator (2005), Minnesota Vikings offensive coordinator (2002-2004).

Linehan was named the 22nd head coach in franchise history by Owner/Chairman Georgia Frontiere on January 19, 2006.

TEAM RANKINGS

Scoring	10th
Passing Offense	4th
Rushing Offense	17th
Passing Defense	8th
Rushing Defense	31st
Turnovers	2nd

RATINGS HISTORY

Category	'07	'06	'05	'04
Overall	87	82	86	**88**
Offense	89	90	90	**98**
Defense	**84**	73	75	75

Bold = Highest Year

87
FIVE-YEAR
AVERAGE

TEAM STRATEGY

2006 STANDINGS

Wins	Losses	Ties	PF	PA	Home	Road	vs. AFC	vs. NFC	vs. Div
8	8	0	367	381	4-4	3-5	2-2	6-6	2-4

TEAM OVERVIEW

The Rams offense is a far cry from the Greatest Show on Turf days of Mike Martz. However, after experimenting with a safety-first, they have put their foot on the gas a bit with great results. Bulger has toned down his game by being careful with the ball, yet set career highs in yards and TD passes.

Steven Jackson was a complete beast in both running and receiving the ball. The Rams all still have plenty of assets at receiver with Torry Holt, Drew Bennett, and Isaac Bruce.

The Rams were terrible against the run last year. They must get better for this team to have a chance at being successful. With only two 90+ rated players on the team, Madden users might struggle on defense.

SCOUTING REPORT

STRENGTHS

Description	Maximizing Potential	Tips for Opponents
Steven Jackson had a huge season not only running the ball, but also catching it out the backfield	Get Jackson involved in the offense early and often. He has the ability to consistently move the chains.	Because the Rams' passing attack is so effective, you really can't load the box up to stop Jackson.
Marc Bulger has steadily become one the best QBs in the game by consistently putting up big numbers.	With Bulger's high accuracy rating, chances are the ball is going to be thrown on target.	It's best to play zone and wait for Bulger to make a mistake by not reading the coverage correctly.
The Rams have one of the top WR trios in the game.	The defense won't be able to double team very often.	If you feel inclined to call double coverage, cover Holt.

WEAKNESSES

Description	Minimizing Risks	Tips for Opponents
Outside of sack artist Leonard Little, the Rams have no other defensive linemen you should fear.	Because the Rams lack any pass rusher except for Little, try moving him around based on your team.	Wherever Little lines up, he must be accounted for at all times. His has a knack for beating his man.
The Rams' linebackers had a hard time defending the run and pass in '06 due to blown coverages.	Any time a passing situation arrives, make sure to call nickel and dime packages to get Short off the field.	If for some reason Short is left on the field, look to attack him first with a speedy tight end.

OFF-SEASON UPGRADES

Type	Round	First Name	Last Name	School/Team	Position	Height	Weight
Free Agent	N/A	Drew	Bennett	Tennessee Titans	WR	6'5"	206
Trade	N/A	Dante	Hall	Kansas City Chiefs	WR	5'8"	187
Free Agent	N/A	Randy	McMichael	Miami Dolphins	TE	6'3"	255
Draft	1st	Adam	Carriker	Nebraska	DE	6'6"	292
Draft	2nd	Brian	Leonard	Rutgers	FB	6'1"	238

FANTASY OUTLOOK

Star Player: Steven Jackson
Round of Draft: 1st

After last season's breakout season, Jackson must now be considered one of the top five fantasy running backs come draft day. Last season, he rushed for over 1,500 yards and caught 90 balls thrown his way.

Star Player: Torry Holt
Round of Draft: 3rd

Holt should be the first receiver off the draft board after posting 1,188 receiving yards during the 2006-07 season. In addition, he managed to get into the end zone 10 times and had 93 receptions.

5-YEAR PLAYER PROGRESSION

First Name	Last Name	Position	'07 Overall	'08 Overall	'09 Overall	'10 Overall	'11 Overall
Torry	Holt	WR	98	98	99	95	92
Orlando	Pace	LT	96	98	97	96	96
Steven	Jackson	HB	96	99	99	99	99
Marc	Bulger	QB	95	98	98	96	96
Adam	Carriker	DT	81	84	87	92	92

FRANCHISE MODE STRATEGY

The Rams have a wealth of talent on the offensive of the ball, so no need to focus your attention there. Instead concentrate on drafting defensive backs, in particularly both safety spots.

Key Franchise Info

Team Salary: $85.6M
Cap Room: $23.4M
Key Rival:
• San Francisco 49ers
NFL Icons: Tory Holt
Philosophy:
• Offense: West Coast
• Defense: Contain Passing
Prestige: Medium
Team Needs:
• Defensive Line
• Defensive Back
Highest Paid Players:
• Orlando Pace
• Torry Holt
Up and Coming Players:
• Joe Klopfenstein
• Adam Carriker

TEAM STRATEGY

ROSTER AND PACKAGE TIPS   KEY PLAYER SUBSTITUTIONS

• **Position:** FB
• **Substitution:** Joe Klopfenstein
• **When:** Global
• **Advantage:** Klopfenstein's 79 CTH rating as an FB should help out the passing game, as he comes out of the backfield giving QB Marc Bulger another asset.

• **Position:** RG
• **Substitution:** Todd Steussie
• **When:** Global
• **Advantage:** With a better OVR rating at 81, Steussie is a better fit at RG than Richie Incognito and should help improve the running game more.

• **Position:** DT
• **Substitution:** Adam Carriker
• **When:** Global
• **Advantage:** Carriker's STR rating of 90 and SPD rating of 76 should help him shed off blockers and break plays up in the backfield easier than La'Roi Glover.

• **Position:** 3RDB
• **Substitution:** Brian Leonard
• **When:** Global
• **Advantage:** Leonard has a better CTH rating at 82 than Stephen Jackson, which should allow him to help out more in the passing game.

ST. LOUIS RAMS / OFFENSE

OFFENSIVE STAR PLAYER #10

Marc Bulger	Quarterback (QB)

Key Attributes

Awareness	94
Speed	57
Throwing Power	91
Throwing Accuracy	97

Over the last few seasons, Bulger has quietly become one of the top single callers in the game. Last season, he posted All Pro numbers by throwing for **4,301** yards and **24** touchdowns. He is good at utilizing the talent around him by spreading the ball to multiple receivers. He threw just **eight** interceptions last season, which is a career low. With another season in the Rams' multiple scheme, he will look to improve on his passing numbers.

Player Weapons: Franchise QB / Accurate QB, Smart QB

OFFENSIVE STRENGTH CHART

○: OVR less than 80   ◑: OVR 90 or greater
◐: OVR between 80-89   ○: Player Weapons

2-Back Set

WR #83 | OL #76 | OL #75 | OL #67 | OL #68 | OL #70 | TE #84 | WR #81
OL #10
OL #44
OL #39

3-Receiver Set

WR #83 | OL #76 | OL #75 | OL #67 | OL #68 | OL #70 | TE #84 | WR #81
WR #80
OL #10
OL #39

RECOMMENDED OFFENSIVE AUDIBLE PACKAGES

I-Form-Twin WR	Strong I-Normal	Split Backs-Normal	Singleback-Empty 5WR	Shotgun-Empty Trips
WR Corner	Counter Weak	HB Blast	Smash Fork	Strong Overload

OFFENSIVE PLAYCOUNTS

Quick Pass:	15	Screen Pass:	9	Pinch:	13
Standard Pass:	88	Hail Mary:	1	Counter:	19
Shotgun Pass:	47	Inside Handoff:	29	Draw:	11
Play Action Pass:	23	Outside Handoff:	12		

TEAM TRIVIA

St. Lous Rams Facts

Turn the page for the answers.

❶ Before moving to St. Louis, where was the Rams franchise located?

❷ Who did the Rams play in Super Bowl XIV?

❸ What nickname was given to the famous defensive line of the 70's?

OFFENSIVE FORMATIONS

Singleback	Split Backs
Singleback	Normal
Big	3WR
Twin TE	**Strong I**
Normal	Normal
Normal Slot	3WR
Trips Bunch	**Weak I**
Base Flex	3WR
4WR Spread	Big
Trips WR	H Twins
Empty 5WR	**Shotgun**
I Form	2RB 3WR
Normal	Normal Slot
Twin WR	4WR
Twin TE	Empty Trips

OFFENSIVE ROSTER LIST   Current / Next Gen

Pos.	#	First Name	Last Name	Overall	Player Weapons
C	67	Andy	McCollum	83	
C	65	Brett	Romberg	67	
FB	44	Madison	Hedgecock	73	
HB	39	Steven	Jackson	96	Feature Back / Power Back, Stiff Arm BC
HB	36	Brian	Leonard	78	
HB	22	Travis	Minor	75	
K	14	Jeff	Wilkins	95	Accurate Kicker
LG	75	Claude	Terrell	82	
LG	66	Mark	Setterstrom	71	
LT	76	Orlando	Pace	96	Road Blocker / Power Blocker
LT	79	Todd	Steussie	82	
QB	10	Marc	Bulger	95	Franchise Quarterback / Accurate, QB, Smart QB
QB	12	Gus	Frerotte	78	
QB	11	Ryan	Fitzpatrick	69	
RG	68	Richie	Incognito	79	
RG	72	Adam	Goldberg	78	
RT	70	Alex	Barron	87	
RT	77	Drew	Strojny	67	
TE	84	Randy	McMichael	89	
TE	82	Joe	Klopfenstein	79	
TE	86	Dominique	Byrd	73	
TE	87	Aaron	Walker	68	
WR	81	Torry	Holt	98	Go-To Guy / Quick Receiver, Hands Spectacular Catch Receiver,
WR	80	Isaac	Bruce	87	Possession Receiver / Quick Receiver, Hands
WR	83	Drew	Bennett	87	Spectacular Catch Receiver
WR	18	Dante	Hall	74	Deep Threat
WR	89	Dane	Looker	72	

Weak I-3WR

WR Streak

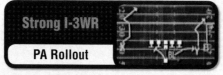

Strong I-3WR

PA Rollout

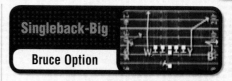

Singleback-Big

Bruce Option

Quarterback Mark Bulger shows great anticipation and touch on his passes.

Bulger also does a great job of getting out of the pocket and leading his wide receivers.

Again, Bulger anticipates the routes of his receivers.

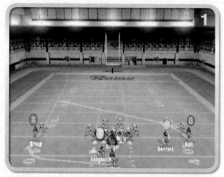

This play allows quarterback Marc Bulger to show that he still has the arm strength to play in the league.

The PA Rollout pass is a very effective strategy to use with Bulger because of the presence of running back Stephen Jackson.

This is a play designed for Issac Bruce to choose which route he wants to run based on the defensive coverage.

As Bulger drops back to pass, he spots wide receiver Issac Bruce in a one-on-one match up with the corner back.

Bulger sells the run. Most defenses will bite on this because of Jackson's efficiency and effectiveness of rushing the football.

There is another route on this play in which Bulger is adept at throwing, and that is the seam route to the tight end.

He gets the ball up and out in front of his receiver, allowing Bruce to run under the ball for a big play for the offense.

As Marc pulls up the pass, he finds a wide open Tory Holt on the deep out route. He delivers a crisp spiral to move the chains.

Bulger can get the ball up high enough for his tight ends to come down with the catch behind the LBs.

TEAM STRATEGY

ST. LOUIS RAMS / **DEFENSE**

TEAM STRATEGY

DEFENSIVE **STAR PLAYER** #91

Leonard Little	Defensive End (LE)

Key Attributes	
Awareness	81
Speed	85
Strength	75
Tackle	76

After having a few down years, **Little** posted his highest sack total since 2003. He got to the quarterback **13** times last season. Little uses his instincts that allow him to be able to anticipate the snap count and blow by slower offensive tackles. He has sideline-to-sideline range that allows him to chase down ball carriers from behind. He has a flair for forcing fumbles, and caused **seven** last season.

Player Weapons: Pass Rusher / Finesse Move D-Lineman

RECOMMENDED DEFENSIVE **AUDIBLE PACKAGES**

4-3-Normal	4-3-Over	Dime-Flat	Nickel-Normal	Quarters-Normal
Storm Blitz	SS Blitz	1 Man DB Strike	Quarters Safe	QB Trap

DEFENSIVE **PLAYCOUNTS**

Man Coverage:	41	Cover 3 Zone:	23	Combo Blitz:	23
Man Zone:	37	Deep Zone:	22	Goal Line:	15
Combo Coverage:	12	Man Blitz:	49	Special Teams:	12
Cover 2 Zone:	14	Zone Blitz:	57		

TEAM **TRIVIA**

St. Louis Rams Facts
Answers:

1. Los Angeles
2. The Pittsburgh Steelers
3. The Fearsome Foursome

DEFENSIVE **FORMATIONS**

4-3	Nickel
4-3-Normal	Nickel-Normal
4-3-Over	Nickel-Strong
4-3-Under	**Quarter**
Dime	Quarter-3 Deep
Dime-3-2-6	Quarter-Normal
Dime-Normal	
Dime-Flat	

DEFENSIVE **STRENGTH CHART**

- ○ : OVR less than 80
- ● : OVR 90 or greater
- ● : OVR between 80-89
- ○ : Player Weapons

DEFENSIVE **ROSTER LIST** Current / Next Gen

Pos.	#	First Name	Last Name	Overall	Player Weapons
CB	34	Fakhir	Brown	84	
CB	26	Tye	Hill	83	Quick Corner / Speed
CB	27	Lenny	Walls	78	
CB	37	Jonathan	Wade	77	
CB	24	Ronald	Bartell	75	
CB	31	Mike	Rumph	75	
CB	23	Jerametrius	Butler	75	
DT	97	La›Roi	Glover	87	
DT	73	Jimmy	Kennedy	82	
DT	90	Adam	Carriker	81	
DT	99	Claude	Wroten	73	
FS	21	O.J.	Atogwe	83	
FS	42	Jerome	Carter	75	
LE	91	Leonard	Little	94	Pass Rusher / Finesse Move D-Lineman
LE	92	Eric	Moore	76	
LOLB	54	Brandon	Chillar	80	
LOLB	56	Raonall	Smith	72	
MLB	51	Will	Witherspoon	91	Defensive Enforcer
MLB	52	Chris	Draft	83	
P	5	Donnie	Jones	79	
RE	96	James	Hall	84	
RE	94	Victor	Adeyanju	78	
ROLB	50	Pisa	Tinoisamoa	87	Playmaker
ROLB	57	Jon	Alston	73	
SS	25	Corey	Chavous	85	
SS	35	Todd	Johnson	76	Big Hitter

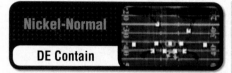

Nickel-Normal
DE Contain

Dime-Flat
QB Contain

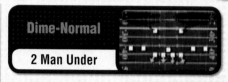

Dime-Normal
2 Man Under

Leonard Little does a good job of taking containment pass rushing lanes to keep quarterbacks in the pocket.

This play allows Little to be disruptive in zone coverage versus the short and intermediate passing attack.

Little has the speed to turn the corner and make plays in the offensive backfield.

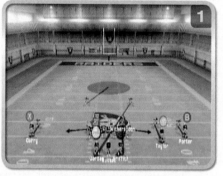

Leonard Little has been at this game for awhile now, chasing down and containing quarterbacks.

Because of his speed, Little can drop back into coverage. The Dime-Flat QB Contain shows off Little's zone coverage skills.

This play allows you to take control of Little, while having safe coverage in the secondary.

This play showcases Little's containment ability. On the snap, Little will take a wide rush and wait on the edge.

Little drops back into coverage on this play and allows the nickel and dime corner backs to contain the QB.

Spread the defensive line. On the snap of the ball, beat the tackle off the line and get a wide rush to create a pocket around the quarterback.

Once the QB makes his move, Little closes in and finishes him off. Little's speed is an asset against the fast quarterbacks in the game.

He sits in the middle and guards all intermediate routes that wide receivers run across his zone area.

Now work back off of the block of the tackle toward the QB. If you can, take the QB down for a loss.

TEAM STRATEGY

199

BALTIMORE RAVENS

Division: AFC North | **Stadium:** M&T Bank Stadium | **Type:** Open | **Capacity:** 68,915 | **Surface:** Grass

2006 STANDINGS

Wins	Losses	Ties	PF	PA	Home	Road	vs. AFC	vs. NFC	vs. Div
13	3	0	353	201	7-1	6-2	10-2	3-1	5-1

TEAM OVERVIEW

The Ravens crushed the opposition in the AFC North last season, but failed to get the job done in the playoffs. Ravens' users rejoiced with the signing of McNair last year, as they finally have a signal caller that can get the job done when they take the stick into their own hands.

Jamal Lewis is gone, but Willis McGahee comes rolling into town as his replacement.

He'll provide more speed and the ability to break a game wide open with a long-range strike.

Defensively, the Ravens are top notch with five 90+ overall defenders on their team. Ed Reed is the key cog in this defense, providing great deep pass coverage and destroying receivers that come over the middle into his space.

COACHING PROFILE

Brian Billick

- **Head Coaching Year:** 9th
- **Experience:** Minnesota Vikings offensive coordinator (1992-1998).

Billick became the head coach of the Baltimore Ravens on January 19, 1999. He led the Ravens to a Super Bowl victory over the New Giants in 2000. Since becoming the head coach of the Ravens, his overall record is 75 wins and 53 losses.

TEAM RANKINGS

Scoring	12th
Passing Offense	11th
Rushing Offense	25th
Passing Defense	6th
Rushing Defense	2nd
Turnovers	1st

RATINGS HISTORY

Category	'07	'06	'05	'04
Overall	88	88	90	75
Offense	89	68	76	70
Defense	90	90	90	75

Bold = Highest Year

86
FIVE-YEAR
AVERAGE

SCOUTING REPORT

STRENGTHS

Description	Maximizing Potential	Tips for Opponents
Over the years, the Ravens had to rely on their defense to win games. They have more options now.	Use a balanced attack when running the Ravens' offense. McNair has solid attributes as a passer.	Now that the Ravens have balance, you have to mix coverages if you plan on beating them.
The Ravens' linebackers have been the heart and soul of the team's defense for years.	Send MLB Ray Lewis in on run blitz schemes to blow up the opposing offensive rushing attack.	Your best bet for success is to run misdirection plays and hope that Lewis gets out of position.
SS Ed Reed can stuff the run and pass.	The Raven's strong CBs let you move Reed up close.	Be aware at all times of where Reed lines up on the field.

WEAKNESSES

Description	Minimizing Risks	Tips for Opponents
The Ravens have lost some talent this past year along the offensive line, so running may not be easy.	Even though the Ravens' line is not as strong, LT Jonathan Ogden remains one of the best in the game.	Load up the left side of the offensive line with extra run defenders, and force the ball carrier to run right.
If we had to pick on one defender in pass coverage, it would be strong safety Dawan Landry.	Manually take control of him to minimize him biting on the play action fake.	If your opponent does not take control of Landry, use play action passes.

TEAM STRATEGY

OFF-SEASON **UPGRADES**

Type	Round	First Name	Last Name	School/Team	Position	Height	Weight
Trade	N/A	Willis	McGahee	Buffalo Bills	RB	6'0"	228
Draft	1st	Ben	Grubbs	Auburn	G	6'3'	314
Draft	3rd	Yamon	Figurs	Kansas State	WR	5'11"	174
Draft	3rd	Marshal	Yanda	Iowa	G	6'4"	304
Draft	4th	Antwan	Barnes	Florida International	LB	6'1"	240

FANTASY **OUTLOOK**

⭐ **Star Player:** Willis McGahee
Round of Draft: 1st

Last season McGahee failed to reach the 1,100-yard mark for first time since the 2004. A change of scenery in Baltimore may be all he needs to get back on track.

⭐ **Star Player:** Todd Heap
Round of Draft: 6th

Heap may not be a top echelon tight end when it comes to fantasy draft day, but once the big three (Gates, Shockey, and Gonzalez) have been selected, he should be next to come off the board.

5-YEAR **PLAYER PROGRESSION**

First Name	Last Name	Position	'07 Overall	'08 Overall	'09 Overall	'10 Overall	'11 Overall
Ed	Reed	S	99	99	99	99	99
Chris	McAlister	CB	97	94	93	89	87
Ray	Lewis	LB	96	95	95	93	92
Willis	McGahee	HB	92	98	99	99	96
Marshal	Yanda	G	74	74	74	75	75

FRANCHISE MODE **STRATEGY**

The Ravens skill positions on offense are in good shape. However, you might consider drafting a quarterback to eventually replace Steve McNair. Also look for a right guard and right tackle in the early rounds of the draft.

Key Franchise Info

Team Salary: $89.9M
Cap Room: $19.1M
Key Rival:
• Pittsburgh Steelers
NFL Icons: Ray Lewis
Philosophy:
• Offense: Ball Control
• Defense: Force the PAss
Prestige: Medium
Team Needs:
• QB (future)
• Offensive Line
Highest Paid Players:
• Jonathan Ogden
• Ray Lewis
Up and Coming Players:
• Le'Ron McClain
• Marshal Yanda

ROSTER AND **PACKAGE TIPS** — KEY PLAYER SUBSTITUTIONS

• **Position:** FB
• **Substitution:** LéRon McClain
• **When:** Passing Situations
• **Advantage:** McClain's CTH rating of 77 allows him to be a threat coming out of the backfield, adding another dimension to the offensive scheme.

• **Position:** RT
• **Substitution:** Ben Grubbs
• **When:** Global
• **Advantage:** Grubbs's RBK and STR ratings should help the running game by adding a big, strong lineman to run behind who can clear holes.

• **Position:** LOLB
• **Substitution:** Dan Cody
• **When:** Global
• **Advantage:** With an 80 SPD rating, Cody can cover receivers in both man and zone coverage better than current starter Jarret Johnson.

• **Position:** PR
• **Substitution:** Yamon Figurs
• **When:** Global
• **Advantage:** Figurs's 97 speed rating makes him one of the fastest players in the league, and should help him make a splash in the return game.

TEAM STRATEGY

BALTIMORE RAVENS / OFFENSE

TEAM STRATEGY

OFFENSIVE STAR PLAYER #9

Steve McNair	Quarterback (QB)

Key Attributes

Awareness	85
Speed	68
Throwing Power	86
Throwing Accuracy	84

McNair did not have one of his best seasons as far as passing stats go, but he did provide the Ravens with the stability they have lacked at quarterback since their Super Bowl team. McNair will be in his second season under center in the Ravens offensive system. With a solid cast of receivers and upgrades in the running the game, McNair's passing numbers should see an improvement this season.

Player Weapon: None

RECOMMENDED OFFENSIVE AUDIBLE PACKAGES

I Form-Twin TE	Strong I-Twin TE	Singleback-Big	Singleback-Slot Strong	Singleback-Trips Bunch
HB Balst	HB Stretch	TE Corner	Double Hook	Drive

OFFENSIVE PLAYCOUNTS

Quick Pass:	10	Screen Pass:	15	Pinch:	15
Standard Pass:	74	Hail Mary:	1	Counter:	22
Shotgun Pass:	30	Inside Handoff:	36	Draw:	18
Play Action Pass:	45	Outside Handoff:	18		

TEAM TRIVIA

Baltimore Ravens Facts

Turn the page for the answers.

1. What team did the Baltimore Ravens originate from?

2. How many Super Bowls have the Ravens won?

3. What former Ravens running back rushed for 2,066 yards in 2003?

OFFENSIVE FORMATIONS

Singleback	Strong I
Big	Normal
Twin TE	Twin WR
Big 3TE	Twin TE
Normal	**Weak I**
Slot Strong	Normal
Trips TE	Twin TE
Trips Bunch	**Shotgun**
4WR	Normal
I Form	Slot Strong
Normal	4WR
Tight Twins	Trips
3WR	
Twin TE	

OFFENSIVE STRENGTH CHART

○: OVR less than 80	○: OVR 90 or greater
●: OVR between 80-89	○: Player Weapons

2-Back Set

WR #85 OL #75 OL #66 OL #62 OL #68 WR #78 TE #86 WR #89
QB #9
FB #37
HB #23

3-Receiver Set

WR #85 OL #75 OL #66 OL #62 OL #68 WR #78 TE #86
WR #87 QB #9 WR #89
HB #23

OFFENSIVE ROSTER LIST Current / Next Gen

Pos.	#	First Name	Last Name	Overall	Player Weapons
C	62	Mike	Flynn	86	
C	63	Ike	Ndukwe	72	
FB	37	LéRon	McClain	83	
FB	33	Justin	Green	82	
HB	23	Willis	McGahee	92	Stiff Arm BC
HB	38	Mike	Anderson	81	Power Back
HB	32	Musa	Smith	81	
HB	34	Cory	Ross	73	
K	3	Matt	Stover	95	Accurate Kicker
LG	66	Ben	Grubbs	82	
LG	60	Jason	Brown	78	
LT	75	Jonathan	Ogden	96	Road Blocker / Crushing Run Blocker, Pass Blocker
LT	73	Marshal	Yanda	74	
QB	9	Steve	McNair	85	
QB	7	Kyle	Boller	79	
QB	11	Troy	Smith	70	
RG	68	Keydrick	Vincent	80	
RG	65	Chris	Chester	75	
RT	78	Adam	Terry	74	
RT	69	Brian	Rimpf	67	
TE	86	Todd	Heap	94	Possesion, Quick Receiver
TE	83	Daniel	Wilcox	78	
WR	89	Mark	Clayton	87	
WR	85	Derrick	Mason	86	Possession Receiver / Hands, Possession Receiver,
WR	87	Demetrius	Williams	80	
WR	84	Clarence	Moore	74	
WR	16	Yamon	Figurs	71	Speed
WR	81	Devard	Darling	70	

Singleback-Normal
Mason Option

Quarterback Steve McNair is the NFL tough man champion as he works his way through pain. He still throws a great short pass.

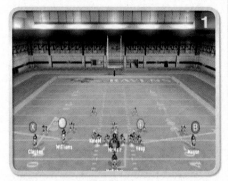

The Singleback-Normal Mason option has an option call for Mason. Mark Clayton, who lines up opposite of Mason, will run the comeback route.

McNair does not have the arm strength that he once possessed, so throwing the short and intermediate passes keeps his efficiency and passer rating up.

Look to McNair to hit the short routes such as the comeback route that Clayton runs here as a way to keep the ball moving.

Singleback-Slot Strong
Double Hook

McNair also has a nice spiral for the short and intermediate middle area.

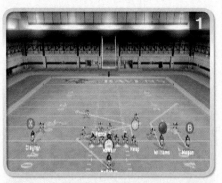

This contains the comeback route that McNair has great success in throwing. But it also contains an angle route for the running back.

Throwing to the half back over the short and intermediate middle area of the field is a good use of what's left of McNair's arm.

Hit running back Willis McGahee out of the backfield on the angle route, and then let him work for yards after the catch.

Shotgun-Slot Strong
Sprint Rt Option

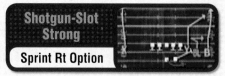

McNair is strong, confident, and can still break tackles if he needs to when running the football out of the pocket.

While it can be used to pass, we like to use it in the red zone to highlight McNair's running ability

Running back Willis McGahee will pull and block the edge on this play. This is a great play to use in the red zone with McNair.

He is still a threat in the red zone, and will tuck it down and run the ball across the goal line for a score.

TEAM STRATEGY

BALTIMORE RAVENS / DEFENSE

DEFENSIVE **STAR PLAYER**   #52

Ray Lewis — Linebacker (MLB)

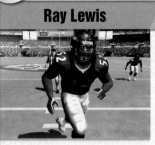

Key Attributes

Awareness	94
Speed	83
Strength	78
Tackle	94

Some will say that **Lewis** is past his prime, and that might be somewhat true. However, he still has enough gas in the tank to put fear into the opposing offense's run and pass game. Last season, Lewis tied the team in solo tackles with **83**. In addition, he managed five sacks and three interceptions. Expect another Pro Bowl type of season from Lewis with his aggressive style and his uncanny knack for making impact plays.

Player Weapons: Defensive Enforcer / Big Hitter, Brick Wall Defender, Smart Linebacker

RECOMMENDED DEFENSIVE **AUDIBLE PACKAGES**

3-4-Normal	3-4-Normal	3-4-Solid	4-3-Normal	46-Normal
2 Man Clamp	OLB Dogs Fire	2 Rambo Swap	Zone Blitz	Mike Blitz

DEFENSIVE **PLAYCOUNTS**

Man Coverage:	41	Cover 3 Zone:	21	Combo Blitz:	23
Man Zone:	28	Deep Zone:	22	Goal Line:	15
Combo Coverage:	13	Man Blitz:	49	Special Teams:	12
Cover 2 Zone:	15	Zone Blitz:	57		

TEAM **TRIVIA**

Baltimore Ravens Facts

Answers:

1 Cleveland Browns

2 One

3 Jamal Lewis

DEFENSIVE **FORMATIONS**

3-4	Nickel
3-4-Normal	Nickel-1-1-5 Prowl
3-4-Over	Nickel-3-3-5
3-4-Under	Nickel-Normal
4-3	**Quarter**
4-3-Normal	Quarter-3 Deep
4-3-Under	Quarter-Normal
46	
46-Bear	
46-Normal	
Dime	
Dime-3-2-6	
Dime-Flat	
Dime-Normal	

DEFENSIVE **STRENGTH CHART**

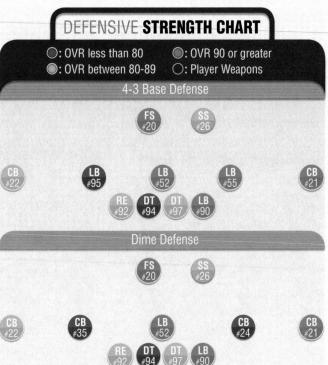

◯: OVR less than 80   ●: OVR 90 or greater
◑: OVR between 80-89   ○: Player Weapons

4-3 Base Defense

FS #20   SS #26

CB #22   LB #95   LB #52   LB #55   CB #21

RE #92   DT #94   DT #97   LB #90

Dime Defense

FS #20   SS #26

CB #22   CB #35   LB #52   CB #24   CB #21

RE #92   DT #94   DT #97   LB #90

DEFENSIVE **ROSTER LIST**   Current / Next Gen

Pos.	#	First Name	Last Name	Overall	Player Weapons
CB	21	Chris	McAlister	97	Shutdown Corner / Press Coverage, Smart, Shutdown Corner
CB	22	Samari	Rolle	87	Containment Corner
CB	24	David	Pittman	71	
CB	35	Corey	Ivy	71	
CB	36	B.J.	Sams	66	
CB	29	Derrick	Martin	66	
DT	97	Kelly	Gregg	89	Run Stopper
DT	94	Justin	Bannan	77	
DT	71	Andrew	Powell	67	
FS	20	Ed	Reed	99	Hit Man / Smart Safety
FS	28	Jamaine	Winborne	73	
LE	90	Trevor	Pryce	93	Run Stopper / Power Move D-Lineman
LE	93	Dwan	Edwards	70	
LOLB	55	Terrell	Suggs	91	Playmaker / Finesse Move D-Lineman
LOLB	56	Gary	Stills	64	
MLB	52	Ray	Lewis	96	Defensive Enforcer / Big Hitter, Brick Wall Defender, Smart Linebacker,
MLB	57	Bart	Scott	91	Heavy Hitter / Big Hitter
MLB	51	Mike	Smith	68	
MLB	50	Antwan	Barnes	65	
P	4	Sam	Koch	77	
RE	92	Haloti	Ngata	87	Run Stopper / Power Move D-Lineman
RE	98	Attiyah	Ellison	71	
ROLB	95	Jarret	Johnson	76	
ROLB	53	Dan	Cody	75	
SS	26	Dawan	Landry	87	
SS	42	Gerome	Sapp	75	

4-3-Normal
2 Man Under

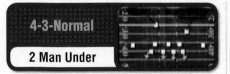

Lewis is aggressive and plays with a high level of intensity.

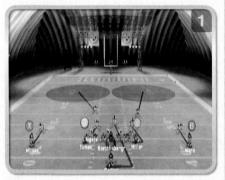

Ray Lewis is no longer the youngster that he was, but he's not to be overlooked or downplayed.

The 4-3-Normal 2 Man Under allows Lewis to easily diagnose plays out of the Singleback formation.

Against straight ahead run plays, Lewis hits the hole like no other and still has the power to stack up running backs and send them packing.

4-3-Under
Tango Swap 3

Lewis is an explosive hitter and tackler that plays with a mean streak.

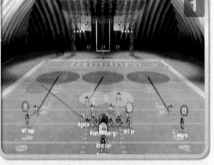

Lewis has improved an area of his game every year. This past year, he had the most sacks he has had in a season.

The play allows you to display Lewis's pass rush ability on a right side pass rush stunt with him and outside line-backer Jarrett Johnson.

Once around the pass protection and into the backfield, the quarterback has a whole lot of pain to deal with as Lewis will not let up on tackling.

3-4-Normal
2 Man Clamp

Lewis carries the Ravens' defense, and helps everyone around him by making big plays all over the field.

The 3-4-Normal 2 Man Clamp drops the inside linebacker into the curl area to defend intermediate passing routes.

Lewis has improved his coverage ability over the years and has snagged down quite a few interceptions.

Lewis's instincts would make one think he plays offense as he anticipates and jumps passing routes.

TEAM STRATEGY

205

WASHINGTON REDSKINS

Division: NFC East | **Stadium:** FedEX Field® | **Type:** Open | **Capacity:** 91,665 | **Surface:** Grass

2006 STANDINGS

Wins	Losses	Ties	PF	PA	Home	Road	vs. AFC	vs. NFC	vs. Div
5	11	0	307	376	3-5	2-6	2-2	3-9	1-5

TEAM OVERVIEW

The Redskins mortgaged the future in 2006 by dumping draft picks and grabbing at high-priced free agents. Injuries killed them, but with a healthy lineup in *Madden NFL 07*, they can be a lot of fun to play with. Jason Campbell will lead the show and provide good mobility at QB.

HB Clinton Portis still has plenty of game. He has big play speed, agility, and can run over blockers. Santana Moss provides a deep threat with Brandon Lloyd playing the role of possession receiver.

The heart and soul of the Redskins' defense is safety Sean Taylor. Taylor had a poor campaign in 2006, but should be back to his old ways this season. London Fletcher provides veteran leadership to what should be a solid defense.

SCOUTING REPORT

STRENGTHS

Description	Maximizing Potential	Tips for Opponents
The Redskins can have a potent passing attack with up-and-coming starter Jason Campbell.	The duo of Antwaan Randle El and Santana Moss can give defensive coordinators headaches if Campbell gets going.	Defend the deep ball because Randle El and Moss have the speed to get downfield and make big plays.
Clinton Portis is a work-horse. Give him the ball and keep pressure off your young quarterback.	If you have proven that you can get the ball to your receivers, then pound the rock with Portis.	Do not fall into the trap of bringing eight in the box. Do not get beat deep with Moss and Randle El.
Top draft choice LaRon Landry will help in the secondary.	The Redskins can play more man-to-man defense now.	With Landry playing safety, it will be harder to beat the Redskins deep.

WEAKNESSES

Description	Minimizing Risks	Tips for Opponents
Jason Campbell is still a work in progress. A blitzing defense will give him problems.	With the likes of a Clinton Portis, call play action pass plays to keep the defense honest.	If the Redskins get in third and long situations, go ahead and blitz to rattle Jason Campbell.
The Redskins do not have a star at the defensive end position. Opposing QBs can find the open receiver.	Allow your MLB to blitz up the middle if your defensive ends cannot bring a lot of pressure on the QB.	A lackluster pass rush will make it easy for opposing teams to move the ball up and down the field.

TEAM STRATEGY

COACHING PROFILE

Joe Gibbs

- **Head Coaching Year:** 16th
- **Experience:** Redskins head coach 1981-1992. Won three Superbowls in that time.

Joe Gibbs returned to coah the Redskins on January 7, 2004. Since coming back the team is 21-27. Gibbs is still the most successful coach in Redskins history.

TEAM RANKINGS

Scoring	20th
Passing Offense	21st
Rushing Offense	4th
Passing Defense	23rd
Rushing Defense	27th
Turnovers	23rd

RATINGS HISTORY

Category	'07	'06	'05	'04
Overall	**89**	77	82	75
Offense	**90**	69	90	67
Defense	**88**	87	86	82

Bold = Highest Year

82
FIVE-YEAR AVERAGE

OFF-SEASON **UPGRADES**

Type	Round	First Name	Last Name	School/Team	Position	Height	Weight
Released	N/A	Derrick	Blaylock	New York Jets	RB	5'10"	210
Free Agent	N/A	David	Macklin	Arizona Cardinals	LB	5'10"	206
Released	N/A	Fred	Smoot	Minnesota Vikings	CB	5'11"	174
Draft	1st	LaRon	Landry	LSU	S	6'1"	213
Draft	5th	Dallas	Sartz	USC	LB	6'5"	237

FANTASY **OUTLOOK**

Star Player: Clinton Portis
Round of Draft: 1st

If you draft Portis in the first round, you better have a back-up plan, just in case he goes down due to injury. We suggest grabbing teammate LaDell Betts later in the draft as insurance.

Star Player: Chris Cooley
Round of Draft: 9th

Not very flashy, but Cooley gets the job done year after year. Over the last three seasons, he has gotten in the end zone no fewer than six times.

5-YEAR **PLAYER PROGRESSION**

First Name	Last Name	Position	'07 Overall	'08 Overall	'09 Overall	'10 Overall	'11 Overall
Jason	Campbell	QB	81	80	79	77	77
Clinton	Portis	HB	92	93	93	93	92
Santana	Moss	WR	89	90	91	93	93
Sean	Taylor	S	92	91	92	92	91
LaRon	Landry	S	85	83	83	83	84

FRANCHISE MODE **STRATEGY**

The Redskins can use some help at quarterback. Starter Jason Campbell has yet to live up to expectations, and back-up veteran Mark Brunell is past his prime. Another need is a right outside linebacker.

Key Franchise Info

Team Salary: $97.3M
Cap Room: $11.6M
Key Rival:
• Dallas Cowboys
NFL Icons: Clinton Portis
Philosophy:
• Offense: Establish Runs
• Defense: Shut Down Runs
Prestige: Low
Team Needs:
• Quarterback
• Defensive Line
Highest Paid Players:
• Chris Samuels
• Clinton Portis
Up and Coming Players:
• LaRon Landry
• Rocky McIntosh

ROSTER AND **PACKAGE TIPS** — KEY PLAYER SUBSTITUTIONS

Singleback-Big

I Form-Close

Weak I-H Wing TE

4-3-Normal

• **Position:** WR
• **Substitution:** Antwaan Randle El
• **When:** Global
• **Advantage:** Randle El's 93 speed weapon will allow him to stretch defenses and take some of the attention away from Santana Moss.

• **Position:** LG
• **Substitution:** Casey Rabach
• **When:** Global
• **Advantage:** Rabach has an OVR rating of 78, four points higher than the starter Taylor Whitley, and makes for a better fit on the offensive line.

• **Position:** C
• **Substitution:** Ross Tucker
• **When:** Global
• **Advantage:** Tucker's STR rating of 89 will help him clear the road for oncoming tacklers and make huge holes for the running game.

• **Position:** ROLB
• **Substitution:** Lemar Marshall
• **When:** Global
• **Advantage:** Marshall has a better OVR rating at 83 at ROLB than current starter Rocky McIntosh. Plus, his speed will allow him to cover better

WASHINGTON REDSKINS / OFFENSE

TEAM STRATEGY

OFFENSIVE STAR PLAYER #26

Clinton Portis — Halfback (HB)

Key Attributes
Acceleration	95
Agility	94
Break Tackle	88
Speed	94

When healthy, **Clinton Portis** is one the premier running-backs in the NFL. He set a team record for rushing yards in 2005 when he gained **1,516** yards in his first year with the Redskins. Even though Portis was hurt last season and wound up going on injured reserve with six games remaining, he still led the Redskins with rushing touchdowns (**7**). Look for Portis and his to be back in the mix this season.

Player Weapons: Feature Back / Elusive Back

RECOMMENDED OFFENSIVE AUDIBLE PACKAGES

Singleback-Big Jumbo Wing	Singleback-Trips WR	Singleback-4WR Stack	Singleback-Big Twin WR	Shotgun-Wing Trips
Counter H Strg	Slot Middle	Corner Cross	Slot Under	Vertical TE Cross

OFFENSIVE PLAYCOUNTS

Quick Pass:	13	Screen Pass:	7	Pinch:	9
Standard Pass:	96	Hail Mary:	2	Counter:	23
Shotgun Pass:	12	Inside Handoff:	33	Draw:	12
Play Action Pass:	17	Outside Handoff:	13		

TEAM TRIVIA

Washington Redskins Facts
Turn the page for the answers.

1. Which former Redskins quarterback is now the starter in Miami?
2. What was the original name of the Washington Redskins?
3. In 1981, the Redskins hired Joe Gibbs. What team did he come from?

OFFENSIVE FORMATIONS

Singleback	I Form
Big	Close
Big Twin WR	3WR
Twin TE	Twin TE
Twin TE WR	**Split Backs**
Big TE Flip	3WR
Deuce Wing	**Strong I**
Big Jumbo Wing	H Twin TE
Normal TE Flip	**Weak I**
Strg TE Flip	H Wing TE
Trips Bunch	H Twin TE
Stack Doubles WK	**Shotgun**
4WR Stack	Normal Slot
4WR Spread	Wing Trips
Trips WR	

OFFENSIVE STRENGTH CHART

- ○: OVR less than 80
- ◑: OVR between 80-89
- ●: OVR 90 or greater
- ○: Player Weapons

OFFENSIVE ROSTER LIST — Current / Next Gen

Pos.	#	First Name	Last Name	Overall	Player Weapons
C	61	Casey	Rabach	83	
C	68	Ross	Tucker	80	
FB	45	Mike	Sellers	79	
HB	26	Clinton	Portis	92	Feature Back / Elusive Back
HB	46	Ladell	Betts	85	
HB	31	Rock	Cartwright	76	
HB	23	Derrick	Blaylock	74	Speed Back
K	6	Shaun	Suisham	79	
LG	62	Mike	Pucillo	74	
LG	72	Taylor	Whitley	74	
LT	60	Chris	Samuels	93	Road Blocker / Crushing Run Blocker, Pass Blocker
LT	75	Calvin	Armstrong	67	
QB	17	Jason	Campbell	81	
QB	8	Mark	Brunell	79	
QB	15	Todd	Collins	74	
RG	77	Randy	Thomas	94	Pass Blocker / Pass Blocker
RG	63	William	Whitticker	67	
RT	76	Jon	Jansen	91	Road Blocker / Crushing Run Blocker
RT	71	Todd	Wade	80	
TE	47	Chris	Cooley	88	
TE	87	Todd	Yoder	68	
WR	89	Santana	Moss	89	Deep Threat / Speed
WR	82	Antwaan	Randle El	82	
WR	85	Brandon	Lloyd	82	Possession Receiver / Spectacular Catch Receiver
WR	83	James	Thrash	75	

TEAM STRATEGY

Strong I- Twin TE	Singleback- Big Jumbo Wing	I Form-3WR
HB Blast	**TE Motion Cntr**	**HB Blast**

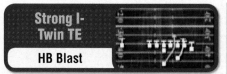

Clinton Portis was thought to be a system back when he carried the ball in Denver, but he has proven otherwise since becoming a Redskin.

When a team has a back with the skill-set that Portis possesses, they need to let him showcase his abilities as often as possible.

Clinton Portis has the speed to run the ball on the outside, but he is very well-equipped to pound out the hard yards between tackles.

The HB Blast is a great running play out of a solid formation that provides blocking for Clinton Portis at multiple levels of the defense.

This play is designed to take advantage of how good Portis is with running stretch-type plays. This counter works the same way.

This play is designed to give Portis the ball and let him follow the FB into the left "B" gap. It is a straight-ahead play, a true tone-setter.

With the ball in his hands, Portis starts out to the right and delivers a stiff arm to the oncoming defender to eliminate him in the play.

Any time the defense sees a wall of blockers in front of Portis, it's not a good thing. Portis can turn this into points with just a few steps.

Even if the defense has called the right play, keep Portis straight toward the hole, and he will make it through every time.

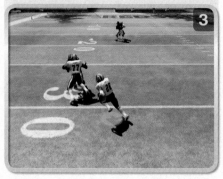

Portis is a mis-match for any defender in the open field. He is to fast, strong and elusive.

Portis is a patient runner and uses the blocks to maximize his rushing yards.

Portis can break up the sideline now that he has made it through the hole.

TEAM STRATEGY

WASHINGTON REDSKINS / DEFENSE

DEFENSIVE STAR PLAYER #21

Sean Taylor Safety (FS)

Key Attributes

Awareness	65
Speed	90
Strength	71
Tackle	84

Safeties hit, and **Sean Taylor** is made from the mold of Ronnie Lott and Steve Atwater. Taylor has great speed and instincts, and you can always find him around the ball. He plays exceptionally well in run support, but his strength is also his weakness, as he can get beat deep because he is looking in the backfield too much. Nonetheless, he is a playmaker, and led the defense with **111** tackles last season.

Player Weapons: Hit Man / Big Hitter

RECOMMENDED OFFENSIVE AUDIBLE PACKAGES

4-3-Normal	4-3-Normal	Nickel-3-3-5	Nickel-Normal	Nickel-Normal
Free Fire	Mid Rush	LB Ram Dogs	9 Velcro	Over Storm Brave

DEFENSIVE PLAYCOUNTS

Man Coverage:	41	Cover 3 Zone:	23	Combo Blitz:	23
Man Zone:	37	Deep Zone:	22	Goal Line:	15
Combo Coverage:	12	Man Blitz:	49	Special Teams:	12
Cover 2 Zone:	14	Zone Blitz:	57		

TEAM TRIVIA

Washington Redskins Facts

Answers:

1. Trent Green
2. The Boston Braves
3. The San Diego Chargers

DEFENSIVE FORMATIONS

4-3	Nickel
4-3-Normal	Nickel-3-3-5
4-3-Over	Nickel-Normal
4-3-Under	Nickel-Strong
Dime	**Quarter**
Dime-3-2-6	Quarter-3 Deep
Dime-Normal	Quarter-Normal

DEFENSIVE STRENGTH CHART

- ○: OVR less than 80
- ◐: OVR between 80-89
- ●: OVR 90 or greater
- ○: Player Weapons

4-3 Base Defense

FS #21 SS #30

CB #22 LB #52 LB #59 LB #53 CB #24

RE #93 DT #64 DT #96 LE #99

Dime Defense

FS #21 SS #30

CB #22 CB #27 LB #59 CB #38 CB #24

RE #93 DT #64 DT #96 LE #99

DEFENSIVE ROSTER LIST Current / Next Gen

Pos.	#	First Name	Last Name	Overall	Player Weapons
CB	24	Shawn	Springs	88	Containment Corner
CB	22	Carlos	Rogers	87	Quick Corner / Press Coverage Corner
CB	27	Fred	Smoot	83	
CB	38	David	Macklin	79	
CB	32	Ade	Jimoh	64	
DT	96	Cornelius	Griffin	89	Run Stopper
DT	64	Kedric	Golston	79	
DT	95	Joe	Salaveá	71	
DT	94	Anthony	Montgomery	67	
DT	73	Ryan	Boschetti	65	
FS	21	Sean	Taylor	92	Hit Man / Big Hitter
FS	20	Pierson	Prioleau	80	
FS	37	Reed	Doughty	69	
LE	99	Andre	Carter	85	
LE	97	Renaldo	Wynn	82	
LOLB	53	Marcus	Washington	93	Defensive Enforcer / Brick Wall Defender
LOLB	50	Khary	Campbell	73	
MLB	59	London	Fletcher	94	Playmaker / Brick Wall Defender, Smart Defender
MLB	98	Lemar	Marshall	83	
P	4	Derrick	Frost	76	
RE	93	Phillip	Daniels	83	
RE	92	Demetric	Evans	73	
ROLB	52	Rocky	McIntosh	77	
ROLB	55	Dallas	Sartz	68	
SS	30	LaRon	Landry	85	Coverage Safety / Big Hitter
SS	23	Omar	Stoutmire	81	
SS	39	Vernon	Fox	75	

4-3-Normal
Buzz Weak

The talk around Sean Taylor is always about how good he is in run support and what an aggressive hitter he is.

The 4-3 Buzz Weak is a 3 deep designed defense. This play asks Sean Taylor to play the deep middle of the field .

When the safety has deep middle responsibility, he will protect against the deepest threat. Taylor is making sure to keep an eye on the tight end.

Taylor elevates to defend the pass in the air. He has good speed and jumping ability.

4-3-Normal
Safety Blitz

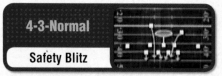

Taylor is such a good hitter and great in run support, it is no surprise to see him being used in the blitz game.

This play is designed to let Sean Taylor and the strong safety come down into the tackle box and add pressure to the offense.

When the offense starts the play, Sean Taylor is already a step away from crossing the line of scrimmage. He is a very aggressive hitter.

Taylor strikes fear in the runningback's mind with a bone crushing hit.

Quarter-Normal
Robber FS Lurk

Taylor is great in pass coverage. It is a shame that he is not used as much this way. He can turn the Redskins' secondary into a lockdown group.

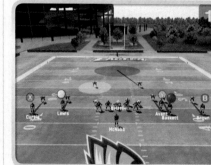

The defense is designed to use Taylor as the robber safety. His assignment is to patrol the underneath middle zone and prevent any completions in this zone.

The play ends early for the offense, as the quarterback thought he saw an opening over the middle, only to have Taylor step in and intercept the ball.

He runs this interception back for a touchdown.

TEAM STRATEGY

211

NEW ORLEANS SAINTS

Division: NFC South | **Stadium:** Superdome | **Type:** Dome | **Capacity:** 72,675 | **Surface:** Turf

COACHING PROFILE

Sean Payton

- **Head Coaching Year:** 2nd
- **Experience:** 20 years in the league. Assistant Dallas head coach 2003-2006

Sean Payton was named NFL Coach of the Year in his rookie year as a head coach. He led the Saints to a 10-6 record and a first round play-off bye. Payton wins everywhere he goes and the Saints' fans have witnessed that first hand.

TEAM RANKINGS

Scoring	5th
Passing Offense	1st
Rushing Offense	19th
Passing Defense	3rd
Rushing Defense	23rd
Turnovers	22nd

RATINGS HISTORY

Category	'07	'06	'05	'04
Overall	86	72	76	78
Offense	87	83	88	87
Defense	84	65	72	65

Bold = Highest Year

80
FIVE-YEAR AVERAGE

2006 STANDINGS

Wins	Losses	Ties	PF	PA	Home	Road	vs. AFC	vs. NFC	vs. Div
10	6	0	413	322	4-4	6-2	1-3	9-3	4-2

TEAM OVERVIEW

The Saints made a amazing comeback from NFC doormat to Division champions. Using Drew Brees to solidify the quarterback position was rewarded by a Pro Bowl performance and league best yardage total from their signal caller. Offense isn't in short supply with the Saints.

The Saints have speed to burn at many positions and they toasted their fair share of defenses last season. Reggie Bush can move all over the field to attack the defense and create mismatches.

The Saints' defense isn't amazing, but it is solid enough to keep players from looking elsewhere for their go-to team. You'll get good pressure off the defensive line from Smith and Grant. Lack of speed at corner is a concern.

SCOUTING REPORT

STRENGTHS

Description	Maximizing Potential	Tips for Opponents
QB Drew Brees proved all his skeptics wrong when he came back to have a Pro Bowl year last year.	Brees led the league last season in yards passing, and was third in passer rating and touchdowns.	Brees has all kinds of assets at his disposal. Your best bet is to mix up your defensive calls.
Reggie Bush and Deuce McAllister combined to make one lethal one-two punch last season.	Both backs can be used in the passing game and the running game. Bush's speed makes him dangerous.	Be weary of down and distance and try to stay one step ahead of your opponent.
Receiver Marques Colston was a sleeper pick last year.	Colston managed to garner 70 receptions in 2006.	Frequently double-team him with a corner and safety.

WEAKNESSES

Description	Minimizing Risks	Tips for Opponents
One of the Saints' only glaring weaknesses is their safeties. Strong safety Jay Bellamy is on the decline.	Bullocks's lack of experience is a hindrance on the entire secondary.	Exploit these two whenever possible and attack them deep with multiple combination routes.
Other than left tackle Jammal Brown, the Saints are fairly weak up front with their offensive line.	Left guard Jon Stinchcomb needs to prove he's worth the money the Saints are paying for him.	With such a mediocre offensive line, you can rely more on your defensive front four to provide a pass rush.

TEAM STRATEGY

Overall Rating **88**
Offense **88**
Defense **86**

OFF-SEASON **UPGRADES**

Type	Round	First Name	Last Name	School/Team	Position	Height	Weight
Free Agent	N/A	Jason	David	Indianapolis Colts	CB	5'8"	180
Free Agent	N/A	Eric	Johnson	San Francisco 49ers	TE	6'3"	256
Free Agent	N/A	Olindo	Mare	Miami Dolphins	K	5'11"	190
Draft	1st	Robert	Meachem	Tennessee	WR	6'2"	214
Draft	3rd	Usama	Young	Kent State	CB	5'11"	196

FANTASY **OUTLOOK**

⭐ **Star Player:** Reggie Bush
Round of Draft: 1st

Bush didn't put up big numbers as a runner, but he did produce jaw-dropping numbers as a receiver out of the backfield and in the slot. If he gets more touches as a ball carrier, watch out.

⭐ **Star Player:** Drew Brees
Round of Draft: 2nd

Brees is another player who doesn't often get talked about as one of the best at his position, despite putting up elite numbers. After Manning is drafted, Brees should go next.

5-YEAR **PLAYER PROGRESSION**

First Name	Last Name	Position	'07 Overall	'08 Overall	'09 Overall	'10 Overall	'11 Overall
Drew	Brees	QB	95	98	98	98	99
Reggie	Bush	HB	89	89	89	92	94
Marques	Colston	WR	88	88	90	90	90
Will	Smith	DE	94	95	95	97	97
Robert	Meachen	WR	82	82	82	82	83

FRANCHISE MODE **STRATEGY**

The Saints are set on offense, so no need to draft there in the first few rounds of the draft. Instead, concentrate on the defensive side of the ball. Both safety positions need to be upgraded, so that's a good place to start.

Key Franchise Info

Team Salary: $78.3M
Cap Room: $30.6M
Key Rival:
• Atlanta Falcons
NFL Icons: None
Philosophy:
• Offense: Establish Runs
• Defense: Shut Down Runs
Prestige: Medium
Team Needs:
• Offensive Line
• Defensive Line
Highest Paid Players:
• Drew Brees
• Deuce McAllister
Up and Coming Players:
• Antonio Pittman
• Robert Meachem

TEAM STRATEGY

ROSTER AND **PACKAGE TIPS**   KEY PLAYER SUBSTITUTIONS

• **Position:** HB
• **Substitution:** Reggie Bush
• **When:** Global
• **Advantage:** Bush is one of the fastest players in the league at 98 SPD. His versatility as a run and pass threat will help to keep the defense honest.

• **Position:** TE
• **Substitution:** Billy Miller
• **When:** Global
• **Advantage:** Miller's SPD rating of 82 allows him to stretch defenses at the seams, providing another asset for QB Drew Brees in this potent offense.

• **Position:** SS
• **Substitution:** Jay Bellamy
• **When:** Defend Run
• **Advantage:** Bellamy's 80 AWR rating will help him react to plays better and quicker than current starter Roman Harper. Plus, he's got a better OVR rating at 82 than Harper.

• **Position:** WR
• **Substitution:** Reggie Bush
• **When:** 4WR Formations
• **Advantage:** Bush's speed is simply amazing. Lining him up at WR can force the defense to focus on him, thus opening up the running game for Deuce McAllister.

NEW ORLEANS SAINTS / OFFENSE

OFFENSIVE STAR PLAYER #9

Drew Brees — Quarterback (QB)

Key Attributes

Awareness	94
Speed	63
Throwing Power	88
Throwing Accuracy	86

In a year when all the news of the off-season was set on Reggie Bush, **Drew Brees** stepped in as the Saints' quarterback and led them to the organization's first ever NFC Championship Game. On the way, Brees gained **4,418** passing yards with **26** touchdown passes. His leadership took the team to an impressive **10-6** record after finishing 3-13 the previous year. He also had an impressive completion percentage, finishing the year at **64.3** percent.

Player Weapons: Precision Passer / Accurate QB, Smart QB

RECOMMENDED OFFENSIVE AUDIBLE PACKAGES

I Form-Normal	Strong I-Normal	Singleback-4WR	Singleback-Empty Trey	Shotgun-5WR Bunch
FB Fake HB Toss	Slant Hook	Smash Post	HI Lo Read	Spacing Switch

OFFENSIVE PLAYCOUNTS

Quick Pass:	23	Screen Pass:	10	Pinch:	13
Standard Pass:	60	Hail Mary:	1	Counter:	16
Shotgun Pass:	43	Inside Handoff:	30	Draw:	9
Play Action Pass:	21	Outside Handoff:	11		

TEAM TRIVIA

New Orleans Saints Facts

Turn the page for the answers:

1. The Saints played their first NFL season in which year?

2. What Saints' head coach gave up all the team's draft picks to draft Ricky Williams?

3. What famous Saint played in the first nationally broadcast primetime college football game?

OFFENSIVE FORMATIONS

Singleback	Full House
Big	Normal Wide
Twin TE	**Strong I**
Twin TE WR	Normal
Normal	Twin WR
Tight Doubles	Twin TE
Slot Strong	**Weak I**
4WR	Normal
Empty Trey	Twin WR
I Form	Twin TE
Normal	**Shotgun**
Big	Normal
Twin TE	Slot Strong
Split Backs	4WR
Normal	Empty 4WR

OFFENSIVE STRENGTH CHART

- ◐ : OVR less than 80
- ● : OVR 90 or greater
- ◑ : OVR between 80-89
- ○ : Player Weapons

2-Back Set

WR #19, OL #70, OL #67, OL #52, OL #73, OL #78, TE #82, QB #9, FB #44, HB #25, WR #12

3-Receiver Set

WR #19, OL #70, OL #67, OL #52, OL #73, OL #78, TE #82, WR #85, QB #9, WR #12, HB #25

OFFENSIVE ROSTER LIST — Current / Next Gen

Pos.	#	First Name	Last Name	Overall	Player Weapons
C	52	Jeff	Faine	84	
C	76	Jonathan	Goodwin	69	
FB	44	Mike	Karney	90	
HB	26	Deuce	McAllister	89	Power Back / Power Back, Stiff Arm BC
HB	25	Reggie	Bush	89	Feature Back / Elusive Back, Hands
HB	24	Antonio	Pittman	78	
HB	27	Aaron	Stecker	73	
K	2	Olindo	Mare	83	
LG	67	Jamar	Nesbit	80	
LG	65	Andy	Alleman	78	
LT	70	Jammal	Brown	92	Pass Blocker / Pass Blocker
LT	64	Zach	Strief	68	
QB	9	Drew	Brees	95	Precision Passer / Accurate QB, Smart QB
QB	10	Jamie	Martin	70	
RG	73	Jahri	Evans	84	
RG	79	Rob	Petitti	79	
RT	78	Jon	Stinchcomb	77	
RT	74	N/A	N/A	68	
TE	82	Eric	Johnson	82	
TE	80	Mark	Campbell	79	
TE	83	Billy	Miller	77	
WR	12	Marques	Colston	88	Possesion Receiver, Spectacular Catch
WR	19	Devery	Henderson	84	Deep Threat / Speed
WR	85	Robert	Meachem	82	Deep Threat
WR	18	Terrance	Copper	75	
WR	81	David	Patten	73	
WR	84	Michael	Lewis	71	

Singleback-Tight Doubles
Slot Corner

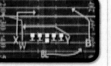

Singleback-Empty Trey
Hi Lo Read

Shotgun-Empty 4WR
Slot Crossers

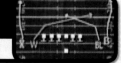

Drew Brees is a very accurate quarterback that puts nice touches on the football. His QB mechanics are top of the line.

Brees has a knack for getting rid of the ball on time and making the correct read on the defender.

Another play that displays Brees's quarterback smarts is the Shotgun-Empty 4WR Slot Crossers.

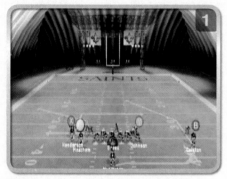

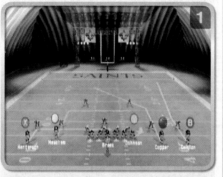

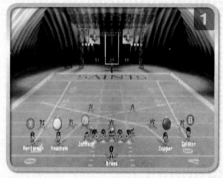

This play highlights the corner route, the deep in route, the drag, and a deep post route. The swing pass to the HB is available against the blitz.

Brees is better able to show off his mechanics with the Singleback-Empty Trey Hi Lo Read. This play calls for a hi/lo read on the middle linebacker.

This play features two crossing routes in the middle as well as two vertical routes on the outside. It is a good play against all coverages.

The Singleback-Tight Doubles Slot Corner shows off Brees's accuracy, touch, and his mechanics. He does not need to hold the ball long on this play.

As Brees drops back to pass, he notices the linebacker creeping on the shallow route by the left flanker.

As he drops back to pass, Brees finds his right slot receiver on the crossing route in the intermediate area and delivers a crisp pass.

He finds the slot receiver open on the corner route and delivers an accurate pass on the sideline where only his receiver can get it.

Thus, he delivers the pass to the left slot on the deep in route and shows off his mechanics with the hi/lo read.

Brees's pass is delivered so that the slot receiver has a chance to run after the catch and pick up yardage.

215

NEW ORLEANS SAINTS / DEFENSE

DEFENSIVE STAR PLAYER #94

Charles Grant — Defensive End (LE)

Key Attributes

Acceleration	77
Agility	75
Break Tackle	10
Speed	75

The Saints' Mr. Reliable is on the defensive line, and his name is **Charles Grant**. Grant has been playing for six years, and has yet to miss a single game. When a team has a high performer like Grant and don't have to worry about him being there, it makes having consistent performances easy. Grant finished last year with **6** sacks and **2** fumble recoveries. His play also made it possible for opposite defensive end Will Smith to rack up **10.5** sacks.

Player Weapon: None

RECOMMENDED DEFENSIVE AUDIBLE PACKAGES

4-3-Normal	4-3-Normal	4-3-Over	Dime-Flat	Dime-Normal
Under Ram Buck	Zip Shoot Gut	Safety Blitz	Zone Man X	Fincher Blitz

DEFENSIVE PLAYCOUNTS

Man Coverage:	41	Cover 3 Zone:	23	Combo Blitz:	23
Man Zone:	37	Deep Zone:	22	Goal Line:	15
Combo Coverage:	12	Man Blitz:	49	Special Teams:	12
Cover 2 Zone:	14	Zone Blitz:	57		

TEAM TRIVIA

New Orleans Saints Facts

Answers:

1 1967

2 Mike Ditka

3 Archie Manning

DEFENSIVE FORMATIONS

4-3	Nickel
4-3-Normal	Nickel-3-3-5
4-3-Over	Nickel-Normal
4-3-Under	Nickel-Strong
Dime	**Quarter**
Dime-3-2-6	Quarter-3 Deep
Dime-Normal	Quarter-Normal

DEFENSIVE STRENGTH CHART

- ●: OVR less than 80
- ●: OVR between 80-89
- ●: OVR 90 or greater
- ○: Player Weapons

4-3 Base Defense

FS #29 · SS #20

CB #42 · LB #58 · LB #51 · LB #55 · CB #34

RE #91 · DT #66 · DT #99 · LE #94

Dime Defense

FS #29 · SS #20

CB #42 · CB #22 · LB #51 · CB #21 · CB #34

RE #91 · DT #66 · DT #99 · LE #94

DEFENSIVE ROSTER LIST — Current / Next Gen

Pos.	#	First Name	Last Name	Overall	Player Weapons
CB	34	Mike	McKenzie	87	
CB	42	Jason	David	84	
CB	22	Fred	Thomas	82	
CB	21	Jason	Craft	80	
CB	28	DeJuan	Groce	75	
CB	38	N/A	N/A	74	
DT	99	Hollis	Thomas	86	Run Stopper
DT	66	Brian	Young	85	
DT	96	Antwan	Lake	71	
DT	77	Rodney	Leisle	69	
FS	29	Josh	Bullocks	83	Coverage Safety
FS	43	Kevin	Kaesviharn	79	
LE	94	Charles	Grant	91	
LE	98	Willie	Whitehead	76	
LOLB	55	Scott	Fujita	84	
LOLB	56	Alfred	Fincher	78	
MLB	51	Brian	Simmons	84	Playmaker
MLB	53	Mark	Simoneau	80	
P	6	Chris	Hanson	83	
P	7	Steve	Weatherford	80	
RE	91	Will	Smith	94	Pass Rusher / Finesse Move D-Lineman
RE	93	Rob	Ninkovich	73	
ROLB	58	Scott	Shanle	85	
ROLB	54	Troy	Evans	70	
SS	20	Jay	Bellamy	82	
SS	41	Roman	Harper	80	

4-3-Normal
DE Contain

Charles Grant is one of the larger-framed defensive ends in the league, but he has great speed.

Charles Grant is really making a name for himself on the Saints' defensive line. He shares bookend duties with Pro Bowler Will Smith.

The 4-3-Normal DE Contain allows Grant to get outside and contain the quarter-back. This is a good play to call against scramblers like Michael Vick.

When the quarterback makes his move, Grant is there to make the stop in the backfield. He also gets help from his teammates.

4-3-Normal
Zip Shoot Gut

Because of his big body, Grant is able to drop back into coverage and make plays on the football.

Grant has the ability to contain the quarterback, but he also has the skills to drop back into coverage and mirror certain passing routes.

Grant generally plays on the strong side over the tight end, so this is a good call against the quick pass to the tight end.

Grant gets a jump on the pass and breaks it up. He's not the greatest catcher in the world; perhaps that's why he plays on defense.

4-3-Over
Zone Blitz

This play sends a blitz on the weak side and drops Grant off into cover-age on the strong side.

This play is a three-deep zone blitz that uses Grant's size to defend routes. Call this play in third and long situations.

This is a good play to use to bring pres-sure from the left side and let Grant dis-play some coverage ability on the right.

Again, he will defend the intermediate and short routes showing off his good change of direction skills.

217

SEATTLE SEAHAWKS

Division: NFC West | **Stadium:** Qwest Field™ | **Type:** Open | **Capacity:** 67,000 | **Surface:** Turf

2006 STANDINGS

Wins	Losses	Ties	PF	PA	Home	Road	vs. AFC	vs. NFC	vs. Div
9	7	0	335	341	5-3	4-4	2-2	7-5	3-3

TEAM OVERVIEW

The Seahawks would like to take a mulligan for the 2006 season. Injuries plagued the offense, and kept them from ever finding their rhythm. The ever-accurate Matt Hasselbeck is back in the saddle, and should have Holmgren's offense clicking on all cylinders.

Shaun Alexander is the key cog in the wheel for the offense. If he can stay healthy, his vision and ability to shed tackles will have the running game working at maximum effectiveness. Marcus Pollard will give the QB a new target for moving the chains as well.

The defense must get more pressure on the QB so that the secondary doesn't give up so many big plays. Peterson and Tatupu are the core of this defense, so use them!

COACHING PROFILE

Mike Holmgren

- **Head Coaching Year:** 9th
- **Experience:** Green Bay Packers head coach (1992-1998), San Francisco 49ers offensive coordinator (1989-1991).

Mike Holmgren was named as the Seahawks' sixth head coach on January 8, 1999. Holmgren has coached in some capacity: Joe Montana, Steve Young and Brett Favre.

TEAM RANKINGS

Scoring	14th
Passing Offense	20th
Rushing Offense	14th
Passing Defense	16th
Rushing Defense	22nd
Turnovers	27th

RATINGS HISTORY

Category	'07	'06	'05	'04
Overall	**90**	86	**90**	83
Offense	**91**	89	**91**	82
Defense	88	76	**89**	79

Bold = Highest Year

88
FIVE-YEAR
AVERAGE

SCOUTING REPORT

STRENGTHS

Description	Maximizing Potential	Tips for Opponents
Shawn Alexander still remains one of the elite running backs in the game, but injury is a concern.	Don't overuse Alexander. Instead, keep him fresh by giving Maurice Morris more carries.	Alexander has lost a bit of speed, so he is not going to break off long runs like he used to.
Deion Branch is the team's home run hitter, even though his numbers may say otherwise.	Call plays that have Branch running deep patterns, so he can use speed to blow by the pass coverage.	If the CB covering Branch does not have the speed to keep up, you will have to play zone or give him help.
Julian Peterson is one of the prime players at his position.	Blitz Peterson to disrupt the passing game.	You must account for Peterson at all times on the field.

WEAKNESSES

Description	Minimizing Risks	Tips for Opponents
Tight end Marcus Pollard is still serviceable, but is no longer considered a deep threat in the passing game.	Consider going four wide to get faster receivers on the field if you need to convert a long yardage situation.	If Pollard is on the field, you don't have to assign a fast defender to him.
The Seahawks do not have a pass rushing threat along the defensive line.	Don't expect to get a lot of pressure from the front four. Opposing players must blitz.	Until they show you that they can get consistent pressure, send all five eligible receivers out on routes.

TEAM STRATEGY

OFF-SEASON **UPGRADES**

Type	Round	First Name	Last Name	School/Team	Position	Height	Weight
Free Agent	N/A	Deon	Grant	Jacksonville Jaguars	S	6'2"	210
Free Agent	N/A	Patrick	Kerney	Atlanta Falcons	DE	6'5"	273
Free Agent	N/A	Marcus	Pollard	Detroit Lions	TE	6'3"	247
Draft	2nd	Josh	Wilson	Maryland	CB	5'9"	188
Draft	3rd	Brandon	Mebane	California	DT	6'1"	305

FANTASY **OUTLOOK**

Star Player: Shaun Alexander
Round of Draft: 1st

Alexander didn't have the type of season owners expected. He should be selected in the first round on draft day, but be sure to draft another back right after him in the second round in case he is not productive.

Star Player: Matt Hasselbeck
Round of Draft: 7th

Just like Alexander, Hasselbeck did not put up the same type of numbers owners are used to because of injuries. If he is able to remain healthy, he should bounce back and put up numbers like he did in 2005.

5 YEAR **PLAYER PROGRESSION**

First Name	Last Name	Position	'07 Overall	'08 Overall	'09 Overall	'10 Overall	'11 Overall
Walter	Jones	T	98	98	98	99	98
Shaun	Alexander	HB	96	95	92	88	-
Julian	Peterson	LB	94	96	95	93	92
Matt	Hasselbeck	QB	92	93	94	95	97
Baraka	Atkins	DE	78	78	78	78	77

FRANCHISE MODE **STRATEGY**

If you plan on including the tight end in your offensive passing attack, then you will want to look for help here. Marcus Pollard has lost a step or two, so a replacement will be needed sooner rather than later.

Key Franchise Info

Team Salary: $87.4M
Cap Room: $21.5M
Key Rival:
• Oakland Raiders
NFL Icons: Shaun Alexander
Philosophy:
• Offense: Vertical Passing
• Defense: Disrupt Passing
Prestige: Medium
Team Needs:
• Tight End
• Defensive Back
Highest Paid Players:
• Julian Peterson
• Shaun Alexander
Up and Coming Players:
• Baraka Atkins
• Darry Tapp

TEAM STRATEGY

ROSTER AND **PACKAGE TIPS** KEY PLAYER SUBSTITUTIONS

• **Position:** LE
• **Substitution:** Baraka Atkins
• **When:** Global
• **Advantage:** Atkins's 77 speed rating gives Seattle another pass rush threat coming off the edge to generate some heat with the front four.

• **Position:** CB
• **Substitution:** Kelly Jennings
• **When:** Global
• **Advantage:** A speed rating of 94 and jump rating of 93 will allow him to be able to cover most of the receivers in the NFL effectively.

• **Position:** CB
• **Substitution:** Josh Wilson
• **When:** Global
• **Advantage:** Wilson's 95 speed rating means that he should not get burnt very often. If he does, though, his speed should allow him to catch up to the WR.

• **Position:** 3RDB
• **Substitution:** Maurice Morris
• **When:** Global
• **Advantage:** Morris is faster and has a better catch rating than Shaun Alexander, which should prove to be helpful in crucial third down situations.

SEATTLE SEAHAWKS / **OFFENSE**

TEAM STRATEGY

OFFENSIVE **STAR PLAYER** #37

Shaun Alexander	Halfback (HB)

Key Attributes

Acceleration	92
Agility	88
Break Tackle	95
Speed	89

Alexander had a down year in '06, primarily due to injuries and inconsistent play along the offensive line. Because of those reasons, he wasn't able to get through the holes as decisively as he is accustomed to. He is expected to be healthy again in '07 and should be able regain some of his MVP Form of '05 when he led the league in rushing and touchdowns. If he does regain his form, the Seahawks should end up making the playoffs.

Player Weapons: Feature Back / Power Back, Stiff Arm BC

RECOMMENDED OFFENSIVE **AUDIBLE PACKAGES**

Far-Tight-Twins	Near-Pro	I Form-TE Flat	Singleback-4WR Spread	Singleback-Bunch Swap
HB Counter	Texas	Pump-N Go	949 Yara	Bunch Fade

OFFENSIVE **PLAYCOUNTS**

Quick Pass:	32	Hail Mary:	1	Counter:	19
Standard Pass:	103	Inside Handoff:	32	Draw:	9
Shotgun Pass:	26	Outside Handoff:	6	FB Run:	20
Screen Pass:	12	Pinch:	14		

TEAM **TRIVIA**

Seattle Seahawks Facts

Turn the page for the answers.

❶ In which division did the Seahawks play in their NFL debut season of 1976?

❷ Which team defeated Seattle in their first-ever AFC Championship game appearance?

❸ Who set a career Seahawk record for receiving yardage?

OFFENSIVE **FORMATIONS**

Singleback	Split Backs
Big	Pro
Normal	Pro Spread
Tight Doubles	**Far**
Slot Strong	Pro
Bunch Swap	Tight Twins
4WR Spread	3WR
4WR Flex	**Near**
Trey Open	Pro
Empty Trey	Close
I Form	Jumbo
Normal	**Strong I**
Twin WR	Normal
3WR	**Weak I**
Big	Twin WR

OFFENSIVE **STRENGTH CHART**

◐: OVR less than 80   ●: OVR 90 or greater
◓: OVR between 80-89   ○: Player Weapons

2-Back Set

WR #84 OL #71 OL #67 OL #65 OL #62 OL #75 TE #88   WR #83
QB #8
FB #38
HB #37

3-Receiver Set

WR #84 OL #71 OL #67 OL #65 OL #62 OL #75 TE #88   WR #83
WR #18   QB #8   WR #83

HB #37

OFFENSIVE **ROSTER LIST** Current / Next Gen

Pos.	#	First Name	Last Name	Overall	Player Weapons
C	65	Chris	Spencer	84	
C	66	Austin	King	69	
FB	38	Mack	Strong	96	Crushing Run Blocker
FB	49	Josh	Parry	73	
HB	37	Shaun	Alexander	96	Feature Back / Power Back, Stiff Arm BC
HB	20	Maurice	Morris	82	
HB	30	Marquis	Weeks	74	
K	3	Josh	Brown	90	Big Foot Kicker
LG	67	Rob	Sims	83	
LG	77	Floyd	Womack	81	
LT	71	Walter	Jones	98	Road Blocker / Crushing Run Blocker, Pass Blocker
LT	68	Tom	Ashworth	84	
QB	8	Matt	Hasselbeck	92	Precision Passer / Smart QB
QB	15	Seneca	Wallace	81	Speed QB
QB	11	David	Greene	71	
RG	62	Chris	Gray	84	
RT	75	Sean	Locklear	83	
RT	74	Ray	Willis	69	
TE	88	Marcus	Pollard	80	
TE	85	Will	Heller	64	
WR	83	Deion	Branch	88	Go-To Guy / Possession, Quick Receiver, Hands
WR	84	Bobby	Engram	83	
WR	18	D.J.	Hackett	79	
WR	81	Nate	Burleson	77	
WR	87	Ben	Obomanu	69	

OFFENSE / KEY OFFENSIVE PLAYS

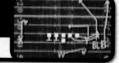

Near-Close
Post Drag

Near-Jumbo
HB Counter

Singleback-Trey Open
HB Screen

Shaun Alexander wastes little motion as he moves on pass routes. This play shows off his fluidity in movement as he runs passing routes.

Alexander is a big, physical, north-south runner that has great vision to see holes.

Alexander has a second gear when he gets in the open field.

Near-Close Post Drag allows Shaun Alexander to show that he has fully recovered from his foot injury from a year ago.

This is a staple running play that can spring Alexander free for major yardage.

Shaun Alexander has a lot of great open field moves. Bring that out in your offensive attack with this play.

Send Alexander in motion before the snap. Hike the football before he sets on the outside. This will get him a free release, especially against press man coverage.

Alexander receives the football and follows the blocks of his fullback and right guard; they pull left and take out any defender that shows his face.

Alexander sets up behind his blockers here. Hasselbeck does a fantastic job of selling the pass as he almost gets sacked by the defense.

Let Alexander burn the linebackers and throw it to him deep. There is no stopping Alexander on this play against man coverage.

Once around the edge, Alexander becomes a north-south runner as he turns on the jets and picks up as many yards as possible.

He gets down the field and uses his ability to embarrass the defense. One missed tackle is all he needs.

TEAM STRATEGY

221

SEATTLE SEAHAWKS / **DEFENSE**

DEFENSIVE **STAR PLAYER**   **#59**

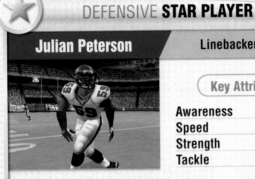

Julian Peterson	Linebacker (ROLB)

Key Attributes

Awareness	84
Speed	86
Strength	74
Tackle	89

Peterson is a multipurpose defensive playmaker, who uses his athleticism to make plays all over the field. He uses his speed to shoot through gaps to get to the ball carrier in the backfield to blow up the run. Last season he had a total of **89** tackles. His forte is getting after the quarterback as a pass rusher. He led the team in sacks with **10**. He is adept at dropping back in pass coverage, making him an every down linebacker.

Player Weapons: Defensive Enforcer / Brick Wall Defender

RECOMMENDED DEFENSIVE **AUDIBLE PACKAGES**

4-3-Normal	4-3-Over	Dime-3-2-6	Dime-3-2-6	Dime-Normal
Herndon Blitz	SS Blitz	2 Deep LB Blitz	QB Trap	Tatupu Blitz

DEFENSIVE **PLAYCOUNTS**

Man Coverage:	41	Cover 3 Zone:	23	Combo Blitz:	23
Man Zone:	37	Deep Zone:	22	Goal Line:	15
Combo Coverage:	12	Man Blitz:	49	Special Teams:	12
Cover 2 Zone:	14	Zone Blitz:	57		

TEAM **TRIVIA**

Seattle Seahawks Facts

Answers:

❶ NFC West

❷ The Los Angeles Raiders

❸ Steve Largent

DEFENSIVE **FORMATIONS**

4-3	Nickel
4-3-Normal	Nickel-3-3-5
4-3-Over	Nickel-Normal
4-3-Under	Nickel-Strong
Dime	**Quarter**
Dime-3-2-6	Quarter-3 Deep
Dime-Normal	Quarter-Normal
Dime-Flat	

DEFENSIVE **STRENGTH CHART**

- ○ : OVR less than 80
- ● : OVR 90 or greater
- ◐ : OVR between 80-89
- ○ : Player Weapons

4-3 Base Defense

FS #24   SS #25

CB #21   LB #59   LB #51   LB #56   CB #23

RE #97   DT #91   DT #99   LE #94

Dime Defense

FS #24   SS #25

CB #21   CB #31   LB #51   CB #27   CB #23

RE #97   DT #91   DT #99   LE #94

DEFENSIVE **ROSTER LIST**   Current / Next Gen

Pos.	#	First Name	Last Name	Overall	Player Weapons
CB	23	Marcus	Trufant	90	Quick Corner / Shutdown Corner
CB	21	Kelly	Jennings	82	
CB	31	Kelly	Herndon	81	
CB	27	Jordan	Babineaux	80	
CB	26	Josh	Wilson	76	
CB	33	Rich	Gardner	65	
DT	99	Rocky	Bernard	87	
DT	91	Chartric	Darby	83	
DT	90	Marcus	Tubbs	82	
DT	95	Russell	Davis	82	
DT	92	Brandon	Mebane	77	
DT	93	Craig	Terrill	77	
FS	24	Deon	Grant	89	
FS	42	Mike	Green	83	
LE	94	Bryce	Fisher	85	
LE	96	Baraka	Atkins	78	
LE	79	Brandon	Green	67	
LOLB	56	Leroy	Hill	85	
LOLB	57	Kevin	Bentley	78	
MLB	51	Lofa	Tatupu	93	Playmaker / Big Hitter, Brick Wall Defender, Smart Linebacker
MLB	53	Niko	Koutouvides	76	
P	1	Ryan	Plackemeier	89	
RE	97	Patrick	Kerney	89	
RE	55	Darryl	Tapp	78	
ROLB	59	Julian	Peterson	94	Defensive Enforcer / Brick Wall Defender
ROLB	58	Marquis	Cooper	71	
SS	25	Brian	Russell	84	
SS	28	Michael	Boulware	80	

4-3-Normal

2 Man Under

Julian Peterson has the ability to turn and run with tight ends. This play shows off his ability to play man coverage.

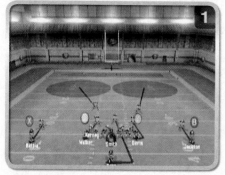

A few years ago and prior to a serious injury, he was a hot commodity at outside linebacker because of his ability to play every position on the defense.

Call 4-3-Normal 2 Man Under to allow Peterson to use his coverage skills to keep tight ends in check. He will run with them step for step.

When they go for the football, Peterson has the hitting ability, and they know how to knock the ball loose and force an incomplete pass.

4-3-Over

Zone Blitz

Peterson is best when he is close to the line of scrimmage. He has a quick first step.

The only adjustments that are needed is to first shift the defensive line to the left. Second, hot blitz Peterson and then shift the linebackers to the left.

This gives Peterson that free release on the edge that is needed for the defense to have a shot at the big play sack.

Peterson gets in and takes the QB out from his blindside. Often, Peterson can cause the quarterback to fumble in this situation.

Nickel-Normal

Peterson Blitz

A play that shows off Peterson's quick first step, closing ability, and gap-reading intelligence is the Nickel-Normal.

The only adjustments made to this play are a left defensive line shift and a moving of Peterson up front on the line.

On the snap, Peterson gets a jump and runs downhill through the "A" gap. His progress is unimpeded by the offensive line.

The quarterback never had a chance on this one, as Peterson got a clean pass to take him out.

PITTSBURGH STEELERS

Division: AFC North | **Stadium:** Heinz Field™ | **Type:** Open | **Capacity:** 64,450 | **Surface:** Grass

TEAM STRATEGY

2006 **STANDINGS**

Wins	Losses	Ties	PF	PA	Home	Road	vs. AFC	vs. NFC	vs. Div
8	8	0	353	315	5-3	3-5	5-7	3-1	3-3

COACHING **PROFILE**

Mike Tomlin

- **Head Coaching Year:** 1st
- **Experience:** Minnesota Vikings defensive coordinator (2006).

Tomlin became the 16th head coach in Steelers history when he replaced Bill Cowher on January 22, 2007. Tomlin, 34, was selected by Vikings head coach Brad Childress to be his defensive coordinator.

TEAM **RANKINGS**

Scoring	12th
Passing Offense	9th
Rushing Offense	10th
Passing Defense	20th
Rushing Defense	3rd
Turnovers	27th

RATINGS **HISTORY**

Category	'07	'06	'05	'04
Overall	89	**91**	74	86
Offense	**90**	89	73	85
Defense	89	**95**	82	84

Bold = Highest Year

86
FIVE-YEAR
AVERAGE

TEAM **OVERVIEW**

After winning Super Bowl XL, the Steelers went through a miserable season of turmoil and defeat. Big Ben is back in full health and provides a solid presence behind center. He has two good assets to throw to in Hines Ward and Santonio Holmes.

The running game is in great shape with the speedy Willie Parker and bulldozer Dan Kreider leading the way. The offensive line is especially strong on the left side and should have no problems creating rushing lanes.

Despite losing Joey Porter in the off-season, the Steelers still return a formidable defense. Troy Polamalu will make plays all over the field, crushing WRs, plugging gaps in the run game, and blitzing the QB from every angle.

SCOUTING **REPORT**

STRENGTHS

Description	Maximizing Potential	Tips for Opponents
Willie Parker has established himself as one of the premier runningbacks in the league.	Run counters and toss plays to take advantage of Parker's ability to get outside and bust off long runs.	Whatever you do, don't let Parker get outside of tackles where he can use his speed and acceleration.
Whenever Polamalu lines up near the line of scrimmage, good things happen for the Steelers defense.	Move Polamalu up into the box and let him go after the quarterback. Your opponent will have to adjust.	Make sure you know where Polamalu is located on each and every play.
Hines Ward continues to be the team's go-to receiver.	Any time you need to pick up a first down, look for Ward.	Double up on Ward and force Big Ben to look elsewhere.

WEAKNESSES

Description	Minimizing Risks	Tips for Opponents
Outside of Hines Ward, the Steelers have no other reliable receivers when the game is on the line.	Move Ward around so the defense has to locate him on the field. Create match-up problems on every down.	Focus most of your attention on Ward. Rotate pass coverage in his direction.
The Steelers cornerbacks are solid, but none of them can lock down an elite receiver.	Try to avoid leaving the Steelers cornerbacks in one-on-one coverage. Call Cover 2, Cover 3, and Cover 4.	If the Steelers' cornerbacks are left on an island, look to expose them by going deep.

Steelers

OFF-SEASON **UPGRADES**

Type	Round	First Name	Last Name	School/Team	Position	Height	Weight
Free Agent	N/A	Nick	Eason	Cleveland Browns	DE	6'3"	305
Free Agent	N/A	Sean	Mahan	Tampa Bay Buccaneers	C	6'3"	301
Free Agent	N/A	Najeh	Davenport	Green Bay Packers	RB	6'1"	247
Draft	1st	Lawrence	Timmons	Florida State	LB	6'3"	232
Draft	2nd	LaMarr	Woodley	Michigan	DE	6'3"	269

FANTASY **OUTLOOK**

★ **Star Player:** Willie Parker
Round of Draft: 1st

Despite the Steelers passing woes, he was able to post impressive numbers by rushing for nearly 1,500 yards and getting into the end zone 16 times. Despite a new coach this year, his numbers shouldn't drop.

★ **Star Player:** Hines Ward
Round of Draft: 4th

Ward still remains the Steelers go-to receiver even though his numbers were down last season. If Big Ben comes back healthy, Ward's numbers will go up to the levels fantasy owners have come to expect.

5 YEAR **PLAYER PROGRESSION**

First Name	Last Name	Position	'07 Overall	'08 Overall	'09 Overall	'10 Overall	'11 Overall
Troy	Polamalu	S	97	98	99	99	99
Hines	Ward	WR	91	91	90	-	-
Willie	Parker	HB	90	91	93	98	99
Ben	Roethlisberger	QB	88	89	90	91	91
Lawrence	Timmons	LB	82	83	84	83	85

FRANCHISE MODE **STRATEGY**

Hines Ward needs someone to line up on the opposite side of the field so that he won't be double-teamed as often. Look for a receiver in the first or second round who has some speed to stretch the field vertically.

Key Franchise Info

Team Salary: $86.8M
Cap Room: $22.1M
Key Rival:
• Cleveland Browns
NFL Icons: Hines Ward
Philosophy:
• Offense: Vertical Passing
• Defense: Disrupt Passing
Prestige: Medium
Team Needs:
• Receiver
• Defensive Back
Highest Paid Players:
• Marvel Smith
• Hines ward
Up and Coming Players:
• Lawrence Timmons
• Matt Spaeth

TEAM STRATEGY

ROSTER AND **PACKAGE TIPS** — KEY PLAYER SUBSTITUTIONS

Singleback-Big

• **Position:** HB
• **Substitution:** Najeh Davenport
• **When:** Short Yardage
• **Advantage:** Davenport's STR and BTK ratings should help him gain those tough, short yards when they count the most (whereas Willie Parker could not).

I Form-Normal

• **Position:** WR
• **Substitution:** Santonio Holmes
• **When:** Global
• **Advantage:** Holmes is faster and has a better catch rating than Cedrick Wilson, which should help take the focus off of Hines Ward.

I Form-Twin WR

• **Position:** C
• **Substitution:** Chukky Okobi
• **When:** Global
• **Advantage:** With a higher STR, OVR, and RBK rating than Sean Mahan, Okobi should be able to shed blockers and create holes for the running game.

3-4-Normal

• **Position:** ROLB
• **Substitution:** Lawrence Timmons
• **When:** Global
• **Advantage:** With a better OVR and SPD rating than James Harrison, Timmons is better suited to cover receivers and backs, and help out the run game.

PITTSBURGH STEELERS / OFFENSE

OFFENSIVE STAR PLAYER #7

Ben Roethlisberger — Quarterback (QB)

Key Attributes

Awarenesss	84
Speed	68
Throwing Power	90
Throwing Accuracy	85

Roethlisberger didn't have the type of season he was hoping for after helping the Steelers to a Super Bowl victory in 2005. With the off-season injuries he had in 2006, he never really got on track. Although he posted his highest total in pass yardage during his three year career, he never looked like he was comfortable lining up behind center. With a new head coach, expect Big Ben to be at the top of his game in '07.

Player Weapon: Cannon Arm

OFFENSIVE STRENGTH CHART

○: OVR less than 80　　◉: OVR 90 or greater
◉: OVR between 80-89　　○: Player Weapons

2-Back Set

WR #10　OL #77　OL #66　OL #56　OL #73　OL #78　TE #83　WR #86
QB #7
FB #35
HB #39

3-Receiver Set

WR #10　OL #77　OL #66　OL #73　OL #78　TE #83
WR #80　QB #7　WR #86
HB #39

RECOMMENDED OFFENSIVE AUDIBLE PACKAGES

I Form-Normal	I Form-Big	Singleback-Trips Bunch	Singleback-Normal Slot	Shotgun-Trips Bunch
Comet Pass	FB Fake HB Toss	Smash Slot Post	FL Z Clearout	Twin Fades

OFFENSIVE PLAYCOUNTS

Quick Pass:	7	Screen Pass:	12	Pinch:	15
Standard Pass:	71	Hail Mary:	1	Counter:	16
Shotgun Pass:	41	Inside Handoff:	37	Draw:	17
Play Action Pass:	43	Outside Handoff:	21		

TEAM TRIVIA

Pittsburgh Steelers Facts

Turn the page for the answers.

① In which year did Art Rooney Sr. purchase the NFL franchise that would become the Pittsburgh Steelers?

② Who originally suggested that the Steelers use the Steelmark logo on their helmets?

OFFENSIVE FORMATIONS

Singleback	I Form
Big	Normal
Twin TE	Twin WR
Twin TE WR	Big
Normal Slot	Twin TE
Trips Bunch	**Shotgun**
Slot Strong	2RB Flex
Strong I	Normal
Normal	Wing Trips
Twin WR	Trips Bunch
Jumbo	4WR
Weak I	
Normal	
Twin WR	
Twin TE	

OFFENSIVE ROSTER LIST — Current / Next Gen

Pos.	#	First Name	Last Name	Overall	Player Weapons
C	56	Chukky	Okobi	81	
C	61	Sean	Mahan	78	
FB	35	Dan	Kreider	90	Crushing Run Blocker
HB	39	Willie	Parker	90	Speed Back / Speed
HB	44	Najeh	Davenport	82	Power Back
HB	32	Kevan	Barlow	79	
K	3	Jeff	Reed	79	
LG	66	Alan	Faneca	96	Road Blocker / Crushing Run Blocker
LG	62	Marvin	Philip	68	
LT	77	Marvel	Smith	89	Run Blocker / Crushing Run Blocker
LT	79	Trai	Essex	73	
QB	7	Ben	Roethlisberger	88	Cannon Arm
QB	16	Charlie	Batch	79	
QB	2	Brian	St.Pierre	64	
RG	73	Kendall	Simmons	85	
RG	68	Chris	Kemoeatu	70	
RT	78	Max	Starks	81	
RT	74	Willie	Colon	70	
TE	83	Heath	Miller	86	
TE	89	Matt	Spaeth	77	
TE	84	Jerame	Tuman	72	
WR	86	Hines	Ward	91	Go-To Guy / Possesion, Quick Receiver, Hands
WR	10	Santonio	Holmes	80	Deep Threat
WR	80	Cedrick	Wilson	77	
WR	85	Nate	Washington	76	
WR	15	Willie	Reid	71	

OFFENSE / KEY OFFENSIVE PLAYS

Singleback-Normal Slot
FL Middle

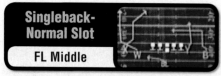

Big Ben has a big time arm and can make all the throws.

This play features a deep route passing combination that shows off Ben Roethlisberger's arm strength.

Once you drop back and read the field, look for a single match-up. Wide receiver Antonio Holmes gets one-on-one with Samari Rolle.

Big Ben is able to launch the pass deep and exploit the one-on-one coverage. Ben is a big arm quarterback that can make big plays in big games.

Singleback-Trips Bunch
PA Ctr

Ben's quickness allows him to get out of the pocket and make throws on the run.

This play allows Steelers' users to highlight another aspect of Big Ben's game—out of pocket passing.

This play gets Ben to sell the fake. Once the fake is sold, Ben can get out of the pocket and throw the deep pass or any pass on the run.

Ben hooks up with one of his favorite targets, Hines Ward, on the deep corner route. Mobility and passing on the run are key to making Ben a success.

Shotgun-2RB Flex WR
Post Corner

Not only can Ben make throws on the run, but he can tuck the ball and run.

This features the post corner route. We chose this play, however, to highlight something else about Big Ben.

In his first two years in the league, Ben did a great job of dropping back in the pocket and reading the pass rush.

He often got out of the pocket and ran down the field. This is important in Roethlisberger's game.

TEAM STRATEGY

PITTSBURGH STEELERS / DEFENSE

DEFENSIVE STAR PLAYER #43

Troy Polamalu — Strong Safety (SS)

Key Attributes

Awareness	80
Speed	93
Strength	68
Tackle	85

Polamalu is one of the premier safeties in the league. He has the knack for coming up with game-changing plays that swing the momentum in the Steelers' favor. His ability to play up in the box allows him to make plays against the opposing offense's running game. He will take chances on the field that often result in him forcing a turnover. Look for another great season from one of the top defensive playmakers in the game.

Player Weapons: Hit Man / Big Hitter, Smart Safety

RECOMMENDED DEFENSIVE AUDIBLE PACKAGES

4-3-Normal	4-3-Over	Dime-3-2-6	Dime-3-2-6	Dime-Normal
Herndon Blitz	SS Blitz	2 Deep LB Blitz	QB Trap	Tatupu Blitz

DEFENSIVE PLAYCOUNTS

Man Coverage:	46	Cover 3 Zone:	24	Combo Blitz:	10
Man Zone:	36	Deep Zone:	16	Goal Line:	15
Combo Coverage:	9	Man Blitz:	48	Special Teams:	12
Cover 2 Zone:	24	Zone Blitz:	60		

TEAM TRIVIA

Pittsburgh Steelers Facts
Answers:

1. 1933
2. Cleveland's Republic Steel

DEFENSIVE FORMATIONS

3-4	Nickel
3-4-Normal	Nickel-2-4-5
3-4-Over	Nickel-3-5-5
3-4-Under	**Quarter**
3-4-Solid	Quarter-3 Deep
Dime	Quarter-Normal
Dime-3-2-6	
Dime-Normal	

DEFENSIVE STRENGTH CHART

- ○: OVR less than 80
- ●: OVR between 80-89
- ○: OVR 90 or greater
- ○: Player Weapons

4-3 Base Defense

FS #25 · SS #43
CB #24 · LB #94 · LB #51 · LB #53 · CB #26
RE #99 · DT #76 · DT #98 · LE #91

Dime Defense

FS #25 · SS #43
CB #24 · CB #20 · LB #51 · CB #21 · CB #26
RE #99 · DT #76 · DT #98 · LE #91

DEFENSIVE ROSTER LIST — Current / Next Gen

Pos.	#	First Name	Last Name	Overall	Player Weapons
CB	26	Deshea	Townsend	84	
CB	24	Ike	Taylor	83	Quick Corner
CB	20	Bryant	McFadden	82	
CB	21	Ricardo	Colclough	78	
CB	37	Anthony	Madison	64	
DT	98	Casey	Hampton	97	Power Move D-Lineman
DT	76	Chris	Hoke	82	
DT	96	Shaun	Nua	62	
FS	25	Ryan	Clark	81	
FS	23	Tyrone	Carter	74	
LE	91	Aaron	Smith	89	Run Stopper
LE	69	Ryan	McBean	72	
LOLB	53	Clark	Haggans	88	
LOLB	97	Arnold	Harrison	75	
LOLB	55	LaMarr	Woodley	71	
MLB	51	James	Farrior	95	Heavy Hitter / Brick Wall Defender, Smart Defender, Big Hitter
MLB	50	Larry	Foote	87	
MLB	57	Clint	Kriewaldt	78	
MLB	54	Rian	Wallace	69	
P	9	Daniel	Sepulveda	82	
RE	99	Brett	Keisel	82	
RE	90	Travis	Kirschke	75	
RE	93	Nick	Eason	69	
ROLB	94	Lawrence	Timmons	82	
ROLB	92	James	Harrison	76	
SS	43	Troy	Polamalu	97	Hit Man / Big Hitter, Smart Safety
SS	27	Anthony	Smith	72	

DEFENSE / KEY DEFENSIVE PLAYS

3-4-Normal

2 Man Under

Troy Polamalu is the Steelers best defender. He can play everywhere.

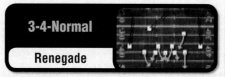

3-4-Normal

Renegade

Not only does Troy have the gift to cover the pass, but he also has the bulk to play in the box.

Nickel-2-4-5

Polamalu Blitz

Another play that shows his ability to play in the box and rush the passer is the Nickel-2-4-5 Polamalu Blitz.

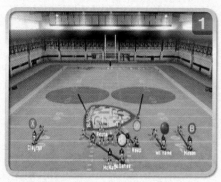

This gives both safeties the assignment of covering the deep portion of the football field (from the hash marks to the sidelines).

This is an all-out blitz with only three men dropping into coverage. Troy is the pass rusher from the secondary on this play.

This is a special play that calls Troy's number to rush the passer. Troy lines up in the box on this play to get a jump on the quarterback.

Troy Polamalu has the speed and the range to play from the hash to the sideline, helping out on almost any passing route.

Polamalu has made a name for himself not only in pass coverage but by coming up in the box and stuffing running plays.

The play stacks the line with defenders. But on the snap, many drop out in man coverage. Polamalu goes after quarterback Steve McNair.

He always finds himself around the football at the right time, whether changing for an interception or a big hit to jar the ball lose and force an incomplete pass.

The 3-4-Normal Renegade allows the Steelers' defensive coordinator to bring Polamalu up in the box to stop the run in its tracks.

Once he is into the backfield, Troy knows how to finish off the QB. He tackles him low with Hit Stick 2.0.

TEAM STRATEGY

229

HOUSTON TEXANS

Location: AFC South | **Stadium:** Reliant Stadium | **Type:** Retractable Roof | **Capacity:** 69,500 | **Surface:** Grass

2006 STANDINGS

Wins	Losses	Ties	PF	PA	Home	Road	vs. AFC	vs. NFC	vs. Div
6	10	0	267	366	4-4	3-6	6-6	0-4	3-3

TEAM OVERVIEW

This expansion franchise has still not managed to dig its way out of the cellar. Will year six be the change? Probably not, but they are moving in the right direction. The reins of the offense have been handed over to Matt Schaub who has looked impressive, but only has 161 regular-season tosses onhis resume.

Ahman Green comes in at the latter part of his career, but still has plenty of gas left in the tank. He should provide a spark to the running game and take some pressure off of Schaub.

The Texans' defense is nothing to write home about. Texans' players should take special care against the deep ball as they have two very low-rated safeties minding the fort in center field.

SCOUTING REPORT

STRENGTHS

Description	Maximizing Potential	Tips for Opponents
The Texans acquired quarterback Matt Schaub, a three-year backup to Michael Vick, from the Falcons.	Schaub was a highly sought after free agent and is known around the league as an accurate passer.	Schaub has plenty of potential, but is unproven as a starter in this league. Confuse him with multiple looks.
They were really busy this off-season, also acquiring free agent veteran running-back Ahman Green.	Green, a former five-time Pro-Bowler, is trying to return to that form after an injury-plagued season last year.	Green is one of the few assets the Texans have on offense. Focus on stopping the run.
Andre Johnson is the Texans other asset.	Johnson led the league in receptions last season.	Concentrate your defensive scheme on stopping him.

WEAKNESSES

Description	Minimizing Risks	Tips for Opponents
The Texans finished the season ranked 25th in the league in total defense allowed last season.	The Texans are trying to build from scratch, which leaves them with huge holes in their defense.	Attack their secondary with flurries of combination routes and floods to confuse them.
Left tackle Jordan Black is one of the weaker starting left tackles in the game.	With some good play calling and attention to detail, you can confuse Black and get him to give up a sack.	Try getting your best defensive end lined up against Black in crucial third and long situations.

COACHING PROFILE

Gary Kubiak

- **Head Coaching Year:** 2nd
- **Experience:** Offensive coordinator of the Denver Broncos.

Gary Kubiak has the fans in Houston optimistic after finishing with a 6-10 record. Don't laugh; this was a four game improvement over the 2005 season and he has proved to free agents that the Texans are on the rise.

TEAM RANKINGS

Scoring	28th
Passing Offense	27th
Rushing Offense	21st
Passing Defense	22nd
Rushing Defense	20th
Turnovers	21st

RATINGS HISTORY

Category	'07	'06	'05	'04
Overall	85	83	73	72
Offense	85	81	81	70
Defense	84	79	72	73

Bold = Highest Year

79
FIVE-YEAR
AVERAGE

OFF-SEASON UPGRADES

Type	Round	First Name	Last Name	School/Team	Position	Height	Weight
Free Agent	N/A	Jordan	Black	Kansas City Chiefs	T	6'5"	310
Free Agent	N/A	Danny	Clark	New Orleans Saints	LB	6'2"	245
Free Agent	N/A	Ahman	Green	Green Bay Packers	RB	6'0"	218
Draft	1st	Amobi	Okoye	Louisville	DT	6'2"	302
Draft	3rd	Jacoby	Jones	Lane	WR	6'3"	210

FANTASY OUTLOOK

Star Player: Andre Johnson
Round of Draft: 3rd

Johnson is the team's one offensive asset that puts the fear in the opposing defense. With his speed, he is a sure bet to pick up a ton of yardage and score a few touchdowns along the way.

Star Player: Ahman Green
Round of Draft: 5th

Green is expected to carry the workload as the team's featured runningback. Anything less than 1,100 yards rushing and 10 touchdowns will be considered a letdown.

5 YEAR PLAYER PROGRESSION

First Name	Last Name	Position	'07 Overall	'08 Overall	'09 Overall	'10 Overall	'11 Overall
Andre	Johnson	WR	93	93	93	94	94
Matt	Schaub	QB	83	85	85	86	88
Demeco	Ryans	LB	89	89	91	91	92
Dunta	Robinson	CB	87	88	90	89	88
Amobi	Okoye	DT	81	81	82	81	81

FRANCHISE MODE STRATEGY

The Texans have several holes that need to be filled. If a blue chip receiver or left tackle falls in your lap on draft day in the first round, snag them. Safety is another position of need for the first three rounds.

Key Franchise Info

Team Salary: $83.4M
Cap Room: $25.5M
Key Rival:
• Tennessee Titans
NFL Icons: Andre Johnson
Philosophy:
• Offense: Ball Control
• Defense: Force the Pass
Prestige: Very Low
Team Needs:
• Offensive Line
• Defensive Line
Highest Paid Players:
• Andre Johnson
• Mario Williams
Up and Coming Players:
• Amobi Okoye
• Chris Taylor

TEAM STRATEGY

ROSTER AND PACKAGE TIPS — KEY PLAYER SUBSTITUTIONS

- **Position:** WR
- **Substitution:** Jacoby Jones
- **When:** Global
- **Advantage:** Jones's 91 SPD rating will help him attack safeties deep and take some of Andre Johnson in the passing game. His speed will also help him keep defenses from overloading the box.

- **Position:** LT
- **Substitution:** Ephraim Salaam
- **When:** Global
- **Advantage:** Salaam's 82 OVR rating plus Run Blocker player weapon make him a force to be reckoned with in the running game, clearing holes along the way.

- **Position:** RG
- **Substitution:** Steve McKinney
- **When:** Global
- **Advantage:** McKinney's 83 OVR helps secure an otherwise below average offensive line, and helps to give QB Vince Young more time to find WRs downfield.

- **Position:** RT
- **Substitution:** Eric Winston
- **When:** Global
- **Advantage:** Winston's 66 SPD rating will allow him to block faster DEs better, and also will allow him to get out to block defenders quicker on pulling plays.

HOUSTON TEXANS / **OFFENSE**

OFFENSIVE **STAR PLAYER** #80

Andre Johnson — Wide Receiver (WR)

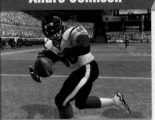

Key Attributes

Awareness	85
Acceleration	94
Catching	89
Speed	95

The Texans have one of the best receivers in the AFC in **Andre Johnson**. Johnson keeps proving that he is a solid receiver racking up **103** catches for **1,147** yards and **5** touchdowns. His performance year in and year-out earned him another trip to the Pro-Bowl and validates him as a proven receiver. Even though Johnson doesn't have a true complementary receiver, he gets the job done.

Player Weapons: Go-To Guy / Possession Receiver, Spectacular Catch Receiver

OFFENSIVE **STRENGTH CHART**

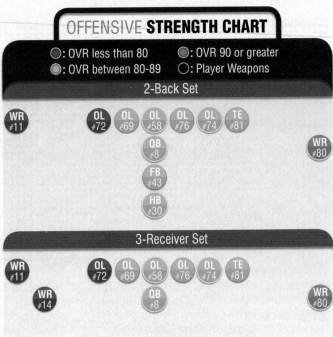

⬤ : OVR less than 80   ◯ : OVR 90 or greater
◉ : OVR between 80-89   ◯ : Player Weapons

2-Back Set

WR #11   OL #72 OL #69 OL #58 OL #76 OL #74 TE #81   WR #80
QB #8
FB #43
HB #30

3-Receiver Set

WR #11   OL #72 OL #69 OL #58 OL #76 OL #74 TE #81   WR #80
WR #14   QB #8
HB #30

RECOMMENDED OFFENSIVE **AUDIBLE PACKAGES**

I Form-Normal	Strong I-Normal	Singleback-Big	Sngleback-4WR	Shotgun-4WR
HB Counter	Middle Cross	TE Cross	Slot Middle	Slot Post

OFFENSIVE **PLAYCOUNTS**

Quick Pass:	15	Screen Pass:	8	Pinch:	14
Standard Pass:	89	Hail Mary:	2	Counter:	17
Shotgun Pass:	22	Inside Handoff:	35	Draw:	11
Play Action Pass:	23	Outside Handoff:	9		

TEAM **TRIVIA**

Houston Texans Facts

Turn the page for the answers.

❶ In what year did the Texans become an NFL Expansion team?

❷ Who was the first pick by the Texans in the 2002 NFL draft?

❷ What stadium was their first home game held in?

OFFENSIVE **FORMATIONS**

Singleback	Strong I
Big	H Pro
Big Twin WR	H Twins
Big Wing	**Weak I**
Big 3TE	H Pro
Normal Slot	H Twins
Slot Strong	**Near**
Trips Bunch	Normal Offset Wk
Tight Flex	Slot Strong
4WR Spread	Trips TE
Trey Open	4WR
Empty 5WR	
I Form	
Normal	
Big	

OFFENSIVE **ROSTER LIST** Current / Next Gen

Pos.	#	First Name	Last Name	Overall	Player Weapons
C	58	Mike	Flanagan	89	Pass Blocker
C	57	Drew	Hodgdon	71	
FB	43	Jameel	Cook	82	
HB	30	Ahman	Green	88	Speed Back
HB	36	Ron	Dayne	82	Power Back / Power Back
HB	33	Wali	Lundy	79	
HB	27	Chris	Taylor	78	
HB	35	Samkon	Gado	74	
K	3	Kris	Brown	79	
LG	69	Chester	Pitts	81	
LG	71	Atlas	Herrion	67	
LT	72	Jordan	Black	76	
LT	77	Charles	Spencer	72	
QB	8	Matt	Schaub	83	Precision Passer
QB	18	Sage	Rosenfels	75	
RG	76	Steve	McKinney	83	
RG	70	Fred	Weary	74	
RT	74	Ephraim	Salaam	85	Run Blocker
RT	73	Eric	Winston	77	
TE	81	Owen	Daniels	83	
TE	88	Jeb	Putzier	76	
TE	87	Mark	Bruener	76	
WR	80	Andre	Johnson	93	Go-To Guy / Possession Receiver, Spectacular Catch Receiver
WR	11	Andre	Davis	75	
WR	14	David	Anderson	73	
WR	12	Jacoby	Jones	72	
WR	13	Jerome	Mathis	72	Deep Threat / Speed
WR	83	Kevin	Walter	70	

OFFENSE / KEY OFFENSIVE PLAYS

Singleback-Normal Slot
Johnson Option

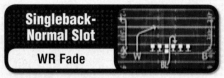
Singleback-Normal Slot
WR Fade

Singleback-4WR
WR Screen

Andre Johnson is a big-bodied wide receiver who is intelligent, explosive, and has a quick first step off the line of scrimmage.

Johnson is the best playmaker the Texans have on offense.

This play shows off Johnson's ball skills as he catches the ball early and is given the opportunity to make moves on the defense.

This allows Johnson to choose the best route to run given the situation. Johnson sees one-on-one coverage.

On option routes, he may choose to run a streak, curl, slant, or an out. On the WR Fade play, he has one emphasis—to get deep.

Johnson's game doesn't only consist of deep and option routes. He is also a good player to use on wide receiver screens.

Andre Johnson is a physical wide receiver that can make some nice plays for his offense, both in the short area as well as deep down the field.

CBs will make a mistake by stepping up to press this big receiver. Johnson does a good job of jabbing cornerbacks that try to press him.

Johnson cannot really hide his body, but the blockers set the screen up for him so that the defender loses him in the traffic.

Therefore he chooses to burn past the corner back on the streak route and into the red zone for a big play for the offense.

On the fade route, Johnson uses the jab against press coverage and then uses his speed to outrun the cornerback and make a big-time catch for his ball club.

Once he gets the ball, he can use his speed to outrun the defense.

TEAM STRATEGY

HOUSTON TEXANS / DEFENSE

DEFENSIVE STAR PLAYER #59

DeMeco Ryans — Linebacker (MLB)

Key Attributes

Awareness	82
Speed	80
Strength	75
Tackle	93

Ryans flew under the radar last year with all the hype around Mario Williams; regardless, it was an impressive performance by this second round pick. Ryans led the Texans with an impressive **155** tackles. His consistent performance over the length of the season made it a sure thing for him to win the Defensive Rookie of the Year award. The Texans feel they have a star in the making here, and Ryans will continue to develop into one of the better linebackers in the NFL.

Player Weapon: Brick Wall Defender

RECOMMENDED DEFENSIVE AUDIBLE PACKAGES

4-3-Normal	4-3-Normal	4-3-Under	4-3-Under	Dime-Normal
Buzz Weak	Storm Blitz	Zone Blitz	Over 3 Strong	Quarter Zone

DEFENSIVE PLAYCOUNTS

Man Coverage:	41	Cover 3 Zone:	23	Combo Blitz:	23
Man Zone:	37	Deep Zone:	22	Goal Line:	15
Combo Coverage:	12	Man Blitz:	49	Special Teams:	12
Cover 2 Zone:	14	Zone Blitz:	57		

TEAM TRIVIA

Houston Texans Facts

Answers:

❶ 2002

❷ Quarterback David Carr

❷ Reliant Stadium

DEFENSIVE FORMATIONS

4-3	Nickel
4-3-Normal	Nickel-3-3-5
4-3-Over	Nickel-Normal
4-3-Under	Nickel-Strong
Dime	**Quarter**
Dime-3-2-6	Quarter-3 Deep
Dime-Normal	Quarter-Normal

DEFENSIVE STRENGTH CHART

● : OVR less than 80   ● : OVR 90 or greater
● : OVR between 80-89   ○ : Player Weapons

4-3 Base Defense

FS #24   SS #26

CB #20   LB #56   LB #59   LB #52   CB #23

RE #90   DT #91   DT #92   LE #98

Dime Defense

FS #24   SS #26

CB #20   CB #21   LB #59   CB #38   CB #23

RE #90   DT #91   DT #92   LE #98

DEFENSIVE ROSTER LIST Current / Next Gen

Pos.	#	First Name	Last Name	Overall	Player Weapons
CB	23	Dunta	Robinson	87	Quick Corner / Press Coverage Corner
CB	20	Dexter	McCleon	81	
CB	38	DeMarcus	Faggins	77	
CB	21	Jamar	Fletcher	77	
CB	34	Von	Hutchins	74	
CB	32	Fred	Bennett	73	
DT	91	Amobi	Okoye	81	
DT	92	Jeff	Zgonina	81	
DT	99	Travis	Johnson	79	
DT	95	Anthony	Maddox	77	
FS	24	C.C.	Brown	78	
FS	22	Jason	Simmons	73	
LE	98	Anthony	Weaver	85	
LE	94	Ndukwe	Kalu	80	
LOLB	52	Kailee	Wong	80	
LOLB	53	Shantee	Orr	78	
MLB	59	DeMeco	Ryans	89	Brick Wall Defender
MLB	55	Danny	Clark	76	
P	7	Chad	Stanley	76	
RE	90	Mario	Williams	85	Pass Rusher
RE	93	Jason	Babin	77	
ROLB	56	Morlon	Greenwood	86	
ROLB	51	Shawn	Barber	83	
SS	26	Glenn	Earl	79	
SS	31	Brandon	Harrison	73	

DEFENSE / **KEY DEFENSIVE PLAYS**

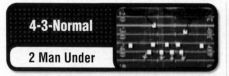

4-3-Normal

2 Man Under

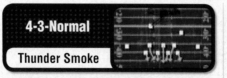

4-3-Normal

Thunder Smoke

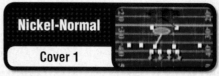

Nickel-Normal

Cover 1

DeMeco Ryans plays with intelligence, quickness, and good technique.

Ryans has good ball instincts and rarely makes a mistake or takes a wrong gap to the football.

Ryans is quick enough to cover tight ends and drop into zone coverage.

Against Singleback sets, the 4-3-Normal allows him to run downhill and make plays.

Not only can Ryans stuff the run, he can also rush the passer. This play gets the second-year linebacker a clean shot at the quarterback.

The Nickel-Normal Cover 1 drops the middle linebacker into curl/hook zone coverage to guard the short and intermediate routes.

Ryans's instincts come in as the offense attempts to run right at him. He's not afraid to get physical and exert his will on the offense.

We make one adjustment, and that's to move Ryans over to the right and down closer on the line of scrimmage.

Ryans drops back into coverage and mirrors the nearest wide receiver. On this play, that is Titans' tight end Ben Troupe.

He attacks the runner before the runner has a chance to attack him, and stops this HB dive play for a one yard gain.

Now we take the leash off Ryans and allow him to attack the offense. DeMeco Ryans is a young player who is continuing to improve his game.

Ryans knocks down the pass intended for Troupe, and makes a big play.

TENNESSEE TITANS

Division: AFC South | **Stadium:** The Coliseum | **Type:** Open | **Capacity:** 68,798 | **Surface:** Grass

2006 STANDINGS

Wins	Losses	Ties	PF	PA	Home	Road	vs. AFC	vs. NFC	vs. Div
8	8	0	324	400	4-4	4-4	5-7	3-1	4-2

TEAM OVERVIEW

This team is going to be interesting this season. Vince Young has a huge burden on his shoulders as the cover guy for *Madden NFL 08* and the franchise hope for the Tennessee Titans. Unfortunately, he doesn't have much help on offense so if they win, it'll be because he makes it happen.

Madden NFL 08 players will be drawn to Young for his mobility and rocket arm. When they see what he has to work with, they will probably bail out on this team. David Givens is the only real asset on a team short on speed at receiver.

The Titans have one star on defense in Keith Bulluck. He had better make plays all over the field, because the right side of the defensive line isn't going to give him much help.

COACHING PROFILE

Jeff Fisher

- **Head Coaching Year:** 14th
- **Experience:** Assisted defensive coordinator of the '85 Bears after an ankle injury put him on reserve.

Jeff Fisher is the most-tenured coach in the NFL. Fisher holds the franchise mark for wins with 105 over his 11-year coaching career, and ranks fifth among NFL head coaches.

TEAM RANKINGS

Scoring	16th
Passing Offense	30th
Rushing Offense	5th
Passing Defense	27th
Rushing Defense	30th
Turnovers	13th

RATINGS HISTORY

Category	'07	'06	'05	'04
Overall	85	69	**92**	88
Offense	85	80	**89**	82
Defense	**86**	68	85	84

Bold = Highest Year

83
FIVE-YEAR
AVERAGE

SCOUTING REPORT

STRENGTHS

Description	Maximizing Potential	Tips for Opponents
When you think of the Titans, you immediately think of last year's offensive Rookie of the Year Vince Young.	As a dual threat QB, Vince was able to lead the Titans to winning six of their final seven games last season.	Vince is a mobile QB, so be prepared to stop him both running and passing. Be sure to use QB Contain.
Seven year veteran linebacker Keith Bulluck is the anchor for the Titans' defense.	Bulluck once again led the Titans in tackles last season, compiling 144 tackles and 2 sacks.	Bulluck has the speed to keep up with most tight ends in the league. Force him to cover a WR instead.
The other anchor for the Titans is Chris Hope.	Hope was the Titans' 2nd leading tackler last season with 121.	Try to pound the ball to force Hope up in support.

WEAKNESSES

Description	Minimizing Risks	Tips for Opponents
Vince Young's unorthodox throwing style causes him to be a little bit less accurate than he'd like to be.	Young only completed 52 percent of his passes last year, not exactly quarterback of the Year Performance.	Fluster Young, but remember to keep him contained. Try to get him to throw off-balance.
The Texans failed to help their passing game through the draft or free agency this off-season.	Young doesn't have a go-to receiver and really can't rely on any of his receivers to make the catch.	Your secondary should be fine in man-to-man coverage, so you can focus on containing Young.

TEAM STRATEGY

OFF-SEASON **UPGRADES**

Type	Round	First Name	Last Name	School/Team	Position	Height	Weight
Free Agent	N/A	Ryan	Fowler	Dallas Cowboys	LB	6'3"	250
Free Agent	N/A	Nick	Harper	Indianapolis Colts	CB	5'10"	182
Free Agent	N/A	Bryan	Scott	New Orleans Saints	S	6'1"	219
Draft	1st	Michael	Griffin	Texas	S	6'0"	202
Draft	2nd	Chris	Henry	Arizona	RB	5'11"	230

FANTASY **OUTLOOK**

Star Player: Vince Young
Round of Draft: 6th

When looking at Young's passing numbers, they don't jump out. However, his rushing numbers do, and that's why he will be drafted by some owner's team as starting quarterback.

Star Player: LenDale White
Round of Draft: 8th

White looks to be the featured running back in Tennessee's backfield. If he manages to break 1,200 yards and gets in the end zone eight or more times, then he will be one of the biggest steals come draft day.

5 YEAR **PLAYER PROGRESSION**

First Name	Last Name	Position	'07 Overall	'08 Overall	'09 Overall	'10 Overall	'11 Overall
Vince	Young	QB	87	92	94	95	95
Lendale	White	HB	79	79	79	79	77
Keith	Bulluck	LB	96	96	95	93	-
Jonathan	Orr	WR	73	73	73	74	74
Michael	Griffin	S	82	81	81	82	82

FRANCHISE MODE **STRATEGY**

The Titans have many needs, so you can pretty much draft whoever the top player is on the board. Running back, receiver, offensive line, defensive line, and linebacker are all team needs.

Key Franchise Info

Team Salary: $71.6M
Cap Room: $37.3M
Key Rival:
• Indianapolis Colts
NFL Icons: None
Philosophy:
• Offense: Establish Run
• Defense: Shut Down Runs
Prestige: Medium
Team Needs:
• Running Back
• Receiver
Highest Paid Players:
• Vince Young
• Keith Bulluck
Up and Coming Players:
• Lendale White
• Randy Starks

TEAM STRATEGY

ROSTER AND **PACKAGE TIPS** KEY PLAYER SUBSTITUTIONS

• **Position:** FB
• **Substitution:** Bo Scaife
• **When:** Global
• **Advantage:** Scaife's SPD and CTH ratings will help make him another target out of the backfield for QB Vince Young to help open up the passing game.

• **Position:** RE
• **Substitution:** Travis LaBoy
• **When:** Global
• **Advantage:** LaBoy's AWR will help him make better, smarter plays than Antwan Odom, like recognizing screen passes.

• **Position:** PR
• **Substitution:** Chris Davis
• **When:** Global
• **Advantage:** Davis's 92 OVR rating as a kick return man should ease the doubt of the possibility of a fumble.

• **Position:** RG
• **Substitution:** Jacob Bell
• **When:** Global
• **Advantage:** Bell's high PBK rating of 89 should help provide quarterback Vince Young the confidence in knowing he'll have more time to throw the football.

TENNESSEE TITANS / **OFFENSE**

TEAM STRATEGY

OFFENSIVE **STAR PLAYER** #10

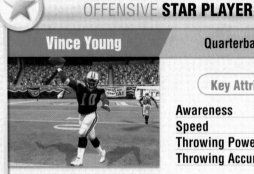

Vince Young	Quarterback (QB)

Key Attributes

Awareness	65
Speed	90
Throwing Power	92
Throwing Accuracy	84

Success has become **Vince Young's** middle name. He was a winner in college and also in his first season as a pro. Young overcame the shadow that Steve McNair cast when he left before the start of last season, and he started to build a foundation on his playing ability. As he matures, the outlook can only get better. He finished last season throwing for **2,199** yards and **12** touchdowns with **13** interceptions.

Player Weapons: Scrambler / Speed QB

RECOMMENDED OFFENSIVE **AUDIBLE PACKAGES**

I Form-Normal	I Form-Big	Singleback-Normal Slot	Singleback-Tight Flex	Shotgun-Trips TE
HB Middle	Titans 24 Blast	WR Drag	Quick Fade	HB Swing

OFFENSIVE **PLAYCOUNTS**

Quick Pass:	18	Screen Pass:	7	Pinch:	7
Standard Pass:	80	Hail Mary:	1	Counter:	17
Shotgun Pass:	39	Inside Handoff:	35	Draw:	14
Play Action Pass:	24	Outside Handoff:	13		

TEAM **TRIVIA**

Tennessee Titans Facts

Turn the page for the answers.

1. What was the team's first season as the Tennessee Titans?

2. Before being called the Tennessee Titans, what was the team's name?

3. What Super Bowl did the Titans lose to the Rams on a last second, game-saving tackle?

OFFENSIVE **FORMATIONS**

Singleback	Strong I
Big	H Pro
Big Twin WR	H Twins
Big Wing	**Weak I**
Big 3TE	H Pro
Normal Slot	H Twins
Slot Strong	**Near**
Trips Bunch	Normal Offset Wk
Tight Flex	Slot Strong
4WR Spread	Trips TE
Trey Open	4WR
Empty 5WR	
I Form	
Normal	
Big	

OFFENSIVE **STRENGTH CHART**

- ○: OVR less than 80
- ●: OVR 90 or greater
- ◐: OVR between 80-89
- ○: Player Weapons

2-Back Set

WR #81 · OL #71 · WR #76 · OL #68 · OL #75 · OL #60 · TE #84 · WR #87 · QB #10 · FB #45 · HB #25

3-Receiver Set

WR #81 · OL #71 · WR #76 · OL #68 · OL #75 · OL #60 · TE #84 · WR #25 · QB #10 · WR #87 · HB #25

OFFENSIVE **ROSTER LIST** Current / Next Gen

Pos.	#	First Name	Last Name	Overall	Player Weapons
C	68	Kevin	Mawae	89	
C	54	Eugene	Amano	73	
C	64	Leroy	Harris	71	
FB	45	Ahmard	Hall	79	
HB	25	LenDale	White	79	Power Back
HB	29	Chris	Henry	77	
HB	35	Quinton	Ganther	74	
K	2	Rob	Bironas	81	Big Foot Kicker
LG	76	David	Stewart	75	
LG	73	Justin	Geisinger	68	
LT	71	Michael	Roos	81	
LT	70	Daniel	Loper	72	
QB	10	Vince	Young	87	Scrambler / Speed QB
QB	5	Kerry	Collins	79	
QB	13	Tim	Rattay	77	
RG	75	Benji	Olson	88	Run Blocker
RG	67	Isaac	Snell	68	
RT	60	Jacob	Bell	79	
RT	64	Seth	Wand	76	
TE	84	Ben	Troupe	83	
TE	80	Bo	Scaife	80	
TE	88	Ben	Hartsock	73	
WR	87	David	Givens	83	
WR	81	Brandon	Jones	77	
WR	12	Justin	Gage	76	
WR	11	Paul	Williams	74	
WR	85	Jonathan	Orr	73	
WR	17	Chris	Davis	72	

Singleback-Big Wing

PA Boot Lt

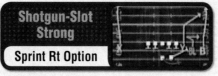

Shotgun-Slot Strong

Sprint Rt Option

Shotgun-4WR

Hail Mary

Vince Young's quick feet help him move in and out of the pocket and make precision throws.

Young is continuing to develop as a passer and this play helps him progress as a player.

Young has the uncanny ability to see the open field when he is outside of the pocket.

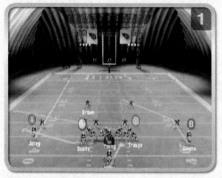

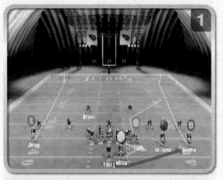

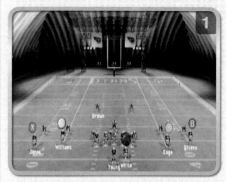

This play allows second-year quarterback Vince Young to sell a run fake and then get on the perimeter to make plays in the passing game.

Vince Young is still learning the game. While in the process, he is using his legs to make plays in both the run and passing game.

The Shotgun-4 WR Hail Mary is a play in which the QB generally chucks the ball up deep and prays for something good to happen.

Young sells the fake and fools the defense into thinking it is a run, and then bootlegs to the left side of the field.

The Shotgun-Slot Strong Sprint Rt Option gets Vince out of the pocket and onto the edge of the defense. He spots his tight end here.

We like to call this play for Vince Young for a different reason. The wide receivers will run the defenders off deep.

Here, he finds tight end Ben Troupe on the crossing route and throws him a bullet for first down yardage.

He hits Ben Troupe on the deep corner route for a huge gain. Getting Vince Young on the edge is a nightmare for the defense.

Then we create our own play for Vince Young to use his legs and pick up as many yards as possible.

TEAM STRATEGY

239

TENNESSEE TITANS / DEFENSE

DEFENSIVE STAR PLAYER #53

Keith Bulluck — Linebacker (ROLB)

Key Attributes

Awareness	86
Speed	86
Strength	73
Tackle	90

Teams can be sure of one thing when they line up to face the Titans **Keith Bulluck** will be around the ball. Bulluck is still proving that he is the leader of the defense, while adding a fifth straight season leading the defense in tackles. He finished last year with **143** tackles, and should do much of the same this year because of his athletic ability in pass coverage and his instinct to get to the ball carrier quickly on runs.

Player Weapons: Defensive Enforcer / Big Hitter, Brick Wall Defender

RECOMMENDED DEFENSIVE AUDIBLE PACKAGES

4-3-Normal	4-3-Under	Dime-3-2-6	Dime-Flat	Dime-Flat
SS Snake 3 Stay	Str Snake 3 Deep	Fire Blitz	4 Deep Safe	Zone Blitz

DEFENSIVE PLAYCOUNTS

Man Coverage:	41	Cover 3 Zone:	23	Combo Blitz:	23
Man Zone:	37	Deep Zone:	22	Goal Line:	15
Combo Coverage:	12	Man Blitz:	49	Special Teams:	12
Cover 2 Zone:	14	Zone Blitz:	57		

TEAM TRIVIA

Tennessee Titans Facts

Answers:

1. 1999
2. The Tennessee Oilers
3. Super Bowl XXXIV

DEFENSIVE FORMATIONS

4-3	**Nickel**
4-3-Normal	Nickel-Normal
4-3-Over	Nickel-Strong
4-3-Under	**Quarter**
46	Quarter-3 Deep
46-Bear	Quarter-Normal
Dime	
Dime-3-2-6	
Dime-Normal	
Dime-Flat	

DEFENSIVE STRENGTH CHART

○: OVR less than 80   ◑: OVR 90 or greater
◐: OVR between 80-89   ○: Player Weapons

4-3 Base Defense

FS #33 — SS #24

CB #21 — LB #53 — LB #55 — LB #50 — CB #20

RE #91 — DT #90 — DT #92 — LE #93

Dime Defense

FS #33 — SS #24

CB #21 — CB #31 — LB #55 — CB #26 — CB #20

RE #91 — DT #90 — DT #92 — LE #93

DEFENSIVE ROSTER LIST Current / Next Gen

Pos.	#	First Name	Last Name	Overall	Player Weapons
CB	20	Nick	Harper	85	
CB	21	Reynaldo	Hill	82	
CB	31	Cortland	Finnegan	75	
CB	26	Andre	Woolfolk	74	
CB	30	Eric	King	73	
DT	92	Albert	Haynesworth	88	Run Stopper
DT	90	Randy	Starks	78	
DT	94	Jesse	Mahelona	75	
FS	33	Michael	Griffin	82	
FS	28	Lamont	Thompson	78	
FS	38	Bryan	Scott	75	
LE	93	Kyle	Vanden Bosch	88	
LE	95	Josh	Savage	64	
LOLB	50	David	Thornton	87	
LOLB	51	Robert	Reynolds	72	
MLB	55	Stephen	Tulloch	74	
MLB	52	Ryan	Fowler	63	
P	15	Craig	Hentrich	85	
RE	91	Travis	LaBoy	79	
RE	98	Antwan	Odom	75	
ROLB	53	Keith	Bulluck	96	Defensive Enforcer / Big Hitter, Brick Wall Defender
ROLB	51	Gilbert	Gardner	73	
ROLB	49	LeVar	Woods	72	
SS	24	Chris	Hope	91	Big Hitter
SS	23	Donnie	Nickey	73	
SS	37	Calvin	Lowry	73	

4-3-Normal
Cover 2

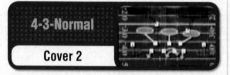

Nick Harper is a solid cornerback that is adept at the fundamentals of cornerback play.

This play drops both safety defenders to the deep half (hash mark to the sideline) of the football field while leaving both cornerbacks in the flats.

Nick Harper is an excellent Cover 2 corner. He jumps up to play the flats quickly against the pass

Once he reads there is no threat in the flats area, he immediately jumps to the intermediate area to defend the pass.

4-3-Normal
2 Man Under

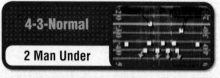

Harper shows good press coverage technique, but does not run with receivers very well.

The 2 Man Under is a good base man coverage scheme to use to allow your cornerbacks to run man-to-man with wide receivers.

Harper does a good job of jamming WRs at the line of scrimmage; however, he does not have the foot speed to keep up with the burners.

This play is good if you want to run man coverage with Harper giving you a good jam at the line of scrimmage. The safety helps nullify the deep pass against him.

4-3-Normal
Hill Blitz

Harper takes little time to reach top speed. This play shows his ability to blitz the edge and close in on the passer.

This quarter half zone blitz scheme sends the cornerback on a pass rush. Defenders cover the buzz, hook, and deep third areas.

Harper is allowed to rush the passer with this play call. On the snap, he gets a clean jump off the edge.

Once he gets into the backfield, he does a good job of consistently taking down the QB.

TEAM STRATEGY

MINNESOTA VIKINGS

Division: NFC North | **Stadium:** The Metrodome™ | **Type:** Dome | **Capacity:** 64,121 | **Surface:** Turf

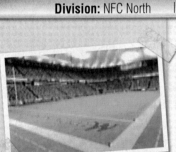

TEAM STRATEGY

COACHING PROFILE

Brad Childress

- **Head Coaching Year:** 2nd
- **Experience:** Philadelphia Eagles offensive coordinator (2003-2005).

Childress was named the seventh head coach in Vikings history on January 6, 2006. Brad Childress is considered a third generation West Coast Offense disciple and is part of the Bill Walsh coaching tree.

TEAM RANKINGS

Scoring	26th
Passing Offense	18th
Rushing Offense	16th
Passing Defense	31st
Rushing Defense	1st
Turnovers	10th

RATINGS HISTORY

Category	'07	'06	'05	'04
Overall	86	**90**	85	78
Offense	87	**92**	90	82
Defense	**87**	80	84	71

Bold = Highest Year

84
FIVE-YEAR AVERAGE

2006 STANDINGS

Wins	Losses	Ties	PF	PA	Home	Road	vs. AFC	vs. NFC	vs. Div
6	10	0	282	327	3-5	3-5	0-4	6-6	2-4

TEAM OVERVIEW

The Vikings had the league's best run defense in 2006, but a disastrous performance by the offense led to a dismal season. Childress has cleaned house on offense, but it remains to be seen whether Tarvaris Jackson will be able to handle the quarterbacking duties.

The running game appears to be in fine shape with the one-two punch of Chester Taylor and rookie Adrian Peterson. WR is a weak spot on this team with rookie Sidney Rice bringing the most to the table.

The Vikings' defense is solid all around. Forget trying to run up the middle on them. You will also want to stay away from the right side of the field, with Winfield and Sharper roaming the sidelines.

SCOUTING REPORT

STRENGTHS

Description	Maximizing Potential	Tips for Opponents
Both Chester Taylor and Adrian Peterson have the potential to run for over 1,000 yards each.	Call plays for Taylor that have him running between the tackles. Call plays for Peterson that get him outside.	When Taylor lines up in the backfield, call inside run defenses that shoot the linebackers through the gaps.
Right outside linebacker Chad Greenway is the team's best pass rushing threat.	Greenway's speed rating is 85, making him a valuable asset when calling plays that bring the heat.	Outside of Greenway, they don't have any other linebacker who poses a threat as a pass rusher.
The Vikings left side of the offensive line is one of the best in the game.	Call plays that take the backs to the left.	Overload to this side and force the back right.

WEAKNESSES

Description	Minimizing Risks	Tips for Opponents
Neither Tarvaris Jackson or Brooks Bollinger are going to put any fear into the opposing secondary.	Run the ball as much as possible with Taylor and Peterson. This will keep you in short yardage situation.	On first down, load the box with nine defenders and force the Vikings' HBs to beat you with their legs.
Adding to the Vikings' problems at QB, the team does not have a true number one receiver on their roster.	Slants, drags, curls, and other short pass routes are your best bet at moving the ball through the air.	Call a lot of bump-n-run-to slow down the receivers. They don't have the ability to get off the press quickly.

OFF-SEASON **UPGRADES**

Type	Round	First Name	Last Name	School/Team	Position	Height	Weight
Free Agent	N/A	Mike	Doss	Indianapolis Colts	S	5'10"	207
Free Agent	N/A	Visanthe	Shiancoe	New York Giants	TE	6'4"	250
Free Agent	N/A	Bobby	Wade	Tennessee Titans	WR	5'10"	190
Draft	1st	Ben	Grubs	Auburn	G	6'3"	314
Draft	2nd	Yamon	Figures	Kansas State	WR	5'11"	174

FANTASY **OUTLOOK**

⭐ **Star Player:** Chester Taylor
Round of Draft: 4th

The biggest problem with drafting Taylor is rookie Adrian Peterson is going to steal some of his attention. If you draft Taylor, then you better make sure you grab Peterson as well in the next round.

⭐ **Star Player:** Adrian Peterson
Round of Draft: 5th

He isn't expected to be the starter at running back on opening day, but he will get his share of carries. If he outplays Taylor in the first half of the season, he should end up becoming the team's full-time starter.

5 YEAR **PLAYER PROGRESSION**

First Name	Last Name	Position	'07 Overall	'08 Overall	'09 Overall	'10 Overall	'11 Overall
Steve	Hutchinson	G	97	97	97	96	98
Kevin	Williams	DT	97	97	99	99	99
Chester	Taylor	HB	87	87	87	85	82
Adrian	Peterson	HB	85	87	90	91	92
Chad	Greenway	LB	82	81	81	78	77

FRANCHISE MODE **STRATEGY**

If a franchise quarterback should land in your lap in the first round, don't hesitate to draft him. After all a franchise quarterback sells tickets and ultimately helps win championships.

Key Franchise Info

Team Salary: $94.9M
Cap Room: $14.0M
Key Rival:
• Green Bay Packers
NFL Icons: None
Philosophy:
• Offense: Ball Control
• Defense: Force the Pass
Prestige: Very Low
Team Needs:
• Quarterback
• Receiver
Highest Paid Players:
• Steve Hutchinson
• Troy Williamson
Up and Coming Players:
• Sidney Rice
• Adrian Peterson

TEAM STRATEGY

ROSTER AND **PACKAGE TIPS** — KEY PLAYER SUBSTITUTIONS

• **Position:** HB
• **Substitution:** Adrian Peterson
• **When:** Global
• **Advantage:** Peterson's high SPD and BTK ratings should make him a threat to go the distance anytime he touches the ball coming out of the backfield.

• **Position:** WR
• **Substitution:** Sidney Rice
• **When:** Global
• **Advantage:** At the height of 6'4" and having a JMP rating of 92, Rice should have absolutely no problem going up and making the catch deep down the field.

• **Position:** RT
• **Substitution:** Marcus Johnson
• **When:** Global
• **Advantage:** Johnson has better RBK and PBK ratings than Ryan Cook, which should help solidify the offensive line.

• **Position:** LE
• **Substitution:** Ray Edwards
• **When:** Passing Situations
• **Advantage:** Edwards's SPD rating of 77 will help add another pass rusher to the defensive front for those crucial third downs.

MINNESOTA VIKINGS / OFFENSE

OFFENSIVE STAR PLAYER #29

Chester Taylor — Halfback (HB)

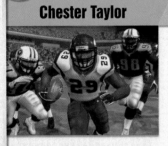

Key Attributes

Acceleration	93
Agility	94
Break Tackle	82
Speed	89

In his first season as a full time starter for the Vikings, **Taylor** had a productive season at runningback. He managed to rush for **1,216** yards and was able to get in the end zone **6** times. Taylor uses his vision, patience, and instincts to find open holes along the offensive line to pick up positive yardage. He also has a solid pair of hands that allows him to be a valuable asset in the Vikings' aerial attack.

Player Weapon: Power Back

OFFENSIVE STRENGTH CHART

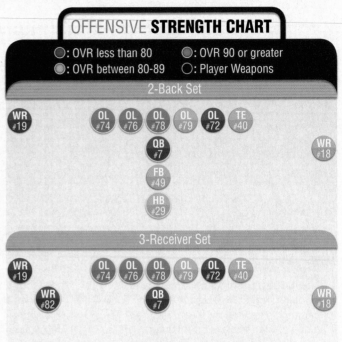

○ : OVR less than 80   ● : OVR 90 or greater
● : OVR between 80-89   ○ : Player Weapons

2-Back Set

WR #19 | OL #74 | OL #76 | OL #78 | OL #79 | OL #72 | TE #40
QB #7
WR #18
FB #49
HB #29

3-Receiver Set

WR #19 | OL #74 | OL #76 | OL #78 | OL #79 | OL #72 | TE #40
WR #82
QB #7
WR #18
HB #29

RECOMMENDED OFFENSIVE AUDIBLE PACKAGES

I Form-Normal	I Form-Big	Singleback-Big	Singleback-Slot Strong	Shotgun-4WR
TE Flat	HB Lead Toss	HB Stretch	FL Drag	HB Screen

OFFENSIVE PLAYCOUNTS

Quick Pass:	11	Screen Pass:	14	Pinch:	10
Standard Pass:	100	Hail Mary:	1	Counter:	17
Shotgun Pass:	13	Inside Handoff:	30	Draw:	15
Play Action Pass:	34	Outside Handoff:	10		

TEAM TRIVIA

Minnesota Vikings Facts

Turn the page for the answers.

❶ What year did the Minnesota Vikings win their first Division title?

❷ How many Super Bowls have the Vikings played in?

❸ What former Vikings receiver now plays for the New England Patriots?

OFFENSIVE FORMATIONS

Singleback	Far
Big	Pro
Normal	**Strong I**
Slot Strong	Normal
Trips Bunch	3WR
4WR Flex	Twin TE
Trips WR	**Weak I**
Empty 5WR	Close
I Form	Tight Twins
Normal	**Shotgun**
Close	2RB 3WR
Big	4WR
Split Backs	
Normal	
3WR	

OFFENSIVE ROSTER LIST Current / Next Gen

Pos.	#	First Name	Last Name	Overall	Player Weapons
C	78	Matt	Birk	92	Pass Blocker
C	66	Norm	Katnik	68	
FB	49	Tony	Richardson	89	
HB	29	Chester	Taylor	87	Power Back
HB	28	Adrian	Peterson	85	Power Back
HB	30	Mewelde	Moore	77	Elusive Back
HB	35	Ciatrick	Fason	75	
K	8	Ryan	Longwell	86	
LG	76	Steve	Hutchinson	97	Run Blocker / Crushing Run Bocker
LG	63	Brian	Daniels	72	
LT	74	Bryant	McKinnie	93	Pass Blocker / Pass Blocker
LT	75	Chase	Johnson	64	
QB	7	Tarvaris	Jackson	77	Scrambler
QB	9	Brooks	Bollinger	73	
RG	79	Artis	Hicks	80	
RG	64	Anthony	Herrera	71	
RT	72	Marcus	Johnson	76	
RT	62	Ryan	Cook	74	
TE	40	Jim	Kleinsasser	81	
TE	81	Visanthe	Shiancoe	75	
TE	45	Richard	Owens	66	
WR	18	Sidney	Rice	80	Spectacular Catch Receiver
WR	19	Bobby	Wade	79	
WR	14	Aundrae	Allison	76	
WR	82	Troy	Williamson	76	Deep Threat
WR	12	Billy	McMullen	75	
WR	16	Cortez	Hankton	70	

Strong I-HB

Off Tackle

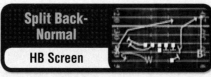

Split Back-Normal

HB Screen

Singleback-Big

HB Counter

Chester Taylor is a productive back that can run the ball between the tackles or on the outside.

Taylor is not only a good back when running the ball between the tackles or on sweeps, he is also a solid back when used in the pass game.

Defenses know Taylor has great speed, so it is necessary to use him on a counter to make sure the defense has to defend against him honestly.

This play is designed to let Taylor follow his fullback off tackle and work his way up the field. With his explosiveness and vision, this play is perfect.

This screen play is designed to pull the cornerback away to allow for the needed space to make the screen pass to Taylor a success.

This play is designed to beat defenses that try to shift into an over or under formation or for defenses that like to over-pursue.

As Taylor makes it to the outside, he has his eyes upfield, steadily reading and setting his blocks up downfield.

The receiver clears the defender out and leaves an open area for the screen pass. Taylor is shown making the catch in the open field.

The defense bit on the counter step, and now Taylor is making his way around the corner as shown here, with the right guard leading the way.

Taylor makes a quick juke, and in doing so, helps himself pick up additional yards on the play.

Taylor's agility makes it easy for him to turn upfield and put on the speed.

Taylor beats the defenders around the corner and explodes downfield. The defense must play him honest.

TEAM STRATEGY

245

MINNESOTA VIKINGS / DEFENSE

DEFENSIVE STAR PLAYER #26

Antoine Winfield	Cornerback (CB)

Key Attributes

Acceleration	91
Awareness	90
Catching	67
Speed	90

One of the better tackling defensive backs in the NFL, **Winfield** ranked second on the team in total tackles with **97**. He was also tied for first among the team in interceptions with **4**. He uses a tough, aggressive style of play to give opposing receivers fits getting off the line of scrimmage. He may not be an elite cornerback, but he brings his workmanlike mentality to game every week and gets the job done in pass coverage and as a run stopper.

Player Weapons: Containment Corner / Press Coverage Corner, Smart Corner

RECOMMENDED DEFENSIVE AUDIBLE PACKAGES

4-3-Normal	4-3-Under	Dime-3-2-6	Ncikel-Normal	Nickel-Normal
Free Fire	Buzz Duo	DB Dogs 1	Over Storm Brave	Quarter Half

DEFENSIVE PLAYCOUNTS

Man Coverage:	36	Cover 3 Zone:	18	Combo Blitz:	11
Man Zone:	30	Deep Zone:	15	Goal Line:	15
Combo Coverage:	8	Man Blitz:	36	Special Teams:	12
Cover 2 Zone:	18	Zone Blitz:	53		

TEAM TRIVIA

Minnesota Vikings Facts

Answers:

1 1968

2 Four

3 Randy Moss

DEFENSIVE FORMATIONS

4-3	Nickel
4-3-Normal	Nickel-3-3-5
4-3-Over	Nickel-Normal
4-3-Under	Nickel-Strong
Dime	**Quarter**
Dime-3-2-6	Quarter-3 Deep
Dime-Normal	Quarter-Normal
Dime-Flat	

DEFENSIVE STRENGTH CHART

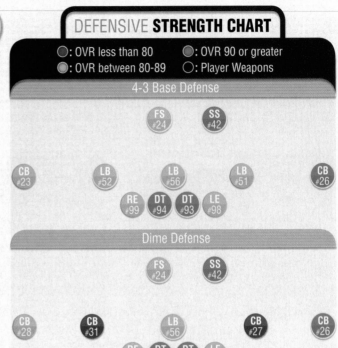

○: OVR less than 80　　◐: OVR 90 or greater
◑: OVR between 80-89　　○: Player Weapons

4-3 Base Defense

FS #24　　SS #42

CB #23　　LB #52　　LB #56　　LB #51　　CB #26

RE #99　　DT #94　　DT #93　　LE #98

Dime Defense

FS #24　　SS #42

CB #28　　CB #31　　LB #56　　CB #27　　CB #26

RE #99　　DT #94　　DT #93　　LE #98

DEFENSIVE ROSTER LIST   Current / Next Gen

Pos.	#	First Name	Last Name	Overall	Player Weapons
CB	26	Antoine	Winfield	91	Containment Corner / Press Coverage, Smart Corner
CB	23	Cedric	Griffin	86	
CB	31	Marcus	McCauley	78	
CB	27	Ronyell	Whitaker	71	
CB	37	Mike	Hawkins	66	
DT	93	Kevin	Williams	97	Finesse Move D-Lineman, Power Move D-Lineman
DT	94	Pat	Williams	93	Power Move D-Lineman
DT	97	Spencer	Johnson	71	
FS	24	Dwight	Smith	86	Coverage Safety
FS	25	Tank	Williams	79	
LE	95	Kenechi	Udeze	80	
LE	98	Darrion	Scott	80	
LE	92	Jayme	Mitchell	75	
LOLB	51	Ben	Leber	81	
LOLB	59	Heath	Farwell	66	
MLB	56	E.J.	Henderson	85	Heavy Hitter
MLB	50	Vinny	Ciurciu	66	
P	5	Chris	Kluwe	77	
RE	99	Erasmus	James	82	
RE	91	Ray	Edwards	77	
RE	96	Brian	Robison	77	
ROLB	52	Chad	Greenway	82	Playmaker
ROLB	54	Dontarrious	Thomas	81	
ROLB	57	Rufus	Alexander	75	
SS	42	Darren	Sharper	93	Smart Safety
SS	21	Mike	Doss	82	

TEAM STRATEGY

4-3-Normal

Cover 2

4-3-Normal

Man QB Spy

Nickel-Normal

NB Blitz

Antoine Winfield is an aggressive corner that is really good in run support. This play lets him showcase his ability to read and react.

The Vikings' defense trusts Winfield to hold it down in man coverage, and he has no problem proving to his teammates just how trustworthy he is.

When a defense has a talented player like Winfield on the field, it is important to also get him involved in other aspects of the defense.

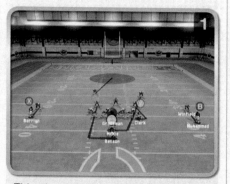

The defense is designed to keep everything in front of it. This is why the Cover 2 is so hard to beat. Winfield excels in this scheme.

This play covers the outside receivers in man-to-man coverage, while covering the center of the field with underneath and deep zone coverage.

The defense is designed to bring pressure from the nickelback while keeping the rest of the defense in man-to-man coverage.

A lot of Cover 2 corners sit in their stance on an angle Winfield sees the run and he has fought through the receiver to attack the RB.

Winfield recognizes a play action fake even this early because of how the receiver is releasing off the ball. He quickly turns to bail and gets back.

Winfield can easily be packaged in at the NB position and bring that unexpected pressure, as seen here as he sprints in at the snap.

Winfield elevates his stock with plays made against the run. He takes this runningback down easily.

Winfield has great hopes, and shows the jump ball is not going to work against him.

When he comes from the nickel position it results in a sack of the quarterback.

TEAM STRATEGY

247

FRANCHISE MODE

Franchise mode is back again in *Madden NFL 08*, and is sure to provide franchise junkies with hours of rewarding gameplay. Franchise mode puts you in the driver's seat as you take on the functions of owner, GM, coach, and player. You step right behind the desk of an NFL front office, making personnel and on field adjustments as well as dealing with contracts and the Salary Cap.

In this chapter we'll take you through the ins and outs of owning and running an NFL team in *Madden NFL 08*. We'll provide you with draft day advice (for those of you who like the Fantasy Draft), salary cap information, a rundown on free agency, and tips for making the most of your NFL budget.

STARTING A FRANCHISE

As you begin a new franchise, you will have to make some basic decisions, such as the number of players in your league and whether you want to use a Fantasy Draft or just take control of a current team. You'll then determine whether you want the Trade Deadline to be in effect. This will restrict you from making trades part way through the season. Otherwise, you'll be able to make trades all season long.

With the Fantasy Draft turned on, all of the current NFL players are placed in one monster-sized pool. This is one of the best ways to play Franchise Mode, as you'll have 49 rounds to assemble your own dream team. This gives you the ultimate flexibility to build a team that will fit your own unique style of play. Do you want to play a Run-N-Gun style offense with a mobile QB? Or would you rather get a franchise running back and a bunch of road graders to break open massive running lanes through the defense? You're in control!

Lastly, you will select a coach and team to begin with. If you are doing a Fantasy Draft, this will not matter too much, as you will build your own team from scratch. Pick the team you've always wanted to play for. In the event that you have turned off the Fantasy Draft, you will be working with the current personnel of the team you pick. This gives you a bunch of options. You can go with a current powerhouse and try to keep the dynasty going, or you can take a down-and-out franchise and build it into a winner. You can play the game to make money, or play to win championships. Again, the choice is yours!

FANTASY DRAFT

Before you commit to playing in a Fantasy Draft league, you need to be aware that it is going to take some serious time if you want to be hands-on the whole way. Fortunately, you can stop, save, and come back to it later. We really recommend doing this so that you will be fresh throughout the process. Fourty-nine rounds is a lot of drafting. To be fully prepared, you must know the player breakdown you will need at the end of the day. The draft works in a snaking order – that is, the team that picks first in one round will pick 32nd in the subsequent round, then back to first and so on. If you pick 16th in the first round, you'll be back in the same spot coming and going each time through.

You can pick any player you want that is available at your turn. You will, however, have to meet some requirements before you can begin play. Be sure to get the following (at minimum).

#	Offense
3	Quarterbacks (QB)
3	Halfbacks (HB)
1	Fullback (FB)
4	Wide Receivers (WR)
2	Tight Ends (TE)
4	Offensive Tackles (LT,RT)
4	Offensive Guards (LG,RG)
2	Centers (C)

#	Defense
4	Defensive (LE, RE)
3	Defensive Tackles (DT)
4	Outside Linebakers (LOLB,ROLB)
2	Middle Linebackers (MLB)
4	Cornerbacks (CB)
2	Free Safeties (FS)
2	Strong Safeties (SS)

#	Special Teams
1	Kicker (K)
1	Punter (P)

FANTASY DRAFT NOTES

Remember that this isn't a traditional NFL setup in which there will be a large pool of talented free agents at the end of the day that you can use to fill gaps. Most if not all players will be taken, and you have no excuse not to get some depth at every position.

When drafting, a good rule of thumb is to go fast and young. You can develop many of the other attributes of your players,

but speed can't be coached up. A player's SPD rating will only budge a point or two during their career. Obviously, young players give you more time to develop them into superstars, but it is still useful to have a couple of cagey vets as well.

Get your franchise off to a quick start by drafting the best available player in the first couple of rounds. After that you can worry about adding depth and filling in the gaps in your roster.

PHILOSOPHY

Creating teams using your own *philosophy*

Your first Fantasy Draft can be overwhelming, so we have created a draft-priority list to help you draft an entire team with your first 25 picks. Once you get the hang of things, we encourage you to experiment with this list to build your own style of team with your own priorities. Should you ever get stuck, you can come back to our notes to bail you out of trouble.

Round	Position	Notes
1	Quarterback	You can't win without scoring. The QB is the leader of the O and is critical with the new vision and precision passing features of *Madden NFL 08*. Look for a quarterback with an accurate arm and high awareness rating. If you like to run, find a QB that also has decent speed.
2	Defensive End	A dominating presence here can put a ton of pressure on your opponent. Think speed!
3	Offensive End	An elite left tackle will go a long way towards keeping your franchise quarterback protected.
4	Cornerback	A shut-down cover guy gives you all kinds of options with your defensive scheme.
5	Halfback	We need a versatile back who has speed and is able to catch the ball. He doesn't need to be a bruiser, because we plan on spreading the defense out and allowing him to use his speed and shiftiness to get his yards.
6	Wide Receiver	We need a good receiver, but he doesn't need great speed, just solid hands. We plan on throwing a lot of quick passes; he needs to be able catch the ball.
7	Defensive Tackle	This player will work in conjection with the DE to get pressure up the middle and shut down the run.
8	Defensive End	Another quick, agile body on defense.
9	Offensive Tackle	Look at his speed and agility rating. These attributes will be needed to keep the left end off of the quarterback.
10	Middle Linebacker	The QB of the defense. Get someone with great awareness and speed here.
11	Tight End	Get a serviceable run-blocker here. Grab a pass catcher if one is still handy.
12	Outside Linebacker	Outside linebackers need to be fast, especially the ROLB. Draft the fastest one and don't worry about his other attributes.
13	Center	Look for a center with high awareness and pass blocking ability. These two attributes will go a long way in protecting the QB up the middle.
14	Cornerback	Your second corner has to be good in a league full of three-wide sets.
15	Strong Safety	This guy needs to be strong and a big hitter.
16	Wide Receiver	Look for a pure-speed guy here. Hands don't hurt, either.
17	Defensive Tackle	Prioritize size for the second interior D-lineman. Stuff the run.
18	Outside Linebacker	Speed and tackling ability are precious commodities here.
19	Offensive Guard	The second guard will probably have to be average at best.
20	Free Safety	Look for speed and good catch ratings here. He's the last line of defense on the deep ball.
21	Fullback	Get a sledgehammer of a blocker here. There's nothing fancy about the FB position.
22	Halfback	Backups are essential at all positions, but none more so than HB.
23	Offensive Guard	You've got the QB and now you've got two guys to protect him.
24	Kicker	Most decent kickers perform about the same. Any middle of the road guy will do here.
25	Punter	Grab a punter with power.

There—twenty-five picks later you're on your way to a solid lineup! Use the Draft-Breakdown screen to assess your needs as you move into the later rounds of the draft. Be sure to get the required number of players at each position. Otherwise, one small injury could spell disaster.

FRANCHISE MODE

MOCK DRAFT

Here are the results of our mock draft. We picked 9th in the first round and 24th in the second round. 9th in the 3rd round and 24th in the 4th round, etc.

Round	First Name	Position	Overall	Age
1	Champ Bailey	CB	99	29
3	Ed Reed	FS	99	28
4	Antonio Gates	TE	97	27
5	Ray Lewis	MLB	96	32
17	Jason Hanson	K	92	37
6	Chris Snee	G	90	25
7	Kelly Gregg	DT	89	30
8	Brian Kelly	CB	87	31
2	Vince Young	QB	87	24
9	Marion Barber	HB	87	24
10	Nick Ferguson	SS	86	32
11	Darren Howard	DE	86	29
12	Eddie Kennison	WR	85	34
13	Maurice Williams	T	85	28
25	Brian Simmons	MLB	84	32
15	Jeremy Newberry	C	84	31
14	Igor Olshansky	DE	84	25
16	Travelle Wharton	T	83	26
18	Le'Ron McClain	FB	83	22
19	Na'il Diggs	OLB	82	29
20	Chris Bober	G	82	29
21	Chad Greenway	OLB	82	24
22	Micah Knorr	P	81	32
26	Seth Payne	DT	81	32
27	Darrelle Revis	CB	81	22

Round	First Name	Position	Overall	Age
29	L.J. Shelton	T	80	31
28	Pierson Prioleau	FS	80	30
23	Travis Taylor	WR	80	29
30	Nick Greisen	OLB	79	28
31	Rex Hadnot	C	79	27
34	Adrian Peterson	HB	78	28
24	Hank Baskett	WR	78	25
33	Jeff King	TE	78	23
32	Baraka Atkins	DE	78	22
37	Patrick Ramsey	QB	77	28
36	Anthony Adams	DT	77	27
35	Brandon Jones	WR	77	25
39	Lennie Friedman	G	76	29
38	Jerome McDougle	DE	76	27
41	DeJuan Groce	CB	75	27
40	Vernon Fox	SS	75	26
42	Jesse Chatman	HB	75	25
46	David Thomas	TE	75	24
47	Marques Tuiasosopo	QB	74	28
43	Phil Bogle	G	74	27
49	Keith Smith	CB	73	27
48	Matt Ware	TE	73	24
44	Robert Reynolds	OLB	72	26
45	Mark LeVoir	T	70	25

DRAFT HIGHLIGHTS

One of the options you have is to let the CPU simulate the draft for you. If you are impatient or just short on time, you can make the first couple of picks (❶) and then let the CPU finish things off. We did that with our mock draft. We like to make at least the first 4-5 rounds worth of picks so we can choose our superstar players and dictate the feel of our team.

We picked up a monster secondary. With Champ Bailey and Ed Reed anchoring this unit, we can run just about any defensive coverage in the game. Ray Lewis patrols the middle of the field and should be able to plug holes in the run game.

On offense, we gave some love to *Madden NFL 08* cover man Vince Young as we put him behind the helm of our offense. He is not without help either, as he has stud TE Antonio Gates to bail him out of trouble if need be.

Our team has a pretty good mix of veteran and young players. We have 12 guys in the 30 or older bracket, and 15 guys 25 or younger. As a rule, we like to go for younger and cheaper if we have two possible players with similar abilities. For straight simulated franchises, you are better off with more veteran players.

This team is really built around the defense. Early picks were used to lock down Bailey and Reed to give us a one-two punch in the secondary that is second to none. We don't have a lot of speed at DE, so that will be one of the things we will look to shore up in our first offseason. Our starting linebackers (Simmons, Lewis, and Greenway) all have good speed. With our strong secondary behind them, they'll be used in the pass rush game early and often.

We don't have a ton of stars on the offensive side of the ball, but we have more than enough firepower to get the job done. Young will have veteran targets in Kinnison and Gates, with Barber providing a stable presence in the run game. We don't have much speed at wideout so that will be a future need that we try to address. We will play ball control offense, using Young's legs to break down the defense and get Gates in mismatch situations with the linebackers.

We used the latter rounds to build our depth. Be sure to keep an eye on your late-round draft picks. You need to make sure that you sign inexpensive players to fill out your roster. Keep as much cap room free as possible; you'll need it in year two.

In the final equation, we came in 19.8 million under the cap, giving the team some flexibility to sign future draft choices and free agents as they come available.

PLAYER MANAGEMENT

The Player Management screen (2) under Roster options gives you the ability to deal with your team player by player. You can release players, trade them, put them on the trading block, and check on career statistics. Here, we assign Champ Bailey to be our team captain, as well as check out his roles on the team (more on this later).

PLACE ON TRADE BLOCK

The trading block (3) allows you to take a player on your team and see what others are willing to give you for them. This is a great way to passively trade players. Throw a guy up on the block and display what you are willing to take in return. You can choose by position/rating or draft pick.

We put Jerome McDougle up for a fourth round draft pick. He's deep on our bench and his $12M contract is tying up our funds. We are able to pawn him off on the Bears.

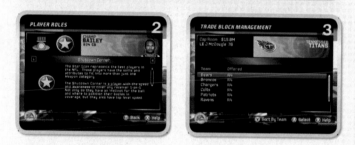

TRAINING CAMP

Before each season, you will have the option of running drills to work on the skills of different players (4). The type of drill you run affects players differently. You run through the mini-camp drills to gain new attribute points. After you complete a level successfully, you have the option of trying the next level for more points. Be careful: if you fail in a drill, you won't get any improvement points. Practice the mini-camp drills outside of Franchise mode before you put your skills to the test. For example, we were able to add 4 points to Ray Lewis's tackle rating during these drills.

FRANCHISE SIMULATION

Once you get past training camps, it's time to get ready for the gridiron. Coach's Corner allows you to manage a variety of coaching options like hot routes, packages, substitutions, and philosophy. If you plan on simming your seasons, then you will want to take some time to adjust your coaching philosophy.

We like to stick with our default 4-3 defensive alignment, but move our sliders a bit more to the aggressive side on defense. With our secondary, we can afford to attack a bit more than normal. Offensively, we favor the run and look to play with a balanced attack.

THE PHILOSOPHY

The My Week menu option lets you control your weekly schedule as a coach. From this screen (1) you can adjust rosters, practice, check email messages, and study your opponent.

Gameplan mode is back again and can be found under the Study Opponent submenu. In Weekly Gameplan mode, you can take your squad on the field and practice against your opponent's specific tendencies. You'll have different offensive and defensive plays to work with each week. By performing well in Gameplan mode, you will see benefits on the field when running against those schemes.

Our favorite part of the Study Opponent menu is the Positional Breakdown screen. This gives you a preview of the other team's strengths and weaknesses. Use this screen (2) to get an idea of what the other team will throw your way. If you have performed a Fantasy Draft to start the season, then this is especially useful. With star players spread all over the NFL, you can use this feature to figure out what you will be facing come game time. You'll get three keys and an overview of their starting line-ups.

After you get some games under your belt, be sure to check out the statistical breakdowns. This will give you an idea of what is working for you in both the run, and passing games.

STATS/INFO

The Stats/Info screen (3) replaces the old Storyline Central from *Madden NFL 07*. You still can check out both the national and local beat papers for news.

The local paper provides menus where you can view Depth Charts, Injury Reports, Player Stats, and Team Info. This is a nice way to navigate the menus as well as read some pretty cool articles about your team. All in all, it really helps make Franchise mode more immersive.

Be sure to look out for little clues that affect your franchise. You'll get tips on players that are nearing the end of their contracts, as well as players that are unhappy with their current situation.

TOTAL CONTROL SIMULATION

Once you get into the season, you have several different options for processing your game. One of the ways making its return from last year is Total Control Simulation. With Total Control Simulation, you can call the plays and see the result in text format. This allows you to be the coach and quickly work through games that you don't want to play in live action. The really nice part about this mode is that you can jump into the game anytime you want. The option also exists to have the CPU fully simulate that game without you having to call plays or be in control of your team. This is the standard simulation mode from years past.

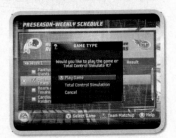

SPAWN GAMES

Madden NFL 08 comes fully equipped with support for spawned franchise games this year. You can spawn a game to play it on your PSP, play it online, or just play it offline outside of Franchise mode. When you spawn a game, you are basically just taking one of your franchise games and separating it from the franchise. When the game is completed, you can merge the results back into your franchise.

INTO THE SEASON

After training camp and the pre-season, you can check out your team's player progression. It is a good idea to play some of your pre-season games and really focus in on a couple of players. By focusing reps on the younger players, you can rapidly increase their abilities. Veteran players will not see as much of an improvement.

For purposes of this guide, we simmed the regular season all the way through. Remember that the trade deadline is at week 6. If you are going to make any changes, you don't want to do a sim of the full season. You are better off simming one game at a time and adjusting your lineup accordingly.

Time to head Into the Season

Our team came out with a 10-6 record to win the AFC South. Thanks to our power packed defense, we made it all the way to the Super Bowl and picked up the Lombardi Trophy as world champs!

SEASON HIGHLIGHTS

	First Name	Last Name	Season Stats
Offense	Vince	Young	1,726 yards passing, 16 TDs, 1,244 yards rushing
	M	Marber	1,244 yards rushing, 8 TDs
	Antonio	Gates	71 receptions, 607 yards
	E	Kinnison	58 receptions, 8 TDs
Defense	D	Howard	10 sacks
	Ray	Lewis	131 tackles, 5 sacks
	D	Revis	4 interceptions
Special Teams	Champ	Bailey	22.7 yards return / kick return average
	J	Hanson	27/33 field goals made, 107 points

OWNER'S BOX

With *Madden NFL 08*, you get to be the player, coach, GM, and owner. This is a completely different side to the game and opens up a lot of variety for gameplay. You can play the game from the perspective of making as much money as possible as the owner. Put a good enough team on the field to fill the seats, but keep your salaries down to bank plenty of cash. The Owner's Box lets you take a peek inside what it is like to be the owner of an NFL franchise you control every aspect of your team from concession prices to stadium upgrades.

The Owner's Box view gives you a quick look at your franchise's health, including Fan Support, Cash Assets, Attendance, and Record. You can consult with your Board of Advisors for suggestions and readings of your fans' feelings. The advisors aren't always right, so take their advice with a grain of salt. Don't forget that advertising can help fill the seats, but

there is a cost trade off. Try to keep things in balance as much as possible.

The Set Prices screen allows you to do just that. You can set prices for individual concession stand items, tickets, parking and merchandise. Once you can afford a solid advertising

OWNER'S BOX

budget, you can fill the seats up with a lesser team. Be sure not to go overboard and outprice your customers. They'll let you know you've gone too far by not attending games as often.

One of the more valuable screens in the Owner Box is the Franchise/Team info page. This page gives you a ton of useful facts about your franchise, especially in comparison to other teams in the league. Our franchise currently is in a great cash position. We have the 25rd lowest team salary in the league and are $21.0 million under the cap. We'll have plenty of money to resign players and pay our top draft choices.

The other useful feature on this page is the Positional Ratings. Now you can get a good idea of where your talent stacks up compared to the rest of the league. As you can see, we are close to the league average at most positions with our strengths at DB and QB. Young is riding on a high after his playoff performance and Super Bowl win. We are

lagging behind on the defensive line, but we can address that at free agency or the draft.

Finally, don't forget to take a peak at your team's Income and Expenses from time to time. As an Owner, one of your jobs is to make money. Winning is important, but so is a healthy bottom line. Cash in the bank means upgrades to your stadiums that can attract more fans and give them a better experience. More cash means more advertising so you can fill up the stands.

ADVANCE TO OFF-SEASON

OFF-SEASON SCHEDULE

You will have a ton of things that need to be done in the off-season to get ready for the next go around. Below, we give you some strategies on how to best perform each of these tasks.

You can let the CPU sign your coaching staff if there are any holes to fill. You have ultimate control of the team in the long run–no need to waste time here unless you really like to tightly manage your team. We like to manage our own staff. In these off-season, we pick up a new offensive coordinator as our former left for a head coaching position.

OFF-SEASON CUT LOGIC

After going through player retirements (we lost Eddie Kinnison here), the CPU uses intelligent logic to determine when to cut players loose. You may take a cap hit, but will save money in the long run by dropping overpriced talent. We did a pretty good job of dropping our dead weight early on so EA has no recommendations for us.

RESTRICTED FREE AGENTS

With Restricted Free Agents, we have the right to first match any offers from other teams to our players. If it's a guy you want to hang on to, be sure to match the offer sheet and get him back under contract. Denver snatches up one of our young wideouts, but he is replaceable. Too much money for an overall rating of 77.

RE-SIGN PLAYERS

This part gets pretty tricky. You have to pony up the dough or watch your players take a walk. Any players you don't sign will hit free agency. You can at times sign them back, but it gets pretty expensive. You have to be really careful here to not get in over your head. This part of the off-season is made very tricky when you do a Fantasy Draft. If you planned things right from the start, you should be okay here. Just sign the guys you really want and let lesser talent fall by the wayside. Take a look at restructuring the deals for some of your key players that still have time left on their contracts. It's usually much more cost effective to get them earlier rather than later. Remember, you have the draft coming, so you don't need to sign guys low on the depth chart for a lot of money. Sign your older players to short-term contracts in case their ratings fall off dramatically as they age.

FREE AGENT SIGNING

After re-signing and/or releasing your current players, you move into Free Agency. Now it is time to put that cash flow to work as you add the missing pieces to your team.

We make a big splash by signing Lance Briggs to a big contract. Our linebacking core now has enough mojo to match our secondary. We also grab a couple of wide receivers to fill the needs we had there. They aren't top notch starts, but we do have some speed to work with at last.

PRE-DRAFT SCOUTING SYSTEM

As you prepare for the draft it is very important to scout the incoming talent as much as possible (**1**).

You begin the scouting process with the College All Star Game. This is your opportunity to take the field with the incoming draft class and try them on for size. Go into battle with either the East or West All Stars so you can see the talent on the field for yourself (**2**). This is a great way to get a feel for the ability of the next NFL Rookie Class. You can't see ratings, though, so you'll have to go by feel.

Next comes the opportunity to work out specific players. You get to put 8 players through their paces. You actually take control of the player and run them through position specific drills. For example, if you want to work out the defensive end, you take him through the Rush QB drill. The higher you score, the more you find out about the player.

We ran Terry Linton through this drill (**3**) and discovered he had amazing tackling ability. Hopefully, we will be able to snag him in round 1.

You only get eight workouts, so use them wisely. You aren't going to nab a Top 5 Player if you don't have a high draft pick. Don't waste time scouting them. We pick last so we are looking at 1st Round/2nd Round guys.

A good strategy is to pick the top three positions you need to upgrade, and scout three guys at each spot. With this info in front of you, you can be fairly confident in your choices. Be sure you think about what order you will draft these players in. If you know you are going to pick a WR in the first round, don't bother to scout a QB that is projected for Top-5 or Top-10 picks. Look for 2nd rounders to scout since the other guys will be gone when it comes your turn again.

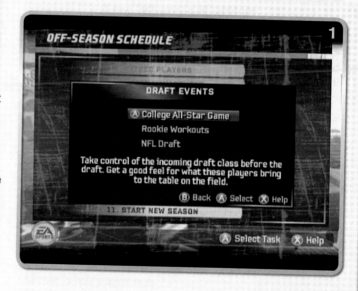

Scouting players is not an exact science, but with hard facts and some reading between the lines, it can be done successfully.

WHAT TO LOOK FOR

Keep your eyes peeled...

The table to the right is an easy guide to which ratings are most important by position. Having a wide receiver with great awareness might be nice, but we'll take a speed guy with hands. Defensive ends need to be quick off the edge, but they don't need a great jump rating. To avoid confusion in your drafting, refer to the rating priority for each position. One note: speed is an added factor to consider at every position except kicker and punter.

As you proceed through the draft, you will be put on the clock to make your picks. Take your time, but don't miss out on your pick.

Sometimes the CPU will offer a trade as well. We were able to dump our 32nd and 64th picks for a Number 6 overall. We are able to finally nab what we hope will be a game changing wide receiver with 4.29 speed.

Position	Rating Priority
QB	THP, THA, AWR
HB	SPD, BTK, ACC
FB	RBK, PBK
WR	SPD, CTH
TE	CTH, RBK
T	PBK, RBK
G	RBK, PBK
C	RBK, PBK
DE	SPD, TAC
DT	STR, TAK
OLB	SPD, AWR
MLB	TAK, AWR
CB	SPD, JMP

Position	Rating Priority
FS	AWR, TAK
SS	TAK, AWR
K/P	KAC, KPW

NFL SUPERSTAR MODE

Superstar mode has evolved a bit from last year's version. EA has maintained the core things that really worked and dropped a couple of items that didn't tie in so well with what gamers really want.

THE GOAL

In NFL Superstar Mode, you take control of a football player just exiting college and diving into the NFL draft (1). You have total control over just about every aspect of your player: agents, contracts, on the field control, workouts, and even movie roles.

The goal of the game this year is quite simple: build an NFL Hall of Fame–worthy player and take him to the pinnacle of the sport.

REGISTRATION AND BUILD

Step one is to register for the draft and put in your personal information (2). You can pick your name, height, weight, handedness, and college. Try to set your height and weight at a reasonable level for your position. We wanted to be a prototype fullback, so we chose 6'0", 240 lbs. If you want to get creative, you can play around with having an oversized player in your position. Maybe a 275 lb QB to stand in the pocket and shake off defenders before delivering a 60 yard missile to your receiver.

After registration, it's time to customize the appearance of your player (3). You can be flabby, ripped, or some combo in between. Instead of using DNA to determine your player's abilities, you get to select ratings yourself. You are given a batch of points to use to pick your ratings. The higher the rating, the more points it will cost you. You can also choose Randomize to have the CPU give you a good skill set for your position.

GETTING STARTED

Once you have birthed your new Superstar, you will be transported to the My Apartment screen (4). As an unsigned rookie, we don't have much cash flow to purchase a primo pad. No problem though; You will upgrade your digs when you sign your deal in year 3. This screen serves as your Superstar menu system, allowing you to do everything you need to do as an NFL player.

My Schedule presents you with a calendar view of the upcoming events (5). Things like training camp, games, movie offers, and interviews are all laid out for you here. You can skip ahead if you want or take things day by day.

Your Cell Phone contains messages from your mentor, agents, and others involved in your life. Your mentor provides you with timely advice to help you know how to manage yourself as a professional. Your coach sends you information about your play and even admonishes you a bit if you get crazy with the media.

My Web is your information central. Here you can find out how your career is progressing, view stats, and check out potential endorsement deals. If you can't find it anywhere else, you can usually find it here. Rosters, Depth Charts, and your Hall of Fame Resume can all be checked here.

City Map allows you to go to different places in your town (6). You can swing by your agent's office to set up a press conference, fix your wig, or hit the tattoo parlor for some fresh ink. As your player improves, you can hire an agent that gives you access to the Performance Institute.

The Mirror allows you to adjust your appearance. Add a visor to your helmet, tape up your ankles, and get some elbow pads here (7). You'll be able to change your equipment for both Artificial and Grass Turf games for the ultimate in realism.

Finally, the Rookie Handbook allows you to save your Super-star, as well as change Gameplay and System settings. You can set audibles and other coaching options from this screen at the same time.

ROAD TO THE **DRAFT**

Now that you know your way around your pad, it's time to get ready for the draft. Step one is to hire an agent to represent you in contract negotiations. When you visit the Agent Directory (❶), you can see who is interested in you, as well as view their ratings in several different categories. If you are all about the bucks, look for a top negotiator. You don't usually have much in the way of choices to start with. We picked a weasely-looking guy named Jeremy Powers as our representative. Once you become an NFL stud, you'll have agents knocking at your door. After a couple of years, look for an agent that can get you into the Performance Institute.

There are three parts to the pre-draft process (❷). First you take an IQ test that will help establish the mental capacity of your player. This is a combination of intelligence and attitude test that will help NFL teams gauge your personality. You have to answer questions within the time period. Do your best, but keep an eye on the clock.

The interview part of the pre-draft process allows you to fur-ther establish the character of your player (❸). You can talk like a company man, or toot your own horn and boast about your skills. Being an outspoken media hog can be fun, but it has drawbacks as well. Don't become a distraction to your team or your ability to lead will suffer. You won't be a first round pick no matter what as the 2007 1st rounders roll through first. You'll usually fall somewhere in the 2nd to 3rd round, but you might go even lower.

The final aspect of the pre-draft process involves individu-al workouts and the combine (❹). You get to perform position specific drills as well as the all-important 40-yard dash. The drills can be kind of tricky since you have to do them from the new 3rd-person perspective. Perform well in the drills, and you can improve your attributes before the draft.

You have two choices when it comes to draft day. EA Sports has now given you the ability to get picked by your favorite team, or you can just take your chances. We were picked up at the top of the 3rd round by the Houston Texans. We hope to bring some power to the backfield as we pave the way for Ahman Green.

NFL SUPERSTAR MODE

259

ADVANCING YOUR CAREER

Once you get started, go to My Web (①) and check out your Home Page. This will give you a scouting report on your player.

From the website you can also see your Franchise Resume, Career Stats, and Game Stats. Find out about your Agent, view your Personas, and check out your other awards.

Personas is a cool feature that tracks key moments of your career. Your web guy puts up paintings as you achieve various goals in your career. You'll start out with the draft pick persona but can pick up other things as time goes along.

Now that you have reached the big time, it's time to play your games. You have three options here: play every game plus work out in every practice, sim them all, or go for a combination. If you really want to see your player take off quickly, play as many games with him as you can.

Remember, in game mode you will play from the third person. The coach will call the plays and you will perform them on the field. Unless you are the team QB, you won't be able to make adjustments on the line.

As our FB grows in his skills, we will have greater influence over our team (②). New roles give us different ways to bolster the ratings of our teammates. We can increase the line's ability to block and improve our own run-blocking ability. You will see your assignment drawn on the field for that play.

PLAYER ROLES

EA Sports continues to develop the roles feature of NFL Superstar. Different roles allow you to elevate your play and even that of others on your team.

For example, the "Blocking Back" role increases RB blocking and O-Line pass blocking (③). It also decreases the awareness of the defensive line. Your player can have more than one role, but you will only be able to activate one at a time during a game. As the game goes on and you perform well, your sphere of influence increases.

NFL SUPERSTAR MODE

Gameplan

Each week you have the opportunity to take reps (snaps) in both Practice and Gameplan modes. You are graded in your practices; positive plays can result in ratings boosts for you player. Make sure you take enough snaps to get graded and earn those extra points.

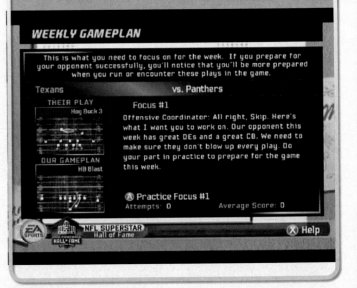

CONTRACT **TIME**

After Season 2, our contract was up and it was time to meet with our agent. We have the option of resigning or trying our hand at Free Agency. We have had a good time with the Texans and decide to stick around. We tell our agent to make it happen.

At some point, we will dump our agent for a guy with a little more pull. We want better endorsements and access to the Performance Training Institute.

Before game day each week, you can visit the Performance Training Institute from the City Map and work on your skills. You'll be able to pick one of the minigame drills for your position and work out. Success will give you a performance boost for your next game. These drills are tough but can mean valuable increases for your player.

After 5 years in the pros, we have established ourselves as the elite FB in the game. In addition to several Pro Bowl appearances, we own numerous roles including: Bruiser, Receiving RB, Blocking Back, and Mentor. As a new contract approaches, it's time to cash in.

Seattle comes calling to the tune of $19.88 million per year, which sounds pretty good to us. We are off to the Pacific Northwest to keep our career going toward the Hall of Fame.

Off-Season

During the off-season, you'll be presented with other opportunities, like being invited to star in a movie. You will receive a minute or so to learn your lines, then it's crunch time. You'll see the script and have to choose your line from a set of choices. The better you do, the better your reviews. If you rock the joint, you'll earn the "Movie Star Persona." Not too many guys are movie stars and Hall of Famers.

Our first year brought us a bit of fame and fortune, so we moved up to the My Loft screen. This works just like My Apartment, but looks nicer. Our ratings improved and now we are a 99 overall FB and a Pro Bowler.

261

MADDEN NFL ONLINE

With broadband Internet available in just about every place in the country, online play has become one of the biggest draws for competitive gamers. Human players bring a completely different approach to this game than a CPU opponent. If you can't defend the HB Dive, a human opponent will run it 20 times in a row until you figure it out; the CPU won't. You'll encounter all manner of play styles. Some will blitz you every down and go deep on just about every play. Others will run a variable gameplan and wait for you to make mistakes that they can exploit for points.

ONLINE OFFENSIVE STYLES

During the course of online play, you will typically run into one of these standard styles of play.

GROUND POUNDER

The Ground Pounder/Clock Baller is one of the more frustrating gamers to go up against (①). When playing a *Madden* Challenge with 2-minute quarters, this is a potent strategy. Online, however, it can be like Chinese water torture to go up against. If players get frustrated with their passing game, they will focus on poundng the rock to keep the score close.

The player that runs the ball to drain the clock is worried only about scoring and using up so much time that you have to rush your offense. When trying to defend against the Ground Pounder, make sure to keep good pursuit angles. The majority of Ground Pounders watch for the defense to over pursue, then take advantage of cut back lanes or out of position players. The Clock Baller is a different monster. Skill-wise they are easier to deal with than the Ground Pounder but they are more frustrating. Try to get out with an early lead and force them to play catch up. The other option is to slow things down. As long as you don't mess up your own rhythm doing this, it might push your opponent out of his gameplan.

The player that runs the ball to drain the clock is one of the most frustrating opponents you will compete against.

THE GUNSLINGER

With the exception of *Madden NFL 05*, the passing game reigns supreme in most seasons. Some players like to run a high-percentage, west-coast style of offense (②). They will work the curls, slants and flats to dink and dunk down the field. There are balanced players who run short, medium, and deep routes to move the ball. Finally there are the lobbers. These guys like to roll out, force you to honor the run, and then heave it deep to their receivers. They take control of the intended receiver and use their stick skills to make the catch. The Patriots and Randy Moss will be a sure favorite this year for the long ball.

If you have played this game online the last few years, you know what we are talking about.

West Coast Offenses can be dangerous because they use all their receivers and it's hard to figure out where they are going to go with the ball. If you are playing against this type of player, you are better off not blitzing. Use your defenders to fill the short passing lanes by dropping defensive linemen or by bringing up safeties. These players are hard to sack, because

the ball is not in the quarterback's hand very long. If for some reason the passing lanes are blocked, these players will struggle and hold on to the ball longer, trying to buy time in the pocket. This is when you will get coverage sacks.

The second type of player is one who throws short, medium, and deep. These are the hardest players to defend against, as balanced players always are. They use all their receivers just like dink and dunkers but are not afraid to go up top every once in a while. Use all the tools at your disposal to try to throw them off of their game. Disguise your defenses by using the defensive playmaker, coverage audibles, manually moving defenders, and blitzing at the right time.

Most of your lobbers don't work at reading pass coverages. They rely on their stick skills to get the job done. You have to work on your stick ability or you have no hope of slowing them down. Go into practice mode and put yourself on defense. Practice against the Hail Mary play and work on manual defense.

MADDEN ONLINE

MOBILE QB **ATTACK**

One of the most difficult players to deal with in this game is the player that has a quarterback that can run and pass (❸). We have seen this year in and year out with the domination of Michael Vick on the Video gridiron. This player is going to try to break contain, get out to the edge, and force you to make a choice. Do you pull off coverage and defend the run, or do you stay back to guard the pass. *Madden NFL 08* cover man Vince Young is sure to get some looks as well with his size and speed making for a deadly combination.

One of the best ways to defend this type of player is by using Man/Zone coverages. Coverages with man on one side and zone on the other gives the offensive player a false read to whichever side they roll and make reverse field plays harder. Also try to blitz a mobile quarterback, forcing him to the short side of the field. If the offense lines up on the right side of the hash, then you should blitz from the left. The final way to handle this type of player is to constantly bring pressure from the right, forcing the QB left. This is taking into consideration that most players are more comfortable looking right first. You will be surprised how many sacks you can get just by attacking a right-handed player from that side. Use defensive playmaker to put your end in QB Contain to slow down the QB's rollout game.

NO HUDDLE **OFFENSE**

We mentioned before how frustrating it is to deal with the Clock Baller. Well, meet his evil twin Mr. No Huddle (❹). There are two different techniques used by this player. One tactic is to no huddle you right from the first snap. This player normally has all of his audibles set and will attack you with everything he has preset. He is going to try to hit you again and again to get the quick score.

The second type will no huddle you once they see they have your defense in a bad defense or out of position. If you do not stop this player right away, then the frustration can be endless. There is nothing like being caught in the wrong defense while the offense just keeps hitting you with the same play, over and over and over again.

What do you do if you have used all of your time outs? It doesn't even have to get that far. When you feel that your defense is out of position and you don't want to use a time out, go offside while the team is coming to the line. This will let you pick a new play and force the offense to go to the play selection screen. Sometimes a time out is worth more than 5 yards, especially when it is early in the drive.

You also have defensive playmaker routes available to you so you can make quick adjustments on the fly. Finally, manually take control of a defender and put him in the weak spot to force your opponent to make a new play call.

Most of your lobbers don't work at reading pass coverages. They rely on their stick skills to get the job done.

One of the most difficult players to deal with in this game is the player that has a quarterback that can run and pass.

This player normally has all of his audibles set and will attack you with everything he has preset. He will try to hit you again and again to get the quick score.

ONLINE DEFENSIVE STYLES

Defensively, you typically encounter three different types of players online.

MAX COVERAGE

This type of defense takes the rubber band approach. We will bend, but won't break (**1**). You will find this to be effective online because it allows the defense to sit back and wait for the offense to come to them. Hopefully there is a change of possession by downs, or there is a mistake such as an interception or fumble. On offense, you will need to be extremely patient. Take what the defense gives you and dink your way down the field if you have to. The real key is converting in the red zone. Be sure to work on your red zone offense so that you can play beyond the twenties. One variation you will see is the All Coverage defense. Basically, the defensive player will playmaker everybody into coverage with the exception of a lineman or two. Dropping 10 men into coverage is not unheard of here. Take what you can get on every play and take your time in the pocket because there won't be much of a pass rush.

You will find the Max Coverage defensive style to be effective online.

MAX PRESSURE

Players who run attacking-style defenses are aggressive. They like to live on the edge and dictate the tempo of the game (**2**). They are willing to give up the big play on offense in return for a big play on defense. They are going to blitz, blitz, and blitz some more. Expect to see lots of bump-n-run coverage

You will find plenty of players online who use this same defensive style. There are all types of aggressive players. One uses blitz packages based on the framework of the game. They use shifts, defensive playmaker options, and may move a player or two to bring the heat. The other type of player plays a more freelance style of defense. They tend to move several defenders all over the field and not play within the framework of the game. Often they will move defenders off the screen creating unrealistic defenses or move players on the line to linebacker depth to shoot defenders through gaps to put instant heat on the quarterback.

These are what are referred to as Nano Blitz Packages. The pressure comes on the quarterback within a nanosecond of the snap. These can be set up by shifts and using the defensive playmaker hot routes.

If you play against an opponent who knows how to set up high pressure defenses, be prepared to use your slide protection and leave extra blockers in. Leaving the tight end in is a great way to counter nanos because he changes the way the rest of the offensive line pass blocks. You can also motion a player behind the line and snap the ball so that he blocks.

Beat up this defender by going to the flats and grabbing those quick gains. Remember, if he blitzes, he is leaving a gap somewhere in the coverage.

Expect to see lots of bump-n-run coverage with this style.

Balanced Coverage players understand how the defense works.

BALANCE COVERAGE

A player who calls a good mixture of plays on defense is the hardest player to beat (**3**). They understand how the defense works and generally know what each defense is designed to do. They use a good mixture of zone, man, and blitz packages to keep the offense guessing. They will even throw in some all coverage from time to time to keep you honest.

These players will set up some nanos within the framework of the game to keep the offense on its toes, but it's not their whole game plan.

If you really want to be a top player while playing online, you need to be this type of player. Learning who covers who and who does what can make the difference in stopping your opponent.

THE *MADDEN NFL 08* COMMUNITY

For your *Madden NFL 08* fix.

Each year the community grows with leaps and bounds. 2007 was no exception as the community upped the ante with podcasts, blogs, videos and social networking pages popping up all over the place.

These incredible online resources provide news, discussion forums and loads of tips for improving your game. You can meet new players, participate in leagues and shoot the breeze in the online version of the good old company watercooler.

EA Sports continues to push this game into the mainstream with the EA Sports *Madden* Challenge and *Madden* Nation reality TV show. More and more players are forming teams that are willing to travel all over the country to put their skills to the test.

Tournament play is a completely different beast than the online experience. If you are looking to dive into the *Madden* Challenge or other *Madden NFL 08* Tournaments, there are a couple of things that you need to know before game day.

MADDEN NFL 08

❶ **Take it as a learning experience.** Unless you currently play with tournament seasoned players, you might take it on the chin in your first event. Playing online and playing face-to-face in that kind of environments is a whole new game. You will see things you may have never encountered before. Try to find events that have a Round Robin format so you will receive a guaranteed number of games.

❷ **Register early.** Many events offer a discount for players that register early. Tournament play doesn't come cheap so get every break you can. Many of the *Madden* Challenge locations fill up quickly, so get in right away. You'll have an easier time advancing in the events in the early part of the year when the game is still new.

❸ **Come up with a nickname for yourself.** Just about every serious tournament player has a nickname. If you just play as "Joe," everybody in the room will know you are new to the scene.

❹ **Try to find a league or team to join as soon as possible.** This will give you a steady group of guys to

play with as well as a crew to cheer you on at events. Teams are becoming a bigger and bigger part of the tournament world.

❺ **Make sure you know the rules before the event.** Most quality tournaments will have a web page with a description of the rules. Pay special attention to use of motion, audibling from one formation to another (called audibling down), substitutions guidelines and glitches/AI exploits that have been outlawed.

❻ **Practice playing games with the actual tournament rules.** Most of the games that you will play only have two minutes per quarter. This totally changes up the way you play the game. Be sure to get in a ton of games with your crew to get used to proper time management.

❼ **Make sure you have a backup game plan/playbook** for players that might have scouted your game. Using a variety of formations and different sets of plays can throw off the competition and make it difficult for your opponent to stop you.

COMMUNITY WEBSITES

If you are into this game, fire up your web browser and go take a look at these sites.

Worth Checking Out

• **Madden-tips.blogspot.com**
The biggest blog on the net. The Madden Tips Blog provides the most up to date information about what is going on in the community possible. Add its RSS feed to your favorite reader for info piped right to your desktop.

• **Maddentips.com**
VG Sports is the home of the serious competitive baller. With a strong forum following, you will be able to hook up with leagues, find out about tournaments, and get help with your game. VG has a balance of sim-style & free-style players.

• **Maddenmania.com**
MM is the elder statesman of the community. With an emphasis on sim-style play, MM boasts the biggest community forum on the net. Be sure to check out their radio podcasts.

• **Maddenwars.com**
A competition between 6 teams to secure all 32 NFL stadiums to better the advancement of the group. Madden Wars is played on EA's servers and the stats are kept on the site. Madden Wars is about competing against some of the best Str8/SIM guys you will find online and having fun in the process.

• **Maddenplanet.com**
Establish in 1996, MP has been serving the community for a decade now. Maddenplanet.com now runs a Video Blog on the home page of their site, and boasts over 26,000 forum members.

MADDEN ONLINE

EA SPORTS™ FANTASY FOOTBALL

FANTASY FOOTBALL 101

Welcome to Fantasy Football from Prima Games. But what is Fantasy Football? Believe it or not, there are some football fans out there who do not take part in this truly unique experience. If you are one of those fans, then the following Fantasy Football 101 is the quick-start guide you are looking for. For those of you who read our Fantasy Football Draft Guide from last year, much of this intro will look familiar.

So what is Fantasy Football? Simply put, Fantasy Football is a way for football fans to assemble their "dream team" to play against other fans' teams. Each football player chosen will accrue points based on how their real life counterpart performs on the field on any given week. Say, for example, you chose Peyton Manning and Willie Parker to be on your team, your team will then gain points based on their on-field performances that week.

Typically, participants will draft their fantasy players before the NFL season begins and settle on a scoring system for their league scoring systems vary from league to league. Picking the right combination of players will differ based on your league's scoring system and, of course, your personal preference and projections.

Sounds like too much to take on? Well, don't worry, Prima is here to ease the pain and initiate you rookies, as well as provide a comprehensive study guide for fantasy football newbies and seasoned veterans alike. So strap on some pads, put on your helmet, and lace up your cleats because football season is coming up and it waits for no one.

STARTING A LEAGUE

Most important in creating a Fantasy Football league is deciding *who* you will play with. The best way to do this is to find a few (7-9) other football enthusiasts and settle on a few things. A new league will require the following:

• **A commissioner** — This person will be in charge of the league. The "commish" will set the rules, scoring system, draft date, number of players, trade deadlines (if any) and various other details pertaining to the league as a whole. This person should be well-versed in how a pigskin season develops. If your league does not have a single person who can decide such matters, as most beginner leagues don't, then it may be best to make these decisions as a group and appoint one person to manage the league.

• **A draft date** — This date should be convenient to most participants in the league. Typical drafts take anywhere from 1-2 hours, so make sure that you not only have the date clear, but also a few spare hours to dedicate to the draft.

If some participants cannot make the draft date, then they should create a draft list that places their desired players in numerical order of importance. As the players are chosen, their list dictates which player they will draft in their absence. For example, Jookie lists Peyton Manning as his number one choice and Larry Johnson as his second, but Pogi chose Peyton Manning before it was Jookie's turn to pick. Jookie will then choose Larry Johnson by default. This method of absentee drafting can be tricky, so plan carefully if you can't make it to your draft.

• **A schedule** — The schedule will decide which two fantasy football teams will face off from week to week. Some leagues will have divisions where you will only play in your division, while other leagues may allow for everyone to play against every other team throughout the course of the season.

Some leagues are not run in traditional "one player versus another" fashion. "Head to head" leagues face off with a real win/lose schedule. The points garnered serve as tiebreakers in case two teams have the same win/loss ratio. "Points" leagues do not have any teams facing off against each other. Each team accrues points per game, as the name implies, and the lead is determined by which team accrues the most points throughout the season. What kind of league you will be playing in should also affect your draft. Plan accordingly.

• **A weekly line-up** — This is your team. The league commissioner (or the entire league itself) will decide what kind of line-up you play from each week. Will you have three wide receivers or two? How many tight-end positions will you need to fill? Should you pick more than one running back to fill that two-back slot?

Keep both your weekly line-up, and your league's scoring system in mind when preparing for the draft. If your league is going to be a touchdown heavy league with two running back slots per team, for example, then you will want to find RB's who are more prone to getting touchdowns than heavy yardage.

• **Transaction deadlines** — Though not all leagues will allow trades after a certain week, most will restrict the amount of transactions a participant can make throughout the season. If you can't get that star WR you were eye-balling before the draft, and you have an extra pick, consider picking up a highly sought-after player for trading early in the season.

FORGOING THE "NEWBIE" HASSLE

If you still can't manage to scrounge up a few friends to start a league, feel free to browse online. There are hundreds of Fantasy Football leagues out there waiting to take on new participants. As with most new things you take on, make sure to research and find one that best suits your needs. Public leagues will often host introductory leagues for rookies.

Luckily, many online Fantasy Football sites are very beginner friendly. Many sites, like Yahoo's Fantasy Football page, have everything from adjustable scoring system templates to stat trackers, and everything in between. Many will even include week to week player performance analysis, offer advice as to who to play and when, and even offer detailed information about how your players perform against their rival team for that week. Unfortunately, a lot of that information will come at some additional cost.

WHY SHOULD I PUT THIS GUIDE TO USE?

Chances are that if you're taking part in a Fantasy Football league, then you're already a football fan. If so, Fantasy Football will not only further engross you in Football from week to week, but will also help you build upon your football knowledge.

Most participants tend to gravitate toward a certain NFL team. Playing Fantasy Football, however, will make each and every game throughout the season more interesting. You will find yourself cheering for that rival NFL team solely because your star running back is playing, even if your star running back is playing against your favorite team.

If you choose to do so, you may even have a trophy for the league champion at the end of the season, monetary or otherwise. If you *do* manage to round up a few friends to form a league, there is a good chance that it may become a yearly thing. So make sure you're in it to win it.

COURTESY OF EA's *MADDEN NFL 08*

So now that you're all caught up on Fantasy Football basics, huddle up with Prima's Official Fantasy Football Guide and Prima's Official Madden NFL 08 Strategy Guide, and plan out your strategy. Not only does *Prima's Official Fantasy Football Guide* provide you with all the vital information you will need to assemble the best possible team you can, but this year's *Madden* guide will also help as a useful reference guide for possible player statistics as it boasts the most up-to-date stats for all NFL teams and their stars.* We will see you on the football field!

(* All stats and information provided in these guides was compiled before the NFL season started and is current as of printing date.)

2006 NFL STATISTICS

QUARTERBACKS • SORTED BY TD's

NAME	TEAM	RATING	COMP	ATT	PCT	YDS	Y/G	AVG	TD	INT
Peyton Manning	IND	101	362	557	65	4397	274.8	7.9	31	9
Carson Palmer	CIN	93.9	324	520	62.3	4035	252.2	7.8	28	13
Drew Brees	NOR	96.2	356	554	64.3	4418	276.1	8	26	11
Tom Brady	NWE	87.9	319	516	61.8	3529	220.6	6.8	24	12
Eli Manning	NYG	77	301	522	57.7	3244	202.8	6.2	24	18
Marc Bulger	STL	92.9	370	588	62.9	4301	268.8	7.3	24	8
Rex Grossman	CHI	73.9	262	480	54.6	3193	199.6	6.7	23	20
Philip Rivers	SDG	92	284	460	61.7	3388	211.8	7.4	22	9
Jon Kitna	DET	79.9	372	596	62.4	4208	263	7.1	21	22
Michael Vick	ATL	75.7	204	388	52.6	2474	154.6	6.4	20	13
Tony Romo	DAL	95.1	220	337	65.3	2903	181.4	8.6	19	13
J.P. Losman	BUF	84.9	268	429	62.5	3051	190.7	7.1	19	14
Donovan McNabb	PHI	95.5	180	316	57	2647	264.7	8.4	18	6
Ben Roethlisberger	PIT	75.4	280	469	59.7	3513	234.2	7.5	18	23
Matt Hasselbeck	SEA	76	210	371	56.6	2442	203.5	6.6	18	15

RUNNING BACKS • SORTED BY TD's RUSHING

NAME	TEAM	RUSH	YDS	Y/G	AVG	TD	FUM	REC	YDS	Y/G	AVG	TD
LaDainian Tomlinson	SDG	348	1815	113.4	5.2	28	1	56	508	31.8	9.1	3
Larry Johnson	KAN	416	1789	111.8	4.3	17	2	41	410	25.6	10	2
Marion Barber III	DAL	135	654	40.9	4.8	14	0	23	196	12.3	8.5	2
Steven Jackson	STL	346	1528	95.5	4.4	13	2	90	806	50.4	9	3
Willie Parker	PIT	337	1494	93.4	4.4	13	5	31	222	13.9	7.2	3
Corey Dillon	NWE	199	812	50.8	4.1	13	2	15	147	9.2	9.8	0
Maurice Jones-Drew	JAC	166	941	58.8	5.7	13	1	46	436	27.3	9.5	2
Rudi Johnson	CIN	341	1309	81.8	3.8	12	2	23	124	7.8	5.4	0
Deuce McAllister	NOR	244	1057	70.5	4.3	10	1	30	198	13.2	6.6	0
Brandon Jacobs	NYG	96	423	28.2	4.4	9	1	11	149	9.9	13.5	0
Jamal Lewis	BAL	314	1132	70.8	3.6	9	2	18	115	7.2	6.4	0
Mike Bell	DEN	157	677	45.1	4.3	8	0	20	158	10.5	7.9	0
Frank Gore	SFO	312	1695	105.9	5.4	8	5	61	485	30.3	8	1
Brian Westbrook	PHI	240	1217	81.1	5.1	7	2	77	699	46.6	9.1	4
Travis Henry	TEN	270	1211	86.5	4.5	7	1	18	78	5.6	4.3	0

WIDE RECEIVERS • SORTED BY TD's RUSHING

NAME	TEAM	REC	YDS	Y/G	AVG	LNG	YAC	TD
Terrell Owens	DAL	85	1180	73.8	13.9	56	4.7	13
Marvin Harrison	IND	95	1366	85.4	14.4	68	3.2	12
Plaxico Burress	NYG	63	988	65.9	15.7	55	3.7	10
Torry Holt	STL	93	1188	74.3	12.8	67	3	10
Darrell Jackson	SEA	63	956	73.5	15.2	72	4	10
T.J. Houshmandzadeh	CIN	90	1081	77.2	12	40	3.8	9
Reggie Wayne	IND	86	1310	81.9	15.2	51	2.5	9
Chris Henry	CIN	36	605	46.5	16.8	71	4.9	9
Marques Colston	NOR	70	1038	74.1	14.8	86	5.4	8
Javon Walker	DEN	69	1084	67.8	15.7	83	5.1	8
Lee Evans	BUF	82	1292	80.8	15.8	83	4.5	8
Donald Driver	GNB	92	1295	80.9	14.1	82	5.9	8
Reggie Brown	PHI	46	816	51	17.7	60	4.5	8
Steve Smith	CAR	83	1166	83.3	14	72	5.7	8
Chad Johnson	CIN	87	1369	85.6	15.7	74	3.8	7

TIGHT ENDS • SORTED BY TD's

NAME	TEAM	REC	YDS	Y/G	AVG	TD
Antonio Gates	SDG	71	924	57.8	13	9
Alge Crumpler	ATL	56	780	48.8	13.9	8
Jeremy Shockey	NYG	66	623	41.5	9.4	7
Desmond Clark	CHI	45	626	39.1	13.9	6
Chris Cooley	WAS	57	734	45.9	12.9	6
Todd Heap	BAL	73	765	47.8	10.5	6
Tony Gonzalez	KAN	73	900	60	12.3	5
L.J. Smith	PHI	50	611	38.2	12.2	5
Heath Miller	PIT	34	393	24.6	11.6	5
Owen Daniels	HOU	34	352	25.1	10.4	5
Tony Scheffler	DEN	18	286	22	15.9	4
Dan Campbell	DET	21	308	19.3	14.7	4
Chris Baker	NYJ	31	300	18.8	9.7	4
Jerramy Stevens	SEA	22	231	21	10.5	4
Dallas Clark	IND	30	367	30.6	12.2	4

KICKERS • SORTED BY POINTS

NAME	TEAM	0-19	20-29	30-39	40-49	50+	FGM	FGA	PCT	XPM	XPA	PTS
Robbie Gould	CHI	0-0	6-6	14-16	12-14	0-0	32	36	88.9	47	47	143
Nate Kaeding	SDG	0-0	7-7	11-12	7-9	1-1	26	29	89.7	58	58	136
Jeff Wilkins	STL	1-1	11-11	6-6	11-16	3-3	32	37	86.5	35	35	131
Matt Stover	BAL	0-0	12-13	9-9	6-7	1-1	28	30	93.3	37	37	121
Josh Scobee	JAC	0-0	5-6	7-7	14-18	0-1	26	32	81.3	41	41	119
Jason Hanson	DET	1-1	12-12	6-6	7-8	3-6	29	33	87.9	30	30	117
Joe Nedney	SFO	2-2	11-12	8-10	7-9	1-2	29	35	82.9	29	29	116
Neil Rackers	ARI	0-0	11-11	9-9	7-10	1-7	28	37	75.7	32	32	116
John Carney	NOR	1-1	9-9	7-8	5-6	1-1	23	25	92	46	47	115
Jason Elam	DEN	0-0	10-10	10-10	6-8	1-1	27	29	93.1	34	34	115
Shayne Graham	CIN	0-0	9-9	8-9	6-8	2-4	25	30	83.3	40	42	115
Adam Vinatieri	IND	1-1	3-3	12-13	9-10	0-1	25	28	89.3	38	38	113
Josh Brown	SEA	0-0	10-10	5-7	7-9	3-5	25	31	80.6	36	36	111
Dave Rayner	GNB	0-0	11-12	6-9	8-11	1-3	26	35	74.3	31	32	109
Jay Feely	NYG	0-0	7-7	10-11	6-8	0-1	23	27	85.2	38	38	107

TEAM DEFENSE • SORTED BY POINTS ALLOWED PER GAME

TEAM	PTS/G	YDS/G	RUSH YDS/G	PASS YDS/G	INT	INTTD	FFUM	DEF TD	SACK
Baltimore Ravens	12.6	264.1	75.9	188.2	28	5	12	6	60
New England Patriots	14.8	294.4	94.2	200.2	22	0	13	0	44
Chicago Bears	15.9	294.1	99.4	194.8	24	1	23	3	40
Jacksonville Jaguars	17.1	283.6	91.3	192.4	20	1	8	1	35
Miami Dolphins	17.7	289.1	101.1	187.9	8	2	22	3	47
New York Jets	18.4	331.6	130.3	201.4	16	0	13	1	35
San Diego Chargers	18.9	301.6	100.8	200.8	16	0	17	3	61
Denver Broncos	19.1	326.4	113.3	213.1	17	2	17	2	35
Carolina Panthers	19.1	296.1	108.6	187.5	14	2	14	2	41
Buffalo Bills	19.4	329.6	140.9	188.7	13	2	13	4	40
Kansas City Chiefs	19.7	328.9	120.5	208.4	15	0	19	0	32
Pittsburgh Steelers	19.7	300.3	88.3	212.1	20	2	13	2	39
New Orleans Saints	20.1	307.3	128.9	178.4	11	0	12	0	38
Minnesota Vikings	20.4	300.2	61.6	238.6	21	3	13	5	30
Philadelphia Eagles	20.5	328.1	136.4	191.7	19	4	18	5	40

EA SPORTS™ FANTASY FOOTBALL

269

PROJECTIONS: QUARTERBACKS

EA SPORTS™ FANTASY FOOTBALL

1. Peyton Manning (Indianapolis)

Barring an injury that occurs during an enthusiastic dancing moment, I think we can count on one of the NFL's all-time greatest quarterbacks putting up some astounding numbers in the stat column. The fact is that Peyton is bionic. Consider a 31/9 touchdown to interception ratio last year, the fact that he's had the top QB ratio in the NFL for the past 3 years while averaging almost 2 touchdowns per game, and the fact that Joseph Addai and the Colts' offensive line were banging on all cylinders last year (4.8 YPC). Expect your computer to blow up at least once when looking up his game stats this year.

2. Tom Brady (New England)

Put Randy Moss, Donté Stallworth, Reche Caldwell, and Benjamin Watson on the same field with Tom Brady throwing up passes for them, and you have a very dangerous offense. New England proves time and time again that they are amongst the NFL's elite, and with Brady as their unwavering leader they can make any defender's knees shake more than a paint mixer. The Pats have gone out and made some great additions to their passing game in the off-season, and even if Brady's numbers don't swell, another 3,500 yard, 24 touchdown performance will earn your fantasy team a lot of points.

3. Carson Palmer (Cincinnati)

Palmer has a very strong arm, is well-poised, and has some very powerful teammates. He threw for over 4,000 yards, and 28 touchdowns last year, and that was coming off of a knee injury he sustained in the 2005 playoffs. Not to mention the fact that the Bengals have one of the most threatening wide receiver duos in the league in Chad Johnson, and T.J. Houshmandzadeh. Don't let it catch you off guard if these guys rack up some yardage courtesy of Mr. Palmer.

4. Drew Brees (New Orleans)

You probably weren't too surprised while watching Brees put up a 26/11 touchdown to interception ratio last year, or while he threw his way beyond 4,400 yards with a 64% completion percentage in his first year with the Saints. Usually it goes like this: experience brings composure, composure brings better play, and better play brings lots of numbers for statisticians, which in turn means lots of fantasy points for you. Brees will only get more comfortable with the Saints' offense. Reggie Bush is arguably the best receiving running back in the league, Marques Colston and Devery Henderson aren't too shabby at the wide receiver position either (combining for over 1,800 receiving yards last year), and the addition of tight end Eric Johnson and rookie wide receiver Robert Meachem can mean only one thing: Lots of passing yards.

5. Marc Bulger (St. Louis)

Every year since 2003 he has been on pace to break 4,000 passing yards, and barring injury he'll probably complete that feat just like he did last year. He put up 24 touchdowns with only throwing 8 interceptions, and a 63% completion percentage (which by no means an easy task). He's an efficient quarterback, with a very strong and deep receiving core (Bruce, Holt, Bennett), and plays on the same team as freight train running back Steven Jackson. Bulger always comes to play, and will make a great addition to any fantasy team.

6. Donovan McNabb (Philadelphia)

One of the NFL's premier quarterbacks will continue to control defenses. He put up 18 touchdowns last year while throwing for 2,600 yards and maintaining a 95.6 quarterback rating. Reggie Brown is developing into a viable NFL receiver, Brian Westbrook has proven to be the best receiving running back in the league, and LJ Smith is one of the top-receiving tight ends around. It will be interesting to see what McNabb can do with Kevin Curtis (Philly's recent pickup from the Rams), but most likely it will involve lots of numbers.

7. Philip Rivers (San Diego)

His numbers will continue to swell this year as he enters into his second year of having the starting QB job over in San Diego. Last year, Rivers proved himself worthy of the starting job by throwing almost 3,400 yards and 22 Touchdowns with only 9 Interceptions. The addition of Craig Davis from LSU will most likely be very beneficial, and the continuing dominance of LT will take attention away from the Chargers' passing game.

8. Eli Manning (New York Giants)

In the last two years, Eli has shown us just how good the Manning family is at playing quarterback. He's posted at least 3,200 yards and 24 touchdowns each season, and he's only getting better. The addition of USC product Steve Smith to the receiving core, and existence of viable options in Plaxico Burress, Amani Toomer, and man-beast Jeremy Shockey will only further encourage his development as one of the NFL's top quarterbacks.

9. Tony Romo (Dallas)

Romo became one of last year's biggest surprises. You might not be able to count on him holding for the kicker anymore, but they don't give out fantasy points for that, now do they? Almost 3,000 passing yards and 19 touchdowns for someone that is coming off the bench are impressive stats to say the least. He's only going to get more comfortable throwing to Terrell Owens, Jason Witten, and Terry Glen. Watch for him to add a little padding to his stats from last year.

10. Vince Young (Tennessee)

This guy is a winner. He's known for taking anything that defenses give him and exploiting it to the fullest. After a dismal start, Young led the Titans to an 8-3 record to finish the regular season, and I would suspect that his skills are only going to expand. Tennessee went receiver hunting in the draft (Williams, Davis, and Filani), and this youth is what makes them dangerous. Watch out for this sleeper to explode out of the gates.

1. LaDanian Tomlinson (San Diego)

After a league-leading 1,815 rushing yards and 28 rushing touchdowns last year I see no reason why his numbers will be any different this year. Not to mention the motivation he'll have to run through tackles after last year's disappointing playoff loss. Did you see how upset he was that the New England Patriots danced at the 50-yard line? I've watched quite a few of his games and never have seen him that upset. Something tells me he has bottled that anger up for defenses this year. Another good sign for LT this year is Norv Turner will be calling the shots as the new head coach. Norv helped create an offense for San Francisco, over the past couple of seasons, and their running back, Frank Gore, thrived in that system. Could LT actually be better this year? Well, I know he won't be any worse.

2. Larry Johnson (Kansas City)

Just behind LaDanian Tomlinson in total rushing yards was Larry Johnson. He's the definition of "workhorse" when it comes to carrying the ball. He set an NFL record last year with 416 carries and remained relatively healthy throughout the season. He's a big, strong running back who will carry about the same amount this year, but his goal line opportunities should go up. He still had a respectable 17 touchdowns, but that pales in comparison to 28 by LT. Last year's quarterback, Trent Green, is gone, leaving either Damon Huard or sophomore Brodie Croyle at the helm. Either way, you have rather experienced quarterbacks, so head coach Herm Edwards will probably elect to keep the ball in LJ's hands as much as possible. That's good news for those lucky enough to draft this stud.

3. Frank Gore (San Francisco)

Where'd he come from? The answer is the University of Miami. Not many know this, but Frank beat out Willis McGahee as the 2002 Hurricanes starter before crumbling to a torn ACL. Because of his injuries, he fell in the 2005 draft and became a steal in the third round. Much to the San Francisco 49ers' delight, their gamble looks to have paid off after last season. The 49ers are still grooming Alex Smith at quarterback and don't want him throwing too much, guaranteeing that Gore will touch the ball more than others. The only concern fantasy owners should have about this kid is that he hasn't had much success around the goal line. He only had 8 touchdowns, in part because he battled a tendency to fumble around the end zone, but he did seem to be better toward the end of the year. If he shows improvement at hanging onto the ball, (5 fumbles lost last year) his number of chances in the red zone and at touchdowns will increase.

4. Stephen Jackson (St. Louis)

As predicted last year, Mike Martz' exodus as head coach has been a good thing for Stephen Jackson. He had over 1,500 yards rushing and 13 touchdowns. He was third in total rushes behind only Larry Johnson and LaDanian Tomlinson. It's a comforting feeling for any fantasy owner when the team will give him the ball that much. Because the Rams are so balanced in their offense, opposing defenses can't focus all of their attention solely on stopping the run. Once the team gets into the red zone, they're not afraid to give it to such a powerhouse in Jackson because he has proven he will run right over and through his opponents. A repeat performance from last year is a given.

5. Willie Parker (Pittsburgh)

A team that's never afraid to get down and dirty has to have a running game to back it up. Bill Dudley, Franco Harris, and Jerome Bettis are a few of the best running backs ever to wear the yellow and black. Willie Parker is trying to be the next running back in line of greats, but he's different from the previously mentioned backs. Parker is more explosive and can break a run wide open as illustrated by his 76 yard jog last year. He still gets the famous fans waving the "terrible towel" because they, as well as opposing defenses, know the threat waiting in the backfield. An average of 93 yards per game and almost 1 touchdown per game, make him a viable starting running back for any team.

6. Brian Westbrook (Philadelphia)

Nicknamed "B-Rabbit" by the offensive line coach (Juan Castillo) and "The Wizard" by the Eagles radio announcer (Merrill Reese), Brian Westbrook is elusive and magical at the same time. If I were official enough to give him a nickname, it would be "Mr. Everything" because as a running back he does so much for the team. Brian had over 1200 yards on only 240 carries (5.1 yards per carry), 699 yards on 77 receptions, 5 punt returns, and 11 touchdowns. If there were a "utility man" position on a football team, Brian's nameplate would be solidly glued to it. It's a testament to his athletic ability and reliability that the team and his quarterback look to go to him so often. The total number of offensive plays for the Eagles' offense was 499 and Brain touched the ball on 317 of those. I think it's safe to say "Mr. Everything" is fitting, isn't it?

7. Rudi Johnson (Cincinnati)

For a team that threw 520 times last season, you'd expect their running game to be malnourished. Not so for the Bengals, who have emerged as one of the most potent offenses in the NFL. Their star running back carried the ball 341 times for over 1,300 yards and 12 rushing touchdowns. One thing about this team is that they'll always have opportunities to score and Rudi's usually right in the mix. He's probably not going to bust any long runs for touchdowns, but he's going to pound away at the defense and open things up for the passing game. The Bengals have a true 1-2 punch with such established passing and running games.

8. Maurice Jones-Drew (Jacksonville)

This may be a surprise for some, but those are the ones who didn't have him or face him in fantasy football last year. From week 10 through 17, Maurice ran in 10 touchdowns, he was on fire. Prior to that, he was sharing time with the often-injured Fred Taylor. I think the back half of last season was prove that Fred Taylor's best days are behind him and the future for the Jaguars and Maurice are brighter than ever. When he runs, he's dangerous and anyone lucky enough to make the pick in their draft will be rewarded with entertainment and points all year.

9. Reggie Bush (New Orleans)

Waving at Brian Urlacher on his way to the end zone didn't help the Saints in their loss to the Bears in the playoffs, but it showed the flash of greatness that everyone's on the edge of their seats to witness. He'll learn that the NFL isn't a place to show—up great linebackers, but he'll also be looking over his shoulder at many of them on his way to scoring 6. The Saints will find more ways to get Reggie Bush involved in their offense because it's quite evident that there's something VERY special about this talent out of USC. He won't have the most rushing or receiving yards, but he'll have touchdowns and that's what we look for right? If I pick Reggie up in the draft though, I will be pleading with the television not to get cute with the likes of Urlacher or Shawne Merriman because they will catch him at some point when he's least expecting it and I need my running back on the field, not on the sidelines, or worse, wearing an oxygen mask.

10. Willis McGahee (Baltimore)

A bit inconsistent with Buffalo this running back has all the abilities to be a top 5 running back. He's down to 10th overall because of a slump last season, but with a fairly conservative offense in the Baltimore Ravens he'll see more consistency and carries on his new team. In the Ravens 10-year franchise history they've had solid running backs along with Conference Championships and a Super Bowl. Now it's time for Willis to show that his place in history with this team will be a valuable one. We predict a comeback for Willis and he may be undervalued here. Watch him closely and don't let him slip too far.

EA SPORTS™ FANTASY FOOTBALL

PROJECTIONS: WIDE RECEIVERS

1. Chad Johnson [Cincinnati]

"Ocho Cinco" is one of the NFL's elite at his position and in 2006 became the first Bengal to lead the NFL in receiving yards with 1,369. Even though he started the season slowly, he showed his skill by catching 37 passes, for 765 yards and five touchdowns in a five-game stretch. With Carson Palmer as his quarterback, Rudi Johnson doing his thing, and Chris Henry out for eight games, expect Johnson to see a lot of passes.

2. Steve Smith [Carolina]

Steve Smith followed up his awesome 2005 "Triple Crown" season with 83 catches for 1,166 yards and 8 touchdowns last season. Smith was a little banged up and missed two games, quarterback Jake Delhomme went down as well for three games. A new season, a new three-year contract extension and a healthy Delhomme is great news for Smith, who remains as the Panthers' number one offensive option.

3. Marvin Harrison [Indianapolis]

He joined the 1,000 reception club, averages 93 receptions a year, and has caught at least one pass in every single game of his career. Marvin Harrison may be getting older, but he is still one of the best wide receivers in the NFL. He almost guarantees at least 1,100 yards and double—digit touchdowns each year. Last season, Harrison had six games where he had 100 yards or more and eight games where he had at least eight receptions. His quarterback, Peyton Manning. They hold the NFL record for most receptions between a quarterback and wide receiver.

4. Torry Holt [St. Louis]

Last season, Holt became the fastest player in NFL history to reach 10,000 receiving yards. Even though he had a low year for his standards, Holt still finished with 93 receptions for 1,188 yards and 10 touchdowns. He had knee surgery in the off-season but do not let this fool you. He has the skills to have another solid year with at least 90+ receptions, 1,300+ yards and double-digit touchdowns.

5. Terrell Owens [Dallas]

"TO" produced last year, catching 85 passes for 1,180 yards and league-leading 13 touchdowns. Owens loves getting in the end—zone because he has scored 13 or more touchdowns in six of his last nine seasons. Despite his antics on and off the field and the surgery on his finger, Owens will excel, especially if quarteback Tony Romo continues to develop.

6. Reggie Wayne [Indianapolis]

Wayne notched his third straight 1,000-yard season in 2006 with 1,310. He set career highs in receptions and yards and made his first Pro Bowl. In two of the last three seasons, he has scored at least 9 touchdowns. Even though Marvin Harrison is the Colts' top receiver, Peyton Manning has shown that he has confidence in Wayne especially when deep pass plays are involved.

7. Larry Fitzgerald [Arizona]

"Fitz" missed three games last season due to a hamstring injury. He finished the 2006 season with 69 receptions for 946 yards and 6 touchdowns. Fitz is healthy and with Matt Leinart as quartetback, the Cardinals look to pass more. This means more opportunities for Fitz and his teammate Anquan Boldin.

8. Javon Walker [Denver]

After missing nearly all of the 2005 season with a knee injury, Walker returned with 69 receptions, 1,084 yards and 8 touchdowns in his first season with the Broncos. He also ran 9 times for 123 yards and one touchdown. Walker is the go-to wide receiver for the Denver offense and with the acquisition of running back Travis Henry and the development of quartetback Jay Cutler, their offense can only get better.

9. Roy Williams [Detroit]

Williams had career highs with 82 receptions and 1,310 yards. He also scored 7 touchdowns and has had 7 or more touchdowns in each of his first three seasons. With the Mike Martz' offense and wide receiver rookie Calvin Johnson, Williams will get numerous opportunities to get the ball due to less double-teaming.

10. T.J. Houshmandzadeh [Cincinnati]

Considered to be one of the most underrated wide receivers in the NFL, Houshmandzadeh finished the 2006 season with 90 receptions for 1,081 yards and 9 touchdowns, all career highs. He missed the first two games and he played with four cracked bones in his back in the last month of the season! Houshmandzadeh and Chad Johnson are considered by some to be the best receiving duo in the league.

PROJECTIONS: TIGHT ENDS

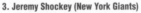

1. Antonio Gates (San Diego)

There should be no question as to why this guy is named the top fantasy tight end. Antonio Gates put up another stellar performance last season, totaling 71 receptions for 924 yards and 9 touchdowns, and touchdowns in 8/16 games. That kind of performance places him among the top wide receivers in the game and at the top of every tight end ranking list across the country. Antonio Gates will continue to thrive and put together another fantasy-worthy season.

2. Alge Crumpler (Atlanta)

Last season, Alge Crumpler led the Falcons in receptions (56), receiving yards (780 yards), and touchdowns (8), and continues to be Vick's favorite target. Crumpler was second only to Antonio Gates in TE fantasy points last season. New head coach Bobby Petrino looks to open up the Falcons' passing game, something that should only help Crumpler as Vick will still look to his favorite target in most situations, including the endzone.

3. Jeremy Shockey (New York Giants)

Finishing with 66 receptions, 623 receiving yards, and 7 touchdowns last season, Shockey continues to be a viable fantasy tight end despite his nagging injuries. This season, the Giants have a new offensive coordinator who hopes to get Shockey more involved downfield. Should he stay healthy and his ankle not act up, Shockey will have the opportunity to return to the phenomenal numbers he put up in the '05 season.

4. Tony Gonzales (Kansas City)

Tony G still remains a top tight end candidate, putting up numbers of 73 receptions for 900 yards, and 5 touchdowns. This marks the fourth year in a row he has recorded 70-plus receptions for 900 yards or more with no reason to think he won't do it again this season. Although Trent Green is no longer feeding him the ball, Tony G's sure hands and large frame will be an attractive target for any quarterback in Herm Edwards' conservative offense.

5. Todd Heap (Baltimore)

Todd Heap's consistency puts him high on the list again this year. Very similar to his '05 numbers, Heap logged 73 receptions for 765 yards and 6 touchdowns last season, and managed to play all 16 games. And, you can bet that the Ravens would like to see more of a deep passing game, Steve McNair will still rely on Heap as an outlet and hurry-up option. Look for a repeat performance from Heap again this year in a seemingly unchanged Billick offense.

6. Kellen Winslow (Cleveland)

7. Chris Cooley (Washington)

8. L.J. Smith (Philadelphia)

9. Vernon Davis (San Francisco)

10. Randy McMichael (St. Louis)

PROJECTIONS: KICKERS

1. Nate Kaeding (San Diego)

Nate Kaeding, last season's point leader for kickers is primed for another great year. Cleaning up for the Chargers' powerful offense, led by Rivers and Tomlinson, he had a career year, with career bests in field goals, extra points and field goal percentage. While he didn't get a lot of chances to show off his strong leg last year he had only one attempt from beyond 50 yards, which he made, and only missed three from 49 yards and closer. There is no reason to think he wont have another solid year.

2. Adam Vinatieri (Indianapolis)

"Mr. Clutch," has made his living for years by winning the big games. Last season he battled a few injuries that led to his lower numbers and accuracy, including missing two in the championship game. He is solid, only missing two attempts from 49 yards in, there is no reason to doubt him returning to form for the Colts and their dominate offense.

3. Jason Elam (Denver)

The mad bomber from the Rockies, is once again primed to have one of his patented consistent seasons. He can be counted on for at least one 50-yard plus bomb per season; he's done it for 15 years. He's reliable, only missing two from less than 50 yards, and will be crucial for Denver with their young quarterback leading the offense.

4. Jeff Wilkins (St. Louis)

Playing in a dome has its benefits and a potent offense in a weak division doesn't hurt either. With 100 plus fantasy points in three of the last four seasons, Wilkins is a solid pick. Wilkins missed five from less than 50 yards, but hit all three of his 50-yard plus attempts, which is nice for the leagues that reward such feats.

5. Matt Stover (Baltimore)

Not quite ready for his walker yet, the old man of the league, now that Morten Anderson finally hung it up, Stover is still a solid fantasy pick. He's accurate and reliable, almost 90 percent for the past four seasons, and led the league last season with 93 percent. While he doesn't get a lot of attempts from 50 yards plus, he's 75 percent when does get the opportunity, including his lone chance last season.

6. Robbie Gould (Chicago)

7. David Akers (Philadelphia)

8. Josh Scobee (Jacksonville)

9. Joe Nedney (San Francisco)

10. Neil Rackers (Arizona)

PROJECTIONS: DEFENSE

1. Baltimore Ravens

From year to year, you can count on a few things to stay constant in the NFL. New England will be a high-powered offense, LT will put up great numbers, and the Baltimore Ravens will have one of the NFL's best defenses. Granted, some might argue that the Ravens' defense is getting a bit long in the tooth, but there's no arguing with the type of season they had last year. They only allowed four teams to score 20 or more points the entire season, and kept every other team close to single digits.

2. Chicago Bears

The Chicago Bears' trip to the Super Bowl last year had a lot less to do with offense than defense. While their quarterback, Rex Grossman, was surrounded by doubt and second-guessing, their defense was solid, strong, and unforgiving. Talk of Lance Briggs' dissatisfaction with the Bears did little to weaken Chicago's defensive wall. Rest assured, Briggs can go, but as long as Urlacher stays, the Bears' defense will remain strong.

3. San Diego Chargers

Many people were surprised by the emergence of the San Diego defense last year. With the help of Shawne Merriman and Shaun Phillips, the San Diego defense proved they could cause havoc for the opposition. Not only did Merriman lead the NFL in sacks with 17, he did so in only 12 games. The other Shaun? He racked up 11.5 sacks. Sure, they let defensive stalwart Donnie Edwards go to the Chiefs, but if there's one thing the Chargers' defense has it's depth.

4. Pittsburgh Steelers

They may have lost Joey Porter to Miami, but as long as Troy Polamalu is on the field, opposing quarterbacks will have to think twice before launching the ball in his direction. Polamalu's speed and soft hands are matched only by his keen ability to read quarterbacks and be at the right place at the right time. Luckily, the Steelers have also retained the services of their defensive coordinator Dick LeBeau, so they'll continue to be consistent.

5. New England Patriots

Here are a few reasons that the Pats aren't higher on this list; Teddy Bruschi is the heart and soul of the Pats "D", but concerns about injury and age are finally catching up. and Asante Samuel's future in New England is in doubt, there seems to be very little to bank on in New England, right? Wrong! Sure there are plenty of question marks when it comes to New England's defense, but Adalius Thomas, Ty Warren, and Vince Wilfork will do plenty to turn those question marks into exclamation points.

6. Jacksonville

7. Carolina

8. Denver

9. Philly

10. Miami

EA SPORTS™ FANTASY FOOTBALL

PROJECTIONS: SLEEPERS

QUARTERBACK

Jon Kitna had his best season to date last year. He seems to mesh well with the Lions' offensive strategy. He's got several things that should make him attractive to fantasy owners: first, he doesn't have a serious contender for the starting position so you can expect, short of injury, that he'll start every game. Second, while Mike Martz' offense is often turnover-prone, it's also much more likely to hit the big play. Third, defensive-minded new head coach Marinelli is likely to do a lot to keep Kitna on the field and in the game. Finally, Calvin Johnson + Roy Williams + Mike Furrey = really tired cornerbacks.

RUNNING BACK

Ahman Green's best years came under the coaching of Mike Sherman in Green Bay. Now the two are reunited in Houston as top running back and offensive coordinator respectively. The Texans have made a number of significant off-season moves, including picking up a more stable quarterback and a number of defensive additions. Expect Green's rushing numbers to be augmented by the short, safe passing scheme of Schaub and Kubiak and his time on the field to increase as the Texans' defense improves.

WIDE RECEIVER

As the Chargers' offense comes into its own, quarterback Philip Rivers gets more and more confidence. This will translate into more passing, more completions, and better wide receiver stats. Eric Parker has been the top wide receiver in San Diego for the past few years, but last season was a solid warm-up for **Vincent Jackson**. Many are predicting a breakout year from him this season. It might be pushing it to put him in with the wide receiver starters in your draft, but he's a solid choice for a late round pickup or a steal during waivers.

TIGHT END

The tight-end position is probably the most predictable for fantasy owners. Antonio Gates is the class of the field and, after the top five, the drop-off is significant. Teams rarely change their strategies to focus on tight ends and the position is less injury-prone than many others. All of this means that there will rarely be any big surprises coming from tight ends. In fact, the last time a tight end made a big splash in the league was when rookie Jeremy Shockey joined the Giants. This year, a different rookie, **Greg Olsen**, signed with Chicago. I'm not saying he's going to be the next Shockey, but if anyone can shake up the tight-end status quo, it's likely to be Olsen. He has the size (6' 4") and hands to make some big plays in the red zone and his quarterback Grossman prefers the short yardage game over airing it out.

KICKER

Second year starter, **Stephen Gostkowski** only has room to improve this season. He delivered the points for New England and the lucky fantasy owners who took a chance with him. The Pats offensive upgrades could lead to a bunch of new PAT (point after touchdowns) attempts for Gostkowski, and his mediocre field goal percentage has had an entire off-season to improve.

DEFENSE

Many teams, including San Francisco, Seattle, and St. Louis, made important defensive additions during the off-season. Look for all of these to make steady improvement. However, expect the **Vikings** to break into the top tier for fantasy owners. Minnesota, already number 1 against the run, beefed up their secondary with the additions of Mike Doss and Tank Williams. In addition, 2006 top draft pick Chad Greenway and impressive defensive end Erasmus James will both be returning from injuries. The Vikings were a fantasy scoring machine last year with five touchdowns and more than 30 turnovers. This season could see a Purple Reign.

ROOKIE PROSPECT

Of all the rookies this season, **Brandon Jackson** has the best chance of starting and making a significant contribution to his team. The second round pick out of Nebraska is listed as the Packers' number two running back behind unproven Vernand Morency. Jackson is a compact, fast rusher who should fit in well with the Packers' offense. He also managed to catch quite a few passes in his last year at Nebraska and he could become a good dump-off target for a scrambling Bret Favre.

DRAFT STRATEGY

TOUCHDOWN LEAGUES vs. YARDAGE LEAGUES

The object of fantasy football is to assemble a team that will whoop up on everyone else's team. The team with the most points wins, so finding out what type of league you're playing in is key. In fantasy football terms, there are two fundamental types of leagues, a Touchdown League and a Yardage League.

• **TOUCHDOWN LEAGUE** — The Touchdown League is just what it sounds like. Your team compiles points based on the players' scoring touchdowns. There are usually two categories for accumulating points. Touchdowns thrown account for 4 points in most leagues, whereas, touchdowns run in or re-ceived are worth 6 points. Quarterbacks usually score more touchdowns than running backs and receivers, accounting for the scoring discrepancy. In this type of league it's important to find guys who score often, not necessarily guys who gain a lot of yardage. A great example can be drawn from the Dallas Cowboys' Marion Barber III running game last year. Julius Jones was the primary running back, racking up yardage like a madman to the five yard line, but from there Marion Barber III would take over and score touchdowns with very little yardage. In this league, Barber III would be the favorable choice.

• **YARDAGE LEAGUE** — The Yardage League is a more balanced scoring system using not only touchdowns as points, but also a compilation of yardage totals. Touchdown points are usually similar to that of Touchdown leagues, except there are often "bonus" points associated with the distance of the touchdown scored. For example, a 60-yard touchdown received may be worth 10 points, whereas a 5-yard touchdown received would be worth 6 points. Aside from touchdown points, the points are generated from total yardage thrown, run or received. For example, some leagues are set up to give rushing and receiving points for every 10 or 20 yards. Each increment of 10 or 20 yards would garner a certain point value. As well, the quarterback position may be similarly scored, except for a larger integer between yardages. For example, most leagues will give specified points to a quarterback for every 25 to 50 yards thrown. Again, "bonuses" are usually set-up in the scoring system to reward players gaining yardage past certain milestones set up by the league commissioner. In this type of league, look for players who get the ball often. Scoring a lot of touchdowns is always good, but it's equally important to find someone with the possibility of adding "bonuses" to your point totals through compiled yardage.

Note: With the flexibility of online leagues, it is possible that your league can be a hybrid of the two major league formats. Speak with your other Fantasy Football participants to decide on what league format works best for you.

HOW TO GET READY

Be prepared! Do your homework and know what you want to do. Have a game plan on draft day. Most owners will often have printouts of complete statistics by key positions, scribbled notes of top-ten players at each position, the prior year's fantasy results from another league, or a fantasy football magazine that does the work for them...ahem...a Prima guide! Whatever strategy you bring, just make sure you have some study materials to thumb through while you're preparing for your next pick. But you should be fully aware of the opposing owners' draft strategy too.

WATCHING THE OPPOSING OWNERS

One of the biggest mistakes owners make is not being aware of their counterparts. Most leagues have a draft board or complete the draft online. Either way, it should be possible to view the other owners' picks. Scanning everyone else's team is key to not making mistakes.

Let's say you had three picks and you selected 2 running backs and 1 wide receiver, but you obviously still need a quarterback. Your next pick shouldn't necessarily be a quarterback. If all the other teams have already drafted their quarterback, then they won't be looking to add a back-up until later in the draft. They'll most likely be going after running backs and receivers. So, your next choice should probably be another running back, receiver or even the best tight end, kicker, or defense, if still available. What you're doing is taking another great player away from opposing teams while solidifying yours. None of the owners are going to take that quality quarterback still on the board, because they've already filled that position. You can then pick up that quarterback slightly later in the draft without essentially "wasting" a prime pick.

Another strategy is to "steal" players that an opposing owner may need. It may not be the most necessary pick for you at the time, but you can always make trades and it may give you another option at that position. The idea is that you shouldn't be so consumed by your team that you fail to see the strengths and weaknesses of other teams. Doing this may cripple another team into choosing a weaker player at the needed position. Effective, yes. Dirty, maybe. Illegal, no. Play to win.

BYE WEEKS

Don't be that guy! Inevitably there's someone in the draft who picks players of the same position that have the same bye week. Unfortunately we had one of those in our league, but it was his first time and that's what you get for not reading our strategy. It's simple though; get an NFL schedule with bye weeks and write down a list of weeks with the teams on a bye for that week. If you pick players of the same position with the same bye week, you'll go into that week either having to dump a player or two whom you want to keep in order to pick up some players, or you'll be forced to play that week with one or two empty spots. You want to be able to spread out the bye weeks throughout the year so that you're not left with a depleted team in any given week. You could argue that you're playing the most talented team for 16 weeks, but you're simply giving away one of those weeks if a majority of your team is out. Any bench player should be able to come in during the starter's bye week to get you some points. Don't be stuck scrambling last minute to put a team together when all you needed was a list of the teams' bye weeks on piece of paper for draft day.

MOCK DRAFT

To illustrate the draft process and to provide some possible draft strategies, we have set up a mock draft. The following is the draft that took place between eight knowledgeable Fantasy Football veterans.

MOCK DRAFT **LEAGUE SETTINGS**

We set up an average league scenario of 16 players, 10 starter positions and a 6-player bench. This year we added the popular running back/wide receiver "flex" position where on any given week an extra running back or wide receiver may be played. We chose a touchdown heavy league where all touchdowns count as 6 points no matter who scores them or the length of touchdown. There are point allotments for the amount of yards a player passes (1 pt per 50 yrds), receives (1 pt per 20 yrds), and rushes (1 pt per 20yrds).

Defense scores are based on points allowed, interceptions, sacks, and fumble recoveries. Points will also be deducted for thrown interceptions.

You will find that this is a pretty standard and universal scoring method with online Fantasy Football leagues.

(See www.primagames.com for complete mock draft rules and scoring breakdown, as well as weekly updates.)

TEAM BREAKDOWNS • Each team consists of 10 starting positions and 6 bench players.

STARTING POSITIONS		BENCH SLOTS
QB		
WR		
WR		
WR		
RB		
RB		
RB/WR		
TE		
K		
D		

EA SPORTS™ FANTASY FOOTBALL

ROUND	MACSTER	DANNIL	ZAGS	JOOKIE	SPAZZ	PAPPA G	RED STAR	POGI
Round 1	LaDainian Tomlinson	Steven Jackson	Peyton Manning	Larry Johnson	Drew Brees	Shaun Aleander	Rudi Johnson	Frank Gore
Round 2	Chad Johnson	Steve Smith	Maurice Jones-Drew	Willie Parker	Edgerrin James	Joseph Addai	Carson Palmer	Tom Brady
Round 3	Reggie Wayne	Marvin Harrison	Terrell Owens	Torry Holt	Reggie Bush	Antonio Gates	Brian Westbrook	Jeremy Shockey
Round 4	Marc Bulger	Willis McGahee	Marques Colston	Javon Walker	Darrell Jackson	T.J. Houshmandzadeh	Randty Moss	Larry Fitzgerald
Round 5	Laurence Maroney	Travis Henry	Clinton Portis	Anquan Boldin	Tony Gonzalez	Plaxico Burress	Ronnie Brown	Cedric Benson
Round 6	Vernon Davis	Roy Williams	Marion Barber III	Alge Crumpler	Donte' Stallworth	Brandon Jacobs	Santana Moss	Donald Driver
Round 7	Baltimore Defense	Michael Vick	Kellen Winslow Jr.	Andre Johnson	Ben Watson	Lee Evans	Bears Defense	Chris Chambers
Round 8	Hines Ward	Donovan McNabb	Pittsburgh Defense	Ahman Green	New England Defense	Laveranues Coles	Todd Heap	San Diego
Round 9	Deuce McAllister	Deion Branch	Marshawn Lynch	Tony Romo	Adam Vinatieri	Phillip Rivers	Mark Clayton	Vince Young
Round 10	Mushin Muhammad	Reggie Brown	Calvin Johnson	Matt Leinart	Mike Furrey	Matt Stover	Cadillac Williams	Shayne Graham
Round 11	Jeff Wilkins	Thomas Jones	Nate Kaeding	Jamal Lewis	Warrick Dunn	Adrian Peterson	Braylon Edwards	Lendale White
Round 12	L.J. Smith	Robbie Gould	Joey Galloway	Denver Defense	Matt Hasselback	San Francisco Defense	Vincent Jackson	Chris Cooley
Round 13	Isaac Bruce	Minnesota Defense	Jacksonville Defense	Joe Horn	Julius Jones	DeAngelo Williams	Jason Elam	Philadelphia
Round 14	Alex Smith	Jon Kitna	Desmond Clark	Jason Whitten	Arnaz Battle	J.P. Losman	Trent Green	Jerricho Cotchery
Round 15	Derrick Mason	Randy McMichael	Eli Manning	Greg Jennings	Brandon Jackson	Bernard Berrian	Dallas Clark	Matt Jones
Round 16	Mike Bell	Owen Daniels	Marty Booker	Neil Rackers	Kevin Curtis	Miami Defense	Michael Turner	Lamont Jordan

DRAFT SYNOPSIS

1st PICK • JIM "MACSTER" KNIGHT

Number 1. In fantasy drafts, this is the ultimate and I got it. Easy choice right? After getting my first pick, I had to break my normal draft strategy. For better or worse, I generally go top tier quarterback first. Usually Peyton Manning if I pick early enough, but by the luck of the draw, I had to throw that strategy out. So I jumped on the LT bandwagon and will hopefully ride it out to the end. One is the loneliest number, especially while waiting for my turn to come back around, I watched several top tier quarterbacks and running backs disappear, so when it was my turn again, I went for productivity and took two top tier receivers, Chad Johnson and Reggie Wayne. Chad, also known as "Ocho Cinco," may have started slow last year but he blew up in the second half of the season. Wayne is just money. He made 9 touchdowns and 1,300 yards while playing opposite arguably the best receiver in the game, Marvin Harrison. There was no way I could pass that up.

On my next turn, I snatched up Mark Bulger to fill my starting quarterback slot. With St. Louis playing in the weak West and having bolstered their offense, he's primed to have a productive season yet again. Later on I picked up Alex Smith for the week that Bulger is off. Smith has shown the potential to

be a better than average quarterback in the league, hopefully in Week 9 he will show that. Laurence Maroney was my pick after Bulger. He had a decent rookie campaign while sharing time in the backfield and now he's the man, hopefully he'll do even better.

With my next set of picks, I grabbed my tight end, Vernon Davis. A promising young player, who looks like a star in the making. Then I went out on a limb and took the Baltimore Ravens defense. While it may be early to pick a defense, I wanted to make sure I had a good one. From there I was just filling holes. I picked up a group of solid performers at wide receiver, with Hines Ward, Mushin Muhammad, Derrik Mason, and Issac Bruce. All interchangeable when the need arises. I also selected Deuce McAllister and Mike Bell to back up my running back slots for the season. Both are solid point earners. Near the end I was able to pick up L.J. Smith as a back-up tight end, which I think is a steal and a capable replacement for Davis if he's not cutting it. Then I picked up Jeff Wilkins for a solid kicker. Overall I think I did quite well. Some nice pieces and some expendable pieces for those pesky bye weeks. Can't wait to get this started.

EA SPORTS™ FANTASY FOOTBALL

2nd PICK • DAN "DANNIL" RANSOM

This year's draft came up on us fast. Not only did we not have a great deal of time to prepare, but we were drafting in the very early days of training camps. Taking this into account, I wanted to step away from my usual conservative draft strategy and take a few risks. Conservative draft picks in June often end up being risky by September anyway. I focused my picks on one key element: potential.

With the number two pick, most owners would have gone for Peyton Manning or Larry Johnson. I took Steven Jackson. Stay with me here. Johnson's a great back, but last year kind of evened out for him. His carries went way up, but his yardage stayed about the same and he had a few less touchdowns. Meanwhile, Jackson is on his way up. His stats, both rushing and receiving keep going up and with an aging receiving core, Bulger may find Jackson and tight-end McMichael –– a steal for me in the 15th round –– to be his best targets. Manning was a different issue for me. After years of knocking on the door, he finally got a Superbowl ring, and MVP to boot. I've got no empirical facts to back me up, but that just seems like a classic time for a let down. If I was the fifth or sixth pick, I probably would have grabbed him anyway, but my gut screams that he's due for an off season.

I drafted a solid receiving core with Steve Smith, Marvin Harrison, and Roy Williams and for running backs I really like McGahee and Travis Henry's chances to improve this season. Henry was a 1,200-yard back with the Titans and now he's in Denver, where they build 1,000-yard rushers on an assembly line. He should do even better this year with the Broncos' zone-blocking scheme. McGahee, meanwhile, moves from a struggling offensive team to the team that led to Jamal Lewis's recent success. His average numbers have the chance to jump into the big time this year.

I'm less happy with my picks at quarterback, but drafting this early in the summer makes the injury-prone position unpredictable at best. I went with two quarterback with something to prove: McNabb is faced with his team's decision to draft a quarterback in the first round and is rebounding from last season's injury. All reports available before the draft spoke of his impressive performance in training camp. Michael Vick, while he hasn't quite gotten back to the stats that made him the league's poster boy for the next generation of quarterbacks in 2002, has seen steady improvement in his passing numbers each year since 2004. Additionally, the signing of Joe Horn should only help his receiving core. As far as the off-field problems go. I'm a cat person.

3rd PICK • ANDY "ZAGS" ROLLERI

Going into this draft I wanted to get a well-rounded team with scoring threats in every position and I was looking for players who typically don't miss a lot of games due to injury.

With my first pick I went against current trends and took a quarterback rather than a top running back. The only reason I didn't feel worried about this was because the quarterback was Peyton Manning, you know, Super Bowl champion Peyton Manning. Thirty one touchdowns in 2006, Peyton Manning. Never misses a game Peyton Manning. Winning the Super Bowl will only help Peyton this year, look for him to deliver his customary 25-30 touchdowns.

Running backs were coming off the board fast, so with my second pick I grabbed Maurice Jones-Drew. He splits time with Fred Taylor, so that is a concern, but he had a breakout season in 2006 and the oft-injured Taylor is getting up there in years. The Jags seemed happy to give Jones-Drew the ball near the goal line, so as long as that remains the case this will be a good pick.

Last season I picked up Terrell Owens with my second draft pick and he came through with 13 touchdowns. So this year I decided to wait until round three to pick him up. T.O. is one of the most volatile players in the league, but no one can doubt his talent. If he can continue his hot play with Tony Romo, he should be good for another double-digit TD season.

As a rookie, Marques Colston scored 8 touchdowns in just 14 games. He quickly became Drew Brees' favorite target. Look for them to connect even more this season.

Clinton Portis's 2006 season was shortened by injury. Though he played in only 8 games, he still managed to put the ball in the end zone 7 times. Washington has a run-happy offense and with the QB spot in Washington still in flux, look for Portis to see a lot of the ball. If he can stay healthy, he should put up big numbers.

Round 6 and tight ends were starting to come off the board and my guy was still available with only a few picks before my turn. As I dug into my pizza, a tasty cheese if you care, I noticed that a few more people had taken players so I rose and announced that I'd be taking Alge Crumpler with my pick. A steal this late and my second rated tight end overall. But as I

rose, the others in the draft room started grumbling.

The source of the commotion? It wasn't quite my pick yet. In my excitement I didn't notice that there was one more spot before my turn. So what did Jeff do? Of course he took Crumpler. Maybe he wanted a tight end and maybe Crumpler was high on his list, but I think it was done out of spite and a desire to make me look the fool. Either way I was a little rattled and with my sixth pick I took.... Marion Barber III. He is not the #1 running back in Dallas, Julius Jones has that distinction. And while Barber carried the ball 132 times less than Jones, he scored 14 touchdowns to Jones's 4. Barber is a short yardage specialist and since this league is a touchdown league, he is a great pick in the 6th round.

Having regained my composure, I took tight end Kellen Winslow Jr. with my next pick. And no matter how often you ask me, I'll swear that he was the tight end I wanted all along.

Pittsburgh is a defense-minded team that always forces turnovers. In 2006 they forced 13 fumbles and intercepted the ball 20 times. A new coach will do nothing to change the defensive nature of the team, so look for them to have another good season.

With picks nine and ten I went young and picked Marshal Lynch and Calvin Johnson, two young studs who could really have an impact this season. If either catches fire I can move them into the starting lineup.

Kickers were starting to go, so when my turn came up I went with a solid pro that is consistently in the top tier of kickers, Nate Keating.

By round 12 I was just filling spots and looking for bye week help. Joey Galloway, the Jacksonville Jags, Desmond Clark, Eli Manning and Marty Booker are all accomplished players who at any time can catch fire and move into my starting team.

Overall I'm pleased with my picks. I managed to get a top quarterback and receiver though my running backs are not as strong as I had hoped, and as the season moves along, that could be my weak point. I think this year more than the last few I will need to keep a close eye on my starting lineup and make changes as the weeks move along.

4th PICK • JEFF "JOOKIE" BARTON

This year I was fortunate enough to draft toward the front of the pack. I was not so far up that I had to make any real decisions on my first pick; simply take who was left out of the top four picks. I knew L.T. would go first, followed by Larry Johnson, Peyton Manning, and Stephen Jackson/Frank Gore. When Stephen Jackson went second, to my surprise, I knew I had just landed Larry Johnson or Peyton Manning. Then Peyton was selected and my choice was easy. Larry Johnson making it to the fourth pick was like a birthday gift from the football gods. I'll take it! Don't expect this to happen in many draft situations, as L.J. is easily considered the number 2 draft this season. At the fourth selection, you are more apt to select Stephen Jackson, Frank Gore, or Peyton Manning.

My draft strategy this year was to try to use my first two selections for top running backs. With an increasing amount of teams sharing the running back workload, especially in goal line situations, there seems to be fewer premier backs to choose from this season. I figured drafting two of the top featured backs early would save me from having to rely on one of the many unproven backs or a split-back situation. Should these backs be gobbled up by my draft brothers, then I would take one of the elite wide outs sure to be available. However, the sun shined in my direction a second time; Willie Parker, another on my top pick list, managed to slip through the first round and into my lap.

With two premier backs now in my stable, I wanted to turn to wide outs. Unless you are able to snag Peyton, Brees, or Palmer, quarterbacks can wait a few rounds. Using your first few rounds to collect a couple of star wide receivers is better

use of your picks. I selected Torry Holt (STL), Javon Walker (DEN), and Anquan Boldin (ARZ) with my next three picks. All of whom are similar in play; big, fast play-makers with great hands and the potential to gain yards after catch and get their share of end zone dances.

I took a gamble in the quarterback position. Both of my quarterbacks, Romo and Leinart, are young, extremely talented and have plenty of weapons surrounding them, but have yet to prove consistency. To top it off, they both have a bye week of week 8 (as does half my team). My theory here is that by the halfway point in the season, I will know better as to whom my clear starter is and can use the other as trade material. I like both and think they both scream with potential. Mark my words; look for Leinart to have a break-out season!

As for the remainder of my picks, I took the best available at the time to flesh out my roster. I got a bargain in wide receiver Andre Johnson, selected in the middle rounds as well as running back Ahman Green, although he is yet to prove himself in the new offense of Houston. I managed to also pick up Alge Crumpler and Jason Witten as tight ends. They also share the same bye week, but again, I will test the waters before letting one go to fill the void in week 8. Finally, I selected a kicker. In this league, and in most leagues, there are only 8 to 12 teams. Only a fool would select more than one kicker, so I'm guaranteed to get a top 10 kicker (a top 8 kicker in this league). I simply don't waste the earlier round picks.

5th PICK • MARIO "SPAZZ" DEGOVIA

Sadly, I was the goat of the draft. It was not surprising. It was my preordained destiny considering I'd never done a fantasy draft before and only recently began paying more attention to the NFL so that I could keep up with my co-workers' conversations during the season. When it came time to draft day for our fantasy league I was surrounded by veterans of the game, and without much prep work under my belt I felt like a hambone at a starved wolf convention. The feeling intensified as I saw my opponents pulling out graphs, stacks of magazines, laptops, highlighters, Bill Parcells, annotated sheets of stats, and monogrammed stopwatches. I had to scrounge a pad of paper and a pen, having forgotten both before walking into this meat grinder.

I had a borrowed rankings magazine at my elbow and the good graces of Pappa G to help me (even after stealing Warrick Dunn from him). My strategy, therefore, was simply to not suck as badly as possible. And I got some good picks. There are those who question the sanity of Edgerrin James as my second choice, but Tony Gonzalez is solid, no question. Plus Hasselbeck as a back-up quarterback isn't going to get my man-card revoked and I was proud of snapping up Brees and Bush.

That pride was almost completely washed away when, around pick 14, I started paying attention to bye weeks. Check it out for yourself; weeks 6 and 8 are going to be horror shows for Team Bliss (as in the phrase, "Ignorance is…").

I had to scramble, choosing Brandon Jackson to fill in for week 8 and Kevin Curtis to be able to field at least two wide receivers in week 6. Jookie pointed out that by week 8 things can change dramatically with trades and such. Even so, I may end up short one wide receiver and a kicker in week 6, so I have to pray that the Saints will have a record breaking game that Sunday against Seattle. Oh please, football gods, look upon this wretched newbie with favor. Of course, I have two wide receivers on the same team, and upon reflection that seems dumb. So, to the rookie fantasy player I have this to say about strategy: there's always next year.

Overall I'm fine with my team but (according to Andy) that's mainly because I don't know any better. As I mentioned, I'm happy about Brees and Bush, I like Vinatieri going into the playoffs last year with 100% FG (Field Goal) completion, and being a 49ers fan (never, NEVER play fantasy football with your heart, they say) my heart is with Darrell Jackson. And who doesn't like the New England defense? I don't have a hands-off team. Even as a rank amateur at this I can see that if I want to be competitive I'm going to have to make some fancy moves and pay close attention. I'm so dead.

Well, at least I got one or two "attaboys" during the picks. As I marked Mike Furrey on the white board I heard a quiet "good pick" from someone. And the hiss of anguish from Pappa G when I grabbed Warrick Dunn was satisfying.

6th PICK • PAUL "PAPPA G" GIACOMOTTO

Delicious New York-style pizza covered eight greasy plates and plenty of excitement was evident throughout the "war room". You can imagine how quickly excitement turned to disgust as I saw the number 6 on the back of my plate. For a moment the pizza didn't taste so good. I said, "for a moment." Once I came to grasp my position in the draft, I started to strategize who might be available. As I saw the top couple running backs and quarterbacks scratched off my list it was my turn to make the uncomfortable walk to the draft board. I feel like a got a great value pick with Shaun Alexander. His numbers were down last season because he didn't play the full season due to injury. He's been one of the top two running backs over the past five years, so I'm expecting he's healthy enough to return to form and guarantee me two touchdowns per week. I'm anticipating more touchdowns from the next two players I grabbed, Joseph Addai and Antonio Gates. Joseph Addai is the featured back for the world champion Colts and should give me 12-15 touchdowns this year. Antonio Gates may've been a little early in the third round, but the top players were gone and wide receivers were flying off the board. It was imperative rather take a 2nd tier

receiver it was time to take everyone's top tight end. I felt no urgency to get a quarterback even though six had already been chosen. There are 2-3 quarterbacks who are top tier, and after that it's a bit muddy. Leaving the urge to get a quarterback, I selected another running back. Brandon Jacobs will be the feature back now that Tiki Barber has retired from the New York Giants. My wide receivers were picked later, but TJ Houshmandzedah and Plaxico Burress are solid picks as starters, while quality back-ups like Lee Evans and Laveranues Coles will serve well. At this point I decided it was time to snag quarterback Philip Rivers to bookend Antonio Gates in San Diego. An active and accurate kicker in Matt Stover made me nod and San Francisco's young and aggressive defense filled my guilty pleasure to get a position from my favorite team (it's not advised to EVER pick with your heart). I rounded out my team with rookie Adrian Peterson, speedster DeAngelo Williams, slinger JP Losman, deep threat Bernard Berrian, and Miami's solid defense. I'm pleased with my team after picking 6th in the draft. On paper I might rank one or two teams higher than my own, but I'm a motivator and expect the team to give me everything they've got. Stay tuned and enjoy your fantasy football season.

When I saw the starting lineup I knew that the bulk of my picks would have to be running backs and wide receivers. Of course, that didn't mean that I would focus solely on two positions for the entire draft. Luckily the NFL has a lot of depth at those two positions. Quarterbacks? Not so much. It's a given that Peyton Manning will go in the first round of most drafts, leaving only a handful of other quarterbacks that are worthy of being picked in the early rounds. After nabbing Rudi Johnson with my first pick, I knew that if I didn't grab Carson Palmer with my second pick, I'd end up having to pick up a quarterback with a lot less potential. Unfortunately, that meant that later in my draft I'd have to pick up a running back and quarterback duo that didn't have byes in the same week.

Because our league is only eight players deep, I knew that I'd be able to get a good kicker no matter what. So instead of picking a kicker and filling up my roster, I decided to build depth on my roster before picking a kicker. That's where two hometown heroes came in. With the arrival of Norv Turner in San Diego, I'm looking to (bona fide sleeper) Vincent Jackson to emerge as San Diego's number one wide out and Michael Turner to pick up a few more carries. Turner "the Burner" won't be a starting RB on my team, but if he becomes a larger part of the San Diego offense this year, he'll be a great RB to have in a pinch. After all, this might be his final year in San Diego, so he'll want to put on a show every chance he gets

for prospective teams. If you're playing in a keeper league, Michael Turner is a great pick up; he'll definitely be a strong starter on another team next year.

Of my draft, two other picks stand out; Randy Moss and Ronnie Brown. In retrospect, I might have taken Randy Moss a bit early. Only time will tell. However, rumors of Moss running the 40 at sub 4.3 speeds and now that he's on a Super Bowl-caliber team with a Top 3 quarterback throwing to him, shot his potential is through the roof. Will his attitude get in the way? Maybe. Who knows?

I was truly happy and 100 percent secure when I picked up Ronnie Brown, though. In fact, I felt he dropped a bit low in the draft. Cam Cameron's move to Miami can only increase Ronnie Brown's production. And while some might have given up on Ronnie's new quarterback, Trent Green, I haven't. I don't think he'll have a turnaround like Drew Brees when he left San Diego for New Orleans, but I do think that Trent Green will continue being a productive quarterback.

When all was said and done, I was able to pick up Braylon Edwards, Cadillac Williams, and Dallas Clark as bench-fillers. In some other leagues, those three players could be starters in second and third positions. On my team, they're insurance against empty bye weeks and decent depth.

For my first pick, I wanted a running back. L. T., Steven Jackson, L. J., Shaun Alexander, and Rudi Johnson were all gone, so I went with Frank Gore. Gore came out of nowhere last season. He led the NFC with 1,695 yards, had 9 touchdowns and even had 61 receptions! Because of the snaking pattern we use for the draft, I got the next pick and I had this nagging feeling that I should take a quarterback. Peyton Manning and Drew Brees were off the boards, and I was debating whether I should go with Carson Palmer or Tom Brady. Tom Brady is my man. He does a lot with so little. He has had inferior receivers, but in the last five years has averaged at least 3,500 yards and 20 TDs. The Patriots went out and got him three quality receivers in Donté Stallworth, Wes Welker, and the very talented Randy Moss.

Pappa G took tight end Antonio Gates in the third round and that made me wonder if I should get a tight end or a wide receiver. I got both. I went with Jeremy Shockey and Larry Fitzgerald. I know that Shockey only had 623 yards, but he had seven touchdowns. I'm banking that the Giants' new offensive coordinator Kevin Gilbride will get Shockey the ball more. Larry Fitzgerald was injured for three games last year, but he looked comfortable playing with Matt Leinart. Another running back is what I needed and I went with Cedric Benson. Benson is now the man for the Bears with the departure of Thomas Jones to the Jets. Donald Driver and Chris Cham-

bers were my next two picks. Driver is coming off a solid season and he is still Brett Favre's favorite target. Chambers, on the other hand, is a risky pick. He had one of his worst seasons ever, but with Cam Cameron heading up the team and bringing his offensive wizardry, I hope Chambers rebounds. I wanted to round out my starting lineup, so I decided to get a defense. Chicago was taken so I went with San Diego. San Diego led the league with 61 sacks and had three defensive touchdowns. Shawne Merriman, Shaun Phillips and Jamal Williams, with new defensive coordinator Ted Cottrell, will make this defense even better. Next, I needed to get a backup QB, and Madden 2008 cover boy Vince Young was my choice. There will be no curse this year! As the kicker, I chose Shayne Graham. He has averaged at least 123 points a season and should do well with the Bengals' high-powered offense.

My starting lineup had 2 players out for Week 4 and 3 players out for Week 9 so the rest of my picks were to cover for bye weeks and solidify my lineup. LenDale White, Chris Cooley, Philadelphia defense, Jerricho Cotchery, Matt Jones, and LaMont Jordan filled out the rest of the team. I took the only Raider in the whole draft. Was it out of pity? No! Jordan is a high-risk pick but there is a possibility that he may do well despite Dominic Rhodes being there.

MINI-GAMES

Mini-games are one of the #1 keys to improving your gameplay. Each of the drills works on a different skill set so make sure to spend a good amount of time with each one. These are also great to use as a pre-game warm before you go online to play.

DL Trench Fight

Challenge	Team	Player	Bronze	Silver	Gold	Notes
Rookie	Houston	Weaver	7	8	9	3 checkpoints
Pro	Eagles	Cole	9.75	11.75	14	4 checkpoints
All-Pro	49ers	Douglas	17.5	20.5	24	5 checkpoints
All-Madden	NY Giants	Strahan	22.5	26	30	6 checkpoints

Advance down the field, defeating blocks to grab a series of flags as quickly as possible.

• In this drill you'll need to use your rip, shove, and spin moves to take on a series of offensive linemen. Beat the linemen and grab the flags to complete the drill.

• In the early levels you can sprint right past the blocker much of the time. As you get to the All-*Madden* level, you are going to need to use more fakes to get past the defenaders. Don't get hung up on them, or you'll lose valuable time.

POSITIONS

Rookie: 1 OL each
Pro: 1 OL, 1 OL, 1 OL, 1 OL
All-Pro: 2 OL, 1 OL, 2 OL+1 RB, 1 OL, 2 OL
All-Madden: OL, 3 OL, 1 OL+1 RB, 1 OL+1 RB, 3 OL, 1 OL

RB Ground Attack

Challenge	Team	Player	Bronze	Silver	Gold	Notes
Rookie	Redskins	Portis	800	1400	2100	2 defenders
Pro	Vikings	Taylor	750	1300	1900	3 defenders
All-Pro	Chiefs	Johnson	700	1100	1500	3 defenders
All-Madden	Chargers	Tomlinson	600	900	1200	4 defenders

It sounds simple, and it is. Take the ball and run with it. Use any blockers, the blocking dummies, and every special move you've got to make the most of each carry.

• You will see the designed route for the play right before the snap. You are usually better off following your fullback in the beginning and then making a move once he engages. If he misses his block, be prepared to use the blocking dummies to get free.

• Once your fullback has taken care of a man, the rest of the play hinges on your ability to size up angles, use the special moves, and generally show off your "stick skills." Stiff-arm works for defenders that are coming at you from the side, while juke is best in a head-on situation with the defender right in front of you. The spin is a great move if a guy or two is beating you to a spot. Don't neglect the Truck Stick if you have a bigger back going up against a small defender.

SCORING

+ 10 points per yard gained
- 20 point penalty per yard lost
+ 30 point bonus for each touchdown
- *Online only:* 100-point penalty for each fumble
+ *Online only:* 100-point penalty for each tackle broken

DB Swat Ball

Challenge	Team	Player	Bronze	Silver	Gold	Notes
Rookie	Falcons	Hall	300	600	900	3 targets
Pro	Buccaneers	Barber	300	575	800	4 targets
All-Pro	Ravens	McAlister	300	525	725	5 targets
All-Madden	Broncos	Bailey	300	500	600	5 targets

A passing machine fires 20 balls at one of several stationary targets, indicating the target just before the release. Your job is to knock down—or preferably, intercept—as many as possible.

• In order to succeed at this drill, you have to be good with your speed burst, strafe, and catch buttons. Speed burst toward the target and then hit the strafe button as you get into position. Once you have squared your shoulders to the ball, it is much easier to pick up the interception. Even if you miss the catch, you will at least get the swat.

• Use the swat button only on passes that seem to be out of reach or are directly over your shoulder. These types of catches are very difficult for DBs, and the swat is the way to go.

• After each pass, try to get back into the center of the screen as quickly as possible. This will put you in position to get to as many of the targets as possible.

SCORING

+ **10 points** for the first pass defended
+ **20 points** for the second pass defended (consecutively)
+ **30 points** for the third pass defended (consecutively)
+ **40 points** for the fourth and all subsequent passes defended
+ **Double points** for an interception

Coffin Corner

Challenge	Team	Player	Bronze	Silver	Gold	Notes
Rookie	Bills	Moorman	250	650	900	—
Pro	Packers	Ryan	250	600	800	—
All-Pro	Seahawks	Plackemeier	250	500	700	—
All-Madden	Saints	Weatherford	250	375	500	—

Pin the imaginary opponent deep by landing six punts in either corner of the field.

• Here's one of the easiest mini-games in the series. Just kick the ball toward either corner and work on your touch to score max points. The less power you put into the kick, the slower the kick meter moves. Kick to the short side of the field; you'll have and easier time judging the angle.

• Kicking low laser-beamlike shots reduces the effect of the wind. This is especially important on the higher levels, where the wind is raging and the meter is moving very quickly.

• Repetition and learning the physics of power and the wind factor are the keys here. Practice enough, and soon you'll feel like you're just throwing darts out there (well, except that you're kicking footballs).

SCORING

+ **50 points** for the landing in the yellow area
+ **100 points** for the landing in the orange area
+ **200 points** for the landing in the red area
+ ***Online only:* Variable bonus** for each area, increasing with proximity to the front pylon

Clutch Kicking

Challenge	Team	Player	Bronze	Silver	Gold	Notes
Cardinals	Lions	Rackers	900	1500	2200	–
Pro	Josh	Scobee	900	1500	2200	–
All-Pro	Lions	Hanson	900	1500	2100	–
All-Madden	Colts	Vinatieri	900	1500	2100	–

You are on the clock as you try to hit as many field goals as possible in one minute. Hit the center to maximize your points.

• With the new kicking meter, it is going to take some reps to get comfortable with your kicking game. This drill puts you under pressure and moves you all over the field as you go for three pointers. Remember to check the wind and adjust for the hash marks when firing at your target.

• As in the punt drill, try reducing the loft on your kicks. Real kickers would never do this because of the risk of the kick being blocked, but that's not a concern here. Lower kicks mean less wind effect. Lower kicks travel faster, and will allow you to get off more kicks than if you boom big floaters out there.

SCORING

+ **75 points** for hitting the yellow area
+ **150 points** for hitting the orange area
+ **300 points** for hitting the red area
+ *Online only:* **Bonuses** awarded for each area, increasing with proximity to the center

Chase and Tackle

Challenge	Team	Player	Bronze	Silver	Gold	Notes
Rookie	Jets	Vilma	800	1475	2000	–
Pro	Titans	Bulluck	1000	1725	2250	–
All-Pro	Browns	Davis	650	1100	1500	–
All-Madden	Bears	Urlacher	650	1100	1500	–

Take control of a defender and stop the running back in his tracks.

• You want to avoid contact with the blockers if you are going to be able to make the stop. The sweep plays are the easiest to defend. Get out in front of the blocking, but watch out for the cut back move.

• The CPU will test your pursuit with spins and jukes. Every time you think you've got them beat to the corner; he'll cut back against the grain. Pursue gradually and with a careful angle to avoid getting burned. User your hit stick when possible to try to create fumbles.

• The best strategy involves waiting for the FB to hit the line of scrimmage while you track the ball carrier. Also try to shoot the gap right after the snap. Sometimes you'll rack up fumble bonuses because you'll disrupt the handoff. It's risky, because if you whiff you could give up a big play and get hit with a TD penalty.

SCORING

+ **10 points** for each yard the RB is stopped short of the end zone, if the computer-controlled player makes the tackle
+ **20 points** for each yard the RB is stopped short of the end zone, if the user-controlled player makes the tackle
+ **100-point bonus** for forcing a fumble
- **250-point penalty** for allowing a touchdown

Pocket Presence

Challenge	Team	Player	Bronze	Silver	Gold	Notes
Rookie	Steelers	Roethlisberger	900	1200	1400	–
Pro	Cowboys	Romo	800	1100	1325	–
All-Pro	Dolphins	Green	600	850	1100	–
All-Madden	Colts	Manning	450	675	950	–

This drill simulates pressure from all sides, and you've got to make the correct reads while the tennis balls are being shot at you. If you get hit with a ball, you're "sacked."

• This drill really forces you to have top-notch situational awareness. Just like a real QB, you can't be focused on what's right in front of you, or you'll never throw to the right guy. Try to pick up on the yellow tennis balls and where they're coming from, but always be watching to see what target icon has popped up.

• You need to stay in the target area as much as possible. You will be notified if you drift too far out of play. If you fail to get pack in the zone, the drill ends. Make small movements in the pocket. You don't want to overuse your stick.

SCORING

+ **25 points** for the first target hit in succession
+ **50 points** for the second target hit in succession
+ **75 points** for the third target hit in succession
+ **100 points** for the fourth and all subsequent targets hit in succession
- **10-point penalty** for throwing to the wrong target
- **10-point penalty** for throwing to any target when none is indicated
- **10-point penalty** for being hit by a tennis ball
- **Variable penalty** for leaving the pocket

Precision Passing

Challenge	Team	Player	Bronze	Silver	Gold	Notes
Rookie	Panthers	Delhomme	500	750	1000	–
Pro	Raiders	Russell	500	750	1000	–
All-Pro	Rams	Bulger	500	750	1000	–
All-Madden	Bengals	Palmer	500	750	1000	–

Throw at the right moment/trajectory so your pass goes through the ring and to the receiver.

• This drill simulates throwing through passing lanes. Usually there's only a small window to get the ball by the defense, and the rings simulate that window. Timing and how hard you throw the pass are the keys to performing well here. On the comebacks, ins, and outs, try throwing more of a bullet just as the receiver is making his break. The slants and posts are easy—you should just throw it a couple of steps before the receiver reaches the ring.

• Be sure to use the vision cone to maximize your accuracy. You can lock onto the route's pre-snap so that you can just concentrate on your timing once the drill starts. Deep routes require more loft on the ball. You also will want to control the receivers and make the user catch for maximum points.

SCORING

+ **25 points** for throwing the ball through a bronze-colored ring
+ **50 points** for throwing the ball through a silver-colored ring
+ **75 points** for throwing the ball through a gold-colored ring
+ **20 point bonus** if the receiver catches the ball
+ **Bonus** for user controlled receptions
+ **Bonus** for catch and turn—controlled receptions

MINI-GAMES

285

MADDEN CARDS

MADDEN CHALLENGE TASKS

This chapter includes all the information you need to keep track of your *Madden* Card book. From the *Madden* Challenge tasks to your player checklist and special cards, we've got you covered. See which ones you want to go after and target those tasks first. Good luck!

Challenge	Level 1	Level 2	Level 3	Level 4	Level 5
Rookie	2	2	2	2	2
Pro	2	2	2	2	2
All-Pro	2	2	2	2	2
All-Madden	2	2	2	2	2

MADDEN CARDS

1 LEVEL 1
Challenge Description

- Make a field goal of **40** yards or more
- Punt the ball **50** yards or more
- Hold CPU under **7** points (min qtr: 4)
- Score **21** points in a game (max qtr: 6)
- One reception by **3** different players
- Recover a fumble on defense
- Sack the opposing QB
- Throw **2** TD passes with one player
- Gain **200** yards of total offense (max qtr: 6)
- Break a **20**-yard run
- Complete **5** consecutive passes
- Complete a **30**-yard pass
- No dropped passes all game (min qtr: 4)
- No offensive fumbles all game (min qtr: 4)
- No interceptions thrown all game (min qtr: 4)
- No sacks allowed all game (min qtr: 4)
- Score **35** pts. on the Panthers at Carolina (max qtr: 6)
- Hold Patriots to **21** pts. in New England (min qtr: 5)
- Intercept a pass on defense
- Record **3** tackles with one player

2 LEVEL 2
Challenge Description

- **30**-yard PR avg. for one player (min ret: 2)
- Defeat the CPU by **28** points (max qtr: 6)
- Gain **100** receiving yards with one player
- **20**-yard rec avg. for one player (min rec: 3)
- Throw for **300** yards with one player
- Complete **80%** of your passes (min att: 5)
- Commit no penalties in a game (min qtr: 4)
- Record **2** sacks with one player
- Record **5** tackles with 2 different players
- **30**-yard KR avg. for one player (min ret: 2)
- Score **42** points in a game (max qtr: 6)
- **10**-yard rush avg. for one player (min att: 5)
- Catch **2** TD passes with one player
- Score **3** rushing TDs with one player
- Throw **4** TD passes with one player
- Complete **10** consecutive passes
- Defeat the '90 Giants with a regular team
- Force **3** turnovers in one game on defense
- Hold CPU under **150** total off. yds. (min qtr: 4)
- Gain **100** rushing yards with one player

3 LEVEL 3
Challenge Description

- Punt the ball out of bounds inside the **5**-yard line
- Shut out the CPU (min qtr: 4)
- **10** rushing attempts by 2 different players
- Gain **150** receiving yards with one player
- Gain **400** yards of total offense (max qtr: 6)
- Complete **15** consecutive passes
- Gain **450** yards of total offense against the Eagles
- Recover **2** fumbles on defense with one player
- Record **3** sacks with one player
- Record **8** tackles with one player
- Kick and recover an onside kick
- Score **63** points in a game (max qtr: 6)
- Make **10** receptions with one player
- Gain **100** rushing & **50** rec. yds. w/one player
- Gain **150** rushing yards with one player
- Break a **40**-yard run
- Complete a **60**-yard pass
- Gain **150** rushing yds. vs. '75 Vikings (max qtr: 6)
- Intercept **2** passes with one player
- Deflect **4** passes with one player

4 LEVEL 4
Challenge Description

- Make a field goal of **50** yards or more
- Make **6** two-point conversions in one game
- Gain **100** rushing yds. with **2** different players
- Gain **200** receiving yards with one player
- Complete **25** passes with one player
- Throw for **500** yards with one player
- Achieve **20** first downs (max qtr: 6)
- Return a fumble for a touchdown on defense
- Cause **6** turnovers on defense
- Record a safety on defense
- Punt the ball **65** yards or more
- Defeat the CPU by **56** points (max qtr: 6)
- Gain **100** receiving yds. with two different players
- Gain **200** rushing yards with one player
- **40** rushing att. by one player (max qtr: 6)
- Gain **650** yards of total offense (max qtr: 6)
- Complete a pass to **7** different receivers
- Break a **60**-yard run
- Record **7** sacks with one player
- Return an interception for a touchdown

5 LEVEL 5
Challenge Description

- Gain **200** PR yards with one player
- Return a punt for a touchdown
- Complete **100%** of your passes (min att: 5)
- Gain **100** rushing & **100** passing yards with one player
- **20**-yard rush avg. for one player (min att: 3)
- Gain **250** rushing yards with one player
- Break an **80**-yard run
- Play injured and score a touchdown
- Intercept **5** passes on defense
- Record **2** safeties in one game
- Gain **200** KR yards with one player
- Return a kickoff for a touchdown
- Score **84** points in a game (max qtr: 6)
- Gain **100** receiving yards with three different players
- Gain **100** rushing & **150** passing yards with one player
- Gain **200** passing yards with two different players
- Break **10** tackles with one player
- Complete **20** consecutive passes
- Complete a **90**-yard pass
- Hold CPU to zero total offensive yards (min qtr: 4)

MADDEN CARD CHECKLIST

Note: Each card in *Madden NFL 08* is listed on the following pages, with the variations for each player/coach explained below.

Player Card

Bronze: This card gives a 25% ratings boost for **one play**.
Silver: This card gives a 25% ratings boost until the end of the **current quarter**.
Gold: This card gives a 25% ratings boost until the end of the **current half**.

Coach Card

Bronze: This card boosts the awareness of your team for **one play**.
Silver: This card boosts the awareness of your team until the end of the **current quarter**.
Gold: This card boosts the awareness of your team until the end of the **current half**.

PLAYER CHECKLIST

The Player Checklist spans *Madden* Cards 1-155

Card	Player	Card	Player	Card	Player	Card	Player
1	Rex Grossman	41	Larry Johnson	80	Byron Leftwich	118	Terrell Suggs
2	Olin Kreutz	42	Tony Gonzalez	81	Fred Taylor	119	Ray Lewis
3	Tommie Harris	43	Willie Roaf	82	John Henderson	120	Chris McAlister
4	Brian Urlacher	44	Derrick Johnson	83	Marcus Stroud	121	Ed Reed
5	Lance Briggs	45	Peyton Manning	84	Rashean Mathis	122	Clinton Portis
6	Nathan Vasher	46	Marvin Harrison	85	Curtis Martin	123	Santana Moss
7	Carson Palmer	47	Reggie Wayne	86	Laveranues Coles	124	Chris Cooley
8	Rudi Johnson	48	Dwight Freeney	87	Justin McCareins	125	Chris Samuels
9	Chad Johnson	49	Cato June	88	Jonathan Vilma	126	Deuce McAllister
10	TJ Houshmandzadeh	50	Drew Bledsoe	89	Kevin Jones	127	Donte Stallworth
11	David Pollack	51	Terry Glenn	90	Roy Williams	128	Joe Horn
12	Odell Thurman	52	Jason Witten	91	Kalimba Edwards	129	Dwight Smith
13	Deltha O'Neal	53	DeMarcus Ware	92	Shaun Rogers	130	Matt Hasselbeck
14	Willis McGahee	54	Roy Williams	93	Brett Favre	131	Shaun Alexander
15	London Fletcher	55	Daunte Culpepper	94	Samkon Gado	132	Jerramy Stevens
16	Takeo Spikes	56	Chris Chambers	95	Nick Barnett	133	Walter Jones
17	Nate Clements	57	Randy McMichael	96	Jake Delhomme	134	Lofa Tatupu
18	Jake Plummer	58	Jason Taylor	97	DeShaun Foster	135	Michael Boulware
19	Tatum Bell	59	Zach Thomas	98	Steve Smith	136	Ben Roethlisberger
20	Al Wilson	60	Donovan McNabb	99	Mike Wahle	137	Willie Parker
21	Champ Bailey	61	Brian Westbrook	100	Julius Peppers	138	Hines Ward
22	John Lynch	62	Jevon Kearse	101	Chris Gamble	139	Heath Miller
23	Charlie Frye	63	Jeremiah Trotter	102	Tom Brady	140	Alan Faneca
24	Reuben Droughns	64	Brian Dawkins	103	Corey Dillon	141	Troy Polamalu
25	Braylon Edwards	65	Michael Vick	104	Deion Branch	142	David Carr
26	Andra Davis	66	Warrick Dunn	105	Richard Seymour	143	Domanick Davis
27	Carnell Williams	67	Alge Crumpler	106	Tedy Bruschi	144	Andre Johnson
28	Joey Galloway	68	Keith Brooking	107	Rodney Harrison	145	Dunta Robinson
29	Simeon Rice	69	DeAngelo Hall	108	LaMont Jordan	146	Drew Bennett
30	Derrick Brooks	70	Alex Smith	109	Jerry Porter	147	Chris Brown
31	Ronde Barber	71	Kwame Harris	110	Randy Moss	148	Brandon Jones
32	Kurt Warner	72	Bryant Young	111	Derrick Burgess	149	Kyle Vanden Bosch
33	Anquan Boldin	73	Derek Smith	112	Marc Bulger	150	Keith Bulluck
34	Larry Fitzgerald	74	Eli Manning	113	Steven Jackson	151	Travis Taylor
35	Bertrand Berry	75	Tiki Barber	114	Torry Holt	152	Jermaine Wiggins
36	LaDainian Tomlinson	76	Plaxico Burress	115	Isaac Bruce	153	Antoine Winfield
37	Keenan McCardell	77	Jeremy Shockey	116	Orlando Pace	154	Darren Sharper
38	Antonio Gates	78	Michael Strahan	117	Jonathan Ogden	155	Donald Driver
39	Shawne Merriman	79	Osi Umenyiora	118	Terrell Suggs		
40	Trent Green						

COACH **CHECKLIST** The Coach Checklist spans *Madden* Cards 156-187

	Card	Team	Coach		Card	Team	Coach		Card	Team	Coach		Card	Team	Coach
❐	155	Bears	Lovie Smith	❐	163	Chiefs	Herm Edwards	❐	171	Jaguars	Jack Del Rio	❐	179	Ravens	Brian Billick
❐	156	Bengals	Marvin Lewis	❐	164	Colts	Tony Dungy	❐	172	Jets	Eric Mangini	❐	180	Redskins	Joe Gibbs
❐	157	Bills	Dick Jauron	❐	165	Cowboys	Dallas Coach	❐	173	Lions	Rod Marinelli	❐	181	Saints	Sean Payton
❐	158	Broncos	Mike Shanahan	❐	166	Dolphins	Nick Saban	❐	174	Packers	Mike McCarthy	❐	182	Seahawks	Mike Holmgren
❐	159	Browns	Romeo Crennel	❐	167	Eagles	Andy Reid	❐	175	Panthers	John Fox	❐	183	Steelers	Bill Cowher
❐	160	Bucs	Jon Gruden	❐	168	Falcons	Jim Mora Jr.	❐	176	Patriots	NE Coach	❐	184	Texans	Gary Kubiak
❐	161	Cardinals	Dennis Green	❐	169	49ers	Mike Nolan	❐	177	Raiders	Art Shell	❐	185	Titans	Jeff Fisher
❐	162	Chargers	Marty Schottenheimer	❐	170	Giants	Tom Coughlin	❐	178	Rams	Scott Linehan	❐	186	Vikings	Brad Childress

SPECIAL **CHECKLIST** The Special Checklist spans *Madden* Cards 188-283.

	Card	Type	Name	Variation	Description
❐	188	Cheat	1st and 15	Bronze	Requires your opponent to get 15 yards to reach a first down for one drive.
❐	188	Cheat	1st and 15	Silver	Requires your opponent to get 15 yards to reach a first down for the quarter.
❐	188	Cheat	1st and 15	Gold	Requires your opponent to get 15 yards to reach a first down for the half.
❐	189	Cheat	1st and 5	Bronze	When played: Your remaining yards for first down will be set to 5 for one play.
❐	189	Cheat	1st and 5	Silver	Your remaining yards for first down will be set to 5 for the quarter.
❐	189	Cheat	1st and 5	Gold	When played: Your remaining yards for first down will be set to 5 for the half.
❐	190	Cheat	Unforced	Bronze	When played: Your opponent will fumble every time he tries to juke for 1 play.
❐	190	Cheat	Unforced	Silver	When played: Your opponent will fumble every time he jukes during the quarter.
❐	190	Cheat	Unforced	Gold	When played: Your opponent will fumble every time he tries to juke for the half.
❐	191	Cheat	Extra Credit	Bronze	Awards 2 points for every interception and 1 point for every sack.
❐	191	Cheat	Extra Credit	Silver	Awards 3 points for every interception and 2 points for every sack.
❐	191	Cheat	Extra Credit	Gold	Awards 4 points for every interception and 3 points for every sack.
❐	192	Cheat	Tight Fit	Bronze	When played: Your opponent's uprights will be made very narrow for 1 play.
❐	192	Cheat	Tight Fit	Silver	When played: Your opponent's uprights will be made very narrow for the quarter.
❐	192	Cheat	Tight Fit	Gold	When played: Your opponent's uprights will be made very narrow for the half.
❐	193	Cheat	5th Down	Bronze	When played: You will get 5 downs to make a first (one use).
❐	193	Cheat	5th Down	Silver	When played: You will get 5 downs to make a first for the quarter.
❐	193	Cheat	5th Down	Gold	When played: You will get 5 downs to make a first for the half.
❐	194	Cheat	3rd Down	Bronze	When played: Your opponent will only get 3 downs to make a first.
❐	194	Cheat	3rd Down	Silver	When played: Your opponent will only get 3 downs to make a first for the quarter.
❐	194	Cheat	3rd Down	Gold	When played: Your opponent will only get 3 downs to make a first for the half.
❐	195	Cheat	Human Plow	Bronze	When played: Your broken tackles will increase by 25% for the game.
❐	195	Cheat	Human Plow	Silver	When played: Your broken tackles will increase by 50% for the game.
❐	195	Cheat	Human Plow	Gold	When played: Your broken tackles will increase by 75% for the game.
❐	196	Cheat	Super Dive	Bronze	When played: Your diving distance increases by 25% for the game.
❐	196	Cheat	Super Dive	Silver	When played: Your diving distance increases by 50% for the game.
❐	196	Cheat	Super Dive	Gold	When played: Your diving distance increases by 75% for the game.
❐	197	Cheat	Da Boot	Bronze	When played: You will receive unlimited field goal range for 1 play.
❐	197	Cheat	Da Boot	Silver	When played: You will receive unlimited field goal range for the quarter.
❐	197	Cheat	Da Boot	Gold	When played: You will receive unlimited field goal range for the half.

	Card	Type	Name	Variation	Description
☐	198	Cheat	Da Bomb	Bronze	When played: You will receive unlimited pass range for 1 play.
☐	198	Cheat	Da Bomb	Silver	When played: You will receive unlimited pass range for the quarter.
☐	198	Cheat	Da Bomb	Gold	When played: You will receive unlimited pass range for the half.
☐	199	Cheat	Lame Duck	Bronze	When played: Your opponent will throw a lob pass for 1 play.
☐	199	Cheat	Lame Duck	Silver	When played: Your opponent will throw lob passes for the quarter.
☐	199	Cheat	Lame Duck	Gold	When played: Your opponent will throw lob passes for the half.
☐	200	Cheat	Mistake Free	Bronze	When played: You can't fumble or throw an interception for 1 play.
☐	200	Cheat	Mistake Free	Silver	When played: You can't fumble or throw an interception for the quarter.
☐	200	Cheat	Mistake Free	Gold	When played: You can't fumble or throw an interception for the half.
☐	201	Cheat	Fumblitis	Bronze	When played: Your opponent's fumbles will increase by 25% for the game.
☐	201	Cheat	Fumblitis	Silver	When played: Your opponent's fumbles will increase by 50% for the game.
☐	201	Cheat	Fumblitis	Gold	When played: Your opponent's fumbles will increase by 75% for the game.
☐	202	Cheat	BINGO!	Bronze	When played: Your defensive interceptions will increase by 25% for the game.
☐	202	Cheat	BINGO!	Silver	When played: Your defensive interceptions will increase by 50% for the game.
☐	202	Cheat	BINGO!	Gold	When played: Your defensive interceptions will increase by 75% for the game.
☐	203	Cheat	Mr. Mobility	Bronze	When played: Your QB can't be sacked for 1 play.
☐	203	Cheat	Mr. Mobility	Silver	When played: Your QB can't be sacked for the quarter.
☐	203	Cheat	Mr. Mobility	Gold	When played: Your QB can't be sacked for the half.
☐	204	Cheat	Touchy	Bronze	When played: Your opponent's penalties will increase by 50% for 1 play.
☐	204	Cheat	Touchy	Silver	When played: Your opponent's penalties will increase by 50% for the quarter.
☐	204	Cheat	Touchy	Gold	When played: Your opponent's penalties will increase by 50% for the half.
☐	205	Cheat	Bad Spot	Bronze	When played: The ref will spot the ball 1-2 yards short for 1 play.
☐	205	Cheat	Bad Spot	Silver	When played: The ref will spot the ball 1-2 yards short for the quarter.
☐	205	Cheat	Bad Spot	Gold	When played: The ref will spot the ball 1-2 yards short for the half.
☐	206	Cheat	Toast	Bronze	When played: Your ability to burn a DB will increase by 25% for the game.
☐	206	Cheat	Toast	Silver	When played: Your ability to burn a DB will increase by 50% for the game.
☐	206	Cheat	Toast	Gold	When played: Your ability to burn a DB will increase by 75% for the game.
☐	207	Cheat	Jam	Bronze	When played: Your ability to jam a WR will increase by 25% for the game.
☐	207	Cheat	Jam	Silver	When played: Your ability to jam a WR will increase by 50% for the game.
☐	207	Cheat	Jam	Gold	When played: Your ability to jam a WR will increase by 75% for the game.
☐	208	Cheat	Pocket Protect	Bronze	When played: Your pass blocking effectiveness will increase by 25% for the game.
☐	208	Cheat	Pocket Protect	Silver	When played: Your pass blocking effectiveness will increase by 50% for the game.
☐	208	Cheat	Pocket Protect	Gold	When played: Your pass blocking effectiveness will increase by 75% for the game.
☐	209	Cheat	Penetration	Bronze	When played: Your line penetration will increase by 25% for the game.
☐	209	Cheat	Penetration	Silver	When played: Your line penetration will increase by 50% for the game.
☐	209	Cheat	Penetration	Gold	When played: Your line penetration will increase by 75% for the game.
☐	210	Cheat	QB On Target	Bronze	When played: Your QB Accuracy will be 100% for 1 play.
☐	210	Cheat	QB On Target	Silver	When played: Your QB Accuracy will be 100% for the quarter.
☐	210	Cheat	QB On Target	Gold	When played: Your QB Accuracy will be 100% for the half.
☐	211	Cheat	Coffin Corner	Bronze	When played: Your punt will go out of bounds at the max distance for 1 play.
☐	211	Cheat	Coffin Corner	Silver	When played: Your punt will go out of bounds at the max distance for the quarter.
☐	211	Cheat	Coffin Corner	Gold	When played: Your punt will go out of bounds at the max distance for the half.
☐	212	Cheat	Wind Gust	Bronze	When played: Field goal kicks will receive a gust in your favor for 1 play.
☐	212	Cheat	Wind Gust	Silver	When played: Field goal kicks will receive a gust in your favor for the
☐	212	Cheat	Wind Gust	Gold	When played: Field goal kicks will receive a gust in your favor for the half.

MADDEN CARDS

	Card	Type	Name	Variation	Description
❐	213	Cheat	Hands of Glue	Bronze	When played: Your catching ability will increase by 25% for the game.
❐	213	Cheat	Hands of Glue	Silver	When played: Your catching ability will increase by 50% for the game.
❐	213	Cheat	Hands of Glue	Gold	When played: Your catching ability will increase by 75% for the game.
❐	214	Cheat	Hands of Stone	Bronze	When played: Your opponent's catching ability will decrease by 25% for the game.
❐	214	Cheat	Hands of Stone	Silver	When played: Your opponent's catching ability will decrease by 50% for the game.
❐	214	Cheat	Hands of Stone	Gold	When played: Your opponent's catching ability will decrease by 75% for the game.
❐	215	Cheat	Couch Potato	Bronze	When played: Your opponent's fatigue will increase by 25% for the game.
❐	215	Cheat	Couch Potato	Silver	When played: Your opponent's fatigue will increase by 50% for the game.
❐	215	Cheat	Couch Potato	Gold	When played: Your opponent's fatigue will increase by 75% for the game.
❐	216	Cheat	Time Out	Bronze	When played: You will get unlimited timeouts for the current quarter.
❐	216	Cheat	Time Out	Silver	When played: You will get unlimited timeouts for the current half.
❐	216	Cheat	Time Out	Gold	When played: You will get unlimited timeouts for the current game.
❐	217	Cheat	Ouch!	Bronze	When played: Your opponent's injuries will increase by 25% for the game.
❐	217	Cheat	Ouch!	Silver	When played: Your opponent's injuries will increase by 50% for the game.
❐	217	Cheat	Ouch!	Gold	When played: Your opponent's injuries will increase by 75% for the game.
❐	218	Cheat	Worker's Comp	Bronze	Awards points (based on severity) whenever a player gets injured this quarter.
❐	218	Cheat	Worker's Comp	Silver	Awards points (based on severity) whenever a player gets injured this half.
❐	218	Cheat	Worker's Comp	Gold	Awards points (based on severity) whenever a player gets injured this game.
❐	219	Cheat	Passerby	Bronze	When played: Your QB can throw past the line of scrimmage for 1 play.
❐	219	Cheat	Passerby	Silver	When played: Your QB can throw past the line of scrimmage for the quarter.
❐	219	Cheat	Passerby	Gold	When played: Your QB can throw past the line of scrimmage for the half.
❐	220	Stadium	Super Bowl XLI	Gold	When obtained: The Super Bowl XXXIX stadium will be unlocked at Stadium Select.
❐	221	Stadium	Super Bowl XLII	Gold	When obtained: The Super Bowl XL stadium will be unlocked at Stadium Select.
❐	222	Stadium	Super Bowl XLIII	Gold	When obtained: The Super Bowl XLI stadium will be unlocked at Stadium Select.
❐	223	Stadium	Super Bowl XLIV	Gold	When obtained: The Super Bowl XLIII stadium will be unlocked at Stadium Select.
❐	224	Stadium	Aloha Stadium	Gold	When obtained: Aloha Stadium (Pro Bowl) will be unlocked at Stadium Select.
❐	225	Team	'58 Colts	Gold	When obtained: The '58 Colts will be unlocked at Team Select.
❐	226	Team	'66 Packers	Gold	When obtained: The '66 Packers will be unlocked at Team Select.
❐	227	Team	'68 Jets	Gold	When obtained: The '68 Jets will be unlocked at Team Select.
❐	228	Team	'70 Browns	Gold	When obtained: The '70 Browns will be unlocked at Team Select.
❐	229	Team	'72 Dolphins	Gold	When obtained: The '72 Dolphins will be unlocked at Team Select.
❐	230	Team	'74 Steelers	Gold	When obtained: The '74 Steelers will be unlocked at Team Select.
❐	231	Team	'76 Raidres	Gold	When obtained: The '76 Raiders will be unlocked at Team Select.
❐	232	Team	'77 Broncos	Gold	When obtained: The '77 Broncos will be unlocked at Team Select.
❐	233	Team	'78 Dolphins	Gold	When obtained: The '78 Dolphins will be unlocked at Team Select.
❐	234	Team	'80 Raiders	Gold	When obtained: The '80 Raiders will be unlocked at Team Select.
❐	235	Team	'81 Chargers	Gold	When obtained: The '81 Chargers will be unlocked at Team Select.
❐	236	Team	'82 Redskins	Gold	When obtained: The '82 Redskins will be unlocked at Team Select.
❐	237	Team	'83 Raiders	Gold	When obtained: The '83 Raiders will be unlocked at Team Select.
❐	238	Team	'84 Dolphins	Gold	When obtained: The '84 Dolphins will be unlocked at Team Select.
❐	239	Team	'85 Bears	Gold	When obtained: The '85 Bears will be unlocked at Team Select.
❐	240	Team	'86 Giants	Gold	When obtained: The '86 Giants will be unlocked at Team Select.
❐	241	Team	'88 49ers	Gold	When obtained: The '88 49ers will be unlocked at Team Select.
❐	242	Team	'90 Eagles	Gold	When obtained: The '90 Eagles will be unlocked at Team Select.
❐	243	Team	'91 Lions	Gold	When obtained: The '91 Lions will be unlocked at Team Select.

Card	Type	Name	Variation	Description
☐ 244	Team	'92 Cowboys	Gold	When obtained: The '92 Cowboys will be unlocked at Team Select.
☐ 245	Team	'93 Bills	Gold	When obtained: The '93 Bills will be unlocked at Team Select.
☐ 246	Team	'94 49ers	Gold	When obtained: The '94 49ers will be unlocked at Team Select.
☐ 247	Team	'96 Packers	Gold	When obtained: The '96 Packers will be unlocked at Team Select.
☐ 248	Team	'98 Broncos	Gold	When obtained: The '98 Broncos will be unlocked at Team Select.
☐ 249	Team	'99 Rams	Gold	When obtained: The '99 Rams will be unlocked at Team Select.
☐ 250	Cheerleader	Bears Cheerleaders	Gold	When played: This pumps up the crowd for the Bears.
☐ 251	Cheerleader	Bengals Cheerleaders	Gold	When played: This pumps up the crowd for the Bengals.
☐ 252	Cheerleader	Bills Cheerleaders	Gold	When played: This pumps up the crowd for the Bills.
☐ 253	Cheerleader	Broncos Cheerleaders	Gold	When played: This pumps up the crowd for the Broncos.
☐ 254	Cheerleader	Browns Cheerleaders	Gold	When played: This pumps up the crowd for the Browns.
☐ 255	Cheerleader	Bucs Cheerleaders	Gold	When played: This pumps up the crowd for the Buccaneers.
☐ 256	Cheerleader	Cardinals Cheerleaders	Gold	When played: This pumps up the crowd for the Cardinals.
☐ 257	Cheerleader	Chargers Cheerleaders	Gold	When played: This pumps up the crowd for the Chargers.
☐ 258	Cheerleader	Chiefs Cheerleaders	Gold	When played: This pumps up the crowd for the Chiefs.
☐ 259	Cheerleader	Colts Cheerleaders	Gold	When played: This pumps up the crowd for the Colts.
☐ 260	Cheerleader	Cowboys Cheerleaders	Gold	When played: This pumps up the crowd for the Cowboys.
☐ 261	Cheerleader	Dolphins Cheerleaders	Gold	When played: This pumps up the crowd for the Dolphins.
☐ 262	Cheerleader	Eagles Cheerleaders	Gold	When played: This pumps up the crowd for the Eagles.
☐ 263	Cheerleader	Falcons Cheerleaders	Gold	When played: This pumps up the crowd for the Falcons.
☐ 264	Cheerleader	49ers Cheerleaders	Gold	When played: This pumps up the crowd for the 49ers.
☐ 265	Cheerleader	Giants Cheerleaders	Gold	When played: This pumps up the crowd for the Giants.
☐ 266	Cheerleader	Jaguars Cheerleaders	Gold	When played: This pumps up the crowd for the Jaguars.
☐ 267	Cheerleader	Jets Cheerleaders	Gold	When played: This pumps up the crowd for the Jets.
☐ 268	Cheerleader	Lions Cheerleaders	Gold	When played: This pumps up the crowd for the Lions.
☐ 269	Cheerleader	Packers Cheerleaders	Gold	When played: This pumps up the crowd for the Packers.
☐ 270	Cheerleader	Panthers Cheerleaders	Gold	When played: This pumps up the crowd for the Panthers.
☐ 271	Cheerleader	Patriots Cheerleaders	Gold	When played: This pumps up the crowd for the Patriots.
☐ 272	Cheerleader	Raiders Cheerleaders	Gold	When played: This pumps up the crowd for the Raiders.
☐ 273	Cheerleader	Rams Cheerleaders	Gold	When played: This pumps up the crowd for the Rams.
☐ 274	Cheerleader	Ravens Cheerleaders	Gold	When played: This pumps up the crowd for the Ravens.
☐ 275	Cheerleader	Redskins Cheerleaders	Gold	When played: This pumps up the crowd for the Redskins.
☐ 276	Cheerleader	Saints Cheerleaders	Gold	When played: This pumps up the crowd for the Saints.
☐ 277	Cheerleader	Seahawks Cheerleaders	Gold	When played: This pumps up the crowd for the Seahawks.
☐ 278	Cheerleader	Steelers Cheerleaders	Gold	When played: This pumps up the crowd for the Steelers.
☐ 279	Cheerleader	Texans Cheerleaders	Gold	When played: This pumps up the crowd for the Titans.
☐ 280	Cheerleader	Titans Cheerleaders	Gold	When played: This pumps up the crowd for the Texans.
☐ 281	Cheerleader	Vikings Cheerleaders	Gold	When played: This pumps up the crowd for the Vikings.
☐ 282	Cheerleader	Hall of Fame AFC	Gold	If you have this card, the Hall of Fame AFC legends will be unlocked at Team Select.
☐ 283	Cheerleader	Hall of Fame NFC	Gold	If you have this card, the Hall of Fame AFC legends will be unlocked at Team Select.

DEPTH CHARTS

Bears

Pos.	D	First Name	Last Name
3DRB	0	Cedric	Benson
C	0	Olin	Kreutz
C	1	Anthony	Oakley
CB	0	Nathan	Vasher
CB	1	Charles	Tillman
CB	2	Ricky	Manning
DT	0	Tommie	Harris
DT	1	Anthony	Adams
DT	2	Antonio	Garay
HB	0	Cedric	Benson
HB	1	Adrian	Peterson
LT	0	John	Tait
LT	1	John	St. Clair
MLB	0	Brian	Urlacher
MLB	1	Rod	Wilson
QB	0	Rex	Grossman
QB	1	Brian	Griese
QB	2	Kyle	Orton
RT	0	Fred	Miller
RT	1	Mark	LeVoir
TE	0	Desmond	Clark
TE	1	Greg	Olsen
TE	2	John	Gilmore
WR	0	Muhsin	Muhammad
WR	1	Bernard	Berrian
WR	2	Mark	Bradley

Bengals

Pos.	D	First Name	Last Name
3DRB	0	Chris	Perry
C	0	Eric	Ghiaciuc
C	1	Alex	Stepanovich
CB	0	Deltha	O'Neal
CB	1	Johnathan	Joseph
CB	2	Leon	Hall
DT	0	Domata	Peko
DT	1	John	Thornton
DT	2	Michael	Myers
HB	0	Rudi	Johnson
HB	1	Chris	Perry
HB	2	Kenny	Irons
LT	0	Levi	Jones
LT	1	Adam	Kieft
MLB	0	Ahmad	Brooks
MLB	1	Caleb	Miller
QB	0	Carson	Palmer
QB	1	Doug	Johnson
RT	0	Willie	Anderson
RT	1	Scott	Kooistra
TE	0	Reggie	Kelly
TE	1	Ronnie	Ghent
TE	2	Tab	Perry
WR	0	Chad	Johnson
WR	1	T.J.	Houshmandzadeh
WR	2	Tab	Perry

Bills

Pos.	D	First Name	Last Name
3DRB	0	Marshawn	Lynch
C	0	Melvin	Fowler
C	1	Aaron	Merz
CB	0	Terrence	McGee
CB	1	Jason	Webster
CB	2	Kiwaukee	Thomas
DT	0	Larry	Tripplett
DT	1	Kyle	Williams
DT	2	Darwin	Walker
HB	0	Marshawn	Lynch
HB	1	Anthony	Thomas
LT	0	Jason	Peters
LT	1	Brad	Butler
LT	2	Kirk	Chambers
MLB	0	Paul	Posluszny
MLB	1	John	DiGiorgio
QB	0	J.P.	Losman
QB	1	Craig	Nall
QB	2	Trent	Edwards
RT	0	Langston	Walker
RT	1	Terrance	Pennington
TE	0	Robert	Royal
TE	1	Kevin	Everett
TE	2	Josh	Reed
WR	0	Lee	Evans
WR	1	Peerless	Price

Broncos

Pos.	D	First Name	Last Name
3DRB	0	Mike	Bell
C	0	Tom	Nalen
C	1	Mark	Fenton
CB	0	Champ	Bailey
CB	1	Dré	Bly
CB	2	Domonique	Foxworth
DT	0	Gerard	Warren
DT	1	Alvin	McKinley
DT	2	Marcus	Thomas
HB	0	Travis	Henry
HB	1	Mike	Bell
HB	2	Cecil	Sapp
LT	0	Matt	Lepsis
LT	1	Erik	Pears
MLB	0	D.J.	Williams
MLB	1	Nate	Webster
QB	0	Jay	Cutler
QB	1	Patrick	Ramsey
RT	0	Adam	Meadows
RT	1	Ryan	Harris
TE	0	Daniel	Graham
TE	1	Stephen	Alexander
TE	2	Tony	Scheffler
WR	0	Javon	Walker
WR	1	Brandon	Marshall

Browns

Pos.	D	First Name	Last Name
3DRB	0	Jason	Wright
C	0	LeCharles	Bentley
C	1	Hank	Fraley
CB	0	Leigh	Bodden
CB	1	Eric	Wright
CB	2	Gary	Baxter
DT	0	Ted	Washington
DT	1	Shaun	Smith
DT	2	Ethan	Kelley
HB	0	Jamal	Lewis
HB	1	Jason	Wright
HB	2	Jerome	Harrison
LT	0	Kevin	Shaffer
LT	1	Joe	Thomas
MLB	0	Andra	Davis
MLB	1	D'Qwell	Jackson
QB	0	Charlie	Frye
QB	1	Brady	Quinn
QB	2	Derek	Anderson
RT	0	Ryan	Tucker
RT	1	Kelly	Butler
TE	0	Kellen	Winslow
TE	1	Steve	Heiden
TE	2	Darnell	Dinkins
WR	0	Braylon	Edwards
WR	1	Joe	Jurevicius

Buccanners

Pos.	D	First Name	Last Name
3DRB	0	Michael	Pittman
C	0	John	Wade
C	1	Nick	Mihlhauser
CB	0	Ronde	Barber
CB	1	Brian	Kelly
CB	2	Phillip	Buchanon
DT	0	Chris	Hovan
DT	1	Ellis	Wyms
DT	2	Ryan	Sims
HB	0	Carnell	Williams
HB	1	Michael	Pittman
LT	0	Luke	Petitgout
LT	1	Anthony	Davis
MLB	0	Barrett	Ruud
MLB	1	Antoine	Cash
QB	0	Jeff	Garcia
QB	1	Chris	Simms
QB	2	Bruce	Gradkowski
RT	0	Jeremy	Trueblood
RT	1	Donald	Penn
TE	0	Anthony	Becht
TE	1	Alex	Smith
TE	2	Jerramy	Stevens
WR	0	Joey	Galloway
WR	1	Michael	Clayton
WR	2	Ike	Hilliard

Cardinals

Pos.	D	First Name	Last Name
3DRB	0	Edgerrin	James
C	0	Al	Johnson
C	1	Nick	Leckey
CB	0	Antrel	Rolle
CB	1	Roderick	Hood
CB	2	Eric	Green
DT	0	Darnell	Dockett
DT	1	Alan	Branch
DT	2	Gabe	Watson
HB	0	Edgerrin	James
HB	1	Marcel	Shipp
HB	2	J.J.	Arrington
LT	0	Mike	Gandy
LT	1	Oliver	Ross
MLB	0	Gerald	Hayes
MLB	1	Monty	Beisel
QB	0	Matt	Leinart
QB	1	Kurt	Warner
RT	0	Levi	Brown
RT	1	Brandon	Gorin
TE	0	Leonard	Pope
TE	1	Ben	Patrick
TE	2	Tim	Euhus
WR	0	Larry	Fitzgerald
WR	1	Anquan	Boldin
WR	2	Bryant	Johnson

Chargers

Pos.	D	First Name	Last Name
3DRB	0	LaDainian	Tomlinson
C	0	Nick	Hardwick
C	1	Cory	Withrow
CB	0	Quentin	Jammer
CB	1	Drayton	Florence
CB	2	Antonio	Cromartie
DT	0	Jamal	Williams
DT	1	Ryon	Bingham
DT	2	Brandon	McKinney
HB	0	LaDainian	Tomlinson
HB	1	Michael	Turner
HB	2	Darren	Sproles
LT	0	Marcus	McNeill
LT	1	Roman	Oben
LT	2	Jeromey	Clary
MLB	0	Matt	Wilhelm
MLB	1	Stephen	Cooper
QB	0	Philip	Rivers
QB	1	Billy	Volek
QB	2	Charlie	Whitehurst
RT	0	Shane	Olivea
RT	1	Cory	Lekkerkerker
TE	0	Antonio	Gates
TE	1	Brandon	Manumaleuna
WR	0	Eric	Parker
WR	1	Vincent	Jackson

Chiefs

Pos.	D	First Name	Last Name
3DRB	0	Larry	Johnson
C	0	Casey	Wiegmann
C	1	Rudy	Niswanger
CB	0	Ty	Law
CB	1	Patrick	Surtain
CB	2	Benny	Sapp
DT	0	Ron	Edwards
DT	1	Alfonso	Boone
DT	2	Turk	McBride
HB	0	Larry	Johnson
HB	1	Michael	Bennett
HB	2	Kolby	Smith
LT	0	Damion	McIntosh
LT	1	Kevin	Sampson
MLB	0	Napoleon	Harris
MLB	1	William	Kershaw
QB	0	Damon	Huard
QB	1	Brodie	Croyle
QB	2	Casey	Printers
RT	0	Chris	Terry
RT	1	Will	Svitek
TE	0	Tony	Gonzalez
TE	1	Jason	Dunn
TE	2	Michael	Allan
WR	0	Eddie	Kennison
WR	1	Samie	Parker
WR	2	Dwayne	Bowe

Colts

Pos.	D	First Name	Last Name
3DRB	0	Joseph	Addai
C	0	Jeff	Saturday
C	1	Dylan	Gandy
CB	0	Marlin	Jackson
CB	1	Kelvin	Hayden
CB	2	Tim	Jennings
DT	0	Anthony	McFarland
DT	1	Corey	Simon
DT	2	Raheem	Brock
HB	0	Joseph	Addai
HB	1	DeDe	Dorsey
HB	2	Kenton	Keith
LT	0	Tarik	Glenn
LT	1	Charlie	Johnson
MLB	0	Gary	Brackett
MLB	1	Rob	Morris
QB	0	Peyton	Manning
QB	1	Jim	Sorgi
QB	2	John	Navarre
RT	0	Ryan	Diem
RT	1	Tony	Ugoh
RT	2	Michael	Toudouze
TE	0	Dallas	Clark
TE	1	Bryan	Fletcher
WR	0	Marvin	Harrison
WR	1	Reggie	Wayne
WR	2	Anthony	Gonzalez

Cowboys

Pos.	D	First Name	Last Name
3DRB	0	Marion	Barber
C	0	Andre	Gurode
C	1	Cory	Procter
CB	0	Terence	Newman
CB	1	Anthony	Henry
CB	2	Aaron	Glenn
DT	0	Jason	Ferguson
DT	1	Jay	Ratliff
DT	2	Montavious	Stanley
HB	0	Julius	Jones
HB	1	Marion	Barber
HB	2	Tyson	Thompson
LT	0	Flozell	Adams
LT	1	Pat	McQuistan
LT	2	Doug	Free
MLB	0	Bradie	James
MLB	1	Akin	Ayodele
MLB	2	Bobby	Carpenter
QB	0	Tony	Romo
QB	1	Brad	Johnson
RT	0	Marc	Colombo
RT	1	James	Marten
TE	0	Jason	Witten
TE	1	Anthony	Fasano
WR	0	Terrell	Owens
WR	1	Terry	Glenn
WR	2	Patrick	Crayton

Dolphins

Pos.	D	First Name	Last Name
3DRB	0	Ronnie	Brown
C	0	Samson	Satele
C	1	Drew	Mormino
C	2	Johnathan	Ingram
CB	0	Andre	Goodman
CB	1	Will	Allen
DT	0	Keith	Traylor
DT	1	Paul	Soliai
DT	2	Fred	Evans
HB	0	Ronnie	Brown
HB	1	Lorenzo	Booker
HB	2	Jesse	Chatman
LT	0	Vernon	Carey
LT	1	Anthony	Alabi
MLB	0	Zach	Thomas
MLB	1	Channing	Crowder
MLB	2	Donnie	Spragan
QB	0	Trent	Green
QB	1	Cleo	Lemon
QB	2	John	Beck
RT	0	L.J.	Shelton
RT	1	Mike	Rosenthal
TE	0	David	Martin
TE	1	Justin	Peelle
WR	0	Chris	Chambers
WR	1	Marty	Booker
WR	2	Ted	Ginn Jr.

Eagles

Pos.	D	First Name	Last Name
3DRB	0	Brian	Westbrook
C	0	Jamaal	Jackson
C	1	Nick	Cole
CB	0	Lito	Sheppard
CB	1	Sheldon	Brown
CB	2	William	James
DT	0	Mike	Patterson
DT	1	Brodrick	Bunkley
DT	2	Montae	Reagor
HB	0	Brian	Westbrook
HB	1	Correll	Buckhalter
HB	2	Ryan	Moats
LT	0	William	Thomas
LT	1	Winston	Justice
MLB	0	Jeremiah	Trotter
MLB	1	Omar	Gaither
QB	0	Donovan	McNabb
QB	1	A.J.	Feeley
QB	2	Kelly	Holcomb
RT	0	Jon	Runyan
RT	1	Patrick	McCoy
TE	0	L.J.	Smith
TE	1	Matt	Schobel
TE	2	Brent	Celek
WR	0	Reggie	Brown
WR	1	Kevin	Curtis
WR	2	Greg	Lewis

Falcons

Pos.	D	First Name	Last Name
3DRB	0	Warrick	Dunn
C	0	Todd	McClure
C	1	Doug	Datish
CB	0	DeAngelo	Hall
CB	1	Lewis	Sanders
CB	2	Chris	Houston
DT	0	Rod	Coleman
DT	1	Grady	Jackson
DT	2	Jonathan	Babineaux
HB	0	Warrick	Dunn
HB	1	Jerious	Norwood
HB	2	Jamal	Robertson
LT	0	Wayne	Gandy
LT	1	Frank	Omiyale
LT	2	Leander	Jordan
MLB	0	Keith	Brooking
MLB	1	Jordan	Beck
QB	0	Michael	Vick
QB	1	Joey	Harrington
QB	2	D.J.	Shockley
RT	0	Todd	Weiner
RT	1	Quinn	Ojinnaka
TE	0	Alge	Crumpler
TE	1	Dwayne	Blakley
WR	0	Michael	Jenkins
WR	1	Joe	Horn
WR	2	Roddy	White

49ers

Pos.	D	First Name	Last Name
3DRB	0	Frank	Gore
C	0	Eric	Heitmann
C	1	David	Baas
CB	0	Nate	Clements
CB	1	Walt	Harris
CB	2	Shawntae	Spencer
DT	0	Ronald	Fields
DT	1	Aubrayo	Franklin
DT	2	Isaac	Sopoaga
HB	0	Frank	Gore
HB	1	Michael	Robinson
HB	2	Maurice	Hicks
LT	0	Jonas	Jennings
LT	1	Joe	Staley
MLB	0	Patrick	Willis
MLB	1	Derek	Smith
MLB	2	Brandon	Moore
QB	0	Alex	Smith
QB	1	Trent	Dilfer
QB	2	Shaun	Hill
RT	0	Kwame	Harris
RT	1	Adam	Snyder
TE	0	Vernon	Davis
TE	1	Billy	Bajema
WR	0	Darrell	Jackson
WR	1	Arnaz	Battle
WR	2	Ashley	Lelie

Giants

Pos.	D	First Name	Last Name
3DRB	0	Brandon	Jacobs
C	0	Shaun	O'Hara
C	1	Grey	Ruegamer
CB	0	Sam	Madison
CB	1	Corey	Webster
CB	2	Aaron	Ross
DT	0	Fred	Robbins
DT	1	Barry	Cofield
DT	2	William	Joseph
HB	0	Brandon	Jacobs
HB	1	Reuben	Droughns
HB	2	Derrick	Ward
LT	0	David	Diehl
LT	1	Guy	Whimper
MLB	0	Antonio	Pierce
MLB	1	Chase	Blackburn
QB	0	Eli	Manning
QB	1	Anthony	Wright
QB	2	Jared	Lorenzen
RT	0	Kareem	McKenzie
RT	1	Jon	Dunn
TE	0	Jeremy	Shockey
TE	1	Kevin	Boss
TE	2	Amani	Toomer
WR	0	Plaxico	Burress
WR	1	Amani	Toomer
WR	2	Steve	Smith

Jaguars

Pos.	D	First Name	Last Name
3DRB	0	Maurice	Jones-Drew
C	0	Brad	Meester
C	1	Dan	Connolly
CB	0	Rashean	Mathis
CB	1	Brian	Williams
CB	2	Terry	Cousin
DT	0	Marcus	Stroud
DT	1	John	Henderson
DT	2	Rob	Meier
HB	0	Fred	Taylor
HB	1	Maurice	Jones-Drew
HB	2	Alvin	Pearman
LT	0	Khalif	Barnes
LT	1	Maurice	Williams
MLB	0	Mike	Peterson
MLB	1	Tony	Gilbert
QB	0	Byron	Leftwich
QB	1	David	Garrard
QB	2	Quinn	Gray
RT	0	Tony	Pashos
RT	1	Richard	Collier
TE	0	George	Wrighster
TE	1	Jermaine	Wiggins
TE	2	Marcedes	Lewis
WR	0	Reggie	Williams
WR	1	Ernest	Wilford
WR	2	Matt	Jones

Jets

Pos.	D	First Name	Last Name
3DRB	0	Leon	Washington
C	0	Nick	Mangold
CB	0	Andre	Dyson
CB	1	Darrelle	Revis
CB	2	Hank	Poteat
DT	0	Dewayne	Robertson
DT	1	Sione	Pouha
DT	2	C.J.	Mosley
HB	0	Thomas	Jones
HB	1	Leon	Washington
HB	2	Cedric	Houston
LT	0	D'Brickashaw	Ferguson
LT	1	Ed	Blanton
LT	2	Jacob	Bender
MLB	0	Jonathan	Vilma
MLB	1	Victor	Hobson
MLB	2	David	Harris
QB	0	Chad	Pennington
QB	1	Kellen	Clemens
QB	2	Marques	Tuiasosopo
RT	0	Anthony	Clement
RT	1	Adrian	Jones
RT	2	Na'shan	Goddard
TE	0	Chris	Baker
TE	1	Sean	Ryan
TE	2	Jerricho	Cotchery
WR	0	Laveranues	Coles

Lions

Pos.	D	First Name	Last Name
3DRB	0	Kevin	Jones
C	0	Dominic	Raiola
C	1	Blaine	Saipaia
CB	0	Fernando	Bryant
CB	1	Stanley	Wilson
CB	2	Travis	Fisher
DT	0	Shaun	Rogers
DT	1	Cory	Redding
DT	2	Shaun	Cody
HB	0	Kevin	Jones
HB	1	Tatum	Bell
HB	2	T.J.	Duckett
LT	0	Jeff	Backus
LT	1	Jonathan	Scott
MLB	0	Paris	Lenon
MLB	1	Teddy	Lehman
QB	0	Jon	Kitna
QB	1	Dan	Orlovsky
QB	2	Drew	Stanton
RT	0	George	Foster
RT	1	Rex	Tucker
TE	0	Dan	Campbell
TE	1	Eric	Beverly
WR	0	Roy	Williams
WR	1	Calvin	Johnson
WR	2	Mike	Furrey

Packers

Pos.	D	First Name	Last Name
3DRB	0	Vernand	Morency
C	0	Scott	Wells
C	1	Tyson	Walter
CB	0	Al	Harris
CB	1	Charles	Woodson
CB	2	Patrick	Dendy
DT	0	Corey	Williams
DT	1	Ryan	Pickett
DT	2	Colin	Cole
HB	0	Brandon	Jackson
HB	1	Vernand	Morency
HB	2	Noah	Herron
LT	0	Chad	Clifton
LT	1	Tony	Moll
MLB	0	Nick	Barnett
MLB	1	Abdul	Hodge
QB	0	Brett	Favre
QB	1	Aaron	Rodgers
QB	2	Ingle	Martin
RT	0	Mark	Tauscher
TE	0	Bubba	Franks
TE	1	Donald	Lee
TE	2	Clark	Harris
WR	0	Donald	Driver
WR	1	Greg	Jennings
WR	2	Robert	Ferguson

Panthers

Pos.	D	First Name	Last Name
3DRB	0	DeAngelo	Williams
C	0	Justin	Hartwig
C	1	Ryan	Kalil
CB	0	Chris	Gamble
CB	1	Ken	Lucas
CB	2	Richard	Marshall
DT	0	Kris	Jenkins
DT	1	Ma'ake	Kemoeatu
DT	2	Damione	Lewis
HB	0	DeShaun	Foster
HB	1	DeAngelo	Williams
HB	2	Nick	Goings
LT	0	Travelle	Wharton
LT	1	Rashad	Butler
MLB	0	Dan	Morgan
MLB	1	Adam	Seward
QB	0	Jake	Delhomme
QB	1	David	Carr
RT	0	Jordan	Gross
RT	1	Jeremy	Bridges
TE	0	Michael	Gaines
TE	1	Jeff	King
TE	2	Dwayne	Jarrett
WR	0	Steve	Smith
WR	1	Dwayne	Jarrett
WR	2	Keary	Colbert

Patriots

Pos.	D	First Name	Last Name
3DRB	0	Kevin	Faulk
C	0	Dan	Koppen
C	1	Gene	Mruczkowski
CB	0	Asante	Samuel
CB	1	Ellis	Hobbs
CB	2	Tory	James
DT	0	Vince	Wilfork
DT	1	Mike	Wright
DT	2	Le Kevin	Smith
HB	0	Laurence	Maroney
HB	1	Sammy	Morris
HB	2	Kevin	Faulk
LT	0	Matt	Light
LT	1	Wesley	Britt
MLB	0	Adalius	Thomas
MLB	1	Tedy	Bruschi
MLB	2	Junior	Seau
QB	0	Tom	Brady
QB	1	Matt	Cassel
QB	2	Matt	Gutierrez
RT	0	Nick	Kaczur
RT	1	Ryan	O'Callaghan
TE	0	Benjamin	Watson
TE	1	Kyle	Brady
TE	2	Wes	Welker
WR	0	Randy	Moss
WR	1	Donte	Stallworth

Raiders

Pos.	D	First Name	Last Name
3DRB	0	Dominic	Rhodes
C	0	Jake	Grove
C	1	Jeremy	Newberry
CB	0	Nnamdi	Asomugha
CB	1	Fabian	Washington
CB	2	Duane	Starks
DT	0	Warren	Sapp
DT	1	Terdell	Sands
DT	2	Anttaj	Hawthorne
HB	0	LaMont	Jordan
HB	1	Dominic	Rhodes
HB	2	Justin	Fargas
LT	0	Barry	Sims
LT	1	Mario	Henderson
MLB	0	Kirk	Morrison
MLB	1	Robert	Thomas
QB	0	JaMarcus	Russell
QB	1	Andrew	Walter
QB	2	Josh	McCown
RT	0	Robert	Gallery
RT	1	Cornell	Green
TE	0	Zach	Miller
TE	1	Tony	Stewart
TE	2	John	Madsen
WR	0	Jerry	Porter
WR	1	Ronald	Curry
WR	2	Travis	Taylor

Rams

Pos.	D	First Name	Last Name
3DRB	0	Steven	Jackson
C	0	Andy	McCollum
C	1	Brett	Romberg
C	2	Dustin	Fry
CB	0	Fakhir	Brown
CB	1	Tye	Hill
CB	2	Jonathan	Wade
DT	0	La'Roi	Glover
DT	1	Adam	Carriker
DT	2	Claude	Wroten
HB	0	Steven	Jackson
HB	1	Travis	Minor
HB	2	Brian	Leonard
LT	0	Orlando	Pace
LT	1	Todd	Steussie
MLB	0	Will	Witherspoon
MLB	1	Chris	Draft
QB	0	Marc	Bulger
QB	1	Gus	Frerotte
QB	2	Ryan	Fitzpatrick
RT	0	Alex	Barron
RT	1	Drew	Strojny
TE	0	Randy	McMichael
TE	1	Joe	Klopfenstein
TE	2	Dominique	Byrd
WR	0	Torry	Holt
WR	1	Isaac	Bruce

Ravens

Pos.	D	First Name	Last Name
3DRB	0	Musa	Smith
C	0	Mike	Flynn
CB	0	Chris	McAlister
CB	1	Samari	Rolle
CB	2	Corey	Ivy
DT	0	Kelly	Gregg
DT	1	Justin	Bannan
DT	2	Andrew	Powell
HB	0	Willis	McGahee
HB	1	Musa	Smith
HB	2	Mike	Anderson
LT	0	Jonathan	Ogden
LT	1	Marshal	Yanda
MLB	0	Ray	Lewis
MLB	1	Bart	Scott
MLB	2	Mike	Smith
QB	0	Steve	McNair
QB	1	Kyle	Boller
QB	2	Troy	Smith
RT	0	Adam	Terry
RT	1	Brian	Rimpf
TE	0	Todd	Heap
TE	1	Daniel	Wilcox
TE	2	Quinn	Sypniewski
WR	0	Derrick	Mason
WR	1	Mark	Clayton
WR	2	Demetrius	Williams

Redskins

Pos.	D	First Name	Last Name
3DRB	0	Ladell	Betts
C	0	Casey	Rabach
C	1	Ross	Tucker
CB	0	Shawn	Springs
CB	1	Carlos	Rogers
CB	2	Fred	Smoot
DT	0	Cornelius	Griffin
DT	1	Kedric	Golston
HB	0	Clinton	Portis
HB	1	Ladell	Betts
HB	2	Derrick	Blaylock
LT	0	Chris	Samuels
LT	1	Calvin	Armstrong
MLB	0	London	Fletcher-Bake
MLB	1	Lemar	Marshall
MLB	2	HB	Blades
QB	0	Jason	Campbell
QB	1	Mark	Brunell
QB	2	Todd	Collins
RT	0	Jon	Jansen
RT	1	Jason	Fabini
TE	0	Chris	Cooley
TE	1	Todd	Yoder
TE	2	Brandon	Lloyd
WR	0	Santana	Moss
WR	1	Brandon	Lloyd
WR	2	Antwaan	Randle El

Saints

Pos.	D	First Name	Last Name
3DRB	0	Reggie	Bush
C	0	Jeff	Faine
C	1	Jonathan	Goodwin
CB	0	Mike	McKenzie
CB	1	Jason	David
CB	2	Fred	Thomas
DT	0	Hollis	Thomas
DT	1	Brian	Young
DT	2	Kendrick	Clancy
HB	0	Deuce	McAllister
HB	1	Reggie	Bush
HB	2	Aaron	Stecker
LT	0	Jammal	Brown
LT	1	Zach	Strief
MLB	0	Brian	Simmons
MLB	1	Mark	Simoneau
QB	0	Drew	Brees
QB	1	Jamie	Martin
QB	2	Tyler	Palko
RT	0	Jon	Stinchcomb
RT	1	Rob	Petitti
TE	0	Eric	Johnson
TE	1	Mark	Campbell
TE	2	Billy	Miller
WR	0	Marques	Colston
WR	1	Devery	Henderson
WR	2	Robert	Meachem

Seahawks

Pos.	D	First Name	Last Name
3DRB	0	Shaun	Alexander
C	0	Chris	Spencer
C	1	Austin	King
CB	0	Marcus	Trufant
CB	1	Jordan	Babineaux
CB	2	Josh	Wilson
DT	0	Rocky	Bernard
DT	1	Chartric	Darby
DT	2	Marcus	Tubbs
HB	0	Shaun	Alexander
HB	1	Maurice	Morris
HB	2	Marquis	Weeks
LT	0	Walter	Jones
LT	1	Tom	Ashworth
MLB	0	Lofa	Tatupu
MLB	1	Niko	Koutouvides
QB	0	Matt	Hasselbeck
QB	1	Seneca	Wallace
QB	2	David	Greene
RT	0	Sean	Locklear
RT	1	Ray	Willis
TE	0	Marcus	Pollard
TE	1	Will	Heller
TE	2	D.J.	Hackett
WR	0	Deion	Branch
WR	1	D.J.	Hackett
WR	2	Bobby	Engram

Steelers

Pos.	D	First Name	Last Name
3DRB	0	Verron	Haynes
C	0	Sean	Mahan
C	1	Chukky	Okobi
CB	0	Deshea	Townsend
CB	1	Ike	Taylor
CB	2	Bryant	McFadden
DT	0	Casey	Hampton
DT	1	Chris	Hoke
DT	2	Shaun	Nua
HB	0	Willie	Parker
HB	1	Najeh	Davenport
HB	2	Kevan	Barlow
LT	0	Marvel	Smith
LT	1	Trai	Essex
MLB	0	James	Farrior
MLB	1	Larry	Foote
MLB	2	Clint	Kriewaldt
QB	0	Ben	Roethlisberger
QB	1	Charlie	Batch
QB	2	Brian	St.Pierre
RT	0	Max	Starks
RT	1	Willie	Colon
TE	0	Heath	Miller
TE	1	Jerame	Tuman
WR	0	Hines	Ward
WR	1	Santonio	Holmes
WR	2	Nate	Washington

Texans

Pos.	D	First Name	Last Name
3DRB	0	Ahman	Green
C	0	Mike	Flanagan
C	1	Drew	Hodgdon
CB	0	Dunta	Robinson
CB	1	DeMarcus	Faggins
DT	0	Travis	Johnson
DT	1	Amobi	Okoye
DT	2	Jeff	Zgonina
HB	0	Ahman	Green
HB	1	Ron	Dayne
HB	2	Wali	Lundy
LT	0	Jordan	Black
LT	1	Ephraim	Salaam
MLB	0	DeMeco	Ryans
MLB	1	Danny	Clark
QB	0	Matt	Schaub
QB	1	Sage	Rosenfels
QB	2	Bradlee	Van Pelt
RE	0	Mario	Williams
RT	0	Eric	Winston
RT	1	Brandon	Frye
TE	0	Owen	Daniels
TE	1	Jeb	Putzier
TE	2	Mark	Bruener
WR	0	Andre	Johnson
WR	1	Kevin	Walter
WR	2	Jacoby	Jones

Titans

Pos.	D	First Name	Last Name
3DRB	0	Chris	Brown
C	0	Kevin	Mawae
C	1	Eugene	Amano
CB	0	Nick	Harper
CB	1	Michael	Griffin
CB	2	Kelly	Herndon
DT	0	Albert	Haynesworth
DT	1	Randy	Starks
DT	2	Jesse	Mahelona
HB	0	Chris	Brown
HB	1	Chris	Henry
LT	0	Michael	Roos
LT	1	Daniel	Loper
MLB	0	Stephen	Tulloch
MLB	1	Ryan	Fowler
MLB	2	Robert	Reynolds
QB	0	Vince	Young
QB	1	Kerry	Collins
QB	2	Tim	Rattay
RT	0	Jacob	Bell
RT	1	Seth	Wand
TE	0	Ben	Troupe
TE	1	Bo	Scaife
TE	2	Ben	Hartsock
WR	0	David	Givens
WR	1	Brandon	Jones

Vikings

Pos.	D	First Name	Last Name
3DRB	0	Mewelde	Moore
C	0	Matt	Birk
C	1	Norm	Katnik
CB	0	Antoine	Winfield
CB	1	Cedric	Griffin
CB	2	Marcus	McCauley
DT	0	Kevin	Williams
DT	1	Pat	Williams
DT	2	Spencer	Johnson
HB	0	Chester	Taylor
HB	1	Adrian	Peterson
HB	2	Mewelde	Moore
LT	0	Bryant	McKinnie
LT	1	Chase	Johnson
MLB	0	E.J.	Henderson
MLB	1	Vinny	Ciurciu
QB	0	Tarvaris	Jackson
QB	1	Brooks	Bollinger
QB	2	Tyler	Thigpen
RT	0	Ryan	Cook
RT	1	Marcus	Johnson
TE	0	Jim	Kleinsasser
TE	1	Visanthe	Shiancoe
TE	2	Richard	Owens
WR	0	Bobby	Wade
WR	1	Sidney	Rice
WR	2	Troy	Williamson

ROSTER ATTRIBUTES

The following offensive and defensive lists include every player who is rated approximately 70 or above in his position, and have been sorted by overall rating. However, the overall rating is just a starting point. Each list includes additional attributes related to the position. Consider these attributes when you search for the perfect player to complement your team.

OFFENSIVE / PLAYER LIST

ROSTER ATTRIBUTES

C Centers

Overall Rating	First Name	Last Name	Speed	Aware	Run Block	Pass Block
98	Olin	Kreutz	62	92	93	90
96	Jeff	Saturday	58	95	88	97
92	Tom	Nalen	64	90	91	86
92	Casey	Wiegmann	61	92	90	90
92	Matt	Birk	54	92	90	93
91	Todd	McClure	58	87	94	85
90	LeCharles	Bentley	54	80	93	90
90	Nick	Hardwick	60	82	92	89
90	Brad	Meester	55	87	92	90
89	Andre	Gurode	53	83	90	87
89	Mike	Flanagan	55	86	89	93
89	Kevin	Mawae	60	90	87	90
88	Nick	Mangold	63	75	89	87
88	Dan	Koppen	54	86	87	91
86	Mike	Flynn	59	88	85	88
85	Eric	Heitmann	51	82	90	90
85	John	Wade	52	87	87	88
85	Jamaal	Jackson	57	74	89	88
84	Hank	Fraley	48	88	88	86
84	Shaun	O'Hara	53	84	88	86
84	Dominic	Raiola	60	80	86	86
84	Justin	Hartwig	57	79	90	85
84	Jeremy	Newberry	49	75	90	89
84	Jeff	Faine	58	73	86	86
84	Chris	Spencer	60	64	89	88
83	Scott	Wells	58	80	86	85
83	Andy	McCollum	46	90	87	87
83	Casey	Rabach	53	80	88	87
82	Ryan	Kalil	64	64	84	86
81	Eric	Ghiaciuc	52	72	89	85
81	Jake	Grove	55	74	85	83
81	Chukky	Okobi	53	74	86	83
80	Melvin	Fowler	54	76	85	84
80	Ross	Tucker	53	74	84	86
79	Rex	Hadnot	57	66	88	82
78	Sean	Mahan	54	73	84	85
77	Jason	Whittle	47	75	87	81
77	Al	Johnson	54	68	87	80
77	Grey	Ruegamer	44	70	88	84
77	Wade	Smith	55	65	84	85
76	Alex	Stepanovich	46	75	85	83
75	Nick	Leckey	55	73	80	83
73	Dylan	Gandy	56	53	82	88
73	Tyson	Clabo	58	58	85	80
73	Eugene	Amano	58	64	82	81
72	Tyson	Walter	48	69	82	82
72	Ike	Ndukwe	57	60	83	76
71	Drew	Hodgdon	52	62	80	82
71	Leroy	Harris	51	62	83	78
70	Mark	Fenton	50	60	81	77

FB Fullbacks

Overall Rating	First Name	Last Name	Speed	Aware	Catch	Run Block
98	Lorenzo	Neal	65	90	62	85
96	Mack	Strong	81	75	68	67
91	Justin	Griffith	80	66	70	66
90	Jeremi	Johnson	72	72	68	66
90	Ovie	Mughelli	64	70	64	76
90	Mike	Karney	68	70	72	68
90	Dan	Kreider	63	80	54	84
89	Tony	Richardson	74	73	70	62
88	Terrelle	Smith	62	75	52	82
87	Kyle	Johnson	77	65	72	64
87	Greg	Jones	85	68	55	56
86	Jason	McKie	72	80	67	66
86	Mike	Alstott	80	90	60	50
86	Cory	Schlesinger	70	75	74	58
86	Zack	Crockett	84	74	55	55
85	Bryan	Johnson	65	75	66	67
85	Jim	Finn	65	80	66	66
85	Shawn	Bryson	87	67	72	52
83	Heath	Evans	80	63	68	58
83	Le'Ron	McClain	65	52	77	60
82	Alan	Ricard	65	71	50	82
82	B.J.	Askew	85	70	65	55
82	Justin	Green	64	54	70	69
82	Jameel	Cook	75	64	70	60
80	Ryan	Neufeld	62	69	66	63
80	Obafemi	Ayanbadejo	75	65	62	62
80	Lousaka	Polite	64	67	62	67
80	Brad	Hoover	75	68	65	55
79	Paul	Smith	78	72	60	60
79	Ben	Utecht	74	68	84	48
79	Mike	Sellers	64	62	57	71
79	Ahmard	Hall	73	60	65	60
78	Brandon	Miree	81	55	60	58
77	Lawrence	Vickers	80	55	60	52
77	Darian	Barnes	65	70	58	66
74	Moran	Norris	72	55	64	55
74	Thomas	Tapeh	80	49	70	50
73	Madison	Hedgecock	71	59	63	60
73	Josh	Parry	65	60	50	69
72	Oliver	Hoyte	74	55	57	60
71	Andrew	Pinnock	71	64	58	55
70	Greg	Hanoian	70	60	52	60
70	Derrick	Wimbush	88	60	68	42
68	Boomer	Grigsby	74	52	48	65

HB Halfbacks

Overall Rating	First Name	Last Name	Speed	Agility	Run Aware	Break Tackle
99	LaDainian	Tomlinson	96	98	95	91
97	Larry	Johnson	93	90	91	97
96	Steven	Jackson	89	92	91	95
96	Shaun	Alexander	89	88	95	95
94	Brian	Westbrook	94	98	90	80
92	Frank	Gore	92	93	89	91
92	Edgerrin	James	88	90	90	87
92	Willis	McGahee	92	89	87	94
92	Clinton	Portis	94	94	86	88
91	Rudi	Johnson	87	84	85	96
90	Willie	Parker	96	91	87	84
89	Ronnie	Brown	92	90	78	87
89	Warrick	Dunn	95	97	87	66
89	Maurice	Jones-Drew	94	95	64	93
89	Fred	Taylor	93	93	87	86
89	Deuce	McAllister	88	85	85	93
89	Reggie	Bush	98	99	74	76
88	Travis	Henry	89	89	86	89
88	Carnell	Williams	93	94	77	84
88	Joseph	Addai	93	92	67	82
88	Thomas	Jones	90	90	82	88
88	Ahman	Green	90	85	86	88
87	Michael	Turner	92	85	79	92
87	Marion	Barber	88	88	77	88
87	Kevin	Jones	93	88	78	85
87	Laurence	Maroney	90	90	68	90
87	Chester	Taylor	89	94	84	82
86	Cedric	Benson	87	87	81	85
86	Jamal	Lewis	85	84	80	97
86	Julius	Jones	91	93	77	81
86	LaMont	Jordan	87	83	80	87
85	Brandon	Jacobs	87	87	67	97
85	DeShaun	Foster	92	92	75	86
85	Ladell	Betts	88	89	82	86
85	Adrian	Peterson	93	93	66	84
84	Jerious	Norwood	94	88	70	81
84	DeAngelo	Williams	93	94	68	80
83	Dominic	Rhodes	89	91	76	78
82	Marshawn	Lynch	91	91	60	84
82	Priest	Holmes	87	84	91	76
82	Reuben	Droughns	85	78	82	89
82	Leon	Washington	91	94	68	76
82	Tatum	Bell	95	87	72	80
82	Vernand	Morency	92	93	72	77
82	Maurice	Morris	91	90	75	75
82	Najeh	Davenport	86	83	67	94
82	Ron	Dayne	84	82	82	91
81	Chris	Perry	90	91	65	75
81	Mike	Bell	87	84	68	87
81	Michael	Pittman	86	85	76	82
81	Mike	Anderson	84	75	83	90
81	Musa	Smith	87	83	68	87
80	Anthony	Thomas	85	78	82	88
80	Brandon	Jackson	90	92	60	78
79	Kenny	Irons	91	94	52	76
79	Correll	Buckhalter	86	79	76	88
79	Sammy	Morris	87	83	70	80
79	Kevin	Faulk	88	92	85	65
79	Justin	Fargas	93	89	70	70
79	Michael	Bush	87	85	52	88

HB Halfbacks (continued)

Overall Rating	First Name	Last Name	Speed	Agility	Run Aware	Break Tackle
79	Kevan	Barlow	84	80	72	88
79	Wali	Lundy	87	87	62	77
79	LenDale	White	86	83	49	92
78	Michael	Robinson	87	88	52	83
78	Adrian	Peterson	88	89	67	80
78	Cecil	Sapp	85	82	66	83
78	Marcel	Shipp	84	79	77	86
78	T.J.	Duckett	83	81	72	91
78	Nick	Goings	86	82	76	77
78	Brian	Leonard	85	87	62	81
78	Antonio	Pittman	90	91	56	74
78	Chris	Taylor	87	90	58	82
77	Darren	Sproles	92	94	58	68
77	Chris	Henry	93	92	46	75
77	Mewelde	Moore	88	90	72	67
76	Dwayne	Wright	84	82	54	85
76	Michael	Bennett	97	86	70	67
76	Lorenzo	Booker	92	96	64	55
76	Ryan	Moats	92	94	63	72
76	Cedric	Houston	85	78	70	85
76	Rock	Cartwright	85	78	68	85
75	Maurice	Hicks	87	87	68	75
75	Kenneth	Darby	88	88	50	76
75	Jesse	Chatman	90	84	60	75
75	Tony	Hunt	85	80	60	87
75	Alvin	Pearman	87	90	59	72
75	LaBrandon	Toefield	86	84	62	84
75	Brian	Calhoun	95	89	52	70
75	Travis	Minor	88	88	74	65
75	Ciatrick	Fason	86	84	54	85

LG Left Guard

Overall Rating	First Name	Last Name	Strength	Aware	Run Block	Pass Block
97	Steve	Hutchinson	97	87	98	88
96	Brian	Waters	94	87	94	91
96	Alan	Faneca	95	93	97	92
94	Mike	Wahle	88	87	93	90
93	Kris	Dielman	92	86	96	90
92	Eric	Steinbach	88	87	89	95
91	Larry	Allen	98	95	97	84
90	Ruben	Brown	93	96	91	86
89	Ben	Hamilton	85	80	90	88
89	Vince	Manuwai	93	78	90	92
88	Edwin	Mulitalo	96	87	96	84
88	Logan	Mankins	92	78	90	89
86	Derrick	Dockery	97	82	95	84
85	Kyle	Kosier	86	82	85	89
85	Pete	Kendall	87	82	88	89
84	Dan	Buenning	89	79	88	86
84	Reggie	Wells	87	79	85	86
83	Matt	Lehr	85	78	86	86
83	Rick	DeMulling	86	77	86	90
83	Rob	Sims	91	79	87	85
82	Chris	Bober	87	79	87	89
82	Chris	Liwienski	90	85	86	85
82	Todd	Herremans	88	74	88	87
82	Claude	Terrell	91	74	91	80

297

ROSTER ATTRIBUTES

LG Left Guards (continued)

Overall Rating	First Name	Last Name	Strength	Aware	Run Block	Pass Block
82	Ben	Grubbs	89	66	87	84
81	Terrence	Metcalf	90	70	87	84
81	Ryan	Lilja	87	74	85	88
81	Floyd	Womack	96	73	92	84
81	Chester	Pitts	89	76	87	83
80	Rich	Seubert	87	77	86	86
80	Russ	Hochstein	88	74	87	86
80	Jamar	Nesbit	89	79	84	88
79	Justin	Blalock	94	57	88	83
79	Daryn	Colledge	82	62	81	88
78	Samson	Satele	86	62	78	87
78	Jason	Brown	94	68	87	80
78	Andy	Alleman	87	62	82	80
77	Milford	Brown	91	74	87	80
76	Lennie	Friedman	86	74	86	83
75	David	Stewart	85	66	85	85
74	Max	Jean-Gilles	95	60	90	81
74	Toniu	Fonoti	92	68	86	82
74	Mike	Pucillo	88	69	84	82
74	Taylor	Whitley	88	67	83	83
73	Andrew	Whitworth	93	64	87	82
73	Ben	Wilkerson	85	60	85	77
73	Paul	McQuistan	93	60	86	79
72	Brian	Daniels	85	59	80	80
71	Patrick	Estes	85	56	82	83
71	Chris	Myers	85	59	84	82
71	LG	#63	84	52	78	79

LT Left Tackles (continued)

Overall Rating	First Name	Last Name	Strength	Aware	Run Block	Pass Block
83	Travelle	Wharton	87	75	86	89
82	Vernon	Carey	92	75	91	84
82	Todd	Steussie	89	89	89	79
81	Mike	Gandy	88	78	85	87
81	Roman	Oben	91	77	86	88
81	David	Diehl	88	75	91	86
81	Barry	Sims	87	82	86	85
81	Michael	Roos	89	73	90	86
79	Joe	Staley	84	66	83	87
79	Adrian	Jones	82	73	83	88
78	Anthony	Davis	92	73	89	85
78	Damion	McIntosh	91	79	85	82
77	Oliver	Ross	90	72	85	85
77	Doug	Free	85	63	84	85
76	Jordan	Black	89	70	88	83
75	John	St. Clair	88	75	86	79
75	Winston	Justice	89	49	89	89
74	Marshal	Yanda	84	60	82	86
73	Rashad	Butler	83	62	79	85
73	Trai	Essex	85	60	84	86
72	Erik	Pears	85	69	84	77
72	Kevin	Sampson	86	67	85	82
72	Guy	Whimper	85	55	82	84
72	Jonathan	Scott	87	68	80	82
72	Charles	Spencer	92	62	87	79
72	Daniel	Loper	82	65	80	88
70	Allen	Barbre	85	54	78	82

LT Left Tackles

Overall Rating	First Name	Last Name	Strength	Aware	Run Block	Pass Block
98	Walter	Jones	97	95	97	97
96	Tarik	Glenn	95	94	94	98
96	Orlando	Pace	95	96	90	97
96	Jonathan	Ogden	98	95	98	92
94	Marcus	McNeill	94	85	97	94
93	William	Thomas	95	89	95	95
93	Chris	Samuels	97	87	95	92
93	Bryant	McKinnie	93	87	88	98
92	Jammal	Brown	92	85	91	95
91	Levi	Jones	90	84	91	95
91	Chad	Clifton	91	89	92	95
90	John	Tait	91	89	91	94
90	Matt	Lepsis	88	87	94	88
90	Matt	Light	86	92	87	95
89	Flozell	Adams	97	90	97	87
89	Marvel	Smith	97	86	95	87
88	Jason	Peters	93	84	92	88
88	Kevin	Shaffer	92	85	95	86
88	Wayne	Gandy	92	88	90	90
88	Jeff	Backus	90	86	92	90
87	D'Brickashaw	Ferguson	90	74	88	92
86	Luke	Petitgout	88	86	88	93
85	Jonas	Jennings	94	85	92	84
85	Joe	Thomas	87	74	88	90
85	Khalif	Barnes	90	72	91	89
85	Maurice	Williams	93	80	91	89
84	Tom	Ashworth	85	87	85	89

QB Quarterbacks

Overall Rating	First Name	Last Name	Speed	Aware	Thow Power	Throw Accur.
99	Peyton	Manning	59	99	96	98
98	Tom	Brady	60	98	92	96
97	Carson	Palmer	56	92	97	96
95	Donovan	McNabb	77	83	96	89
95	Marc	Bulger	57	94	91	97
95	Drew	Brees	63	94	88	96
92	Matt	Hasselbeck	64	90	89	93
89	Michael	Vick	93	73	97	78
89	Brett	Favre	53	88	98	88
88	Philip	Rivers	64	82	87	94
88	Chad	Pennington	56	88	86	96
88	Ben	Roethlisbergr	68	84	90	85
87	Vince	Young	90	65	92	84
86	Jay	Cutler	68	71	95	88
86	Eli	Manning	61	85	91	86
86	Jake	Delhomme	64	82	88	89
85	Rex	Grossman	59	80	94	87
85	Daunte	Culpepper	72	72	96	81
85	Steve	McNair	68	85	86	84
84	Alex	Smith	73	71	89	87
84	Matt	Leinart	60	77	89	88
84	Tony	Romo	73	75	89	86
84	Jon	Kitna	54	84	89	88
83	Trent	Green	49	84	86	91
83	David	Carr	68	70	92	85
83	Matt	Schaub	63	74	88	90
82	Brian	Griese	54	83	87	88

QB Quarterbacks (continued)

Overall Rating	First Name	Last Name	Speed	Aware	Thow Power	Throw Accur.
82	Jeff	Garcia	64	84	82	87
82	Byron	Leftwich	50	75	97	86
82	David	Garrard	70	70	92	82
82	JaMarcus	Russell	74	58	99	82
81	J.P.	Losman	70	69	92	83
81	Charlie	Frye	72	70	85	86
81	Kurt	Warner	46	88	87	88
81	Billy	Volek	55	80	87	88
81	Jason	Campbell	69	69	91	83
81	Seneca	Wallace	85	69	86	80
80	Damon	Huard	57	80	86	88
80	Brad	Johnson	46	86	85	89
79	Trent	Dilfer	45	83	89	86
79	Kelly	Holcomb	52	82	83	87
79	Josh	McCown	76	66	90	80
79	Kyle	Boller	69	72	92	77
79	Mark	Brunell	59	77	87	85
79	Charlie	Batch	50	80	87	85
79	Kerry	Collins	47	79	93	82
78	Anthony	Wright	69	73	87	80
78	Gus	Frerotte	52	80	87	84
77	Craig	Nall	60	68	89	84
77	Patrick	Ramsey	55	75	92	81
77	Brady	Quinn	62	68	86	87
77	Chris	Simms	63	70	88	83
77	Tim	Rattay	52	74	86	87
77	Tarvaris	Jackson	78	58	91	80
76	Joey	Harrington	62	70	88	81
76	Kellen	Clemens	66	60	91	84
76	Aaron	Rodgers	66	62	91	82
75	Kyle	Orton	55	74	87	80
75	Brodie	Croyle	55	65	91	85
75	Matt	Cassel	64	70	86	81
75	Andrew	Walter	54	64	92	84
75	Sage	Rosenfels	60	70	87	82
74	John	Beck	64	57	90	86
74	A.J.	Feeley	54	74	87	81
74	Marques	Tuiasosopo	71	64	84	78
74	Todd	Collins	50	79	86	80
73	Derek	Anderson	48	66	93	83
73	Charlie	Whitehurst	62	62	81	88
73	Kevin	Kolb	66	52	89	86
73	Brooks	Bollinger	65	65	81	84
72	Cleo	Lemon	65	64	84	80
72	Tim	Hasselbeck	52	70	82	84
72	Quinn	Gray	71	63	85	77
72	Drew	Stanton	70	50	90	83
71	Doug	Johnson	47	75	86	80
71	Trent	Edwards	60	60	87	82
71	Bruce	Gradkowski	70	55	83	86
71	D.J.	Shockley	85	42	90	78
71	Dan	Orlovsky	55	63	86	84
71	Ingle	Martin	78	48	88	78
71	David	Greene	54	64	82	86
70	Jim	Sorgi	62	68	84	78
70	Troy	Smith	80	52	88	74
70	Jamie	Martin	50	74	84	80
69	Ryan	Fitzpatrick	60	64	86	76
67	Shaun	Hill	55	60	79	84
67	Jeff	Rowe	64	53	83	80

RG Right Guards

Overall Rating	First Name	Last Name	Strength	Aware	Run Block	Pass Block
95	Shawn	Andrews	97	84	98	88
94	Randy	Thomas	92	87	89	97
91	Damien	Woody	92	85	93	89
90	Mike	Goff	94	90	94	85
90	Kynan	Forney	87	84	88	91
90	Chris	Snee	92	80	92	89
90	Chris	Naeole	95	85	96	84
89	Leonard	Davis	98	85	92	83
88	Benji	Olson	93	87	93	87
87	Davin	Joseph	88	74	89	86
87	Marco	Rivera	92	87	90	87
87	Brandon	Moore	89	79	89	87
87	Stephen	Neal	87	81	86	89
85	Roberto	Garza	92	78	89	89
85	Kendall	Simmons	90	75	88	85
84	Jahri	Evans	89	75	89	88
84	Chris	Gray	88	82	88	86
83	Justin	Smiley	87	72	87	84
83	Jake	Scott	87	78	87	85
83	Steve	McKinney	85	80	83	88
82	Bobbie	Williams	93	80	89	83
82	John	Welbourn	91	72	92	82
82	Cooper	Carlisle	87	75	89	83
81	Stockar	McDougle	94	75	91	87
80	David	Baas	88	65	88	87
80	Leander	Jordan	89	73	85	83
80	Keydrick	Vincent	93	76	90	80
80	Artis	Hicks	89	73	85	86
79	Evan	Mathis	86	64	83	86
79	Geoff	Hangartner	87	68	87	86
79	Richie	Incognito	87	61	88	80
79	Rob	Petitti	90	70	86	82
78	Arron	Sears	91	54	87	83
78	Adam	Goldberg	88	70	82	89
76	Montrae	Holland	92	70	89	81
76	Seth	McKinney	84	70	81	82
76	Deuce	Lutui	94	58	87	85
75	Josh	Beekman	86	64	87	80
75	Anthony	Alabi	87	65	86	78
75	Chris	Chester	86	45	83	84
74	Duke	Preston	85	65	83	82
74	Chris	Kuper	82	60	84	78
74	Manuel	Ramirez	94	59	84	79
74	Jason	Spitz	88	60	87	82
74	Fred	Weary	86	66	84	80
73	Brad	Butler	88	65	84	80
73	Fred	Matua	84	58	80	82
73	Elton	Brown	90	62	84	80
73	Kevin	Boothe	87	66	85	80
72	Ed	Blanton	85	62	82	83
71	Jeromey	Clary	82	60	85	80
71	Anthony	Herrera	87	65	85	76
70	Stacy	Andrews	89	52	86	76
70	Matt	Ulrich	87	62	81	76
70	Chris	Kemoeatu	95	45	89	78
69	Tre	Stallings	85	60	83	79
69	Dan	Stevenson	84	65	81	79
69	Matt	Lentz	86	56	83	80
69	D'Anthony	Batiste	88	62	81	78
68	Scott	Young	86	52	83	75

ROSTER ATTRIBUTES

RT Right Tackles

Overall Rating	First Name	Last Name	Strength	Aware	Run Block	Pass Block
95	Willie	Anderson	97	94	98	93
92	Mark	Tauscher	93	90	93	93
92	Jordan	Gross	89	83	94	95
91	Jon	Jansen	97	90	98	86
90	Ryan	Diem	95	80	91	97
90	Jon	Runyan	97	92	98	85
90	Todd	Weiner	92	86	94	92
88	Shane	Olivea	90	83	94	91
87	Fred	Miller	93	87	92	89
87	Kareem	McKenzie	95	82	94	88
87	Alex	Barron	91	75	92	91
85	Ryan	Tucker	94	85	92	86
85	Ephraim	Salaam	89	82	92	87
84	Mike	Rosenthal	90	83	91	88
84	Rex	Tucker	88	85	88	87
83	Sean	Locklear	85	76	88	89
82	Kwame	Harris	88	74	88	89
82	Levi	Brown	91	72	89	86
82	Marc	Colombo	92	77	90	84
82	Tony	Pashos	92	82	90	86
82	George	Foster	94	68	91	88
81	Adam	Meadows	85	84	85	86
81	Max	Starks	91	74	91	86
80	Langston	Walker	93	77	88	84
80	L.J.	Shelton	95	80	87	84
80	Anthony	Clement	92	81	88	84
80	Barry	Stokes	90	85	83	85
80	Todd	Wade	90	80	89	84
79	Jeremy	Trueblood	91	74	87	85
79	Kevin	Barry	96	70	92	80
79	Nick	Kaczur	92	73	81	87
79	Jacob	Bell	89	65	86	89
78	Adam	Snyder	91	69	88	86
78	Jeremy	Bridges	86	76	88	84
77	Chris	Terry	87	72	87	83
77	Robert	Gallery	88	70	87	81
77	Cornell	Green	91	73	87	83
77	Jon	Stinchcomb	82	72	81	89
77	Eric	Winston	84	65	85	85
76	Kelly	Butler	87	67	86	85
76	Brandon	Gorin	89	74	84	82
76	Seth	Wand	89	72	86	83
76	Marcus	Johnson	89	60	90	86
75	Scott	Kooistra	90	72	83	84
75	Tony	Ugoh	89	62	87	80
74	Ryan	O'Callaghan	94	70	88	79
74	Adam	Terry	87	58	84	87
74	Ryan	Cook	87	64	84	82
73	Ryan	Harris	85	64	80	82
73	James	Marten	86	62	79	84
72	Jon	Dunn	87	60	86	82
71	Quinn	Ojinnaka	83	65	82	82
70	Mark	LeVoir	90	55	87	83
70	Terrance	Pennington	90	66	85	79
70	Willie	Colon	84	60	79	83
69	Ray	Willis	89	60	81	80
68	RT	#74	85	51	79	81
67	Will	Svitek	84	55	83	80
67	Drew	Strojny	91	55	82	79
67	Brian	Rimpf	85	57	84	78

TE Tight Ends

Overall Rating	First Name	Last Name	Strength	Aware	Catch	Pass Block
97	Antonio	Gates	74	84	90	55
96	Tony	Gonzalez	69	94	92	55
94	Todd	Heap	68	86	88	58
93	Kellen	Winslow	70	75	86	58
92	Alge	Crumpler	74	85	86	60
92	Jeremy	Shockey	71	84	85	54
90	Jason	Witten	71	80	85	59
89	Randy	McMichael	71	74	83	57
88	Benjamin	Watson	70	74	82	53
88	Chris	Cooley	67	80	87	54
87	L.J.	Smith	69	76	82	58
86	Vernon	Davis	70	55	85	53
86	Desmond	Clark	66	80	85	55
86	Daniel	Graham	73	69	78	60
86	Heath	Miller	68	72	87	56
85	Dallas	Clark	66	72	83	54
83	Greg	Olsen	63	60	82	55
83	Jerramy	Stevens	65	70	80	58
83	Jermaine	Wiggins	77	80	88	52
83	Owen	Daniels	66	70	80	55
83	Ben	Troupe	67	70	79	55
82	George	Wrighster	72	73	75	58
82	Eric	Johnson	66	80	85	55
81	Reggie	Kelly	74	73	76	65
81	Alex	Smith	68	68	81	55
81	Dan	Campbell	73	78	76	64
81	Bubba	Franks	78	80	72	66
81	Kyle	Brady	82	84	63	75
81	Jim	Kleinsasser	78	70	70	66
80	Marcedes	Lewis	73	62	80	57
80	Marcus	Pollard	68	79	77	56
80	Bo	Scaife	63	70	83	54
79	Robert	Royal	70	72	75	58
79	Stephen	Alexander	65	77	77	57
79	Tony	Scheffler	68	68	76	55
79	Jason	Dunn	75	72	67	70
79	David	Martin	69	71	73	60
79	Matt	Schobel	69	69	76	59
79	Chris	Baker	65	68	75	60
79	Joe	Klopfenstein	67	66	79	55
79	Mark	Campbell	66	68	75	65
78	Anthony	Becht	78	76	65	70
78	Scott	Chandler	62	62	80	61
78	Bryan	Fletcher	65	72	82	49
78	Anthony	Fasano	73	56	77	62
78	Jeff	King	74	63	72	62
78	Daniel	Wilcox	74	74	77	55
77	Steve	Heiden	73	75	72	59
77	Leonard	Pope	68	45	77	59
77	Kevin	Boss	70	60	80	55
77	Billy	Miller	65	70	78	52
77	Matt	Spaeth	64	72	82	53
76	Brandon	Manumaleuna	80	70	72	59
76	Kris	Wilson	66	68	79	53
76	Donald	Lee	70	67	70	56
76	Zach	Miller	63	66	80	50
76	John	Madsen	68	68	76	48
76	Jeb	Putzier	68	68	74	58
76	Mark	Bruener	80	82	55	82
75	Darnell	Dinkins	72	65	71	60

Overall Rating	First Name	Last Name	Speed	Accel.	Aware	Catch
98	Chad	Johnson	96	97	60	96
98	Steve	Smith	97	99	63	95
98	Torry	Holt	94	96	55	99
97	Marvin	Harrison	94	97	51	99
95	Terrell	Owens	93	96	77	89
94	Larry	Fitzgerald	88	90	72	97
94	Anquan	Boldin	89	92	78	94
94	Reggie	Wayne	89	95	57	97
94	Randy	Moss	97	95	55	91
93	Javon	Walker	92	94	67	92
93	Roy	Williams	93	92	70	91
93	Donald	Driver	91	92	56	95
93	Andre	Johnson	95	94	73	89
92	T.J.	Houshmandz	91	91	67	96
91	Laveranues	Coles	97	95	53	92
91	Hines	Ward	87	88	72	94
90	Lee	Evans	98	99	52	88
90	Plaxico	Burress	92	90	70	88
89	Darrell	Jackson	90	92	63	88
89	Terry	Glenn	94	93	45	93
89	Santana	Moss	98	98	44	88
88	Braylon	Edwards	93	94	66	87
88	Joey	Galloway	97	97	48	87
88	Chris	Chambers	94	93	62	84
88	Marques	Colston	87	90	72	90
88	Deion	Branch	93	95	48	90
87	Muhsin	Muhammad	86	85	70	93
87	Mike	Furrey	88	88	62	92
87	Calvin	Johnson	95	95	74	85
87	Isaac	Bruce	90	91	42	92
87	Drew	Bennett	89	88	63	88
87	Mark	Clayton	92	95	45	89
86	Bernard	Berrian	97	98	48	87
86	Joe	Horn	87	85	64	90
86	Donte	Stallworth	97	97	55	87
86	Derrick	Mason	87	90	46	93
85	Chris	Henry	93	94	59	88
85	Eddie	Kennison	90	89	54	89
85	Reggie	Brown	90	92	58	87
85	Jerricho	Cotchery	89	92	58	88
84	Rod	Smith	84	85	62	89
84	Bryant	Johnson	92	93	55	87
84	Kevin	Curtis	96	97	50	86
84	Greg	Jennings	93	95	50	87
84	Devery	Henderson	98	99	49	82
83	Brandon	Marshall	89	90	70	82
83	Joe	Jurevicius	84	84	70	87
83	Michael	Jenkins	89	87	65	86
83	Amani	Toomer	87	85	65	85
83	Matt	Jones	93	90	67	80
83	Bobby	Engram	87	91	46	86
83	David	Givens	86	83	70	87
82	Patrick	Crayton	90	90	48	94
82	Marty	Booker	86	84	67	85
82	Reche	Caldwell	90	91	52	85
82	Wes	Welker	88	92	52	88
82	Jerry	Porter	91	92	64	82
82	Antwaan	Randle El	93	97	52	79
82	Brandon	Lloyd	88	90	44	90
82	Robert	Meachem	93	94	61	84

Overall Rating	First Name	Last Name	Speed	Accel.	Aware	Catch
81	Brandon	Stokley	90	90	54	85
81	Eric	Parker	91	92	44	84
81	Vincent	Jackson	91	88	76	81
81	Dwayne	Bowe	91	90	68	80
81	Reggie	Williams	88	89	70	78
80	Ashley	Lelie	92	93	42	82
80	Arnaz	Battle	88	90	62	81
80	Ted	Ginn Jr.	98	99	51	77
80	Ernest	Wilford	85	85	69	81
80	Dwayne	Jarrett	87	88	64	86
80	Travis	Taylor	88	88	58	83
80	Demetrius	Williams	90	94	60	82
80	Santonio	Holmes	93	94	56	79
80	Sidney	Rice	89	90	60	85
79	Peerless	Price	92	93	47	80
79	Roscoe	Parrish	94	97	43	82
79	Josh	Reed	85	87	55	86
79	Michael	Clayton	87	87	66	79
79	Craig	Davis	93	91	51	83
79	Anthony	Gonzalez	95	96	55	82
79	Jabar	Gaffney	87	89	42	87
79	Ronald	Curry	89	91	57	80
79	Doug	Gabriel	87	87	68	80
79	D.J.	Hackett	88	91	58	80
79	Bobby	Wade	90	92	48	81
78	Jason	Hill	92	91	54	82
78	Mark	Bradley	91	93	60	76
78	Ike	Hilliard	86	86	46	83
78	Hank	Baskett	87	88	64	82
78	Roddy	White	93	94	60	78
78	Robert	Ferguson	91	87	67	77
78	Kelley	Washington	90	90	66	77
77	David	Boston	88	85	75	80
77	Maurice	Stovall	88	90	67	77
77	Malcom	Floyd	87	88	62	82
77	Samie	Parker	94	95	36	78
77	Derek	Hagan	87	88	60	82
77	Kelly	Campbell	93	94	44	77
77	Laurent	Robinson	92	93	52	81
77	Dennis	Northcutt	90	95	45	75
77	Chad	Jackson	91	92	50	82
77	Nate	Burleson	91	93	46	75
77	Cedrick	Wilson	91	91	49	78
77	Brandon	Jones	90	90	56	82
76	Rashied	Davis	92	93	53	75
76	Tim	Carter	94	93	52	77
76	Travis	Wilson	87	88	65	79
76	Greg	Lewis	93	92	49	81
76	Brian	Finneran	85	82	65	80
76	Steve	Smith	92	93	56	77
76	Shaun	McDonald	93	94	42	78
76	Nate	Washington	88	92	52	77
76	Justin	Gage	86	87	65	76
76	Aundrae	Allison	93	96	52	78
76	Troy	Williamson	96	95	52	70
75	Taylor	Jacobs	90	89	45	79
75	Devin	Hester	100	99	52	70
75	Tab	Perry	88	87	60	79
75	David	Kircus	88	86	52	80
75	Rod	Gardner	86	85	68	76

DEFENSIVE / PLAYER LIST

ROSTER ATTRIBUTES

CB Cornerbacks

Overall Rating	First Name	Last Name	Speed	Accel.	Aware	Catch
99	Champ	Bailey	98	98	97	82
97	Chris	McAlister	94	97	94	71
96	Ronde	Barber	88	95	97	78
95	Rashean	Mathis	94	93	84	80
95	Asante	Samuel	91	94	92	79
94	Lito	Sheppard	92	94	92	78
93	Nate	Clements	93	94	91	69
93	DeAngelo	Hall	98	98	78	80
93	Al	Harris	90	94	95	63
93	Nnamdi	Asomugha	91	92	90	74
92	Patrick	Surtain	90	95	92	79
91	Ty	Law	88	89	94	81
91	Antoine	Winfield	90	91	90	67
90	Nathan	Vasher	90	90	85	84
90	Dre'	Bly	93	96	88	82
90	Marcus	Trufant	94	98	80	68
89	Charles	Tillman	88	91	82	73
89	Terence	Newman	96	97	80	74
89	Sheldon	Brown	91	94	84	75
89	Charles	Woodson	87	90	90	70
89	Fabian	Washington	98	96	84	67
88	Walt	Harris	88	90	92	69
88	Chris	Gamble	92	94	74	79
88	Ken	Lucas	92	92	79	72
88	Shawn	Springs	89	90	90	67
87	Brian	Kelly	88	91	86	68
87	Quentin	Jammer	94	91	76	67
87	Sam	Madison	88	90	92	67
87	Brian	Williams	88	89	83	74
87	Samari	Rolle	90	92	93	72
87	Carlos	Rogers	91	92	80	64
87	Mike	McKenzie	89	93	88	63
87	Dunta	Robinson	96	97	72	69
86	Deltha	O'Neal	94	93	75	78
86	Anthony	Henry	88	90	80	71
86	Andre	Dyson	94	94	78	74
86	Cedric	Griffin	89	92	78	68
85	Johnathan	Joseph	97	96	68	66
85	Terrence	McGee	94	95	78	67
85	Gary	Baxter	85	86	84	70
85	Tory	James	86	85	82	77
85	Nick	Harper	87	86	82	77
84	Ricky	Manning	90	92	74	78
84	Antrel	Rolle	89	92	70	70
84	Antonio	Cromartie	94	92	62	74
84	Marlin	Jackson	87	90	77	65
84	Ellis	Hobbs	91	92	77	68
84	Fakhir	Brown	88	89	82	66
84	Jason	David	88	95	80	78
84	Deshea	Townsend	88	90	86	64
83	Domonique	Foxworth	93	96	74	65
83	Will	Allen	98	97	79	55
83	Tye	Hill	98	97	69	66
83	Fred	Smoot	92	94	77	70
83	Ike	Taylor	94	94	72	59
82	Leigh	Bodden	88	90	80	64
82	Roderick	Hood	90	91	78	62
82	Fernando	Bryant	94	93	80	64
82	Richard	Marshall	93	94	64	70
82	Fred	Thomas	87	87	84	66

CB Cornerbacks (continued)

Overall Rating	First Name	Last Name	Speed	Accel.	Aware	Catch
82	Kelly	Jennings	94	93	70	64
82	Bryant	McFadden	89	92	76	62
82	Reynaldo	Hill	89	91	76	69
81	Shawntae	Spencer	91	92	70	65
81	Jason	Webster	87	87	80	64
81	Drayton	Florence	91	92	72	64
81	Corey	Webster	87	91	73	64
81	David	Barrett	87	86	73	70
81	Justin	Miller	95	97	62	68
81	Darrelle	Revis	90	92	67	68
81	Chad	Scott	87	88	76	63
81	Kelly	Herndon	88	90	74	64
81	Dexter	McCleon	89	89	80	68
80	Leon	Hall	92	92	64	69
80	Kenny	Wright	88	89	78	60
80	Aaron	Glenn	87	88	83	65
80	Aaron	Ross	90	92	65	67
80	R.W.	McQuarters	90	92	81	64
80	Jason	Craft	91	91	74	65
80	Jordan	Babineaux	89	87	73	64
79	Keiwan	Ratliff	88	93	68	76
79	Daven	Holly	93	93	69	72
79	Eric	Green	89	90	70	68
79	Kelvin	Hayden	90	94	60	70
79	Travis	Daniels	87	90	72	62
79	William	James	91	90	67	64
79	Chris	Houston	96	95	56	65
79	Travis	Fisher	91	92	70	65
79	Randall	Gay	88	89	72	68
79	David	Macklin	87	87	76	62
78	Terry	Cousin	88	90	80	57
78	Duane	Starks	91	90	78	62
78	Lenny	Walls	87	85	76	57
78	Ricardo	Colclough	91	93	63	69
78	Marcus	McCauley	92	93	59	65
77	Kiwaukee	Thomas	87	88	76	62
77	Phillip	Buchanon	97	94	64	68
77	Daymeion	Hughes	87	89	66	70
77	Jonathan	Wade	96	98	50	68
77	DeMarcus	Faggins	90	92	70	62
77	Jamar	Fletcher	87	92	70	72
76	Ashton	Youboty	92	92	59	57
76	Sammy	Davis	90	92	65	64
76	Lewis	Sanders	87	87	68	64
76	Stanley	Wilson	94	93	62	65
76	CB	#35	95	96	52	62
76	Josh	Wilson	95	93	57	60
75	Donald	Strickland	88	91	65	62
75	Karl	Paymah	93	90	62	57
75	Scott	Starks	92	92	64	66
75	A.J.	Davis	92	94	57	60
75	Stanford	Routt	97	94	56	64
75	Ronald	Bartell	92	92	57	60
75	Mike	Rumph	88	87	64	60
75	Jerametrius	Butler	90	90	66	64
75	DeJuan	Groce	90	91	72	64
75	Cortland	Finnegan	92	93	61	58
74	Dante	Wesley	89	89	70	58
74	Steve	Gregory	88	89	59	64
74	Andre	Goodman	93	90	67	58

CB Cornerbacks (continued)

Overall Rating	First Name	Last Name	Speed	Accel.	Aware	Catch
74	CB	#38	94	96	54	60
74	Von	Hutchins	90	92	65	60
74	Andre	Woolfolk	92	91	60	62
73	Matt	Ware	87	89	56	65
73	Tim	Jennings	95	95	55	62
73	Keith	Smith	91	91	60	65
73	Patrick	Dendy	88	89	64	64
73	Fred	Bennett	92	91	53	61
73	Eric	King	90	93	64	65
72	Jereme	Perry	89	90	60	60
72	Alan	Zemaitis	87	85	55	63
72	Benny	Sapp	93	93	62	55

DT Defensive Tackles

Overall Rating	First Name	Last Name	Speed	Strength	Aware	Tackle
97	Tommie	Harris	78	91	83	82
97	Jamal	Williams	54	98	91	91
97	Casey	Hampton	58	98	86	97
97	Kevin	Williams	71	91	84	86
96	John	Henderson	62	95	83	93
96	Marcus	Stroud	65	94	82	88
95	Shaun	Rogers	60	96	83	92
94	Rod	Coleman	75	84	84	84
94	Kris	Jenkins	64	93	79	88
93	Pat	Williams	50	96	93	96
92	Vince	Wilfork	64	93	78	87
89	Warren	Sapp	68	82	90	77
89	Kelly	Gregg	56	88	88	88
89	Cornelius	Griffin	65	86	81	87
88	Anthony	McFarland	62	90	76	86
88	Cory	Redding	69	87	76	82
88	Albert	Haynesworth	63	92	66	88
87	Darnell	Dockett	71	87	71	82
87	Corey	Williams	67	87	70	84
87	Ma'ake	Kemoeatu	50	96	77	94
87	La'Roi	Glover	64	82	91	81
87	Rocky	Bernard	64	87	70	85
86	John	Thornton	62	86	80	85
86	Darwin	Walker	66	83	77	83
86	Ted	Washington	44	97	88	90
86	Chris	Hovan	66	84	75	80
86	Corey	Simon	59	87	74	87
86	Dewayne	Robertson	64	87	69	84
86	Hollis	Thomas	48	93	86	89
85	Larry	Tripplett	65	84	76	83
85	Gerard	Warren	61	92	70	85
85	Jason	Ferguson	55	90	80	87
85	Mike	Patterson	63	86	70	82
85	Brian	Young	63	85	83	78
84	Brodrick	Bunkley	65	96	55	78
83	Tank	Johnson	70	84	69	77
83	Alvin	McKinley	56	91	74	86
83	Keith	Traylor	47	93	85	87
83	Grady	Jackson	43	96	80	92
83	Chartric	Darby	67	80	71	83
82	James	Reed	62	85	74	85
82	Ryan	Pickett	62	85	68	83

DT Defensive Tackles (continued)

Overall Rating	First Name	Last Name	Speed	Strength	Aware	Tackle
82	Terdell	Sands	51	93	72	85
82	Jimmy	Kennedy	58	90	69	85
82	Marcus	Tubbs	60	92	64	82
82	Russell	Davis	56	90	71	86
82	Chris	Hoke	57	90	75	90
81	Raheem	Brock	76	76	70	80
81	Ian	Scott	63	86	70	82
81	Damione	Lewis	64	84	72	80
81	Adam	Carriker	76	90	60	74
81	Amobi	Okoye	66	88	58	80
81	Jeff	Zgonina	55	83	86	82
80	Kendrick	Clancy	54	88	70	87
80	Fred	Robbins	54	88	75	86
80	Justin	Harrell	64	89	60	80
79	Michael	Myers	64	84	68	80
79	Domata	Peko	62	89	62	80
79	Ryan	Sims	62	84	66	82
79	Ron	Edwards	58	88	70	80
79	Montae	Reagor	65	79	72	79
79	Marcus	Bell	48	92	72	85
79	Rob	Meier	62	80	72	83
79	Kedric	Golston	61	84	65	80
79	Travis	Johnson	65	84	57	80
78	Ellis	Wyms	65	80	69	81
78	Alan	Branch	62	94	56	82
78	William	Joseph	64	82	69	79
78	Barry	Cofield	67	84	62	78
78	Shaun	Cody	64	80	65	79
78	Randy	Starks	62	87	61	82
77	Isaac	Sopoaga	55	95	55	84
77	Anthony	Adams	61	83	68	80
77	Tim	Anderson	55	84	72	83
77	Marcus	Thomas	65	86	51	78
77	Dan	Klecko	66	80	70	77
77	Kindal	Moorehead	58	83	70	79
77	Justin	Bannan	55	86	72	80
77	Brandon	Mebane	65	90	54	73
77	Craig	Terrill	62	83	70	78
77	Anthony	Maddox	67	86	62	76
76	Kyle	Williams	59	84	66	79
76	Shaun	Smith	59	89	60	77
76	Colin	Cole	56	89	63	83
75	John	McCargo	66	82	55	77
75	Ethan	Kelley	56	86	68	83
75	Quinn	Pitcock	61	85	60	77
75	Jonathan	Babineaux	67	79	57	75
75	Jesse	Mahelona	57	91	54	83
74	Ronald	Fields	56	88	61	79
74	Demetrin	Veal	64	80	64	79
74	Alfonso	Boone	54	87	70	78
74	Tank	Tyler	54	96	52	78
74	Paul	Soliai	62	93	55	74
73	Joe	Cohen	60	91	52	78
73	Aubrayo	Franklin	54	87	64	81
73	Jay	Ratliff	66	83	54	77
73	C.J.	Mosley	59	83	63	78
73	Claude	Wroten	63	84	49	82
72	Gabe	Watson	57	91	49	85
72	Jay	Alford	63	84	58	70
72	Sione	Pouha	62	87	50	77

ROSTER ATTRIBUTES

303

ROSTER ATTRIBUTES

FS Free Safeties

Overall Rating	First Name	Last Name	Speed	Strength	Aware	Tackle
99	Ed	Reed	93	56	92	67
97	Bob	Sanders	93	65	88	86
97	Brian	Dawkins	90	70	90	80
96	John	Lynch	84	70	98	92
92	Sean	Taylor	90	71	65	84
90	Mike	Brown	87	56	84	71
89	Deon	Grant	89	57	78	65
87	Eugene	Wilson	90	62	79	70
86	Madieu	Williams	88	63	66	72
86	Marlon	McCree	85	68	82	73
86	Ken	Hamlin	88	65	65	85
86	Mike	Minter	86	63	82	83
86	Stuart	Schweigert	90	62	73	76
86	Dwight	Smith	90	63	71	69
85	Brodney	Pool	90	61	66	68
84	Greg	Wesley	84	65	72	75
83	Danieal	Manning	91	64	62	71
83	Renaldo	Hill	87	55	79	62
83	Reggie	Nelson	93	55	60	66
83	Erik	Coleman	87	54	74	72
83	O.J.	Atogwe	88	65	70	74
83	Josh	Bullocks	90	58	64	66
83	Mike	Green	86	59	76	78
82	Will	Demps	86	66	75	77
82	Nick	Collins	93	64	60	73
82	Brandon	Meriweather	92	58	60	66
82	Michael	Griffin	91	60	61	70
81	Terrence	Holt	84	55	76	64
81	Gerald	Sensabaugh	87	62	68	68
81	Ryan	Clark	87	58	68	75
80	Ko	Simpson	89	61	60	76
80	Will	Allen	85	58	65	70
80	Jason	Allen	92	66	59	68
80	Pierson	Prioleau	84	60	80	78
79	Mark	Roman	88	58	66	70
79	Pat	Watkins	89	54	54	68
79	Chris	Crocker	90	56	60	76
79	Daniel	Bullocks	87	57	66	68
79	Kevin	Kaesviharn	80	60	81	65
79	Tank	Williams	87	67	65	84
78	Aaron	Francisco	87	60	68	64
78	Eric	Weddle	90	56	57	67
78	Deke	Cooper	87	65	68	70
78	C.C.	Brown	86	64	66	73
78	Lamont	Thompson	87	59	60	60
77	Sam	Brandon	88	54	66	72
77	Jimmy	Williams	93	70	52	65
77	Rashad	Baker	86	55	66	63
76	Dashon	Goldson	88	58	60	63
76	Keith	Davis	82	62	70	72
76	Greg	Blue	87	68	54	77
75	John	Wendling	89	65	52	69
75	Mike	Adams	85	54	62	65
75	Jerome	Carter	86	64	62	75
75	Bryan	Scott	85	65	61	70
74	Ethan	Kilmer	91	60	47	67
74	Tanard	Jackson	88	52	54	60
74	C.J.	Gaddis	92	67	50	71
74	Eric	Smith	87	67	55	74
74	Marviel	Underwood	86	60	62	69

LE Left Defensive Ends

Overall Rating	First Name	Last Name	Speed	Strength	Aware	Tackle
98	Julius	Peppers	87	84	77	76
94	Leonard	Little	85	75	81	76
93	Michael	Strahan	76	85	88	82
93	Aaron	Kampman	75	85	83	83
93	Trevor	Pryce	69	93	89	87
92	Adewale	Ogunleye	84	78	80	74
91	Charles	Grant	75	81	77	82
90	Luis	Castillo	65	94	80	90
90	Robert	Mathis	85	69	76	74
89	Jevon	Kearse	85	70	77	74
89	Ty	Warren	68	88	82	86
89	Aaron	Smith	69	86	86	85
88	Shaun	Ellis	68	89	80	85
88	Kyle	Vanden Bosch	72	81	80	82
86	Bryant	Young	64	88	94	88
86	Kenard	Lang	74	75	83	80
86	Kevin	Carter	66	86	87	83
86	Tamba	Hali	74	84	65	80
85	Chike	Okeafor	77	73	85	75
85	Andre	Carter	76	75	77	76
85	Bryce	Fisher	74	78	74	81
85	Anthony	Weaver	67	84	76	83
84	Orpheus	Roye	63	88	82	87
84	Marcus	Spears	69	82	69	82
84	Eric	Hicks	73	77	86	77
83	Chris	Kelsay	72	76	80	79
83	Ryan	Denney	69	83	80	80
83	Greg	Spires	74	73	74	78
83	Dewayne	White	74	75	67	74
83	Tommy	Kelly	64	84	66	81
82	Renaldo	Wynn	63	86	86	85
81	Jamaal	Anderson	79	72	52	74
81	Paul	Spicer	66	82	76	82
81	Tyler	Brayton	70	77	70	79
80	Bryan	Robinson	60	82	83	85
80	John	Engelberger	69	78	76	78
80	Ndukwe	Kalu	75	69	78	76
80	Kenechi	Udeze	70	77	62	75
80	Darrion	Scott	69	79	64	74
78	Melvin	Oliver	68	86	56	79
78	Tim	Crowder	82	80	47	66
78	Turk	McBride	65	85	52	76
78	Josh	Thomas	72	75	65	75
78	Matt	Roth	72	74	62	73
78	Juqua	Thomas	73	72	66	71
78	Baraka	Atkins	77	78	58	70
77	Ray	McDonald	68	83	48	74
76	Jerome	McDougle	77	68	65	70
76	Eric	Moore	75	67	58	75
76	Willie	Whitehead	64	82	70	78
75	Rodney	Bailey	65	78	71	75
75	LE	#49	75	70	53	70
75	Jayme	Mitchell	68	82	49	76
73	Jonathan	Fanene	67	79	62	73
73	Chauncey	Davis	74	66	45	74
73	Adrian	Awasom	72	77	55	73
73	Kenyon	Coleman	72	76	59	70
73	Jared	DeVries	65	78	72	74
72	Frostee	Rucker	61	72	61	72
72	Joe	Tafoya	67	74	68	73

LOLB — Left Outside Linebackers

Overall Rating	First Name	Last Name	Speed	Strength	Aware	Tackle
98	Shawne	Merriman	87	86	83	90
94	Joey	Porter	85	76	88	90
93	Marcus	Washington	83	76	85	91
91	Terrell	Suggs	86	76	79	87
89	Cato	June	84	66	82	86
88	Rosevelt	Colvin	80	78	85	86
88	Clark	Haggans	75	82	89	88
87	Karlos	Dansby	85	73	72	86
87	Derrick	Johnson	87	69	76	84
87	Daryl	Smith	79	75	77	87
87	David	Thornton	77	74	85	87
86	Willie	McGinest	77	76	90	85
85	Leroy	Hill	83	73	77	87
84	Mathias	Kiwanuka	82	77	76	84
84	Thomas	Davis	87	69	62	85
84	Scott	Fujita	82	73	77	83
83	Warrick	Holdman	78	76	79	84
83	Greg	Ellis	76	78	88	84
83	Boss	Bailey	87	71	66	79
81	Michael	Boley	81	68	69	82
81	Clint	Ingram	84	69	64	83
81	Sam	Williams	81	74	78	80
81	Ben	Leber	78	73	77	85
80	Manny	Lawson	90	72	58	79
80	Alex	Lewis	85	65	68	82
80	Brady	Poppinga	76	76	78	83
80	Brandon	Chillar	77	73	74	82
80	Kailee	Wong	75	72	84	82
79	Hunter	Hillenmeyer	73	74	77	87
79	Ryan	Nece	79	67	75	81
79	Anthony	Spencer	81	80	70	79
79	Chris	Gocong	78	75	75	79
78	D.D.	Lewis	77	73	74	80
78	Bryan	Thomas	78	75	78	82
78	Tim	Shaw	87	68	60	77
78	Alfred	Fincher	77	75	73	84
78	Kevin	Bentley	78	73	70	80
78	Shantee	Orr	77	74	72	83
77	David	Pollack	77	76	68	78
77	Rashad	Jeanty	76	72	73	81
77	Mario	Haggan	77	69	72	82
77	Reggie	Torbor	81	67	70	80
75	Parys	Haralson	76	72	70	80
75	Robert	McCune	85	72	58	79
75	Arnold	Harrison	77	74	68	80
73	Rocky	Boiman	74	73	72	78
73	Stewart	Bradley	74	76	72	75
73	Jorge	Cordova	76	74	59	80
73	Khary	Campbell	77	68	68	78
72	Raonall	Smith	83	64	67	72
72	Robert	Reynolds	76	72	66	78
71	Korey	Hall	77	72	60	75
71	LaMarr	Woodley	78	80	59	77
70	Carlos	Polk	73	72	67	78
70	LOLB	#55	79	85	50	72
69	Darrell	McClover	86	60	61	68
69	Roy	Manning	77	71	55	74
69	David	McMillan	79	74	52	77
69	Brandon	Johnson	85	69	43	72
69	Kris	Griffin	78	63	54	76

MLB — Middle Linebackers

Overall Rating	First Name	Last Name	Speed	Strength	Aware	Tackle
98	Brian	Urlacher	88	77	93	94
97	Zach	Thomas	75	78	98	97
96	Ray	Lewis	83	78	94	94
95	Antonio	Pierce	85	76	91	94
95	James	Farrior	79	80	91	94
94	Jonathan	Vilma	85	72	88	95
94	London	Fletcher	80	68	92	97
93	Lofa	Tatupu	84	77	87	94
91	Jeremiah	Trotter	76	80	91	92
91	Keith	Brooking	81	79	90	91
91	Mike	Peterson	85	71	90	91
91	Will	Witherspoon	86	72	86	92
91	Bart	Scott	81	80	88	90
90	D.J.	Williams	86	79	82	89
90	Andra	Davis	77	78	87	93
89	Nick	Barnett	81	77	82	93
89	Dan	Morgan	84	73	85	90
89	Mike	Vrabel	74	82	90	90
89	DeMeco	Ryans	80	75	82	93
88	Derek	Smith	74	76	90	91
88	Kirk	Morrison	80	79	81	93
87	Tedy	Bruschi	74	78	92	88
87	Larry	Foote	77	75	84	89
86	Angelo	Crowell	78	75	85	89
86	Bradie	James	79	79	80	90
85	Patrick	Willis	87	77	76	87
85	Gerald	Hayes	73	80	83	90
85	Gary	Brackett	81	72	84	88
85	Channing	Crowder	79	77	77	90
85	E.J.	Henderson	73	81	78	92
84	Odell	Thurman	84	76	74	89
84	D'Qwell	Jackson	82	75	77	88
84	Akin	Ayodele	82	74	79	87
84	Junior	Seau	74	74	92	84
84	Brian	Simmons	82	71	85	85
83	Rob	Morris	74	76	82	87
83	Victor	Hobson	75	79	82	87
83	Chris	Draft	78	74	82	85
83	Lemar	Marshall	84	71	79	86
82	Brandon	Moore	78	79	77	85
81	Omar	Gaither	80	70	77	86
80	Jeff	Ulbrich	75	74	82	84
80	Barrett	Ruud	75	76	75	88
80	Napoleon	Harris	83	73	75	85
80	Mark	Simoneau	80	73	79	84
79	Nate	Webster	79	68	77	85
79	Bobby	Carpenter	84	70	72	86
79	Brad	Kassell	72	72	80	86
79	Paris	Lenon	77	72	78	84
78	Chaun	Thompson	85	70	72	84
78	Monty	Beisel	76	74	78	83
78	Clint	Kriewaldt	70	79	75	88
77	Leon	Williams	83	76	65	86
77	David	Harris	83	77	68	85
76	Ahmad	Brooks	78	72	72	82
76	Donnie	Spragan	75	73	74	85
76	Abdul	Hodge	81	74	68	87
76	Niko	Koutouvides	75	74	70	84
76	Danny	Clark	79	76	73	81
75	Caleb	Miller	77	75	72	83

ROSTER ATTRIBUTES

MLB Middle Linebackers (continued)

Overall Rating	First Name	Last Name	Speed	Strength	Aware	Tackle
75	Teddy	Lehman	84	69	73	81
75	Robert	Thomas	79	68	75	80
74	Matt	Wilhelm	75	74	74	81
74	Anthony	Schlegel	70	82	66	87
74	Larry	Izzo	69	69	80	80
74	Stephen	Tulloch	78	70	67	84
71	Buster	Davis	81	69	65	80
71	Stephen	Cooper	76	72	70	78
71	Jordan	Beck	83	73	59	82
70	Rod	Wilson	80	68	66	79
70	Brandon	Siler	82	71	62	80
70	Tony	Gilbert	70	75	65	83
69	Rian	Wallace	73	74	62	83
68	Anthony	Waters	80	75	60	76
68	William	Kershaw	77	76	62	78
68	Adam	Seward	74	76	63	80
68	Mike	Smith	76	69	66	79
66	Antoine	Cash	78	63	64	78
66	Vinny	Ciurciu	70	68	70	79
65	Antwan	Barnes	88	71	52	77
63	Derrick	Pope	77	70	55	78
63	Chase	Blackburn	73	68	60	79

P Punters

Overall Rating	First Name	Last Name	Aware	Kick Power	Kick Accur.	Tackle
98	Shane	Lechler	78	95	91	18
94	Brian	Moorman	76	94	90	19
93	Scott	Player	92	89	92	22
93	Mat	McBriar	70	95	89	10
89	Jason	Baker	78	90	90	14
89	Ryan	Plackemeier	68	93	88	40
88	Hunter	Smith	76	89	91	14
87	Brad	Maynard	89	87	90	12
87	Ben	Graham	60	93	88	39
87	Josh	Miller	80	88	91	25
86	Todd	Sauerbrun	69	92	87	26
86	Nick	Harris	75	92	86	13
85	Andy	Lee	69	89	90	35
85	Josh	Bidwell	79	90	87	23
85	Craig	Hentrich	86	90	86	12
84	Jon	Ryan	66	94	84	31
83	Dave	Zastudil	67	91	86	12
83	Chris	Hanson	74	90	86	12
82	Kyle	Larson	66	90	87	27
82	Dustin	Colquitt	64	90	87	29
82	Michael	Koenen	64	93	84	14
82	Daniel	Sepulveda	65	92	85	55
80	Mike	Scifres	60	91	85	22
80	Steve	Weatherford	74	89	85	23
79	Dirk	Johnson	71	88	86	33
79	Jeff	Feagles	96	83	88	19
79	Donnie	Jones	62	90	85	23
78	Adam	Podlesh	65	89	85	30
77	Sam	Koch	60	90	84	33
77	Chris	Kluwe	64	86	88	20
76	Derrick	Frost	62	87	86	10
76	Chad	Stanley	73	85	87	19

RE Right Defensive Ends

Overall Rating	First Name	Last Name	Speed	Strength	Aware	Tackle
97	Richard	Seymour	71	92	91	88
96	Dwight	Freeney	87	74	80	75
94	Will	Smith	83	81	79	80
93	Derrick	Burgess	82	75	85	79
92	Aaron	Schobel	74	81	84	84
92	Simeon	Rice	84	70	92	74
92	John	Abraham	80	77	77	81
90	Bertrand	Berry	79	78	80	79
90	Osi	Umenyiora	84	73	72	77
89	Mike	Rucker	74	78	88	83
89	Patrick	Kerney	74	78	88	82
88	Alex	Brown	83	74	74	75
88	Jared	Allen	79	75	74	79
88	Reggie	Hayward	77	78	77	79
87	Mark	Anderson	80	73	68	79
87	Justin	Smith	74	82	80	79
87	Haloti	Ngata	63	94	69	87
86	Robert	Geathers	80	73	72	74
86	Trent	Cole	79	73	72	76
86	Darren	Howard	73	81	77	80
86	Kabeer	Gbaja Biamila	81	70	72	72
85	Mario	Williams	82	79	58	70
84	Marques	Douglas	71	78	76	80
84	Gaines	Adams	84	72	45	75
84	Igor	Olshansky	62	90	73	86
84	Bobby	McCray	79	72	74	71
84	Jarvis	Green	68	84	67	83
84	James	Hall	73	80	75	80
83	Vonnie	Holliday	63	88	84	86
83	Cullen	Jenkins	66	82	72	81
83	Phillip	Daniels	65	85	82	86
82	Elvis	Dumervil	79	71	64	70
82	Ebenezer	Ekuban	72	75	78	78
82	Robaire	Smith	62	87	77	85
82	Kimo	vonOelhoffen	60	88	88	88
82	Bobby	Hamilton	65	82	82	84
82	Brett	Keisel	73	80	73	76
82	Erasmus	James	78	72	62	72
81	Jarvis	Moss	82	67	48	73
81	Kalimba	Edwards	78	70	64	72
79	Chris	Canty	70	80	65	77
79	Travis	LaBoy	75	70	65	73
78	Charles	Johnson	78	80	55	71
78	Victor	Adeyanju	77	79	45	75
78	Darryl	Tapp	74	74	50	80
77	Anthony	Hargrove	75	67	65	71
77	Quentin	Moses	78	70	51	70
77	Jason	Babin	78	67	60	71
77	Ray	Edwards	77	73	45	71
77	Brian	Robison	76	77	52	72
76	Dan	Bazuin	76	77	54	70
76	Jacques	Cesaire	69	82	62	78
76	Jason	Hatcher	73	84	40	72
75	Patrick	Chukwurah	75	68	65	76
75	Victor	Abiamiri	74	75	51	70
75	Justin	Tuck	75	66	46	71
75	Travis	Kirschke	60	86	72	83
75	Antwan	Odom	75	69	54	69
74	Chase	Page	63	86	56	77
73	Damane	Duckett	60	84	64	79

ROLB Right Outside Linebackers

Overall Rating	First Name	Last Name	Speed	Strength	Aware	Tackle
96	Keith	Bulluck	86	73	86	90
95	Lance	Briggs	80	79	89	93
95	Jason	Taylor	84	78	94	89
95	Adalius	Thomas	87	80	86	85
94	Derrick	Brooks	82	70	92	89
94	Donnie	Edwards	83	66	90	90
94	Julian	Peterson	86	74	84	89
92	Demarcus	Ware	86	78	76	90
91	Takeo	Spikes	80	79	91	90
90	Ian	Gold	86	68	84	84
89	Eric	Barton	78	75	84	90
89	Ernie	Sims	86	77	70	90
89	A.J.	Hawk	87	73	78	85
87	Kamerion	Wimbley	84	77	72	86
87	Pisa	Tinoisamoa	87	67	75	84
86	Ed	Hartwell	75	83	82	92
86	Morlon	Greenwood	85	67	81	85
85	Landon	Johnson	81	68	77	86
85	Shaun	Phillips	82	73	79	85
85	Thomas	Howard	87	70	68	84
85	Scott	Shanle	78	73	78	87
84	Demorrio	Williams	86	67	75	81
83	Kendrell	Bell	76	81	80	89
83	Kawika	Mitchell	79	77	74	84
83	Jon	Beason	81	66	69	86
83	Shawn	Barber	82	67	79	80
82	Tully	Banta Cain	78	71	78	83
82	Paul	Posluszny	82	70	71	80
82	Na'il	Diggs	79	73	75	87
82	Lawrence	Timmons	85	74	61	82
82	Chad	Greenway	85	70	63	85
81	Dontarrious	Thomas	85	71	68	82
79	Matt	McCoy	82	68	69	83
79	Nick	Greisen	73	77	77	86
78	Matt	Stewart	73	76	77	83
78	Gerris	Wilkinson	81	73	62	80
77	Rocky	McIntosh	82	68	57	84
76	Keith	Ellison	83	70	58	76
76	Jamie	Winborn	80	65	70	78
76	Kevin	Burnett	85	75	54	79
76	David	Bowens	74	80	78	80
76	James	Anderson	85	67	62	79
76	Jarret	Johnson	74	80	76	84
76	James	Harrison	76	81	65	83
75	Michael	Okwo	74	73	65	80
75	Pat	Thomas	80	74	62	80
75	Eric	Alexander	74	75	66	82
75	Dan	Cody	80	73	62	80
75	Rufus	Alexander	80	65	64	75
74	Calvin	Pace	74	76	70	80
73	Quincy	Black	87	66	54	75
73	Keyaron	Fox	82	65	56	76
73	Stephen	Nicholas	79	66	60	77
73	Tracy	White	76	72	70	77
73	Jon	Alston	87	75	46	80
73	Gilbert	Gardner	77	69	66	74
72	Darryl	Blackstock	81	73	64	75
72	LeVar	Woods	73	72	72	78
71	Donte	Curry	78	65	68	76
71	Marquis	Cooper	85	63	56	72

SS Strong Safeties

Overall Rating	First Name	Last Name	Speed	Strength	Aware	Tackle
97	Troy	Polamalu	93	68	80	85
96	Adrian	Wilson	88	72	83	88
95	Kerry	Rhodes	87	69	84	88
94	Roy	Williams	85	75	85	90
93	Darren	Sharper	88	60	86	76
92	Rodney	Harrison	82	72	92	92
91	Chris	Hope	88	68	80	86
90	Gibril	Wilson	89	67	76	84
89	Donovin	Darius	86	75	82	90
88	Donte	Whitner	92	65	68	82
88	Sean	Jones	90	65	70	76
87	Jermaine	Phillips	87	69	78	87
87	Lawyer	Milloy	82	69	89	82
87	Michael	Huff	93	64	70	79
87	Dawan	Landry	86	65	76	78
86	Nick	Ferguson	83	67	81	82
86	Antoine	Bethea	89	67	69	81
85	Corey	Chavous	85	54	88	60
85	LaRon	Landry	94	69	62	82
84	Michael	Lewis	87	68	74	86
84	Dexter	Jackson	85	54	84	67
84	Brian	Russell	85	55	80	64
83	Sean	Considine	86	64	70	78
82	Kenoy	Kennedy	85	69	72	91
82	Jay	Bellamy	83	61	80	79
82	Mike	Doss	86	60	73	80
81	Adam	Archuleta	85	69	74	84
81	Omar	Stoutmire	84	63	82	76
80	Travares	Tillman	84	64	75	72
80	Roman	Harper	85	62	70	77
80	Michael	Boulware	84	67	62	81
79	Sabby	Piscitelli	92	56	62	68
79	Glenn	Earl	86	65	68	74
78	Bernard	Pollard	86	72	60	78
78	Yeremiah	Bell	86	60	67	70
76	Keith	Lewis	87	57	65	72
76	Jon	McGraw	86	60	66	74
76	Marquand	Manuel	85	64	64	70
76	Todd	Johnson	83	68	68	82
75	Chris	Harris	86	58	64	65
75	Curome	Cox	86	62	68	73
75	Bhawoh	Jue	88	52	64	68
75	James	Sanders	82	70	64	74
75	Gerome	Sapp	83	63	73	71
75	Vernon	Fox	85	62	70	69
74	Clinton	Hart	84	55	68	70
74	Rashad	Washington	84	64	64	71
73	Brandon	Harrison	87	68	54	72
73	Donnie	Nickey	85	60	68	66
73	Calvin	Lowry	84	60	64	71
72	Marvin	White	89	56	51	74
72	Brannon	Condren	91	64	50	69
72	Abram	Elam	86	65	61	75
72	Idrees	Bashir	87	50	70	58
72	Tyrone	Culver	87	58	58	68
72	Darnell	Bing	86	71	48	76
72	Anthony	Smith	87	52	64	63
71	Coy	Wire	85	60	62	80
71	Kevin	McCadam	85	55	79	57
71	Aaron	Rouse	89	57	53	65

ROSTER ATTRIBUTES

NEXT GENERATION

PLAYER WEAPONS

Just like the current generation consoles, the next generation consoles also get the Player Weapons treatment. What is a Player Weapon, you ask? Essentially, it is an elite player who can turn the tide of a game single-handedly. It could be a smart quarterback who has the ability to read the defense, or a shutdown corner who lock-down an opposing receiver. The more Player Weapons your team has, the better your chance of winning; it's that simple. All the offensive, defensive, and even special teams can have Player Weapons on their side. By learning each Player Weapon and the counter, it will put you on the path to success.

PLAYER WEAPONS PLAY CAM ART

Use the Player Weapons play cam art to view where all the Player Weapons are on the field on both sides of the ball. It's a great way to view match ups, and attack weaknesses of your opponent's team.

KNOW YOUR PLAYER WEAPONS

One thing is for sure: EA made it a priority to show you who the Player Weapons are in the game. From the player intros in the beginning of the game to the flashy player information rosters screen, you will always know who your Player Weapons are.

RISK AND REWARDS BY POSITION

There are some different Player Weapons on the next generation consoles than there are on the current generation. In this section, we list all 24, plus give you some info on rewards and risks in the game.

SMART QB

REWARD

Smart Quarterbacks read the defense and reveal their play art.

RISK

Calling a diverse range of plays is the best way to counter a Smart QB.

ACCURATE QB

REWARD

An Accurate Quarterback puts the ball exactly where you want it, and rarely makes an errant throw.

RISK

A quarterback's accuracy isn't guaranteed when throwing deep or on the run.

CANNON ARM QB

REWARD

Cannon Arms throw the farthest and add the most velocity to their passes.

RISK

When throwing deep, these quarterbacks are more likely to overthrow the ball.

SPEED

REWARD

These players are the fastest in the league.

RISK

None.

SPECTACULAR CATCH RECEIVER

REWARD

These receivers perform the most amazing catches in the league.

RISK

Spectacular Catches will often leave the receiver vulnerable to Big Hitters.

ELUSIVE BACK

REWARD

Elusive Backs are true tackle escape artists.

RISK

These backs are generally smaller players and are vulnerable to Big Hitters.

SHUTDOWN CORNER

REWARD

These corners work great at shutting down receivers.

RISK

Shutdown Corners are best in man coverage, there are no guarantees in zone.

HANDS

REWARD

These players have an excellent chance of catching the ball.

RISK

Receiver Spotlight makes it harder for these receivers to get open.

PASS BLOCKER

REWARD

Pass blockers buy the quarterback more time to find an open receiver.

RISK

Finesse Move Defensive Linemen can penetrate even the best pass blockers.

QUICK RECEIVER

REWARD

Quick Receivers are superb at shaking defenders, and always beat the press.

RISK

Shutdown Corners can match these receivers on every cut.

STIFF ARM BALL CARRIER

REWARD

Stiff arm backs have the best and strongest stiff arm moves in the business.

RISK

Stripping the ball is the best way to counter a Stiff Arm Ball Carrier.

CRUSHING RUN BLOCKER

REWARD

Crushing Run Blockers pancake defenders and always lead the backs to daylight.

RISK

Power Move Defensive Linemen can negate the strength of a Crushing Run Blocker.

POSSESSION RECEIVER

REWARD

These players are great at catching in traffic and rarely drop the ball.

RISK

Big Hitters take many of the Possession Receivers' advantages away.

POWER BACK

REWARD

These backs truck through defenders, and when tackled, consistently fall forward.

RISK

Use a Big Hitter to take the Power Back's legs out from underneath him.

ACCURATE KICKER

REWARD

Accurate Kickers hardly ever miss, plain and simple.

RISK

None.

BIG FOOT KICKER

REWARD

Big Foot Kickers and punters kick and punt farther than anyone in the game.

RISK

None.

BRICK WALL DEFENDERS

REWARD

These guys are tackle machines; they consistently wrap up ball carriers.

RISK

These defenders have a tough time wrapping up Power and Elusive Backs.

POWER MOVE D-LINEMAN

REWARD

These lineman use their brute strength to bull rush the offense.

RISK

Crushing Run Blockers can prevent these linemen from entering the backfield.

FINESSE MOVE D-LINEMAN

REWARD

These players are great pass rushers.

RISK

Pass Blockers take the edge away from these defensive linemen.

SMART SAFETY

REWARD

Smart Safeties read the offense's play and reveal all their play art.

RISK

Calling a diverse range of plays is the best way to counter a Smart Safety.

SMART CORNER

REWARD

Smart corners read the offense's play and reveal the receiver's play art.

RISK

Calling a diverse range of plays is the best way to counter a Smart Corner.

PRESS COVERAGE CORNER

REWARD

These corners are excellent for pressing a receiver at the line of scrimmage.

RISK

Pressing a Quick Receiver leaves the corner exposed to getting beat deep.

BIG HITTER

REWARD

The hit stick works best with Big Hitters and increases the chance of a fumble.

RISK

It's harder to force the fumble when the ball carrier is covering the ball.

SMART LINEBACKER

REWARD

Smart linebackers read the offense and reveal the play art between the tackles.

RISK

Calling a diverse range of plays is the best way to counter a Smart Linebacker.

PLAYERS BY POSITION

Smart QBs (Awareness 92+)	Cannon Arm QBs (Throw Power 95+)	Accurate QBs (Throw Accuracy 94+)	Speed QB's (Speed 85+)
Peyton Manning	JaMarcus Russell	Peyton Manning	Michael Vick
Tom Brady	Brett Favre	Marc Bulger	Vince Young
Marc Bulger	Carson Palmer	Drew Brees	Seneca Wallace
Drew Brees	Byron Leftwich	Tom Brady	
Carson Palmer	Michael Vick	Carson Palmer	Elusive Back (Elusiveness 92+)
Matt Hasselbeck	Donovan McNabb	Chad Pennington	Reggie Bush
	Peyton Manning	Philip Rivers	LaDainian Tomlinson
	Jay Cutler		Brian Westbrook
	Daunte Culpepper		Darren Sproles
	Rex Grossman		Maurice Jones-Drew
			DeAngelo Williams
			Warrick Dunn
			Clinton Portis

NEXT GENERATION

Power Back (Trucking 90+)

- Larry Johnson
- Brandon Jacobs
- Jamal Lewis
- Rudi Johnson
- Steven Jackson
- Shaun Alexander
- Marion Barber
- Willis McGahee
- Michael Turner
- Maurice Jones-Drew
- Ronnie Brown
- Laurence Maroney
- Ron Dayne
- LaDainian Tomlinson
- Deuce McAllister
- Frank Gore

Stiff Arm Ball Carrier (Stiff Arm 95+)

- Willis McGahee
- Jamal Lewis
- Laurence Maroney
- Larry Johnson
- Steven Jackson
- LaDainian Tomlinson
- Rudi Johnson
- Deuce McAllister
- Shaun Alexander
- Edgerrin James
- Anquan Boldin
- Terrell Owens
- Kevin Jones

Quick Receiver (Running Route 91+)

- Marvin Harrison
- Torry Holt
- Reggie Wayne
- Jeremy Shockey
- Chad Johnson
- Larry Fitzgerald
- Kellen Winslow
- Hines Ward
- Todd Heap
- Darrell Jackson
- Anquan Boldin
- Terrel Owens
- Deion Branch
- Steve Smith
- Donald Driver
- Javon Walker

Quick Receiver (Running Route 91+)

- Isaac Bruce
- Terry Glenn
- T.J. Houshmandzadeh
- Tony Gonzalez
- Antonio Gates

Possession Receiver (Catch in Traffic 90+)

- Hines Ward
- Anquan Boldin
- Steve Smith
- T.J. Houshmandzadeh
- Andre Johnson
- Larry Fitzgerald
- Marvin Harrison
- Reggie Wayne
- Kellen Winslow
- Laveranues Coles
- Chad Johnson
- Deion Branch
- Marques Colston
- Jason Witten
- Wes Welker
- Derrick Mason
- Donald Driver
- Javon Walker
- Tony Gonzalez
- Antonio Gates
- Todd Heap
- Alge Crumpler
- Jeremy Shockey

Spectacular Catch Receiver (Spec Catch 90+)

- Plaxico Burress
- Randy Moss
- Brandon Lloyd
- Dwayne Jarrett
- Chris Chambers
- Chad Johnson
- Javon Walker
- Sidney Rice
- Larry Fitzgerald
- Marvin Harrison
- Calvin Johnson
- Roy Williams
- Andre Johnson
- Braylon Edwards
- Matt Jones

Spectacular Catch Receiver (Continued)

- Matt Jones
- Torry Holt
- Drew Bennett
- Malcolm Floyd
- Anquan Boldin
- Reggie Wayne
- Todd Heap
- Antonio Gates
- Marques Colston

Hands (90+ Catching)

- Tony Gonzalez
- Antonio Gates
- Marvin Harrison
- Reggie Wayne
- Torry Holt
- Larry Fitzgerald
- Hines Ward
- Steve Smith
- Chad Johnson
- Anquan Boldin
- Mushin Muhammad
- Terry Glenn
- Donald Driver
- Derrick Mason
- Isaac Bruce
- Laveranues Coles
- T.J. Houshmandzadeh
- Roy Williams
- Deion Branch
- Joe Horn
- Javon Walker
- Patrick Crayton
- Mike Furrey
- Reggie Bush
- Jerricho Cotchery
- Brian Westbrook

Shutdown Corner (Man Coverage 92+)

- Champ Bailey
- Al Harris
- Lito Sheppard
- Nate Clements
- Asante Samuel
- Chris McAlister
- Rashean Mathis
- Patrick Surtain

Shutdown Corner (Continued)

- Marcus Trufant
- Dré Bly
- Nnamdi Asomugha

Smart Corner (Play Recognition 90+)

- Champ Bailey
- Ronde Barber
- Lito Sheppard
- Rashean Mathis
- Chris McAlister
- Asante Samuel
- Nathan Vasher
- Walt Harris
- Antoine Winfield
- Al Harris
- Charles Woodson
- Ty Law

Press Coverage Corner (Press 92+)

- Al Harris
- Champ Bailey
- Ronde Barber
- Nate Clements
- Chris McAlister
- Asante Samuel
- Dunta Robinson
- Charles Tillman
- Quentin Jammer
- Charles Woodson
- Carlos Rogers
- Rashean Mathis
- Antoine Winfield

Smart Safety (Play Recognition 90+)

- Brian Dawkins
- John Lynch
- Ed Reed
- Bob Sanders
- Rodney Harrison
- Troy Polamalu
- Darren Sharper

NEXT GENERATION

Smart Linebacker (Play Recognition 90+)

Derrick Brooks
Donnie Edwards
Zach Thomas
Brian Urlacher
Tedy Bruschi
Ray Lewis
Lofa Tatupu
James Farrior
Antonio Pierce
Jonathan Vilma
London Fletcher-Baker
Mike Peterson
Junior Seau
Jeremiah Trotter

Big Hitter (Hit Power 88+)

Sean Taylor
Shawne Merriman
John Lynch
Roy Williams
Brian Urlacher
Rodney Harrison
Brian Dawkins
Donovin Darius
Ray Lewis
Joey Porter
Keith Bulluck
Todd Johnson
Lance Briggs
Bart Scott
James Farrior
Takeo Spikes
Tory Polamalu
D.J. Williams
Chris Harris
Jermaine Phillips
Ken Hamlin
Kenoy Kennedy
Greg Wesley
Mike Minter
Ed Hartwell
Julius Peppers
Lofa Tatupu
LaRon Landry
Patrick Willis
Ernie Sims
Marlon McCree

Brick Wall Defender (Tackle 91+)

Zach Thomas
London Fletcher-Baker
Jonathan Vilma
Ray Lewis
James Farrior
Lofa Tatupu
Kirk Morrison
A.J. Hawk
Antonio Pierce
Andra Davis
Shawne Merriman
Lance Briggs
Jeremiah Trotter
Keith Brooking
Mike Peterson
Marcus Washington
Julian Peterson
Brian Urlacher
DeMeco Ryans
Derrick Brooks
John Lynch
Ernie Sims
Joey Porter
Keith Bulluck
Roy Williams
DJ Williams
Rodney Harrison

Finesse Move D-Lineman (Finesse Moves 92+)

Julius Peppers
Shawne Merriman (LB)
Terrell Suggs (LB)
Leonard Little
Jason Taylor (LB)
Dwight Freeney
Osi Umenyiora
Robert Mathis
DemMarcus Ware (LB)
Will Smith
Adewale Ogunleye
Derrick Burgess
Kamerion Wimbley (LB)
Jevon Kearse
Kevin Williams
Tommie Harris
Jared Allen
Joey Porter (LB)

Finesse Move D-Lineman (Continued)

Adalius Thomas (LB)
John Abraham
Bertrand Berry
Warren Sapp

Power Move D-Lineman (Power Moves 92+)

Casey Hampton
Jamal Williams
Marcus Stroud
Shaun Rogers
Richard Seymour
John Henderson
Shawne Merriman (LB)
Luis Castillo
Kevin Williams
Kris Jenkins
Ted Washington
Trevor Pryce
Rod Coleman
Pat Williams
Aaron Kampman
Tommie Harris
Vince Wilfork
Aaron Schobel
Bryant Young
Michael Strahan
Shaun Ellis
Haloti Ngata

Crushing Run Blocker (Run Block Stength 95+)

Larry Allen
Jonathan Ogden
Jon Jansen
Flozell Adams
Willie Anderson
Leonard Davis
Walter Jones
Jon Runyan
Chris Samuels
Shawn Andrews
William Thomas
Steve Hutchinson
Marvel Smith
Nick Hardwick
Marcus McNeil
Alan Faneca
Brian Waters
Vince Manuwai

Crushing Run Blocker (Continued)

Derrick Dockery
Kris Dielman
Lorenzo Neal
Mack Strong
Dan Kreider
Ovie Mughelli

Pass Blocker (Pass Block Stength 94+)

Bryant McKinnie
Tarik Glenn
Jonathan Ogden
Chris Samuels
Orlando Pace
William Thomas
Walter Jones
Randy Thomas
Jeff Saturday
Olin Kreutz
Eric Steinback
Joe Thomas
Jordan Gross
Matt Light
Jamaal Brown
Marcus McNeill
Levi Jones
Ruben Brown

Accurate Kicker (Kick Accuracy 92+)

Adam Vinatieri
Matt Stover
Jeff Wilkins
Rian Lindell
Robbie Gould
Shayne Graham
Jason Elam
Jason Hanson
Nate Kaeding

Big Foot Kicker (Kick Power 93+)

Sebastian Janikowski
Neil Rackers
Jason Elam
Matt Bryant
Josh Brown
Rob Bironas
Dave Rayner
John Kasay

Big Foot Kicker (Continued)	Speed (Speed 96+)	Speed (Continued)	Speed (Continued)
Mat McBriar (Punter)	Devin Hester	Bethel Johnson	Yamon Figurs
Shane Lechler (Punter)	Reggie Bush	Devery Henderson	Johnathan Joseph
Jon Ryan (Punter)	Tye Hill	DeAngelo Hall	Stanford Routt
Brian Moorman (Punter)	Ted Ginn Jr.	Fabian Washington	Justin Miller
Ben Graham (Punter)	Joey Galloway	Jerome Mathis	Allen Rossum
Michael Koenen (Punter)	Champ Bailey	Lee Evans	Michael Bennett
	Randy Moss	Donte Stallworth	Bernard Berrian
	Santana Moss	Steve Smith	Willie Parker
	Will Allen	Laveranues Coles	

RING OF A CHAMPION

Rings are 3D objects that represent your overall gamer level. The more rings you have, the higher your gamer level. Collect rings by playing games and completing tasks. Tasks can be completed in any order and have points associated with them. Rings also contain stats that the gamer can view via a card that sits alongside the rings. As you move up in skill and experience, you collect more trophies. This allows you to be able to customize each of the five rings with as much as you like, as well as adding or changing team logos and colors to those of your choice. When going online you can view your opponent's rings and he can also view yours. This allows you to see how well you match up with your opponent and to see how good he is.

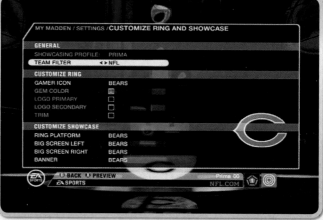

RISKING GAME TROPHIES

You can choose to risk a preexisting Game Trophy or create a new one. The Game Trophy keeps track of games played, game winners, and stats for all games that an individual Game Trophy is put at risk on, or off-line.

The winner of the Game Trophy will have it displayed in their Showcase, the loser will not be able to see the trophy although the history of the game played will be maintained in that trophy history.

FRANCHISE MODE

ranchise mode is back on the Xbox 360/PS3 and this year it includes an brand new "owner" component. You start off by choosing your favorite teams with their current-day rosters, and then try to stay on top for up to three full decades. To begin a franchise, choose the number of users, select the team for each user, and choose what options you want to play your franchise with.

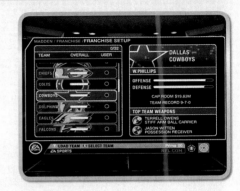

Here is list of some of franchise mode updates you will find in Franchise Mode for the next generation systems.

FRONT OFFICE MODE

You take over a team as the owner. You are responsible for your team's finances, stadium, and scouting players all in an effort to build your team to one ultimate goal: to win a championship.

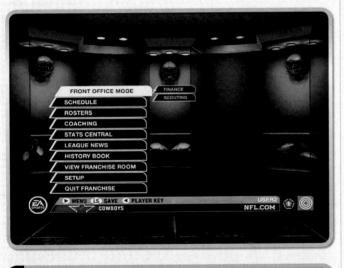

SCOUTING

First you must hire a scouting agency to scout players. Once you do, you will want to scout players all season long leading up to the draft. The longer the scouting period goes, the better the indication of how a player will pan out for your team.

BUSTS AND GEMS

How many times have you drafted a player in the first or second round only for him to turn into a bust? Conversely how many times have you wanted to pull the trigger on a quarterback in seventh round from a small school, but then decided not to because you weren't sure if he would even make the team?

Now you can do your homework and find a diamond in the rough just like the real NFL Scouts do. If you don't do your homework, you might end up regretting it by selecting what you thought was a surefire hit in the first round, only to find out later that he is a bust.

SUPERSIM

If you don't want to play a full game because you are blowing out the CPU controller or vice versa, no problem. The SuperSim feature allows you to sit back and watch the game in progress at any point. One nice feature is that if for some reason the CPU comes back, you can always jump right back in and take control. This feature is also available at the schedule screen. This allows you to start simming the game without actually playing it. If your team gets behind, you can join in and make things right.

IMPORT DRAFT CLASS

You can now import any *NCAA Football 08* draft class into *Madden NFL 08* on the Xbox 360/PS3, for those of you who like to play the college game. This is really a nice feature because you get to watch your college players become stars in the NFL.

SUPERSTAR MODE

You have won the Super Bowl as an owner, but have you ever seen yourself picking off a game-saving pass and taking the rock all the way in for a score as you high step into the end zone? Now you can, because Superstar Mode makes its debut on the next generation consoles. Create a Superstar either from scratch, by importing an NCAA Legend from *NCAA Football 08*, or by choosing a rookie from the 2007 draft class and guiding his life from pre-draft workouts through his entire career. Can your Superstar have a fantastic NFL career and make it all the way to the Pro Football Hall of Fame in Canton?

SUPERSTAR MODE UPDATE

PLAY AS: SUPERSTAR

You will now be able to select a rookie from the 2007 Draft Class and determine the outcome of his career. Guide him through his first training camp and then to his first Super Bowl victory.

IMPORT NCAA LEGEND

Your legend has graduated from college, but that does not mean his football career is over. Import him in *Madden NFL 08*'s Superstar Mode, and take him to the Hall of Fame.

OFF-SEASON WORKOUTS

Just because the season is over doesn't mean you take the summer off. You can now take part in the organized team activities. It is in your Superstar's best interest to attend as many of these as possible, as ratings and influence points are at stake.

MINI GAMES

Develop your skills in six mini-games intended to test your speed, strength, and skills. Each mini-game has a distinctive set of controls explained onscreen before the event begins. Your performance goes a long way toward increasing your Gamer Level and Ring Builder Meter.

FORTY-YARD DASH

Get your player across the line as quickly as possible. Right before the drill starts, push back on either analog stick to get into the ready stance. On the fourth beep, the game starts. Make your player run by alternately pushing the sticks back then releasing them. As you pick up speed, you enter the Zone where time slows down. Right before you cross the finish line, pull the right trigger to lean over the line and cut tenths of a second off of your time.

NEXT GENERATION

BENCH PRESS

To lift the bar, push the two analog sticks up together and release them once you hit the green zone. After you release, the weights drop. Push up on the sticks again when entering the blue zone. Your stamina will decrease over time and if you hit the red zone. Press LT and RT (for 360) or L2 and R2 (for PS3) quickly when the weights are falling to recover and increase your stamina.

The next four all involve getting on the field and making plays against a CPU opponent. Pick your favorite team and take on the challenge to complete passes, rush for yards, make blocks, receive passes, and defend in coverage.

QUARTERBACK CHALLENGE

In this drill you have 10 passes to rack up as many points as possible—for catches, yards, and TDs. If you can string them together, you can pick up bonuses for consecutive successes. If your throwing meter runs out before you make a throw, you lose that round. After your 10 passes, the CPU gets 10 with you in coverage.

RUNNINGBACK CHALLENGE

In this drill you have 60 seconds to get as many rushing yards and touchdowns as possible. Use your lead blocker to spring your man for maximum yardage. If you can't put the ball in the end zone, get out of bounds to stop the clock. After you take your shot with the ball, the CPU gets the ball and you play the part of the tackler.

COVERAGE CHALLENGE

This drill has two parts. In round one, you are the wide receiver trying to break open for the pass. You get 10 attempts to make a play on the ball. You might as well run deep routes and go for the extra points that a touchdown will give you. After your reps, you take the part of the cornerback and try to prevent the receiver from making the grab.

LINEMAN CHALLENGE

You begin the drill by controlling an offensive lineman. Get in front of your blockers and lay the wood down on the defense. Use the strafe button to hold your position until you see where your back is going; that way you'll be in the best possible position to make the block. After your reps, you switch and play defense. Use your power moves to make the tackle.

PLAYER WEAPONS IN MINI-CAMP

A new addition to the Mini-challenges is the ability to select Player Weapons on both sides of the ball based on the challenge. For instance, for the Quarterback Challenge you can select one of the three receiver Player Weapons to throw to or you can simply select random. You must also select one of three defensive back Player Weapons or just select random.

MINI GAME TIP

The Quarterback, Runningback, Coverage, and Lineman Challenges are good for helping you learning stick control. We suggest spending a lot of time in these challenges. Don't worry about scores; instead concentrate on working on your stick control. Once you get them down, you will be that much better against a live human opponent.

PRACTICE MODE

Practice mode allows for you to take your favorite team to the lab and run plays without having to worry about hurting your stats or players. Most top players that play *Madden NFL 08* will tell you that this is where they spend most of their time when they are not playing in tourneys or online. This allows them to learn the nuts and bolts of the game. For those that are new to the game, there is no pressure and no play clock. This allows newer players to master a set of plays and learn the new controls in practice mode at their own pace. Use the random play feature to give different looks on both sides of the field.

CREATE A TEAM

Create every aspect of your team including geographical location, uniform, and stadium, then play with them in franchise and exhibition games. If you feel the need to put your favorite high school or college team into the game, no problem: now you can in *Madden NFL 08* on the next generation systems.

To get to the Create-a-Team Menu, select My Madden on the main menu screen.

Once actually in the Create-a-Team Menu, you have three options to choose from. They are as follows:

UNIFORM

The Uniform screen gives you several options for choosing your team's colors for your helmets, pants, and jerseys.

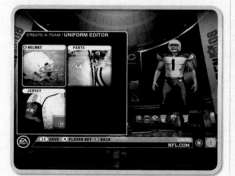

STADIUM

The Stadium option allows you to create the look of your stadium from scratch. You can change sidelines, end zones, environment, lights, roof, edge wall, field, and even a particular section's name. Dawg Pound anyone?

TEAM DATA

Team Data is the last of the options to choose from. Here you can edit your team's info, team type, and logos.

CREATE-A-PLAYER

Create-a-Player is back and better than ever in *Madden NFL 08*. Create an NFL star exactly how you want him, and add him to your team. Users are now able to fully customize the look of their player, but there is a catch. In order to set your player's ratings, you must earn it. Using mini-games, users will now need to actually run the 40-yard dash, complete a bench press as well as a skill game to set their ratings. Also, players will now be able to select Player Type templates where they will be able to pick their player's tendency from the start. This helps take away some confusion when it comes to wanting to set a player up correctly.

- Enter My Madden and select Create-a-Player.

- Once here, you may set some of your player's basic attributes, such as Name, Position, Team and Jersey Number.

- Selecting Bio will allow you to edit your player's biographical data such as birth date, etc.

- Appearance will allow users to change a multitude of physical attributes, such as height, weight, arm size, etc.

- The Accessories menu allows the user to completely trick out their player using all of our new equipment.

- Once you have locked in your player's looks and bio, press the start button.

- This is the Player Types screen. Here, the user is able to select the Player Type that they would like to create. This is essentially the mold that you will be creating your player in.

- Once you have chosen a Player Type, you will be transitioned into the mini-games.

- After completing the mini-games, you will be returned to the overview screen where you will see your player's final ratings. After this, your player is added to that team.

NEW PLAY CALL MENU

When you first get on the sticks in *Madden NFL 08* for the next generation consoles, you will notice there is a new Play Call menu screen. You can still select plays by formation, but instead of having six formations appear on the screen at the same time, there is now list of formations based on the set you call. For instance say you selected the I-Form set tab; you will see formations from that set just below.

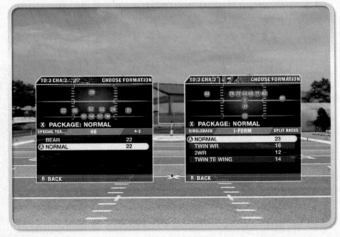

318

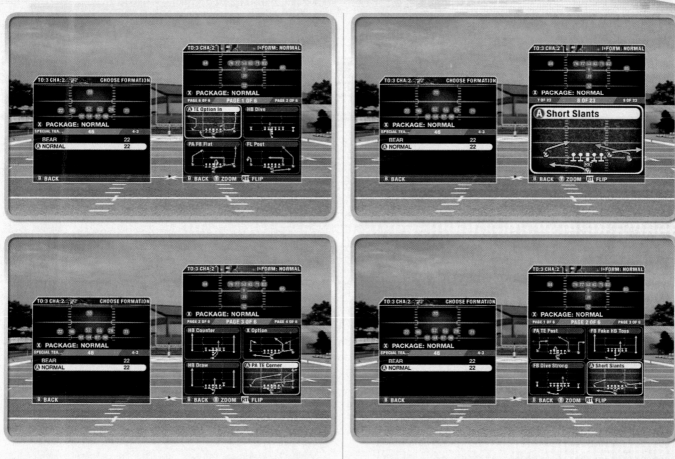

Once you actually select the set and formation you want to call, you will then go into actual Play Call screen. Instead of seeing six plays on the screen like in *Madden NFL 07*, you will now see four. You can even zoom in one play to get a closer look by pressing the zoom button.

To select a play, press down the Ⓐ button for the 360 or ✕ button for the PS3. The play will now be called and you will be taken the field.

To bluff your opponent, press and hold the Ⓐ button for the 360 or ✕ button for the PS3 on the play you want to call. Continue to hold it down and cycle through other plays. Your opponent will not be able to tell what play you called. Once you are done bluffing him, release Ⓐ button for the 360 or ✕ button for the PS3, and they head to the field.

RECEIVER SPOTLIGHT

Receiver Spotlight gives the human-controlled player on defense the ability to neutralize the threat of a particularly good receiver that has been scorching your defense throughout the game. By using the Receiver Spotlight, it puts extra attention on the receiver that has been spotlighted. It puts defenders in position to either swat the ball down or pick off the pass.

HOW TO EXECUTE

Pull the right trigger for the 360 or hold the R2 trigger for the PS3 to enter the spotlight mode before the snap. Press the receiver's pass icon that you would like to have spotlighted.

RECEIVER SPOTLIGHT TIP

Spotlighting a receiver is a great way to neutralize the threat by having solid coverage around him; however, paying too much attention to him might leave other receivers in his area open.

BLOCKING

Anytime you see a big run or pass play on your 10 o'clock news channel, you only see the part where the quarterback makes the throw, or the runningback uses a spin move to be open. Before any of that can happen, the offensive linemen must protect the quarterback or open holes for the running back. Over the years of this series, the offensive blocking has never really been tweaked. For the most part, the blocking was pretty basic. In *Madden NFL 08*, all that has changed with new blocking animations, cut blocking logic, better pass blocking, and double-teams and zone blocking.

NEW BLOCKING ANIMATIONS

EA has captured all new animations to get the offensive linemen off the ball quicker. This includes new kick back steps for pass blockers, new lateral steps for zone blocking, new pulling initial moves, and all new regular run blocking initial moves.

NEW CUT BLOCKING LOGIC

Cut blocking is a vital part of an offense. In *Madden NFL 08* on the next generation, you will see it happen on the field to help protect the quarterback in the pocket or to free up the ball carrier.

- Big Momentum Differences: Basically this means that if a defender is coming at a stationary block, the offensive linemen will consider blocking them.
- Desperation Cuts: If the blocker gets beat, he will still make every effort to try and cut the defender.

BETTER PASS BLOCKING

Offensive linemen do a better job at getting in pass blocking position by getting better depth. This should limit some of the nanos that have plagued the versions of earlier games. Also, an unassigned blocker will move to get in position to help a teammate if they are getting beat.

DOUBLE TEAMS & ZONE BLOCKING

Of all the new blocking improvements, doubles and zone blocking may be the biggest improvement. There are three types of double-teams results you find in *Madden NFL 08*.

- Blocker Success: If the first-level target is blocked properly by being double-teamed, then one of the blockers will move on to the second level target.
- Defender Split: The first-level defender splits the double-team and gets into the backfield.

- Defender Sink: If the first-level defender recognizes a double-team, he may drop to the ground to create a pile. This will free up the second-level defender to make the tackle.

POWER AND FINESSE DEFENSIVE MOVES

One of the wishes that players have voiced over the years is the ability to get pressure on the quarterback while in control of defensive linemen. Power and Finesse Defensive Moves give that ability on the next generation systems, provided that the defensive linemen is a player who can push the pocket, such as Chicago Bears' powerful defensive tackle Tommy Harris or a great finesse pass rusher such as Panthers' defensive end Julius Peppers.

POWER D-LINEMEN

Power move defensive linemen push offensive linemen into the backfield in order to blow up the run, or get to the quarterback to produce sacks by using their brute strength.

To perform a power move, press the RB button on the 360 or the R1 button on the PS3.

FINESSE D-LINEMEN

Finesse move defensive linemen are great pass rushers. They use swims and spins to get past offensive linemen to get to the quarterback.

To perform a finesse move, press the LB button on the 360 or the L1 button on the PS3.

GANG TACKLING NEXT GENERATION CONSOLES

Gang tacking made it to the PS3 version of *Madden NFL 07*, but missed the 360 version. This year both systems get gang tackling, which is a big deal in the player community. For years, players have wanted some type of gang tackling the game; now there is. What gang tackling will do is allow for more than one defender to make the tackle on a ball carrier. How many times over the years have you seen a big, bruising runningback break a tackle by a single defender, and then pick up more yardage. If a few tacklers would have tried to tackle him at the same time, chances are that he would have been able to break off a big run. Now, that's not to say L.T. isn't going to shrug off defenders as he is being gang tackled, because he still will; after all, he is L.T. However, smaller backs are not going to be so lucky. If multiple defenders are attempting to bring the smaller ball carrier down, chances are that he is going to be stopped in his tracks.

NEW RATINGS

Armed with a much more powerful next-gen system, EA Sports has expanded the roster ratings system by adding an additional six more on top of the 19 that were added in *Madden NFL 07*. The new ones deal with receiving and pass coverage.

PLAYER RATINGS

RUSHING RATINGS

TRK – Trucking
ELU – Elusiveness
BCV – Ball Carrier Vision
SFA – Stiff Arm
SPM – Spin Move
JKM – Juke Move

RECEIVER RATINGS

CIT – Catch in Traffic (new)
SPC – Spectacular Catch (new)
RLS – Release (new)
RTE – Route Running (new)

DEFENSIVE LINE/ LINEBACKER RATINGS

PMV – Power Moves
FMV – Finesse Moves
BSH – Block Shedding
PRS – Pursuit

COVERAGE RATINGS

MCV – Man Coverage
ZCV – Zone Coverage
PRS – Press (new)
POW – Hit Power (new)

RUN/PASS BLOCKING RATINGS

PBK – Pass Block
RBK – Run Block
IBL – Impact Blocking
RBS – Run Block Strength
RBF – Run Block Foot Work
PBS – Pass Block Strength
PBF – Pass Block Foot Work

These ratings readily represent EA Tiburon's desire to put the most realistic football experience possible in your hands. Now receivers and defensive backs are even more distinguished on the field.

Be sure to look over the ratings of your linebackers and defensive linemen. When controlling them, you will want to take advantage of your best skill set. If you have great finesse ratings, then use your spin moves to attack the offensive line. If power is your thing, bulldoze that lineman in front of you and knock him on his backside.

Pay attention to how your secondary covers best. If they are highly skilled at zone coverage, stay away from man. If they are strong man defenders, then put them out on an island by themselves and get after the quarterback.

Finally, you can decide to structure your offensive line to either a running machine, or pick guys that can help you in the passing game. Obviously, having balanced guys is the best solution, but sometimes you have to take what you can get in the free agent market. When this is the case, get guys that fit your style of offense best.

TEAM RATINGS

Teams	Overall	Offense	Defense
Bears	91	85	97
Bengals	87	92	74
Bills	67	65	70
Broncos	89	89	89
Browns	67	67	74
Buccaneers	74	75	88
Cardinals	75	79	72
Chargers	95	92	92
Chiefs	80	80	78
Colts	94	99	75
Cowboys	87	88	85
Dolphins	78	71	85
Eagles	87	87	86
Falcons	80	80	78
49ers	82	82	82
Giants	81	82	80
Jaguars	86	78	93
Jets	84	84	81
Lions	76	81	70
Packers	80	80	83
Panthers	85	86	88
Patriots	97	97	94
Raiders	67	59	91
Rams	83	94	75
Ravens	90	76	99
Redskins	81	77	84
Saints	88	96	75
Seahawks	89	90	87
Steelers	88	85	90
Texans	73	70	72
Titans	74	68	79
Vikings	67	62	65

ROSTER ATTRIBUTES

The following offensive and defensive lists include every player who is rated approximately 70 or above in his position, and have been sorted by overall rating. However, the overall rating is just a starting point. Each list includes additional attributes related to the position. Consider these attributes when you search for the perfect player to complement your team.

OFFENSIVE / PLAYER LIST

C Centers

Overall Rating	First Name	Last Name	Run Block Strength	Run Block Footwork	Pass Block Strength	Pass Block Footwork
97	Olin	Kreutz	92	93	95	95
96	Jeff	Saturday	88	87	97	98
92	Tom	Nalen	85	98	84	93
92	Nick	Hardwick	95	82	86	75
92	Matt	Birk	87	96	90	93
91	Kevin	Mawae	90	83	92	80
90	LeCharles	Bentley	92	85	92	82
90	Andre	Gurode	90	75	88	70
90	Brad	Meester	89	88	92	84
89	Todd	McClure	75	95	79	91
89	Nick	Mangold	88	89	89	88
88	Casey	Wiegmann	76	97	79	95
87	Dan	Koppen	89	80	89	78
87	Mike	Flanagan	89	87	88	93
86	Shaun	O'Hara	89	78	83	74
86	Dominic	Raiola	84	88	80	87
86	Mike	Flynn	86	78	86	72
85	Casey	Rabach	89	76	85	80
85	Jeff	Faine	86	90	85	87
84	John	Wade	87	75	87	76
84	Jamaal	Jackson	84	78	84	80
84	Eric	Heitmann	90	77	85	73
84	Chris	Spencer	89	90	82	88
83	Hank	Fraley	91	72	87	70
83	Jake	Grove	87	87	87	83
82	Scott	Wells	82	74	80	75
82	Justin	Hartwig	90	84	88	82
82	Andy	McCollum	86	75	85	77
82	Sean	Mahan	84	79	82	75
80	Melvin	Fowler	84	79	84	76
80	David	Baas	87	75	85	70
80	Jeremy	Newberry	89	80	86	75
80	Chukky	Okobi	86	83	84	75
79	Eric	Ghiaciuc	84	69	78	66
79	Ryan	Kalil	80	90	82	90
78	Al	Johnson	86	69	84	65
77	Ross	Tucker	84	75	80	72
76	Grey	Ruegamer	85	55	80	58
74	Alex	Stepanovich	78	75	82	78
73	Nick	Leckey	84	66	80	65
73	Wade	Smith	84	70	84	60
72	Dylan	Gandy	82	73	85	80
72	Samson	Satele	80	70	86	85
72	Doug	Datish	80	70	82	75
72	Eugene	Amano	82	66	78	65
71	Cory	Withrow	83	78	81	74
70	Blaine	Saipaia	83	70	80	65
70	Ike	Ndukwe	80	60	76	58
70	Leroy	Harris	87	77	86	72
70	Norm	Katnik	85	85	85	85

FB Fullbacks

Overall Rating	First Name	Last Name	Speed	Run Block	Pass Block	Impact Block
98	Lorenzo	Neal	65	85	55	100
94	Jeremi	Johnson	70	72	55	90
94	Mack	Strong	80	66	48	88
93	Dan	Kreider	63	82	65	96
92	Heath	Evans	82	64	59	77
91	Ovie	Mughelli	63	77	52	90
89	Justin	Griffith	80	60	50	80
89	Tony	Richardson	77	64	50	78
88	Mike	Karney	72	64	56	85
87	Jim	Finn	65	70	60	86
85	Terrelle	Smith	62	75	64	92
85	Greg	Jones	85	57	40	70
84	Darian	Barnes	65	66	57	91
83	Kyle	Johnson	77	62	46	78
83	Mike	Sellers	64	71	65	80
83	Jameel	Cook	75	60	54	90
82	Jason	McKie	72	66	53	87
82	Lawrence	Vickers	78	62	45	77
82	Cory	Schlesinger	74	58	54	85
82	Zack	Crockett	76	58	44	75
82	Ahmard	Hall	73	62	52	90
81	Brad	Hoover	75	57	50	66
80	Mike	Alstott	82	50	45	75
80	Lousaka	Polite	63	68	55	85
80	Brandon	Miree	80	56	50	75
79	Shawn	Bryson	89	50	50	62
78	Obafemi	Ayanbadejo	74	62	52	75
78	Ryan	Neufeld	62	62	56	75
78	Ben	Utecht	74	54	44	75
78	Moran	Norris	72	60	45	78
78	Casey	Fitzsimmons	72	60	54	74
78	Justin	Green	72	62	56	70
77	B.J.	Askew	82	58	47	65
77	Oliver	Hoyte	74	62	52	78
77	Madison	Hedgecock	70	64	48	84
76	Thomas	Tapeh	80	50	40	75
76	Le'Ron	McClain	68	57	50	70
76	Vonta	Leach	70	58	50	82
74	Kris	Wilson	78	52	45	65
74	Josh	Parry	65	60	55	76
73	Brad	Cieslak	70	60	55	73
72	Robert	Douglas	76	58	45	70
71	Andrew	Pinnock	73	55	40	75
67	Derrick	Wimbush	88	49	41	55
66	Greg	Hanoian	72	60	45	68

HB Halfbacks

Overall Rating	First Name	Last Name	Speed	Agility	Elusive	Truck
99	LaDainian	Tomlinson	96	99	100	92
96	Larry	Johnson	93	90	85	98
96	Steven	Jackson	90	92	89	97
95	Shaun	Alexander	88	91	82	96
94	Brian	Westbrook	94	98	97	76
93	Frank	Gore	92	93	90	91
92	Willis	McGahee	92	92	79	94
92	Clinton	Portis	94	94	93	88
91	Rudi	Johnson	88	86	76	96
91	Edgerrin	James	88	90	84	89
89	Maurice	Jones-Drew	94	95	96	93
89	Fred	Taylor	92	93	89	86
89	Deuce	McAllister	89	86	72	95
89	Reggie	Bush	98	99	99	73
89	Willie	Parker	97	91	88	84
88	Carnell	Williams	93	94	91	84
88	Ronnie	Brown	93	90	80	90
88	Warrick	Dunn	95	96	94	65
88	Thomas	Jones	90	90	87	88
87	Travis	Henry	89	90	84	87
87	Joseph	Addai	93	93	91	84
86	Marion	Barber	88	87	87	90
86	Julius	Jones	91	93	89	81
86	Chester	Taylor	89	94	88	84
86	Ahman	Green	90	85	76	88
85	Michael	Turner	92	85	77	94
85	Laurence	Maroney	90	90	85	90
85	Adrian	Peterson	93	93	90	85
84	Cedric	Benson	87	87	82	86
84	Jamal	Lewis	87	85	68	96
84	Kevin	Jones	93	88	82	85
84	DeShaun	Foster	92	92	89	84
84	DeAngelo	Williams	93	94	95	80
84	Ladell	Betts	88	89	82	87
83	Marshawn	Lynch	91	92	82	85
83	Jerious	Norwood	96	90	80	84
83	Brandon	Jacobs	87	88	76	98
83	Dominic	Rhodes	89	91	86	80
83	LaMont	Jordan	87	82	74	87
82	Priest	Holmes	85	84	78	76
82	Tatum	Bell	96	87	88	78
80	Kenny	Irons	91	94	87	77
80	Michael	Pittman	87	85	80	85
80	Reuben	Droughns	85	82	64	93
80	Leon	Washington	91	94	91	75
80	Maurice	Morris	91	90	87	75
80	Ron	Dayne	85	83	68	92
79	Correll	Buckhalter	86	84	74	88
79	Vernand	Morency	92	93	88	77
79	Kevin	Faulk	89	92	88	65
79	Chris	Brown	88	86	78	80
78	Mike	Bell	87	85	80	86
78	Sammy	Morris	87	83	79	84
78	Michael	Bush	87	86	77	85
78	Brian	Leonard	85	87	79	84
78	LenDale	White	86	83	67	89
77	Chris	Perry	89	87	85	72
77	Brandon	Jackson	90	93	87	76
77	Najeh	Davenport	86	83	68	89
77	Mewelde	Moore	88	90	89	67

HB Halfbacks (continued)

Overall Rating	First Name	Last Name	Speed	Agility	Elusive	Truck
76	Adrian	Peterson	88	88	86	82
76	Darren	Sproles	92	94	95	65
76	Musa	Smith	87	83	71	87
76	Chris	Henry	94	92	80	83
76	Wali	Lundy	86	87	82	77
75	Anthony	Thomas	86	82	58	88
75	LaBrandon	Toefield	86	84	74	84
75	Justin	Fargas	93	91	78	70
75	Travis	Minor	88	88	87	65
75	Antonio	Pittman	90	91	80	72
75	Kevan	Barlow	85	84	69	86
74	Jerome	Harrison	91	92	90	67
74	Michael	Bennett	97	89	82	65
74	DeDe	Dorsey	88	88	85	72
74	Lorenzo	Booker	92	96	91	50
74	Tony	Hunt	85	80	68	90
74	Maurice	Hicks	88	87	85	75
74	Michael	Robinson	86	88	80	83
74	Alvin	Pearman	87	90	87	72
74	Cedric	Houston	86	78	66	87
74	Nick	Goings	86	82	69	79
74	Mike	Anderson	84	77	55	89
74	Derrick	Blaylock	92	88	84	65
74	Aaron	Stecker	88	89	88	70
74	Verron	Haynes	86	85	70	82
73	Kenny	Watson	87	83	78	75
73	Selvin	Young	90	90	75	80
73	Cecil	Sapp	85	82	68	84
73	Jason	Wright	86	86	84	70
73	Jesse	Chatman	90	84	75	75

LG Left Guard

Overall Rating	First Name	Last Name	Run Block Strength	Run Block Footwork	Pass Block Strength	Pass Block Footwork
98	Steve	Hutchinson	96	90	90	85
97	Alan	Faneca	96	93	90	86
96	Brian	Waters	96	88	91	85
95	Larry	Allen	99	70	92	67
94	Eric	Steinbach	92	92	95	95
94	Kris	Dielman	95	75	87	70
93	Mike	Wahle	89	85	88	93
92	Vince	Manuwai	95	75	92	79
92	Logan	Mankins	88	90	95	97
90	Ben	Hamilton	75	96	80	90
89	Ruben	Brown	91	65	94	55
88	Derrick	Dockery	95	55	87	54
87	Edwin	Mulitalo	92	65	89	55
86	Reggie	Wells	87	79	88	80
86	Pete	Kendall	84	82	88	84
85	Matt	Lehr	85	76	82	73
85	Dan	Buenning	90	74	86	69
85	Ryan	Lilja	79	80	83	82
85	Kyle	Kosier	84	80	86	75
85	Todd	Herremans	88	75	85	78
85	Todd	Wade	92	74	86	69
84	Rich	Seubert	88	70	83	72
84	Rob	Sims	82	73	82	74
84	Chester	Pitts	87	85	85	84

LG Left Guards (continued)

Overall Rating	First Name	Last Name	Run Block Strength	Run Block Footwork	Pass Block Strength	Pass Block Footwork
83	Rick	DeMulling	85	80	86	85
83	Zach	Piller	88	73	87	74
82	Chris	Bober	87	72	84	67
82	Chris	Liwienski	84	86	86	73
82	Jason	Brown	89	75	83	70
82	Jamar	Nesbit	84	72	85	78
82	Floyd	Womack	93	65	89	60
80	Terrence	Metcalf	88	70	83	68
80	Justin	Blalock	92	80	90	70
80	Daryn	Colledge	74	90	77	92
80	Ben	Grubbs	89	86	87	80
79	Qasim	Mitchell	83	68	82	69
79	Mark	Setterstrom	80	88	78	86
79	David	Stewart	84	73	82	70
78	Lennie	Friedman	85	70	79	78
77	Andrew	Whitworth	88	80	88	76
76	Claude	Terrell	90	80	85	70
76	Andy	Alleman	82	78	80	80
75	Ben	Wilkerson	82	78	78	75
75	Brad	Butler	84	75	77	70
75	Joe	Toledo	75	90	75	90
75	Toniu	Fonoti	90	65	87	60
75	Paul	McQuistan	85	70	77	65
75	Mike	Pucillo	85	64	82	60
74	Max	Jean-Gilles	92	62	88	50
73	Chris	Myers	81	71	82	78
73	Tony	Wragge	85	75	84	70

LT Left Tackles (continued)

Overall Rating	First Name	Last Name	Run Block Strength	Run Block Footwork	Pass Block Strength	Pass Block Footwork
83	Joe	Thomas	90	92	93	93
83	Travelle	Wharton	86	92	87	92
83	Barry	Sims	88	75	90	70
82	Roman	Oben	87	65	86	65
82	Todd	Steussie	87	55	86	64
82	Tom	Ashworth	85	75	84	76
82	Michael	Roos	89	80	84	85
79	Oliver	Ross	88	67	84	60
79	Damion	McIntosh	87	65	85	55
79	Ephraim	Salaam	85	80	84	85
78	Anthony	Davis	89	76	84	76
77	Winston	Justice	87	93	90	91
77	Joe	Staley	80	93	87	94
76	Leander	Jordan	86	70	84	65
76	Jordan	Black	87	75	85	70
74	John	St. Clair	87	55	78	60
74	Erik	Pears	85	85	85	85
74	Mike	Gandy	88	64	82	60
74	Doug	Free	84	80	87	85
73	Marshal	Yanda	80	75	85	82
73	Trai	Essex	84	76	78	76
73	Daniel	Loper	80	75	83	74
73	Charles	Spencer	87	75	85	72
72	Pat	McQuistan	86	78	84	74
72	Anthony	Alabi	85	85	85	85
72	Jonathan	Scott	78	85	82	85
71	Kevin	Sampson	84	68	82	60

LT Left Tackles

Overall Rating	First Name	Last Name	Run Block Strength	Run Block Footwork	Pass Block Strength	Pass Block Footwork
98	Walter	Jones	98	95	97	90
97	Jonathan	Ogden	98	79	98	80
96	Tarik	Glenn	93	93	98	98
96	Orlando	Pace	91	92	97	90
95	Jammal	Brown	93	86	97	90
94	Marcus	McNeill	96	88	96	84
94	William	Thomas	95	85	94	92
94	Chris	Samuels	97	84	97	85
94	Bryant	McKinnie	93	87	98	98
93	Levi	Jones	91	95	95	92
93	Chad	Clifton	92	80	96	85
92	Marvel	Smith	98	85	92	74
91	John	Tait	93	75	89	69
91	Matt	Lepsis	83	93	87	88
91	Matt	Light	87	82	94	87
90	Flozell	Adams	97	65	93	59
89	Luke	Petitgout	86	80	92	90
88	Wayne	Gandy	92	71	90	70
88	Jeff	Backus	88	72	93	78
87	Jason	Peters	91	85	87	79
87	Kevin	Shaffer	90	80	88	82
87	Jonas	Jennings	93	66	90	62
87	Khalif	Barnes	92	85	92	90
87	D'Brickashaw	Ferguson	87	95	88	98
84	Vernon	Carey	92	74	90	78
84	David	Diehl	89	78	87	74
84	Maurice	Williams	91	75	90	78

QB Quarterbacks

Overall Rating	First Name	Last Name	Speed	Aware	Thow Power	Throw Accur.
99	Peyton	Manning	59	100	96	98
98	Tom	Brady	61	100	91	96
97	Carson	Palmer	54	96	97	95
95	Drew	Brees	63	95	88	96
94	Donovan	McNabb	76	84	96	89
94	Marc	Bulger	57	94	90	97
92	Matt	Hasselbeck	62	92	90	92
90	Michael	Vick	94	74	97	78
89	Philip	Rivers	64	85	87	94
89	Brett	Favre	53	86	98	86
87	Ben	Roethlisberger	68	82	91	85
87	Vince	Young	90	74	92	80
86	Chad	Pennington	55	84	86	94
85	Jay	Cutler	68	70	95	88
85	Trent	Green	49	87	86	92
85	Eli	Manning	61	84	91	84
85	Jake	Delhomme	63	82	88	88
85	Steve	McNair	68	86	86	85
84	Rex	Grossman	59	74	95	87
84	Jeff	Garcia	75	83	82	86
84	Matt	Leinart	60	78	87	90
84	Tony	Romo	73	75	89	86
84	Jon	Kitna	58	79	89	89
83	Daunte	Culpepper	70	74	95	80
83	Alex	Smith	73	71	89	87
83	Matt	Schaub	62	75	88	90
82	J.P.	Losman	70	69	94	83

NEXT GENERATION

QB Quarterbacks (continued)

Overall Rating	First Name	Last Name	Speed	Aware	Thow Power	Throw Accur.
82	Damon	Huard	57	80	86	88
82	Byron	Leftwich	50	72	97	86
82	David	Carr	68	66	92	87
82	JaMarcus	Russell	72	58	99	84
82	Seneca	Wallace	85	72	84	82
81	Brian	Griese	53	80	87	88
81	David	Garrard	70	70	91	83
81	Jason	Campbell	69	70	91	83
80	Charlie	Frye	72	70	85	86
80	Kurt	Warner	46	84	87	87
80	Brad	Johnson	46	84	85	89
80	Trent	Dilfer	45	83	89	86
80	Mark	Brunell	62	78	86	84
79	Patrick	Ramsey	55	75	92	81
79	Billy	Volek	55	76	87	87
79	Kerry	Collins	47	79	92	82
78	Derek	Anderson	50	69	94	85
78	Kelly	Holcomb	52	82	85	84
78	Josh	McCown	79	64	90	79
78	Charlie	Batch	50	80	86	84
78	Tim	Rattay	52	74	86	87
77	Brady	Quinn	77	62	86	84
77	Chris	Simms	63	70	88	83
77	Brodie	Croyle	55	68	91	85
77	Gus	Frerotte	52	78	86	84
76	Craig	Nall	60	68	88	84
76	A.J.	Feeley	54	70	87	85
76	Joey	Harrington	62	70	88	81
76	Anthony	Wright	69	72	86	78
76	Kellen	Clemens	66	60	90	84
76	Aaron	Rodgers	66	64	90	82
76	Kyle	Boller	69	67	92	76
76	Jamie	Martin	50	78	84	85
76	Tarvaris	Jackson	79	56	92	79
76	Sage	Rosenfels	60	70	87	82
75	Matt	Cassel	64	67	86	81
74	John	Beck	64	57	89	85
74	Kevin	Kolb	66	52	89	86
74	Andrew	Walter	54	62	92	83
73	Doug	Johnson	47	75	86	80
73	Charlie	Whitehurst	62	62	81	88
73	Dan	Orlovsky	55	65	86	84
73	Drew	Stanton	64	54	90	83
73	Todd	Collins	50	75	85	80
73	Brooks	Bollinger	65	65	81	84
72	Chris	Leak	72	54	83	85
72	Bruce	Gradkowski	70	55	83	86
72	Cleo	Lemon	65	65	84	80
72	Tim	Hasselbeck	52	70	82	84
72	Quinn	Gray	71	63	85	77
72	Marques	Tuiasosopo	71	64	84	78
71	Kyle	Orton	55	68	84	80
71	Jim	Sorgi	62	68	84	78
71	David	Greene	54	64	82	86
70	Trent	Edwards	60	55	87	82
70	Casey	Printers	74	52	88	78
70	Bradlee	Van Pelt	73	60	83	77
69	Ingle	Martin	79	48	88	76
69	Ryan	Fitzpatrick	60	64	86	76
69	Troy	Smith	81	52	89	70

RG Right Guards

Overall Rating	First Name	Last Name	Run Block Strength	Run Block Footwork	Pass Block Strength	Pass Block Footwork
96	Shawn	Andrews	99	75	95	64
93	Randy	Thomas	87	93	96	99
92	Kynan	Forney	87	89	92	84
92	Chris	Snee	93	78	88	86
91	Mike	Goff	92	69	89	65
91	Chris	Naeole	94	75	82	60
91	Damien	Woody	92	85	89	80
91	Benji	Olson	92	68	87	66
90	Leonard	Davis	98	68	90	60
89	Kendall	Simmons	92	73	89	71
88	Brandon	Moore	89	84	88	84
87	Roberto	Garza	87	88	87	88
87	Davin	Joseph	89	86	87	86
87	Stephen	Neal	88	72	85	75
86	Justin	Smiley	86	79	89	77
85	John	Welbourn	85	80	85	70
85	Jake	Scott	84	79	79	74
85	Chris	Gray	87	68	84	68
84	Rex	Hadnot	88	80	86	75
84	Stockar	McDougle	91	63	88	61
83	Keydrick	Vincent	91	66	87	55
83	Jahri	Evans	86	77	85	79
82	Bobbie	Williams	90	50	80	52
82	Evan	Mathis	83	85	83	80
82	Richie	Incognito	87	77	82	72
82	Artis	Hicks	88	65	85	70
80	Cooper	Carlisle	82	88	84	85
79	Montrae	Holland	89	65	86	62
79	Seth	McKinney	85	69	85	73
79	Deuce	Lutui	90	86	88	80
79	Russ	Hochstein	84	75	83	78
79	Chris	Chester	83	93	80	87
79	Steve	McKinney	83	25	82	86
78	Duke	Preston	84	83	84	82
78	Jason	Whittle	87	70	84	68
78	Arron	Sears	90	82	89	80
78	Tyson	Clabo	85	85	85	85
78	Jason	Spitz	86	77	80	74
78	Kevin	Boothe	88	69	82	65
77	Josh	Beekman	88	82	83	80
77	Fred	Matua	87	72	85	78
77	Adam	Goldberg	84	64	85	60
77	Fred	Weary	84	73	83	70
76	Adrien	Clarke	84	65	81	63
76	Geoff	Hangartner	83	76	80	77
76	Chris	Kemoeatu	91	71	84	67
75	Elton	Brown	86	63	84	66
74	Stacy	Andrews	86	55	80	55
74	Chris	Kuper	75	89	75	91
74	Manuel	Ramirez	92	65	86	55
74	Allen	Barbre	81	88	83	89
74	Anthony	Herrera	88	55	76	76
72	Dan	Stevenson	81	69	83	67
72	Mansfield	Wrotto	88	68	84	65
71	Mike	Jones	82	65	80	60
71	Scott	Young	84	65	80	64
70	Herbert	Taylor	80	85	84	85
70	Matt	Ulrich	81	67	80	66
70	Matt	Lentz	81	75	83	74
70	Na'shan	Goddard	87	67	84	63

RT Right Tackles

Overall Rating	First Name	Last Name	Run Block Strength	Run Block Footwork	Pass Block Strength	Pass Block Footwork
96	Willie	Anderson	98	85	93	85
92	Mark	Tauscher	91	87	93	88
92	Jordan	Gross	87	95	90	92
91	Todd	Weiner	92	83	92	90
90	Jon	Runyan	96	69	89	64
90	Jon	Jansen	96	60	90	55
89	Ryan	Diem	91	79	89	94
88	Kareem	McKenzie	93	74	90	74
87	Fred	Miller	90	89	88	76
86	Shane	Olivea	91	85	87	78
85	Ryan	Tucker	90	80	88	79
85	Alex	Barron	89	89	92	91
85	Sean	Locklear	86	80	86	80
84	Kwame	Harris	87	87	87	88
84	Anthony	Clement	90	67	86	60
84	George	Foster	92	72	90	65
83	L.J.	Shelton	94	78	88	78
83	Tony	Pashos	92	75	90	65
83	Max	Starks	92	62	88	58
83	Jacob	Bell	87	76	85	72
82	Mike	Rosenthal	88	79	85	78
82	Rex	Tucker	85	80	85	76
82	Jason	Fabini	90	80	88	75
81	Langston	Walker	91	66	89	70
81	Adam	Meadows	82	87	84	88
81	Levi	Brown	93	87	88	83
81	Nick	Kaczur	84	70	83	77
79	Jeremy	Trueblood	87	70	88	78
79	Marc	Colombo	88	65	82	54
79	Adam	Snyder	87	85	86	79
79	Adrian	Jones	84	75	86	70
79	Robert	Gallery	89	85	90	78
79	Jon	Stinchcomb	85	75	88	80
78	Chris	Terry	85	85	85	85
78	Eric	Winston	79	92	79	90
77	Jeremy	Bridges	86	77	84	67
77	Seth	Wand	85	72	83	70
76	Kelly	Butler	86	60	88	64
76	Tony	Ugoh	90	84	86	77
76	James	Marten	82	74	88	70
76	Adam	Terry	86	74	87	73
75	Scott	Kooistra	86	69	84	66
75	Ryan	O'Callaghan	90	60	90	55
75	Cornell	Green	84	77	83	72
74	Brandon	Gorin	85	75	83	73
74	Rob	Petitti	83	65	85	62
74	Ryan	Cook	84	70	85	66
73	Ryan	Harris	80	75	86	75
73	Marcus	Johnson	90	74	87	70
72	Ray	Willis	89	64	87	62
71	Mark	LeVoir	85	85	85	85
71	Quinn	Ojinnaka	80	66	82	70
70	Terrance	Pennington	85	65	79	65
70	Willie	Colon	80	65	82	64
68	Brian	Rimpf	84	65	80	60
67	Cory	Lekkerkerker	85	85	85	85
67	Will	Svitek	85	85	85	85
67	Jon	Dunn	84	65	85	60
66	Michael	Toudouze	83	69	84	67
66	Junius	Coston	84	70	80	60

TE Tight Ends

Overall Rating	First Name	Last Name	Speed	Catch	Run Block	Pass Block
98	Antonio	Gates	86	90	55	50
96	Tony	Gonzalez	84	92	55	50
95	Jeremy	Shockey	84	85	54	50
95	Todd	Heap	81	88	58	52
94	Kellen	Winslow	85	86	58	53
94	Alge	Crumpler	78	88	60	50
92	Jason	Witten	77	85	56	51
90	Chris	Cooley	83	87	54	46
88	Daniel	Graham	80	78	58	49
88	Randy	McMichael	83	82	57	55
87	Dallas	Clark	86	86	56	48
87	L.J.	Smith	81	82	58	52
87	Benjamin	Watson	89	82	53	47
86	Vernon	Davis	92	82	53	46
86	Heath	Miller	82	87	60	50
83	Desmond	Clark	78	86	55	52
83	Owen	Daniels	84	80	55	50
82	Jermaine	Wiggins	70	88	48	45
82	George	Wrighster	78	79	54	52
82	Eric	Johnson	77	87	55	52
82	Marcus	Pollard	74	82	56	52
81	Reggie	Kelly	67	77	65	60
81	Jerramy	Stevens	79	77	58	58
81	Ben	Troupe	84	79	55	48
80	Dan	Campbell	68	76	64	60
80	Bubba	Franks	64	72	60	50
80	Kyle	Brady	59	63	75	62
80	Jim	Kleinsasser	70	70	70	52
79	Greg	Olsen	86	83	52	50
79	Anthony	Becht	62	74	70	62
79	Alex	Smith	79	81	55	52
79	Anthony	Fasano	72	77	62	58
79	David	Martin	79	77	55	50
79	Matt	Schobel	79	80	54	50
79	Marcedes	Lewis	77	80	57	54
79	Chris	Baker	77	78	60	58
79	Zach	Miller	77	84	50	48
79	Mark	Campbell	74	77	65	60
78	Jason	Dunn	64	67	78	64
78	Daniel	Wilcox	75	77	55	54
78	Bo	Scaife	83	84	54	50
77	Joe	Klopfenstein	83	79	55	50
76	Steve	Heiden	69	72	59	55
76	Leonard	Pope	82	77	59	57
76	Mark	Bruener	56	55	82	66
75	Brandon	Manumaleuna	67	72	66	60
75	Visanthe	Shiancoe	78	75	52	48
75	Jeb	Putzier	75	74	58	52
74	Tony	Scheffler	83	76	54	48
74	Donald	Lee	78	75	54	49
74	Jerame	Tuman	62	66	70	65
73	Ronnie	Ghent	66	71	60	55
73	Robert	Royal	75	75	58	54
73	David	Thomas	78	75	57	54
72	Stephen	Alexander	75	77	60	55
72	Ben	Patrick	77	81	52	50
72	Scott	Chandler	76	84	50	45
72	Bryan	Fletcher	81	82	50	48
72	Michael	Gaines	78	78	51	45
71	Justin	Peelle	73	71	58	52

NEXT GENERATION

NEXT GENERATION

WR Wide Receivers

Overall Rating	First Name	Last Name	Speed	Catch	Route Run	Catch Traffic
98	Chad	Johnson	96	95	98	93
98	Marvin	Harrison	94	98	100	95
98	Steve	Smith	97	95	93	95
98	Torry	Holt	94	98	98	86
96	Reggie	Wayne	89	97	97	94
95	Larry	Fitzgerald	88	96	96	95
95	Anquan	Boldin	89	93	92	99
94	Terrell	Owens	93	89	92	82
94	Andre	Johnson	95	90	89	92
93	Donald	Driver	91	95	92	90
93	Randy	Moss	97	90	88	84
92	Javon	Walker	92	90	92	90
92	Roy	Williams	92	92	87	86
92	Hines	Ward	87	94	94	98
91	T.J.	Houshmandzadeh	90	96	91	97
91	Laveranues	Coles	97	92	88	93
90	Lee	Evans	97	89	88	80
90	Plaxico	Burress	92	87	89	82
89	Darrell	Jackson	89	88	92	84
89	Marques	Colston	87	91	87	92
89	Deion	Branch	93	89	92	87
88	Terry	Glenn	93	94	87	80
88	Chris	Chambers	94	88	78	82
88	Isaac	Bruce	88	94	91	86
88	Santana	Moss	98	87	88	81
87	Joey	Galloway	98	87	83	82
87	Joe	Horn	87	88	90	84
87	Calvin	Johnson	96	86	85	84
86	Muhsin	Muhammad	86	91	90	86
86	Braylon	Edwards	92	87	84	80
86	Jerricho	Cotchery	89	91	85	87
85	Bernard	Berrian	97	85	82	72
85	Greg	Jennings	93	87	82	84
85	Drew	Bennett	89	88	84	84
85	Mark	Clayton	92	88	88	82
85	Derrick	Mason	88	90	87	80
84	Eddie	Kennison	91	87	87	80
84	Donte	Stallworth	97	85	79	74
83	Rod	Smith	84	88	85	85
83	Reggie	Brown	90	87	81	82
83	Amani	Toomer	88	86	84	84
83	Mike	Furrey	89	92	78	85
83	Wes	Welker	88	88	82	94
82	Bryant	Johnson	92	87	82	80
82	Patrick	Crayton	91	94	76	79
82	Marty	Booker	86	85	82	85
82	Devery	Henderson	98	84	78	70
82	Bobby	Engram	87	87	84	82
82	D.J.	Hackett	88	86	84	78
82	David	Givens	87	85	82	84
81	Chris	Henry	93	85	77	75
81	Kevin	Curtis	96	84	78	80
81	Santonio	Holmes	93	80	84	70
80	Brandon	Marshall	90	82	78	75
80	Joe	Jurevicius	85	87	78	88
80	Eric	Parker	91	84	82	84
80	Reche	Caldwell	90	86	80	70
80	Jerry	Porter	91	80	77	77
79	Brandon	Stokley	89	85	78	84
79	Vincent	Jackson	92	81	76	75

WR Wide Receivers (continued)

Overall Rating	First Name	Last Name	Speed	Catch	Route Run	Catch Traffic
79	Ted	Ginn Jr.	98	78	79	66
79	Arnaz	Battle	89	88	77	69
79	Travis	Taylor	90	83	82	75
78	Michael	Clayton	86	80	81	78
78	Maurice	Stovall	88	82	76	79
78	Reggie	Williams	88	80	80	70
78	Dwayne	Jarrett	87	83	85	87
78	Ronald	Curry	89	82	80	70
78	Brandon	Lloyd	88	82	77	78
78	Sidney	Rice	89	85	82	81
77	Peerless	Price	92	80	78	79
77	Dwayne	Bowe	91	78	80	79
77	Anthony	Gonzalez	94	82	77	80
77	Michael	Jenkins	89	86	70	67
77	Ernest	Wilford	86	82	80	72
77	Matt	Jones	93	80	76	66
77	Justin	McCareins	90	78	78	80
77	Marcus	Robinson	88	85	78	77
77	Robert	Meachem	93	84	76	68
76	David	Boston	88	80	75	76
76	Ike	Hilliard	87	84	80	75
76	Craig	Davis	93	80	75	82
76	Nate	Burleson	91	77	74	81
75	Doug	Gabriel	87	80	74	71
75	Nate	Washington	88	79	78	76
75	Brandon	Jones	90	85	69	82
75	Bobby	Wade	89	80	80	74
75	Billy	McMullen	87	82	72	74
74	Mark	Bradley	92	78	70	74
74	Josh	Reed	85	86	75	78
74	Laurent	Robinson	91	81	78	80
74	Ashley	Lelie	92	83	68	60
74	Steve	Smith	92	82	80	64
74	Dennis	Northcutt	91	77	82	60
74	Mike	Walker	94	79	76	78
74	Robert	Ferguson	90	76	74	70
74	Jabar	Gaffney	87	85	77	66
74	Antwaan	Randle El	93	79	66	70
74	Cedrick	Wilson	91	78	74	79
74	Troy	Williamson	96	75	70	70
73	Travis	Wilson	89	80	72	78
73	Malcom	Floyd	87	80	69	74
73	Rod	Gardner	86	75	75	78
73	Brian	Finneran	85	80	70	84
73	Jason	Hill	91	82	72	70
73	Kelley	Washington	91	78	70	62
73	Chad	Jackson	91	80	75	72
72	Rashied	Davis	94	76	69	67
72	Tab	Perry	90	82	71	69
72	Samie	Parker	94	78	70	74
72	Derek	Hagan	87	82	75	62
72	Hank	Baskett	87	82	68	67
72	James	Jones	89	75	76	79
72	Keary	Colbert	88	78	76	70
72	Johnnie Lee	Higgins	93	80	71	78
72	Justin	Gage	87	79	70	77
72	Aundrae	Allison	93	81	70	74
71	David	Kircus	88	80	68	71
71	Aaron	Moorehead	85	82	74	64
71	Greg	Lewis	93	81	67	76

CB Cornerbacks

Overall Rating	First Name	Last Name	Speed	Man Cover	Zone Cover	Press
99	Champ	Bailey	98	100	99	98
98	Chris	McAlister	93	94	95	94
97	Rashean	Mathis	94	94	92	88
96	Asante	Samuel	91	94	95	93
95	Ronde	Barber	88	78	99	98
95	Lito	Sheppard	93	95	90	84
95	Al	Harris	88	98	90	99
94	DeAngelo	Hall	98	92	90	70
94	Nate	Clements	92	96	86	97
93	Patrick	Surtain	90	93	90	84
93	Nnamdi	Asomugha	91	94	84	88
92	Nathan	Vasher	92	90	89	83
92	Terence	Newman	96	95	86	74
92	Charles	Woodson	87	89	94	92
92	Antoine	Winfield	89	88	90	94
91	Charles	Tillman	88	91	88	93
91	Marcus	Trufant	94	92	88	82
90	Dre'	Bly	93	92	85	88
90	Ty	Law	88	86	90	84
90	Sheldon	Brown	91	88	92	82
88	Quentin	Jammer	94	87	78	92
88	Anthony	Henry	87	84	88	90
88	Walt	Harris	88	90	88	75
88	Chris	Gamble	92	90	88	75
88	Ken	Lucas	92	84	88	88
88	Carlos	Rogers	91	87	89	92
88	Shawn	Springs	88	85	92	88
87	Sam	Madison	88	84	89	80
87	Samari	Rolle	90	85	88	82
87	Mike	McKenzie	89	86	89	75
87	Ike	Taylor	94	85	85	90
87	Dunta	Robinson	96	84	77	90
86	Ricky	Manning	90	84	85	85
86	Brian	Williams	88	80	85	89
85	Deltha	O'Neal	94	80	85	75
85	Tory	James	86	84	88	84
85	Fabian	Washington	98	87	76	74
84	Brian	Kelly	89	70	90	78
84	Antrel	Rolle	89	79	85	82
84	Andre	Dyson	94	84	75	71
84	Ellis	Hobbs	91	86	84	68
84	Tye	Hill	98	87	80	64
84	Deshea	Townsend	88	84	80	87
84	Nick	Harper	87	77	88	72
83	Gary	Baxter	86	82	84	84
83	Antonio	Cromartie	94	82	76	78
83	Marlin	Jackson	88	78	86	78
83	Fred	Smoot	92	87	80	70
83	Cedric	Griffin	89	84	85	70
82	Johnathan	Joseph	97	80	82	70
82	Terrence	McGee	94	82	80	65
82	Leigh	Bodden	89	80	80	82
82	Roderick	Hood	90	84	85	72
82	Drayton	Florence	91	84	78	75
82	Aaron	Glenn	87	80	85	78
82	Darrelle	Revis	89	82	84	78
82	Fernando	Bryant	93	88	80	68
82	Richard	Marshall	92	86	82	78
82	Jordan	Babineaux	89	84	80	74
82	Bryant	McFadden	89	82	83	74

CB Cornerbacks (continued)

Overall Rating	First Name	Last Name	Speed	Man Cover	Zone Cover	Press
81	Will	Allen	97	85	75	62
80	Leon	Hall	92	80	82	72
80	Domonique	Foxworth	93	82	77	68
80	Lewis	Sanders	88	75	85	80
80	Chris	Houston	96	87	70	90
80	Shawntae	Spencer	91	79	83	61
80	Corey	Webster	87	80	75	79
80	Aaron	Ross	90	80	82	84
80	Fakhir	Brown	88	77	80	81
80	Jason	David	88	75	85	62
80	Kelly	Herndon	88	80	80	80
79	Chad	Scott	86	77	85	80
79	Reynaldo	Hill	89	85	84	58
78	Jason	Webster	87	75	80	70
78	Eric	Wright	92	84	82	75
78	William	James	91	79	82	55
78	Travis	Fisher	91	75	84	72
78	Kelly	Jennings	94	82	80	58
77	Keiwan	Ratliff	88	82	77	55
77	Daven	Holly	93	80	79	60
77	Kenny	Wright	88	78	80	65
77	Phillip	Buchanon	96	85	70	58
77	Kelvin	Hayden	90	75	82	70
77	Travis	Daniels	87	78	72	80
77	Andre	Goodman	93	78	76	65
77	Stanley	Wilson	94	82	74	62
77	Josh	Wilson	95	80	80	78
77	DeMarcus	Faggins	92	78	72	60
76	Daymeion	Hughes	88	78	80	65
76	Hank	Poteat	88	82	80	60
76	Justin	Miller	98	70	76	68
76	Randall	Gay	88	76	82	58
76	Duane	Starks	89	80	82	60
76	David	Macklin	87	66	85	70
76	Fred	Thomas	86	78	82	60
76	Dexter	McCleon	89	70	78	65
75	Kiwaukee	Thomas	87	79	77	58
75	Eric	Green	89	74	76	76
75	Tim	Jennings	96	82	83	52
75	David	Barrett	87	75	82	68
75	Jonathan	Wade	96	78	70	66
75	Marcus	McCauley	92	74	76	82
75	Jamar	Fletcher	87	86	67	48
74	R.W.	McQuarters	89	75	75	58
74	Patrick	Dendy	87	75	85	74
74	Usama	Young	94	78	79	59
74	Fred	Bennett	92	74	78	64
73	Ashton	Youboty	92	78	78	60
73	Jerametrius	Butler	90	78	72	65
73	Ricardo	Colclough	91	76	65	62
73	Cortland	Finnegan	92	68	77	56
72	Karl	Paymah	93	77	75	55
72	Matt	Ware	87	69	79	58
72	David	Irons	91	78	70	72
72	Keith	Smith	93	78	70	54
72	Jarrett	Bush	91	65	75	70
72	Lenny	Walls	87	65	76	82
72	Corey	Ivy	90	66	80	75
72	Jason	Craft	91	70	65	66
71	Dashon	Goldson	88	70	75	65

NEXT GENERATION

329

CB Cornerbacks (continued)

Overall Rating	First Name	Last Name	Speed	Man Cover	Zone Cover	Press
71	Andre	Woolfolk	92	72	70	66
70	Dante	Wesley	89	66	76	68
70	Steve	Gregory	88	70	75	54
70	Benny	Sapp	93	70	70	68
70	Marcus	Maxey	88	78	79	50
70	Willie	Andrews	90	72	82	54
69	Jabari	Greer	91	71	75	49
69	Jereme	Perry	89	72	74	56
69	Joselio	Hanson	87	75	80	50
69	A.J.	Davis	92	76	70	50
69	Will	Blackmon	90	75	70	40
69	John	Bowie	95	70	70	62

DT Defensive Tackles

Overall Rating	First Name	Last Name	Speed	Strength	Power Moves	Finesse Moves
98	Jamal	Williams	54	98	98	67
97	Tommie	Harris	77	91	94	93
97	Kevin	Williams	71	92	95	94
96	Casey	Hampton	55	98	98	67
95	John	Henderson	62	95	97	65
94	Marcus	Stroud	63	95	97	83
94	Shaun	Rogers	62	96	96	79
94	Kris	Jenkins	64	93	95	82
92	Rod	Coleman	74	84	94	90
92	Vince	Wilfork	60	94	94	75
90	Pat	Williams	50	96	96	45
89	Warren	Sapp	67	82	82	94
88	La'Roi	Glover	64	82	84	88
88	Kelly	Gregg	56	88	88	60
88	Cornelius	Griffin	65	86	89	72
86	Anthony	McFarland	62	90	88	76
86	Dewayne	Robertson	64	89	87	82
86	Cory	Redding	69	87	85	78
85	Darwin	Walker	66	83	86	78
85	Darnell	Dockett	71	87	83	85
85	Brian	Young	64	86	84	55
85	Hollis	Thomas	48	94	88	48
85	Rocky	Bernard	64	87	87	86
85	Albert	Haynesworth	63	92	90	72
84	Sam	Adams	47	93	93	52
84	Gerard	Warren	61	92	86	67
84	Ted	Washington	44	96	95	45
84	Jason	Ferguson	55	90	88	54
84	Corey	Williams	68	86	86	84
83	John	Thornton	62	86	86	58
83	Larry	Tripplett	65	84	78	85
83	Corey	Simon	58	87	86	84
83	Keith	Traylor	47	93	88	44
83	Ma'ake	Kemoeatu	50	96	88	60
83	Chartric	Darby	67	82	83	84
82	Raheem	Brock	76	80	78	86
82	Brodrick	Bunkley	65	95	88	80
82	Barry	Cofield	68	88	84	74
82	Ryan	Pickett	62	87	84	70
82	Terdell	Sands	51	94	88	70
82	Adam	Carriker	76	89	88	82
82	Marcus	Tubbs	60	92	87	65

DT Defensive Tackles (continued)

Overall Rating	First Name	Last Name	Speed	Strength	Power Moves	Finesse Moves
82	Chris	Hoke	59	88	86	60
81	Chris	Hovan	66	84	75	86
81	Mike	Patterson	63	87	78	84
81	Ian	Scott	63	86	84	78
81	Grady	Jackson	43	96	90	54
81	Fred	Robbins	54	89	86	64
80	Kyle	Williams	59	85	84	78
80	Justin	Harrell	65	89	88	72
79	Alvin	McKinley	56	91	85	52
79	Rob	Meier	60	85	86	70
79	Randy	Starks	64	87	85	76
79	Amobi	Okoye	66	87	84	87
78	Domata	Peko	61	89	85	74
78	Ryan	Sims	62	84	84	74
78	Ron	Edwards	60	88	80	52
78	Montae	Reagor	65	79	80	75
78	William	Joseph	64	87	82	79
78	Jeff	Zgonina	55	82	79	58
77	Anthony	Adams	61	83	83	66
77	John	McCargo	66	82	86	78
77	Alan	Branch	64	94	89	65
77	Ronald	Fields	56	90	82	64
76	Jimmy	Kennedy	58	88	84	64
76	Marcus	Thomas	65	86	85	83
76	Darrell	Reid	64	82	82	65
76	Shaun	Cody	64	82	79	82
76	Justin	Bannan	56	87	82	78
76	Travis	Johnson	65	84	81	85
75	Alfonso	Boone	54	87	80	50
75	Quinn	Pitcock	61	84	86	83
75	Aubrayo	Franklin	55	89	84	66
75	Marcus	Bell	48	92	83	54
75	Damione	Lewis	64	84	79	77
75	Kedric	Golston	61	84	82	55
75	Kendrick	Clancy	54	90	84	42
75	Anthony	Maddox	67	86	82	58
74	Michael	Myers	64	84	79	67
74	Ellis	Wyms	65	80	78	75
74	James	Reed	62	85	75	50
74	Isaac	Sopoaga	55	95	86	55
74	Brandon	Mebane	63	90	88	75
73	Shaun	Smith	59	89	80	60
73	Gabe	Watson	57	91	87	58
73	Tank	Tyler	54	96	87	68
73	Joe	Cohen	60	91	86	73
73	Kindal	Moorehead	66	83	74	75
72	Kenderick	Allen	64	83	85	50
72	Tim	Anderson	55	84	76	68
72	Rodney	Bailey	65	82	82	62
72	Colin	Cole	56	88	81	58
72	Jesse	Mahelona	57	91	83	66
72	Spencer	Johnson	65	84	79	51
71	Ethan	Kelley	56	86	76	52
71	Jay	Ratliff	67	83	74	72
70	Paul	Soliai	62	93	79	65
70	Jonathan	Babineaux	69	80	72	78
70	Derek	Landri	60	84	78	80
70	Sione	Pouha	62	88	79	60
70	Jordan	Carstens	58	84	78	74
70	Rien	Long	64	78	74	78

NEXT GENERATION

FS Free Safeties

Overall Rating	First Name	Last Name	Speed	Man Cover	Zone Cover	Hit Power
99	Ed	Reed	93	88	98	85
97	Brian	Dawkins	88	70	90	97
96	Bob	Sanders	92	65	84	84
95	John	Lynch	85	60	90	98
90	Mike	Brown	88	65	90	74
90	Sean	Taylor	91	50	78	99
88	Madieu	Williams	88	75	87	75
88	Eugene	Wilson	90	80	87	74
87	Deon	Grant	89	75	85	75
86	Dwight	Smith	90	70	75	59
85	Stuart	Schweigert	90	60	85	78
84	Danieal	Manning	91	75	80	64
84	Marlon	McCree	86	65	74	86
84	Ken	Hamlin	88	65	80	92
84	Will	Demps	86	65	80	80
84	Mike	Minter	86	60	80	90
84	Josh	Bullocks	90	65	80	65
83	Brodney	Pool	90	64	82	70
82	Ko	Simpson	89	78	85	55
82	Terrence	Holt	85	66	82	52
82	Reggie	Nelson	93	65	80	81
82	Erik	Coleman	87	60	75	70
82	Daniel	Bullocks	87	70	85	42
82	Brandon	Meriweather	92	75	80	70
82	Michael	Griffin	92	76	84	82
81	O.J.	Atogwe	88	70	78	74
81	Kevin	Kaesviharn	84	60	80	58
81	Lamont	Thompson	87	70	80	62
80	Will	Allen	87	68	80	50
80	Greg	Wesley	85	62	78	89
80	Renaldo	Hill	87	75	74	57
80	Jason	Allen	92	75	80	70
80	Jimmy	Williams	93	80	82	44
80	Nick	Collins	93	68	74	76
80	Mike	Green	86	70	80	76
80	Ryan	Clark	87	60	74	72
78	Sam	Brandon	88	60	78	79
78	Eric	Weddle	89	65	78	74
78	Pat	Watkins	89	70	80	52
77	Keith	Davis	86	70	75	77
77	Chris	Crocker	89	45	75	83
76	Mark	Roman	88	65	75	52
76	Pierson	Prioleau	84	65	65	78
75	Tanard	Jackson	88	78	80	54
75	Anthony	Smith	87	60	78	44
75	Tank	Williams	87	55	65	82
74	Mike	Adams	85	65	70	68
74	Gerald	Alexander	90	75	80	62
74	Deke	Cooper	87	50	72	54
74	Ronald	Bartell	92	70	75	51
74	Bryan	Scott	85	60	80	83
73	Ethan	Kilmer	89	60	70	60
73	Aaron	Francisco	86	55	75	55
73	Josh	Gattis	89	60	70	74
73	Greg	Blue	87	60	75	84
72	Jarrad	Page	87	65	75	80
72	C.J.	Gaddis	92	76	75	70
72	Eric	Smith	87	70	72	60
71	C.C.	Brown	86	50	65	44
70	Jarrod	Cooper	85	50	72	80

LE Left Defensive Ends

Overall Rating	First Name	Last Name	Speed	Strength	Power Moves	Finesse Moves
98	Julius	Peppers	87	81	86	99
95	Leonard	Little	85	75	75	97
94	Michael	Strahan	75	80	94	90
94	Aaron	Kampman	74	85	94	90
93	Trevor	Pryce	68	93	96	78
92	Luis	Castillo	66	95	98	70
92	Patrick	Kerney	74	78	89	86
91	Aaron	Smith	69	86	89	82
90	Charles	Grant	75	81	85	86
90	Kyle	Vanden Bosch	72	81	88	86
89	Adewale	Ogunleye	83	73	74	94
89	Ty	Warren	68	87	91	78
88	Chike	Okeafor	77	73	80	88
88	Robert	Mathis	85	73	70	94
88	Jevon	Kearse	85	70	68	93
88	Shaun	Ellis	69	89	92	75
86	Kevin	Carter	66	86	86	82
86	Tamba	Hali	72	84	84	85
86	Darren	Howard	73	80	86	82
86	Bryant	Young	64	89	92	68
85	Andre	Carter	76	75	78	86
83	Dewayne	White	74	74	79	85
82	Marcus	Spears	69	82	87	75
82	Eric	Hicks	72	77	87	68
82	Tommy	Kelly	66	86	86	70
81	Kenard	Lang	74	75	82	72
80	Greg	Spires	74	73	74	84
80	Jamaal	Anderson	78	72	82	88
80	Paul	Spicer	67	83	76	79
80	Kenechi	Udeze	70	77	82	83
80	Anthony	Weaver	67	84	85	74
79	Bryan	Robinson	60	82	81	74
79	Chris	Kelsay	72	79	85	70
79	Matt	Roth	72	83	82	78
78	Tim	Crowder	82	82	78	85
78	Renaldo	Wynn	63	86	84	67
78	ND	Kalu	75	69	67	81
77	Ryan	Denney	68	81	86	72
77	Bobby	Hamilton	65	82	66	75
77	Tyler	Brayton	70	77	80	75
77	Darrion	Scott	67	79	77	74
76	John	Engelberger	69	78	77	74
76	Baraka	Atkins	76	77	82	75
75	Orpheus	Roye	63	88	85	57
75	Turk	McBride	65	85	80	81
75	Josh	Thomas	72	75	70	84
72	Melvin	Oliver	68	87	80	60
72	Ryan	McBean	63	86	76	84
70	Patrick	Chukwurah	76	69	55	78
70	Joe	Tafoya	67	74	80	64
70	Chauncey	Davis	74	66	60	82
70	Jared	DeVries	65	78	74	70
69	Frostee	Rucker	65	75	67	82
69	Jerome	McDougle	77	68	63	83
69	Jeremy	Mincey	75	73	72	70
69	Ikaika	Alama-Francis	68	77	72	79
69	Kareem	Brown	60	87	82	74
69	Eric	Moore	75	67	66	81
68	Israel	Idonije	70	75	68	86
68	Derreck	Robinson	65	82	79	72

LOLB Left Outside Linebackers

Overall Rating	First Name	Last Name	Speed	Pursuit	Play Rec.	Man Cover
98	Shawne	Merriman	87	95	76	55
95	Joey	Porter	85	96	85	55
90	Derrick	Johnson	87	96	80	70
90	Marcus	Washington	83	94	85	65
89	Cato	June	84	93	85	75
88	Daryl	Smith	79	88	86	60
88	Terrell	Suggs	87	95	78	60
88	David	Thornton	77	94	84	65
87	Karlos	Dansby	85	90	78	75
86	Angelo	Crowell	79	89	80	60
86	Thomas	Davis	87	90	68	70
86	Rosevelt	Colvin	82	90	85	55
86	Clark	Haggans	77	90	78	60
85	Willie	McGinest	78	88	86	55
85	Leroy	Hill	83	88	78	55
84	Scott	Fujita	82	90	85	55
82	Michael	Boley	84	88	75	60
82	Bryan	Thomas	78	90	70	65
82	Boss	Bailey	87	90	62	70
81	Warrick	Holdman	77	83	82	55
80	Mathias	Kiwanuka	82	87	68	49
79	Greg	Ellis	77	82	84	45
78	Hunter	Hillenmeyer	74	84	78	55
78	D.D.	Lewis	78	86	75	50
78	Manny	Lawson	90	88	68	55
78	Sam	Williams	81	84	68	60
78	Ben	Leber	78	88	78	50
76	Clint	Ingram	84	86	60	48
75	Rashad	Jeanty	75	85	70	60
75	Anthony	Spencer	82	85	60	60
75	Brady	Poppinga	79	84	68	50
74	Mario	Haggan	76	84	75	50
74	Ryan	Nece	79	85	68	55
74	Chris	Gocong	78	85	65	45
74	Alex	Lewis	85	85	55	70
74	Kevin	Bentley	78	84	65	65
74	LaMarr	Woodley	80	85	60	50
74	Gilbert	Gardner	77	85	70	65
73	Rocky	Boiman	74	86	68	55
73	Brandon	Chillar	77	84	70	40
72	Shantee	Orr	78	80	55	55
71	David	Pollack	77	87	64	40
71	Carlos	Polk	74	85	60	45
71	Reggie	Torbor	82	78	65	40
71	Tim	Shaw	87	86	60	45
70	Stewart	Bradley	75	82	58	40
69	Parys	Haralson	78	82	65	35
69	Zak	DeOssie	78	85	60	60
69	Pierre	Woods	75	79	68	60
68	Brendon	Ayanbadejo	74	78	60	55
68	Darrell	McClover	86	83	58	70
68	Abraham	Wright	78	84	60	45
67	Korey	Hall	77	80	60	50
67	Alfred	Fincher	76	84	60	30
66	Rich	Scanlon	72	78	70	40
66	Brandon	Jamison	84	83	62	60
65	Matt	Chatham	70	79	65	40
65	Arnold	Harrison	76	79	58	50
65	Heath	Farwell	72	82	58	54
64	Antwan	Peek	79	75	55	45

MLB Middle Linebackers

Overall Rating	First Name	Last Name	Speed	Pursuit	Play Rec.	Man Cover
99	Brian	Urlacher	88	98	96	80
97	Zach	Thomas	76	98	98	60
96	Ray	Lewis	82	96	89	70
95	Jonathan	Vilma	85	95	90	85
95	London	Fletcher-Baker	80	98	93	68
94	Antonio	Pierce	85	95	92	77
94	Adalius	Thomas	87	95	84	79
94	Lofa	Tatupu	84	95	93	60
93	James	Farrior	79	95	92	55
92	Keith	Brooking	82	94	89	65
92	Mike	Peterson	85	96	90	65
91	Bart	Scott	82	92	86	55
90	D.J.	Williams	86	90	82	72
90	Will	Witherspoon	86	97	84	75
89	Jeremiah	Trotter	75	96	94	35
89	Tedy	Bruschi	75	94	94	60
88	Andra	Davis	77	92	85	50
88	Nick	Barnett	81	90	82	68
88	Dan	Morgan	84	90	85	65
88	Kirk	Morrison	80	94	89	50
88	DeMeco	Ryans	80	93	84	62
85	Gary	Brackett	81	90	87	66
85	Channing	Crowder	79	89	82	65
85	Larry	Foote	77	91	82	62
84	Odell	Thurman	84	88	77	70
84	Patrick	Willis	88	92	80	60
84	E.J.	Henderson	73	88	85	50
83	Bradie	James	79	88	78	55
83	Lemar	Marshall	84	91	84	70
83	Brian	Simmons	80	88	85	60
82	D'Qwell	Jackson	82	88	82	45
82	Derek	Smith	74	92	86	48
82	Brandon	Moore	79	90	78	60
82	Junior	Seau	74	85	94	55
80	Paul	Posluszny	82	90	78	65
80	Barrett	Ruud	76	87	80	48
80	Gerald	Hayes	74	86	75	45
80	Rob	Morris	74	86	85	45
80	Jeff	Ulbrich	74	90	85	40
80	Victor	Hobson	76	87	78	50
79	Akin	Ayodele	82	85	70	50
79	Paris	Lenon	79	88	78	52
78	Ahmad	Brooks	78	85	74	60
78	Napoleon	Harris	84	80	67	57
78	Bobby	Carpenter	86	84	77	68
78	Omar	Gaither	80	88	75	55
78	Chris	Draft	78	88	75	75
76	David	Harris	82	88	78	50
76	Mark	Simoneau	80	83	70	67
75	Chaun	Thompson	85	82	65	60
74	Nate	Webster	79	85	70	55
74	Leon	Williams	83	82	68	45
74	Anthony	Waters	80	85	66	45
74	Clint	Kriewaldt	70	86	80	40
74	Stephen	Tulloch	78	88	64	55
74	Danny	Clark	79	89	78	40
73	Monty	Beisel	76	85	65	55
73	Abdul	Hodge	79	85	75	30
72	Stephen	Cooper	76	85	60	70
72	Matt	Wilhelm	74	82	72	40

MLB Middle Linebackers (continued)

Overall Rating	First Name	Last Name	Speed	Pursuit	Play Rec.	Man Cover
72	Brad	Kassell	72	89	72	35
72	Robert	Thomas	79	85	65	60
72	Ryan	Fowler	75	84	68	45
71	Caleb	Miller	77	83	70	55
71	Buster	Davis	81	88	60	40
71	Teddy	Lehman	82	84	68	45
70	Brandon	Siler	82	84	60	40
70	Donnie	Spragan	75	83	75	35
69	Mike	Smith	76	80	40	85
68	Rod	Wilson	80	78	65	54
68	Larry	Izzo	69	80	40	65
68	Niko	Koutouvides	75	82	65	40
67	Antwan	Barnes	88	88	48	40
67	Vinny	Ciurciu	70	82	55	60
66	William	Kershaw	78	78	50	50
66	Adam	Seward	74	82	62	45
66	HB	Blades	76	85	60	55
66	Robert	Reynolds	74	80	60	30
65	Jordan	Beck	83	82	30	60
65	Rian	Wallace	73	80	65	40
64	Tony	Gilbert	70	78	60	35
63	John	DiGiorgio	74	83	67	49

P Punters

Overall Rating	First Name	Last Name	Aware	Kick Power	Kick Accur.	Tackle
98	Shane	Lechler	78	95	91	18
96	Mat	McBriar	68	97	89	10
94	Brian	Moorman	76	94	90	19
92	Scott	Player	92	89	91	22
91	Hunter	Smith	80	90	91	14
87	Brad	Maynard	89	87	90	12
87	Andy	Lee	66	89	92	35
87	Ryan	Plackemeier	68	92	88	40
86	Todd	Sauerbrun	69	92	87	26
85	Josh	Bidwell	79	90	87	23
85	Ben	Graham	60	92	88	39
85	Nick	Harris	70	92	86	13
85	Jason	Baker	72	90	88	14
85	Craig	Hentrich	86	90	86	12
84	Dustin	Colquitt	70	90	88	29
84	Jon	Ryan	66	94	84	31
83	Dave	Zastudil	67	91	86	12
83	Josh	Miller	76	88	88	25
82	Kyle	Larson	66	90	87	27
82	Michael	Koenen	64	93	84	14
81	Daniel	Sepulveda	62	92	84	55
80	Mike	Scifres	60	91	85	22
80	Dirk	Johnson	76	88	86	33
80	Steve	Weatherford	74	89	85	23
79	Jeff	Feagles	96	83	88	19
79	Adam	Podlesh	65	90	85	30
79	Donnie	Jones	62	90	85	23
79	Chris	Hanson	65	90	85	12
78	Sam	Koch	60	90	85	33
77	Chris	Kluwe	64	87	87	20
76	Derrick	Frost	62	87	86	10
76	Chad	Stanley	73	85	87	19

RE Right Defensive Ends

Overall Rating	First Name	Last Name	Speed	Strength	Power Moves	Finesse Moves
97	Richard	Seymour	71	92	97	82
95	Dwight	Freeney	87	74	76	99
94	Aaron	Schobel	74	81	93	82
94	Derrick	Burgess	80	73	79	95
94	Will	Smith	82	80	86	95
93	John	Abraham	80	77	82	92
92	Bertrand	Berry	79	78	93	85
92	Jared	Allen	79	72	86	92
91	Simeon	Rice	84	70	78	90
88	Reggie	Hayward	77	78	85	88
88	Mike	Rucker	74	78	90	85
87	Justin	Smith	74	82	88	75
87	Osi	Umenyiora	84	73	80	94
86	Kabeer	Gbaja Biamila	81	70	74	90
86	Mario	Williams	84	76	83	90
85	Alex	Brown	83	74	75	88
84	Mark	Anderson	79	76	77	90
84	Gaines	Adams	84	72	85	90
84	Igor	Olshansky	62	90	89	70
84	Vonnie	Holliday	63	88	89	75
84	Cullen	Jenkins	68	82	86	82
84	James	Hall	73	80	78	86
84	Bryce	Fisher	74	78	78	85
83	Robert	Geathers	77	77	74	88
82	Ebenezer	Ekuban	72	75	77	79
82	Bobby	McCray	79	72	75	86
82	Haloti	Ngata	64	94	92	65
82	Brett	Keisel	73	83	85	72
82	Erasmus	James	78	72	82	86
81	Robaire	Smith	62	87	88	70
81	Trent	Cole	80	73	70	88
80	Marques	Douglas	70	80	80	78
80	Kimo	von Oelhoffen	60	88	88	67
80	Phillip	Daniels	65	84	82	72
79	Elvis	Dumervil	79	71	70	86
79	Jarvis	Moss	82	67	75	86
79	Chris	Canty	70	80	83	81
79	Jarvis	Green	68	84	87	70
79	Travis	LaBoy	75	70	75	84
78	Kalimba	Edwards	79	70	68	87
78	Jason	Babin	79	67	85	82
77	Darryl	Tapp	74	74	76	84
76	Dan	Bazuin	77	80	75	77
75	Jimmy	Wilkerson	72	80	70	82
75	Charles	Johnson	76	80	78	84
75	Antwan	Odom	75	76	80	75
74	Paul	Carrington	73	74	66	84
74	Brian	Robison	77	78	74	77
74	Ray	Edwards	77	73	70	86
73	Anthony	Hargrove	75	67	68	82
73	Jacques	Cesaire	69	82	70	78
73	Bo	Schobel	69	79	77	76
73	Victor	Abiamiri	75	76	80	78
73	Stanley	McClover	78	69	64	84
72	Juqua	Thomas	73	72	81	64
72	Quentin	Moses	78	70	70	79
72	Travis	Kirschke	62	85	85	64
71	Ray	McDonald	68	83	82	78
71	Victor	Adeyanju	78	77	72	82
70	Jason	Hatcher	73	84	67	84

ROLB Right Outside Linebackers

Overall Rating	First Name	Last Name	Speed	Pursuit	Play Rec.	Man Cover
97	Keith	Bulluck	86	94	82	75
96	Lance	Briggs	80	95	87	77
96	Jason	Taylor	87	96	89	62
95	Julian	Peterson	86	98	86	80
94	Derrick	Brooks	80	91	93	80
92	Donnie	Edwards	80	90	92	82
92	Takeo	Spikes	83	92	85	61
91	Ian	Gold	87	93	88	78
90	Demarcus	Ware	86	94	78	45
90	A.J.	Hawk	87	94	80	70
88	Ernie	Sims	87	94	68	69
88	Mike	Vrabel	74	90	86	60
86	Kamerion	Wimbley	85	92	78	55
86	Shaun	Phillips	84	92	79	58
85	Kawika	Mitchell	79	92	82	59
84	Morlon	Greenwood	85	89	80	65
83	Ed	Hartwell	75	87	85	45
83	Eric	Barton	78	89	82	55
82	Demorrio	Williams	86	88	80	62
82	Thomas	Howard	87	90	74	65
82	Pisa	Tinoisamoa	87	92	70	60
81	Jon	Beason	82	91	74	65
80	Landon	Johnson	81	86	79	60
80	Kendrell	Bell	76	88	78	55
80	Lawrence	Timmons	85	93	60	70
79	Chad	Greenway	85	90	65	60
78	Tully	Banta Cain	78	86	78	45
78	Na'il	Diggs	78	86	70	70
78	Rocky	McIntosh	82	84	70	67
78	Scott	Shanle	78	90	76	55
78	Shawn	Barber	82	88	60	78
77	Nick	Greisen	73	84	82	40
77	David	Bowens	75	85	74	50
77	Jarret	Johnson	74	87	78	50
76	Matt	Stewart	73	86	78	50
75	Kevin	Burnett	85	86	55	67
75	Matt	McCoy	82	82	68	60
74	Dontarrious	Thomas	85	88	60	50
73	Freddie	Keiaho	84	88	60	65
73	James	Harrison	77	84	65	55
71	Jamie	Winborn	80	82	55	65
71	Quincy	Black	87	85	60	60
70	Michael	Okwo	74	84	70	50
70	Keith	Ellison	83	85	66	60
70	Gerris	Wilkinson	81	78	54	54
70	Justin	Durant	85	84	52	60
70	Rufus	Alexander	80	91	60	75
69	Calvin	Pace	77	85	60	45
69	Eric	Alexander	74	78	60	60
68	Keyaron	Fox	81	82	55	50
68	Stephen	Nicholas	79	84	60	45
67	Darryl	Blackstock	81	84	65	45
67	Dan	Cody	80	78	65	40
66	Leon	Joe	83	84	55	55
66	Dallas	Sartz	76	77	60	48
65	Coy	Wire	85	84	50	65
65	Roderick	Green	81	86	60	35
65	Tracy	White	78	84	60	42
65	Jon	Alston	87	84	35	65
65	Marquis	Cooper	85	82	55	60

SS Strong Safeties

Overall Rating	First Name	Last Name	Speed	Man Cover	Zone Cover	Hit Power
98	Troy	Polamalu	93	65	85	91
97	Adrian	Wilson	89	65	85	81
94	Kerry	Rhodes	88	60	80	82
93	Darren	Sharper	88	82	90	78
92	Roy	Williams	85	40	70	98
92	Chris	Hope	88	65	85	85
90	Gibril	Wilson	88	70	85	82
90	Rodney	Harrison	82	40	70	97
88	Donte	Whitner	92	75	87	80
88	Lawyer	Milloy	82	50	80	86
88	Dawan	Landry	86	70	80	78
87	Sean	Jones	90	68	82	78
86	Michael	Huff	93	80	80	73
85	Antoine	Bethea	89	65	80	79
85	LaRon	Landry	94	60	70	90
85	Brian	Russell	85	64	88	82
84	Nick	Ferguson	85	62	72	83
84	Jermaine	Phillips	87	65	65	90
84	Michael	Lewis	87	60	80	85
83	Sean	Considine	86	51	72	75
83	Corey	Chavous	85	65	82	72
82	Dexter	Jackson	85	70	85	65
82	Michael	Boulware	85	70	80	80
81	Roman	Harper	85	67	85	80
80	Adam	Archuleta	86	50	70	76
80	Bernard	Pollard	86	62	75	82
80	Kenoy	Kennedy	85	45	70	89
79	Yeremiah	Bell	86	65	75	79
79	Mike	Doss	86	55	80	82
79	Glenn	Earl	86	62	83	80
78	Gerald	Sensabaugh	87	60	75	81
78	Omar	Stoutmire	84	60	70	66
76	Quintin	Mikell	84	70	80	76
76	Todd	Johnson	83	40	70	93
74	Chris	Harris	86	70	72	90
74	John	Wendling	89	70	80	60
74	Sabby	Piscitelli	92	70	70	60
74	Travares	Tillman	84	60	70	77
74	Marquand	Manuel	85	55	70	70
74	Jerome	Carter	86	58	68	68
73	Curome	Cox	86	40	74	82
73	Bhawoh	Jue	88	75	70	60
73	Jon	McGraw	87	50	70	81
73	Tyrone	Carter	83	60	84	58
72	Keith	Lewis	87	65	66	55
72	Rashad	Washington	84	60	70	78
72	Gerome	Sapp	83	60	71	68
72	Vernon	Fox	85	65	75	56
72	Jay	Bellamy	82	55	65	55
72	Brandon	Harrison	87	55	65	74
71	Aaron	Rouse	88	50	60	80
70	Clinton	Hart	86	70	65	62
70	Brannon	Condren	91	70	70	76
70	Nate	Salley	85	60	75	65
70	James	Sanders	84	45	65	51
70	Darnell	Bing	86	45	60	84
69	Marvin	White	89	50	60	81
68	Idrees	Bashir	86	60	75	50
68	Eric	Frampton	89	55	75	82
67	Kevin	McCadam	85	35	60	82

NEXT GENERATION